The Marketing Channel

The Wiley Marketing Series

WILLIAM LAZER, *Advisory Editor*
Michigan State University

MARTIN ZOBER, *Marketing Management*

ROBERT J. HOLLOWAY AND ROBERT S. HANCOCK
*The Environment of Marketing Behavior—
Selections from the Literature*

GEORGE SCHWARTZ, *Editor*
Science in Marketing

EDGAR CRANE
*Marketing Communications—
A Behavioral Approach to Men, Messages, and Media*

JOSEPH W. NEWMAN, *Editor*
On Knowing the Consumer

STEUART HENDERSON BRITT, *Editor*
*Consumer Behavior and the Behavioral Sciences—
Theories and Applications*

DONALD F. MULVIHILL AND STEPHEN PARANKA
Price Policies and Practices

DAVID CARSON
International Marketing: A Comparative Systems Approach

BRUCE E. MALLEN
The Marketing Channel: A Conceptual Viewpoint

The Marketing Channel

A Conceptual Viewpoint

BRUCE E. MALLEN

Chairman, Department of Marketing
Sir George Williams University
and
President, International Marketing Consultants, Inc.

JOHN WILEY & SONS, INC.   *New York · London · Sydney*

CONTRIBUTORS*

WROE ALDERSON
Wharton School, University of Pennsylvania

ROLAND ARTLE
The Stockholm School of Economics

LEO ASPINWALL
University of Colorado

F. E. BALDERSTON
University of California at Berkeley

HEMLY H. BALIGH
University of Illinois

THOMAS L. BERG
Columbia University

S. BERGLUND
The Stockholm School of Economics

BRUCE BLOMSTROM
M.I.T. School of Industrial Management

RALPH F. BREYER
Wharton School, University of Pennsylvania

JOHN M. BRION
Marketing Consultant, New York, N.Y.

LOUIS P. BUCKLIN
University of California at Berkeley

ROBERT COLE
University of Illinois

REAVIS COX
Wharton School, University of Pennsylvania

JOHN K. GALBRAITH
Harvard University

RICHARD GETTELL
Fortune Magazine

CHARLES S. GOODMAN
Wharton School, University of Pennsylvania

E. R. HAWKINS
Johns Hopkins University

RICHARD B. HEFLEBOWER
Northwestern University

* Affiliations are indicated as of the date the contributions were originally published.

A. C. HOGGATT
University of California at Berkeley

BERT C. McCAMMON, Jr.
Indiana University

PHILIP McVEY
University of Nebraska

BRUCE E. MALLEN
Sir George Williams University

MILES W. MARTIN
Wharton School, University of Pennsylvania

JOSEPH CORNWALL PALAMOUNTAIN Jr.
Wesleyan University

DAVID A. REVZAN
University of California at Berkeley

GEORGE SCHWARTZ
University of Rochester

STEPHEN D. SILVER
Assistant Economist, Canadian National Railroad

LOUIS W. STERN
Ohio State University

GEORGE J. STIGLER
Columbia University

GERALD B. TALLMAN
M.I.T. School of Industrial Management

GEORGE WADINAMBIARATCHI
University of Western Ontario

MARTIN R. WARSHAW
University of Michigan

ROBERT E. WEIGAND
De Paul University

WARREN J. WITTREICH
Vice-President, National Analysts

PREFACE

The marketing channel as an area of study has led a strange existence. It is perhaps the only major concept in marketing not borrowed from another discipline,* but it is perhaps also the least understood and examined area in the field. While marketing scholars have been incorporating sophisticated concepts from psychology, sociology, economics, mathematics, etc., into their particular specialty, they have neglected this area of relatively pure marketing.

We are all aware of the significant contributions made to the discipline of marketing in the areas of buyer behavior, marketing research, advertising and selling psychology and communication, microeconomic price concepts, marketing management, and marketing logistics. Indeed, even the institutional parts of the channel, for example, wholesalers and retailers, have received considerable attention in the literature. However, the marketing channel as such has not received the intensive study that it warrants. Outside of a number of highly specific channel studies, there has been only one significant general contribution to the field (Richard Clewett [editor] *Marketing Channels For Manufactured Products*), and this was written over a decade ago.

It is the purpose of this book to bring together the most significant conceptual articles, chapters, and papers written in the channel field. A very careful screening process has convinced me that not only do these selections include the more important papers in the field, but that they also almost exhaust the significant conceptual contributions to channel knowledge. Though the reader may be quite encouraged by the level of sophistication and depth of many of these articles, he must be warned that "this is it." Except for a few remaining oases, there is a desert of scholarly contributions.

The selection process used several criteria for inclusion: Is the paper conceptual, or simply a description of current company or industry practices? Is the paper concerned with vertical relationships, or with horizontal relationships? Is the paper concerned with the channel, or with its retail, wholesale, or other institutional parts? Does the paper view the channel from an external macroviewpoint, or from an internal microviewpoint?

If an article could be said to answer in the positive the first part of one or more of these questions, it was considered a possible candidate for selection. Thus, this book emphasizes the social and theoretical viewpoints, though the managerial and trend aspects are covered by some high-grade papers in Part V. It is an analysis of the concept of The Marketing Channel rather than a description of various marketing channels prevalent in specific industries.

The problem of organizing the selections proved to be most difficult. Many changes were made until the final, hopefully optimum, arrangement was arrived at:

I   INTRODUCTION—Basic Concepts and Definitions
II CHANNEL STRUCTURE THEORY

* ". . . the only concept [in marketing] that is . . . [probably] a marketing concept [that is, not borrowed from another discipline] is the one of channels of distribution." Halbert, Michael, *The Meaning and Sources of Marketing Theory* (New York: McGraw-Hill, 1965), p. 10.

I view the channel field as logically consisting of two broad divisions: (a) that of structure and design, and (b) that of relations between the microunits within the channel. The first area is concerned with the vertical arrangement and pattern of the channel. The second area assumes a given structure and is concerned with the power and price interactions between the channel members.

Thus, after an introduction to the basic concepts and definitions of the field, Part II moves into the area of channel origin and structure. This is followed by a discussion, in Part III, of the interacting forces within the channel. Parts IV and V discuss the research and analytical tools as well as the managerial programs that may be applied to the areas discussed under the previous two sections. In addition, Section B of Part V discusses some of the major trends that must be considered.

BRUCE E. MALLEN

July, 1966

ACKNOWLEDGMENTS

I appreciate the opportunity to reproduce material selected from the following sources:

Publishers: American Marketing Association, Harvard University Press, Houghton Mifflin Co., Richard D. Irwin, Inc., Southwestern Publishing Co., University of Illinois, Bureau of Business and Economic Research, and John Wiley and Sons.

Periodicals: *The Accounting Review, American Economic Review, The Business Quarterly, Cost and Management, Harvard Business Review, Journal of Marketing, Journal of Marketing Research, Journal of Political Economy, Journal of Retailing, Management Science, and The Marketer.*

For most selections, the author's affiliation is indicated as of the date the material was published.

I wish to thank all those who, through discussions or their own writings,[*] helped me to formulate, sharpen, and organize my thoughts in the channel area. I am indebted to Dr. W. Lazer of Michigan State University, Dr. I. A. Litvak of McMaster University, and particularly to Dr. S. H. Britt of Northwestern University for their help and encouragement in this project. I am also indebted to my senior students in Marketing 441, "Marketing Channels," who, through their shrewdly innocent questions, often made me realize that I did not know that which I often thought I did, and so contributed to my own eagerness for more knowledge in this area. Finally, I wish to thank Kenneth Beraznik and Miss K. McMorrow for a sometimes difficult mechanical and secretarial assignment respectively well done.

B. E. M.

[*] See, in particular, the excellent overview paper, McCammon, Bert C. Jr., and Robert W. Little, "Marketing Channels: Analytical Systems and Approaches," in George Schwartz, editor, *Science in Marketing*, (New York: John Wiley and Sons, 1965), pp. 321–385.

CONTENTS

PART
I

Introduction—Basic Concepts and Definitions

This section serves two purposes: (a) to give the reader an overview of the channel field and (b) to introduce basic concepts and definitions.

The selections in this section closely define the marketing channel and present several related concepts. Perhaps the most important of these concepts are the "marketing flows"—that which the channel carries. These include the flows of physical possession, ownership, promotion, negotiation, financing, risking, ordering, and payment. Other basic concepts developed in this section include:

Linkages	Channel level
Blockages	Channel segment
Notational systems	Type channels
Channel classes	Enterprise channels
Channel structure	Business unit channels
Trading channels	Single channels
Nontrading channels	Channel groups
Channel formation	Channel growth
Channel dissolution	Isolated channels
Engineered channels	Mixed channels
Integrated channels	

Revzan's essay includes a rather complete overview of the various broad channel categories in the economy, and the reasons why they have the structure they do. This overview includes descriptions of channels for raw materials as well as for industrial and consumer goods and services. Breyer's paper introduces a number of fine definitional points, and reveals the complexity of the term "marketing channel."

The final selection in this section (McVey) questions the concept of the marketing channel itself, and asks whether it is principally an academic's rather than a practitioner's term.

1. Marketing Organization Through the Channel*

DAVID A. REVZAN

This paper serves as a rather thorough introduction to channel concepts and definitions. Included are discussions of linkages, blockages, notational systems, channel classification systems, channel structure, and descriptions of channels for agricultural, extractive, industrial, consumer, and service products. Channels are classified by the number of links, the level of importance, the type of control, the breadth of business penetration, and the types of flows.

Ordinarily, marketing organization would be visualized mainly in its internal aspects: that is, primarily how individual business enterprises engaged in the work of marketing allocate responsibilities among the various personnel in relation to authority; what type of organizational framework is applicable; what span of executive control is visualized; and whether or not decentralization of authority is utilized.

Within the content of this paper, marketing organization is studied only in its external aspects. In this perspective, it is concerned with how agencies related directly, semidirectly, or indirectly to the functions of marketing are so intertwined with each other that some semblance of orderly relationship can be detected. The main vehicle for this orderly relationship, as will be seen, is the channel of distribution. But the concept of marketing organization in these external aspects also connotes the existence of systematic relationship in terms of the geographic units involved. In this sense, it has a very close tie-in with the motion of area structure. Thus, the external view of marketing organization is a result of the concept of level of business activity, of specialization of labor, and of function and process (marketing) as they relate to structure.

Within this context of marketing organiza-

tion, the most important factors acting as influencing agents are: The physical and dollar volume of goods and services to be marketed; the varietal composition of the goods and services included in the preceding; the evaluation of specialized management abilities within the marketing framework; the increasing diversification of types of users of products; the increasing diversifications of locations of buyers and sellers; the increasing diversification of the auxiliary marketing functions; the changing sizes and policies of business firms; and the effects of government activities.

The Meaning of Channel of Distribution

The word "channel" has its origins in the French word for canal. It thus connotes, in its marketing application, a pathway taken by goods as they flow from point of production to points of intermediate and final use. But in these flows there is a further connotation of a sequence of marketing agencies; namely, the wholesale and retail middlemen who perform, type by type, various combinations of marketing functions at various points in the channel in order to facilitate such flows. In addition, there is a connotation of a sequence of facilitating agencies which perform auxiliary functions at one or more points within the channel. Some writers view each functional or subfunctional grouping as giving rise to flows. The channel is, therefore, the vehicle for viewing marketing organization in its external aspects and for bridging the physical and nonphysical gaps which exist in moving goods from pro-

• SOURCE: David A. Revzan, "Marketing Organization through the Channel," *Wholesaling in Marketing Organization* (New York: John Wiley and Sons, 1961), pp. 107–142. David A. Revzan, Professor of Business Administration, University of California (Berkeley).

3

ducers to consumers through the exchange process, including the determination of price.

The channel thus bridges the gap, geographically speaking, between producers and users. In this sense, distance is involved not only in the usual terms of miles (or an equivalent measure) but also in terms of the times involved and the costs of communication and transportation. In addition to time in this aspect, the channel has a function to perform in bridging time gaps in the pure storage sense. Thus, within the channel, certain types of middlemen and certain special agencies arise to carry physical inventories (and to change their physical characteristics) over periods of time. In addition, the channel is useful in bridging gaps in product assortment patterns by matching sellers' inventories—in physical and qualitative aspects—with buyers' inventory intentions. More will be said of this function of channels in later sections. Finally, the channel is a means of bridging gaps in knowledge and in the communication of that knowledge. It becomes, accordingly, a structural arrangement whereby sellers (or their middlemen representatives) search for customer prospects with whom to communicate and to whom sales can ultimately be made, and whereby buyers, in turn, search for sellers carrying the assortments desired from whom purchases ultimately can be made.

The concept of the channel of distribution involves, in addition to these characteristics, sets of vertical and horizontal relationships between various types of wholesale and retail middlemen. As such, it can be used as the keystone for the analysis of various "circuit" and "flow" arrangements centering around these management aspects. Based upon all of these considerations, there can evolve systematic analysis of such problems as: (a) the characteristics of various types of channel structures; (b) the power focus of the management element in each kind of channel structure, (c) comparisons between these as to relative short-run and long-run efficiency; (d) comparative costs of keeping and defending existing channels of distribution as against selecting new types.

From this lengthy definition of the channel and its characteristics, it follows that the channel is composed of the following:

1. A series of more or less complicated connections between business units or groups of business units by means of which the center of marketing activity is effected; namely, the transfer of legal possession or right or use by means of buying and selling activities. At the wholesaling sector there

may be more than one cycle of buying-selling relationships in the channel.

2. A pattern of physical flow of the commodity or commodities involved which may parallel the business connections in (1) or move through different business units arrangements.

3. Further patterns designed to show flows of other auxiliary activities.[1]

The business units involved in channels of distribution, other than the wholesale and retail middlemen as such, may be classified as follows:[2]

I. *Extractive Industry Establishments*
   A. Agriculture.
   B. Forestry.
   C. Fisheries.
   D. Mining (metal, anthracite coal, bituminous coal, crude petroleum and natural gas, and nonmetallic mining and quarrying).
II. *Contract Construction*
III. *Manufacturing Establishments*[3]
IV. *Finance, Insurance, and Real Estate Agencies*
   A. Banking.
   B. Securities brokers, dealers, exchanges.
   C. Finance agencies, n. e. c.
   D. Insurance carriers.
   E. Insurance agents and combination offices.
   F. Real Estate.
V. *Transportation Agencies*
   A. Railroads; freight and passenger.
   B. Local and highway passenger.
   C. Highway freight transportation and warehousing.
   D. Water.
   E. Air.
   F. Pipelines.
   G. Services allied to transportation.
VI. *Communications and Public Utilities Agencies*
   A. Telegraph, telephone, and related.
   B. Radio broadcasting and television.
   C. Utilities—electric and gas.
   D. Local utilities and public service, n. e. c.
VII. *Services*
   A. Hotels and other lodgings.
   B. Personal.
   C. Private households.
   D. Commercial and trade schools and employment agencies.
   E. Business services, n. e. c.
   F. Miscellaneous repair services and hand trades.
   G. Motion pictures.

[1] R. Vaile, E. T. Grether, and R. Cox, *Marketing in the American Economy* (New York: The Ronald Press Co., 1952). These authors speak of *forward flows* of physical possession, ownership and negotiation; *backward flows* of ordering and payment; and *combination flows* of information, financing, and risking.
[2] In this classification scheme, any one of the groups may appear in the channel as an originating seller; as an intermediate or final buyer; as a provider of some primary or auxiliary function within the channel; or in a combination of these.
[3] See the classification used in Chapter 4.

H. Amusement and recreation (except motion pictures).
I. Medical and other health services.
J. Engineering and other professional services, n. e. c.
K. Educational service, n. e. c.
L. Nonprofit organizations, n. e. c.
VIII. *Government and Government Enterprises*
  A. Federal.
  B. State.
  C. County.
  D. Municipal.
  E. Foreign.

The Channel and Linkages and Blockages

In terms of physical analogies, the channel has been referred to as a canal in which is contained the variegated physical flow of goods. But in view of the complex array of business units as classified which may be involved in one or all aspects of channel functions, the channel may be visualized also as a chain-link arrangement in which each business is in effect one link. Thus, the channel may be here visualized as a series of linkages which vary as to the number of links, as to the functions to be performed by each link and the entire set of linkages, and according to the "thickness" and strength of each link. Some links are dominant, whereas others play a subordinate role. Closely related to this is the situation wherein some links are engaged in the primary functions of marketing, whereas others function merely as facilitating or auxiliary links.

It is in the functioning of the channel as a series of linkages that there arises also the phenomenon of blockages. In a sense, blockages may be visualized as the activities of one or more links (business units) in a particular channel to protect the economic status of that channel by placing barriers (blockages) in the way of competing channels. These blockages may consist of such legal devices as an exclusive agency franchise arrangement preventing any links in the channel from handling competitive products; they may consist of various forms of legislation designed to restrict the units permitted to market particular products; they may represent manufacturers control over resale prices; or they may represent collusive activity within or outside the letter and the spirit of the law. Such blockages may have only very temporary success, or they may have elements of permanency, or they may generate their own destruction by giving alternative channels and their own linkages considerably more motivation than might be otherwise expected.

The Relationship of the Channel of Distribution to the "Funnel" Concept

The channel is the concrete marketing organizational framework in which the abstract concept of the funnel is executed. The funnel depends on one or more of the types of channels to be discussed later to become a reality. Depending upon the channel and the sum total of the functioning of its component links, the funnel concept may or may not be completely realized. The sum total of the functioning of all channels becomes the basis, in turn, for the approximation of the funnel concept in its total abstract meaning.

Types of Notation Systems for Channel Diagrams

As a final preliminary to this discussion of types of channels, a word needs to be said about how channel diagrams are constructed. In general, the components of the channel diagram consist of: (a) a box enclosing the title of and the type of agency making up a link; (b) a solid or broken line indicating, accordingly, either physical or nonphysical flows; (c) an arrow indicating the direction of the flow; and (d) a box enclosing the title and type of each using agency at the end of the channel. In addition, notation schemes may be used to indicate and differentiate primary agencies from auxiliary or facilitating agencies. By means of varying widths of lines, the proportionate importance of each segment flow through each agency combination can be shown.

Some simple diagrams may indicate each of these aspects of the notation systems. Figure 1 illustrates some kinds of notation systems which may be used to designate the agencies (links) involved in channel diagrams. Any geometric design is permissible, although in actual practice there is no hard and fast line of distinction. Fig-

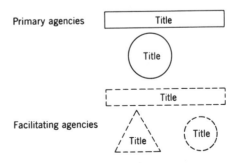

Fig. 1. Notation system for agencies in channel.

Flow of physical movement: ⟶

Flow of nonphysical movements:

Fig. 2. Notation system for types and direction of flows.

ure 2 shows the notation systems typically used for designating the type and direction of flows. Solid lines are the orthodox notational scheme for indicating the physical flow of the commodity or commodities involved. Broken lines generally denote the nonphysical flows and may be further coded to reflect each type of such flows.

In the absence of any standardized notational system, it is obvious that the numerous channel diagrams available show a wide variety of notational framework found in the discussion of types of channels which follows. Any one using channel diagrams ought to be in a position of obtaining from such diagrams the kind of information which may be useful in understanding channel structure.

One other aspect of channel diagram notation may be useful, namely, the indication of the direction and extent of management control. The form used is by Duddy and Revzan[4] (see Figure 3) and is used to explain the evolution of more complex forms of channel organization.

[4] E. A. Duddy and D. A. Revzan, *Marketing: An Institutional Approach*. 2nd ed. (New York: McGraw-Hill, 1953), p. 266.

TYPES OF CHANNELS OF DISTRIBUTION

There are perhaps five important variables which affect the classification of types of channels: (1) Channels may be distinguished according to the number of links (intervening business agencies) involved; (2) channels may be differentiated according to their relative level of importance or their position within the entire framework of marketing; (3) channels may be differentiated according to the type of managerial control manifested; (4) channels may be separated according to the breadth of business penetration which may be presented; and (5) channels may be designated according to the types of flows indicated above.

Obviously, this classification format is so cross-related that any collection of channel diagrams may have to undergo multiple assortment. Presumably, a sixth classification basis could emphasize, by evaluating the five types indicated above, the relative degree of simplicity or complexity found in any given channel situation. But this is a far less satisfactory basis for classification than any of the preceding five indicated.

Channels, by Number of Links

This is the oldest and most orthodox classification scheme used in the marketing literature. Based on the number of links, it distinguishes between direct, semidirect, and indirect channels, and, in addition, has both a commodity

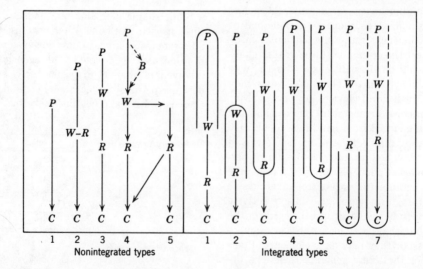

Fig. 3. Progression from simple to complex channels. *Key: P,* producer; *R,* retailer; *B,* broker or selling agent; *W,* wholesaler; *C,* consumer Nos. 1 and 4, producer-owned or controlled; No. 2, wholesaler-owned or controlled; Nos. 3 and 5, retailer-owned or controlled and Nos. 6 and 7, consumer-owned and operated.

and functional aspect. A *direct channel* is characterized by the existence of a single-link pattern; namely, direct contact between manufacturer (or other producer) and user. The producer may assume full responsibility for the marketing functions and for the establishment of communication between himself and the users; or the user may assume full responsibility for the functions and communication. There may be, and usually are, facilitating agencies involved; but the main characteristic is the directness of both the physical and nonphysical flows. The producer may send his salesmen directly to the customers' place of business or residence; the customer may send his buyer to the producer's place of business; or a specialized facility may be used, such as a roadside stand or a mail-order catalog.

Indirect channels represent the opposite spectrum from that of the direct channel. By indirect is meant the insertion between producer and user of more than one type of wholesale middleman if the commodity is of the industrial goods type, and of more than one type of each of wholesale and retail middleman if the commodity is of the consumers' goods category. Indirect channels represent, accordingly, the most complex arrangements from the point of view of both the number of linkages and blockages and the variety of types of middlemen involved.

Semidirect channels represent an intermediate situation between these extremes. Only one type of wholesale middleman may be involved in the case of industrial goods, or only one type of wholesale and of retail middleman may be involved. There is no hard and fast dividing line between the semidirect and indirect channels.

In each of these cases, the characteristics as to number of links are modified by the kinds involved and by the middlemen's adaptations of the functions which need to be performed. For example, both roadside stands and municipal farmers' markets become physical parts of the direct channels for certain kinds of agricultural products. They are not found, on the other hand, in the direct channels either for industrial or manufactured consumers' goods. Again, certain types of organized wholesale market facilities become part of the indirect channels for certain types of agricultural goods but not for the other categories. It may be stated somewhat categorically that the direct channels usually involve the performance of a much wider range of primary and auxiliary functions by the middlemen included than is likely to be the case either for indirect or semidirect channels.

Channels According to Level of Importance

Where a channel exists which makes use of more than one combination of agencies, a differentiation may be made between that part of the channel which is a primary level of importance and that part which is of auxiliary importance.

Channels, by Type of Control

This classification scheme introduces the element of managerial integration, and subdivides channels into producer-controlled, wholesale-middlemen-controlled and retailer-middlemen-controlled. Subclassifications can be introduced by the type of operation found within each group. However, a much more useful subclassification scheme can be based upon the type of horizontal and vertical integration found in the channel.[5]

The horizontally integrated channel includes two types. Type *A* involves a single management which controls a number of units all handling the same general assortments of commodities on the same business plane, *viz.*, production, wholesale market, or retail market. Type *B* involves a similar arrangement of units, but these units together or separately handle either complementary product lines, or completely unrelated lines, or combinations of both. In both types, the controlling management pursues a unified profit policy.

The *vertically integrated* channel is subdivided into two types, and each of these is, in turn, further subdivided into three groups. Type *A* represents a channel arrangement in which the vertically integrated firm controls a number of different operations in production and/or marketing of *similar* commodities on successive business levels. This type is subdivided into: (a) the *backward vertical integration* form, in which the controlling business firm is nearer the ultimate consumer in the channel than any other agency link; (b) the *forward vertical integration* form, in which the controlling business firm is further away from the ultimate consumer in the channel than any other agency link; and (c) the form which is a combination of (a) and (b). Subgroup (a) may be termed retailer-controlled for edible agricultural products and

[5] The discussion which follows is based to a considerable extent upon Werner Z. Hirsch, "Toward a Definition of Integration," *The Southern Economic Journal*, XVII (October 1950), 159–165, and his longer version of the article in typed manuscript form.

manufactured consumers' goods products, while
subgroup (b) may be subdivided into producer-
controlled or wholesale-middleman-controlled.

Type *B* of the vertically integrated channel
consists of the complementary vertically integrated firm which controls a number of different
operations in the marketing and/or production
of complementary products on successive business levels. This type also is subdivided into
three groups as follows: (a) the *divergent forward
variety*, in which a firm begins with one or a few
commodities and then divides these into numerous complementary products as they flow closer
and closer to the consumer; (b) the *convergent
backward variety*, in which a firm "pulls" in
numerous raw materials and services in order
to manufacture and place in the channel one or
just a few commodities; and (c) the *forward
parallel variety*, in which firms merely begin with
a given number of complementary products and
push these along in the channel without any
significant change in number.

There are in addition to these groupings two
types of a combination of the horizontally integrated and vertically integrated channel. Type
A consists of a joint horizontally and vertically
integrated firm which controls a number of vertically integrated units all handling *similar* products at successive levels of the channel. Type *B*
consists of the same kind of arrangement in
which the controlled vertically integrated units
all handle *complementary* products. Each of these
types may be subdivided into the same subgroupings as type *B* of the vertically integrated
channel.

Some discussion may be pertinent at this
point of the main devices used by business firms
to achieve complete or partial integration of the
forms noted. The most obvious and completely
successful device is for the controlling business
unit to acquire the direct ownership and management of all units involved in the channel
of distribution. Control may also be acquired
through ownership of the patents of the basic
machinery used in the production process or
through legal control over an entire product or
family of products. Policies may be dictated
through the many-sided forms of interlocking
directorates or other financial-organizational
controls.

A much more informal but, nevertheless, very
effective control may be achieved by aggressive
sales promotion by any agency in the channel
which is designed to enhance that agency's control over part or all of the channel. These tactics
may establish strong brand preferences which

may "force" the product through the channel
over the opposition of intermediate channel
agencies; or they may open other areas of informal integration. Any agency may attempt to
secure informal integration by prepackaging
policies and by such inventory tactics as full-
line forcing. The extension of credit arrangements and the use of such legal devices as exclusive dealer franchise contracts may act as
the basis for informal integration. The use of
resale price maintenance agreements extends the
manufacturer's control through the length and
breadth of the channel. Finally, such tactics as
sharing-the-market agreements or cartels act as
very potent integrating forces in the channel
until dissolved by the extension of government
regulation.[6]

Channels, by Breadth of Business Penetration

It is obvious that channel structure begins
with the individual channel arrangement which
exists for the product (or products) produced
by a given producing unit. From this beginning
arrangement, there may emerge as many such
channels as there are producing units. Every
change in the number of producing units or in
the number and types of products produced
can lead to changes, in turn, in the number and
format of each of these individual producers'
channels.

These individual producers' channels may be
combined, in turn, into two different group
arrangements. Products of homogeneous marketing characteristics can be grouped together
into a *product family* channel. Thus, all the
individual producers' channels for soaps and
detergents may be grouped into a soap- and-
detergent group channel. Or individual producer channels may be grouped, in turn, into
industry channels, using either the two-digit
basis of classification only or adding the three-
digit and four-digit subgroupings. Finally, product group and/or industry channels may be
further combined into channels for extractive
industry products, channels for industrial goods
products, and channels for manufactured consumers' goods products.

Channels, by Types of Flows

It has been indicated that, so far as flows are
concerned, most marketing studies separate the

[6] At this point, the reader should keep in mind the
relationship between this discussion and the previous discussion of linkages and blockages.

physical from the nonphysical flows. But, as has also been indicated, some writers subdivide the nonphysical flows into several component types. Although not much attention will be given to these subdivisions, the reader should be aware that some writers devote a considerable amount of detailed description and diagrammatic representation to these flows.[7]

THE GEOGRAPHIC STRUCTURE OF CHANNELS OF DISTRIBUTION

Although the usual notation systems used for channels of any of the types discussed in the preceding section do not indicate their geographic characteristics, it should be obvious that channels reflect geographic characteristics. The agencies involved in any channel of distribution represent, among other things, a series of individual decisions by individual business firms as to where to locate a particular establishment. Each establishment in the channel has a geographic zone of influence which represents decisions of some individual firm or group of firms as to what the wholesale and, in the case of consumers' goods, retail trading areas are, measured potentially and in actuality. It has been indicated that these areas change in boundaries with varying degrees of frequency based upon many variables.

Since so much information has to be included in the notation systems for channel diagrams, it should be obvious as to why the geographic aspects are frequently excluded. This exclusion is done for purposes of making the channel diagrams manageable both in physical size and in comprehensibility.

This short section has been included for those readers interested in the full complexity of channel diagrams, and to point out that there is a wealth of complicated geographic data which have not been omitted simply because no notation has been made.[8]

[7] Vaile, Grether, Cox, *op. cit.*, Chapters 5, 7.
[8] R. F. Breyer has a very interesting way in which to diagram a geographic pattern. See his *The Marketing Institution* (New York: McGraw-Hill, 1934), Chapter X, and especially Figs. 14–20 therein. But even these diagrams are only suggestive of the complete range of agencies which can be included in a limited representation of the geographic detail. However, the treatment is in the usual highly imaginative and valuable style of Breyer's writings on marketing organization.

CHANNEL STRUCTURE, THE NATURE OF THE COMMODITY, AND COMMODITY FLOWS

The purpose of this section is to sketch the approach to be taken in succeeding sections in adapting the general outline of channel structure, as discussed in previous sections, to the particular position occupied by wholesale middlemen in channels found in particular commodity situations. It should be apparent that little or no attention can be given here to those types of channels used in marketing the products of individual producing firms.

In the following sections the discussions will center around the channels of distribution for the following industry and product groupings:

I. *Channels of Distribution for Agricultural Products*
   A. Products to be processed.
      1. Moving to industrial users.
      2. Moving to ultimate consumers.
   B. Products moving to ultimate consumers without processing.
II. *Channels of Distribution for Other Extractive Industry Products*
III. *Channels of Distribution for Manufactured Industrial Goods*
   A. Products entering directly into the production of other products.
   B. Products facilitating further production.
   C. Products for nonmanufacturing types of customers.
IV. *Channels of Distribution for Manufactured Consumers' Goods*
   A. Durables.
   B. Semidurables.
   C. Nondurables (except agricultural).
V. *Channels of Distribution for Services*
   A. Business and government services.
   B. Personal services.

In developing the discussion under each subgrouping, it is assumed that the reader has been exposed to the wealth of detail on commodity marketing presented in the better basic marketing textbooks. It is further assumed that he has been exposed to diagrammatic materials which exist for the various commodity and industry channels. With these assumptions in mind, the discussion under each heading will present the following pattern of analysis: (1) The underlying conditions of production which are related to channel structure, (2) the commodity characteristics which bear importantly on the channels of distribution, and (3) the factors that explain the importance of wholesale middlemen in the direct, semidirect, and indirect channels. A final section will deal with the factors that influence the choice of individual manufacturing units for their particular products.

CHANNELS OF DISTRIBUTION—RAW MATERIALS, AGRICULTURAL PRODUCTS

Characteristics of Production

Agriculture is a series of industries involved in producing a wide range of edible and inedible products which have, in turn, wide variations in physical characteristics, in volume moving to market, in value characteristics, and in conditions of production. In terms of producing units, the number of farms in the United States in 1950 totaled 5.4 million, with an average size of only 215 acres. All but one third of these are unimportant as commercial producers; nevertheless, the less important units do contribute variable quantities of agricultural products into the marketing channels. Because of locational dependence upon natural production factors— soil, climate, topography—many farms are at considerable geographic distances from consuming markets. Thus, transportation and storage are of even greater significance than for most manufacturing industries.

Conditions of production range from rudimentary dependency upon manual labor for some crops to a revolutionary increase in the use of machinery at the production and harvesting phases. Fertilizers, medicines, and insecticides, together with various forms of botanical experimentation, have increased sharply the yields of crops per acre and of animals. Yet, the time cycle of production remains relatively rigid, ranging from a few weeks, relatively speaking, for certain truck crops to a period of perhaps 5 years before a citrus fruit tree may reach the maturity period of commercial yield.

It must be emphasized in a discussion of this kind that agricultural production, in a collective sense, is essentially speculative. This is so because of the relative unpredictability of weather conditions (despite recent improvements in forecasting techniques) and, similarly, of such related environmental factors as the presence of plant-destroying insects, and the like. This uncertainty affects both the quality of the crop and animal production involved. Obviously, the shorter the period of harvest, the greater the impact of the risk.

These variables have some very marked effects on the channel structure. For one, a great deal of emphasis must be placed upon the necessity of providing agricultural producers with a variety of alternatives so far as liquidation of output for cash and transfers of ownership are concerned. Structurally, the middlemen in the channel must be attuned especially to the phases of concentration and equalization processes within their respective channel positions. Also, a great deal of specialization must be manifested by these middlemen in the price-determining and risk-bearing aspects of the channel structure. Grading and packaging aspects become magnified in importance, also, as compared with factory production.

Commodity Characteristics

The raw-material agricultural products are divided into foods, fibres, and other groupings. The food group has crops and animals as its initial subdivision. The food crops are mainly as follows: The grains (wheat, corn, oats, barley, rye); fruits and vegetables for canning, preserving, and fast freezing; cane and beet sugar; and the vegetable oils—soybeans, cottonseed, etc. The food animals are the livestock group (cattle, calves, hogs, and sheep); and the poultry group (chickens, turkeys, ducks, etc.). In the fibre group are included both animal and vegetable— cotton, wool, hemp. Finally, the "other" category includes the inedible derivatives from livestock, the industrial uses of grains and soybeans; the production of seed crops and breeding animals; and tobacco.

These raw materials have several characteristics which affect the existing channel structures. They vary widely as to the quantities available to be marketed, as to relative perishability, as to susceptibility to grading and standardization, as to the length of the marketing period, as to the variety of producing conditions, and, finally, as to the stage of development of the manufacturing utilization of raw materials. In general, they vary also as to the need which exists for the utilization in the channel of organized as against nonorganized local and central market facilities.

Factors Explaining the Variable Importance of Wholesale Middlemen

From preceding discussions, the following aspects of the role of wholesale middlemen in the marketing of raw-material agricultural products will have been noted: (1) The existence of certain types of assemblers, such as the grain elevators, local buyers, cooperative shipping associations, which facilitate the performance of the various components of the concentration process; (2) the decision of many agricultural producers to maintain ownership control of their products while using specialists—mainly agent middlemen—to carry on the remaining marketing functions through the channel; (3) the existence of organized central commodity markets which, by virtue of their location relative to agricultural producers, require various types of wholesale middlemen who, as members, represent these producers or represent buyers; (4) the existence of other organized markets with such restrictive membership requirements that more frequently than not wholesale middlemen specialists will be needed; and (5) wholesale middlemen who represent buyers while moving from one agricultural producing area to another.

The resultant of the operation of these forces is a complex mixture of direct, semidirect, and indirect channel arrangements for the same class of raw materials. For the highly perishable raw materials, the role of the nonintegrated wholesale middleman is likely to be at a minimum level because of the necessary close proximity of processing facilities to producing areas. For products such as livestock, there has been an increasing proportion of the output moving through direct channels, but there is a very considerable volume moving through semidirect and indirect channels. In these latter cases, the commission agent, the broker, the cooperative marketing associations, and merchant wholesalers (especially the regular wholesaler) emerge to positions of greatest importance. For export and import trade movements, such wholesale middlemen as exporters, importers, export agents, and import agents assume increased importance. For those commodities sold on the speculative exchanges, the buying and selling brokers assume considerable importance.

Based on the 1954 Census data, it is apparent that, of the total 1954 wholesale sales of raw-material agricultural products, the agent-broker group was most important with 42.7 per cent of the total, duplicated sales volume. The merchant wholesalers group accounted for 34.3 per cent, and the assemblers for the remainder 22.9 per cent. Such integrated middlemen of importance as are found are the cooperative marketing and shipping associations included in the agent-broker and assembler groups. These data do not reflect, of course, the activities of those buyers employed by manufacturers who do not operate separate places of business.

CHANNELS OF DISTRIBUTION— EDIBLE AGRICULTURAL PRODUCTS

Production Characteristics

The production characteristics for these commodities are identical with those listed above for the raw-material category. This is especially so for those types of edible products also classified as raw-material types of products.

Commodity Characteristics

Most of these edible products are, by physical nature, extremely perishable. At the same time, the variable-quality characteristics, noted above, place a very high premium on sales by inspection. The channel structure must provide, accordingly, for rapid physical flows while still permitting such sales by inspection to take place at any transaction center within the channel.

Highly variable relationships exist as to the length of the marketing season for each category of product. Some fresh fruits such as strawberries may be available for only a few weeks of the year, depending, in part, upon the accessibility of a given market to the sources of supply. Other commodities, by virtue of both their growing seasons and the diversity of producing areas together with their ability to be stored for long periods, may be available in "fresh" condition during every week of the year. Examples of such commodities are potatoes, onions, and apples. There are, of course, several gradations between these two extremes.

The fresh, edible products vary according to weight-value relationships. At one extreme are the bulky products of corresponding heavy weights, such as potatoes and cabbage. Generally, but not always, these have the lower relative prices per pound. At the opposite extreme are the fancy fruits and vegetables, relatively lighter in basic selling weights, and usually commanding relatively higher prices, especially when the first shipments of the season take place. These are, of course, only average tendencies, and there are many exceptions.

These categories of commodities vary widely in susceptibility to packaging. Where the products tend to be of very uniform quality and can be assorted by sizes without affecting quality, packaging may enhance the products' value and facilitate movement through the channel. On the other hand, basic physical characteristics together with highly variable runs of sizes and low unit values may make packaging unsuccessful. As the quality and ingenuity of packages and packaging materials continue to improve, and as the demands of self-service marketing continue to require more and more prepackaging, a larger proportion of these products will appear in some form of packaging, including the use of bindings as for bananas and for some forms of lettuce.

Related to the commodity characteristics as they affect the channel structure are certain demand characteristics. First to be noticed is the existence of an important institutional demand as well as ultimate consumer demand. The nature of the institutional demand stemming from restaurants, hotels, dining cars, hospitals, and the like requires a completely different channel structure than do the movements to ultimate consumers either through retail agencies or by means of direct channels. These institutional buyers have different quality and unit purchase requirements than do ultimate consumers. Obviously, the channel will have less need to provide prepackaging for these customers than for ultimate consumers.

Ultimate consumers, as of the present period, have variable reactions to the purchase of fresh products as against utilizing fast-frozen products. With the design of the modern refrigerator and the use of deep-freeze cabinets, many households prefer to stock fast-frozen products in preference to more frequent purchases of the fresh products. As a result, many ultimate consumers have highly fluctuating demands for the fresh products, and this places considerable stress, in turn, on the various types of food stores handling the perishable produce. There is, of course, some underlying foundation by virtue of the fact that some fruits and vegetables do not have any fast-frozen equivalents.

Factors Explaining the Variable Importance of Wholesale Middlemen

There are some conditions which are favorable to the marketing of fresh, edible products through direct channel arrangements, but these are relatively unimportant. Quality considerations, freshness, and the availability of specialized farmers' market facilities are among the reasons why direct channels exist and will be used. But, in view of the varying quantities and varieties of the products to be marketed and the widespread geographical distribution of users, such channel arrangements can do only a fraction of the marketing job.

Accordingly, the bulk of these products must move through considerably more complicated semidirect and indirect channels. The wholesale middlemen tend to be classed in the following functional-process positions in the channel.

1. The *assemblers* group, consisting mainly of those middlemen close to the producers, who conform to the marketing pattern of arranging for partial or complete aspects of the process of concentration. Thus, they may be producer-oriented, as in the case of cooperative shipping associations; or they may be wholesale-market-oriented, as local representatives of central market wholesalers; or they may be representatives of the large-scale retailers, as the corporate chain buyers. They may be used to facilitate the producers' continuous control of legal ownership; or they may provide him with the earliest channel opportunity for liquidation of harvestings for cash while providing for the transfer of ownership.

2. The *central market middlemen* group consisting, on the one hand, of the agent middlemen representing the producers. Of these, depending upon the product and whether or not physical possession of inventories is necessary to the channel structure, the more important would be the auction companies, brokers, commission agents, and cooperative marketing agencies. A second group consists of the orthodox wholesalers, the voluntary chain representatives, and related types all of whom own the fresh products offered for sale. A third group represents, on either an agent or merchant middleman basis, the larger institutional buyers noted above. And a fourth group of wholesaler merchants, especially the orthodox wholesaler and the truck distributor, supply the assortment needed by the nonintegrated or semiintegrated food stores. These middlemen are involved, collectively, in the equalization process and the beginnings of the dispersion process.

3. The final set of middlemen, completing the dispersion process, consists of the various forms of retail and service agencies who sell the products directly to the ultimate consumers or who use the products in the preparation of meals to be served to these consumers.

On a combined basis, the distribution of 1954 sales of edible farm products was as follows: By merchant wholesalers, 49.1 per cent; by assemblers, 21.7 per cent; by agents and brokers, 17.0 per cent; and by manufacturers' sales branches and sales offices, 12.2 per cent. The gross sales value of the products handled was $12.4 billion.

CHANNELS OF DISTRIBUTION—OTHER EXTRACTIVE INDUSTRY PRODUCTS

Production Characteristics

The main categories of products to be considered are petroleum, lumber and forest products, ferrous and nonferrous ores, and coal and coke. Except for the lumber group, the products involved are all located in mines, or their equivalents, below the surface of the earth or of bodies of water. These deposits are not replaceable, as is the case for lumber. And, as already noted for agricultural products, the quality of the raw-material deposits is not controllable to any extent for the commercial market by human beings. As to where these raw materials are located has a considerable bearing upon where the commercial users will locate.

The extraction of these products, including lumber, involves increasingly the use of machinery; and, because of the depletion factor, considerable attention must be devoted to the extraction of all usable deposits of every commercial gradation so far as quality is concerned. In the case of petroleum, very expensive efforts must be made to uncover the deposits wherever they may be in the world. As a result, increasing percentages of our domestic petroleum requirements are being derived from foreign deposits.

Commodity Characteristics

The greater part of these commodities are very bulky and heavy in relation to their values. Thus, the channel must provide a wide range of middlemen devices which reduce the number of times the product must be handled physically. Grading must be done systematically because of the importance of such specifications in the use by various classes and because of the small degree of usefulness these commodities serve in the commercial flows.

Practically all of the categories have experienced distinctly widening varieties of intermediate and final uses, thus increasing sharply the varieties of initial and intermediate users of and customers for the raw materials. Thus, the destructive distillation of lumber yields an increasing number of synthetic-product end uses. In addition to the widening varieties of use for fuel, petroleum, by means of the ever developing petro-chemical industries, is also offering an ever-widening range of uses. Coal, too, in addition to its established use as a fuel, is becoming an important raw-material source for many synthetics. Finally, the metallic ores are becoming the initial ingredients in ever-widening lists of industrial and manufactured consumers' goods products.

Factors Explaining the Variable Importance of Wholesale Middlemen

For such basic raw materials as petroleum and the metallic ores, the largest initial movements of the raw materials are likely to be controlled by those plants which are part of the integrated manufacturer structure. In such cases, the movements are between units of the same business empire, and the pricing process becomes a matter of internal accounting. For products such as coal and lumber, a wider variety of channel alternatives is available. Although large integrated companies may control the forests, and their sales branches and sales offices may control, in part, the initial flows of lumber, these meet only a fraction of the channel needs.

As a result of the diverse intermediate and end uses, wholesale middlemen are necessary who can: (a) locate and maintain contact on a continuous basis with all classes of users and (b) maintain inventories—in addition to those at the forest lumber mill points—from which size, shape, and quality inventory adaptations can be made. Because of weight and transportation cost factors, much intermediate handling is reduced to a minimum by using drop shippers, sales offices, brokers, and manufacturers and sales agents.

In the case of coal, there are somewhat the same channel considerations as for lumber, but the industrial uses of the product are far more important than lumber. As a result, the mining companies have their own sales branches and sales offices which assume considerably greater levels of importance than for lumber. The broker and sales agents, in addition, assume increased importance.

Based upon 1954 data, the types-of-operation groups handling petroleum and petroleum products were petroleum bulk stations, et al., 89 per cent; merchant wholesalers, 7.9 per cent; and agents and brokers, 3.1 per cent. For the lumber and forest products, the division was as follows: Merchant wholesalers, 72.9 per cent; agents and brokers, 15.9 per cent; and sales branches and sales offices, 11.3 per cent. Finally, for coal and coke, the distribution was: merchant wholesalers, 40.9 per cent; agents and brokers, 30.1 per cent; and sales branches and sales offices, 29 per cent.

CHANNELS OF DISTRIBUTION— MANUFACTURED INDUSTRIAL GOODS

Production Characteristics

It is apparent that there are wide ranges of importance depending on the types of products produced and on the difference between the highly geographically concentrated industries and those which are dispersed in location. Furthermore, the manufacturing units range from large numbers of small-size units to such integrated giants as the automobile and steel-producing companies.

In addition, there are wide ranges from those companies producing few products of a relatively homogeneous nature to those producing wide varieties of products classified under more than one category. The products produced have wide ranges of end uses as well, and many have both industrial goods and manufactured consumers' goods characteristics. Manufacturing establishments may concentrate on highly technical products made to complex specifications, as in the case of the missile program; or they may produce highly standardized products, as in the case of electric bulbs; or they may produce varying combinations of both.

Commodity Characteristics

The manufactured industrial goods category involves a wide assortment of products. The most useful classification is to distinguish between two categories: (1) those goods which enter directly into, and can be identified in the actual products produced, and (2) those which either facilitate such production or are needed by the various types of institutional customers. In the first category, apart from the primary and secondary raw materials already discussed, would be included the wide array of semiprocessed and fully processed components, ranging in value from a few cents each to thousands of dollars or more; packaging materials which become part of the final products; and directly related services.

In the second category would be included the following: The basic major equipment (or capital goods) and buildings used for the manufacturing, construction, or similar activities; such accessory equipment as small tools, jigs, dies, which are employed in conjunction with the basic major equipment, but which are used up in considerably shorter periods of time; the office equipment needed by any business, government, educational, or other profit and nonprofit units; various kinds of supplies (lubricating, etc.) needed in both the production and the nonproduction aspects of customer activities; such process materials as bleaching chemicals, enzymes, catalytic chemicals; transportation and storage services; shipping containers;

stationery, office supplies, etc.; and all types of accounting and statistical machines, including computers.

These commodities may be, as noted, highly standardized, or they may involve manufacturer, buyer, or other specifications. They may be highly technical in nature, requiring salesmen with scientific and engineering training, or they may be of such general nature as to require no such specialized knowledge for selling and servicing. They may be durable and last for decades, as in the case of buildings and railroad equipment, or they may be completely used up by each application. As a result, each category has highly varying periods of customer reordering as compared with other categories. Because of these characteristics, sales negotiations may be of very routine nature, or they may involve, on the other hand, key executives as the negotiating agents and months and even years of negotiation. Technical servicing requirements may range from none to very highly skilled arrangements. Many products are covered by intricate patent and/or cross-licensing agreements, while other types have no such protection. Wide varieties of packaging characteristics are to be noted, together with wide ranges of susceptibility to manufacturer brand identification. Obviously, many products lose their brand identification by being components of other final products.

Factors Explaining the Variable Importance of Wholesale Middlemen

Generally, the following factors will be of some help in understanding the high significance of direct channels: (1) The small number of potential users for certain types of industrial goods, requiring very close and continuous contact by the manufacturer if no potential or actual sales opportunities are to be overlooked; (2) a large average unit sale which requires long periods of time for completion of negotiations;[9] (3) concentration of actual and potential customers in very compact geographic areas, thus permitting intensive use of a relatively small sales force; (4) the need for considerable technical advice and assistance in making the initial sales, and in the continuous postsales servicing period; (5) the need for providing key executives on the selling side to match the organizational levels of the buyers; (6) the impact of reciprocity

[9] Visualize, for example, the time periods involved in the sale of jet planes to airline companies, or complete, streamlined trains to the railroads.

in making industrial goods sales; (7) the impact of the greater incidence of integration among industrial goods sellers and buyers; and (8) the length of time required to introduce buyers either to new uses of existing products, or to revolutionary types of new products (such as electronic computers).

On the other hand, there are many factors which underlie the use of many types of merchant and/or agent middlemen in semidirect and indirect channels:

1. The need for specialized knowledge of and contact with specific markets on a widely distributed geographical basis, thus involving a relatively large force of marketing representatives.

2. The inability of many manufacturers, because of financial and manpower reasons, to perform any or all of the marketing task for their product line.

3. The frequent need for guaranteeing products which originate from relatively unknown manufacturing sources.

4. The existence of a "thin" market in the geographic and sales sense. In order to spread the costs of the channel under such conditions, the use of wholesale middlemen handling competing and/or noncompeting lines of products may well be the only satisfactory solution.

5. The existence of a large, widespread market in which customers place frequent orders consisting of many items needing rapid delivery service.

6. The existence of well-known, standardized products requiring less technical and intensive sales arrangements.

7. The existence of large numbers of small buyers who frequently require financial assistance in making purchases.

As a result of the diversity of characteristics and factors affecting the channel structure for manufactured industrial goods, it is true, undoubtedly, that the relative importance of the direct channels has been overstated. Data for 1954 show that the merchant wholesalers group accounted for better than $2 out of every $5 of total gross sales, and that the wholesalers and agent-broker groups combined were just about equal in importance to the manufacturers' sales branches and sales offices group.

For individual kinds of business, however, much wider variations are apparent. Thus, within the limits of census data, sales branches and sales offices apparently accounted for the distribution of all textile mill products (excluding consumers' goods), instruments and related products (excluding tires and tubes), and leather and leather products. They also accounted for above-average percentages in the chemical and metal products groups. On the other hand, the merchant wholesalers' group was very impor-

tant in the wholesale sales of scrap and waste materials, plumbing-heating equipment and supplies, and farm supplies. In addition, they had above-average importance for the machinery equipment and supplies, millwork and construction materials, and paper and allied products kinds of business.

CHANNELS OF DISTRIBUTION— MANUFACTURED CONSUMERS' GOODS

Production Characteristics

It is in this commodity category of channel structure that one finds the greatest diversity of manufacturing units—size ranges, geographical patterns, variety of output, value added, and other measures considered. The producing units range all the way from the numerous individualistic garment manufacturers, with unstable financial structures, unknown brand names, and variable marketing output, to the large, integrated giants. The range of products produced in a single manufacturing plant may consist of one or two to as many as hundreds, especially if the variations in brand names and packages also are considered. The time period of production may range from highly concentrated seasonal periods to an annual cycle.

As to location, the plants producing manufactured consumers' goods range from production-point clusterings, as in the case of meat-slaughtering establishments, to ultimate consumer market orientation, as in the illustrations of bread and bakery products, ice cream, and soft drinks. Every gradation of locational preference is likely to be found, and, once again, the marketing channel structure must reflect an adaptation to these wide ranges. The geographical, chronological, and communication gaps between producers and ultimate consumers create very complex problems for marketing organization.

Commodity Characteristics

The variety of manufactured consumers' goods moving through marketing channels is staggering. No matter which classification scheme is used, it is not difficult to detect sharp increases in the last decade or so in: (a) varieties of products within existing classification categories; (b) identification (brand) names used; (c) varieties of packages for existing categories; and (d) new classification categories. Among other effects, for example, the impact of the foreign automobiles has been the cause to multiply, suddenly and substantially, the buying alternatives. Similarly, the manufacturing of filter-tip cigarettes, together with standard versus king size, and changes in types of packaging are illustrative of explosions in the variety of existing products. On the other hand, the synthetic-fibre and stereophonic-sound-equipment products are examples of new categories which extend existing categories.

In terms of durability, manufactured consumers' goods have a wide range from very perishable to very durable. To many consumers, a loaf of bread has a life of only one to two days, despite the fact that the product may be placed in a deep-freeze unit for use at later dates. On the other hand, a suite of furniture or a rug may last for two or more decades, especially with proper maintenance. Items such as pharmaceuticals may have dosages prescribed which use up the entire amount of the product within a day or a few days. For the various types of durables, there is no comparable notion of dosage.

So far as units of sale are concerned, there exists, once again, a very wide range. Some products are purchased one at a time, whereas others may be purchased by the dozen, bushel, gross, or some similar measure of quantity. Physically, the unit may vary in weight from a single ounce or less to several thousand pounds. The channel structure receives highly unequal impacts from such variations even so far as the delivery function itself is concerned.

Again, extremely wide ranges in unit product values are apparent. Manufactured consumers' goods range in price from fractional cents per unit to thousands of dollars (as in the case of automobiles, motor boats, or jewelry). Even within the same category of product use, sharp variations in unit values are apparent, e.g., perfumes, women's apparel, and jewelry.

Increasingly, the impact of the channel itself is to magnify the importance of packaging for manufactured consumers' goods. Because of over-all physical size some products, such as automobiles, cannot be packaged. In such cases, it is questionable anyway whether or not the package would have any marketing significance. But, in some cases, startling innovations in packaging materials have led, in turn, to startling innovations in prepackaged products. Two examples may be given: the transparent wrappings for meats and certain other manufactured foods, and the cellophane wrappings for men's white shirts which facilitate self-service retailing.

Closely related to, and affected by, the variations in durability noted above is the characteristic of frequency of purchase. Some products, because they are used up physically in the consumption process, have high rates of frequency of purchase, e.g., meats, toothpaste. Other products, as noted, may last for decades. In one case, accordingly, the channel and the middlemen therein devote considerable marketing efforts to maintain their shares or to increase their shares of existing consumption. They attempt, also, to develop new users. In the furniture case, the channel must devote most of its time to selling those persons involved in the formation of new households while the replacement market assumes reduced importance.

Among the more important characteristics affecting channel structure is the factor of relative weight and bulkiness. Manufactured consumers' goods range in physical size and bulk from the very small sewing needle or tablet of medicine to very bulky items such as refrigerators, certain items of furniture, and automobiles. As a result, once again variable combinations will be found of wholesale middlemen selling with and without inventories of merchandise physically present.

Finally, wide ranges are found in the elasticity of demand for manufactured consumers' goods and in the availability of substitutes. The consumers' goods range all the way from vital necessities to complete luxuries, with corresponding effects on the elasticities of demands. In terms of substitutability, the products range from conditions of having hundreds of brands of direct or semidirect substitutes to conditions of no substitutes, as in the case of a rare gem.

Factors Explaining the Variable Importance of Wholesale Middlemen

The complexities of the channel structure for manufactured consumers' goods almost rival those already described for agricultural products. With the exception of the assemblers group, opportunities exist for the use of all types of merchant wholesalers and agent middlemen. All forms of channels from the most simple and direct to the most complicated indirect patterns characterize the flow of manufactured consumers' goods.

The importance of direct channels is limited, relatively, to a few cases of specialty items and to such marketing arrangements as the various types of "of-the-month" clubs. In the case of the specialties, the basis for the direct channel is found in the unique nature of the merchandise coupled, as in the case of Fuller brushes, with a desire to control the complete channel. In the case of the "of-the-month" clubs, in addition to the factor of unique merchandise, there may be offered the features of low prices and the expert advice of a board in selecting each monthly choice.

Of much greater importance are the semi-direct channels. These channels have two distinct structural patterns. The first consists of those manufacturer-controlled channels where, because of the unique nature of the product, of the variety of goods produced, of service, or because of financial considerations, the manufacturers use sales branches and/or sales offices in selling to the various classes of retail customers. In the second form, the retailers, by virtue of backward vertical integration, contact manufacturers directly.

But by far the most important segment of these channel structures consists of the indirect channels. The explanation lies, in part, in the fact that the marketing task to be performed matches very closely the analysis given in explaining the funnel concept of wholesaling and its strategic importance in marketing. This would include the need of many small manufacturers for brokers or selling agents (or their equivalent) in contacting the orthodox wholesaler and other types of merchant wholesalers. Another aspect is to be found, once again, in the close relationship of this particular problem and the importance of the basic marketing processes. A final explanation lies in the complexity of the geographical distribution of retail and ultimate consumers to be reached.

Data exist showing the relative importance of the three types-of-operation groups. On an over-all basis for selected manufactured consumers' goods, the merchant wholesalers had 52 per cent of the gross wholesale sales, whereas the sale branches and sales offices had nearly twice as much of the remaining compared with the agents and brokers group. The merchant wholesalers were very much of above-average importance in the following kinds of business: gift and art goods; jewelry; hardware; beer, wine, distilled spirits; amusements, sporting goods, toys; and tobacco. The kinds of business in which the manufacturers' sales branches and sales offices had above-average sales were: automotive; drugs; electrical appliances, radios, TV sets; books, magazines, newspapers; and tobacco. Finally, the agents and brokers were relatively most important for the dry-goods and apparel groups, and the groceries-confectionery-meats groups.

CHANNELS OF DISTRIBUTION— SERVICES

A discussion of channels of distribution for services opens a field of discussion which has been hardly touched upon in the existing literature.[10] Many of the personal services are either marketed through direct channels from source to user, as in the case of medical, dental, and legal services, or simply involve the use of a retail-type establishment, as in the case of the apparel cleaning, shoe repairing, and barber and beauty shop kinds of business. Some personal services such as motion pictures and baseball require expensive, highly specialized types of establishments. But the discussion here is concerned mainly with other types of channels which involve a much wider range of channel considerations.

Production Characteristics

Most of the types of services being considered here have no concept of production in the ordinary sense in which the term is used for the manufacture of tangible goods. The closest parallel exists in the case of utilities services where there are plants which generate electricity. In most cases, however, the creation of the service is inherent in the professional, semiprofessional, skilled, and unskilled talents of one or more persons. In this sense, also, most of the services cannot be produced in advance of use and stored. The locational aspects of most services becomes, again, a considerably different geographical problem than the location of manufacturing industries.

Commodity Characteristics

Although many services are intangible in and of themselves, they become intertwined, nevertheless, in a particular physical environment. Examples are the institutional aspects of the modern commercial and savings banks, the plush offices of advertising agencies and management consulting firms, and the elaborate facilities of storage and transportation agencies. Most services are highly perishable in the sense that

[10] There are, of course, estimates of expenditures for selected services in the natural income statistics and data for selected services in the *Census of Business.*

the originator cannot, in most instances, store them until they can be marketed. Grading and standardization specifications are nonexistent, and knowledge of quality must depend to a great extent, accordingly, on word-of-mouth promotion. Packaging, at least in the tangible-commodity meaning, is also nonexistent. Pricing and price determination assume far different aspects because of the haziness of what costs are, in most cases, and because of the absence of any systematic price-determining markets.

Factors Explaining the Variable Importance of Wholesale Middlemen

Because of some of the characteristics noted above, it would be expected that the more professional the type of service considered, the greater would be the impact of direct channels of distribution. This is true, however, only where the marketing area is limited or where codes of ethics prevent any widespread use of advertising, as in the legal and medical professions. But in the case of many types of entertainment, various types of management or booking office services exist to establish contracts with the entertainment places used, to publicize the event, to arrange for transportation of the entertainers, and to handle the financial aspects. In the marketing of securities, there do exist organized stock exchanges which rival the organized commodity markets in structure; and within these exchanges there are the important buying and selling brokers.

For the travel industry, including the hotels as well as the transportation agencies, increasing use is being made of travel agents, as well as of the agencies' own controlled sales office, in reaching the wide array of business, government, institutional, and ultimate consumer customers. For such specialized financial problems as one finds in the textile industry, there exist special middlemen known as *factors* who have had a long history of use both in Europe and the United States.[11]

Many services, however, are based either upon individual proprietorship or upon partnership forms of organizations. In such cases, the business must depend upon the ability of its principals to build up a wide, personal acquaint-

anceship with potential users. This is true, for example, of many corporation lawyers, public accounting firms, advertising agencies, and management consulting firms. Advertising, except for the strict limitations noted in the professional services, may be used. Great dependency must be placed upon so servicing customers that a very important word-of-mouth reputation is created. Where these agencies are organized on either partnership or corporate basis, the withdrawal of an execution may involve a considerable diversion of business from the existing firm to a newly created firm. . . .

FACTORS EXPLAINING THE USE OF PARTICULAR CHANNELS BY INDIVIDUAL MANUFACTURERS

Finally, a summary explanation needs to be given of the factors which help to explain the use of particular channels of distribution by individual manufacturers for their products. These factors are divided into basic external considerations and selective internal considerations peculiar to the individual manufacturer. The division, however, is not a hard and fast one, but is meant to be merely suggestive.

Basic External Considerations

These considerations may be subdivided into volume of sales, order, market, product, and channel subclassifications. Volume of sales considerations bring into the channel discussion a marketing research approach: the estimation of total sales potentialities for the product or products to be marketed; the percentage of this estimated total sales which the individual manufacturer can expect to realize, subdivided by product lines and geographic units; and the productivity of various individual channel alternatives in realizing these estimates.

The order characteristics summarize the variables which have been discussed for the various channel patterns. These involve, among other things, the influence of the dollar amount of the average sales order, the relative frequency of ordering, the regularity with which orders are placed, the number of separate product items in each order, and the extent to which solicitation by salesmen may or may not be necessary for repeat sales.

Under market considerations are included all of the pertinent factors explaining the composition of the manufacturers' customers. Included are such factors as: Who are the customers?

---

[11] The modern factors, such as the Walter Heller Company in Chicago, not only purchase a concern's accounts receivable but also frequently offer a quality of professional managerial advice rivaling that of the consulting firms. See the bibliography for appropriate references.

How many are there? What is the geographical distribution? What are their product dislikes and preferences? What type of person influences the purchase? What is the density of distribution? Is it necessary to have personal acquaintanceships in order to make sales?

The product characteristics include the following: (1) Is the product relatively new in the channel or has it an established marketing position? (2) how rapidly does product style or design change? (3) the relative value of the product; (4) the product's weight in relation to such value; (5) the need for promptness in delivery; (6) whether or not technical knowledge is needed for the sale and in installing and servicing the product; (7) the nature and extent of the repair service required, if any; (8) whether or not the product is standardized; and (9) the type of product involved—industrial or consumers' goods.

Finally, increasing attention must be given by the manufacturer to channel characteristics. Pertinent to this analysis is the use of analytical tools and techniques to determine channel costs relative to the functions performed; the effect of channel alternatives on profits; and the attitude of the middlemen in the channel alternatives towards the manufacturer's product or product line.

Internal Considerations

There are, finally, certain selective internal management considerations. One of these considerations involves whether or not the industry, of which the manufacturer is a member, uses orthodox or traditional channel arrangements. If the answer is in the affirmative, then the individual manufacturer must decide whether or not to conform with the industry pattern. In making this decision, he must be guided, in part, by an evaluation of the success achieved by competitors in using nonorthodox channels and, in part, by some of the external considerations.

The manufacturer must consider, also, what functions he needs from the channel; how well his financial and manpower resources will permit him to exercise the degree of channel control he desires; the extent and type of cooperation desired from middlemen in the channel; a critical evaluation of the significant channel trends taking place; and, finally, whether or not there are executive channel preferences or prejudices.

2. Some Observations on "Structural" Formation and the Growth of Marketing Channels*

RALPH F. BREYER

This paper introduces a number of channel definitions and concepts which will aid in any discussion and research on marketing channels. Included are such concepts as trading versus nontrading channels, channel level versus channel segment, type channels, enterprise channels, business-unit channels, single channels, channel groups, channel formation and dissolution, measures of overall channel growth, isolated channels, engineered channels, integrated and mixed channels.

Embedded everywhere in the enormous complex of activities and agreements that characterize the marketing institution is an elemental piece of structure, the so-called marketing channel. In the broadest sense of the term, not only *trading* concerns engaged primarily in selling and buying—producers, wholesalers, retailers, brokers, selling agents, commission houses, etc. —but also *nontrading* concerns engaged principally in other types of marketing activity— commercial banks, transportation and storage companies, insurance companies, and so on— are found in a marketing channel. In this essay, we are concerned only with the trading channel, which consists of various sequences of the former group of "concerns." This channel is, of course, a system, and we shall often refer to it as such. For purposes of this essay, it is sufficient merely to define the term "system" in a broad sense:

"A system is a set of objects together with relationships between the objects and between their attributes."

Being composed of both human beings and machines, the channel is what is often termed a "man-machine" system. This essay is an attempt to answer the following two questions: When does a channel come into existence? What are the more useful indices of overall channel growth? Standing alone, the observations on channel structure presented in this article should help somewhat in the development of more precise concepts than can be used in the study of the marketing channel phenomenon.[1]

To qualify as a channel in this essay, the vertical sequence of trading concerns must bridge the *entire* gap between production and the consumer.[2] The vertical positions of the trading concerns are referred to as "levels"—the producer level, the broker level, the wholesaler

• SOURCE: Ralph F. Breyer, "Some Observations on Structural Formation and the Growth of Marketing Channels," in Cox, Alderson, Shapiro (editors), *Theory in Marketing* (Homewood, Ill.: Richard D. Irwin, Second Series, 1964) pp. 163–175. Ralph F. Breyer, Professor of Marketing Wharton School, University of Pennsylvania
* This essay is part of a study of marketing channels conducted under a grant of Ford Foundation research funds made available to the author by the Wharton School.

[1] This monograph summarizes one part of a broader study of marketing channels which has not yet been completed. In the context of the entire study, the material presented here should take on more meaning and value.
[2] This phrase sounds somewhat "clumsy." If we changed it to "production and consumption," it would literally mean that marketing is carried on right up to the actual time and place of consuming the goods, which is, of course, rarely true. On the other hand, "producer and consumer" fails to indicate specifically that marketing starts *after* production is completed. However, when speaking of channel structure, we are generally dealing with trading *concerns* and shall hereafter use the phrase "producer and consumer" in a sense synonymous with "production and consumer."

level, etc. Any vertical section short of the entire length of the channel is termed a "segment"— producer-to-wholesaler, or wholesaler-to-retailer, or producer-to-wholesaler-to-retailer, and so on. Upon occasion, we shall refer to "type" channels, "enterprise" channels, and "business-unit" (often shortened to "unit") channels. The first is a channel identified solely by *types* of concerns, such as manufacturers, brokers, wholesalers, and retailers; the second, by specific independent *ownerships*, termed enterprises. The business-unit channel is defined in terms of each separately named and/or spatially separated *operating unit* of a trading concern (or enterprise). Thus, two trading businesses under *one* ownership, even though located at the same place, would each constitute a "business-unit" in a channel if they operated under different trade names. A branch warehouse located at some point other than the headquarters of the parent trading concern would also constitute a separate business unit.[3]

The need for the "business-unit" concept is most obvious in a completely integrated trading channel. Although such a channel is composed of but one enterprise and would be represented as a $P-C$ channel, the goods may actually be "moved"[4] from the producer's plant to one of its wholesale warehouses and then to one of its retail stores and finally to the consumer. Obviously, in structural terms, the $P-C$ designation is entirely inadequate, as it does not show those business units owned by the producer that are operated at the wholesale and retail levels. In terms of business units, the channel is a $P-W_p-R_p-C$ channel, the subscripts indicating ownership by the producer in this case. Where only partial structural integration exists, as, for example, a warehouse owned by a retailer that received all shipments from producers, the enterprise channel concept should be expressed by $P-R-C$, but structurally, the channel should be represented by $P-W_R-R-C$. Although, strictly speaking, a channel so structured is a hybrid containing enterprise and business-unit elements, it will be termed a "business-unit channel" as long as it contains at least one business unit. The term "trading concern" or "concern" can refer to a nonintegrated ownership such as

---

[3] Even though this branch house did no selling but merely received, stored, and shipped the goods, it would still be considered part of the *trading* channel, because it is an integral part of the *trading* concern.
[4] The term "moved" is employed here as a synonym of "marketed" and is *not* restricted to physical movement of the merchandise.

P in the channel immediately above, or to the concern R which also owns the warehouse W_R, or to the business unit W_R itself, or to all collectively, depending upon the context.

For the time being, we shall ignore the "type" channel and assume that the enterprise and business-unit channel happen to be identical. Therefore, we will deal with them as one channel. Usually, we shall use the $P-W-R-C$ channel (producer to wholesaler to retailer to consumer) for illustrative purposes.

A trading channel is formed when trading relations making possible the passage of title and/or possession (usually both) of goods from the producer to the ultimate consumer is consummated by the component trading concerns of the system. Let us assume that producer P_1 franchises or agrees to permit a wholesaler, W_1, to handle his product, and W_1, in turn, franchises or agrees to permit a retailer, R_1, to retail this same product. A trading channel exists once the terms of the franchises or agreements spanning the whole gap from producer to consumer are concluded between concerns assumed to possess the necessary marketing capabilities. Theoretically, not a single unit of the product(s) may be actually marketed by this specific sequence of trading concerns. Nevertheless, in a practical and important sense a channel was formed, since the capacity to "move" the product(s) was brought into being by establishing the requisite trading relations between competent concerns. Except for certain industrial goods, such explicit agreements between the retailer and the *consumer* at the terminal segment of a channel are rare.

Let us now assume that a dealer, R_1, receives an order from an industrial consumer for an industrial product manufactured by P_1; a product R_1 has never handled before. Knowing that he cannot deal directly with P_1, R_1 contracts to buy the product from a wholesale distributor, W_1, who also has not handled this product before. W_1 then contracts to purchase it from P_1. As soon as these contracts (orders) are consummated, including the contract (order) between R_1 and the consumer, a trading channel has been formed even though the parties had never traded with one another before and a set of trading relations was not explicitly agreed upon. In this case, the channel system was initiated by the closing of contracts containing firm orders to buy certain amounts of specific goods. This is true even though the product may not actually move through the channel and no passage of title may occur for six months, because the product must be manufactured to order. Although there is no explicit agreement upon trading relations, the establishment of such relations is implicit in the act of entering into sales-purchase contracts.[5]

The two illustrations provided involve channel formation, because the *intent* is that goods shall move. In the example given in the prior paragraph, suppose that the parties had already established trading relations and were trading in *other* goods under these "agreements." Could we say then that the trading channel for the *new* product already exists? If the *new* product does not require any changes in those trading-relation agreements, we would say "yes." If it does require such alterations, the answer is "no." In any case, one must recognize that although explicitly established trading relations may cover a group of products, a separate and distinct channel exists for each product that actually flows down this particular sequence of trading concerns. In this sense, a new channel is formed *productwise* when a new product moves through an established sequence.[6] A channel is formed, of course, wherever a single product or group of products moves through a new combination of trading concerns. This is true even where the goods are merely consigned or leased at various stages of the channel.

INDIVIDUAL CHANNEL FORMATION

Individual channels usually exist as components of a channel group. Such a group is characterized by a network of trading interconnections which link the trading concerns or units of the group. A single new trading-relation agreement is sufficient to establish at least one new channel in such a channel group. To avoid getting bogged down at this stage with the intricacies of channel groups, we shall first take up the *single* channel. A single channel is one that has but one trading concern or trading unit at each level. At times, we shall talk of this channel as if it were "isolated" or "free-standing" rather than one of the constituent channels of a channel group. The "isolated" single channel is defined as one with trading concerns or units that

trade *only* with one another. Having finished with the single channel, we will then move on to the channel *group* (network), treated as a given, integrated, "structured" system of which the single channel is a mere subsystem. To qualify as a channel *group*, at least one trading concern or trading unit must have established trading relations with a minimum of two other trading concerns or units operating on the same level. (Whether we should include the consumer, who is, of course, a part of the channel, in these formulations is optional. For some industrial products it may be worthwhile or even imperative. In this essay, unless otherwise stated, the consumer is excluded from the channel in all subsequent discussions.)

One can maintain that a channel exists when and only so long as goods actually flow. It appears more useful, however, to view a channel system as being formed as soon as new trading relations are established and as continuing to exist so long as these trading relations hold.[7] The actual flow of a product through a channel is almost always intermittent. This is true even for large groups of products that are highly seasonal. If we insisted upon an actual flow of goods, we should, strictly speaking, have to accept the view that the channel is dissolved during even brief periods of a few days when no product(s) move through all or part of the channel and, conversely, a new channel is born on each resumption of the flow. Or, less strictly interpreted, such a requirement would compel us to stipulate the maximum time interval of the intermittency permitted before the channel would be classified as having dissolved. This would perforce be a rather arbitrary decision. On the other hand, we must consider the situation where agreements on trading relations continue in force but no goods have "moved" through the channel for an abnormally long period of time. In such case, we might term this a "passive channel system" in contrast to an "active channel system" where intermittency in goods flow is "reasonable" or "normal." When one of the trading concerns of a channel stops handling the product(s), such action, of course, dissolves the channel.

The formation and dissolution of marketing channel systems is a ubiquitous phenomenon which we shall examine first under the assumption that we have a reasonably large, fixed pattern of trading concern, that is, a large fixed

---

[5] At times, the goods may be consigned to a trading unit or leased to a consumer. In such cases, sale purchase contracts of the product per se may never materialize (i.e., lease without purchase option) or are delayed (i.e., consignment sale or lease with purchase option). Here, explicit agreement on trading relations is almost always required.
[6] A further discussion of this situation is found in the following section.

[7] Here, the term "channel system" refers to a single channel, either "isolated" or a constituent of a channel group.

number of producers, of wholesalers, and of retailers available for a $P-W-R-C$ channel structure. We can discern at once at least three different situations. In a highly flexible situation, the trading concerns can and readily do switch their sources of supply or their outlets with minimum inconvenience and cost. If one resource or outlet is readily substituted, such action destroys one channel and creates a second. If a resource or outlet is added or dropped without substitution, there is a net gain (or loss) of one channel. A very considerable part of all consumer-goods marketing, especially that of low unit value, constant demand items, is characterized by flexible trading relations with changes in suppliers and outlets comparatively frequent and widespread.

In contrast to the situation just discussed above is one where more or less continuing trading relations prevail over a considerable period of time. Such stability may be due to true, in contrast to pseudo, franchise arrangements and exclusive distribution agreements. If such arrangements do not embrace the entire channel, they still leave much flexibility for channel formation or dissolution in the remaining segments. But where such agreements exist, the qualifications of both outlet and supplier are carefully examined in advance; fairly detailed stipulations are usually set forth in a written agreement; and substantial commitments respecting selling methods, advertising, service, merchandising help, etc., are made. These tend to cement the relationship more firmly so that dissolution of the channel by abrogation of the agreement is less easily accomplished, and channel formation is generally a slower process. In any case, many such contracts require thirty to ninety days' notice of an intention to cancel.

Finally, only a qualified flexibility respecting channel formation and dissolution exists in the fully integrated channel where production, wholesaling, and retailing units are all owned by one concern.[8] Such complete integration involves a very considerable investment. A large organization must be developed, and great control exercised throughout the length of the channel. Consequently, the substitution of an outside, independently owned, trading concern for one of the owner's own units is much less likely.

[8] If the producer's plant cannot or does not supply all the goods handled by its wholesale and retail units, then so far as these goods are concerned, the channel is not fully integrated and hence considerable flexibility may exist.

In this case, as well as where only part of the channel is integrated, the enterprise channel, contrary to our prior stipulation, does differ from the business-unit channel. There is some degree of flexibility in adding or dropping certain of the *business units* owned by any one concern, and such action *could* result in the formation and dissolution of *business-unit* channels. However, since changes in the business-unit channel require considerable investment (or, conversely, the liquidation of a sizeable investment with some possibility of loss), the degree of flexibility in an integrated channel will be rather low, unless the owning agency is supported by considerable financial resources. Where only certain segments of the channel are integrated, the other segments are free of the constraints previously mentioned.

It should be emphasized here that "flexibility" has been used to refer primarily to the ease with which channels are formed and dissolved. Although it is usually the case, such of the channels that exist where conditions are highly flexible may not be of shorter life than those established under less flexible conditions.

For a marketing channel to exist, there generally must be at some time a flow of goods from producer to consumer. "Goods" may mean just one product or several products taken together. In its ultimate sense, the channel concept should be centered on the *single* product. Where several different products flow through the same set of trading concerns, there are an equal number of separate channels productwise. Also, each new product that is introduced creates a new channel productwise, even though no new trading relations are explicitly established. Similarly, the dropping of one product dissolves at least one channel productwise. This view of a channel is justified by the following factors: consumers and traders buy *individual* products; different products may possess markedly different marketing characteristics (selling, merchandising, servicing, pricing, costs, etc.); and individual product identification by such factors as brand or trademark constitutes the nucleus for a unique pattern of competitive effort, even though there will be many other aspects of competition between products.

We have previously assumed that the trading-concern population is fixed in size and pattern. In reality, however, some trading concerns are always going out of business and others entering. With the advent of one new trading concern—manufacturer, wholesaler, or retailer in our $P-W-R-C$ structure—at least one and almost always a considerable number of new channels are formed. Conversely, one or more channels are destroyed as each concern exists. Thus, new concerns and new products are great channel multipliers, with the number of channels increasing much faster than the number of firms or products.

Let us now turn to the "type" channel and contrast it with the enterprise and business-unit channels previously considered. As soon as a new *type* of trading concern enters a given marketing sector, at least one and perhaps several new "type" channels are created. The proliferation of new "type" channels resulting from the development of a new type of marketing agency is, however, much more limited than the increase in enterprise and unit channels that occurs when a new trading concern or trading unit makes its appearance. "Type" channels may range from broad to narrow, depending upon the "type" classification under which the trading concerns are grouped. The *P–W–R–C* channel is obviously very broad as *all* of the varying kinds of pertinent producers are included in *P*, all wholesalers in *W*, all retailers in *R*, and all consumers in *C*. On the other hand, a *multiple-line* manufacturer to a *full-line, full-service* wholesaler to a *limited-line, limited-service* dealer to the consumer would be a much narrower "type" channel. "Types" could be based on the distinctive product or product group handled—an *automobile* manufacturer, a *grocery* wholesaler, a *lumber* dealer—but since we generally have a certain product or product group in mind when analyzing channels, such classification comes into the picture automatically. Even so, where product-mix problems at various levels in the channel are important, the "product" classification is inadequate because such mixes may vary widely within any one such classification.[9]

"Type" channel systems are hardy, and often compete sharply with one another. In this struggle, some wax, others wane, and the "type" channels which fall in either category may vary from one sector of marketing to another. But it is rather seldom that the "type" channel, especially those based on the broader "type" classifications, go out of existence altogether. Also, the formation of a new "type" channel is a rather infrequent occurrence. Such changes of

"type" channels are of much greater consequence than the formation and dissolution of enterprise and business-unit channels, because of the direct effect on a large train of individual trading concerns.

MEASURES OF OVERALL GROWTH FOR THE INDIVIDUAL CHANNEL

Perhaps the best measure of overall growth or decline of a marketing channel (or channel group) could be developed from some kind of sophisticated input-output analysis. Such an analysis is a complex and time-consuming undertaking. What we need at the moment is a more readily computed measure of overall growth. The two best measures appear to be (a) the physical units of product "moved" through the channel and (b) the dollar spread of the channel for a given time period. Both are at best approximate and are none too satisfactory measures. The physical unit measures the "put-through" of the channel system, as that term is generally used in engineering. Such a measure has the advantage of eliminating price fluctuations. But where the channel handles several products with varying characteristics, it may be impossible to devise a single unit of measure. Moreover, such a measure would not take into account material changes from year to year in the total "service delivered"[10] by the channel for its customer, the consumer. These services, for example, include such factors as product warranties, consumer credit extension, lessening of "outs" at the retail level (which may well require producer and/or wholesaler cooperation), etc.[11]

The dollar spread of the channel should reflect such "service" changes. It would be computed by subtracting from the *retail* dollar volume of the channel—a figure which is the same as the total sales of the retailer R_1—the production costs of the producer P_1 plus the net

---

[9] "Sorting" concepts, originally developed by Wroe Alderson, are very important in this connection. See Wroe Alderson, *Marketing Behavior and Executive Action* (Homewood, Ill.: Richard D. Irwin, 1957), Chap. vii, "Matching and Sorting—The Logic of Exchange."

[10] The phrase "service delivered" constitutes *all* of the marketing services performed in getting the goods from producer to consumer. It includes that done by the *nontrading* agencies, even though they are not part of the *trading* channel. The justification for this interpretation is that it is the *trading* channel (or more accurately, the individual *trading* concerns that compose it) that authorizes and pays for such "nontrading" marketing work.

[11] Variations of service extended by the trading concerns to one another are not relevant, as these merely involve alterations in allocation of such services among the traders. It is true that such reallocations may bring about lower cost, but this is not at the moment a pertinent issue.

profits of the producer allocable to production in contrast to marketing. This subtrahend is here termed "production takeout." The allocation of net profit to production would admittedly be quite arbitrary. Perhaps the best method would be to allocate it in the ratio which direct production costs bore to direct marketing costs. This would avoid the difficult task of apportioning overhead between production and marketing. To cancel out the effects of price changes, appropriate deflators would have to be used.

Let us assume retail dollar volume could not be obtained directly, a condition which is much more likely to prevail when channel groups rather than single, isolated channels are studied. One might then derive the retail dollar volume figure by using producer dollar sales volume with wholesaler and retailer margins expressed as percentages of the producer sales dollar; or, if more convenient, by using the wholesaler dollar sales volume and the retailer margin expressed as a percentage of it. Having established the dollar spread figure for the channel, one can compute both absolute and relative growth of the channel. Should relative growth alone be desired, the retail dollar volume alone could be used with the assumption that the percentage which the "production takeout" bore to the retail dollar volume remained the same from year to year.[12]

In all of these computations of channel growth, adjustments would have to be made for any differences in inventories at each level of the channel at the beginning and at the end of the period.

CHANNEL GROUP FORMATION

Only one factor justifies the attention given to the single, *isolated* channel, a phenomenon almost nonexistent in practice. Knowledge of such a channel is helpful in understanding certain "structural" features of those multiple-channel networks of marketing which were previously termed channel-group systems. Single channels do, of course, exist in practice but as components of a channel group. In fact, we can view a channel group as being made up of a collection of individual channels. These single channels, however, are not isolated because each one of their trading concerns has trade dealings

with two or more concerns within the given channel group, and often with outside concerns as well. If channel members deal solely with other trading concerns *within* the given channel group, that channel group is then an "isolated" one. Such "isolated" channel groups exist, and some are very important. The channel group that handles the domestic distribution (and this study is confined to domestic marketing) of the automobiles of one domestic manufacturer is, for example, an isolated one, although with the advent of foreign-made cars this situation is rapidly disappearing.

The channel group is obviously more than a mere collection of individual channels. It is in the nature of a network, the structural configurations of which are well known. The formation of the single, isolated channel is structurally defined in the sense that as soon as the requisite trading relations between the full complement of trading concerns spanning the gap from producer to consumer has been consummated, the channel is formed. By definition, no trading concerns or units may be added or subtracted. But for the channel *group* there is no such definite and fixed point marking the completion of its formation. The channel group configurations that merit analysis are generally the resultant of the interplay of the interests of the various trading concerns embraced by the group. Hence, we would generally "set up" a channel group for study by establishing the interests of one or another trading concern or the common interest of a group of trading concerns as the central focus of the study, such as the interest of a particular producer, or wholesaler, or retailer, or of a certain group of producers making a certain product, or of a group of producers, wholesalers, and retailers all of whom are members of a joint product certification program. The identification of this central focus of interest serves to map the pertinent channel group. The primary interest of a sizeable producer is to establish that network of channels[13] for the marketing of his product(s) which will most effectively exploit the ultimate potential markets and at the same time promise him maximum long-run profits.[14] But for almost any product, qualitative, quantitative, and geographic changes in market-demand patterns, product innovations, entrepreneurial innovations (new types of trading concerns), etc., continually occur. This causes a constant flux

---

[12] In fact, if "production takeout" percentage and all margin percentages downstream remained the same, one could use the producer dollar volume or wholesaler dollar volume figure alone for the computation of *relative* growth (or decline).

[13] See, however, the second following paragraph.
[14] Assuming, for simplicity's sake, that this is his only objective, which is rarely true.

in the channel composition of the group as it responds to such alterations.

A producer who seeks 100% distribution makes practically no effort to shape his channel-group structure. Instead, he tries to "pump" his product(s) through whatever channels he can with the hope that nearly all potential ones will finally take on the product(s). The configuration of such a channel group will be highly sensitive to changes in such factors as market conditions and competitive tactics. With the possible exception of some staple manufactured products, such channel groups will exhibit a relatively high degree of instability. Agricultural staples are marketed through highly unstable channel groups. The same holds true for manufactured products sold through agents at some stage in their flow down the channels of the group. If the channel group is a $P-B-W-R-C$ one, and B represents brokers, then the channel configuration will probably be very unstable, as the producers make successive offerings and brokers sell now to certain wholesalers, now to others. A channel is formed every time a wholesaler buys for the first time. When wholesalers who previously purchased refuse to buy, a channel is dissolved if the period of intermittency of purchase is "unreasonably" long.

Very often, however, producers of branded and vigorously promoted items will select the channel group that handles their product(s) with great care and exercise some degree of control over the different trading concerns. Broad gauge marketing policies, objectives, and plans are developed, and an attempt is made to fashion the channel group accordingly. Such "engineered" channel groups are found especially where selective or exclusive distribution policies are followed. In such instances, the formation of the channel group is a comparatively well thought-out and carefully applied process. In this process, however, emphasis is not usually centered as much on *channel* formation as on the individual trading concerns or units to be included. This is true because the trading concern or trading unit is the primary "activating" unit and possesses a closely knit specialized organization with central direction and control. Also, each such concern or unit generally constitutes a common center used by a large number of individual constituent channels of the given channel group. Moreover, as will be made clear in a subsequent paragraph, a trading concern or unit is at times only *directly* interested in its *immediate* sources of supply and its *immediate* customers. If the producer decides to add or

drop such an individual concern, then *ipso facto* at least one and usually several channels are respectively formed or dissolved. Of course, there are times when unauthorized trading concerns get hold of the producer's product(s), in which case the channel so formed might be termed a "bastard channel." In varying degrees and at varying times, wholesalers and retailers also attempt *full-span* "engineering" of their channel group.

MEASURES OF OVERALL GROWTH FOR THE CHANNEL GROUP

As was true for the single, isolated channel, the most useful measures of overall growth of the channel group are the number of physical units of product(s) put through the channel group and the dollar spread for the channel group. Adaptations and cautions similar to those expressed for the single, isolated channel are also relevant. The application of either of these measures to the channel group is generally more complicated than their application to the single, isolated channel. Usually, a number of the trading concerns in such a group will also be dealing with outside trading concerns. Such dealings must be excluded from the computations, because only those goods which "moved" through channels, all of whose trading concerns are a part of the group, can be considered in measuring that channel group's put-through. Consequently, the nonisolated channel-group measurement of growth would require considerable product coding and many separate records. Even in an isolated channel group, where none of the trading concerns deal with concerns outside the group, if the retail dollar volume figures required for computing dollar channel spread by the use of relative margins is to be derived, such margins would need to be properly weighted. In any case, the considerable differences in growth or decline generally present in the various parts of the channel group would be lost in the *overall* measure for the group. Hence, a great deal of "subgroup" or "subsystem" analysis would be required.[15]

The number of consumers served by the channel group, the types of consumers served, the geographical area of the consumer market, the number of products handled, the number of

[15] See, for example, Reavis Cox and Charles S. Goodman, "Marketing of Housebuilding Materials," *Journal of Marketing*, July, 1956, pp. 36–61. In this original study, the authors develop seven measures of work done in each marketing "flow."

trading concerns in the group, and the number of constituent channels in the group have but limited usefulness as measures of overall channel-group growth.[16] Contrary to appearances, it is not easy to use the number of products handled as a measure of growth. All parts of the channel group may not handle each and every product, and the number of items not universally carried may fluctuate from time to time.

The number of individual constituent channels and the number of trading concerns and/or trading units are two possible measures of growth that would not apply to the single channel. However, both have very little usefulness, as they give ambiguous measures of channel-group growth. For instance, an increase in the number of constituent channels might be caused by the following factors: an increase in the interconnections between the same number of trading concerns handling the same products; an increase in the number of products handled by all or part of the channel group; or an increase in trading concerns or units. Also, growth in the number of trading concerns or units in a channel group may or may not mean an increase in the volume handled or on increased number of constituent channels.

To measure the growth of the individual constituent channels of a channel group would seldom be worthwhile. It would always be more difficult than measuring the growth of single, isolated channels. Products are not easily traced through the many channel routes that tie into *each* trading concern or trading unit. Moreover, a specific trading concern, especially in the non-integrated channel group, usually has little direct interest in the growth or decline of each specific channel of which it is a part. Its attention is rarely focused beyond its immediate supplier upstream and its immediate outlet downstream. As stated before, however, the measurement of growth by subgroups of channels of a channel group, based on "type" of

channel, product(s) handled, geographic areas, etc., might well be worthwhile.[17]

A complicating factor in all cases are the changes that occur over time in the composition of the channel group. Some trading concerns drop out and others come into the group. Consequently, the year-to-year measures of growth or decline are not made with reference to an identical channel-group structure. Even where the set of trading concerns remains the same, the pattern of the interconnections between them, i.e., the individual constituent channel pattern, may be altered. This is especially true for those groups where freedom and ease in changing connections are not restricted by selective or exclusive distribution arrangements.

INTEGRATED AND MIXED CHANNEL GROUPS

The formation of fully integrated channel groups is, of course, completely controlled by the single ownership. Although the constituent business units may have limited freedom in determining with whom they will deal, all changes in the structure are dictated by the owner. The channel structure pattern of such a group is comparatively stable. The same measures of growth would apply to it as apply to nonintegrated groups and could probably be computed with less difficulty, because the records kept by the owner would cover the entire channel group. Much the same can be said for the integrated portions of partially integrated channel groups.

Finally, a channel group, unlike the one used for illustrative purposes, may be composed of two or more types of channels. Such a group has already been termed "mixed." A channel group with a mixed structure will be more adaptable to the requirements of varying marketing situations. In addition, it is generally known that some of the most severe competition in marketing occurs between the various types of channel groups. Much the same situation with respect to formation and growth exists for the "mixed" and the "simple" (one-type) channel group.

[16] The author developed a method for establishing such costs for channels and channel groups in his study "Quantitative Systemic Analysis and Control: Study No. 1—Channel and Channel Group Costing," 1949, although his purpose at the time was not the use of such costs for measuring growth.

[17] Here, the channel group is a "mixed" one in that it contains more than one type of channel, such as a channel group with both P–W–R–C and P–R–C types.

3. Are Channels of Distribution
What the Textbooks Say?

PHILLIP McVEY

McVey maintains that the role of the middleman is obscured by oversimplfiied treatment in marketing literature and census data. In this article he examines channel-building from the standpoint of the middleman's relative freedom to make choices, while serving as a purchasing agent for his customers.

Perhaps Wroe Alderson said as much as is safe to say when he described a marketing channel as a group of firms which "constitute a loose coalition engaged in exploiting joint opportunity in the market."[1]

THEORY AND ACTUALITY

Certainly too much is said about channel relationships in many published textbooks for businessmen and students, if one is to look for proof in current marketing practice. The picture usually given is one of long lists of various types of middlemen and facilitating agencies, which differ minutely but precisely in functions performed. Alignments of particular types are presented as "right" or "customary" for a given commodity or type of producer. Furthermore, it is often implied that it is the producer who selects all the links in the channel and establishes the working arrangements with them, down to and including the outlet which sells his goods to the final user.

Several popular college textbooks in marketing illustrate this manufacturer-oriented ap-

proach to channel planning.[2] One reason for fairly standard treatment of channel-building is that the growth of marketing knowledge has proceeded from a description of the activities of existing business firms, leaning heavily on data provided by the U.S. Censuses of Wholesale and Retail Trade. The framework appears orderly and well planned. But little recognition is given to the probability that some channel sequences "just grew" like Topsy, without direction or intent of known parents.

The Census method of counting, whereby each separate establishment is assigned to a single traditional category on the basis of a *major-portion-of-dollar-volume* rule, tends to produce more orderliness in the picture than probably exists. It tends to obscure a great deal of "promiscuous distribution" and channel-jumping. The Census rule, like the Procrustean bed of Greek mythology, effectively reduces the number of categories into which firms are sorted, and avoids hybrid, nondescript classifications.

Yet hybridity is too common among marketing firms to be ignored. For example, almost any wholesaler will do some business at retail; similarly, it is not uncommon for a broker to find

• SOURCE: From *Journal of Marketing*, vol. 24, January, 1960, pp. 61–65. Phillip McVey: Associate Professor of Marketing, University of Nebraska.
[1] Wroe Alderson, "The Development of Marketing Channels," in Richard M. Clewett (editor), *Marketing Channels for Manufactured Products* (Homewood, Illinois: Richard D. Irwin, 1954), p. 30.

[2] Examples are found in: T. N. Beckman, H. H. Maynard, and W. R. Davidson, *Principles of Marketing*, sixth edition (New York: The Ronald Press Company, 1957), pp. 44–45. C. F. Phillips and D. J. Duncan, *Marketing Principles and Methods*, third edition (Homewood, Illinois: Richard D. Irwin, 1956), p. 562. M. P. McNair, M. P. Brown, D. S. R. Leighton, and W. B. England, *Problems in Marketing*, second edition (New York, McGraw-Hill, 1957), p. 66.

himself holding title to a given lot of goods, thus becoming temporarily a merchant middleman. A realistic classification may require the use of relative terms to identify types of operation, according to a range of variables—for example, the *degree* to which a firm caters to a given customer group, or the *frequency* with which a function is performed.

Further study of marketing textbooks may lead a reader to conclude that: (a) middlemen of many types are available to any manufacturer in any market to which he wishes to sell, and within each type there is an ample selection of individual firms; (b) the manufacturer habitually controls the selection and operation of individual firms in his channel; and (c) middlemen respond willingly as *selling agents* for the manufacturer rather than as *purchasing agents* for a coveted group of customers to whom the middlemen sell.

Yet none of these conclusions is entirely valid.

In a product line such as fashion apparel, a garment maker may have an extremely limited choice of types of middlemen: the selling agent, the broker, the direct-buying retailer, or the chain store buying office. The general absence of service wholesalers from this line of trade is not correctible by manufacturers' *fiat*.

In a particular market area, the choice may be even more limited. Of individual firms of a given type, there may be no choice at all. These limitations arise, of course, because of the free choices made by the middlemen as to locations, customer groups, and product assortments they elect to sell.

IS THE "CHANNEL" AN ACADEMIC CONCEPT?

Integrated action up and down a channel is a rare luxury in marketing. Why? It may be that the "channel of distribution" is a concept that is principally academic in usage and unfamiliar to many firms selling to and through these channels.

Instead of a channel, a businessman is likely to concern himself merely with suppliers and customers. His dealings are not with all of the links in the channel but only with those immediately adjacent to him, from which he buys and to which he sells. He may little know nor care what becomes of his products after they leave the hands of some merchant middleman who has paid him for them and released him to return to problems involving his special functions. A manufacturer may not even consider himself

as standing at the head of a channel, but only as occupying a link in a channel that begins with his suppliers.

Policies

Choice of a channel is not open to any firm unless it has considerable freedom of action in matters of marketing policy. Other areas of policy seem to be treated with more respect. For example, it is well recognized that a *price* policy is an authoritarian privilege open only to those sellers who possess power to withhold goods from the market in considerable quantities, or who have the choice of alternative markets and the means to solicit them. Usually a differentiated product is necessary. Therefore, a wheat farmer can seldom have anything resembling a price policy.

Likewise, a *design* policy is meaningful only when variations in product characteristics have been understood and accepted by customers to be of significance. Manufacturers of semi-finished or component parts, or of textile "gray goods" cannot enjoy this luxury in most cases.

Similarly, the selection of a multi-stage channel is not the prerogative of a manufacturer unless his franchise is coveted by the middlemen he seeks, as being more valuable to them than their franchise would be to him.

Names such as Sears, Roebuck & Company, Macys, or Kroger mean a great deal more to the customers of these retailers than do the brand names of most of the items sold in their stores. These firms control the channels for many products, even to the point of bringing into existence some manufacturing firms needed to fill gaps in their assortments. In the same manner some national wholesalers, holding the reins of a huge distributive system, are more powerful than either their suppliers or their customers. In such extreme cases the power position is obvious. The big company, regardless of its position in the channel, tries to make its plans and policies effective by taking the initiative for co-ordinated action.

UNCERTAINTY AMONG SMALLER FIRMS

As to the many thousands of middle-size and small companies that truly characterize American marketing, the power position is speculative, vacillating, and ephemeral. Strength in certain market areas, the temporary success of a product, ability to perform a certain needed type of financing or promotional effort—these and similar factors enable companies to assume power.

On the other hand, financial reverses, an unfortunate sales campaign, or even the lack of accurate market news—these factors can shift power elsewhere, possibly to another link in the channel or to another firm in the same link. In any case, the opportunity of any firm is contingent upon the willingness of others to use it as a link in the channel.

Comparison with Advertising Media

Selection of middlemen has been likened to the selection of advertising media. In both instances the task is to find a vehicle which has an existing coverage (or circulation) which coincides with the market desired. A region blanketed with a neat mosaic of distributors' territories will appear on a map much like the same region covered by television stations.

However, there is an important difference. Seldom does an advertising medium restrict its availability. The advertiser's product need not be sold first to the medium on the grounds of self-interest. Only occasionally will a middleman accept any product he is offered. The requirement that he invest his own money and effort forces him to be selective in terms of probable outcome or profit. No seller can afford to neglect the task of selling *to* the middlemen he seeks, as well as *through* them. Nearly every comprehensive campaign of consumer advertising allots substantial effort to dealer promotion and distributor promotion. Indeed, much consumer advertising is undertaken primarily for the stimulating effect it will have upon middlemen.

Middlemen's Reactions

Middlemen's reactions to new-product offerings probably deserve more attention from manufacturers than usual. Wholesalers and retailers, as well as agent middlemen, enjoy an excellent position from which to make keen judgments of a product's probable successes within local markets. Free from the manufacturer's proclivity to "fall in love with the product," but not primarily concerned with its ultimate usage characteristics, middlemen who are alert merchandisers can look at the product with an eye to salability alone.

Yet it is common practice for manufacturers to force acceptance with a heavy barrage of consumer advertising, introductory high-markup offers, free merchandise, combination deals, co-operative advertising schemes, and the like. These may have the effect of "mesmerizing" middlemen, and of clouding the issue of the product's own rate of initial acceptance.

Lack of effective vertical communication in most channels is a serious deterrent. Possibly no other proof of the weakness of manufacturers' control over channels is so convincing as their inability to obtain facts from their own ultimate and intermediate markets. Information that could be used in product development, pricing, packaging, or promotion-planning is buried in non-standard records of middlemen, and sometimes purposely secreted from suppliers.

Channels research is one of the most frustrating areas of marketing investigation, since it requires access to data collected by firms which are independent, remotely situated, and suspicious. Unless given incentive to do so, middlemen will not maintain separate sales records by brands sold. Extracting the needed figures by preferred units of measure is often a hopeless task. To get such data, one producer of pipe tools adopted a device commonly used with electric appliances: a "warranty registration" questionnaire attached to the tools. Ostensibly designed to validate users' damage claims, its true purpose was to discover where, when, how, and by whom the tools had been sold.

Communication downward from the manufacturer is also faulty, placing in doubt the claim that all links in the channel are bound together by common objectives. For example, it is seldom practical to disclose a forthcoming promotional plan in all its details and to ask the middlemen whether the plan will be timely, acceptable, and supportable by their efforts. To do so would jeopardize the advantage of surprise, usually a significant competitive stratagem. Yet the value of synchronized, coordinated action on any new plan by all firms in the channel is obvious.

MIDDLEMEN'S VIEWS

Channel Building

To the extent that any middleman can do so, he should think of himself primarily as a purchasing agent for his customers, and only secondarily as a selling agent for his suppliers. The planning of his product line will proceed from an analysis of a finite customer group in which he is interested . . . to the selection of goods capable of satisfying those needs . . . and then to the choice of available suppliers who can provide those goods. Of course, he may actually begin his assortment with one or more basic products, chosen by him as a way of defining the area of customer needs in which he elects to deal.

From that point on, however, his chief stock in trade becomes not the franchises of important suppliers, but rather his customer group. He is interested in selling any product which these customers desire to buy from him. The attractiveness of any new offering by a supplier is not to be judged by the size of the markup or commission, nor the unusual nature of the product, nor details of its manufacture, nor the promises of manufacturer's advertising support.

The key question is: Does it fit the line? That is, does it complement the other products that he sells, in terms of salability to precisely the same group of buyers? His list of customers is probably less subject to intentional revision than are many other aspects of his business. Is it not at this point, then, that channel building starts?

Some unusual product combinations may result from this approach. A manufacturers' agent selling baby garments in the Southwest took on a line of printed business forms, which the small retailers on whom he called were seeking. An Omaha wholesaler successfully added grocery products to his liquor business. A Cleveland distributor of welding equipment rejected a portable farm welder offered by his principal supplier, since he had no contact with farmers, but was interested in carrying a line of warehouse tractors and lift trucks.

Approach to New Prospects

In some cases a middleman may deem it worth-while to shift from his current customer group to a new list of prospects, in order to find a market for a particularly promising new product. In the main, however, he will not do so. His approach to new prospects is based on their close similarity to those now on his customer list. To all these persons he attempts to become known as a helpful specialist in a well-defined set of recurring needs. The scope of his line, and the interrelation of products in it, must be known to the bulk of his customers. Scrambled merchandising, or stocking of unrelated items, will tend to split his market into many small groups.

Assortment Sales

Furthermore, the middleman attempts to weld all of his offerings into a family of items which he can sell in combination, as a packaged assortment, to individual customers. His selling efforts are directed primarily at obtaining orders for the assortment, rather than for individual items. Naturally the greatest *numbers* of his transactions will seldom be made in this way; but often his greatest volume and more profitable sales to "blue-chip" accounts will be assortment sales.

Catering to assortment sales has considerable significance to channel operation, because the kind of sales service which a middleman can offer a single-product supplier is affected thereby. Since he is relatively disinterested in pushing individual items, the middleman is criticized for failure to stress a given brand, or for the poor quality of his salesmen's product knowledge, his disuse of suppliers' advertising materials, his neglect of certain customers (who may be good prospects for individual items but not for the assortment), and even for his unrefined systems of record keeping, in which brand designations may be lost.

THE MIDDLEMAN AS AN INDEPENDENT MARKET

The middleman is not a hired link in a chain forged by a manufacturer, but rather an independent market, the focus of a large group of customers for whom he buys. Subsequent to some market analysis of his own, he selects products and suppliers, thereby setting at least one link in the channel.

After some experimentation, he settles upon a method of operation, performing those functions he deems inescapable in the light of his own objectives, forming policies for himself wherever he has freedom to do so. Perhaps these methods and policies conform closely to those of a Census category of middleman, but perhaps they do not.

It is true that his choices are in many instances tentative proposals. He is subject to much influence from competitors, from aggressive suppliers, from inadequate finances and faulty information, as well as from habit. Nonetheless, many of his choices are independent.

As he grows and builds a following, he may find that his prestige in his market is greater than that of the suppliers whose goods he sells. In some instances his local strength is so great that a manufacturer is virtually unable to tap that market, except through him. In such a case the manufacturer can have no channel policy with respect to that market.

PART

II

Channel Structure Theory

A key area in the study of channels is that of selection and design. How do channels come to be structured as they do? Why does a channel take on one particular shape and form rather than another? How does a company go about selecting a channel of distribution? How should it do this?

Before any of the above questions can be answered in depth, one more set of questions must be asked and answered. Why do marketing channels exist in the first place? What is their role in the economic life of a nation? What is their origin? Why do they come to be? In other words, what is their *raison d'etre?*

No man has contributed more to this area than Wroe Alderson. Aldersonian sorting theory lays the foundation for answering this whole battery of questions. We can see in the first and third articles in this section the development of Aldersonian thought over the years, from his concept of matching to his concepts of transactions and transvections. These concepts, plus others such as routinization, search, intermediate sort, collection, and dispersing, all help one to understand the essence of the marketing channel. Thus, one must look to the process of sorting out—accumulation, allocation, assorting—to answer the question of channel being.

Others have also contributed significantly to these fundamental questions. Among these are Stigler, Bulkin, McCammon, and Aspinwall. Stigler's application of external economics created by middlemen, Bulkin's concept of postponement and speculation, McCammon's concept of innovative competition, Aspinwall's depot, goods and parallel system theories—all these authors and their concepts, in addition to a couple more, will give the reader insight into the fundamental problems of origin, structure, design, and selection of marketing channels. An understanding in this area is essential to a thorough grasp of the sections to follow, i.e. channel relations, measurement, and management.

4. Factors Governing the Development of Marketing Channels

WROE ALDERSON

Alderson discusses the origin of marketing channels, the way specialization is achieved through exchange, centralized exchange, creation of time and place utility, the role of sorting, the routinization of transactions, and the search problem through the channel.

Everyone is affected by marketing channels, but few have had the occasion to try to understand them. Even the marketing specialist is likely to be limited to his own product field in his detailed knowledge of channels. It is true that there have been public investigations of channels from time to time, often prompted by a wave of indignation against the "middleman." Legislators and public officials are called upon to make decisions affecting channels without an adequate background concerning their place in the economy. Channels in one field are declared to consist of too many stages, and the conclusion is drawn that they are necessarily inefficient. In another field it is asserted that channels are too highly integrated, with obvious implications as to the growth of monopoly.

The purpose of this paper is to discuss some of the underlying factors which are manifested in the development of channels generally. The first section of the paper will show how intermediaries arise in the process of exchange and will explain how the independent but co-ordinated agencies known as marketing channels contribute to economic efficiency. The second section will assess the forces which bring about change and adjustment in the structure of marketing channels. Finally, there are questions of public policy related to productivity in marketing and the hazards of monopoly. The third and fourth sections of this paper present some salient facts about marketing channels in relation to these issues.

THE ORIGIN OF MARKETING CHANNELS

Human culture is characterized by the existence of an assortment of goods available to the individual for his personal use or similarly available to a family or household. This assortment may include articles of clothing or adornment, stocks of foods or fuel, kitchen utensils, weapons, and tools. In a sense every item in the assortment may be regarded as a tool or instrument designed for specific uses. The significance of the assortment of goods in the possession of the individual is that it provides the means or capacity for the various kinds of activities in which he may expect to engage.

It is rational for the individual to be prepared for all of the activities which are normal for his culture or for his station in life. Thus if any item in his basic assortment should be about to be used up or worn out, he will be interested in replacing it. As his status or other factors in his situation change, he may need to add new items to his assortment. An example of a crucial change of status which may require additional items is that from bachelorhood to married life. The point is that in either primitive or advanced cultures the individual and the household maintain the power to act by replenishing or extending the assortment of goods in their possession.

In a primitive culture most of the goods used

• SOURCE: Reprinted from Richard M. Clewett, ed., *Marketing Channels for Manufactured Products.* Copyright 1954 by Richard D. Irwin. Used by permission. Wroe Alderson, Professor of Marketing Wharton School, University of Pennsylvania

within a household are produced by the members of the household. The term "produce" should be interpreted broadly enough here to include not only fabrication but the collection of natural objects not already in the possession of someone else. At an early stage in the development of economic activities it is found that some of the needs of a household or a tribe can be met more efficiently by exchange than by production. One family might be more skillful than another in making pots, while the second might be more skillful in making baskets. The first might be able to make two pots and the second two baskets faster than either could make one of each. If both families produce a surplus of the article they can make best and then they engage in exchange, both may get better quality goods at lower cost.

Exchange through Intermediaries

This is a very elementary example of the advantages of specialization in production and of the way that specialization is promoted through exchange. The purpose here is to show why exchange takes place through intermediaries and to consider the additional advantages which are gained through the development of middlemen and their alignment into marketing channels. To that end we may picture a slightly more complex exchange economy consisting of five households. Each is producing a surplus of some article used by all five. These articles might be pots, baskets, knives, hoes, and hats. In each case a surplus of four units is produced, and these units are then exchanged with the other households to obtain needed articles. Ten separate exchanges would be required, as shown in Figure 1.

Now suppose that this pattern of decentralized exchange is replaced by a central market. All come together at an appointed place on the second Thursday in April, each bringing his surplus. This may be a time when they are coming together anyway to celebrate the spring festival of their rain god. The increased con-

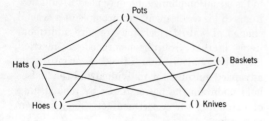

Fig. 1

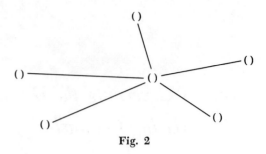

Fig. 2

venience with which the exchange is accomplished is indicated by Figure 2.

Only five trips are required instead of ten. Each participant has his surplus in readiness for exchange. This may not always be true in the case of decentralized exchange. When the potmaker visits the basketmaker to offer his wares, there may not be any finished baskets on hand and ready for exchange. In a primitive culture the goods and the parties to the transaction must be brought together at the same time and place in order for exchange to occur. The example given shows how much more easily this is accomplished through a central market. Here in its most elementary form is the creation of time and place utility, a concept which is generally associated with marketing. Time and place utility have held little interest for the general economist but deserve a more intensive analysis from the viewpoint of the marketing economist.

Centralized Exchange and Possession Utility

The next step in the evolution of exchange is for the market to be operated by an individual who may be called a dealer. Each of the five producers now engage in exchange with the dealer rather than with each other. The basketmaker, for example, trades his surplus to the dealer and receives back the items he requires to replenish his assortment. He may acquire a pot, a knife, a hoe, and a hat in a single transaction rather than through four separate transactions with the respective producers of these articles. In this way he saves time either to make more baskets or to devote to other pursuits. Possibly he will make five baskets instead of four, and the dealer will retain one basket in payment for his services.

Our simplified model of exchange now embraces what has been called "possession utility" as well as "time and place utility." Effort is involved in the act of exchange itself. The dealer has created possession utility by bringing about the transfer of goods from producer to consumer with less effort than would be involved in direct trading. *Economic analysis of the factors in price equilibrium generally rests on the assumption that exchange transactions are costless. Marketing analysis directed toward an understanding of trade channels must begin with a recognition of the costs involved in the creation of time, place, and possession utility.*

The saving might not be very important in the example given of a primitive economy consisting of only five producers. Cutting the number of transactions in half might not make a perceptible increase in productivity, and trading with each other might be valued in itself as a congenial form of social intercourse. The number of transactions necessary to carry out decentralized exchange is $n(n-1)/2$ where n is the number of producers and each makes only one article. Since the number of transactions required is only n if the central market is operated by a dealer, the ratio of advantage is $(n-1)/2$. Thus if the number of producers is raised from 5 to 25 the ratio of advantage in favor of an intermediary increases from 2 to 12. With 125 producers the ratio of advantage is 62. The figure 125 is a tiny fraction of the number of articles which must be produced to maintain satisfactory assortments in the hands of all of the consuming units in our complex modern culture. Even at this preliminary level of analysis, the ratio of advantage in favor of intermediary exchange is overwhelming. Exchange arises out of considerations of efficiency in production. Exchange through intermediaries arises out of considerations of efficiency in exchange itself.

Creation of Time and Place Utility

Intermediaries can increase the efficiency of exchange even when the producers and consumers under consideration are located in the same compact community. The advantages are greater when large distances intervene. Place utility takes on new aspects when the potmaker and the basketmaker are hundreds or even thousands of miles apart. When buyer and seller are so far apart, one or the other must make the initiative in closing the gap. One of them must call on the other if they are to negotiate face to face. One side or the other must assume the cost of moving the goods. Transportation and communication systems arise to bridge the distance. The railroads and trucking companies are in effect new types of specialized intermediaries serving buyer and seller more cheaply than they could serve themselves. It was no less an

authority than Alfred Marshall who said that economic progress consists largely in finding better methods for marketing at a distance.[1] The number of intervening marketing agencies tends to go up as distance increases. Many eastern companies who sell directly to wholesalers in other parts of the country sell through manufacturers' agencies on the Pacific Coast. This type of arrangement was even more common in the past but has been dropped in some instances as communication with the Pacific region has improved. Distance, for the present purpose, is not to be measured in miles but in terms of the time and cost involved in communication and transportation. In this sense there are points 300 miles inland in China which are further away from Shanghai than is San Francisco. Tariffs and the formalities of customs clearance are also a form of distance. As a result, specialized import and export firms commonly enter into foreign trade in addition to other types of intermediaries.

Production and consumption may also be separated widely in time. The wheat crop which is harvested in June is destined to be consumed as bread or other foodstuffs over a period of a year or more thereafter. To bridge this gap in time is to create utility for both producer and consumer. One wishes to be paid as soon as the crop is harvested. The other wants bread as needed without having to maintain a stock of wheat in the meantime. Specialized intermediaries such as grain elevators and warehouses enter the picture and help to create time utility through storage. Banks, insurance companies, and other specialized institutions help to minimize the costs and the risks of owning goods in the period between production and consumption. Retailers and wholesalers create time utility simply by holding stocks of goods available to be drawn upon by buyers. Without these facilities the only course open to the buyer would be to place an order with the producer and wait until the article could be produced and delivered. To be able to obtain the article at once instead of waiting is the essence of time utility. Another way of creating time utility is by selling on credit either to consumers or to other types of buyers. Through the installment purchase of an automobile, for example, the consumer is able to begin enjoying the use of the car long before it would be possible for him to pay it in full. An automobile used partly for business, or other items entering into a

[1] Alfred Marshall, *Principles of Economics* (8th ed.; London: Macmillan & Co., 1920), p. 397.

further stage of production, may help to raise the money needed for purchasing the product.

Technological Distance and the Discrepancy of Assortments

Producer and consumer are often a long way apart not only in time and space but in other ways. A product has a very different meaning for its producer and for the ultimate consumer buyer. For the consumer it has the possibility of contributing to what might be called the potency of his assortment. That is the range of capacity for future action provided by all of the goods in his possession. The consumer judges the product in relation to anticipated patterns of behavior and considers how it will fit in with other products he expects to use. If it is a mechanical refrigerator it must fit into the space available for it in his kitchen or pantry, and be equipped to utilize the supply of electricity or domestic gas. If it is a tie, the wearer does not want the color to clash with the colors of his other clothing. The specifications of the ideal product from the consumer viewpoint are determined by use requirements, including the requirement of not detracting from the value in use of other items already in the assortment.

The goods that a producer has for sale are the expression of his skills and resources. Ideal specifications from his viewpoint would be those which made most effective use of his plant capacity and of the available labor and raw materials. If he makes more than one product his stock of finished goods may be regarded as an assortment in the sense that it constitutes a supply with diverse characteristics. In some cases the separate items will be quite unrelated from the viewpoint of the uses they serve. They may have nothing in common except that they were produced from the same materials or by similar processes. Two items may be linked even more closely, one being a primary product and the other a by-product. In any case it is a wholly different thing for goods to be found together because of convenience in production as compared to an assortment of goods that are all complementary in use.

The most convenient or constructive association of goods changes at each stage in the flow of merchandise from producer to consumer. This fact has been generalized as the "discrepancy of assortment."[2] Goods are associated

[2] David R. Craig and Werner K. Gabler, "The Competitive Struggle for Market Control," *Annals of the American Academy of Political and Social Science*, May, 1940.

for transportation because of physical handling characteristics and common origin and destination. Goods are associated for storage in terms of the length of time they are to be stored and the conditions needed to preserve them. Between the producer's stock of finished goods and the assortment in the hands of the consumer there may be other stocks or assortments maintained by retailers and wholesalers. The composition of these intermediate stocks is determined by the requirements of the functions performed.

The discrepancy of assortments places severe limitations on vertical integration of marketing agencies. A retail grocer typically relies on different wholesale soures for meat, produce, and packaged groceries. The requirements for storage, handling, and other aspects of the wholesale function are quite different in these three product fields. The retailer may provide the consumer who wants to buy peaches with a choice of fresh, canned, or frozen. Yet the routes by which the three items reached the grocery store would normally be quite different at both the wholesale and production levels. If it were not for the discrepancy of assortments, marketing channels might be more frequently integrated from top to bottom. Most fundamental of these discrepancies is that between producer stocks and consumer assortments. The product appears in a very different setting at these two levels and may be said to belong to the technology of production at one stage and the technology of use at the other. In addition to distance in time and space, marketing channels serve to bridge the technological gap (which may be regarded as a third form of distance between production and consumption).

Aspects of Sorting in Marketing

Fundamental to the adjustment effected through marketing channels are the four processes which may be bracketed under the name of "sorting." Most elementary of the forms of sorting is "sorting out." That means breaking down a heterogeneous supply into separate stocks which are relatively homogeneous. Sorting out is typified by the grading of agricultural products or by pulling out rejects in some manufacturing operations. A second form of sorting is accumulation, or bringing similar stocks together into a larger homogeneous supply. Accumulation of such stocks is essential to mass production and continuous manufacturing operations. Automatic machines are built with only a limited range of tolerance for variations in the materials processed.

The other two aspects of sorting are those which predominate in the distribution of finished manufactured goods. The first of these may be called "allocation." It consists in breaking a homogeneous supply down into smaller and smaller lots. This process in marketing is generally coincidental with geographical dispersal and successive changes in ownership. Allocation at the wholesale level has sometimes been called "breaking bulk." Goods received in carload lots are sold in case lots. A buyer in case lots in turn sells individual units.

The final aspect of sorting and the one which is most fundamental for this discussion may be called "assorting." That means building up assortments of items for use in association with each other. Both consumer buyers and industrial buyers enter the market for the purpose of building up assortments. Sellers undertake to facilitate assorting as carried on by buyers. Retail stores usually arrange goods in display according to categories of use rather than by producers or points of origin. Thus a consumer entering a department store can readily locate a department displaying all types of dresses. She does not have to go to a cotton department handling cotton sheets, rugs, awnings, and bandages in order to locate a cotton dress. Allocation and assorting go hand in hand in the channels of distribution. Purchase by the consumer is the common end point. It represents the completion of the process of allocation carried on by sellers and the culmination of economic activity in the replenishment or extension of the assortments in the hands of consumers.

Wholesaling is a manifestation of sorting as an essential marketing process. Goods are received from numerous suppliers and delivered to numerous customers. The essence of the operation is to transform the diversified supplies received into outgoing assortments on their way to customers. The justification for an independent wholesaling operation rests largely on the ratio of advantage growing out of this intermediate sorting. It has been pointed out elsewhere that this advantage goes up in relation to the product of the number of suppliers and the number of customers.[3]

The ultimate in intermediate sorting is seen in the freight classification yard. Trains of cars

[3] Wroe Alderson, "Scope and Function of Wholesaling in the United States," *Journal of Marketing*, September, 1949.

arrive over various routes. These trains are broken up and recombined according to the routes over which they will depart. Let us assume a simplified case in which 5 railroads come into the same terminal point. There are 5 production centers on each line or 25 in all. A train coming in over route A consists of 100 loaded cars. Twenty cars are picked up at each production center on route A, each destined for one of the centers on other lines. The same volume of freight originates on each of the other routes. Each of the production centers ships and receives 20 carloads of freight. Yet because of resorting at the central interchange the entire movement of 500 cars is completed by each of the 5 trains making a round trip over its own line. Note that there are no two cars for which both origin and destination coincide.

To summarize the case presented so far, intermediaries arise in the process of exchange because they can increase the efficiency of the process. The justification for the middleman rests on specialized skill in a variety of activities and particularly in various aspects of sorting. The principle of the discrepancy of assortments explains why the successive stages in marketing are so commonly operated as independent agencies. While economists assume for certain purposes that exchange is costless, transactions occupy time and utilize resources in the real world. Intermediary traders are said to create time, place, and possession utility because transactions can be carried out at lower cost through them than through direct exchange. In our modern economy the distribution network makes possible specialized mass production on the one hand and the satisfaction of the differentiated tastes of consumers on the other.

Routinization of Transactions

There is a final factor to be considered in explaining why a sequence of marketing agencies hangs together in such a way as to deserve the designation of channel. That is the fact that the cost of moving goods from one level to the next can be minimized if the transaction can be reduced to a routine. For a transaction to be routinized it must happen according to rules, and both sides must understand the rules. Even more fundamental is the need for confidence growing out of the established relationships of buyer and seller. Performance on each side rests on the belief that the other side will behave as expected. Out of long acquaintance each becomes a point of reference for habitual behavior by the other.

It is well to remember here certain linguistic coincidences. The word "customer" comes from the same root as the word "customary." Both derive from "custom," meaning habit or established practice. The word "routine" is readily traced to "route," which means a customary course or way. A related word is "channel," a variation on the word *canal* in Old French. Thus channel means a fixed and clearly marked route. In marketing practice there could be no channels without routines. Some advocates of the free market tend to regard all such institutional structures as restrictions on economic freedom. We will try to show later that marketing channels are essential to effective competition and to the orderly and efficient movement of goods.

One of the functions of advertising is to contribute to the routinization of repetitive transactions. A brand name comes to stand in the place of a set of product specifications. This avoids the need for specifying in detail what is wanted for every successive purchase of the same article. Routine handling of actual transactions is promoted when the majority of buyers come to prefer one brand or another. Thus discussion of product specifications is largely eliminated except from those transactions in which the buyer is considering a change. Channels of communication parallel and supplement the channels for the physical movement of goods.

Effective Search through Marketing Channels

The discussion of sorting heretofore assumes that the goods desired by buyers and the customers desired by sellers are readily available. Actually, a perfect market in that sense does not always exist. A buyer with a particular need starts looking for a product with the desired specifications with no assurance that a product of this precise character exists. The same is true for the producer who has increased his production but cannot be certain that customers are to be found to absorb his surplus. This aspect of market behavior may be called "searching." To the extent that buyers and sellers must cope with uncertainty they are engaged in a double search. If the search is successful it leads to the completion of the sorting processes of allocation and assorting which have already been considered.

What is called "shopping" is searching as carried on by consumers. The shopper starts out with some conception of what is wanted, more or less clearly defined. As a shopping trip proceeds, the shopper gains knowledge as to what is available. At each stage the shopper has the option of taking something which is fairly satisfactory or continuing with the search. Usually the shopper does not search at random but goes to the most likely place first. The organization of retailing by separate lines of trade facilitates searching by consumers. The retailer, in buying new items for his store, may be regarded as representing the consumer in searching among sources of supply which are not readily available to the consumer. Thus channels facilitate searching as well as sorting. The same thing is true from the side of the producer who ordinarily searches for new customers through existing channels.

The search problem was analyzed from the military viewpoint during World War II. Principles of efficient search were developed governing such situations as airplanes searching for submarines. Searching in the market place absorbs effort, and this effort can be employed with varying degrees of productivity. The need for efficiency creates a need for specialists in searching as well as in sorting. Particularly is this true if the good to satisfy a need does not actually exist or the demand which can absorb a surplus has yet to be aroused. Special knowledge is required to locate the production facilities which can turn out a new product or the segment of the market which can most readily be induced to accept it. Such activities as product development and marketing research are expanding rapidly in the attempt to meet these problems.

The tendency to maximize productivity in economic activity leads to specialization in marketing as it does in production. A sequence of marketing agencies hangs together to constitute a channel for a given product. Cohesion is promoted by the advantages of the routine handling of transactions made possible by mutual confidence. The successive agencies tend at the same time to remain under separate ownership and control because of the discrepancy of assortments, the principle by which the natural association of products differs at each level. Both sorting and searching, the fundamental marketing functions, are facilitated by the existence of marketing channels. Exchange is inherently dynamic and tends to evolve a structure through which an increasing volume of transactions can be executed at the same or lower cost.

5. *Channels of Distribution in Developing Economies*

GEORGE WADINAMBIARATCHI

This article discusses the relationship between the channels of distribution available in a country and the stage of economic development in that country. Wadinambiaratchi concludes that the channel structures reflect the stage of economic development. From an examination of marketing structure in nine areas, he feels that a complex channel structure reflects a high level of economic development.

The relationship between the channels of distribution available in a country, and the stage of economic development in that country, may prove useful as a theoretical concept for marketing. An explanation, through such a concept, of the differences and similarities between marketing structures in different countries may help in the more successful transferring of marketing techniques between countries at different stages of economic development.

To the business man an awareness and an understanding of the underlying factors would prove useful when considering a plan for international marketing in general, and the building up of an international marketing organization in particular. A knowledge of what gives rise to channel structures would help a business man not only to design a marketing organization abroad, but also to appreciate what has to be done to change the underlying factors to get a channel structure more suitable for his requirements.

It is hoped that the usefulness of the information in this article would not be limited to international marketers. Economists can better understand the underlying economic structure with a proper appreciation of the significance of the institutional superstructure. National planners, too, could benefit by the relationship thus established between the infra- and superstructures.

Few persons would dispute the fact that marketing techniques in general, and any specific distribution methods are not the same in all countries. It has been said that marketing is the most backward part of the economic system in underdeveloped countries. This has a significant implication for international marketers. Michaelis[1] puts the position very succinctly:

"A modern factory can be transplanted from the United States to Asia, Africa or Latin America. The machines will function the same way and the products will be identical . . . Our distribution methods—developed to a high degree of sophistication in our intensely competitive market place—cannot be directly transplanted . . . I would be the last to suggest that American marketing techniques will, or necessarily should, ever fit India's particular requirements. Rather I would plead that—together with India and with other developing nations—we explore what portions of our experience and know-how in marketing that can be adapted to their needs."

I will first review some economic and social-psychological writings in the area and suggest that their explanations are inadequate. Then I will define the concept of channels of distribution and the concept of, and measure for economic development. Thereafter, I will review some marketing studies in nine areas and will attempt to show that, with the countries ranked

• SOURCE: Wadinambiaratchi, George, "Channels of Distribution in Developing Economies," *The Business Quarterly*, Vol. 30 (Winter, 1965), pp. 74–82. George Wadinambiaratchi, Doctoral Student, University of Western Ontario.

[1] Michael Michaelis, "Distribution in Developing Economies," *Boston Conference on Distribution*, 1961.

in order of economic development, there is a discernible pattern of channel development. My conclusion is that the channel structures reflect the stage of economic development in the country.

REASONS FOR DIFFERENCES IN MARKETING SYSTEMS

I question the validity of the present hypotheses regarding economic development and marketing structures. Most of the literature on the subject of marketing and economic development are written from the economists' point of view. Higgins[2] for instance, says:

"Certainly the progress of underdeveloped countries depends not only on their attainments in agriculture and manufacturing but also on the development of an efficient marketing system."

Many writers have argued for better marketing and distribution systems in order that economic development may be accelerated. The economists' argument appears to run in a circle: the country must have a proper distribution and marketing structure that will lead to higher economic development and higher incomes—this then will lead to the growth of a middle class—which in turn will lead to a necessity for further improvements in manufacturing and better distribution, and so on.

This argument seems to imply a causal relationship in that better marketing systems produce higher levels of economic development. Myers and Smalley[3] who were connected with a study on the nature of this causality report,

"Particularly vexing was the attempt to establish growth and behavioural hypotheses. Was, for example, the development of the marketing system in the United States a function of general economic growth and thus fully explainable by the familiar economic determinants? Or, was marketing itself among the fundamental agents of American economic growth?

Leighton[4] advances the hypothesis that there

is no simple cause and effect relationship, but rather a system of reinforcements that move the system upwards: changes in social structure lead to changes in economic institutions (including better distribution) which in turn lead to further changes in social structure and so on. Other writers also believe that the cultural and social fabric of a country determines the type of marketing system.

Socio-psychological, cultural, and anthropological determinants of marketing systems are referred to by many writers: (a) attitude and behavior; (b) attitudes about profits and desire for independence; (c) consumer attitudes to mass produced goods and haggling; and (d) entrepreneurship.

I propose that these socio-psychological, cultural and anthropological influences can be explained in terms of economic factors. Dalton[5] quotes Karl Polanyi as saying that:

"Primitive economy is 'embedded' in society in the sense that the economic system functions as a byproduct of non-economic institutions: that economy as a cohesive entity, a separate set of practices and relationships apart from social organization, does not exist in primitive life."

In such primitive economies there are no market or technological constraints, no economic directives, no jargon of the market place. Production and distribution are an integral part of the structure of social obligations and it is the introduction of money as a means of exchange that divorces distribution from these social obligations. As the new system starts operating it is only a limited number of peripheral items that enter into the "market place." Sellers get only a minor portion of their income from such market activities, and buyers only a part of their daily-used goods and services via the market place. If, then, some of the features of the primitive pre-money economy persist (e.g., in the belief of retailers in underdeveloped countries that price competition is unethical) they do so only because the money economy has not disrupted all the social obligations of the earlier era.

Psychologists claim that, in the long run, the values, attitudes, and motives of the people will determine the speed of economic development.

[2] Benjamin Higgins, *Economic Development*, New York, N.Y., Norton and Co., 1959, p. 82.
[3] Kenneth H. Myers and Orange A. Smalley, "Marketing History and Economic Development," *Business History Review*, Autumn, 1959.
[4] David S. R. Leighton, "Social Change in Western Europe and its Implications for Marketing," *Revue Economique et Sociale*, December, 1962.
[5] George Dalton, "Traditional Production in Primitive African Economics," *Quarterly Journal of Economics*, August, 1964.

It would then be reasonable to say that these values, attitudes and motives, which reflect the sociological, psychological, cultural, and anthropological influences in that country, are reflected in the stage of economic development of that country. Economic development, is thus, a product of these factors in the economy; and economic development can be treated as a proxy variable for the socio-psychological, cultural and anthropological variables.

While some writers are posing the question as to why the underdeveloped countries are quicker to pick up modern production methods than modern methods of marketing, others claim that in these countries production has been encouraged and marketing has been willfully neglected. It is possible that the emphasis on technology is a hangover from classical economics extended to the belief that a product turned out by a high degree of technological skill will sell itself.

The present paper is concerned with the channels of distribution, what the marketing men speak of as the *channel structure*, the types of marketing institutions that form the structure. Here, marketers are concerned with the number and type of middlemen between the manufacturers and retailers. They are also concerned with the breadth of distribution at the retail level (extensive or selective). Economists speak of better distribution in the sense that they would want the product to be available in all parts of the country. It would seem that the economists' conception of distribution comes close to that of the marketer only when the latter is considering regional as opposed to national distribution.

This paper is *not* concerned with cause and effect relationships. It is not concerned with the time dimension, i.e., change of the channels of distribution over time. Rather, it is concerned with the channel structure available at any point in time, and with how it reflects the environmental factors at that time.

Definition of Channels of Distribution

At this stage it is necessary to define the concept of channels as relevant to the present study. Channels of distribution have been variously defined: (a) in terms of a pipeline for goods from manufacturers to consumer; (b) as a combination of agencies between manufacturer and user; and (c) as intermediary sellers between original source of supply and ultimate consumer. For the purposes of this paper, a channel of

distribution may be conceived of as "a course taken in the transfer of title to a commodity."

The channels are meant to include (a) the field sales and distribution operation of a manufacturer; (b) merchants who assume title and resell on their own account; and (c) agents and brokers who do not take title but are in some way instrumental in transferring ownership. Vertically, the channels are meant to include mail order houses, merchant and general wholesalers, manufacturers' agents, jobbers, and brokers. At the retail level, the horizontal channels are meant to include all types of retail outlets from the itinerant peddlar through the corner grocer and specialty store to the department store. Today, governments of different countries are in the business sector at both the middleman and retail levels. Such government organizations would also be included in the channel structure.

Economic Development

For the purpose of this paper economic underdevelopment will be viewed in line with Fisher's[6] conception.

"Countries or areas have been defined as underdeveloped if they have a relatively low rank in per capita real income. Such areas are also characterized by low per capita production, low level of value added by manufacturing, and relatively great emphasis on agricultural and other primary industries. Natural resources are still largely in the potential stage awaiting capital, skilled management and labour, or large markets for their development."

For the purpose of this paper economic development was measured on the basis of the criteria enumerated in Appendix A.

Review of Marketing Studies

Marketing studies in nine areas (Appendix B)—Brazil, Egypt, India, Japan, the Middle East, Puerto Rico, Tropical Africa, Turkey, and Venezuela—appear to lend support to the hypothesis that marketing channels appear to reflect the stage of economic development.

Using data on (a) per capita income, (b) per

[6] Joseph L. Fisher, "The Role of Natural Resources," in Harold F. Williamson and John A. Buttrick, *Economic Development: Principles and Policies*, Englewood Cliffs, N.J., Prentice-Hall, 1961, pp. 22–62.

capita generation of electricity, (c) percentage urban population, (d) manufacturing as a percentage of GNP, (e) private consumption expenditure as a percentage of national income, and (f) infant mortality rates, and using a modified form of the Bridgeman Method[7] the countries, when ranked in order of the stage of economic development achieved, ranked as follows: Japan, Brazil, Venezuela, Puerto Rico, Turkey, Egypt, India, and Tropical Africa (Middle East was excluded).

It was found then, that:

(a) The more developed countries have more levels of distribution (Figure 1), more specialty stores and supermarkets, more department stores, and more stores in the rural areas.

(b) The influence of the foreign import agent declines with economic development.

(c) Manufacturer-wholesaler-retailer functions become separated with economic development.

(d) Wholesaler functions approximate those in North America with increasing economic development.

(e) Financing function of wholesalers declines and wholesale mark-ups increase with increasing development.

(f) The number of small stores decline and the size of the average store increases with increasing development.

(g) The role of the peddlar and itinerant trader, and the importance of the open-garden-fair declines with increasing development, and

(h) Retail margins improve with increasing economic development. (See Table 1.)

[7] P. W. Bridgeman, *Dimensional Analysis*, New Haven, Yale University Press, 1962, pp. 21–22: The advantages of using this method are believed to be twofold: (a) when dimensions are multiplied and a ratio obtained, a pure number—i.e. a number without dimensions—is produced and can therefore be directly compared; (b) the number thus obtained is proportional to the magnitude of the values. The standard Bridgman method uses the product of the values of each dimension, raised to a power representing the importance of the particular dimension. By the standard method, the importance of each value is recognized. For the purpose of this study, it is recognized that it is not possible, in the present state of economic literature, to weight the different criteria for their importance in reflecting economic development. Thus, they are given equal weight.

Table 1. Summary of Marketing Features

	Japan	Brazil	Venezuela	Puerto Rico	Turkey	Egypt	India	Trop. Africa
A. Number of levels in channels	5	2			1	1 to 3	2	2
B. Influence of foreign import agent						Dying out		Very strong
C. Size of wholesalers	Very large		Small	Small	Small	Small	Small	Small
D. Wholesalers own retail outlets				No	Yes	Yes	Yes	
E. Background integration	Yes			No			Yes, some	
F. Wholesalers plan local distribution	Yes				Yes	Yes		
G. Wholesalers have active sales force	Yes		Yes		Yes	Yes	No	
H. Wholesalers provide warehousing field storage, delivery	Yes		Yes	Yes	Yes	Yes	Storage only	
I. Wholesalers order E.O.Q.	Yes		Yes	Yes	Yes	No	No	
J. Wholesaler lends marketing advice	Yes							
K. Wholesalers financing retailers	Important		Important	Important	Very important	Very important	Important	Very important
L. Wholesaler markups	Very high			Very high		5%	1.5 to 4%	Very high
M. Specialty stores and supermarkets		Yes, in cities	Yes					
N. Department stores		Yes, in cities	Yes, in cities			Yes, in cities		
O. Stores in rural areas		General store					None	
P. Stores of small size							Very large number	Very large number
Q. Size of retail store							Small	Very small
R. Peddlars and itinerant traders		Yes	Yes	Yes		Yes	Very important	Very important
S. Open garden fairs		Yes					Yes	Yes
T. Price competition		None	None	None		Little	Little	Little
U. Consumer credit			Very important	Very important		Little		
V. Retail margins			25–50%	24%		35–40%	10%	

*Channels Reflect the Stage
of Economic Development*

The present paper attempts to show that the marketing structure in a country reflects the stage of economic development in that country. Erickson[8] appears to hold a similar view:

8 Leo G. Erickson, "Analyzing Brazilian Consumer Markets," *Business Topics*, Summer, 1963.

"In marketing, as in other areas of social and economic activity, institutions and methodology do not arise simply through chance. Rather they are a reflection of the particular environment in which they are found. The institutions which are engaged in marketing, and the methods used to market output, reflect the environmental factors which are lumped together and called the market."

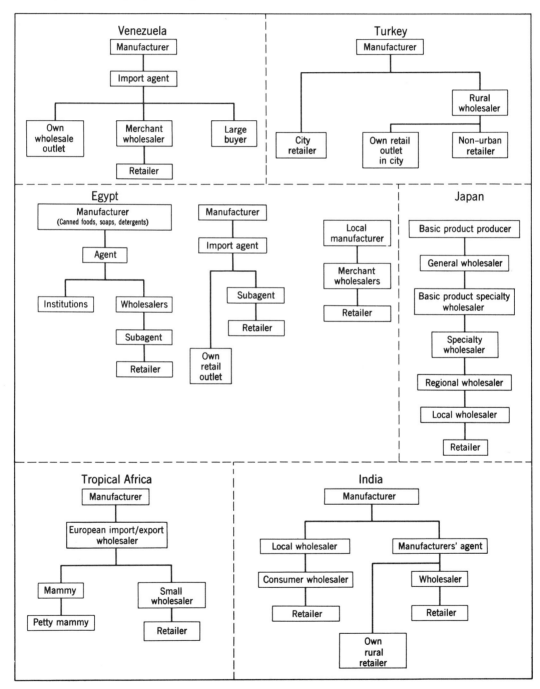

Fig. 1. Levels of distribution.

When economists speak of the adequacy of a marketing structure to develop an economy, or when the sociologist or psychologist speaks of suitable sociological or psychological climates necessary to accelerate economic development, they are referring to causal relationships, or what was referred to earlier as behavioural hypotheses. These involve time dimensions in the sense that the marketing structure of today, or the sociopsychological climate of today determines the stage of economic development of tomorrow or the day after. This paper attempts to establish that marketing structures are reflections of the stage of economic development, more specifically that there is a regular pattern of distribution that is more or less unique at each stage of economic development.

One can delve back several hundred years searching for the *reflection hypothesis* as stated above. Halbert[9] says;

"In every culture studied by anthropologists or historians, some form of exchange has existed. That exchange should develop is predetermined by two factors that are to be found in any organized human society—specialization and motivation . . . when specialization is coupled with motivation, exchange naturally occurs. Anything so vital a part of society tends to be institutionalized, acculturated and ritualized. This is borne out by anthropological studies in which every culture examined shows some ritualistic aspects associated with the problems and practices of exchange. In fact in early societies most of the exchange structure was integrated with the religious and other ritualistic aspects of the system . . . . the importance of the exchange function in culture increased until at the present time we have in many parts of the world cultures that could be described as marketing societies rather than as agricultural or manufacturing societies."

The studies reviewed appear to substantiate the hypothesis that marketing structures reflect the stage of economic development. "Egyptian channels of distribution, with but a few exceptions, are at about the same stage as were those of the United States in the early 1800's." Samli states it more pointedly, ". . . the Turkish wholesaler resembles the American wholesaler

of the 1800's or early 1900's when the American economy was not one of abundance." It has been claimed that American wholesaling and the American economy developed on parallel lines and that early American wholesaling was very closely associated with the import-export trade (like in the underdeveloped countries today). Stewart, in the conclusion to his study on the Middle East says,

"The fact that the market is increasing only slowly probably accounts for the persistence of distribution methods developed for another age and for the continued concentration of many disparate lines in the hands of a single agent. . . ."

It would appear that the middleman is despised all over the world. But the reasons appear to be different, as between the less developed and more developed countries. People in India do not want middlemen because the poor people in India could not afford his services.

In the U.S. middleman are not welcome for slightly different reasons. Courtney[10] says:

"All middlemen have one thing in common —they are too often looked upon by the general public as anachronistic appendages, useless leeches on the economy, adding cost but not value to the goods they handle. . . . Why do wholesalers continue to be criticized? . . . misunderstanding about marketing in general, a negative image of wholesaling . . . claims of a number of individual manufacturers coupled with the more recent direct buying and 'discount' or 'wholesale' selling efforts of some retailers."

Witness that the same institution is rejected in both cases on economic grounds, but in one instance as "too expensive" or "oppressive" for underdeveloped areas, and as "past their usefulness" in the affluent economy.

At the retail level, the number and variety of stores available (i.e. the breadth of retail channels) in any country could, it appears, be explained in economic terms. Taylor, referring to Brazil says:

"If the area in which the community is located is prosperous, two or three general stores may be found, but if the community is located

[9] Michael H. Halbert, "The Requirements for a Theory in Marketing," in Reavis Cox, Wroe Alderson, and Stanley J. Shapiro (Eds.), *Theory in Marketing*, Homewood, Ill., Richard D. Irwin, 1964, pp. 17–18.

[10] Paul L. Courtney, "The Wholesaler as a Link in the Distribution Channel," *Business Horizons*, Special Issue, February, 1961, p. 90.

in a depressed area, only one outlet serves the entire community . . . . The existence of the limited-line store is dependent on the size and economic level of the community . . . in regions of lower economic level, the number of establishments follows the density of population in terms of purchasing power."

Confirmation of this belief comes from at least two other studies. Stewart says of the Middle East, "Product composition, of course, emanates primarily from the patterns of income distribution and tastes," and Edward Marcus says of Tropical Africa, "In a market as changing as the African one, it becomes extremely important to keep in constant touch with the final consumer and to follow the impact of income changes on his taste for material goods." Hirsch[11] observes that there is no clear cut specialization of distribution activities either vertically by successive levels of distribution or horizontally by types of goods handled, in many underdeveloped countries. He maintains that this blurring of functions causes overlapping within, rather than a shortening of, the chain of distribution, and explains;

"The situation may simply be a reflection of the relative lack of specialization prevalent in a low-income economy. More specifically because of such factors as the prevalent market structure, the low cost of labour, and lack of fixed prices, it may often make economic sense for a merchant to widen the nominal distribution level at which he operates." (p. 287).

And again,
"The lack of horizontal differentiation seems to be . . . a result of businessmen's reactions to various economic factors" (p. 289).

Hirsch predicts there will be a gradual trend towards specialization with a growing market and with a differentiation in production.

The number and size of the outlets in underdeveloped countries appear to be a function of (a) size of the family—most establishments are owner managed; (b) availability of own capital to entrepreneur—neither credit institutions nor persons are prepared to lend; and (c) consumer purchases—daily shopping and absence of transportation, both due to low incomes, necessitate location of small stores at frequent intervals.

[11] Leon V. Hirsch, *Marketing in an Underdeveloped Economy: The North Indian Sugar Industry,* Englewood Cliffs, N.J., Prentice-Hall, 1962.

It has also been found that seasonality of consumer incomes leads to the necessity for credit and that daily purchases in small quantities require extensive sales help. The redundancy of traders in distribution appears, then, to be a fault of the economy rather than of the distribution system as such.

It has been suggested that improved transportation and communications facilities were basic prerequisites to "provide the vehicles for aggressive demand creation and satisfaction." These are, of course, sadly lacking in developing countries and hence do result in the absence of some of the methods of modern distribution seen in North America. One study reports how the mail order venture of Sears in Mexico, in 1949, had to be abandoned as "there was no satisfactory method of distribution which could combine the advantages, common to all of us here, of parcel post and C.O.D."

CONCLUSION

As was argued earlier in the paper, the social, psychological, cultural, and anthropological climates in a community determine the institutions in that community. These institutions in turn limit and direct the economy of the community. Thus, given the institutional settings of the underdeveloped countries, it should be possible to understand their marketing structures, in terms of their economic development.

The facts as stated in this paper would seem to indicate that the unfortunate position of the channels of distribution in developing countries is only a natural stage of the evolution: first from a non-monetary subsistence economy to a monetary economy, and later from an economy of scarcity, where demand exceeds supply, to one of comfort, if not opulence, where supply more than meets demand. It would seem then that the hypothesis that "the channels of distribution in a country reflect the stage of economic development in that country" is well founded.

The implications of this hypothesis to the business man is that the market structure or institutions he plans are limited by the environmental factors. And these environmental factors are accounted for in that all-encompassing factor called economic development. He can introduce changes in the channels or in the type of institutions in the channels either (a) in response to changes in the environment, or (b) by attempting to change the environment, first, by changing the socio-psychological, cultural, or anthropological variables as affecting the people in the country, and second, by changing the economic environment itself.

APPENDIX A

Measures of Economic Development

(A) Per Capita Income. Some economists do not believe that per capita income is a suitable measure of economic development because (a) a large real national income is normally a prerequisite for an increase in real per capita incomes, (b) if population increases as fast as real national income, then per capita incomes will not show any increase; and (c) if per capita income is the measurement, the population problem may be concealed, since population has already been divided out.

However, the assumption that economic development reflects an improved adjustment of humans to their physical environment seems very reasonable. Increased national income per capita would, then, ordinarily result from a more effective use of resources and techniques.

Some economists have argued that per capita incomes are not directly comparable between countries. However, in the absence of a correction factor that could be successfully used, and because other measures of development were also being used, per capita incomes could be included as a measure.

(B) Per Capita Generation of Electricity. Most models for economic growth have among their variables one that accounts for technological progress. As electricity has become the form in which energy is most economically stored and transmitted, the production and use of electricity is highly indicative of the level of a country's technology. Per Capita generation of electricity can be used as a measure of economic development.

(C) Percentage Urban Population. Economic development is generally accompanied by other economic and social changes such as the urbanization of the population. A desire to share in the higher consumption standards in the cities operates as a motivating force that impels peasant agricultural labour to migrate into towns. Although it may not be very accurate in a comparison between the more highly developed countries, the percentage breakdown of the population as rural and urban should indicate the comparative degree of economic development in the underdeveloped areas.

(D) Manufacturing As A Percentage of GNP. The degree of industrialization is widely recognized as an important index of economic development. As such, the share of industrial output in the gross national product could be used to compare the stage of economic development achieved. This is particularly useful in the developing economies, where the attempt has been made to move from the lopsided economy producing agricultural goods for the primary goods exporting markets, towards a more balanced economy that features some degree of local manufacturing.

(E) Private Consumption as a Percentage of National Income. Per capita consumption as a percentage of per capita incomes is higher in underdeveloped than in developed countries. Put in another way, the average propensity to consume is very high in underdeveloped areas. A so-called underdeveloped economy has a relatively high average marginal propensity to consume, at least, in comparison to one of the countries bordering the North Atlantic. It is possible, though, that due to the great inequalities of incomes, in underdeveloped countries, the average propensity to consume may be lower than what in fact it is. Private consumption expenditures as a percentage of National Income is a useful measure of economic development.

(F) Infant Mortality Rates. With the improvement in health services the mortality rate falls and life expectancy at birth increases. Declining mortality rates and industrialization have gone together, both in the West and in the East. A serious problem in underdeveloped countries has been the high infant mortality rates, so that a reduction of the rate could be considered a good index of economic development. A word of caution is in order: mortality rates may be falling, not because of development, but because of modern medical methods and scientific techniques. In the instance of all countries, the relationship between economic development and a declining infant mortality rate need not be causal. However, both phenomena, normally, tend to appear together. Therefore, infant mortality rates would be useful as a measure of economic development.

APPENDIX B

Area Marketing Studies Analyzed

Donald A. Taylor, "Retailing in Brazil," *Journal of Marketing*, July, 1959.

Harper W. Boyd, Abdel Aziz El Sherbini and Ahmed Fouad Sherif, "Channels of Distribution for Consumer Goods in Egypt," *Journal of Marketing*, October, 1960.

Ralph Westfall and Harper W. Boyd, "Marketing in India," *Journal of Marketing*, October, 1960.

Lawrence P. Dowd, "Wholesale Marketing in Japan," *Journal of Marketing*, January, 1959.

Charles F. Stewart, "The Changing Middle East Market," *Journal of Marketing*, January, 1961.

Richard H. Holton, "Marketing Structure and Economic Development," *Quarterly Journal of Economics*, August, 1953.

Edward Marcus, "Selling the Tropical African Market," *Journal of Marketing*, July, 1961.

Mildred R. Marcus, "Merchandise Distribution in Tropical Africa" *Journal of Retailing*, Winter, 1959–60.

A. Coskun Samli, "Wholesaling in an Economy of Scarcity: Turkey," *Journal of Marketing*, July, 1964.

Harper W. Boyd, Richard M. Clewett, and Ralph L. Westfall, "The Marketing Structure of Venezuela" *Journal of Marketing*, April, 1958.

6. Toward a Formal Theory of Transactions and Transvections

WROE ALDERSON AND MILES W. MARTIN

This abridged article presents the initial steps in the formalization of a partial theory of marketing. The partial theory pertains to the movement of goods and information through marketing channels, and the theory utilizes two basic concepts of marketing system behavior, namely, transactions and transvections.

A transvection is in a sense the outcome of a series of transactions, but a transvection is obviously more than that. The transactions as such are limited only to the successive negotiations of exchange agreements. A transvection includes the complete sequence of exchanges, but it also includes the various transformations which take place along the way. The pair of shoes in the hands of the consumer is obviously a very different thing from the raw materials in the state of nature. The student of transvections is interested in every step by which this flow through the marketing system was accomplished.

Other contrasts can be drawn between a transaction and a transvection with respect to their use in planning and decision-making. Transactions involve a transfer in ownership or use privileges covering not only sales but all forms of short-term rent and lease agreements. It is assumed that further transformations will take place under the new ownership, but ordinarily this is not required under the terms of the exchange agreement. In market planning there is necessarily substantial emphasis on means of motivating these further transformations following a transfer of ownership.

If planning is approached from the trans-vection standpoint, on the other hand, it is often convenient to consider first what might take place if the product remained under a single ownership throughout. This provides a way of specifying the transformations which are really essential in order to complete the transvection and the sorts or assignments which must intervene to link any pair of successive transformations. While the transaction concept is valuable for market planning, the transvection concept is more fundamental. Beginning from the perspective of the transvection, for example, will be useful in shaping the character of the transactions which need to occur at successive stages.

TRANSACTIONS

The discussion of transactions will begin with a statement which might be called the Law of Exchange. This law states the conditions under which an exchange can take place, but it does not assert that the exchange actually occurred, since there are fortuitous factors which could interfere with the exchange in a given case. In the expression $x \simeq y$, it is merely asserted that x is exchanged for y, the sign for Libra, or the balance, being adopted to represent exchangeability. The Law of Exchange, stated verbally, would be:

Given that x is an element of the assortment A_1 and y is an element of the assortment A_2, x is exchangeable for y if and only if these three conditions hold:

• SOURCE: Wroe Alderson and Miles W. Martin, "Toward a Formal Theory of Transactions and Transvections," *Journal of Marketing Research*, Vol. 2 (May, 1965), pp. 117–127; from pp. 119, 122–126. Wroe Alderson, Professor of Marketing, Wharton School, University of Pennsylvania, Miles W. Martin, Assistant Professor of Statistics and Operations Research, Wharton School.

(a) x is different from y

(b) The potency of the assortment A_1 is increased by dropping x and adding y

(c) The potency of the assortment A_2 is increased by adding x and dropping y

In symbols the Law of Exchange would be stated as follows:

$$x \backsimeq y$$

if, and only if,

$$x \neq y(xeA_1 \text{ and } yeA_2),$$
$$P(A_1 - x + y) > P(A_1),$$

and
$$P(A_2 + x - y) > P(A_2);$$

where $x \backsimeq y$ means x is exchangeable for y,

$x \neq y$ means x is different from y,

xeA_1 means x is an element of A_1,

$P(A_1)$ means the potency of A_1.

This formulation makes no explicit reference to the cost of executing an exchange transaction. For a complete statement of the Law of Exchange, it should be stated explicitly that the increase in the potency of the assortment A_1, brought about by the transaction, should be greater than the cost of the transaction assignable to A_1, and that the same thing should be true for the assortment A_2. This corollary of the Law of Exchange might be stated symbolically as follows:

$x \backsimeq y$ implies that

$$C[P(A_1 - x + y) - P(A_1)] > C_{A_1}(Tr),$$
$$C[P(A_2 + x - y) - P(A_2)] > C_{A_2}(Tr);$$

where the increase in potency is assumed to be measurable in dollars, C, and where $C_{A_1}(Tr)$ is the cost of the transaction to the owner of assortment i.

At a first level of consideration, x and y might be regarded as two different products in a primitive economy, such as a basket and a hat, with exchange taking place on a barter basis. Given a medium of exchange, y might be regarded as an amount of money paid by the buyer to obtain the article. The definitions of buyer and seller need not detain us except to note a very general distinction. The buyer in a transaction is adding a less liquid item to his assortment, while the seller is adding a more liquid asset, very likely with the intent of exchanging this in turn for more specialized assets later on.

We are now in position to state three propositions with more obvious relevance to the problem of planning a marketing system. The first is concerned with the optimality of exchange in a particular exchange situation. Viewing exchange from the standpoint of one of the decision makers, we can say that exchange is optimal if he prefers it to any available alternative. Similarly, for the decision maker on the other side of the transaction, it will be optimal for him if he prefers it to any available alternative. It is assumed that if a concrete situation offers an exchange opportunity, the number of alternatives realistically available to either side is not infinite in number but limited to only a few. Faced with a decision, an individual must be guided by his present knowledge of alternatives and the ordering according to his preferences within that set.

Subject to these constraints, it may be said that exchange is optimal if the individual decision maker I_1 prefers x to any of the available alternatives V_1 to V_n and if the decision maker I_2 prefers y to any of the available alternatives W_1 to W_n. It is scarcely necessary to go through the procedure of stating this proposition symbolically since it would follow the pattern previously illustrated. The principle of optimality rests on the Law of Exchange and its corollary. The principle would hold only where the conditions were consistent with the previously stated propositions. The exchange of x for y is preferred by each decision maker precisely because it offers the greatest increase in the potency of his assortment.

The next proposition to be asserted is that a set of transactions in series can replace direct sales by the supplier to the ultimate consumer if the transactions are optimal at each step. Let us assume initially that a sale is made directly by the supplier to the ultimate consumer. Now let us assume that a single intermediary intervenes between these two. If the exchange between the supplier and the intermediary is optimal, it means that the supplier prefers this exchange to dealing directly with the consumer. Similarly, if the exchange between the consumer and the intermediary is optimal, it means that the consumer prefers this transaction to a direct exchange with the supplier. This sequence of two transactions would therefore be eligible to replace the direct exchange between supplier and consumer.

If one intermediary can intervene between the supplier and the consumer, it follows that a second intermediary can intervene between the supplier and the first intermediary or between the first intermediary and the consumer, provided that the principle of optimality still obtains. Similarly, other intermediaries could be added to the chain as long as the principle of optimality was not violated.

Two major problems in planning the flow of transactions pertain to the case of transactions in series, which has just been discussed, and the case of parallel transactions occurring at the same level of distribution as, for example, between the supplier and the first intermediary. One of the aims of planning is to reduce the cost of individual transactions, particularly the cost of negotiation. The choices are to negotiate each of the parallel transactions separately or to negotiate a rule under which all transactions of a given type can be routinized. This can be reduced to a clear-cut decision based on the relative costs of negotiating individual transactions as compared to the cost of negotiating a rule, plus the cost of negotiating the routinized transactions to be controlled by the rule. A formula for this calculation might be stated in words as follows:

Routinize if the cost of rule negotiation plus the cost of negotiating the routinized transactions while the rule holds is less than the total cost of negotiating the individual transactions without the rule.

The calculation would start by estimating the number of transactions which will probably occur while the rule is in force, and multiplying this number by the average cost of a routinized transaction. If this cost is less than the cost of negotiating the same number of individual transactions, it would be worthwhile to negotiate the adoption of a rule. This, of course, assumes that the difference is greater than the cost of negotiating the rule. Generally, the saving would have to be substantial to force the decision-maker on either side to initiate the process of negotiating a rule. There are, of course, many practical cases in which literally thousands of transactions are to be covered by the rule, so that the condition of overall cost-saving would be fully satisfied.

TRANSVECTIONS

The marketing process is the continuous operation of transforming conglomerate resources as they occur in nature into meaningful assortments in the hands of consumers. Symbolically, the marketing process or operation might be shown as follows:

$$O(C) = \sum_{1}^{n} \underset{t_0 \to t_1}{\Delta} (A_1, A_2, \ldots, A_n, W),$$

where C means conglomerate,

$\underset{t_0 \to t_1}{O(C)}$ means the marketing operation performed on C during time period t_0 to t_1,

$\underset{t_0 \to t_1}{\Delta} (A_i)$ means the increment in assortment A_i during time period t_0 to t_1,

W means waste.

In words, this proposition states that applying the operation O to the conglomerate C over the period from t_0 to t_1 results in increments to the assortments held by consumers, plus an allowance for waste.

A transvection by contrast with the continuing market process refers to a single unit of action of the marketing system. This unit of action is consummated when an end product is placed in the hands of the ultimate consumer, but the transvection comprises all prior action necessary to produce this final result, going all the way back to conglomerate resources. The definition of a transvection can be shown symbolically as $T_v = STSTS \cdots TS$ where S is a sort and T is a transformation.

The statements so far about transvections indicate a need for two simple but fundamental proofs. The first is a proof that the sum of all transvections would correspond to an exhaustive description of the marketing process. The only difficulty here is in the selection of a long enough time period. By definition every sale of an end product has a transvection behind it. Thus, all the end products sold during a given year with their corresponding transvections would be approximately the same as the total marketing process for that year. Even if a four- or five-year period was considered, there would always be transvections beginning in the period which would terminate in a subsequent period. This is not so much a problem of proof as a problem of defining the marketing process and a transvection in such a way that they can be reconciled with each other.

The other problem is more clearly a problem of logical proof. That grows out of the definition of a transvection as shown in symbolic form. As shown in the formula, there is a continuous alternation between sorts and transformations. It will now be asserted that this alternation is inherent in the nature of a transvection. Before attempting to prove this assertion, it will be necessary to define and discuss both sorts and transformations.

SORTS AND TRANSFORMATIONS

First let us consider sorts or sorting, a concept with which the senior author has been identified for some time. Sorting is reclassification resulting in the creation of subsets from a set or of a set from subsets. Earlier treatments have identified four aspects of sorting, one of which is allocation, possibly the most fundamental concept for economics. It now seems possible to compress these types of sorting from four to two to achieve greater simplicity. Most characteristically, sorting suggests sorting out, which means breaking down a heterogeneous set into homogeneous subsets. Sorting out can also be called assignment, since it means assigning each member of a set to the appropriate subset. Assignment is the more general term, while allocation can still be employed to designate the special case in which the original set is regarded as homogeneous.

The other basic type of sorting is assorting. This means drawing members from subsets to form a heterogeneous set or assortment. Again the formation of a homogeneous set can be recognized as a special case designated as "assembly" or "accumulation." Assignment is the sorting perspective of the supplier or purveyor of goods. The broader term purveyor, rather than supplier, is adopted to avoid the implication that there is a supplier who necessarily disposes of the goods through a sales transaction. Assorting is the sorting perspective of the buyer or procurement agent. For the sake of simplicity, the notion of assignment will be generally adopted in the discussions of transvections as if the process was under the management of purveyors throughout.

The proposition that there is an alternation of sorts and transformations throughout the course of a transvection implies that an action of assignment always intervenes between a transformation just completed and the one which is to follow. That this is necessarily true will become clear when the term transformation is more fully explained. A transformation is a change in the physical form of a product or in its location in time and space which is calculated to increase its value for the ultimate consumer who adds it to his assortment. In other words, transformations add form, space, and time utility. Marketing theory is not concerned with the techniques of creating form utility but only

in their marketing implications. For example, marketing theory might need to distinguish between very broad categories of production such as refining and combining.

With respect to time and place utility, marketing is concerned with detailed techniques as well as broad perspective. Sorting might assign some goods to transportation by vehicles suitable for long hauls and others to vehicles designed for short hauls. Similarly, in the creation of time utility, some goods might be stored in one way while other similar or dissimilar goods could be stored more appropriately in a different type of facility. Credit is another way of creating time utility and again there is always an assignment problem prior to the selection of a mode of transformation.

Against this background, the formal proof of the alternating sequence might take the following form: Two sorts cannot follow each other in sequence in any significant sense since sorting out is the act of placing the members of a set in relevant subsets. If members are sorted into subsets and then moved from one subset to another, it is to be regarded as inefficient or exploratory sorting and not two successive sorts in a sequence. Similarly, two transformations cannot appear successively without an intervening sort. Different facilities are required for fabrication, shipment, storage and credit. Thus, there has to be an intervening assignment to the appropriate facilities. In very rare cases facilities might be combined, as in further aging or agitation of a product while in transit. The point, however, is that assignment always precedes the use of a facility and that typically separate facilities are required for each transformation. There are, of course, possibilities for breaking down the sequence of transformation still further with additional intervening sorts, and this topic will now be treated briefly.

A distribution network quickly becomes too complicated for complete evaluation of marketing effectiveness. The concept of the transvection offers a means of piecemeal analysis for planning purposes without violating the principle of the total systems approach. Looking at a transvection in relation to a given end product, it can be bounded or marked off from other related transvections. A network may consist largely of divergent paths, particularly if the basic production process is one of refining, with the end product distributed to thousands of consumers. A network may consist largely of convergent paths, particularly if the basic production process is one of combining materials and components and the ultimate consumer is government or a few large industrial buyers. In either case, there are a number of branching points on the main path along which the product flows through the network.

The bounding of the transvection means evaluation of additions or subtractions at each branching point along the way. Take the relatively simple case of a pair of shoes in which the principle component is leather. At each branching point at which lines converge, the costs of other components such as shoe findings must be added in. At each branching point where lines diverge, there may be waste or by-products to be evaluated. Waste may carry a cost penalty for disposal while by-products may contribute revenue to the main stream.

OPTIMAL NUMBER OF STEPS IN A TRANSVECTION

Against this background a basic principle for the evaluation of transvections may be stated. A transvection has the optimal number of steps if costs cannot be decreased, either by increasing or decreasing the number of steps. First, let us take a hypothetical case in which the only types of transformation pertain to spatial location. Assume that a natural product is being distributed and that it is snapped up immediately by consumers available at the terminal points. Even in this illustration, in which the creation of form and time utility are ruled out, there is still a problem of optimality for the number of steps in a transvection. Suppose an item is to be moved a distance of twenty-five miles. Obviously it would be a very poor solution to send a truck from Point x to Point y for direct delivery if the item was a small parcel making up a very tiny fraction of a truck load. The cost of direct delivery might easily exceed the value of the product at the point of origin.

Suppose now that two trucks are available for a delivery system. One truck picks up parcels from an area regarded as a collection area. The parcels are brought into a center where they are sorted into a sequence for most efficient delivery and then go onto another truck for this purpose. It could easily have required ten trucks previously to handle direct delivery for all origin and destination points for what can now be handled by two trucks.

Some existing parcel delivery networks are far more complex. A pickup truck collects parcels and brings them into a minor sorting center. Here most of the packages may be assigned to a large over-the-road vehicle which carried them to a major sorting center or hub. At this point they are assigned to other large trucks and carried to minor sorting centers. Here they will once more be assigned to small trucks for delivery to their final destination.

For any given system it is possible to compare two network plans. Suppose the following relationship holds: daily cost of transportation facilities, plus daily cost of sorting, under Plan A (4 sorts) > Plan B (5 sorts). It is clear that cost figures should be marshalled to test the possibility that Plan C (6 sorts) would cost still less. The number of possibilities is quite limited so that it would usually suffice to test only two plans against the network already in force, namely, those with one less sort and one more sort.

Actually the situation is not static but dynamic, because of changing technologies both of transportation and sorting. Mechanical sorting equipment has made great strides recently, thus creating the possibility that more sorts would lead to greater efficiency. There are practical limits to the length of a transvectional chain. At some point the cost of delay in the system would outweigh any further savings to be made through additional sorts. When transformations are considered more generally rather than dealing with transportation only, the same kind of reasoning still holds in principle. A detailed analysis might be required for the given network, since the possible patterns may now be large though finite. For example, fabrication may involve both refining and combining. It may be efficient to separate these two by hundreds of miles even though additional sorts and transformations are introduced. An improvement in storage facilities may make it possible to store the product closer to the consumer or even to move it into the consumer's assortment more promptly. It is this last step in the forwarding of goods which may be accomplished through various forms of consumer credit.

Some networks and choices of technologies may involve hundreds of possibilities as to the design of the transvection. While a computer may be needed to test all the possibilities, including differences in number of warehouses and spatial dispersion of production, the test of optimality is in principle the same for all types of transvections. There are considerations as to movement of information and movement of people which lie beyond the scope of this article. Suffice it to say that there is a large segment of marketing in which it is more efficient to bring the people to the goods rather than the goods to the people. There are also many opportunities for reducing the cost of moving goods or people by moving information instead. Mr. Halbert has drawn some interesting parallels between the movement of goods and the flows and stocks of information. We are primarily concerned here with delineating a transvection which represents the shortest path to market, taking account of the several possible types of movement.

The concept of the transvection as a planning tool has continued to evolve. Even in some of its earlier versions it has had fruitful applications in planning distribution systems for Douglas fir plywood, Irish linen, leather, and dry, edible beans. The results obtained can be illustrated by a study of the latter commodity made for the United States Department of Agriculture. It was observed that beans were bagged and rebagged at several places along the way. Analysis from the transvection viewpoint led to recommendations for eliminating bagging entirely. It was also recommended that sorting into grades be postponed until the terminal market was reached, since earlier sorting increased the number of less than carlot shipments required. Similar recommendations could be obtained more readily today with a more fully developed theory of transvections.

CONCLUSION

This article can well terminate with a final reminder to the reader of what it has attempted to accomplish. It has attempted to contribute more specifically to a theoretical treatment of transactions and transvections. In the case of transvections in particular, the effort has been to show both the extent of the difficulties and the promise of useful results in the development of formal theory.

7. The Division of Labor Is Limited by the Extent of the Market

GEORGE J. STIGLER

In this article Stigler sets the theoretical framework for explaining the role of the specialized firm, such as a middleman performing a specialized function for several other firms, for example, manufacturers. The core reason for the rise of middlemen is that they offer external economies to their suppliers and customers. Eventually, with increasing volume, manufacturers can take over the functions that they formerly allowed middlemen to perform.

Economists have long labored with the rate of operation of firm and industry, but they have generally treated as a (technological?) datum the problem of what the firm does—what governs its range of activities or functions. It is the central thesis of this paper that the theorem of Adam Smith which has been appropriated as a title is the core of a theory of the functions of firm and industry, and a good deal more besides. I shall (1) make some brief historical remarks on the theorem, (2) sketch a theory of the functions of a firm, (3) apply this theory to vertical integration, and (4) suggest broader applications of the theorem.

I. HISTORICAL INTRODUCTION

When Adam Smith advanced his famous theorem that the division of labor is limited by the extent of the market, he created at least a superficial dilemma. If this proposition is generally applicable, should there not be monopolies in most industries? So long as the further division of labor (by which we may understand the further specialization of labor and machines) offers lower costs for larger outputs, entrepreneurs will gain by combining or expanding and driving out rivals. And here was the dilemma: Either the division of labor is limited by the extent of the market, and, characteristically, industries are monopolized; or industries are characteristically competitive, and the theorem is false or of little significance. Neither alternative is inviting. There were and are plenty of important competitive industries; yet Smith's argument that Highlanders would be more efficient if each did not have to do his own baking and brewing also seems convincing and capable of wide generalization.

In the pleasant century that followed on the *Wealth of Nations*, this conflict was temporarily resolved in favor of Smith's theorem by the simple expedient of ignoring the conditions for stable competitive equalibrium. Ricardo, Senior, and J. S. Mill—and their less famous confreres—announced the principle of increasing returns in manufacturing—for Senior it was even an axiom. The exclusion of agriculture was based on the empirical judgment, not that further division of labor was impossible, but that it was a weaker tendency than that of diminishing returns from more intensive cultivation of a relatively fixed supply of land.

This was hardly a satisfactory solution, and, when Marshall came to reformulate classical economics into a comprehensive and internally consistent system, the dilemma could no longer be ignored. He refused to give up either increasing returns or competition, and he created three theories (of course, not only for this purpose) which insured their compatibility. First, and perhaps most important, he developed the con-

• SOURCE: Reprinted from *The Journal of Political Economy* (June, 1951), LIX, No. 3, 185–193. Copyright 1961 by The University of Chicago. Used by permission. George Stigler, Professor of Economics, Columbia University.

cept of external economies—economies outside the reach of the firm and dependent upon the size of the industry, the region, the economy, or even the whole economic world. Second, he emphasized the mortality of able entrepreneurs and the improbability that a single business would be managed superlatively for any length of time. Third, he argued that each firm might have a partial monopoly—a separate, elastic demand curve for its product—so that, with expansion of its output, the price would usually fall faster than average costs would.

For a time this reconciliation of competition and increasing returns served its purpose, but, as the center of price theory moved toward the firm, Smith's theorem fell into the background. External economies were a rather nebulous category relative to anything so concrete and definite as economists for a time believed the costs of a firm to be. It was pointed out by Professor Knight, moreover, that economies external to one industry may (and perhaps must) be internal to another. The industries in which the economies are internal will tend to monopoly; and, incidentally, it is no longer a foregone conclusion that such economies will be shared with the buyers. Since external economies seemed a refractory material for the popular analytical techniques, they were increasingly neglected.

Marshall's theory of business mortality was also increasingly neglected, with even less explicit consideration. It was not an approach that harmonized well with the economics of a stationary economy, and again the theory was very inconvenient to incorporate into the cost and demand curves (especially if one will not use the concept of a representative firm). If the economies of scale within the firm were as strong as Marshall pictured them, moreover, it was not clear that continuously high-quality entrepreneurship was necessary to achieve monopoly. And could the giant firm not grow quickly by merger as well as hesitantly by internal expansion?

Marshall's third theory of the falling demand curve for the individual firm lost popularity for a generation because it was incompatible with perfect competition rigorously defined, and this became increasingly the standard model of analysis. And, paradoxically, when the falling demand curve was rediscovered and popularized in the 1930's by the proponents of imperfect and monopolistic competition, they used it not to examine the broad movements of industries and of economies but to focus price theory on the physiology and pathology of the firm.

In 1928, to retrace a step, the neglect of increasing returns had gone so far that Allyn Young felt the need to restore perspective by an emphatic indorsement of the fundamental importance of Smith's theorem: "That theorem, I have always thought, is one of the most illuminating and fruitful generalizations which can be found anywhere in the whole literature of economics."[1] His position seemed persuasive, but he did not resolve the technical difficulties of incorporating the extent of the market into competitive price theory. Indeed, he openly avoided this problem, asserting that the firm and perhaps also the industry were too small to serve as units of analysis in this area. And so, although Young's and Marshall's and Smith's position is often given lip service to this day, the tributes are tokens of veneration, not evidences of active partnership with the theory of the firm and the competitive industry.

II. THE FUNCTIONS OF A FIRM

The firm is usually viewed as purchasing a series of inputs, from which it obtains one or more salable products, the quantities of which are related to the quantities of the inputs by a production function. For our purpose it is better to view the firm as engaging in a series of distinct operations: purchasing and storing materials; transforming materials into semifinished products and semifinished products into finished products; storing and selling the outputs; extending credit to buyers; etc. That is, we partition the firm not among the markets in which it buys inputs but among the functions or processes which constitute the scope of its activity.

The costs of these individual functions will be related by technology. The cost of one function may depend upon whether the preceding function took place immediately before or in the immediate vicinity, as when hot ingots are processed with a saving of heat. Or the interrelationships among processes may be remote, as when the entrepreneur must neglect production in order to supervise marketing.

Let us ignore for a moment these interrelationships of costs of various functions, in order to achieve a simple geometrical picture of the firm's costs of production. If the cost of each function depends only on the rate of output of that function, we may draw a unique cost curve for it. Furthermore, if there is a constant proportion between the rate of output of

[1] "Increasing Returns and Economic Progress," *Economic Journal*, XXXVIII (1928), 529.

each function and the rate of output of the final product (as when every 100 pounds of cement is bagged), we may draw the cost curves of all functions on one graph, and the (vertical) sum of these costs of various functions will be the conventional average-cost curve of the firm.

We should expect to find many different patterns of average costs of functions: some falling continuously (Y_1); some rising continuously (Y_2); some conventionally U-shaped (Y_3) (see Figure 1). It is not impossible, of course, that the average cost of some operations first rises and then falls.

Now consider Smith's theorem. Certain processes are subject to increasing returns; why does the firm not exploit them further and in the process become a monopoly? Because there are other functions subject to diminishing returns, and these are, on balance, at least so costly that average cost of the final product does not diminish with output. Then why does the firm not abandon the functions subject to increasing returns, allowing another firm (and industry) to specialize in them to take full advantage of increasing returns? At a given time these functions may be too small to support a specialized firm or firms. The sales of the product may be too small to support a specialized merchant; the output of a by-product may be too small to support a specialized fabricator; the demand for market information may be too small to support a trade journal. The firm must then perform these functions for itself.

But, with the expansion of the industry, the magnitude of the function subject to increasing returns may become sufficient to permit a firm to specialize in performing it. The firms will then abandon the process (Y_1), and a new firm will take it over. This new firm will be a monopoly, but it will be confronted by elastic demands: it cannot charge a price for the process higher than the average cost of the process to the firms which are abandoning it. With the continued expansion of the industry, the number of firms supplying process Y_1 will increase, so that the new industry becomes competitive and the new industry may, in turn, abandon parts of process Y_1 to a new set of specialists.

The abandonment of function Y_1 by the original industry will alter each firm's cost curves: the curve Y_1 will be replaced by a horizontal line (ignoring quantity discounts) at a level lower than Y_1 in the effective region. The cost curve of the product (drawn with broken lines in Figure 1) will be lower, and, on present assumptions, the output at which average costs are a minimum (if only one such output exists) becomes smaller.

Certain functions are also subject to increasing cost; why not abandon or at least restrict the scale of operation of these functions? The foregoing discussion is also applicable here, with one change. When the industry grows, the original firms need not wholly abandon the increasing-cost processes. Part of the required amount of the process (say, engine castings for automobiles) may be made within the firm without high average (or marginal) costs, and the remainder purchased from subsidiary industries.

In order to give a simple geometrical illustration, we have made two assumptions. The first is that the rate of output of the process and the rate of output of the final product are strictly proportional. This will be approximately true of some functions (such as making parts of a single final product), but it will also be untrue of other functions (such as advertising the product). If we drop the assumption, the substance of our argument will not be affected, but our geometrical picture becomes more complicated.[2]

Our second assumption, that the costs of the functions are independent, is more important. Actually, many processes will be rival: the greater the rate of output of one process, the higher the cost of a given rate of output of the other process or processes. Sometimes the rivalry will be technological (as in many multiple-product firms), but almost always it will

[2] We can either draw separate cost curves for the various functions or combine them on one chart, with the scales of the functions chosen so that the optimum amount of each function is shown for the given rate of final output.

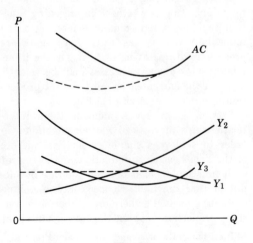

Fig. 1

also be managerial: the wider the range of functions the firm undertakes, the greater the tasks of co-ordination. Other processes will be complementary: the greater the rate of output of one process, the lower the cost of a given rate of output of the other processes. A most curious example of complementarity is the circular flow of materials within a plant; thus, in the course of making steel, steel plants supply a large part of their requirements for scrap.

If, on balance, the functions are rival, then usually the firm will increase its rate of output of the final product when it abandons a function; and I think that this is generally the case. For example, in the famous study of the Lancashire textile industry by Chapman and Ashton, it was found that firms engaged in both spinning and weaving in 1911 had, on average, 47,634 spindles, while those engaged only in spinning had, on average, 68,055 spindles.[3] But this is not necessary—indeed, they found the converse relationship in number of looms—and the effect of the range of functions on the size of the firm requires much study before we can reach safe generalizations.

III. VERTICAL INTEGRATION

Many economists believe that, with the growth of firms (and industries?), functions are usually taken over from previous independent industries. For example, United States Steel Corporation now mines its ores, operates its own ore-hauling railroads and ships, and, at the other end, fabricates barrels, oil-field equipment, and houses. (The number of economic views based chiefly on half-a-dozen giant corporations would repay morbid study.)

Broadly viewed, Smith's theorem suggests that vertical disintegration is the typical development in growing industries, vertical integration in declining industries.[4] The significance of the theorem can therefore be tested by an appeal to the facts on vertical integration.

Unfortunately, there are no wholly conclusive data on the trend of vertical integration. The only large-scale quantitative information at hand comes from a comparison of the 1919

study by Willard Thorp with the 1937 study by Walter Crowder of central offices (companies with two or more manufacturing establishments). In 1919, 602 manufacturing companies, or 13.0 per cent of a moderately complete list of 4,635 companies, had two or more establishments making successive products, that is, the product of one establishment was the raw material of another establishment.[5] In 1937, successive functions were found in 565 companies (or 10.0 per cent of a more complete list of 5,625 companies).[6] In 1919, successive functions were found in 34.4 per cent of all complex central offices (companies with establishments in two or more industries); in 1937, in only 27.5 per cent. Multiplant companies probably grew in relative importance during this period, so it is possible that a larger share of manufacturing output came from vertically integrated firms. But, so far as these multiplant companies are concerned, there seems to have been a tendency away from vertical integration.[7]

If one considers the full life of industries, the dominance of vertical disintegration is surely to be expected. Young industries are often strangers to the established economic system. They require new kinds or qualities of materials and hence make their own; they must overcome technical problems in the use of their products and cannot wait for potential users to overcome them; they must persuade customers to abandon other commodities and find no specialized merchants to undertake this task. These young industries must design their specialized equipment and often manufacture it, and they must undertake to recruit (historically,

[3] S. J. Chapman and T. S. Ashton, "The Sizes of Businesses, Mainly in the Textile Industries," *Journal of the Royal Statistical Society*, LXXVII (1914), 538.

[4] This is not a wholly rigorous implication, however. With the growth of industries specialism of firms may take the form of dealing with a narrower range of products as well as performing fewer functions on the same range of products.

[5] W. Thorp, *The Integration of Industrial Operation* (Washington, 1924), p. 238. I have omitted railroad repair shops and also the 301 companies having establishments which made successive products, because mining establishments were included.

[6] W. F. Crowder, *The Integration of Manufacturing Operations* ("T.N.E.C. Monographs," No. 27 [Washington, 1941], p. 197).

[7] The ratio of "value-added" to value of product is a crude index of the extent of vertical integration *within* establishments. It is interesting to note that in the 17 industries in which this ratio was highest in 1939 in manufacturing, the average number of wage-earners was 16,540. In the 17 industries in which the ratio was lowest, the average number of wage-earners was 44,449. Thus the vertically integrated establishments were in smaller industries than the vertically disintegrated establishments (see National Resources Planning Board, *Industrial Location and National Resources* [Washington, 1943], p. 270).

often to import) skilled labor. When the industry has attained a certain size and prospects, many of these tasks are sufficiently important to be turned over to specialists. It becomes profitable for other firms to supply equipment and raw materials, to undertake the marketing of the product and the utilization of by-products, and even to train skilled labor. And, finally, when the industry begins to decline, these subsidiary, auxiliary, and complementary industries begin also to decline, and eventually the surviving firms must begin to reappropriate functions which are no longer carried on at a sufficient rate to support independent firms.

We may illustrate this general development from the cotton textile machinery industry, much of whose history has recently become available.[8] This industry began as a part of the textile industry: each mill built a machine shop to construct and repair its machines. The subsequent history is one of progressive specialism, horizontal as well as vertical: at various times locomotives, machine tools, the designing of cotton mills, and direct selling were abandoned. When the cotton textile market declined in the 1920's, the machinery firms added new products, such as paper machinery, textile machinery for other fabrics, and wholly novel products, such as oil burners and refrigerators. Indeed, one is impressed that even the longer cyclical fluctuations seem to have affected the extent of specialism in much the same way as have the secular trends.

Of course, this is not the whole story of vertical integration, and it may be useful to sketch some of the other forces at work. The most

[8] G. S. Gibb, *The Saco-Lowell Shops* (Cambridge: Harvard University Press, 1950); T. R. Navin, *The Whitin Machine Works since 1831* (Cambridge: Harvard University Press, 1950).

important of these other forces, I believe, is the failure of the price system (because of monopoly or public regulation) to clear markets at prices within the limits of the marginal cost of the product (to the buyer if he makes it) and its marginal-value product (to the seller if he further fabricates it). This phenomenon was strikingly illustrated by the spate of vertical mergers in the United States during and immediately after World War II, to circumvent public and private price control and allocations. A regulated price of OA was set (Figure 2), at which an output of OM was produced. This quantity had a marginal value of OB to buyers, who were rationed on a nonprice basis. The gain to buyers and sellers combined from a free price of NS was the shaded area, RST, and vertical integration was the simple way of obtaining this gain. This was the rationale of the integration of radio manufacturers into cabinet manufacture, of steel firms into fabricated products, etc.

Although nonprice rationing provides the most striking examples of this force toward vertical integration, private monopolies normally supply the same incentive. Almost every raw-material cartel has had trouble with customers who wish to integrate backward, in order to negate the cartel prices. Since the cartel members are sharply limited in their output quotas, the discounted future profits of a cartel member need not be high, even with very high prices; so it is profitable for buyers to integrate backward by purchase (as well as by seeking noncartelized supply sources). The Rhenish-West-phalian Coal Cartel, for example, was constantly plagued by this problem:

While a few of the members of the original syndicate agreement of 1893 had been steel companies which produced a part of their own coal and coke requirements, the steel industry, for the most part, had relied upon fuel purchased in the market. The stiffening of prices, coupled with the inelastic terms of sale resulting from the operation of the coal syndicate, now caused the steel companies to seek to free themselves from dependence upon the syndicate. ". . . defensive measures were adopted by all clases of consumers. Some of the large industrial consumers . . . acquired their portant companies as the Vereinigte Stahlwerke, Rhenische Stahlwerk-Admiral, Badische Anilin- und Sodafabrik, Norddeutsche Lloyd, Friedrich Krupp, and a number of others representing the electric, gas, railway equipment, rubber,

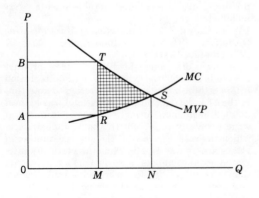

Fig. 2

and other industries. Also some cities such as Cologne and Frankfurt were among them."[9]

Monopoly is a devious thing, and it leads to vertical integration for other reasons also. A firm cannot practice price discrimination in the stages in which it does not operate; only by fabricating cable could the Alumumum Company of America sell cable at less than the ingot price in competition with copper, while maintaining a higher price on less competitive products.[10] Again, it is possible that vertical integration increases the difficulty of entry by new firms, by increasing the capital and knowledge necessary to conduct several types of operation rather than depend on rivals for supplies or markets.

These remarks are not intended to constitute a theory of vertical integration. There is doubt, indeed, that we want a theory of vertical integration except as part of a theory of the functions of a firm. As soon as one tries to classify the variegated details of production, one finds how artificial and arbitrary "vertical" relationships are. Whether one wishes to treat vertical relationships separately or as part of a general theory, however, Smith's theorem promises to be a central part of the explanation.

IV. WIDER IMPLICATIONS

If Smith's theorem is less than a complete theory of the division of functions among industries, it is also something more than this: it sheds light on several aspects of the structure and workings of economies. A few of the implications of the principle of increasing specialization will be discussed very tentatively.

One expects to find some relationship between the functional structure of an industry and its geographical structure—after all, reductions of transportation costs are a major way of increasing the extent of the market. (A reminder is hardly necessary that we are dealing with highly interdependent forces and that unilateral causation is implicitly assumed for simplicity and emphasis.) Localization is one method of increasing the economic size of an industry and achieving the gains of specialization. The auxiliary and complementary industries that must operate in intimate co-operation can seldom do

so efficiently at a distance. I venture that, within a market area, geographical dispersion is a luxury that can be afforded by industries only after they have grown large (so that even the smaller production centers can reap the major gains of specialization) and that it must be sacrified for geographical concentration, once the industry begins to shrink in size.

Closely related to this is the influence of localization upon the size of plant. The individual plants can specialize in smaller ranges of products and functions in highly localized industries (the size of the industry in some sense being held constant). In the United States geographically concentrated industries usually have fairly small plants.[11] There is also some evidence that the plants of an industry are smaller in the larger production centers. For example, in 1937 the average shoe factory in industrial areas had 137 employees, in other areas, 314 employees.[12] The dominance of medium-sized plants in highly localized industries has also been found in England.[13]

During the nineteenth century it was often said that England had the advantage of an "early start"; and this ambiguous statement had an element of truth which Smith's theorem more clearly expresses. As the largest economy in the world, it could carry specialism further than any other country, especially those "general" specialties (like railroads, shopping, banking, etc.) which are not closely attached to any one industry. England's advantage was a big start, as well as an early one.

Those too numerous people who believe that transactions between firms are expensive and those within firms are free will do well to study the organization of England during this period of eminence. In Birmingham, the center of the metal trades, specialism was carried out to an almost unbelievable extent. Consider the small-arms industry in 1860, when Birmingham was still the leading production center of the world:

Of the 5800 people engaged in this manufacture within the borough's boundaries in 1861 the majority worked within a small district round St. Mary's Church. . . . The reason for the high degree of localization is not difficult to discover. The manufacture of guns, as of jewellery, was carried on by a large number of makers

[9] A. H. Stockder, *Regulating an Industry* (New York, 1932), pp. 8, 11, and 36.
[10] D. H. Wallace, *Market Control in the Aluminum Industry* (Cambridge: Harvard University Press, 1937), pp. 218–19, 380.

[11] National Resources Planning Board, *op. cit.*, pp. 250 ff.
[12] *Ibid.*, p. 257.
[13] P. S. Florence, *Investment, Location, and Size of Plant* (Cambridge, 1948).

who specialized in particular processes, and this method of organization involved the frequent transport of parts from one workshop to another.

"The master gun-maker—the entrepreneur—seldom possessed a factory or workshop. . . . Usually he owned merely a warehouse in the gun quarter, and his function was to acquire semi-finished parts and to give these out to specialized craftsmen, who undertook the assembly and finishing of the gun. He purchased materials from the barrel-makers, lock-makers, sight-stampers, trigger-makers, ramrod-forgers, gun-furniture makers, and, if he were engaged in the military branch, from bayonet-forgers. All of these were independent manufacturers executing the orders of several master gun-makers. . . . Once the parts had been purchased from the "material-makers," as they were called, the next task was to hand them out to a long succession of "setters-up," each of whom performed a specific operation in connection with the assembly and finishing of the gun. To name only a few, there were those who prepared the front sight and lump end of the barrels; the jiggers, who attended to the breech end; the stockers, who let in the barrel and lock and shaped the stock; the barrel-strippers, who prepared the gun for rifling and proof; the hardeners, polishers, borers and riflers, engravers, browners, and finally the lock-freers, who adjusted the working parts."[14]

At present there is widespread imitation of American production methods abroad, and "backward" countries are presumably being supplied with our latest machines and methods.

[14] G. C. Allen, *The Industrial Development of Birmingham and the Black Country, 1860–1927* (London, 1929), pp. 56–57, 116–17. Commenting on a later period, Allen says: "On the whole, it can be said that specialization was most apparent in the engineering industries in which output was rapidly expanding; while the policy of broadening the basis [product line] was found, mainly, either in the very large concerns, or in industries in which the decline of the older markets had forced manufacturers to turn part of their productive capacity to serve new demands" (*ibid.*, pp. 335–36). The later history of the gun trade, in which American innovations in production techniques were revolutionary, suggest that the organization in Birmingham was defective in its provision for technical experimentation.

By a now overly familiar argument, we shall often be a seriously inappropriate model for industrialization on a small scale. Our processes will be too specialized to be economical on this basis. The vast network of auxiliary industries which we can take for granted here will not be available in small economies. Their educational institutions will be unable to supply narrowly specialized personnel, they will lack the specialists who can improve raw materials and products. At best, the small economies that imitate us can follow our methods of doing things this year, not our methods of changing things next year; therefore, they will be very rigid. This position has been stated well by one observant citizen of a backward economy, Benjamin Franklin:

"Manufactures, where they are in perfection, are carried on by a multiplicity of hands, each of which is expert only in his own part, no one of them a master of the whole; and if by any means spirited away to a foreign country, he is lost without his fellows. Then it is a matter of extremest difficulty to persuade a complete set of workmen, skilled in all parts of a manufactory, to leave their country together and settle in a foreign land. Some of the idle and drunken may be enticed away, but these only disappoint their employers, and serve to discourage the undertaking. If by royal munificence, and an expense that the profits of the trade alone would not bear, a complete set of good and skilful hands are collected and carried over, they find so much of the system imperfect, so many things wanting to carry on the trade to advantage, so many difficulties to overcome, and the knot of hands so easily broken by death, dissatisfaction, and desertion, that they and their employers are discouraged altogether, and the project vanishes into smoke."[15]

The division of labor is not a quaint practice of eighteenth-century pin factories; it is a fundamental principle of economic organization.

[15] "The Interest of Great Britain in America," edited by V. S. Clark, *History of Manufacturers in the United States* (New York, 1949), I. 152. Clark adds: "In these words Franklin was but reciting the history of the more important colonial attempts to establish a new industry or to enlarge an old one with which he was personally familiar."

8. The Economic Structure of Channels of Distribution

LOUIS P. BUCKLIN*

The purpose of this dissertation is to construct a general theory which could be used to study and predict the structure of a channel of distribution for any product or commodity. The basis for such a theory was found in the synthesis of two familiar concepts: one, the typology of marketing functions and, two, the theory of the firm. The theoretical framework developed from this analysis appeared to be capable of unifying many existing ideas concerning channels and of opening opportunities for formulating new hypotheses about channel structure.

The purpose of this dissertation was to attempt to construct a general theory which could be utilized to study and predict the structure of a channel of distribution for any particular commodity. The structure of a channel may be defined as the number of different types of institutions which perform the activities that produce and move a good to its point of consumption. The kinds of problems that might be solved by such a general theory would include: why five different types of institutions are found in a channel for one good, while ten or twelve make up the channel for another; why two different channel structures exist for the same good; or what changes in existing channels for some commodity should be expected in the future. Such a theory should also be capable of throwing some light upon the kinds of relationships one finds among firms in a channel.

Since the structure of a distribution channel is formed by a set of institutions performing certain kinds of work, the basis for any theory must lie in a methodology which can identify the kinds of work being performed by each institution. The literature of marketing is of help here,

since it is replete with articles which attempt to analyze marketing work into cohesive categories. Unfortunately, there has been little agreement among the proponents of this concept as to how many functions there should be or which activities each should encompass. As a result, it was necessary to construct a new set for the present purpose. This was accomplished by the establishment of four criteria and by the evaluation of different groupings of marketing activities against these criteria. The criteria were:

1. The activities included in each function must be so related as to make it necessary for some firm to organize and direct the performance of either all of them or none of them.
2. The activities must have sufficient scope as to make it possible for the firm to specialize in them to the exclusion of all others.
3. The activities should incur substantial costs.
4. Each marketing activity must be placed in one function and in one function only.

The functions found to meet these criteria were as follows:

1. Transit (T)—all activities required to move goods between two points.
2. Inventory (I)—all activities required to move goods in and out of storage, sort and store them.
3. Search (S)—all activities required to communicate offers to buy and sell and transfer title.
4. Persuasion (P)—activities incurred to influence the beliefs of a buyer or seller.
5. Production (Pr)—activities necessary to create a good with any desired set of specifications.

The first four functions will have a decidedly

• SOURCE: Louis P. Bucklin, "The Economic Structure of Channels of Distribution," in Martin L. Bell (ed.), *Marketing: A Maturing Discipline* (Chicago: American Marketing Association, 1960), pp. 379–85.
* *Louis P. Bucklin*, Assistant Professor of Marketing, University of California.

familiar ring to those acquainted with the literature. The fifth function, production, was included because many marketing activities, such
as the changing of styles and packaging, are
almost inseparably related to production costs.
Further, the general characteristics of the production process will be shown to have an important influence upon channel structure.

By using this set of functions one can identify
the structure of most existing channels. For
example, the familiar manufacturer, wholesaler,
and retailer channel may be symbolically illustrated, using the initial letter of each function,
except production where the first two letters are
used, to denote the performance of a function
by an institution. The description of the channel
is as follows.

$$(\text{PrITSP}) \rightarrow (\text{SITSP}) \rightarrow (\text{SISP}) \leftarrow (\text{STIC})$$

The manufacturer, wholesaler, and retailer
are represented by the bracketed symbols
(PrITSP), (SITSP), and (SISP). This means,
in the case of the manufacturer, that this institution is performing all five marketing functions.
The wholesaler performs only four, but must
search twice, once to contact manufacturers
and once to contact retailers.

The last group of symbols (STIC) represents
the consumer (C). While the consumer is not a
channel institution, his role is important for
two reasons. First, the consumer's rate of use
will have important effects upon the operating
characteristics of other functions in the channel.
Second, the consumer will always perform some
marketing functions and may, on occasion, integrate with a substantial number of functions
that could be performed by channel institutions.

The arrows connecting the institutional symbols represent the direction of search. In the
above case, the arrows indicate that the manufacturer calls upon the wholesaler, the wholesaler upon the retailer, and the consumer upon
the retailer.

Using the concept of marketing functions in
this manner provides a systematic means for
identifying channel structure. In terms of analytic content, however, it pushes no further than
previous functional concepts. In order to make
this system useful it must be placed in a framework which will reveal whether any function
must be performed in a channel and, if so,
whether it ought to be performed by itself or in
conjunction with others.

The quantification of the economic characteristics of functions necessary to accomplish
this task can be obtained through an analysis
of the factors which control cost within the
function. For example, in the channel symbolically described above the product is transported
between a wholesale institution and a retail
institution. The transit costs incurred here may
be mathematically related to distance, physical
characteristics of the product, transportation
technology, the size of individual orders and
the volume of orders carried.

From this mathematical relationship, the familiar long run average cost curve can be readily
derived. The height of the curve will be determined by the distance, physical characteristics
and size of order factors. The shape of the curve
will be dependent upon any economies of scale
that can be realized with greater volume. In
most instances one would expect average costs
for the function to behave in the familiar fashion. Average costs will initially decline to some
minimal point and, then, increase due to managerial inefficiencies at higher operating levels.

For each transit function in a channel a cost
relationship may be determined and an average
cost curve charted in the above manner. Similarly, cost curves may be drawn for each function. Cost curves for institutions performing
several functions may be derived by aggregating
the costs of each function. Modifications in
these aggregate curves will, of course, have to
be made if the firm realizes some economies or
diseconomies from the integration.

When one looks at channel functions from
this point of view it becomes possible to distinguish between two types of channel structures. The first type, to be called the extant
channel, represents the channel structure, and
related costs, for a group of institutions actually
involved in the marketing of some good. The
second type may be termed the normative channel. It is the channel that would exist if all institutions in the extant channel, and all potential
entrants, were fully adapted to current economic conditions. In such a channel there would
be no tendency for new firms to enter, old ones
to exit or to shift functions among themselves.

The focus of this dissertation was placed upon
the analysis of the normative channel. The reason for this is that extant channels are the product of a complex stream of past and present
economic, social, and political forces which are
not always relevant to the future. In order to
determine what the channel structure should be,
or will likely be, it is necessary to discover what
normative channel fits the economic conditions
expected to prevail in the future. By contrasting the structure of a normative channel with

its extant counterpart, one can secure an understanding of the economic forces operating upon existing institutions. Such pressures will continue to exist until change in the extant channel causes its structure to conform to that of the normative, or until the economic conditions creating these forces are altered. A study of the normative channel, consequently, becomes the key to comprehending the behavior of firms in the extant channel.

In order to study the structure of normative channels a step by step analysis was used to sort out the various economic forces operating upon marketing functions and to examine them intensively. The steps consisted of six different, and progressively more complex, environments: perfect competition, pure competition, monopolistic competition caused by spatial differentiation, monopolistic competition caused by product differentiation, and oligopoly. Because of the time limitations it will be impossible to explore the findings in each of these studies. In order to give something of the flavor of the analysis, however, a brief sketch of the channel structures found under perfect competition can be presented.

In perfect competition the conditions of the environment include all the assumptions usually found in traditional economic analysis. In addition, the assumption was included that there was costless and instantaneous communication among all channel institutions and consumers. Also, it was assumed that all production activities would take place at one point and all consumption at another point, any desired distance from the first.

The analysis of normative channel structure has two parts. The first involves a determination of the number and type of each function to be required by a channel handling some commodity under given economic conditions. The second part seeks to discover whether each function will be performed by itself or whether it will be integrated into a firm performing several others.

With respect to the number of functions to be found in a channel under perfect competition, it can be shown that the environmental assumptions eliminate all need for search and persuasion. Costless communication and identical products are the reasons for this. The problem may be further simplified by assuming that production need only take place once in the channel. This leaves the channel structure dependent upon the number of times that inventory and transit are to be performed.

The analysis of this can start from the point that for any good the minimal functional requirements for a channel are one production and one transit function. This may be symbolically written as follows:

$$Pr - T - C$$

Such a channel would move goods immediately from the production line onto some continuously operating transit service and, then constantly into consumption.

While physical distribution systems of this type are rare, a few do exist. The production and supply of electricity is an example. For the most part, however, such a system is apt to be highly unsatisfactory. Elimination of some of the difficulties may be secured by the establishment of inventory functions at the point of production and the point of consumption. This is illustrated as follows:

$$Pr - I - T - I - C$$

In order for the two inventory functions to take their places in the channel, their costs must either be offset by reductions in the expense of performing other functions or their presence must result in an improved service to a consumer willing to pay a higher price for it. Both events are likely to occur. Production costs could be reduced, because that function can now operate at rates dictated by internal economies. Transit function costs could be lowered for the same reason. Finally, the consumer may be able to secure higher levels of satisfaction by having his goods available for consumption at times wholly determined by his needs.

In many cases further use for inventory functions may be found. For example, if the consumer purchases in small quantities, and production takes place in large volume, the transit facilities suitable for picking up the goods from the manufacturer may be uneconomic for delivery.

A central inventory function, as shown in the following case, may serve to save more costs than it adds.

$$Pr - I - T - I - T - I - C$$

When this occurs, it is important to notice that transit is broken into two distinct functions, and costs must now be separately calculated for each.

Additional inventory functions may still be required under other economic conditions. The method of analysis to determine whether these will appear in the structure follows the above approach, and no further elaboration is needed at this point.

The problem of determining which marketing functions will be operated independently and which will be integrated can now be briefly examined. In the present simplified case integration will only occur when the cost of operating two or more of the required functions by a single firm is less, or at least no greater, than when they are undertaken by separate firms. In the long run such savings are only realizable when the inputs required for one function cannot be fully used. Integration may make it possible to put the unused portion of these inputs to work in another function, thus lowering total costs for the performance of both.

Normally, however, one would not expect too much integration in channels operating under perfect competition. The integration of functions is more likely to create diseconomies in management. Further, when the optimal scale of two separate functions is different, then integration would force the firm to operate one, or both, at rates above or below its optimal. Since this would raise the costs above what they would be if the functions were operated by separate firms, the integration cannot persist in the long run.

Time limitations make it impossible to carry this analysis further. It is hoped, however, that the bare bones of the methodology have been so sketched as to suggest how the analysis in the more complex environments would follow. It should be pointed out, however, that abstract and simplified as the above analysis has been, it can be used to indicate reasons for change in actual distribution channels. An exogenous change, for example, in the optimal rate of production can be shown invariably to alter the costs of performing other functions. In many instances it may affect the number of other functions required. Both of these effects may alter the degree of integration of functions in the channel. Similar reactions can be expected when there are exogenous changes in each of the other functions and in consumption. This simple framework, consequently, is capable of convincingly demonstrating this important marketing principle.

In conclusion, the general theory resulting from the approach shown above may be characterized as a synthesis of the familiar concepts of marketing functions and the economists' theory of the firm. It appears to offer a fruitful means for opening opportunities to create new hypotheses concerning channel structure as well as placing many existing ideas into a unified framework. The theory may prove to be a useful guide for empirical work on channels. It, finally, may be ideally suited as a device to aid in the teaching of marketing.

9. Postponement, Speculation, and the Structure of Distribution Channels

LOUIS P. BUCKLIN

While the study of marketing has long been concerned with the creation of time, space, and possession utilities, much of the literature of the field has dealt with the problems of ownership. Issues involving space and time, in particular, have been scarcely touched. The role of time with respect to the character of the structure of distribution channels, for example, has just begun to be charted. The purpose of this article is to derive a principle describing the effect of temporal factors upon distribution systems.

THE CONCEPT OF SUBSTITUTABILITY

Underlying the logic of the principle to be developed is the hypothesis that economic interaction among basic marketing functions, and between these functions and production, provides much of the force that shapes the structure of the distribution channel. These interactions occur because of the capability of the various functions to be used as substitutes for each other within certain broad limitations. This capability is comparable to the opportunities available to the entrepreneur to use varying ratios of land, labor, and capital in the production of his firm's output. The substitutability of marketing functions may occur both within the firm and among the various institutions of the channel, e.g., producers, middlemen, and consumers. This substitutability permits the work load of one function to be shrunk and shifted to another without affecting the output of the channel. These functional relationships may also be seen to be at the root of the "total cost" concept employed in the growing literature of the management of the physical distribution system [3, 9].

A familiar example of one type of substitution

• SOURCE: Louis P. Bucklin, "Postponement, Speculation and the Structure of Distribution Channels," *Journal of Marketing Research*, Vol. 2 (February, 1965), pp. 26–31. Louis P. Bucklin, Assistant Professor of Marketing, University of California (Berkeley).

that may appear in the channel is the use of inventories to reduce the costs of production stemming from cyclical demand. Without the inventory, production could only occur during the time of consumption. Use of the inventory permits production to be spread over a longer period of time. If some institution of the channel senses that the costs of creating a seasonal inventory would be less than the savings accruing from a constant rate of production, it would seek to create such a stock and to retain the resulting profits. The consequence of this action is the formation of a new and alternate channel for the product.

The momentum of change, however, is not halted at this point. Unless there is protection against the full brunt of competitive forces, the institutions remaining in the original, and now high-cost channel, will either be driven out of business or forced to convert to the new system as well. With continued competitive pressure the excess profits, initially earned by the institutions which innovated the new channel, will eventually be eliminated and total channel costs will fall.

In essence, the concept of substitutability states that under competitive conditions institutions of the channel will interchange the work load among functions, not to minimize the cost of some individual function, but the total costs of the channel. It provides, thereby, a basis for the study of distribution channels. By understanding the various types of interactions among the marketing functions and production that could occur, one may determine the type of distribution structure that should appear to minimize the total channel costs including those of the consumer. The principle of postponement-speculation, to be developed below, evaluates the conditions under which one type of substitution may occur.

POSTPONEMENT

In 1950, Wroe Alderson proposed a concept which uniquely related certain aspects of uncertainty and risk to time. He labelled this concept the "principle of postponement," and argued that it could be used to reduce various marketing costs [2]. Risk and uncertainty costs were tied to the differentiation of goods. Differentiation could occur in the product itself and/or the geographical dispersion of inventories. Alderson held that "the most general method which can be applied in promoting the efficiency of a marketing system is the postponement of differentiation . . . postpone changes in form and identity to the latest possible point in the marketing flow; postpone change in inventory location to the latest possible point in time" [1]. Savings in costs related to uncertainty would be achieved "by moving the differentiation nearer to the time of purchase," where demand, presumably, would be more predictable. Savings in the physical movement of the goods could be achieved by sorting products in " large lots," and "in relatively undifferentiated states."

Despite its potential importance, the principle has received relatively little attention since it was first published. Reavis Cox and Charles Goodman [4] have made some use of the concept in their study of channels for house building materials. The Vaile, Grether, and Cox marketing text [10] also makes mention of it. As far as can be determined, this is the totality of its further development.

As a result, the principle still constitutes only a somewhat loose, and possibly misleading, guide to the study of the distribution channel structure. The major defect is a failure to specify the character of the limits which prevent it from being applied. The principle, which states that changes in form and inventory location are to be delayed to the latest possible moment, must also explain why in many channels these changes appear at the earliest. As it stands, the principle of postponement requires modification if it is to be applied effectively to the study of channels.

Postponement and the Shifting of Risk

If one views postponement from the point of view of the distribution channel as a whole, it may be seen as a device for individual institutions to shift the risk of owning goods to another. The manufacturer who postpones by refusing to produce except to order is shifting the risk forward to the buyer. The middleman postpones by either refusing to buy except from a seller who provides next day delivery (backward postponement), or by purchasing only when he has made a sale (forward postponement). The consumer postpones by buying from those retail facilities which permit him to take immediate possession directly from the store shelf. Further, where the consumer first contacts a number of stores before buying, the shopping process itself may be seen as a process of postponement—a process which advertising seeks to eliminate.

From this perspective it becomes obvious that every institution in the channel, including the consumer, cannot postpone to the latest possible moment. The channel, in its totality, cannot avoid ownership responsibilities. Some institution, or group of institutions, must continually bear this uncertainty from the time the goods start through production until they are consumed.

Since most manufacturers do produce for stock, and the ownership of intermediate inventories by middlemen is characteristic of a large proportion of channels, it is clear that the principle of postponement can reach its limit very quickly. As a result, it provides no rationale for the forces which create these inventories. Hence, postponement is really only half a principle. It must have a converse, a converse equally significant to channel structure.

SPECULATION

This converse may be labelled the principle of speculation. It represents a shift of risk to the institution, rather than away from it. The principle of speculation holds that changes in form, and the movement of goods to forward inventories, should be made at the earliest possible time in the marketing flow in order to reduce the costs of the marketing system.

As in the case of postponement, application of the principle of speculation can lead to the reduction of various types of costs. By changing form at the earliest point, one makes possible the use of plants with large-scale economies.

Speculation permits goods to be ordered in large quantities rather than in small frequent orders. This reduces the costs of sorting and transportation. Speculation limits the loss of consumer good will due to stock outs. Finally, it permits the reduction of uncertainty in a variety of ways.

This last point has already been well developed in the literature. It received early and effective treatment from Frank H. Knight [6]. He held that speculators, by shifting uncertainty to themselves, used the principle of grouping, as insurance, to transform it into the more manageable form of a relatively predictable risk. Further, through better knowledge of the risks to be handled, and more informed opinion as to the course of future events, risk could be further reduced.

THE COMBINED PRINCIPLE

From the point of view of the distribution channel, the creation of inventories for holding goods before they are sold is the physical activity which shifts risk and uncertainty. Such inventories serve to move risk away from those institutions which supply, or are supplied by, the inventory. Such inventories, however, will not be created in the channel if the increased costs attending their operation outweigh potential savings in risk. Risk costs, according to the substitutability hypothesis, cannot be minimized if other costs increase beyond the savings in risk.

This discussion shows the principle of speculation to be the limit to the principle of postponement, and vice versa. Together they form a basis for determining whether speculative inventories, those that hold goods prior to their sale, will appear in distribution channels subject to competitive conditions. Operationally, postponement may be measured by the notion of delivery time. Delivery time is the number of days (or hours) elapsing between the placing of an order and the physical receipt of the goods by the buyer [9, p. 93]. For the seller, postponement increases, and costs decline, as delivery time lengthens. For the buyer, postponement increases, and costs decline, as delivery time shortens. The combined principle of postponement-speculation may be stated as follows: A speculative inventory will appear at each point in a distribution channel whenever its costs are less than the net savings to both buyer and seller from postponement.

OPERATION OF THE PRINCIPLE

The following hypothetical example illustrates how the postponement-speculation principle can be applied to the study of distribution channels. The specific problem to be considered is whether an inventory, located between the manufacturer and the consumer, will appear in the channel. This inventory may be managed by the manufacturer, a consumer cooperative or an independent middleman.

Assume that trade for some commodity occurs between a set of manufacturers and a set of customers, both sets being large enough to insure active price competition. The manufacturers are located close to each other in a city some significant distance from the community in which the customers are situated. All of the customers buy in quantities sufficiently large to eliminate the possibility of savings from sorting. Manufacturing and consumption are not affected by seasonal variations. Assume, further, that production costs will not be affected by the presence of such an intermediate inventory.

To determine whether the intermediate inventory will appear, one must first ascertain the shape of the various relevant cost functions with respect to time. In any empirical evaluation of channel structure this is likely to be the most difficult part of the task. For present purposes, however, it will be sufficient to generalize about their character.

The costs incurred by the relevant functions are divided into two broad categories. The first includes those costs originating from activities associated with the potential inventory, such as handling, storage, interest, uncertainty, and costs of selling and buying if the inventory is operated by a middleman. It also includes those costs emanating from transportation, whether the transportation is direct from producer to consumer or routed through the inventory. All of these costs will, in turn, be affected by the particular location of the inventory between the producer and the consumer. In the present instance, it is assumed that the inventory will be located in the consumer city.

In general, this first category includes all the relevant costs incurred by the producer and intermediary, if any. These are aggregated on Figure 1. In this diagram, the ordinate represents the average cost for moving one unit of the commodity from the producer to the consumer. The abscissa measures the time in days for delivery of an order to the consumer after it has been placed. The curve DB measures the

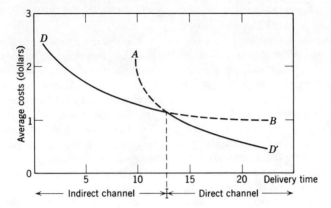

Fig. 1. Average cost of distributing one unit of a commodity to a customer with respect to delivery time in days.

cost of using the speculative inventory to supply the consumer for the various possible delivery times. Curve AD' shows the cost of supplying the consumer direct without use of such an inventory. DD' is the minimum average cost achievable by either direct or indirect distribution of the commodity.

The diagram shows that DD' declines as the delivery time is allowed to increase [7]. With very short delivery times the intermediate inventory is absolutely necessary because only in this way can goods be rushed quickly to the consumer. Further, when virtually immediate delivery is required, the safety stock of the inventory must be kept high in order to prevent temporary stockouts from delaying shipment. Also, delivery trucks must always be available for short notice. These factors create high costs.

As the delivery time to be allowed increases, it becomes possible to reduce the safety stocks, increase the turnover and reduce the size of the facilities and interest cost. Further increases permit continued savings. Eventually, a point will be reached, I in Figure 1, where the delivery time will be sufficiently long to make it cheaper to ship goods directly from the factory to the consumer than to move them indirectly through the inventory. This creates the discontinuity at I as the costs of maintaining the inventory and the handling of goods are eliminated.

In part, the steepness of the slope of DD' will be affected by the uncertainties of holding the inventory. Where prices fluctuate rapidly, or goods are subject to obsolescence, these costs will be high. The extension of delivery time, in permitting the intermediate inventory to be reduced in size, and eventually eliminated, should bring significant relief.

The second category of costs involves those emanating from the relevant marketing functions performed by the customer. Essentially, these costs will be those of bearing the risk and costs of operating any inventory on the customer's premises. These costs are shown as C on Figure 2 with the ordinate and abscissa labelled as in Figure 1.

The shape of C is one that increases with delivery time. The longer the delivery time allowed by the customer, the greater the safety stock he will have to carry. Such stock is necessary to protect against failures in transport and unpredictable surges in requirements. Hence, his costs will increase. The greater the uncertainty cost of inventory holding, the steeper will the slope of this function be.

Determination of the character of the distribution channel is made from the joint consideration of these two cost categories, C and DD'. Whether an intermediate inventory will appear in the channel depends upon the relationship of the costs for operating the two sets of functions and how their sum may be minimized.

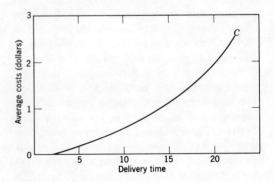

Fig. 2. Average inventory cost for one unit of a commodity to a customer with respect to delivery time in days.

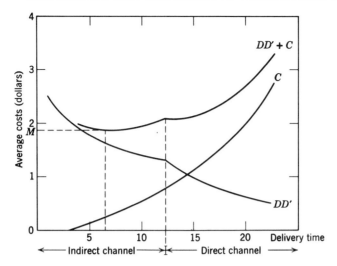

Fig. 3. Total of average distributing and customer inventory costs with respect to delivery time in days.

Functions $DD' + C$ on Figure 3 represent the sum of functions DD' and C. The diagram reveals, in this instance, that costs of postponement are minimized by use of a speculative inventory as the minimal cost point, M, falls to the left of I. If, however, the risk costs to the customer had been less, or the general cost of holding inventories at the customer's home (or plant site, as the case may be) had been lower, then C would be farther to the right. M would also shift to the right. With a sufficient reduction in consumer cost, M would appear to the right of the discontinuity, indicating that direct shipment in the channel would be the means to minimize postponement cost.

SIGNIFICANCE OF THE PRINCIPLE

As developed, the principle of postponement-speculation provides a basis for expecting inventories to be present in channels because of production and distribution time requirements. In particular, it treats the role of speculative inventories in the channel. The concept, as a consequence, extends beyond the physical flow of the goods themselves to the flow of their title. Speculative inventories create the opportunity for new institutions to hold title in the channel. Without such inventories, there may be little economic justification for a title holding intermediary to enter the channel. The economic need to have such an inventory in the physical flow opens the door to a middleman to show whether he is capable of reducing the risk cost of that inventory below the level attainable by either the producer or some consumer cooperative.

The presence of an inventory in the channel for either collecting, sorting, or dispersing does not create the same type of opportunity for a title-taking intermediary to appear in the channel. Such inventories are not speculative in character. They do not need to hold uncommitted stocks of goods available for general sale in order to fulfill their purpose. For example, the REA Express, the parcel post system, freight forwarders, and even the Greyhound Bus Corporation's freight system sort a substantial volume of goods through many nonspeculative type inventories each day. Milk producers establish handling depots where bottled milk is transferred from large, long-distance vehicles to city delivery trucks. Catalogue sellers discharge full truck shipments upon the post offices of distant cities where customers reside. None of these inventories involves the risk of unsold goods. None of these inventories provides the basis for the emergence of a title-holding middleman.

From this perspective, the principle of postponement-speculation may be regarded as a concept which broadens the channel analyst's understanding of the intimate relationship between title and physical flows. The intertwining of the roles of ownership and the holding of speculative stocks provide a fundamental rationale for the position of the merchant middleman. The principle of postponement-speculation, as a consequence, can be employed to provide at least part of the explanation for the number of ownership stages in the channel. This, of course,

is one of the basic questions toward which traditional distribution analysis is directed [5].

In this light, for example, the principle may
be of use in explaining the emergence of an
"orthodox channel of distribution." This concept, developed by Shaw [8], was used to characterize the nature of the distribution channel
through which a large proportion of products
traveled, to wit: the manufacturer-wholesaler-
retailer route. That such a concept should
emerge to characterize products, whose sorting
needs are different because of diverse physical
characteristics and market reach, is of extreme
interest. Similarities among channels for different products imply that forces, which may not
vary significantly among many types of goods,
should be sought as explanatory variables of
channel structure. Since many groups of consumer goods generate similar temporal types of
risk, the principle of postponement-speculation
may provide a major explanation for this
phenomenon.

Testing the Principle

The principle of postponement-speculation
will not be easy to test for a number of reasons.
First of all, it is normative. It is derived from
assumptions of profit maximization and predictions are based upon what firms should do.
Second, it approximates the real world only
when the channel environment is sufficiently
competitive to produce a variety of price-
product-delivery time offers. Finally, it cannot
predict the necessary time delays that occur in
the channel for new facilities to be built or old
ones abandoned.

Despite these problems, a number of hypotheses may be generated from the model and
subjected to evaluation by surveys of existing
channels. These surveys would locate any intermediate, speculative inventory in the channel
and measure the time elapsing between the
placing of an order by, and its delivery to, the
customer. Use of industrial or commodity channels would undoubtedly be the best initial sub-
jects for the surveys. The confounding effects
of collecting, sorting, and dispersing in consumer channels will make the impact of the
principle of postponement-speculation more
difficult to isolate.

Six hypotheses which could be tested in this
manner follow:

1. The shorter the delivery time, the greater the
probability the channel will include an intermediate, speculative inventory.

2. The shorter the delivery time, the closer any
speculative stock will be to the consumer.
3. The shorter the distance between a customer
and a speculative stock, the greater the probability of a second such inventory in the channel.
4. Products which are heavy, bulky, and inexpensive are likely to flow through channels with
more intermediate, speculative inventories than
products with the opposite characteristics.
5. Products which consumers find expensive to
store on their premises, but whose use is both
urgent and difficult to forecast, have a greater
probability of passing through an intermediate,
speculative inventory than products with the
opposite characteristics.
6. The greater the inelasticity of consumer
and/or producer cost with respect to changes in
delivery time, the greater the stability of the most
efficient channel type over time.

All of these hypotheses are subject to the
ceteris paribus limitation. Tests, as a result,
should include only those channels operating
under reasonably similar economic conditions.
This is particularly important with respect to
the distance between the producer and the consumer. Variations in this factor will affect the
cost of providing any given delivery time. Channels which traverse longer distances, in other
words, are likely to require more speculative
inventories than those which move goods less
extensively.

The *ceteris paribus* limitation also contains
an important implication beyond that of the
problems of testing. Consideration of this limitation provides the rationale for the presence
of several different types of channels supplying
the same type of product to a given group of
customers. Producers, for example, provisioning
some market from a distance, may be forced
to use channels distinct from their competitors
located adjacent to the customers. This diversity of channels may also be produced by imperfections in competition as well as variations in
the urgency of demand among consumers in
the market. Those who can easily tolerate delays
in delivery are likely to use a different channel
from those patronized by customers with dissimilar personalities or capabilities.

Implications of the Principle

The principle of postponement-speculation,
in addition to providing a basis for developing
hypotheses for empirical testing, makes it possible to do some *a priori* generalizing concerning
the type of channel structure changes one may
expect to see in the future. Any force, or set of
forces, which affects the types of costs discussed

may be sufficient to move the balance from speculation to postponement, or vice versa.

One type of change, already occurring and which may be expected to spread in the future, rests upon the relationship between the cost of transportation and speed. Rapidly evolving methods of using air transport economically and efficiently are serving to narrow the spread between the cost of high-speed transportation and low-speed transportation. This has effect of reducing the relative advantage of speculation over postponement. Hence, intermediate inventories will tend to disappear and be replaced by distribution channels which have a direct flow.

The increasing proliferation of brands, styles, colors, and price lines is another type of force which will affect the balance. This proliferation increases the risk of inventory holding throughout the entire channel, but particularly at those points closest to the consumer. Retailers will attempt to minimize this risk by reducing the safety stock level of their inventories and relying more upon speedy delivery from their suppliers. The role of the merchant wholesaler, or the chain store warehouse, will become increasingly important in this channel. Indeed, there will probably be increasing efforts on the part of retailers to carry only sample stocks in those items where it is not absolutely necessary for customers to take immediate delivery. General Electric, for example, is experimenting with wholesaler-to-consumer delivery of large appliances. Drugstores, where the role of the pharmacist appears to be slowly changing from one of compounding prescriptions to inventorying branded specialties, will become further dependent upon ultra-fast delivery from wholesalers.

Those stores, such as discount houses, which are successfully able to resist the pressure toward carrying wide assortments of competing brands are likely to utilize channels of distribution which differ significantly from their full-line competitors. Large bulk purchases from single manufacturers can be economically delivered directly to the discount house's retail facilities. Where warehouses are used in discount house channels they can serve stores spread out over a far greater geographical area than would be normally served by a wholesaler. Such stores are also apt to find their market segments not only in middle income range families, but also among those consumers who tend to be heavily presold by manufacturer advertising, or who simply are less finicky about the specific type of item they buy.

A final possible trend may spring from consumers who find that their own shopping costs represent too great an expenditure of effort with respect to the value received from postponement. As a result, such consumers are likely to turn more and more to catalogue and telephone shopping. Improved quality control procedures by manufacturers and better means of description in catalogues could hasten this movement. The acceptance of Sears telephone order services in large cities testifies that many individuals are prone to feel this way. If the movement were to become significantly enlarged, it could have a drastic effect upon the existing structure of distribution.

SUMMARY

The study of distribution channels, and why they take various forms, is one of the most neglected areas of marketing today. Part of the neglect may be due to the absence of effective tools for analysis. The principle of postponement-speculation is offered in the hope that it may prove useful in this regard and stimulate work in the area.

The principle directly treats the role of time in distribution and, indirectly, the role of distance as it affects time. The starting point for the development of the constructs of the principle may be found in the work of Alderson and Knight [2, 3, 7]. Postponement is measured by the change of delivery time in the shipping of a product. Increasing the delivery time decreases postponement costs for the seller, increases them for the buyer and vice versa. Justification and support for the relationships suggested between the costs of marketing functions and delivery time may be found in the recent literature of physical distribution.

The principle reveals the effect upon channel structure of the interaction between the risk of owning a product and the physical functions employed to move the product through time. It holds that, in a competitive environment, the costs of these functions be minimized over the entire channel, not by individual function. The minimum cost and type of channel are determined by balancing the costs of alternative delivery times against the cost of using an intermediate, speculative inventory. The appearance of such an inventory in the channel occurs whenever its additional costs are more than offset by net savings in postponement to the buyer and seller.

REFERENCES

1. Wroe Alderson, *Marketing Behavior and Executive Action*, Homewood, Illinois: Richard D. Irwin, 1957, 424.
2. ——, "Marketing Efficiency and the Principle of Postponement," *Cost and Profit Outlook*, 3 (September 1950).
3. Stanley H. Brewer and James Rosenweig, "Rhochematics," *California Management Review*, 3 (Spring 1961), 52–71.
4. Reavis Cox and Charles S. Goodman, "Marketing of Housebuilding Materials," *The Journal of Marketing*, 21 (July 1956), 55–56.
5. William R. Davidson, "Channels of Distribution—One Aspect of Marketing Strategy," *Business Horizons*, Special Issue—First International Seminar on Marketing Management, February 1961, 85–86.
6. Frank H. Knight, *Risk, Uncertainty and Profit*, Boston: Houghton Mifflin Company, 1921, 238–39, 255–58.
7. John F. Magee, "The Logistics of Distribution," *Harvard Business Review*, 38 (July–August 1960), 97–99.
8. Arch W. Shaw, "Some Problems in Market Distribution," *The Quarterly Journal of Economics*, (August 1912), 727.
9. See Edward W. Smykay, Donald J. Bowersox, and Frank J. Mossman, *Physical Distribution Management*, New York; Macmillan Company, 1961, Ch. IV.
10. Roland S. Vaile, Ewald T. Grether, and Reavis Cox, *Marketing in the American Economy*, New York: Ronald Press Company, 1952, 149–50.

10. Alternative Explanations of Institutional Change and Channel Evolution

BERT C. McCAMMON, JR.

McCammon examines response to change, especially among marketing institutions. While research on the acceptance of new practices has been undertaken on agricultural and drug innovations particularly, such research is lacking in retailing or wholesaling. Barriers to change in the marketing structure are probed, sources of innovation evaluated, and hypotheses about the factors affecting the speed of acceptance of new practices put forth.

INTRODUCTION

Marketing channels and institutions must adapt continuously to their environment in order to avoid "economic obsolescence." Most of the required adaptations are tactical in nature. Channel alignments, for example, can usually be maintained over an extended period of time by effecting a series of minor, though necessary, revisions in marketing practices. Individual firms, under normal conditions, can also maintain their competitive position without significantly altering prevailing policies and procedures. Thus, institutional change in marketing tends to be a process in which firms and channels maneuver for short-run advantage and in which they adapt almost imperceptibly to environmental disturbances.

Periodically, however, a firm's or channel's existence is threatened by a *major* change in marketing practices. The sudden appearance of new products, new methods of distribution, new types of competitors, and new sales approaches, may imperil existing institutional relationships. These abrupt departures from the *status quo* can disrupt prevailing patterns of competition, alter cost-price relationships, and

"enforce a distinctive process of adaptation"[1] on the part of threatened organizations.

Schumpeter, earlier, and Barnet and Levitt, later, argue that this type of competition, usually called innovative competition, is a prerequisite for economic growth.[2] Despite general acceptance of this position, very little is known about the innovative process in marketing. More specifically, we lack a body of theory that explains how new marketing practices are originated and diffused throughout the structure of distribution.

The emergence and acceptance of new practices is a complex process which has been analyzed extensively in the agricultural sector of our economy,[3] and in the medical profession.[4] For example:

"The farmers participating in the diffusion process are relatively easy to identify. Beal and

[1] Joseph Schumpeter, *Business Cycles*, McGraw-Hill, New York, 1939, p. 10.
[2] Joseph Schumpeter, *Capitalism, Socialism, and Democracy*, Harper's, New York, 1947; Edward M. Barnet, *Innovate or Perish*, Graduate School of Business, Columbia University, New York, 1954; Theodore Levitt, *Innovation in Marketing*, McGraw-Hill, New York, 1962.
[3] See for example, E. M. Rogers and G. M. Beal, *Reference Group Influence in The Adoption of Agricultural Technology*, Iowa State University, Ames, 1958.
[4] See for example, J. Coleman, E. Katz, and H. Menzel, "The Diffusion of an Innovation among Physicians," *Sociometry*, December, 1957, pp. 253–270.

Rogers have classified such participants as innovators (the developers or initial accepters of new ideas), early adopters, majority adopters, and laggards. "Indirect" participants, who occupy important positions in the communications network, are classified as key communicators, influentials, and skeptics. Each of these decision makers has a distinctive socio-economic profile and a differentiated mode of behavior. Researchers, by analyzing interaction patterns, can predict the rate at which a new farm practice will be accepted, and they can forecast the probable impact of this innovation on non-adopters."[5]

Unfortunately, comparable analysis has not been undertaken in retailing or wholesaling. The distinguishing characteristics of innovators, early adopters, and other participants in the diffusion process have not been identified, nor have the factors which inhibit or encourage change been isolated. Consequently, the explanation and prediction of institutional change in marketing tends to be a tenuous intellectual exercise.

The diffusion process in marketing is more complex than it is in agriculture because the counter strategies of non-adopters have to be considered as well as the spread of the innovation itself. The phenomenon of transient and selective adoption has to be recognized too. Individual firms may emulate an innovator in the short-run while devising long-run strategies, or alternatively these firms may adopt new practices on a limited or modified basis. Conventional department stores, for example, have recently emulated the discounter by opening self-service branches. This may be an interim strategy in the sense that the branches may change over time so that they eventually bear little resemblance to the original innovation. With respect to selective adoption of new practices, many supermarkets prepack meat but not produce, and numerous department stores operate self-service drug and toy departments while merchandising other lines on a full-service basis. Consequently, it appears that a complex model is needed to analyze the emergence and diffusion of new practices in the marketing structure.

The purposes of this paper are (1) to explore the barriers to change in the marketing struc-

ture, (2) to evaluate the sources of innovation within the structure, and (3) to suggest some hypotheses about the factors which determine rate at which new practices are accepted.

BARRIERS TO CHANGE WITHIN THE MARKETING STRUCTURE

Conventional economic analysis provides a useful frame of reference for explaining institutional change. The firm, in economic theory, attempts to maximize its profits and thus accepts technological improvements as soon as they appear. Innovations under these circumstances are absorbed quickly and the diffusion process is completed in a relatively short period of time. Shifts in channel alignments are also susceptible to economic analysis. Client firms utilize intermediaries because the latter can perform specific functions (in a given location) at a lower cost per unit than can the former. Intermediaries, in this context, are sources of external economies to their clientele. Such economies are possible because intermediaries, by aggregating user requirements, can perform the designated function(s) at an optimum scale, or alternatively, intermediaries, by aggregating user requirements, can more fully utilize existing (though non-optimum) facilities.[6]

As output expands or as *technology changes*, the client firms reach a point at which they can perform the delegated functions at an optimum scale. When this point is reached, functions tend to be reabsorbed, and the channel becomes more completely integrated. This process of reintegration is not necessarily frictionless. The intermediary attempts to avoid being "integrated out" of the channel by changing his method of operation so that it more closely conforms to the client's requirements. Manufacturer's agents in the electronics field, for example, have retained their principals by carrying inventory, and building supply wholesalers continue to sell to large developers by offering goods on a cash and carry basis.

Economic analysis of institutional change can be and has been carried much further.[7] This

[5] S. C. Dodd, "Diffusion is Predictable: Testing Probability Models for Laws of Interaction," *American Sociological Review*, August, 1955, pp. 392–401.

[6] The latter source of economies is often called the "blending principle."

[7] See, for example, R. H. Coase, "The Nature of the Firm," *Economica*, New Series, Volume IV, 1937, pp. 386–405; George J. Stigler, "The Division of Labor Is Limited by the Extent of The Market," *The Journal of Political Economy*, June, 1951, pp. 185–193; R. Artle and S. Berglund, "A Note on

type of analysis, however modified, inevitably assumes that the firm's behavior is determined by cost/revenue considerations, and thus it leaves unanswered some or all of the following questions:

• Why is change resisted by marketing institutions even though it appears to offer economic advantages?
• Why do "uneconomic channels of distribution" persist over extended periods of time?
• Why do some firms accept change rapidly, while others lag in their adaptation or refuse to change at all?

Answers to these and related questions depend upon an analysis of sociological and psychological barriers to change, some of which are discussed below.

Reseller Solidarity[8]

Resellers in many lines of trade often function as a highly cohesive group, bargaining with suppliers and adjusting to their environment collectively as well as individually. Resellers "organized" on this basis must maintain internal harmony and a workable consensus. Consequently, they tend to support traditional trade practices and long established institutional relationships.

Several factors are apparently conducive to group action. Resellers tend to act as a unit when the firms involved are relatively homogeneous. Each of the entrepreneurs in this situation tends to be confronted by similar problems

and has comparable expectations. Thus he identifies with other members of the trade and is willing to work cooperatively with them.

Resellers also tend to engage in collective action when the entrepreneurs have common backgrounds. The owner-managers of drugstores, for example, are often "highly organized" because most of them are pharmacists and are often alumni of the same universities. Business conditions affect reseller solidarity too. There is likely to be more group action during periods of adverse business conditions than during periods of prosperity. Finally, the degree of reseller solidarity that prevails is conditioned by the intensity and complexity of competition. A line of trade, confronted by unusually aggressive competition from outside sources, is more likely to engage in group action than would be the case if this threat did not exist.

The presence of a strong professional or trade association tends to reinforce conservative group behavior. Retail druggists, as an illustration, support long established professional associations which defend existing trade practices. Carpet retailers, on the other hand, are not represented by a trade association, and for this reason, as well others, their industry is characterized by unstable retail prices and by constantly changing institutional arrangements.

To summarize, the presence of group solidarity within the structure of marketing tends to inhibit the rate at which innovation is accepted and thus slows down the diffusion process.

Entrepreneurial Values

The entrepreneur's reaction to change is conditioned by his value hierarchy. Large resellers, as a group, are growth oriented and their decisions are based upon economic criteria. Innovations that promote growth are regarded as being desirable, and technological alternatives are evaluated on the basis of "profitability" analysis.[9] Consequently, the large reseller, given sufficient time to adjust, tends to be responsive to innovation and will either accept it or otherwise react to it on the basis of cost-revenue relationships.

Small resellers often have a markedly different set of values. Wittreich, on the basis of his research, argues that small retailers tend to have

Manufacturers' Choice of Distribution Channel," *Management Science*, July, 1959, pp. 460–471; Edward H. Bowman, "Scales of Operations: An Empirical Study," *Operations Research*, May–June, 1958, pp. 320–328; Louis B. Bucklin, "The Economic Structure of Channels of Distribution," *Marketing: A Maturing Discipline* (Martin L. Bell, Editor), American Marketing Association, 1960, pp. 379–385; and F. E. Balderston, "Theories of Marketing Structure and Channels," *Proceedings, Conference of Marketing Teachers from Far Western States*, University of California, Berkeley, 1958, pp. 135–145.

[8] The discussion in this section is based on the analyses contained in J. C. Palamountain, Jr., *The Politics of Distribution*, Harvard University Press, Cambridge, Massachusetts, 1955, and in E. T. Grether, "Solidarity in The Distribution Trades," *Law and Contemporary Problems*, June, 1937, pp. 376–391.

[9] See Bert C. McCammon, Jr. and Donald H. Granbois, *Profit Contribution: A Criterion for Display Decisions*, Point-of-Purchase Advertising Institute, Inc., New York, 1963.

relatively static expectations.[10] That is, they are interested in reaching and *maintaining* a given scale of operation, and reject opportunities for growth beyond this point. Such retailers tend to view their demand curve as being relatively fixed. Thus, they are inclined to resist innovation because it presumably cannot improve their position and could conceivably disrupt a reasonably attractive *status quo*.

Vidich and Bensman, in their study of life in a small community, reach essentially the same conclusions about the small merchant's behavior.[11] Furthermore, they argue that small retailers are extremely reluctant to invest additional funds in their businesses, almost irrespective of the profits involved. Instead they prefer "secure" investment outlets such as real estate and securities. The small retailers studied by Vidich and Bensman also believed that they had suffered a decline in status during the past three decades, and they resisted any institutional arrangements that would further depress their relative position within the community. This latter condition may partially explain why voluntary and cooperative groups have not been more successful. Retailers participating in these programs sacrifice some of their autonomy, and the loss of this autonomy may be perceived as a loss of status. Wroe Alderson, in another context, has argued that a behavior system will survive as long as it fulfills the status expectations of its participants.[12] Since the small retailer's status is a function of "being in business for himself," the desire to maintain independence may partially explain both the rejection of contractual integration and the persistence of "uneconomic channels."

To summarize, recent research indicates that the small retailer (and presumably other small businessmen) will resist innovation, because they "value" stability more highly than growth.[13] They will also resist innovations that require a substantial investment of funds or that result in a perceived loss of status.

Organizational Rigidity

A well established firm is an historical entity with deeply entrenched patterns of behavior. The members of the organization may resist change because it violates group norms, creates uncertainty, and results in loss of status. Customers may also resent change and threaten to withdraw their patronage. Furthermore the firm has "sunk" costs in training programs, in office systems, and in equipment which it prefers to recover before instituting major revisions in its procedures. Consequently most firms absorb innovation gradually, or react to innovative competition through a series of incremental adjustments.[14] Because of these factors, the diffusion of an innovation through an industry and the distinctive pattern of adaptation it enforces take considerable time.

The firm's reaction to change is also a function of the extent to which the innovator has penetrated the firm's core market. Most firms appeal to a specific group of customers who are uniquely loyal. These customers may patronize the firm for a variety of reasons, but the attraction is such that their patronage is virtually assured. As long as this core market remains intact, the firm can usually maintain sufficient sales to continue operations until it matures strategies to counteract the innovator.[15] If the core market is infringed, however, the firm must either emulate the innovator or develop immediate counter strategies.

To summarize, a firm, because of organizational rigidities, prefers to respond incrementally to innovation. It will gradually imitate the innovating firm or develop counter strategies over an extended period of time. If the innovator has penetrated the firm's core market, however, it must respond quickly to this challenge in order to ensure continued operation.

The Firm's Channel Position[16]

There is a dominant channel of distribution for most lines of merchandise. This channel, as compared with other institutional alignments,

[10] Warren J. Wittreich, "Misunderstanding the Retailer," *Harvard Business Review*, May–June, 1962. pp. 147–159.
[11] Arthur J. Vidich and Joseph Bensman, *Small Town in Mass Society*, Doubleday and Company, Garden City, New York, 1960, pp. 73 and 91–93.
[12] Wroe Alderson, "Survival and Adjustment in Behavior Systems," *Theory in Marketing* (Edited by Reavis Cox and Wroe Alderson), Richard D. Irwin, Homewood, Illinois, 1950, p. 80.
[13] For additional confirmation of this hypothesis, see Louis Kriesberg, "The Retail Furrier, Concepts of Security and Success," *American Journal of Sociology*, March, 1952.

[14] For an interesting discussion of incremental adjustments to innovation, see Alton F. Doody, "Historical Patterns of Marketing Innovation," *Emerging Concepts in Marketing* (William S. Decker, Editor), American Marketing Association, Chicago, 1962, pp. 245–253.
[15] Alderson, *op. cit.*, p. 81.
[16] The discussion in this section is based on the analysis that appears in Louis Kriesberg, "Occupational Controls Among Steel Distributors," *The American Journal of Sociology*, November, 1955, pp. 203–212.

has the greatest prestige and often handles the bulk of the industry's output. Behavior within the channel is regulated by an occupational code which "controls" pricing policies, sales promotion practices, and other related activities. Deviation from the code's prescriptions are punished in a variety of ways, ranging from colleague ostracism to economic sanctions.

Individual firms can be classified in terms of their relationship to the dominant channel of distribution and in terms of their adherence to the occupational code. The *insiders* are members of the dominant channel. They have continuous access to preferred sources of supply, and their relatively high status in the trade is a byproduct of channel membership. The insiders, as a group prescribe the contents of the occupational code and enforce it. They are desirous of the respect of their colleagues, and recognize the interdependency of the firms in the system. In short, the insider has made an emotional and financial commitment to the dominant channel and is interested in perpetuating it.

The *strivers* are firms located outside the dominant channel who want to become a part of the system. These firms have discontinuous access to preferred resources, and during periods of short supply, they may be "short ordered" or not shipped at all. The striver, since he wants to become a member of the system, is responsive to the occupational code and will not engage in deviate behavior under normal economic conditions. Thus he utilizes the same marketing practices as the insider.

The *complementors* are not part of the dominant channel, nor do they desire to obtain membership. As their title suggests, these firms complement the activities undertaken by members of the dominant channel. That is, the complementors perform functions that are not normally performed by other channel members, or serve customers whose patronage is normally not solicited, or handle qualities of merchandise the dominant channel doesn't carry. Thus the complementors are marginally affiliated with the dominant channel and want to see it survive. Their expectations are of a long-run nature and they respect the occupational code.

The *transients* also occupy a position outside the dominant channel and do not seek membership in it. Many transients are mobile entrepreneurs who move from one line of trade to another; other transients are firms that owe their allegiance elsewhere, i.e., they consider themselves to be members of a channel other than the one in question. Therefore they utilize the latter channel's product as an "in and out"

item or as a loss leader, since it is not their market "that is being spoiled" by such activity. All of the transients have short-run expectations and the occupational code is not an effective constraint.

Classification of firms into these four categories explains some of the competitive patterns which have emerged in the ready-to-wear field, in the toy industry, and in the TBA market. Transient firms, in all of these merchandise lines, have disrupted the *status quo* by engaging in deviate competitive behavior. Significantly, none of the four types of firms described above are likely to introduce major marketing innovations. The insiders and the strivers are primarily interested in maintaining existing institutional arrangements. The complementors also have a vested interest in the *status quo*, and the transients are not sufficiently dependent on the product line to develop an entirely new method of distribution. Thus the above analysis suggests that a firm completely outside the system will introduce basic innovations, and historically this has often been the case. Consequently, a fifth category for *outside innovators* is required to explain major structural realignments.

Market Segmentation

As market segments emerge and/or as they are recognized by entrepreneurs, firms that formerly competed directly with each other begin to compete in a more marginal sense. That is, former rivals begin to appeal to different types of customers, and as a result the tactics adopted by one firm may have a negligible potential impact on other firms. Competition, under these circumstances, becomes more fragmented, and the compulsion to accept or react to innovation declines—a condition that slows down the diffusion process.

The discount supermarket, for example, has not increased in importance as rapidly as many of its proponents initially believed, and the bantam supermarket has experienced much the same fate. It appears that these innovative methods of operation appeal to a limited number of market segments, and conventional supermarkets, appealing to other market segments, have not been compelled to react to these new forms of competition.

SOURCES OF INNOVATIVE ACTIVITY

The Channel Administrator

An individual firm usually controls a given marketing channel in the sense that it directs the allocation of resources for all channel members. Manufacturers, farm marketing cooperatives, voluntary groups, and chain store buying offices are illustrations of organizations that direct the activities of other channel members. These decision makers do not set goals for the other firms in the channel, but they do decide what kind of firms shall be combined to form the distribution network for the systems they organize.[17]

The channel administrator often is an innovator, particularly when a new product is being marketed. Manufacturers of new fabricated materials, for example, often have to develop unique institutional arrangements to distribute their products,[18] and the Singer Sewing Machine Company pioneered the use of a franchise agency system and installment credit when it began to market sewing machines during the 1850's.[19] Furthermore channel administrators can be quite responsive to *procedural* innovations. During the last decade, channel administrators have taken the initiative in developing new physical distribution techniques, and they have accepted rather rapidly such innovations as merchandise management accounting, PERT cost analysis, stockless purchasing arrangements, and value analysis.

Channel administrators, however, tend to be well established firms, and thus they are subject to the organizational constraints described above. More specifically, they tend to resist an innovation that involves a major restructuring of the firm's relationship with its customers, since they have the most to lose by such restructuring and the least to gain.

Large firms can overcome their tendency to maintain the *status quo* by underwriting *elite* activities. The elite members of an organization engage in projects that have problematic, long-run payouts rather than certain, short-run yields. The ratio of professional personnel to high status administrators is a rough measure of the use of elite personnel within an organi-zation. The higher the proportion of professional personnel to proprietors, managers, and officials, the more likely is the existence of staff departments preserving long-run interests against the pressure of immediate problems. Stinchcombe, and Hill and Harbison have analyzed the relationship between innovation and the proportion of elite personnel employed.[20] Their findings indicate that innovating industries employ proportionately more professionals than do non-innovating industries.

Furthermore, within a given industry, the firms with proportionately more professionals innovate more rapidly than those with fewer. Significantly, wholesaling and retailing are classified as "stagnant" industries, and the payrolls of these types of firms contain significantly fewer professional employees per hundred administrators than is the case in "progressive" industries. Admittedly, the definitions of "progressiveness" and "stagnation" can be somewhat arbitrary, as can the definition of a "professional" employee. Consequently, the data just cited should be regarded as being suggestive rather than definitive, but the suggestion is unambiguous—retailers and wholesalers could effect economies and develop more productive institutional arrangements if they engaged in additional research and underwrote more elite activities.

The "Outsider"

Institutional innovation, particularly in retailing, has historically occurred *outside* of the established power structure. The retail innovator, in fact, has tended to resemble Eric Hoffer's "The True Believer."[21] J. C. Penney, Richard Sears, King Cullen, and others were discontented "outsiders" who believed that they had discovered a technique of irresistible power. They had an extravagant conception of the potentialities of the future, minimized the problems of managing a large enterprise, and promulgated their merchandising doctrines with an almost evangelical fervor. The premise that the institutional innovator is likely to come

[17] For a more complete discussion of the channel administrator concept, see George Fisk, "The General Systems Approach to the Study of Marketing," The Social Responsibilities of Marketing (Edited by William D. Stevens), American Marketing Association, Chicago, 1961, pp. 207–211.

[18] See E. Raymond Gorey, *The Development of Markets for New Materials*, Division of Research, Graduate School of Business Administration, Harvard University, Boston, 1956.

[19] Andrew B. Jack, "The Channels of Distribution for an Innovation: The Sewing-Machine Industry in America, 1860–1865," *Explorations in Entrepreneurial History*, February, 1957, pp. 113–141.

[20] Arthur L. Stinchcombe, "The Sociology of Organization and The Theory of the Firm," *The Pacific Sociological Review*, Fall, 1960, pp. 75–82. Samuel E. Hill and Frederick Harbison, *Manpower and Innovation in American Industry*, Princeton University Press, 1959, pp. 16–27.

[21] Eric Hoffer, *The True Believer*, New American Library, New York, 1951, pp. 13–20.

from outside the established power structure is also inherent in the wheel of retailing concept which is the most comprehensive theory of innovation yet developed in marketing.[22] Silk and Stern, in their recent study, also conclude that the marketing innovator has traditionally been an "outsider," but they additionally argue that recent innovators have tended to be much more deliberate in their choice processes and much more methodical in their analyses than were their predecessors of several decades ago.[23] In any case, if we accept the assumption that significant innovation tends to occur outside the existing system, then it is important from a social point of view to create a marketing environment in which entry is relatively easy.

ANALYZING INSTITUTIONAL CHANGE

There is a tendency in marketing to refine analysis beyond the point of maximum usefulness, and this is particularly true when the phenomena under investigation are relatively complex. Quite obviously, many of the changes that have occurred in the structure of distribution during the past 50 years can be explained in terms of a relatively simple challenge and response model. The emergence and rapid growth of voluntary and cooperative groups in the food field is a logical response to the expansion of corporate vertical integration, and the rise of the cash and carry wholesaler in the building supply industry is a natural response to the growing importance of the large developer. Thus, if the marketplace is viewed as an area in which firms constantly search for differential advantage and/or react to it, much of what appears to be rather complex behavior can be reduced to fairly simple terms.

Hypotheses

Systems theorists and sociologists have selectively investigated the diffusion of new ideas and practices. The hypotheses that have emerged from this research serve as useful points of origin for subsequent exploration in marketing. More specifically, *marketing analysts should consider*

the following hypotheses when attempting to explain institutional change:

1. The rate of diffusion depends upon the innovation itself. Innovations that involve a substantial capital investment, a major restructuring of the firm's relationship with its customers, and a sizable number of internal realignments are more likely to be accepted slowly than those that involve relatively minor intra- or inter-firm changes.

2. The innovator is likely to be an "outsider" in the sense that he occupies a marginal role in a given line of trade and is on the outskirts of the prevailing sociometric network. Such individuals are interested in innovation because they have the most to gain and the least to lose by disrupting the status quo.

3. A firm will respond incrementally to innovation unless its core market is threatened. If the latter is the case, the response to innovation will proceed swiftly. That is, the firm will parry the innovator's thrust by developing a counter strategy or it will emulate the innovator on a partial or total basis.

4. The higher the entrepreneur's aspirations, the more likely he is to initiate or accept innovation. Alternatively, the lower the entrepreneur's aspirations, the less likely he is to accept innovation, particularly when such acceptance conflicts with his other values.

5. The acceptance of innovation is not always permanent. A firm may emulate an innovator as a part of a transitional strategy. When the firm develops an ultimate strategy, the emulating features of its behavior will be discarded.

6. Innovation will be accepted most rapidly when it can be fitted into existing decision-making habits. Innovations which involve an understanding of alien relationships or which involve new conceptual approaches, tend to be resisted. Many small retailers, for example, have difficulty in accepting the supermarket concept, because it involves a fairly sophisticated understanding of cost-volume relationships.

7. Influentials and innovators are not always the same firms. Institutional innovators, since they tend to be "outsiders," have relatively little influence among their entrepreneurial colleagues. Other firms, occupying central positions in a given line of trade, possess considerable influence, and an innovation will not be adopted widely until these influential firms accept it.

8. Greater energy is required to transmit an innovation from one channel to another than is required to transmit it within a channel. The diffusion of innovation therefore tends to be confined to a given line of trade, before it is adopted by another. The supermarket, as an illustration, became dominant in the food field, before this method of operation was employed by ready-to-wear retailers.

The above hypotheses represent only a small sampling of those developed in other fields. They deserve careful consideration by researchers interested in explaining and predicting institutional change in marketing.

[22] For a careful analysis of the wheel of retailing concept, see Stanley C. Hollander, "The Wheel of Retailing," *Journal of Marketing*, July, 1960, pp. 37–42.

[23] Alvin J. Silk and Louis William Stern, "The Changing Nature of Innovation in Marketing: A Study of Selected Business Leaders, 1852–1958," *Business History Review*, Fall, 1963, pp. 182–199.

11. The Characteristics of Goods and Parallel Systems Theories

LEO ASPINWALL*

Both of the following theories are offered as tentative suppositions designed to provisionally explain marketing facts and guide further investigations. The characteristics of goods theory attempts to arrange all marketable goods in a systematic and useful fashion; the parallel systems theory is designed to explain the parallel relationship between distribution systems and promotion systems of goods.

THE DEVELOPMENT STAGES OF A SCIENCE

The movement towards theory formulation in marketing follows logically the development of a science of marketing. Starting with a definition of science, we find that it consists of a classified body of knowledge. The Oxford Universal Dictionary defines science as "a branch of study which is concerned either with a connected body of demonstrated truths or with observed facts systematically classified and more or less colligated by being brought under general laws, and which includes trustworthy methods for the discovery of new truth within its own domain."

There are six generally recognized stages in the development of a science: (1) observation of phenomena; (2) collection and classification of similar phenomena for the purposes of explanation; (3) selection of several of the most reasonable explanations of these observed similar phenomena. These are called hypotheses, which are tentative theories or suppositions provisionally adopted to explain facts and to guide further investigations. (4) The most reasonable hypotheses are selected and advanced as theories. (5) When theories can, by scientifically

controlled experimentation, recreate the original phenomenon, then a law is established. (6) Finally, when a body of laws is established and supported by a body of related literature, then a science emerges.

SYSTEMATIZATION AS AN AID TO LEARNING

The formulation of the Characteristics of Goods Theory and its closely related Parallel Systems Theory has followed exactly the process described in the foregoing paragraph. These theories are tentative suppositions, provisionally adopted to explain facts and to guide in the investigation of others. Having been charged with the responsibility of teaching marketing for over thirty years, the author has attempted to systematize marketing facts in such a way as to give students a means of relating marketing knowledge to a central thesis. Each central thesis summates in a usable way some closely related areas in marketing. Thus, when a number of such theses are integrated, we have created a model which provides a convenient means by which students can organize and systemize their understanding of marketing.

THEORY AND PRACTICAL EXPERIENCE

As a second and equally important value that stems out of theory formulation in marketing, is the availability of a framework into which current problems of marketing can be fitted for

• SOURCE: Leo Aspinwall, "The Characteristics of Goods and Parallel Systems Theories," in Eugene J. Kelley and William Lazer (editors), *Managerial Marketing*, (Homewood, Ill.: Richard D. Irwin, 1958), pp. 434–450.

* University of Colorado.

purposes of analysis. This means that marketing theories are specialized tools which the marketing practitioner has available for use in solving day-to-day problems, but like any specialized tool, skill is acquired only by repeated use. The marketing practitioner knows full well the importance of actual experience, but to rely on experience might easily lead to serious error, since experience is closely related to conditions that were current at a certain time and which may no longer exist. Marketing theories have an element of timelessness which makes them valuable for analytical purposes: thus a combination of practical experience and marketing theories provides a sound basis for undertaking the solution of current marketing problems.

CHARACTERISTICS OF GOODS THEORY

The characteristics of goods theory attempts to arrange all marketable goods in systematic and useful fashion. It has been tested both in the classroom and in application to business problems. It provides a perspective and frame of reference for organizing marketing facts and for weighing marketing decisions. Previous efforts included the three-way classification of products as convenience goods, shopping goods, and specialty goods. The characteristics of goods theory sets up a continuous scale rather than discrete classes and defines the criteria by which any product can be assigned to an appropriate place on the scale. All of these criteria lend themselves to objective measurement, at least potentially. By contrast, it would be rather difficult to distinguish a shopping good from a convenience good in positive, quantitative terms.

The marketing characteristics of a product determine the most appropriate and economical method for distributing it. To fix its position on the scale, representing the variation in these characteristics, is to take the first major step toward understanding its marketing requirements. To know these characteristics is to be able to predict with a high degree of reliability how a product will be distributed, since most products conform to the pattern. Serious departure from the theoretical expectations will almost certainly indicate the need for change and improvement in distribution methods. These considerations apply both to physical distribution and to the parallel problem of communications including the choice of promotional media and appeals. It follows also that goods having similar characteristics call for similar handling. Finally, if precise weights or

values could be assigned to each characteristic, their combination would determine the unique position of a product on the marketing scale.

The problem-solving process often leads into totally unfamiliar areas which sometimes bring us to a dead end. Only occasionally do these probing excursions uncover new combinations of old ideas that have some relevance to the problem in hand. When such combinations prove to be useful the mind is quick to employ such combinations again for problems of the same general type, so that repeated use tends to formulate a framework of reference which can be readily used for problem solving. Into the framework thus formulated the problem can be fitted so that the relationship of the integral parts can be observed. This may well be a mental sorting operation which seeks to classify problems into similar groups for greater efficiency in the unending task of problem solving.

The characteristics of goods theory is the result of one of these mental excursions, and its repeated use has had the effect of crystalizing the combination of old ideas into a fairly stabilized form. The theory has been revised from time to time through the constructive criticism of my colleagues, but whether it will ever be in final form is doubtful, since the dynamic character of all marketing activity is such that changes are more likely than anything else. Somehow the thought of achieving a final state of equilibrium is rather frightening.

CHARACTERISTICS OF GOODS

The problem of weights or values being assigned to these individual characteristics has been one of the real difficulties in giving the theory a mathematical setting. So far that objective has not been fully achieved. We have been obliged to deal with relative values which might be considered as an intermediary stage in the theory's development. The analogy of an electric circuit may eventually prove useful in formulating a mathematical approach. Getting goods distributed is not unlike moving an electric current through resistance factors, each of which takes a part of the gross margin. When the good finally reaches the consumer's hands, ready for consumption, all of the gross margin has been used. Looking at this idea from the consumer end, the amount of the gross margin the consumer has given up in order to enjoy the utilities the good provides is, in fact, the voltage that the electric current must have in order to pass through the resistance factors and finally reach the consumer.

The decision as to the number and kinds of characteristics to be used was approached by setting up tests which these characteristics should meet. These criteria are:

1. Every characteristic selected must be applicable to every good.
2. Every characteristic selected must be relatively measurable in terms of its relationship to every good.
3. Every characteristic must be logically related to all the other characteristics.

This brings us to the point of defining a characteristic. A characteristic is a distinguishing quality of a good relative to its stable performance in a market and its relationship to the consumers for whom it has want-satisfying capacity. Under this definition five characteristics have been selected, each of which must in turn be defined. These are:

1. Replacement rate—This characteristic is defined as *the rate at which a good is purchased and consumed by users in order to provide the satisfaction a consumer expects from the product.* The replacement rate is associated with the concept of a flow or movement of units of a good from producer to ultimate consumer. The idea is somewhat akin to a turnover rate, except that our understanding of turnover is related to the number of times per year that an average stock of goods is bought and sold. Replacement rate as used here is consumer oriented. It asks how often the consumer buys shoes—once each month, once each six months, or once each year? It does not ask whether or not the shoes have been consumed, but only how often the market must be ready to make shoes available for consumers. This characteristic differentiates the rate or flow of different goods and attempts to envision the market mechanism that will meet the aggregate needs of consumers. This is marketing in motion as dictated by consumer purchasing power.

It may be helpful to introduce a few illustrative cases and at the same time show how the idea of relative measurement is used. Loaves of bread, cigarettes, packets of matches all have high replacement rates in terms of relative measurement. Some people consume bread more often than others, yet the average frequency of all bread eaters in a consumption area determines the replacement rate for bread. In comparison with grand pianos, bread has a high replacement rate and grand pianos have a low replacement rate. Men's shirts and ready-to-wear have medium replacement rates when compared to bread and grand pianos. Here we can visualize fast-moving streams, slow-moving streams and moderately moving streams of different kinds of goods, each with its characteristically different rate of replacement.

2. Gross margin—The definition of gross margin as used here is not different from its use in marketing generally. *The money sum which is the difference between the laid in cost and the final realized sales price* is the gross margin. It is brought to mind at once that there are several gross margins involved in moving goods from factory gates to final consumer. What is meant here is the summation of all the gross margins involved. It is that total money sum necessary to move a good from point of origin to final consumer. It might be thought of as channel costs or as the fare a good must pay to reach its destination. If the amount of gross margin is less than the fare needed, the good will not reach destination. The calculation of the gross margin is a market-oriented function which is based, in the final analysis, on the amount of money a consumer will exchange for a particular good. If the consumer elects to pay a money fund which is less than the production cost and the necessary marketing costs, the good will not be marketed because the gross margin is too low in relation with the other characteristics. The availability of gross margin is the force that operates our marketing system. Suppose a consumer wishes to procure a pack of cigarettes from a vending machine and the machine is set to operate when a twenty-five-cent piece is inserted into the slot. Nothing would happen if a ten-cent piece were dropped into the slot, except that the ten-cent piece would be returned to the customer. The gross margin contained in the twenty-five-cent piece was large enough to bring the consumer the cigarettes he needed.

This may be the appropriate place to call attention to the fact that whenever the flow of goods is arrested for whatever reason, costs begin to take a larger share of the planned gross margin and may actually prevent a good from reaching the final market. Such losses as may have been incurred in the stoppage must be borne by someone, and the calculations made by marketing men are such that loss situations cannot be tolerated, and the flow of goods will be stopped. The secondary action in such a case is that a money flow back to the producer also stops, which in turn closes down production. While this may be oversimplified, it does emphasize the importance of gross margin to the whole economic process.

Certain types of goods are necessarily involved in storage by reason of their seasonal production. Storage assumes the availability of the needed amount of gross margin to pay these costs, otherwise such goods would not be stored. Whatever takes place during the movement of goods from producer to consumer affects gross margin.

This is the first opportunity to test these characteristics against the criteria set up for their selection. It has been shown that the replacement rate is applicable to all goods and that the replacement rate is relatively measurable. Lastly the question must be asked: Is the replacement rate related to gross margin? This is without doubt the most important relationship of all those needing demonstration in this theory. The relationship is inverse. Whenever replacement rate is high gross margin is low and, conversely, when replacement rate is low then gross margin is high. Thus, when goods move along at a lively clip the costs of moving them are decreased. This relationship brings to mind some economic laws which bear on the situation. The theory of decreasing costs seems to apply here to show that marketing is a decreasing-cost industry. This might be stated as follows: As the number of units distributed increases, the cost per unit distributed tends to decrease up to the optimum point. Mass distribution insofar as marketing is concerned has important possibilities. This is amply demonstrated in modern marketing operations. Goods handling in modern warehouses has been studied in this light and warehousing costs have been decreased, which in turn has expedited the flow of goods into consumer's hands. Here again, economic laws operate to induce the seller to pass on savings in marketing costs. Small decreases in gross margin tend to bring forth a disproportionately larger market response.

The relationship of replacement rate and gross margin has thus far been concerned with the increasing side of the relationship. When replacement rate is low and gross margin is relatively higher, it is not difficult to envision higher marketing costs. Almost at once it can be seen that selling costs will be relatively higher per unit. The gross margin on the individual sale of a grand piano or major appliance must bear the cost of direct sales, including salaries and commissions for salesmen who negotiate with prospective buyers and very often make home demonstrations. The fact that shipping costs

are higher in moving pianos is well known. If carlot shipments are used there are likely to be some storage costs involved, and this additional cost must come out of gross margin. It can be shown that high-value goods such as jewelry and silverware reflect this relationship in much the same way. This inverse relationship between replacement rate and gross margin strikes a balance when goods with a medium rate of replacement are involved.

3. Adjustment—An important characteristic which pertains to all goods and which has been named "adjustment" is defined as *services applied to goods in order to meet the exact needs of the consumer*. These services may be performed as the goods are being produced or at any intermediate point in the channel of distribution or at the point of sale. Adjustment as a characteristic of all goods reflects the meticulous demands of consumers that must be met in the market. Even in such goods as quarts of milk there is evidence of adjustment. Some consumers demand milk with low fat content, others require milk with high fat content, to name but one of the items of adjustment which pertains to milk. The matter of size of package, homogenized or regular, and even the matter of added vitamins come under adjustment. The services applied to milk are performed in the processing plant in anticipation of the adjustments the consumer may require. Here slight changes in the form or in size of package are adjustments performed in advance of the sale of the product. This type of adjustment imposes additional costs involving somewhat larger inventories and the use of a greater amount of space, with all that this implies. It can be easily understood that costs are involved whenever adjustments are performed, so that additional amounts of gross margin are necessary. Adjustments made at the point of production become manufacturing costs which only mildly affect the marketing operation, so that the measured amount of adjustment in the marketing channel is relatively low.

Goods with a high replacement rate have low adjustment, but the reverse is true when goods have low replacement rates. Goods with a medium replacement rate have a medium amount of adjustment. Here the inverse relationship between replacement rate and adjustment has been demonstrated, as well as the direct relationship between gross margin and adjustment.

4. Time of consumption—Time of consumption as a characteristic of goods can be defined as *the measured time of consumption during*

which the good gives up the utility desired. This characteristic is related to the replacement rate to a considerable degree, since goods with a low time of consumption are likely to have a high rate of replacement. The inverse relationship is true, but a low time of consumption does not mean that a repetitive purchasing program is maintained by the same consumer. Aspirin gives up its utility in the short period of time during which it is being consumed, but a purchase replacement may not occur until another headache needs attention. The idea of consumption time is more closely related to nondurable goods both in the consumer and industrial classes.

The time of consumption characteristic pertains to all goods, and the amount of this time is relatively measurable, which satisfies the criterion of relationship to all goods and the criterion of relative measurability. The final criterion of relationship to all other characteristics is also met in that low time of consumption is directly related to adjustment and gross margin and inversely related to the rate of replacement.

5. Searching time—The characteristic of searching time can be defined as *the measure of average time and distance from the retail store* and hence convenience the consumer is afforded by market facilities. Suppose the need to purchase a package of cigarettes comes up for immediate attention for a consumer. The amount of effort exerted on his part to procure the needed cigarettes is correlated with the amount of searching time. In this case the amount of inconvenience suffered is usually very low since the market has reacted to the fact that there is a wide and insistent demand for cigarettes. To meet this demand, points of purchase are established wherever large numbers of potential customers are to be found. The result of such market action is that cigarettes can be purchased at many

different places and in many different institutions, and the searching time is low. The old idea expressed in another way: consumers are motivated by a drive for convenience. Out of these relationships we have come to recognize "the span of convenience" for each product. Consumers cannot easily be forced to expend an amount of time and energy that is disproportionate to the satisfaction they expect to receive from the goods in question.

It can easily be seen that for certain goods the searching time will be low, while for certain other goods the searching time will be much larger. The amount of time and energy expended by a customer in the process of furnishing a new home would be very great and, therefore, searching time would be correspondingly high. There is the need for examining, the offerings of many stores, and even though these stores may be located fairly close to each other, in all probability, they will be located at some distance from the consumer's home. The reality of this situation is expressed in the characteristics of the goods. Searching time can be readily envisioned by the fact that we have many more market outlets for cigarettes than we do for grand pianos or furniture and, therefore, market availability for cigarettes is low and for pianos it is high.

Searching time is directly related to gross margin, adjustment, and time of consumption, and is inversely related to replacement rate. Searching time as a characteristic of goods pertains to all goods and for each and every good it is relatively measurable.

This information can now be fitted into a chart which will keep the relationships of the characteristics of goods in position as they pertain to all goods. This chart will show that goods with the same relative amounts of these five characteristics fall into the same broad classifications. Arbitrary names can be fitted to these broad classifications for greater convenience in conveying ideas about goods and the various ways in which they are distributed.

COLOR CONCEPT

This chart introduces an additional element into the characteristics of good theory: the color classification. The idea that goods with similar characteristics are similar to each other lends itself to the establishment of three large classes of goods that can be named in such a manner as to convey the idea of an array of goods. The

Table 1. **Characteristics of Goods Theory**

	Color classification		
Characteristics	Red goods	Orange goods	Yellow goods
Replacement Rate	High	Medium	Low
Gross Margin	Low	Medium	High
Adjustment	Low	Medium	High
Time of Consumption	Low	Medium	High
Searching Time	Low	Medium	High

choice of color names may be inept in some respects, but the idea of an array of goods, based upon the sum of the relative values of characteristics of goods, is important. The length of light rays for red, orange, and yellow, in that order, is an array of light rays representing a portion of the spectrum. For our present purpose it is more convenient to use the three colors only, rather than the seven of the full spectrum. The idea of an infinite graduation of values can be envisioned by blending these colors from red to yellow with orange in between. This is the idea we wish to convey as concerning all goods.

The sum of the characteristics for each and every good is different, and the sum of characteristics for red goods is lower than the sum of the characteristics for yellow goods. The chart shows red goods to have four low values and one of a high value, while yellow goods have four high values and one low.

It is useful to stress this tension between replacement rate and the other four marketing characteristics, since they all tend to decrease as replacement rate increases. That is equivalent to saying that as demand for a product increases, marketing methods tend to develop which reflect economies in the various aspects of marketing costs. It is easily possible, of course, to transform replacement rate into its inverse for use in arriving at a weighted index of the five characteristics. If replacement rate were expressed

as the average number purchases in a year, the measure would be the average number of days between purchases. This measure would be low for red goods and high for yellow, like all of the other characteristics.

A schematic diagram can now be set up which represents all possible graduations in goods from red through orange to yellow. As shown in Figure 1, a simple percentage scale from 0 to 100 is laid out on both coordinates. It is true that the weighted value for any product could be laid out on a single line. Yet there is an advantage in the two-dimensional chart for the purpose of visualizing an array of goods. The scale of values thus really consists of all the points on the diagonal line in the accompanying chart. Since there is an infinite number of points on any line segment, the scale provides for an infinite array of goods. If the chart were large enough, vertical lines could be drawn with each line representing a product now on the market. Even after these lines were drawn there would still remain an infinite number of positions in between. Many of these positions might serve to identify goods which have been withdrawn from the market or others which might be introduced in the future.

Line AB represents a good having an ordinate value of 63, indicating the sum of the characterisics of this good. In the general classification it has 63 per cent yellow characteristics

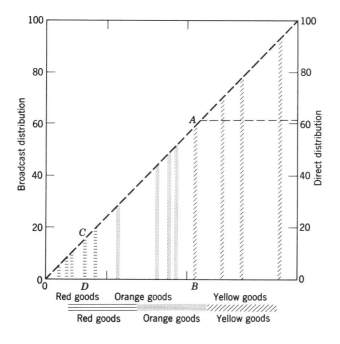

Fig. 1. Schematic array of a few selected goods (plotted in terms of yellow goods.)

and 37 per cent red characteristics. Translated into marketing terms, this good might be ladies' ready-to-wear dresses sold through department stores and shipped directly from the factory to these stores in the larger cities. The smaller cities are served by wholesalers who carry small stocks of these goods along with other dry goods items. Thus the marketing channels utilized for distributing this good would be direct to large department store accounts and semibroadcast through specialty wholesalers serving smaller city accounts.

Line CD in its position near the red end of the scale has a yellow characteristics value of 15 and a red value of 85, which puts this good in the large classification as a red good. The sum of the characteristics value in the scale 0 to 100 is 85 per cent red. This might well be a soap product which is sold mainly by broadcast distribution using a broker, wholesaler, retailer channel. The 15 per cent yellow characteristic might indicate specialty salesmen's activity involving factory drop shipments. The latter type of distribution is more direct and might account for the 15 per cent of direct distribution from the factory to the retailer.

The position of a good on the color scale is not static. Most products fall in the yellow classification when they are first introduced. As they become better known and come to satisfy a wider segment of consumer demand, the replacement rate increases and the good shifts toward the red end of the scale. Thus there is a red shift in marketing which offers a rather far-fetched analogy to the red shift in astronomy which is associated with the increasing speed of movement of heavenly bodies. There is also an opposing tendency in marketing, however, resulting from the constant shrinking of gross margin as a good moves toward the red end of the scale. Marketing organizations, in the effort to maintain their gross margin, may improve or differentiate a good which has moved into the red category, so that some of these new varieties swing all the way back into yellow. Thereafter the competitive drive for volume serves to accelerate the movement toward the red end of the scale again.

The sponsor of a product must decide how it is to be promoted and what channels to use for its physical distribution. He is confronted with a variety of possibilities both for stimulating demand and for moving his product to the consumer. It turns out that there is a parallel relationship between these two aspects of the marketing problem with a distribution system and its appropriate counterpart in promotion usually occurring together. This pairing of systems occurs because the promotion and distribution requirements of a product are both dependent on the marketing characteristics of the goods. The preceding material explained how goods might be arrayed according to their marketing characteristics into groups designated as red, orange, and yellow. It was further shown that this array could be translated into a numerical scale and presented in simple graphic form. The purpose of the present article is to indicate how the position of a product on this scale can be used to identify the parallel systems of promotion and distribution which should be used in marketing the product.

This set of ideas has come to be designated as the parallel systems theory. It is the kind of theory which is intended to be helpful in resolving fundamental practical issues in marketing. Theory alone cannot settle all the details of a marketing plan. It may save much time and effort by indicating the starting point for planning and the appropriate matching of systems of promotion and distribution. The gross margin earned on a product provides the fund which must cover the costs of marketing distribution and marketing promotion. The management of this fund involves many of the most critical decisions with which marketing executives have to deal. Even slight errors of judgment in this regard may spell the difference between profit and loss.

The parallel systems theory begins with a simple thesis which may be stated as follows: The characteristics of goods indicate the manner of their physical distribution and the manner of promotion must parallel that physical distribution. Thus, we have parallel systems, one for physical distribution and one for promotion. The movement of goods and the movement of information are obviously quite different processes. It was to be expected that specialized facilities would be developed for each function. The fact that these developments take place along parallel lines is fundamental to an understanding of marketing. A few special terms must be introduced at this point for use in discussing parallel systems.

A channel for the physical distribution of goods may be either a short channel or a long channel. The shortest channel, of course, is represented by the transaction in which the producer delivers the product directly to its ultimate user. A long channel is one in which the product moves through several stages of location and ownership as from the factory to a regional warehouse, to the wholesaler's warehouse, to a retail store, and finally to the consumer. The parallel concepts in promotion may be compared to contrasting situations in electronic communication. On the one hand, there is the closed circuit through which two people can carry on a direct and exclusive conversation with each other. On the other hand, there is broadcast communication such as radio and television whereby the same message can be communicated to many people simultaneously.

In general, long channels and broadcast promotion are found together in marketing while short channels and closed circuit or direct promotion are found together. The parallel systems theory attempts to show how these relationships arise naturally out of the marketing characteristics of the goods.

CHARACTERISTICS OF GOODS AND MARKETING SYSTEMS

It will be remembered that goods were arrayed according to their marketing characteristics as red, orange, and yellow. Marketing systems can be arrayed in similar and parallel fashion. Red goods call for long channels and broadcast promotion. Yellow goods call for short channels and closed circuit promotion. Orange goods are intermediate as to their marketing characteristics and, hence, are intermediate as to the kind of distribution and promotion systems which they require. There is a continuous gradation from red to yellow and from broadcast to direct methods of marketing.

One of the fundamental marketing characteristics of goods is replacement rate. That is the frequency with which the average consumer in the market buys the product or replenishes the supply of it carried in his household inventory. Red goods are goods with a high replacement rate. A market transaction which occurs with high frequency lends itself to standardization and specialization of function. The movement of goods and the movement of information each becomes clearly marked and separate. Opportunity arises for a number of specialized marketing agencies to participate in distribution, and the result is what has been called the "long channel." Messages to the ultimate user become as standardized as the product itself. This type of information and persuasion does not need to follow the long distribution channel from step to step in its transmission from producer to consumer. Such messages are broadcast to consumers through both electronic and printed advertising media which provide a more appropriate channel.

Yellow goods are low in replacement rate and high in other marketing characteristics such as adjustment. Requirements for this class of goods tend to vary from one user to another. Adjustment embraces a variety of means by which goods are fitted to individual requirements. The marketing process remains relatively costly and a large percentage of gross margin necessarily goes along with high adjustment. The opportunity for standardization and specialization is slight compared to that of red goods. Physical movement and promotion remain more closely associated, with a two-way communication concerning what is available and what is needed finally resulting in the delivery of the custom-made product. A transaction between a man and his tailor would illustrate this type of marketing. Many kinds of industrial equipment are specially designed for the given user and would also be at the extreme yellow end of the scale. The short channel is prevalent in such situations and all promotion or related communication moves through a closed circuit.

Many products lie in the middle range which have been designated as orange goods They have been produced to standard specifications but with the knowledge that they will have to be adapted in greater or less degree in each individual installation. The replacement rate is high enough to offer moderate opportunity for standardization and specialization. At least one intermediary is likely to enter the picture, such as an automobile dealer buying from the manufacturer and selling to the consumer or an industrial distributor serving as a channel between two manufacturers. The car sold to customers may be of the same model and yet be substantially differentiated to meet individual preferences as to color and accessories. Broadcast media are used in promotion but not on the same scale relatively as for soaps or cigarettes. The industrial distributor is often supported in his efforts by specialty salesmen or sales engineers employed by the manufacturer. Advertising of a semibroadcast character is likely to be used. That is to say that messages are specially prepared for various segments of the market for which the appeal of the product is expected to be somewhat different. This approach lies between the standardized message to all users on the one hand and the individualized closed circuit negotiation on the other.

One qualification which may properly be

suggested at this point is that marketing systems are not quite so flexible as this discussion suggests, but must conform to one type or another. Thus a channel for physical distribution could have two steps or three steps but not two and a half. Nevertheless, the picture of continuous variation along a scale is generally valid because of the combinations which are possible. A producer may sell part of his output through wholesalers who service retailers and sell the remainder direct to retailers. The proportions may vary over time so that one channel presently becomes dominant rather than the other. Similarly broadcast promotion may gradually assume greater importance in the marketing mix even though a large but declining amount of adjustment is involved in some individual sales.

MOVEMENT OF GOODS AND MOVEMENT OF INFORMATION

The schematic relationship between goods and marketing systems is shown in Figure 2. This simple diagram depicts the parallels which have been discussed. It will be noted that the segment of the line allowed is greater for orange goods than for red goods and greater for yellow than for orange. It is a readily observable fact that the number of separate and distinct items in any stock of goods increases as replacement rate decreases. A drugstore, for example, has to sell more separate items to achieve the same volume of sales as a grocery store. An exclusive dress shop will need more variation in styles and models than a store operating in the popular price range. Paint brushes, files, or grinding wheels will be made up in a great multiplicity of specifications to serve the industrial market as compared to the few numbers which suffice for the household user. Red goods by their very nature are those in which a single item is bought frequently because it meets the requirements of many occasions for use while in the yellow

goods more numerous items with less frequent sales are required for a more accurate matching of diverse and differentiated use situations.

Figure 3 is intended to demonstrate the relationship between goods and the methods of distribution and promotion. It is not intended to show an accurate mathematical relationship since the data from which it is constructed are not mathematically accurate, but it does implement understanding of the problems with which marketing executives must deal. The reasoning is deductive, moving from the general to the specific and provides a quick basis for reaching an answer which can readily be adjusted to a specific case. The readings from the diagram are in complementary percentages that must be accepted as rough measurements of the kinds and amounts of distribution and promotion. Long channel distribution and broadcast promotion are grouped together as related elements of the marketing mix and designated as "broadcast" for the sake of simplicity. The line representing these two elements in combination slopes downward to the right since this type of expenditure can be expected to be relatively high for red goods and relatively low for yellow goods. Similarly short channel distribution and closed circuit communication are thrown together under the designation of "direct." The line representing direct promotion and distribution slopes upward from left to right.

APPLICATION TO A MANAGEMENT PROBLEM

A short time ago a project was undertaken for a well-known manufacturer whose operation is such that the range of products his company manufactures covers the scale from red goods to yellow goods. In following the reasoning of the characteristics of goods theory and the parallel systems theory he was able to locate a certain product in its position on the base line. He drew the ordinate representing this product and found from the diagram that the distribution indicated was a modified direct distribution and that accordingly a considerable amount of direct promotion should be used. In reviewing what actually was being done with this product he knew that promotion was mostly broadcast while the distribution was a modified direct. Thus, promotion and distribution were not running parallel and such a finding for this product provided a substantial explanation of the poor performance this product was making. Research had confirmed that it was an excellent prod-

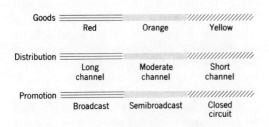

Fig. 2. Relationship between goods and marketing systems.

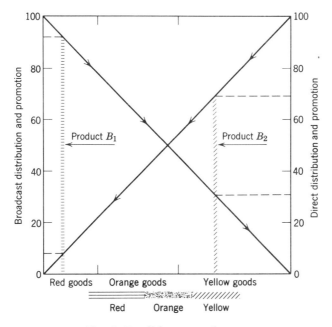

Fig. 3. Parallel systems theory.

uct and that it was priced correctly so that a reasonable volume of sales should have been expected. The planned sales for the product were not realized and to correct this situation a more extensive broadcast promotion program was launched, but from this program little or no increase in sales was realized. At this point the manufacturer decided that it would be worth a try to follow out the indicated promotional and distributional plan shown in the parallel systems theory analysis. A program of direct promotion was initiated and results were immediately forthcoming. The full sales expectations were realized and the manufacturer decided to establish a special division to handle the product which since that time has produced even more sales at costs considerably below the estimated costs.

A somewhat closer look at this case revealed that broadcast promotion was reaching thousands of people who were in no way qualified users of the product and that the type of advertising message was such that qualified users were unable to specify the product even if they wished to do so. A careful study of the problem showed that the direct promotion had produced all of the sales results. Thus the cost of the broadcast promotion had to be borne by qualified users and the result was a higher price than would have been needed if direct promotional means had been employed. The final result of

this operation was that prices were lowered and the profit position for the manufacturer and all institutions in the distribution channel was improved.

Product B_2 in Figure 3, represents the product discussed in the case above located in its correct position. Reading the ordinate value in the vertical scale shows that the product it represents should be distributed 69 per cent direct and that promotion should also be 69 per cent direct. The complementary 31 per cent reading shown indicates that 31 per cent of the distribution should be broadcast and 31 per cent of the promotion should be of the broadcast type. Product B_1 shown on the diagram is product B_2 as it was incorrectly located on the base line array of goods. The incorrect location was based on a measurement of the method of promotion that was being used. Actually this product was being distributed correctly by a modified direct method, and consequently consumers who might have been influenced to use the product had no means by which to exercise their wishes; the product was not available in retail stores in such a way as to make it readily available to qualified customers.

By making analyses of products and their distribution and promotional programs, it will be found that many products are not in conformity with the parallel systems theory, and yet seem to be successful products. This would not of itself disprove the theory. Such results might indicate that better results might be had if the programs were modified in the direction indicated by the theory. This can often be done at a comparatively small cost by using test sales areas in which the adjustment can be made without affecting the national system in which the product may be operating. The results from such experimentation should confirm the analysis made under the parallel systems theory. A large amount of case material has been collected on the parallel systems theory but there seems to be an almost endless variety of cases and there is a need for constantly studying the problem in the light of the improvements in communications and distribution.

CONCLUSION

A further definition for broadcast promotion seems to be needed as well as for direct promotion. Whenever promotional means are used, without knowledge in advance of the identity of prospective users, the promotional means is considered to be broadcast. The firm employing broadcast promotional means relies upon the chance contact with potential customers for the product or service. The broadcast distributional means for such a product are so arranged that the customer for the product who has been reached by this type of promotion can exercise his choice conveniently and quickly. Retail stores are available within a short radius of the consumer who may wish to purchase the product. Thus, the sales gap is shortened both as to time and distance and the effectiveness of the broadcast means of promotion is enhanced. The key fact that makes this type of marketing economical is that while the prospective users are unidentified, they represent a large proportion of the general public which will be exposed to the broadcast message. The opposite of broadcast promotion is direct promotion. The definition of direct promotion turns on the fact that the recipient of the direct communication is known in advance, so that the message reaches the intended purchaser by name and address or by advance qualification of the prospect as to his need and ability to purchase the product. The most direct means would be a salesman who calls upon a selected prospect whose address and name is known in advance, and where judgment has been passed upon his need for the product, and whose ability to pay for the product has been ascertained. The next in order might be a direct first-class letter or telegram sent to a prospect. Then perhaps door-to-door selling or mailing to persons found on selected mailing lists. These selected means of direct promotion used show a widening sales gap between the customer and the product. It is readily seen that broadcast promotion creates the widest sales gap. At the same time it can readily be seen that the marketing radius over which the customer may have to search for the product is increased. Compensating for this increased radius are the more intensive means of promotion that result from direct promotion, which will induce the customer willingly to undertake greater inconveniences of time and distance in order to procure the product.

These definitions relate directly back to the characteristics of goods theory. Whenever a high replacement is involved it becomes physically impossible to effect distribution by direct means. Such a situation calls for mass selling and mass movement of goods wherein all economies of volume selling and goods handling are brought into play. The low gross margin on the individual transaction requires that the aggregate gross margin resulting from mass selling be ample to get the job done. It seems ludicrous to think of fashioning cigarettes to the consumers' needs at the point of sale, putting on filters and adjusting lengths to king size. The gross margin required to do such a job would put cigarettes in the price class of silverware and the number of people who could purchase on that basis would be very small. But mounting a diamond in a special setting is not at all ludicrous, because the gross margin available is large enough to undertake such adjustment. It would be redundant to go through the whole list of characteristics since it is perfectly clear what the relationships would be.

THE ROLE OF THEORY

Theory formulation and development adds a new dimension to the understanding of our field, that of abstractions. The concept of all goods and services being arrayed simultaneously, in accordance with the standards set by the characteristics of goods, at either end of the array, is a pure abstraction. It is a thought pattern that we can conceive mentally, but which in fact does not exist. Yet, such mentally conceived abstractions provide us with an understanding of where in relation to all other goods and services, a certain good exists in the array. This alone provides a quick comparison of the distribution channels of similar goods, and if the product is a new product, suggests the most likely channels to investigate.

The concept of the migration, over a period of time, of a good to new position in the array, suggests that distribution channels change and that the reassessment of the position of a good is essential to sound marketing. Thus, when a certain good entered the field as a strictly pharmaceutical good, it was promoted and distributed in much the same manner as other pharmaceutical goods, but later as its consumer acceptance developed, it was found that its characteristics had changed and that it was necessary to change both the promotion and distribution patterns to affect economic distribution. Here, again, is an abstract idea that provides the basis for understanding the need for change in the distribution pattern of a good as it migrated from one position to another in the array. These illustrations could be carried on endlessly, since every good has its unique and distinctive position in the array, as of a point in time, and literally the variations are limited only by the imagination of the theorist. Finally, the role of theory is the stimulation of creative thinking in any field of scientific investigation. We advance only as our creative thinking pushes outward the horizons of our understanding. This is the true role of theory.

12. The Depot Theory of Distribution

LEO V. ASPINWALL*

This theory helps explain the growth of manufacturer's wholesale branches and the decline of general line wholesaling institutions. It indicates some of the fundamental reasons for the changes that have occurred in the physical handling and storing of goods. This theory extends the flow concept in marketing and contributes to an understanding of the systems approach to marketing management.

The thesis of the depot theory of distribution is that *goods tend to move towards the point of final consumption at a rate established by the ultimate consumer.* The depot theory is concerned with the performance of all direct and supporting storage, handling and transportation activities performed by middlemen in the channel of distribution, on an actual cost of service basis, eliminating merchandising profits. The thesis contains the essentials of the concept of orderly marketing, an objective of all marketing activities.

The depot theory of distribution envisions a steady flow of goods from the point of production to final consumption. The intermediary institutions facilitating this flow are in fact the depots. Depot is a military term and refers to the storage of supplies purely as a service function. The depot theory of distribution considers the performance of the depot function on the basis of costs of services performed.

The import of the depot theory of distribution is the identification of a trend in marketing toward the elimination of merchandising profits. The old idea of a merchant was that he "bought low and sold high." The merchant was an independent enterpriser who bought his goods and then sold them so as to take the difference between the sales price and his cost; this difference, or gross margin, contains all handling costs plus an extra merchandising profit. When transportation facilities and communications were less advanced than they are today, a merchant anticipated the needs of his customers and bought goods in advance of their needs and for this charged a merchandising profit in addition to the cost he had incurred in handling and storing. The merchant's strategy was to attempt to achieve a monopoly position in a limited market. Merchandising profits, under any conditions, are justifiable if the goods or services provide utilities to the consumer. Under less advanced and developed states of communication and transportation real utilities are provided by merchandisers performing these functions. Competition under modern conditions is so intense that merchandising profits are very difficult to obtain.

This current competitive situation points up the depot concept and forecasts the trend in the distribution of products. The depot identifies a function of marketing which performs all storage and handling costs on a cost basis so as to put goods in retailers' hands at lowest possible costs. The competitive retail market demands this policy of management to keep goods flowing into consumption at the rate dictated by consumers; eliminating any stoppage of the flow. Stoppage of the flow causes costs to increase and losses are almost certain to be encountered.

Managing the physical distribution of goods requires utilization of total resources in the most effective manner. Thus, it is necessary to use mass shipments at times in order to take advantage of the rate differential between less than car and full car lots.

• SOURCE: Leo Aspinwall, "The Depot Theory of Distribution," in William Lazer and Eugene J. Kelley, *Managerial Marketing*, Rev. ed. (Homewood, Ill.: Richard D. Irwin, 1962), pp. 652–659.
* University of Colorado.

The depot function involves warehousing activities; large lots are broken into smaller lot shipments. Under the depot theory, goods are stored for the minimum time. The steady flow of goods is maintained between the manufacturer and the consumer. In this theory the amount of gross margin added to the goods is a channel cost representing the cost of services performed by the depot.

It is apparent that in order to provide economic and orderly distribution, goods which are at opposite ends of a scale such as pianos and cigarettes require different distribution patterns. The depot theory is related to the characteristics of goods theory. The latter theory explains that goods, based on the characteristics, are distributed either by a broadcast system or a direct system. Such goods as grand pianos or electronic computers move directly from the manufacturer to the final consumer, with little or no depot function being performed. Goods such as cigarettes or cereals have at least one stop where the depot function is performed in moving from manufacturer to retailer and then to the consumer.

ADVANCING TECHNOLOGY AND MARKETING ADJUSTMENTS

Since the end of World War II, many of the advances in distribution are traceable to materials handling improvements and to new developments in communication. The full impact of recent technological advances has not yet been realized in marketing. The development of the modern data processing, for example, has provided almost instantaneous feed-back information, from the active final sales areas to production centers. As a result, production schedules can be geared more closely to actual sales. This means that inventory risks are minimized at each point in the channel. The quantities and types of goods are adjusted to meet consumer needs more precisely.

The physical transportation of all goods inevitably involves time and costs which means that the physical characteristics of the goods must be taken into account. Valuable high density goods, such as diamonds, are able to bear higher transportation costs than low value bulky type goods, such as coal, which must be moved at lower transportation costs, and which involve more time in transit. Inventory costs occur whenever physical goods are transported. These inventory costs must be added to the factory costs of the goods, along with transportation costs. Even in current marketing practices these costs are added and are not the basis for calculating a merchandising profit by mid-channel operators.

For example, a Chicago packer receives hourly and daily information on the sales of beef in Los Angeles areas. The beef is shipped by air freight over night, so the amount and quality needed for that day's sale arrives early in the morning. Planes fly at high altitude and the need for refrigeration is eliminated. The hanging beef is landed in Los Angeles at the lowest net cost of inventory and transport. Chicago-processed beef is competitive with beef processed in the Los Angeles area. This seems to violate the bulky low-value rule on transportation. However, by eliminating refrigeration costs and landing the beef in Los Angeles without the damage due to bruising which occurs in truck or rail shipments, a firm acceptance for the branded meats of the Chicago packer was earned in the West Coast market. This contract fed, Mid-West beef is taken mainly by hotels and restaurants which cater to upper income customers in Los Angeles. In this instance, cultivation of this profitable segment of the fresh meat market is made possible through the advances in communication and transportation.

The backward integration of retail food is illustrative of the strong tendency to emphasize the depot function and to obtain lowest total physical distribution costs. Large warehouses are built at strategic distribution points. They perform a complete depot function for the stores they support. Even the large delivery trucks are managed on a fleet basis including the provision for all repair services. Trucks are loaded in late afternoon and are dispatched to their destinations during the night hours to avoid day time traffic. Goods are unloaded at the stores during the night and are processed during the early morning hours, before heavy shopping begins. Trucks frequently maintain radio contact with the main warehouse so that in breakdowns goods can be transferred quickly to empty trucks returning to the central warehouse.

The mechanized equipment used minimizes manual handling in depot operations. Goods flow to stocking areas on conveyer belts and roller devices. The stocking areas are located so as to require the least movement of goods. For example, heavy, low-value, bulky goods, such as packaged sugar in one hundred pound bags, have a high replacement rate. The stocking area for these goods are close to the final order assembly. If low-value, bulky items are directed into remote stocking areas, costs would be excessive. Mathematical formuli have been developed to calculate precisely the most economical stocking location.

These activities illustrate the efforts to reduce depot function costs to the lowest possible level. Goods are distributed to retail outlets at the delivered warehouse cost, plus the actual depot function costs. The retail outlet receives these goods F.O.B. warehouse at delivered costs, plus the transportation costs to the retail location. Transportation costs are computed on a ton-mile basis. They are credited to the warehouse as income, supporting truck operations.

The operation of the warehouse is conducted on service cost basis. It is completely devoid of any merchandising profits. Depot activities, therefore, are strictly service operations. The costs of these activities consist of physical handling costs and the costs necessary to support physical facilities including cost of land, buildings and equipment. Additional means are employed in wholesale cooperative organizations designed to minimize taxes, hence reduce depot costs.

The essence of the depot theory of distribution is that goods tend to move towards the point of final consumption at a rate dictated by the final consumer. The consumption rate is governed by costs. Whenever the factory gate price of a product, plus the depot function costs, plus the retailing costs are greater than the estimated utilities received from the product by consumers, the entire flow of an item stops. Such goods in the channel not yet in the hands of retailers are in fact distress merchandise. Losses are involved and information is fed back to the producer who immediately stops production.

The withholding of purchasing power by consumers for reasons other than price results in inventory losses. Design, quality, color and style of goods, are also a basis of market rejection. The increasingly rapid feedback of information limits some of the risks of inventory ownership. The use of computers to process information from geographically separated markets provides immediate market information. This facilitates improved production control. The ideal model of linked information systems, which can never be achieved, would be one where all producers would be served with a unified market information service so that distressed merchandise would be marketed in the most orderly way.

Production complexities are such that it is frequently not possible to respond promptly to changes indicated by market information. Such delays can erase many of the advantages gained by the feed back system.

MERCHANDISING PROFITS ARE CONFINED LARGELY TO RETAILERS AND PRODUCERS

Retail inventories should be maintained at a level sufficient to afford consumers a range of merchandise to meet wants and needs. The maintenance of inventories involves risks for which the retailer must be compensated. If adequate profit margins are not available, retailers will attempt to limit their risks by maintaining inadequate inventories. When wanted goods are not available at convenient retail outlets, the consumer must perform a more extensive search function. The process of seeking out sources may become so inconvenient and burdensome that consumers will either go without, or substitute other goods with approximately the same utilities. The searching process involves the expenditures of time, energy, and money. The limit of the span of convenience is reached whenever the sum of convenience costs is greater than the net satisfactions in utilities of the commodities sought. Areas of profitable retail opportunity may exist in areas lacking these convenience services for consumers. Merchants attempt to locate retail establishments within the span of convenience of as many consumers as possible.

Services performed at the depot enhances the chances of retail survival by affording lower cost goods. Depot operations eliminate payment of profits to wholesalers and warehousemen, and lower the costs of retail operations. Lower merchandise costs seem to indicate increased profit opportunities and tend to encourage more enterprisers to enter retailing. This in turn increases retail competition.

THE PRODUCERS' MERCHANDISING PROFIT

Competition between manufacturers is such that a pure merchandising profit is seldom available. Manufacturers' profits come for the most part from the position of being a reliable supplier. Steel mills, for instance, are operated on the back log of firm orders upon which a normal manufacturing profit is taken. A merchandising profit becomes available when prospects for orders are such that production rates can be increased beyond the breakeven point. The profit position of large integrated industries is in general somewhat better than that of retailers, since there are fewer competing units.

One example of a recent operation of a merchandising profit at the producers' level was the case of the success of the first manufacturer to penetrate the weight reducing food market. The increase in market value of the manufacturer of Metrecal's stock over a comparatively short period of time, indicates the merchandising profit afforded this timely operation.

Product differentiation is a widely used strategy of manufacturers. Brands provide consumers a means of identifying a product which has earned acceptance. Branding is a competitive tactic which attempts to place a manufacturer's product in a special class. The hope is that consumers will seek out the branded product on the basis of satisfactory experience in using the product. The branded product is thus partially removed from the competition of unbranded products as well as from other branded products. Even so, competition and innovation of other brands bid for a share of the market. Such pressures force the branded item away from a merchandising profit and into a position of normal profit.

Market segmentation is also used in connection with the strategy of product differentiation. This means that by design a product is fashioned for a special segment or group of consumers. The high income group who can afford to buy expensive automobiles is the example. The market for cameras is segmented into the professional group and the amateur group. A branded camera designed for professionals does not have to compete with branded cameras intended for the less skilled segment of the camera market. Here too, the forces of competition and innovation move the manufacturer into a normal profit position much akin of the depot concept.

RETAIL COMPETITION GENERATED BY THE DISCOUNT HOUSE

Marketing men had begun to think that the problem of the discount house had been disposed of as a passing innovation in retailing. For a time it was believed the discount house came into being through the availability of distress merchandise in the market. Sharp operators constantly searched the market for opportunities to bid for goods that had stopped moving in the distribution channel and by reason of their accumulation were facing charges of inter-

est on the investment, storage and insurance costs. Owners had to dispose of such goods at whatever price the market would afford. Lines of merchandise accumulated on this basis were not complete and offerings to the public were made from low rent facilities on a cash basis. Price was the main consideration; often well known brands could be found at very low prices. But the discount house now flourishes in an organized way offering standard non-distress merchandise that well-established retailers are undertaking this type of operation on their own account.

At an opening of a large discount house branch in a rapidly growing suburb of Los Angeles, California, over forty thousand (police estimate) people struggled to get into the store. The Los Angeles papers carried a sixteen page insert of offerings including furniture, appliances, groceries, ready-to-wear, shoes and auto accessories, in fact almost everything in the department store range. A three hundred dollar mink cape was offered for ten dollars, to people who had registered and whose names were drawn in a lottery. Well known brands of appliances were offered at prices about half of their established value. The building is located in a prime location within a shopping center which is one of the largest in Southwest Los Angeles. All of this is unorthodox in terms of discount house operations and indicates the vitality of the discount house and is another illustration of a strong trend towards the depot concept of distribution. A merchandising profit under discount house operations arises only through fortuitous circumstance and normal profits are likely to rule, made up of the delivered cost of goods plus handling costs.

Reputable manufacturers now sell directly to discount houses. One case involves a nationally known manufacturer of a complete line of consumer products. The goods, all from the same production line, are branded with four different line brands. Unbranded goods from the production line are sold to discount houses. The discount houses are obliged to buy in case lots and they are not allowed fill-ins from open stock. Here again the depot concept obtains with goods moving directly to the final retail outlet at the lowest possible prices and sold with the handling costs added.

RECAPITULATION

The thesis of the depot theory of marketing distribution is: Goods tend to move towards the point of final consumption at a rate dictated by the ultimate consumer. The theory points to the strong trend in marketing towards the management of marketing activities on a cost of service basis and the consequent diminution of merchandising profits. A merchandising profit is a charge added to the cost of goods for the assumption of inventory risks; it is mainly based upon the anticipations of consumers' needs in advance of the time of consumption. There is a strong element of fortuity in a merchandising profit. Speculation and risk assumption attendant upon inventory ownership is involved in a merchandising profit. It is an increment added beyond the actual service costs incurred in handling the goods.

The operations of the chain super-markets in food distribution, with their backward integration into warehouses and manufacturing, have been cited as an illustration of the depot theory. The operations of the discount house with manufacturers selling directly to these outlets, further emphasizes this trend. The mail-order houses operate on a near discount house basis and the former 5 and 10 chains give evidence of greater attention to merchandising lines outside their former operations, with cut rate practices employed. Careful observers of the current marketing scene have commented on the strong tendency towards low cost handling of goods. The rapid advances in transportation and communication open up new methods of conducting marketing operations, so that the "propensity to consume" is in fact being heightened.

13. Interaction of Channel Selection Policies in the Marketing System

BRUCE MALLEN

This paper argues that every discipline must develop a "knowledge system" in order to develop a general theory and laws. The Marketing System includes market, marketing mix, and company and external elements. All these elements can be shown to affect and interact with the decision area of designing a channel structure.

INTRODUCTION

Knowledge is divided into fields, not because in reality it falls into knowledge-tight compartments but because it makes for convenience and specialization in study. In reality, knowledge is unified. A thorough study of a problem in any one field will almost certainly overlap into another. Even more pertinent, problems in a subdivision of one discipline (field) are bound to involve considerations of other subdivisions of that discipline.

To maintain the convenience of specialization, and at the same time to not lose sight of this unity of knowledge, each field must develop a "knowledge-system." A knowledge-system provides, for each discipline, a perspective on how its parts stand in relation to its whole, and how its whole stands in relation to all other fields of human knowledge.

Business administration is not an exception. Marketing decisions must consider the implications in other areas of business administration as well as those in areas outside of this discipline. Further, for example, channel selection, a marketing subdivision, must consider other subdivisions of marketing and from there move onward to consideration of non-marketing business areas, and eventually consider the social and even natural sciences.

Thus, it is felt that if marketing is to advance as a field of study and perhaps even earn the title of a social science, present and future information and concepts must be put into an organized whole. This organization or structure must be given component parts which are categorized such that they are exhaustive, and yet exclusive of each other. That is, these parts, in total, must account for the entire range of marketing phenomena but yet must not, to any great extent, overlap into each other. Further, this structure must be capable of describing the interaction or dynamics between its component parts.

The necessary structure described above is but an intermediate step in the advancement of marketing as a science. It is felt that it can aid, and indeed is the only feasible way of approaching, a general theory of marketing.

The general outlines of this structure have already been developed; it is the systems approach.[1] It is a goal of marketing science to fill in this outline by describing how each of the system's components, e.g., pricing interacts with the other parts.

• SOURCE: Mallen, Bruce, "Interaction of Channel Selection Policies in the Marketing System," an extension of Bruce Mallen, "A Conceptual Foundation For a General Theory of Marketing," *The Marketer: Journal of the Marketing Association of Canada,* Vol. I (Spring, 1965), pp. 14–16. Bruce Mallen, Chairman, Department of Marketing, Sir George Williams University.

[1] William Lazer and Eugene J. Kelley, *Interdisciplinary Contributions to Marketing Management* (Marketing and Transportation Paper No. 5, Bureau of Business and Economic Research, College of Business and Public Service, Michigan State University, 1959).

THE DEVELOPMENT OF
A MARKETING SCIENCE

The conceptualization of a marketing system, as mentioned, is but one step in the development of a marketing science. There are two before, chaos and experience; and two after, theory and descriptive law. Each of these five steps describes the general way an executive makes a decision, the type of thinking he goes through. Each step is developed from the preceding one. In short, we have an evolution of: chaos–experience–systems–theory–law. These steps are graded and isolated by the degree of rigorism that is used for decision thinking. Thus decision thinking can in the main be artistic, and, if extreme in that direction, it deteriorates to pure guessing, or it can in the main be scientific, and, if extreme in that direction, it deteriorates to a highly inflexible routine. The process is a climb to ever higher levels of rigorous and objective reasoning.

Chaos

The first level is chaos. At this level there appears to be no order in the area of concern. Events take place which seem to have no relationship to other events. Ideas and concepts float around in a bewildering unstructured manner. Decisions may be based on chaos, and this is what is known as pure guessing. There is no sound basis for the decision.

Experience

As the executive continuously makes similar decisions based on chaos, he finds that some lead to success and others to failure. He begins to see some structure in his area of interest. Chaos has now matured into experience. Probably most decisions are made on this second level. This is what is known as informed judgment. Not yet at the articulate stage, experience nevertheless has built an unconscious structure of thought.

System

When this structure is brought to the conscious, a system is evolved. As we have seen, a system is a set of interrelated concepts. It tries consciously, often schematically, to delimit the area of interest. It attempts to put a fence around a section of knowledge and to show the paths that lead from one element to the next in the system. It is more than a checklist, though

it is this also, as it shows the interaction between system elements. It is useful to the decision maker as it forces him to look at all factors and to consider the relationship, one to the other. Though a system puts far more rigor, structure and order into an area of inquiry than do chaos and experience, it still does not attempt to predict. It only shows, in a general way, the interrelations and interactions between the elements. It isolates these system units; it maintains that one affects the other; it suggests how, but it is still indefinite, still not highly structured. There is another stage of development—theory, though systems are still needed in this field.

". . . in marketing we are groping for a more productive approach and for better tools of analysis. We seek presently not so much the end product of systematic generalization (theories) and broad principles, but a conceptual framework (systems) that will assist us in asking the right questions and in fitting facts into an orderly pattern with enlarged and significant meaning."[2]

Theory

By theory is not meant mere speculation, but a set of logically reasoned principles which can successfully be used for prediction. It goes further than a system, for it forecasts the results of a given action. Obviously, the decision maker is on much more solid ground here (if the theory is good) as he can now see the outcome of a decision he may wish to take. Unfortunately, decision makers in marketing do not have the theoretical framework to make use of, as do other fields of study. However, progress, though difficult, is being made.

"Marketing has its particular problems, its own point of view, and its own emerging body of theory. Marketing theory is evolving gradually from the study of a loose collection of data to ideas, concepts, and principles based firmly on empirical evidence. It is growing as a result of the employment of sophisticated and rigorous techniques of investigation and analysis. Moreover, the transference of research attention from gaining answers to problems of immediate attention, to more fundamental considerations of

[2] E. T. Grether, in *Theory in Marketing.* Reavis Cox and Wroe Alderson, Ed. (Homewood: Richard D. Irwin 1959), p. 114.

marketing, has given the development of marketing theory considerable impetus."[3]

Law

Descriptive law (as distinguished from prescriptive or legal law) is the ultimate in scientific explanation. Laws are true over time and place and in the strictest sense are unalterable. There are few, if any, such laws in the social sciences, and even the physical sciences must occasionally "change" their laws to fit reality. The so-called economic laws are really (because of experience and evidence) highly acceptable theories. There is no inherent reason why marketing cannot eventually produce "laws" of this less rigid nature. It is unlikely that rigid laws can ever be developed. (But then, neither is this last statement a law!)

THE MARKETING SYSTEM

A company's marketing plan coordinates and blends many elements. This blend or "marketing mix" includes such variables as products, services, physical distribution, promotion, advertising, personal selling, prices, and marketing channels.

These variables must be related to each other, to company resources and objectives, and to certain exogenous forces in the plan. Each has a definite and logical role to play.

Exogenous forces include governmental, legal, international, ethical, social, cultural, competitive, microeconomic, and geographical factors.

In this "systems" approach to marketing decisions there are a multitude of possible mathematical combinations of which a mix variable can be a part.

A possible dynamic new approach to the study of marketing is to build a body of principles around each variable mix combination. The progression would be from the simple two variable to three and higher variable combinations.

"The marketing management concepts considered in this volume focus on the systems approach to the study of marketing. Marketing managers are concerned with developing an integrated marketing thrust by coordinating all marketing resources to realize predetermined objectives. Such an approach requires that they perceive of the fundamental interrelationships existing between marketing and other business elements, and among various parts of the marketing system, including both the internal and external dimensions of the system. The systems approach affords a valuable basis for the analysis and solution of marketing problems in a period characterized by an explosive rate of change and complex decision situations."[4]

As indicated by Figure 1, the consumer composes the first layer of the marketing system and the 'marketing mix' the second. This latter layer has been divided into a trio classified as communications mix, goods and service mix, and distribution mix. Pricing would fall under the second of these mixes. The goods and service mix also includes product policies while the distribution mix includes location, distribution channels and physical distribution factors. The communication mix is composed of sales promotion, personal selling, marketing intelligence, and advertising.

The third layer includes all nonmarketing factors within a firm: finance, production, purchasing, and establishing corporate objectives. The fourth layer includes the external or exogenous forces mentioned above. These four layers can be referred to as phenomenon—objects of experience which are susceptible of scientific description and explanation. The fifth layer, which completes the marketing system, brings us into metaphysical speculation or noumenon—ultimate forces which affect all phenomenon, but which are nonempirical and thus not susceptible to scientific description.

The marketing system thus moves inward to include all the components of marketing, and outward to consider all of phenomenon's influence on marketing and, indeed, could speculate on metaphysical influences. It is, then a "complete" system, which can eventually serve as a springboard to a general theory of marketing.

THE SYSTEM ELEMENTS WHICH INTERACT WITH CHANNEL SELECTION

This section will describe briefly the various system elements' interaction with channel selection. The market and marketing factors will first be discussed, followed by the company factors, and finally closing with the exogenous forces. This will serve as an example of interaction.

[3] William Lazer and Eugene J. Kelley, *Managerial Marketing*, Rev. ed. (Homewood, Ill. Richard D. Irwin, 1962), p. 694.

[4] Same reference as footnote 3, at p. 683; also of interest pp. 191–198.

Market and Consumer

Under the marketing concept the consumer is the pivotal interaction. The density of the market, its size in terms of number of buying units and of revenue, and its buying habits are all streams of market-channel interaction.

1. The greater the market density, the more direct can be the channel.

2. The greater the market size, the more direct can be the channel.

3. Perhaps the most important question is where the customer expects to find, and will expect to find, the product. If a firm's potential consumers mainly shop at the discount store, then the dis-

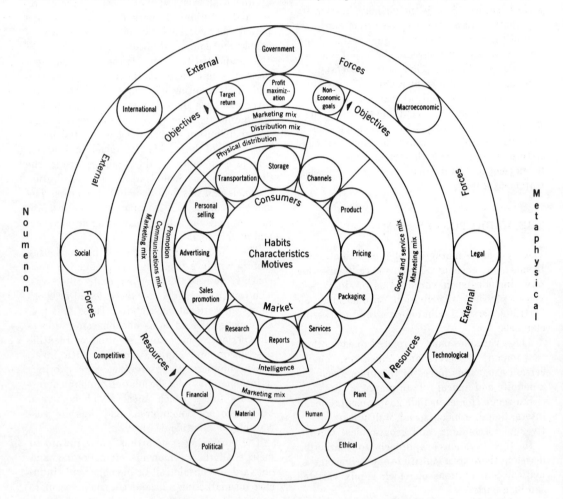

Fig. 1. The conceptual foundation of marketing.

count store should be included in the channel. As will be discussed under the product-channel interaction, the type of goods defined by the way the consumer buys them, (convenience, shopping, or specialty goods) is an important determinant in channel selection.

The factor of buying habits creates difficulties. A product may be, from a technical and production viewpoint, similar to the firm's other products, and so it appears to fit into the product line. But consumers may not have similar buying habits for the product, and hence, it does not fit into the product line from a channel viewpoint.

MARKETING MIX

Product

The uses of a product, its frequency of purchase, rapidity of fashion change or perishability, the service required, its value, and its bulk are all considerations a channel planner must study.

1. The more frequently purchases are made, the more feasible it is for a manufacturer to use direct distribution. However, convenience is important here, and this requires extensive distribution which involves a financial consideration.
2. Fashionable and perishable commodities usually must be placed in the hands of final sellers as quickly as possible. If there is no special marketing institution to handle this, then distribution will be direct.
3. The more technical knowledge required for the sale, installation, maintenance, and repair service, the more direct will the channel be.
4. A high unit cost good will usually be sold more directly as will a bulky one.
5. The life cycle of a product can affect channel selection. A new product may have difficulty in gaining acceptance by middlemen, and may therefore have to use more direct channels than it would need to after it matures.
6. Packaging considerations also interact with channel selection decisions. A self-service route to

the consumer requires a radically different package than a personal selling route.
7. Convenience goods, because they cater to a widely dispersed market, require no service, and usually are of low unit value, utilize indirect and intensive channels.
8. Shopping goods, because consumers' habits (by definition) usually are of high unit value, and often involve a style element, tend to use more direct and selective channels.
9. Industrial goods, aside from supply items, because of user concentration and technical complexities, use direct methods of distribution.
10. Not only the type of product, but also the number of products produced by one firm will influence that firm's channel plans. If a firm makes many similar products, it can better afford to take advantage of the economics accruing from selling more directly. Its salesmen can confront the same customer at the same time with many products, thus spreading the fixed expenses of a sales call. It is important that they not only have multiproducts, but that these products can be sold through the same outlet.

Pricing

Margins are a medium through which channel members may affect each other. Margins can be manipulated by pricing determination, variation (discounts), and changes on the supplier's selling side, and resale price control on the middleman's selling side.

These margins go toward allocating channel and individual expenses and profits. Often well over one-half of the final consumer price is composed of middlemen's margins. There are many factors operating in establishing middlemen's margins including degree of competition, costs of functions performed, desired profits, bargaining power, resale price control power.

Methods used to control prices include direct distribution to consumers, direct distribution to retailers, use of fair trade legislation, sale of goods on consignment, refusal to sell price cutters, distribution through small powerless middlemen, granting of only small trade discounts, advertising resale prices to consumers, suggested and quoted resale prices, and preticketing. Channel policies involving degree of directness, selectivity, choice of middlemen type, and number of channels will all interact with pricing.

Promotion

Promotion and channel selection are determinants of each other.

1. The interaction here is one of more directness and/or intensiveness for less advertising and sales promotion and more personal selling. A firm may feel that it would be more advantageous to sell directly to many retailers, or even consumers, using a large sales force because of a lack of selling effort on the part of wholesalers, even if this method is more costly. Another firm may try to pull its product through a longer channel, and so build up a consumer franchise through much advertising and sales promotion, and a smaller field force.
2. The channel will also influence the target of the promotional impact. With direct channels little of the promotional budget need be aimed at the wholesalers. However, the more indirect the channel, the more must advertising and sales promotion be directed toward these middlemen.
3. Promotion also opens the way to the use of self-service channel members. Promotion substitutes for the lack of salesmen in these stores.

Physical Distribution

Channel of distribution selection and physical distribution, being the two elements that compose the distribution mix, are quite naturally interrelated. Certain types of middlemen, such as service wholesalers, will perform most of the physical distribution functions of transportation and storage, while others, such as agents, will provide very little of these services.

1. Thus, the manufacturer must see how the choice of his channel members will determine the physical functions that he must perform himself. A firm may feel that to use service wholesalers would be more efficient. Conversely, they may rather use agents and thus make certain that reliable inventories will be stocked. Here they provide needed service to retailers, by executing most physical distribution functions themselves.
2. Location of plants and warehouses near markets may enable a firm to use more direct channels.
3. Technological improvements in transportation and material handling allow a company to reach wider markets, and so lead to the results of the channel-market interaction discussed previously.

Marketing Intelligence

The information that a channel planner receives, formal or informal, will, of course, influence channel selection decisions.

1. Marketing research can discover the relative efficiency or potential efficiency among channels. It can give the planner data on the extent of distribution among channel types and can aid in optimizing the extent of coverage required.
2. A study of the operating methods of dealers and distributors in the pricing, promoting, and merchandising areas is another example of channel research.
3. Motivational research on middlemen's attitude towards, and image of, manufacturers is a useful and often necessary step.
4. Cost studies of the relative profitability of one's product to middlemen, as well as optimization studies of the inventory level within the channel, are yet other areas of marketing intelligence which interact with channel selection.
5. Research on consumer buying habits are also valid fields of channel analysis.

COMPANY ELEMENTS

Objectives

The channel planner must work within the framework of the various levels (corporate, departmental) of objectives.

Resources

Resource capacity plays a significant role in channel selection decisions.

1. (a) A strong financial position as well as a strong marketing manpower position allow an organization to engage in costly, though perhaps profitable, direct marketing. Conversely, a weak resource position may force a company to use financially strong middlemen, even if this is not the most profitable route. (b) The strong resource position also enables a firm to better control and direct the channels it does use by building, as mentioned under promotion, a loyal consumer franchise and by providing middlemen with such aids as consignment shipments, servicing, training programs, cooperative allowances, sales promotion media, and better credit terms.
2. Human resources such as the executives concerned with decisions on channels, or the employment of top technical research personnel who are forever developing new products and so new channel problems, influence selection policy. Employees may interact with channel selection in various ways. (a) They could demand company stores at which they can buy their company's products conveniently and less expensively. (b)

High morale among employees makes for high productivity, resulting in low costs, thus enabling a firm to offer bigger margins to channel members, which could mean the use of channels hitherto unavailable. (c) Again, a policy of stable employment will mean stable production, and so high inventories in times of low sales. The firm may need to pass along part of the storage function to channel members. This again could cause a shift in the channel selection decision, e.g., from the use of agent middlemen to the use of service wholesalers.

3. A change in raw material resources, for any reason such as depletion, can alter the product and so the channels.

4. A new expansion of plant capacity may require more aggressive channels to fill the void.

EXOGENOUS FORCES

Competition

There are four distinct types of channel competition. These are:

1. Between channel members—wholesaler versus wholesaler, retailer versus retailer, manufacturer versus manufacturer.

2. Among channel members—wholesaler versus manufacturer, retailer versus wholesaler, manufacturer versus retailer.

3. Between channel members for the use of channel members—manufacturer versus manufacturer for the use of a wholesaler, wholesaler versus wholesaler for the use of a retailer. This is really a special case of Number 1, in that it is one type of competition (non-price) between channel members.

4. Between channels; manufacturer-wholesaler-retailer channel versus manufacturer-retailer channel.

This last form of competition is not one of which the manufacturer usually feels he is a part. From a management viewpoint, it is not a question of competing in the usual sense but rather of carefully watching the changing patterns of distribution. Generally, it appears that direct channels are gaining in this struggle.

Competition for the use of channel members can be as severe as price competition and can set tight limitations on the new and/or financially weak firm. Through a system of vertical integration, franchises, personal relations, and orthodox channels could be closed to the marketer, even if they appear to be the best suited route to the consumer. Even if they are not closed, they may be clogged with so many competitors' products that the channel cannot devote sufficient selling effort to the firm's products.

A company may have, through various methods, been so successful in competition that it has gained a major share of the market, and hence can take advantage of economies by going direct to retailers, or even consumers.

Macroeconomic

The macroeconomic force yields great modification on the number and type of middlemen available. For example, recessive periods tend to kill off the small independent stores, and tend to give rise to door-to-door retailers.

Technology

Some aspects of the technological-channel interaction have already been touched upon under physical distribution and resources. Whole new methods have evolved from technological advances. The rise and improvement of vending machines and the rise of self-service because of packaging and communication (television) improvements, are examples.

International

The marketing explosion in the international area will cause channel decision makers to look for middlemen who specialize in international trade. Importer-exporter merchants and agents will increasingly become areas of interest for domestic producers.

Social and Ethical

Even in channel problems the all pervasive social element shows itself. Thus, distribution through a blackmarket channel involves questions of ethics. Even selling to discounters is still considered unethical in some areas. Of course, almost all new forms of retailing at the time of their birth were considered unethical by the traditional outlets of the time. Department stores and chain stores were no exception.

Government and Legal

Aside from laws and regulations, the government interacts with channel selection decisions in various ways. The government is a customer of many producers. It usually purchases on a bidding basis and this, since bidding is difficult with intervening middlemen, tends to make for direct channels. The government is in some industries a middleman itself (state liquor stores) and in this role affects channel decisions.

Municipalities regulate peddlar and solicitor selling, so that a heavy charge is made in some towns for door-to-door selling, or they may even outlaw such forms of marketing. Obviously, this would influence a selection decision. Direct-to-consumer distribution can also be restricted in some ways by Post Office regulations.

The same Acts which affect pricing influence channel selection through regulation of price discrimination, exclusive dealing, brokerage discounts, allowances for and furnishing of pro-motional services, resale price maintenance, and integration.[5]

"Legislation which influences either the effectiveness with which marketing institutions may compete or the methods and terms employed by sellers can be expected to have repercussions on the use of particular channels of distribution."[6]

[5] For a full treatment of this subject see William F. Brown, "The Effect of Federal Legislation Upon Marketing Channels," in *Marketing Channels*, Richard M. Clewett (Ed.), (Richard D. Irwin, Homewood, Ill., 1954), pp. 470–502; John A. Howard, *Marketing Management* (Richard D. Irwin, Homewood, Ill., 1957), pp. 223–228.

[6] Howard. Same reference as footnote 5, at p. 499.

PART
III

Channel Relationships

A marketing channel is more than a mechanistic arrangement of firms that distribute the goods and services of the economy. It performs more than the mechanical functions associated with sorting and the marketing flows. There is a great deal more to the study of marketing channels than simply obtaining an understanding of its structural anatomy and design: for a marketing channel is also a behavioral system.

One aspect of this system is that the member institutions interact with one another. They lead; they follow; they control; they conflict; they cooperate. However, over and above these interactions, the marketing channel has its own behavior pattern—something more and perhaps different from the sum total of the behavior of its institutional parts. It has its own objéctives, its own actions, and its own criteria of success. It is, in fact, as one scholar has noted, a unit of competition, a unit of action, regardless of internal conflict.

One concept runs like a continuous thread through the fabric of the selections in the first part of this section, i.e., the concept of "power." One sees it in Gettell's concept of pluralistic competition; in Palamountain's concept of distribution politics; in Galbraith's concept of countervailing power; and in Mallen's concept of organizational extension. All of these authors recognize the dynamic flow of conflict and cooperation between channel members, the efforts of one or more members to bend the channel will to *its* will, and the unique effects this may have on the microunits (firms) and the macrounit (channel).

Microeconomic price theory has also contributed to an understanding of the interacting relations amongst channel members. However, traditional theory has had to be adapted to the concept of a sequence of markets between producers and consumers, rather than be satisfied with a direct producer-consumer exchange system. In other words, microeconomic price theory has had to make room for the middleman in order to contribute to the knowledge of marketing channel operations. Not only independent middlemen, but owned middlemen must be included in this area. Thus, an examination of vertical integration is required.

Price itself is a major weapon of control, and in this context, the field of resale price maintenance can prove to be a lucrative source of understanding channel behavior. In addition, one of the most interesting arrangements included in the selections is that of the bilateral market situation.

Clinical Relationships

A. Vertical Power Relationships

14. *Pluralistic Competition*

RICHARD G. GETTELL

This abridged paper discusses the concept of simultaneous cooperation and conflict between and among individuals and business units that characterizes the market place. In this context there are discussed three forms of conflict: market competition, extramarket competition, and structural adjustments. The third form is of most interest to channel students.

Students of marketing have long been frustrated by the gap between the abstract formulations of conventional price theory and the realities of the market place. Efforts to bridge the gap have been made from both directions.

The broadening of the theory of competition by Chamberlin and Robinson has given impetus to a considerable theoretical literature in the field of market imperfections and price policy.

Many marketing practitioners and observers of business practices conducting empirical studies of the competitive struggle among actual business units have tried to draw significant generalizations from the evidence they have uncovered.

In each case, the approach has been piecemeal: either a single new variable has been added as refinement of the theory, or a body of facts has been gathered to illuminate the problems of some small segment of the economy. At best, these are structural elements of a bridge yet to be erected. No general reformulation of the theory or redirection of approach has appeared and gained acceptance.

This essay offers some suggestions as to the directions from which the needed reformulation might be approached. It is based on the notion first articulated by the author of this essay a decade ago[1] that a deeper understanding of modern competition might be attained by the integration of economic and political theory with particular reference to the *identification of the policymaking units* and the *classification and analysis of the areas and tactics of conflict and co-operation among them.*

I. IDENTIFICATION OF THE POLICYMAKING UNIT

The "Entrepreneur," the "Firm," and the "Industry"

The first essential to the formulation of a significant analysis of modern competition is a realistic identification of the individuals and groups who make business policies, and of the interests they represent. Here the student of marketing might profitably borrow from the political theorist and adjust his approach to take fuller account of existing empirical studies

• SOURCE: Richard G. Gettell, "Pluralistic Competition," in *Theory in Marketing*, Reavis Cox and Wroe Alderson (eds.), (Homewood, Ill., Richard D. Irwin, 1950), Chapter 5, from pp. 89–95, 98–99. Richard G. Gettell, Fortune Magazine.

[1] *Pluralistic Competition, with an Illustrative Case Study of the Rubber Tire Industry* (Ph.D. dissertation; University of California, 1940).

of the experience of actual competitors. As will be seen, this will require the rejection of some of the conventional analytical tools and the refashioning of others.

Conventional economic analysis has developed from a philosophical background of rational individualism. It has simplified the complexities of actuality by the use of such concepts as *homo economicus*, the "entrepreneur," the "firm," and the "industry." With these intellectual tools, the policymaker and the unit he represents have been identified; and formal economic analysis has customarily dealt with the problems of competitive policy of units thus conceived.

Theoretical Concepts and Market Activities

Market actualities cast doubt on the validity of some of these concepts. The most cursory examination of modern market activity indicates that rationality in action, as defined by the usual assumptions of economic motivation, is notoriously honored in the breach. Other motivations, from which conventional analysis is abstracted together with irrational or misguided policies,[2] play a large part in contemporary market processes. They give weight to the suspicion that reasoning that fails to consider such phenomena tends to "solve" a problem by assuming it to be nonexistent. The very concept of the "economic man" denies the necessity of studying actual policies and avoids consideration of the essence of market activity—the confused and imperfect decisions of policymakers in a dynamic world.

Empirical studies have sought to find the "entrepreneur," define his functions, and discover his rewards in the world of actuality—and have run afoul of almost insuperable difficulties. The institutional organization of the modern economy is such that ownership, management, and control, and the rewards accruing to each, when they can be identified at all, are often to be found in the hands of different individuals.

The "firm" and the "industry," however precisely conceived on the theoretical level, have no sharply delineated realistic counterparts. By the time one has taken account of such phenomena as the various types of industrial integration, the many tactics of business

"co-operation," divergent channels of distribution, diversification of production, differentiated yet rival products, etc., the clean-cut concept of an independent business unit producing and selling a single commodity[3] in competition with similar units is far removed from the observable facts of the modern market.

The Concept of Pluralistic Activities

It is with respect to the conflict and co-operation among business units, rather than within them, however, that our especial attention will be directed. Here economic reasoning, to gain relevance to the problems of modern competition, must adopt or devise new tools of analysis. Not only must it distinguish between the individual and the unit through which his policies are manifested, but it must also cope with the interdependence of the policies of partially separate units. Perhaps a clue to the more correct identification of policymakers or policymaking units can be found by borrowing a concept that has long been used by the political theorist and incorporating it into economic analysis: the concept of pluralism.

Although the specific use made of the concept of pluralistic activity in political theory is hardly germane to the present discussion, being an attack on a particular concept of sovereignty,[4] the term can be employed here fruitfully to combat the individualism of the conventional economic theory. If "pluralism" is viewed through the eyes of the individual, it can be interpreted to conceive of human activity in some such fashion as follows:

Each individual has a number of different interests of varying importance to him, according to the immediacy with which he believes that these interests affect him. Some may be

---

[2] By which the policymakers may defeat their own ends through the use of measures deliberately undertaken in the belief that they will help to attain these ends—e.g., the unit that starts a price war in which it is defeated.

[3] Or, if producing more than one commodity, able to develop a separate policy for each one.

[4] Cf. F. W. Coker, "The Technique of the Pluralist State," *American Political Science Review*, XV (May, 1921), 186–231, and *Recent Political Thought* (New York: Century, 1934), Chap. XVIII; W. Y. Elliott, "Sovereign State or Sovereign Group," *American Political Science Review*, XIX (August, 1925), 475–99; E. D. Ellis, "The Pluralist State," *American Political Science Review*, XIV (August, 1920), 393–407; M. P. Follett, *The New State* (New York: Longmans, Green & Co., 1918); H. J. Laski, *Authority in the Modern State* (New Haven: Yale University Press, 1919) and *Studies in the Problem of Sovereignty* (New Haven: Yale University Press, 1917); and G. Savine, "Pluralism: A Point of View," *American Political Science Review*, XVII (February, 1923), 34–56.

conflicting, in which case he must choose between them or compromise them, if they cannot be reconciled. In pursuit of his aims, he may ally himself with others who seem to have similar ends in view, in the hope that joint activity, offensively or defensively, may be more effective than independent action.

The individual does not completely submerge himself in the group he joins, for each group is necessarily homogeneous only with respect to the common end of its constituents and may be hetergeneous otherwise. That is, its members may conflict sharply on other issues, having chosen merely to subordinate or temporarily to overlook their differences while in pursuit of their common end. Meanwhile, they reserve the right to combat one another in any area except that for which the alliance has been formed. Further, if it suits his purposes, any member may change the ordering of his allegiances, or break away from some of his alliances and pursue his ends independently.

In the large, however, group activity and group conflicts, rather than independent individual activity, dominate the scene. Nevertheless, since it is the role of the individual to make the initial decisions as to the groups with which he will co-operate, he often tends to represent within himself various of the conflicts that are going on between them.

Pluralistic Competition

The generalized statement of "pluralistic activity" describes a state of affairs closely analogous to the narrower problem at hand. It corresponds to the simultaneous co-operation and conflict between and among individuals and business units that characterize the market place. It accordingly offers a promising analytical framework for the student of modern competition. It suggests that basically the individual must be considered the unit of policymaking, inasmuch as only individuals are capable of making decisions. Since, however, the individual has the option of identifying himself with many groups of differing size and strength to promote his various interests, the joint decisions emerging from these associations of individuals frequently make them the effective policymaking units. Consequently, each individual or group of individuals banded together to promote a common end must be counted as a policymaking unit. In practice, the actual decisions of a group may be made by a single individual or by a few individuals, but all others who follow these deci-

sions become, *ipso facto*, members of the same unit. This means, therefore, that these units can vary in size and scope from a single person, through groups of differing composition, and finally up to all of society. Only at the latter extreme could there be no alternative unit, and hence no element of conflict.

Within these units, which may variously compete and co-operate with one another, the individuals involved may be in conflict as to the control of policy. It thus becomes necessary to distinguish the individual who makes the initial decision as to his ends and the means by which he can best try to achieve them from the effective political unit, the instrumentality through which these decisions are carried into effect.

With reference to the phenomena of market activity that concern the student of modern competition, such a political unit will take the form of a business unit. This would consist in some cases of a single individual but more commonly of any association of individuals which, though its members may be in conflict with respect to the control of its policy, and though they may be individually at odds otherwise because of their allegiance to other groups, serves at any given time as the effective political unit for the promotion of their joint interests as measured in incomes derived from market activity.

This conception of the business unit would permit the study of competitive policies as made by actual groups in the real world, with all their possible differences of composition. With reference to actuality, it would conceive of units that might be formed to pursue the common ends of individuals organized to trade in a single commodity or a group of commodities,[5] in a single market or a number of markets;[6] and it could cover a single tactic or a number of competitive tactics.[7] Further, it could refer not only to legal entities, but also to a part of one,[8] or some alliance of a number of them.[9]

This conception of the effective political unit in the modern market would make it possible for the analyst to cut across the theoretical

---

[5] Ranging from a wheat farmer to a drugstore or a variety store.
[6] Ranging from a local independent retailer to a chain of grocery stores or a mail-order house.
[7] Ranging from mere price setting to all of the alternatives of policy discussed in the following sections.
[8] E.g., the subsidiary of a corporation, the superintendent of a plant in an integrated enterprise, or the local manager of a chain store.
[9] E.g., a trade association or a cartel.

classification of "entrepreneurs," "firms," and "industries," and to identify policymakers in a fashion permitting him to come to grips with the simultaneous elements of conflict and co-operation among individuals and groups in the market that characterize "pluralistic competition."

If pluralistically derived concepts such as these were to be employed by the economic analyst, he would be better able than at present to approximate market realities in his studies of policy. With these concepts as basic tools, he might then be able to develop the necessary refinements to deal separately with, and then perhaps to interrelate, the complexities of atomistic, of nonatomistic but independent, and of interdependent group activities in the market. He might then analyze the differing policies that emerge from group decisions, from individual decisions, and from the passive decisions of those who unconsciously follow others. He would have analytical tools to deal with the congeries of alliances and conflicts among policymaking units that at present elude him. Perhaps eventually, with these concepts as a foundation, he could build up some generalizations and discover whether the empirical evidence indicates that the network of alliances permeating modern market organization tends to serve the social end better or worse than the atomism of politically ineffective units and the relative individualism of independent aggressors.

II. AREAS AND TACTICS OF CONFLICT AND CO-OPERATION

Once the policymaker has been identified, the next essential to the analysis of modern competition is a study of the means by which he endeavors to attain his ends. What are the principal alternatives of policy from which he can choose? What adjustments can he make to his competitive environment? What are the tactics he can employ against or in conjunction with other policymaking units? And how can these tactics be related to the conventional tools of economic analysis?

The simplest cases in the modern market, and those that present the least difficulty in the way of relating them to the models of conventional theory, are to be found in the alternatives of competitive and co-operative tactics open to policymakers directing the activities of homogeneous units.[10] By "homogeneous units" is meant

[10] Admittedly, in the modern market, "homogeneity" and "heterogeneity" are matters of

business units that are similar in their organization and functions and that are presumed to have no internal conflicts of consequence, so that their several policies are devoted solely to the end of maximizing the income of each unit. As a first approximation, these units may be counted as roughly comparable to the theoretically conceived "firm" within an "industry," in so far as they are conceived of as selling similar products or lines of products in the same markets, although we shall see that certain of the conventional assumptions as to their nature and their activities will have to be relaxed to account for phenomena that customarily are not treated in the existing theoretical models.

In this simplified case, with the discussion restricted at first to conflict among independent units, the major alternatives of policy among homogeneous units that must be studied by the analyst of competitive policies would include market competition, extramarket competition, and structural adjustments.

Structural Adjustments

The third major category are structural adjustments that business units may make in attempts to enhance their own efficiency in producing and selling. This is the reverse of extra-market competition. It includes measures that—though they are aimed at the unit's divergence from homogeneity—consist of internal rather than external adjustments. That is' these adjustments are designed to improve the relative market position of the unit, not by direct attacks on similar units, but by internal reorganization of its own functions and activities so as to reduce costs or to achieve greater control of the market.[11] Within this category should be included the policies by which internal economies are realized on the side of production

degree. No actual business unit is totally similar or dissimilar to any other in all respects. At this juncture, the concept of relative homogeneity is employed in order to simplify the exposition. Elements of heterogeneity will be discussed in later pages. Their absence is perhaps the best criterion of homogeneity.

[11] It is important to note that these activities may bring the policymaker directing the business unit into conflict or co-operation with other political units that may be affected by his adjustments— e.g., the labor he hires, the dealers through whom he may sell, and the business units in new markets he may be invading.

—for example, rationalization of production, integration, standardization, relocation of plants, diversification, development of by-products, and various reallocations of the factors, etc. On the selling side, these adjustments could be represented by the various policies through which the channels of distribution are controlled or re-organized and by such tactics as full-line forcing, exclusive dealing, tying agreements, and—when imposed by a single unit—resale price maintenance.

Structural adjustments such as have been suggested here are of great significance to the analyst of the modern market.[12] Unfortunately,

in conventional price analysis, they are frequently assumed away by the use of such logical devices as those of "a given state of the arts," "given technical coefficients," or a tacit presumption that the producer is also the final seller, and in a single market. Much remains to be done in the development of theoretical tools to handle these competitive adjustments, their timing, and their consequences. Not only do they embody important dynamic factors affecting price relationships in the market; they also have serious implications for general stability and efficiency in the economy, since they constitute significant determinants of the volume and the direction of investment.

---

[12] Such adjustments, of course, are important to price analysis, but are not counted as a part of it except as defining "given" conditions of the pricing process. The analyst who is concerned with all of the alternative tactics of conflict among business units cannot take them as "given."

15. Distribution: Its Economic Conflicts

JOSEPH CORNWALL PALAMOUNTAIN, JR.

Palamountain isolates three forms of distributive conflicts (1) Horizontal competition—competition between middlemen of the same type; e.g., discount store versus discount store. (2) Intertype competition—competition between middlemen of different types on the same channel level; e.g., discount store versus department store. (3) Vertical conflict—conflict between channel members who are at different channel levels; e.g., discount store versus manufacturer.

There are three basic forms of distributive conflict. The first, which I shall call horizontal competition, is the conflict among competitors of the same type, e.g., competition between two independent grocers. The second, which for want of a better term I shall call intertype competition, is the conflict among different methods of distribution, e.g., competitive struggle among a mail-order house, a chain variety store, and an independent hardware dealer. And the third is the conflict between different stages in the same line of distribution and can be called vertical struggle. An example of this is conflict over prices and margins between a refiner's bulk station and a filling-station operator.

A. HORIZONTAL COMPETITION

Horizontal competition is the type of competition described in economic theory and usually stressed in economic studies. It is the competition among sellers and among buyers which characterizes the central institution postulated by economic theory, the market. With the construct of perfect competition, economic theory offers a full and internally consistent explanation of the operations of a market. Unfortunately, this explanation is precariously based on certain narrow assumptions—those which are most nearly approximated in such exchanges as agricultural commodity exchanges or stock markets. They are not as valid for modern industrial and commercial activities. Briefly put, they require that the market deal in standardized or homogeneous commodities and that it contain numerous buyers and sellers each of whom knows all pertinent facts and rationally calculates his self-interest and no one of whom is large enough to affect market operations significantly. Prices and quantities are the only important data, and no one buyer or seller can appreciably influence a market price—instead, he adjusts his operations to a price determined by the market.

B. INTERTYPE COMPETITION

Horizontal competition is stressed in economic theory as the mechanism which promotes economic progress by inducing lower costs and prices. In fact, however, it has been less conducive to economic betterment and material progress than has a second and more dynamic type of competition which is often overlooked and seldom stressed in the static framework of economic theory. This competition I call, somewhat clumsily, intertype, and define it as the competition between different methods of distribution. It is really a special application to distribution of what Schumpeter calls the process of "Creative Destruction."

"Capitalism . . . is by nature a form of economic change and . . . never can be stationary. . . . The fundamental impulse that sets and keeps the capitalist engine in motion comes from the new consumers' goods, the new methods of production or transportation, the new markets, the new forms of industrial organization

• SOURCE: Reprinted from *The Politics of Distribution*. Copyright 1955 by the President and Fellows of Harvard College. Used by permission. Joseph C. Palamountain, Jr. Associate Professor of Government, Weslayan University.

that capitalist enterprise creates. . . . The opening up of new markets, foreign or domestic, and the organizational development from the craft shop and factory to such concerns as United States Steel illustrate the same process of industrial mutation . . . that incessantly revolutionizes the economic structure from within, incessantly destroying the old one, incessantly creating a new one. This process of Creative Destruction is the essential fact about capitalism. . . .

". . . it is still competition within a rigid pattern of invariant conditions, methods of production and forms of industrial organization in particular, that practically monopolizes attention. But in capitalist reality as distinguished from its textbook picture, it is not that kind of competition which counts but the competition from the new commodity, the new technology, the new source of supply, the new type of organization . . . —competition which commands a decisive cost or quality advantage and which strikes not at the margins of the profits and the outputs of the existing firms but at their foundations and their very lives. This kind of competition is as much more effective than the other as a bombardment is in comparison with forcing a door, and so much more important that it becomes a matter of comparative indifference whether competition in the ordinary sense functions more or less promptly; the powerful lever that in the long run expands output and brings down prices is in any case made of other stuff."

Within distribution the agents of "Creative Destruction" are the chain store, the mail-order house, the department store, and the supermarket. It is the competition of these new media, and not horizontal competition, that has played a creative role, introducing technological advances and reducing costs. And it is also intertype competition that has frequently performed another duty usually assigned to horizontal competition—protecting the consumer from monopolistic exploitation. The older channels of distribution often failed to do this. The markets in which the wholesaler dealt, both in his purchases and in his sales, were the most competitive, but even these were often dominated by powerful wholesalers. Despite the idyllically competitive picture assumed by those who decry supposed modern trends toward monopoly, in the "good old days" retail markets were often monopolistic. Although the Sherman Act was passed in response to a fear of industrial concentration, "the most effective monopoly of

the time was the small retailer—the general store at the crossroads—whose customers were as dependent on this single source of supply as the desert inhabitant on his oasis. Even the small town provided similar local monopolies in many of the specialized fields where the market could support only a single store."

The consumer was left to the mercy of the local merchant, and it was usually a newer form of distribution which released him from his thralldom. The basic causes of his release were great technological changes. The development of transportation and of manufacturing produced urbanization, which broadened the scope of horizontal competition and, more important, created the department store, which challenged the older general and specialized stores by offering a greater range of selection at lower prices. Similarly, advances in transportation and communication permitted the development of the mail-order house, which freed the rural dweller from much of his dependence on the local general store. "The farmer's only friends are God and Sears-Roebuck." The stories of the chain store and of the supermarket are similar. The automobile made the consumer more mobile, enabling him to range further in the pursuit of price reductions. At the same time, new methods of organizing distributive functions, involving the integration of retailing with wholesaling, the application of new merchandising principles, and the institution of centralized management, produced retail stores that emphasized high volume, fast turnover, and lower prices. Thus it has usually been intertype competition which has played a creative role, offering broader ranges and producing lasting price reductions.

Such economic changes can be expected to have political reflections. In intertype, in contrast to horizontal, competition, the economic bases of conflict permit and encourage grouping of the sort required for effective political actions. We find similar stores, sharing common methods of operation, objectives, and standards of business ethics. More important, they share a *common enemy*.

Here, for example, are some independent druggists. They have learned, consciously or otherwise, to avoid the uncertainties of horizontal price competition with uniform markups or margins and to base competition on service and other intangibles. Location usually assures each druggist a relatively secure market. Then their comfort and security is shattered by the intrusion of chain drugstores, who rely on price competition, lowering their prices by reducing their markups and by purchasing at lower costs. They advertise their lower prices and may dramatize them by using leaders (goods sold below net purchase cost plus average cost of doing business) and loss leaders (goods sold below net purchase cost). They may cut deeply into the volume of each independent druggist, whatever his locational advantage. Thus are created the economic conditions of conflict.

C. VERTICAL CONFLICT

The third general type of conflict is the one which has been most neglected by economic theoreticians. Here we shift our attention from conflicts on the same plane of distribution to the vertical struggle between different levels of distribution, between manufacturer and wholesaler, wholesaler and retailer, or manufacturer and retailer.

Once again our starting point in defining the role of politics will be the analysis of the classical economists. For our purposes the significance of their theories is that they contain an unconscious, contradictory, but illuminating dualism. On the one hand, they believed that society was characterized by a natural harmony of interests. Each man pursued his own self-interest, but, through the mechanism of the impersonal market, this was transmuted into the interest of all. Since economic activities were controlled by the impersonal market, men were free of all but material limitations; since under *laissez-faire* the market was virtually identified with society itself, men were subject to only minimal social restraints. Men lived and worked in natural harmony with their fellows. Yet, on the other hand, classical economics was also a theory of artificial harmony, a theory of the way in which the total product was divided among interdependent yet opposing factors of production, a theory of rent, profits, and wages, a theory of power relations. It was, as Marx pointed out, a theory of economic classes. Indeed, it was almost a theory of irreconcilable class conflict, for whatever one class gained was at the expense of the other classes. Such a society, as Bentham saw, could be held together only if an artificial harmony were imposed upon it.

Economic theory has viewed the relationships between levels of distribution primarily as relationships between buyer and seller, i.e., in terms of the market mechanism. In a market these vertical reationships are defined by objective, material factors. The pivotal datum is price, which is determined by the interaction of conditions controlling supply and demand. Since no one buyer or seller is large enough, or in a strategic enough position, to influence price, no participant stands in any significant relationship to any other. Power is completely absent. Each participant is free from the power or influence of any other, although narrowly limited by material circumstances. While few distributive markets are as devoid of imperfections as this, most do considerably control and channel economic activities. Material conditions of supply and demand are of great importance, especially over time, in defining vertical relationships. Yet the existence of imperfections, by loosening the grip of material determinism and enabling group efforts to influence economic activities, makes our economy a political one.

The very errors of classical analysis best reveal the role of politics. Briefly, they are three in number. First, the classical economists grossly minimized the necessity for rules of business conduct. Second, although they dealt with the process of combining factors of production, they failed to appreciate the probability of organization and grouping. Organization is usually necessary to produce new products and apply new techniques, and grouping may enable men to increase their economic rewards. Such organization or grouping necessarily creates power. Third, not correlating their two analyses of harmony, the early economists failed to see that conditions of mutual dependency, with concomitant power relations, limit the market mechanism. All three errors open the door to politics.

Economic theory usually fails to recognize the extent to which operations even in a fairly perfect market are enabled and channeled by legal regulation. Common law has long played an important role in supporting and protecting market competition. Effective operation of the market requires regulation of such matters as weights and measures, enforcement of contracts, minimum health standards, monopoly practices, deceitful diversion of patronage, misappropriation of trade secrets, and malicious interference with business relations or operations. Even when buyers and sellers are small in scope, their relations on a personal basis, and the channels of distribution simple, there is need for rules of the game. When marketing conditions change, this need increases. For example, the rise of large manufacturing concerns and retail firms has produced major inequalities of bargaining power in many vertical relationships, although older rules assumed substantial equality. Increased scale and scope of marketing operations have reduced the role of custom and increased the need for rules. Newer media have often shattered older forms and customs of marketing, further adding to the uncertainties of vertical relations. These and other changes create a need for either the extension of old rules to cover new situations or the formulation and acceptance of new rules. As was also true in horizontal and intertype competition, the effects are political when they involve the administration of existing economic regulation, the group determination of standards of economic behavior, or direct political pressures for the enactment of new regulatory legislation.

Now, the classical explanation of distribution as a series of markets omits consideration of power. The typical distributive market, however, is imperfectly competitive. Each imperfection partially frees distributors from market constraints. To the extent that they are thus freed, they have some bargaining power over those with whom they deal. A manufacturer who has created consumer preference for his brands enjoys a bargaining advantage in his dealings with distributors. A dealer who benefits from consumer habit and from location is strengthened in his relations with wholesalers. Monopolistic and oligopolistic elements in horizontal competition add uncertainties to vertical relationships and cause their outcome to rest in part on relative bargaining strengths. Furthermore, the increase in size associated with mass distribution has added to the importance of bargaining power. The relations between A & P and a small salmon packer are hardly those contemplated in the concept of a perfectly competitive market.

It is apparent that a principal factor differentiating vertical conflict from horizontal and intertype competition is that it is so directly a power conflict. Power relationships among horizontal competitors occasionally are significant, but this power usually is narrowly limited. Lasting power relations require organization, but organization is difficult, sometimes legally dangerous, and its effects often limited by intertype competition. This latter type of competition is almost devoid of power relationships. With the exception of such haphazard, indirect, and double-edged devices as price wars, there are almost no direct power relationships among different channels. The primary weapon of economic power, the boycott, is directed at a third party and occurs in vertical relationships. In the plane of vertical conflict, however, power relationships are direct, obvious, and important to the extent that the market is imperfect.

Vertical power becomes more apparent when we adopt the second approach of the classical economists. It will be remembered that, in addition to their market analysis, they also regarded production as a *process*. Distribution is a process in much the same sense. Just as production is the transformation of raw materials, labor, and capital into finished goods, so distribution is the transformation of finished goods in the producer's hands into final products in the consumer's hands. Just as mutual dependency characterizes relations among the factors of production, so does it characterize relations among the stages of distribution. The degree of dependency has increased greatly since the late nineteenth century. The very essence of the newer marketing media is their integration of a series of marketing functions which formerly were executed by separate firms. This integration, as we have seen, has been executed from both ends of the distributive chain. Both manufacturers and retailers have acted on the premise that distribution is a process, and have organized it as such, much in the manner that different phases of the manufacturing process are more and more conducted under integrated control and organization. They apply principles of "mass distribution" much as manufacturers apply those of mass production. The older system of distribution, on the other hand, resembles the nonintegrated, Balkanized women's garment industry in which gray goods are often made by one firm, converted by another, cut by another, and assembled and sewn by yet another. In the distribution of some products, such as shoes and tires, manufacturers now perform even the retailing function. Some retail food chains perform all marketing functions and even do some manufacturing and processing.

The reasons for this integration are diverse. There are the efficiencies of mass distribution, an obvious factor in the growth of mail-order houses, department stores, chain stores, and supermarkets, all of which have introduced economies of scale and of uniform and centralized management. And integration from the manufacturing end often results from the development of new products. The last seventy-five years have seen the introduction of many mechanical devices which require considerable capital for their manufacture, intensive efforts for their sale, demonstration and instruction in their uses, and for special services to maintain them. Their distribution is apt to be a unified, integrated flow; otherwise they will be difficult to sell. Indeed, any new product may create for its producer the problem of finding marketing channels. If none are available, he has to encourage their creation or provide his own. In either case, they are likely to be integrated and under his control. Finally, integration is a general policy of many large corporations who try to free themselves from the limitations and uncertainties of their environment. Here integrated marketing is but a part of a broad program of vertical and horizontal integration and control. Most major oil refiners, for example, develop and protect their retail markets by integrating and controlling marketing, just as they protect and develop their sources of supply by integrating and controlling production.

Marketing functions also have often been radically shifted. The crucial function of selection, the choosing of one product from many similar or even identical products, was once performed by the independent wholesaler who decided which line or brand of commodities to carry. Now, with the prevalence of nationally advertised brands, the consumer does much more of the selecting. This increases the dependence of distributors on manufacturers, for they desire to carry popular brands. Large retailers also do much selecting, for many consumers accept the retailer's private brand, buying All-State tires or Ann Page jam without knowing, or caring, who manufactures them. This makes the manufacturer and middleman, if any, dependent on the retailer.

These conditions of dependency and control, revealed by a process analysis, vitiate much of the market analysis of distribution's vertical conflicts. Process analysis reveals power relationships, but power is incompatible with the classical market. There never was absolute equality of bargaining power on opposite sides of distributive markets, but such dominance as did exist was that of the wholesaler. This relative dominance at the mid-point of the distributive flow sharply broke it into two phases, preventing contact between producer and retailer. This structure has now been shattered in many trades. Great increases in the size of either manufacturers or retailers have changed much of distribution from a flow through a series of largely autonomous markets to a single movement dominated by either manufacturer or retailer. Dominance by a manufacturer often reflects the shifting of the selective function to the consumer, for many manufacturers compete more for the patronage of the consumer than for that of the wholesaler and wish to control wholesale and retail levels, since their competitive success is determined at the retail level. A filling station proprietor limited to the sale of Texaco products is largely but an agent of the Texas Company, and his relations with his jobber are not those of a free market. In other channels a large retailer may be dominant and exercise the selective function. His volume may be so great, and his consumer acceptance so strong, that he orders goods to be made under his own specifications and his own label. Manufacturer and middlemen may become almost agents of the retailer.

Furthermore, the impact of intertype competition on the older marketing channels heightens their mutual interdependence. The retailer looks to his wholesalers for aid, and the wholesaler becomes increasingly dependent on his retailers and suppliers. A small manufacturer may be forced to choose sides, to decide either to ally himself with the traditional channels, or to sell only to large retailers.

Finally, power has multiplied in many of the newer marketing channels. Power is a two-sided relationship, and organization tends to breed counterorganization. Dominance by one end of the distributive chain often promotes grouping at the other end, for those subordinated to economic power will naturally tend to organize in attempts to create and use economic or political power. The analogy of the distributive to the manufacturing process applies. What the classical economists overlooked in their analysis of production was the almost inevitable creation of class or group consciousness, although one by no means as simple and monolithic as that described by Marx. Owners or managers, and workers, perceived the similarities of their interests and tried to organize. This organization bred enough power to alter radically the market mechanism. The organization of one productive factor encouraged the organization of another. Thus the organization of capital made the organization of labor more necessary and its advantages, to labor, more apparent. A similar development has occurred within distribution. Reeling from the impact of newer marketing media and from the economic power of large corporate concerns, smaller distributors have become conscious of their group interests. They in turn, have tried to organize and to employ economic and/or political power. This group consciousness sometimes, as in the case of retail druggists, becomes quite intense.

In conclusion, power has come to rival economic factors as the governing element in the vertical relationships of distribution.

16. The Concept of Countervailing Power

JOHN K. GALBRAITH

The thesis put forward in this selection is that big sellers cause the rise of big buyers. These buying channel members offset the power of the selling members and so act as a substitute for competition. The mass retailer is an example of the big buyer.

As with social efficiency, and its neglect of technical dynamics, the paradox of the unexercised power of the large corporation begins with an important oversight in the underlying economic theory. In the competitive model—the economy of many sellers each with a small share of the total market—the restraint on the private exercise of economic power was provided by other firms on the same side of the market. It was the eagerness of competitors to sell, not the complaints of buyers, that saved the latter from spoliation. It was assumed, no doubt accurately, that the nineteenth-century textile manufacturer who overcharged for his product would promptly lose his market to another manufacturer who did not. If all manufacturers found themselves in a position where they could exploit a strong demand, and mark up their prices accordingly, there would soon be an inflow of new competitors. The resulting increase in supply would bring prices and profits back to normal.

As with the seller who was tempted to use his economic power against the customer, so with the buyer who was tempted to use it against his labor or suppliers. The man who paid less than prevailing wage would lose his labor force to those who paid the worker his full (marginal) contribution to the earnings of the firm. In all cases the incentive to socially desirable behavior was provided by the competitor. It was to the same side of the market—the restraint of sellers by other sellers and of buyers by other buyers, in other words to competition—that economists came to look for the self-regulatory mechanism of the economy.

They also came to look to competition exclusively and in formal theory still do. The notion that there might be another regulatory mechanism in the economy has been almost completely excluded from economic thought. Thus, with the widespread disappearance of competition in its classical form and its replacement by the small group of firms if not in overt, at least in conventional or tacit collusion, it was easy to suppose that since competition had disappeared, all effective restraint on private power had disappeared. Indeed this conclusion was all but inevitable if no search was made for other restraints and so complete was the preoccupation with competition that none was made.

In fact, new restraints on private power did appear to replace competition. They were nurtured by the same process of concentration which impaired or destroyed competition. But they appeared not on the same side of the market but on the opposite side, not with competitors but with customers or suppliers. It will be convenient to have a name for this counterpart of competition and I shall call it *countervailing power*.[1]

To begin with a broad and somewhat too dogmatically stated proposition, private economic power is held in check by the countervailing power of those who are subject to it. The

• SOURCE: John K. Galbraith, "The Concept of Countervailing Power," *American Capitalism*, rev. ed. (Boston: Houghton Mifflin Co., 1956), pp. 110–114, 117–123. John K. Galbraith, Professor of Economics, Harvard University.

[1] I have been tempted to coin a new word for this which would have the same convenience as the term competition and had I done so my choice would have been "countervailence." However, the phrase "countervailing power" is more descriptive and does not have the raw sound of any newly fabricated word.

first begets the second. The long trend toward concentration of industrial enterprise in the hands of a relatively few firms has brought into existence not only strong sellers, as economists have supposed, but also strong buyers as they have failed to see. The two develop together, not in precise step but in such manner that there can be no doubt that the one is in response to the other.

The fact that a seller enjoys a measure of monopoly power, and is reaping a measure of monopoly return as a result, means that there is an inducement to those firms from whom he buys or those to whom he sells to develop the power with which they can defend themselves against exploitation. It means also that there is a reward to them, in the form of a share of the gains of their opponents' market power, if they are able to do so. In this way the existence of market power creates an incentive to the organization of another position of power that neutralizes it.

The contention I am here making is a formidable one. It comes to this: Competition which, at least since the time of Adam Smith, has been viewed as the autonomous regulator of economic activity and as the only available regulatory mechanism apart from the state, has, in fact, been superseded. Not entirely, to be sure. I should like to be explicit on this point. Competition still plays a role. There are still important markets where the power of the firm as (say) a seller is checked or circumscribed by those who provide a similar or a substitute product or service. This, in the broadest sense that can be meaningful, is the meaning of competition. The role of the buyer on the other side of such markets is essentially a passive one. It consists in looking for, perhaps asking for, and responding to the best bargain. The active restraint is provided by the competitor who offers, or threatens to offer, a better bargain. However, this is not the only or even the typical restraint on the exercise of economic power. In the typical modern market of few sellers, the active restraint is provided not by competitors but from the other side of the market by strong buyers. Given the convention against price competition, it is the role of the competitor that becomes passive in these markets.

It was always one of the basic presuppositions of competition that market power exercised in its absence would invite the competitors who would eliminate such exercise of power. The profits of a monopoly position inspired competitors to try for a share. In other words competition was regarded as a *self-generating* regulatory force. The doubt whether this was in fact so after a market had been pre-empted by a few large sellers, after entry of new firms had become difficult and after existing firms had accepted a convention against price competition, was what destroyed the faith in competition as a regulatory mechanism. Countervailing power is also a self-generating force and this is a matter of great importance. Something, although not very much, could be claimed for the regulatory role of the strong buyer in relation to the market power of sellers, did it happen that, as an accident of economic development, such strong buyers were frequently juxtaposed to strong sellers. However the tendency of power to be organized in response to a given position of power is the vital characteristic of the phenomenon I am here identifying. As noted, power on one side of a market creates both the need for, and the prospect of reward to, the exercise of countervailing power from the other side.[2] This means that, as a common rule, we can rely on countervailing power to appear as a curb on economic power. There are also, it should be added, circumstances in which it does not appear or is effectively prevented from appearing. To these I shall return. For some reason, critics of the theory have seized with particular avidity on these exceptions to deny the existence of the phenomenon itself. It is plain that by a similar line of argument one could deny the existence of competition by finding one monopoly.

In the market of small numbers or oligopoly, the practical barriers to entry and the convention against price competition have eliminated the self-generating capacity of competition. The self-generating tendency of countervailing

[2] This has been one of the reasons I have rejected the terminology of bilateral monopoly in characterizing this phenomenon. As bilateral monopoly is treated in economic literature, it is an adventitious occurrence. This, obviously, misses the point and it is one of the reasons that the investigations of bilateral monopoly, which one would have thought might have been an avenue to the regulatory mechanisms here isolated, have in fact been a blind alley. However, this line of investigation has also been sterilized by the confining formality of the assumptions of monopolistic and (more rarely) oligopolistic motivation and behavior with which it has been approached. (Cf. for example, William H. Nicholls, *Imperfect Competition within Agricultural Industries*, Ames, Iowa: 1941, pp. 58 ff.) As noted later, oligopoly facilitates the exercise of countervailing market power by enabling the strong buyer to play one seller off against another.

power, by contrast, is readily assimilated to the common sense of the situation and its existence, once we have learned to look for it, is readily subject to empirical observation.

Market power can be exercised by strong buyers against weak sellers as well as by strong sellers against weak buyers. In the competitive model, competition acted as a restraint on both kinds of exercise of power. This is also the case with countervailing power. In turning to its practical manifestations, it will be convenient, in fact, to begin with a case where it is exercised by weak sellers against strong buyers.

The labor market serves admirably to illustrate the incentives to the development of countervailing power and it is of great importance in this market. However, its development, in response to positions of market power, is pervasive in the economy. As a regulatory device one of its most important manifestations is in the relation of the large retailer to the firms from which it buys. The way in which countervailing power operates in these markets is worth examining in some detail.

One of the seemingly harmless simplifications of formal economic theory has been the assumption that producers of consumers' goods sell their products directly to consumers. All business units are held, for this reason, to have broadly parallel interests. Each buys labor and materials, combines them and passes them along to the public at prices that, over some period of time, maximize returns. It is recognized that this is, indeed, a simplification; courses in marketing in the universities deal with what is excluded by this assumption. Yet it has long been supposed that the assumption does no appreciable violence to reality.

Did the real world correspond to the assumed one, the lot of the consumer would be an unhappy one. In fact goods pass to consumers by way of retailers and other intermediaries and this is a circumstance of first importance. Retailers are required by their situation to develop countervailing power on the consumer's behalf.

As I have previously observed, retailing remains one of the industries to which entry is characteristically free. It takes small capital and no very rare talent to set up as a seller of goods. Through history there have always been an ample supply of men with both and with access to something to sell. The small man can provide convenience and intimacy of service and can give an attention to detail, all of which allow him to co-exist with larger competitors.

The advantage of the larger competitor ordinarily lies in its lower prices. It lives constantly under the threat of an erosion of its business by the more rapid growth of rivals and by the appearance of new firms. This loss of volume, in turn, destroys the chance for the lower costs and lower prices on which the firm depends. This means that the larger retailer is extraordinarily sensitive to higher prices by its suppliers. It means also that it is strongly rewarded if it can develop the market power which permits it to force lower prices.

The opportunity to exercise such power exists only when the suppliers are enjoying something that can be taken away; i.e., when they are enjoying the fruits of market power from which they can be separated. Thus, as in the labor market, we find the mass retailer, from a position across the market, with both a protective and a profit incentive to develop countervailing power when the firm with which it is doing business is in possession of market power. Critics have suggested that these are possibly important but certainly disparate phenomena. This may be so, but only if all similarity between social phenomena be denied. In the present instance the market context is the same. The motivating incentives are identical. The fact that it has characteristics in common has been what has caused people to call competition competition when they encountered it, say, in agriculture and then again in the laundry business.

Countervailing power in the retail business is identified with the large and powerful retail enterprises. Its practical manifestation, over the last half-century, has been the rise of the food chains, the variety chains, the mail-order houses (now graduated into chain stores), the department-store chains, and the co-operative buying organizations of the surviving independent department and food stores.

This development was the countervailing response to previously established positions of power. The gains from invading these positions have been considerable and in some instances even spectacular. The rubber tire industry is a fairly commonplace example of oligopoly. Four large firms are dominant in the market. In the thirties, Sears, Roebuck & Co. was able, by exploiting its role as a large and indispensable customer, to procure tires from Goodyear Tire & Rubber Company at a price from twenty-nine to forty per cent lower than the going market. These it resold to thrifty motorists for from a fifth to a quarter less than the same tires carrying the regular Goodyear brand.

As a partial consequence of the failure of the government to recognize the role of countervailing power many hundreds of pages of court records have detailed the exercise of this power by the Great Atlantic & Pacific Tea Company. There is little doubt that this firm, at least in its uninhibited days, used the countervailing power it had developed with considerable artistry. In 1937, a survey by the company indicated that, for an investment of $175,000, it could supply itself with corn flakes. Assuming that it charged itself the price it was then paying to one of the three companies manufacturing this delicacy, it could earn a modest sixty-eight per cent on the outlay. Armed with this information, and the threat to go into the business which its power could readily make effective, it had no difficulty in bringing down the price by approximately ten per cent.[3] Such gains from the exercise of countervailing power, it will be clear, could only occur where there is an exercise of original market power with which to contend. The A & P could have reaped no comparable gains in buying staple products from the farmer. Committed as he is to the competition of the competitive model, the farmer has no gains to surrender. Provided, as he is, with the opportunity of selling all he produces at the impersonally determined market price, he has not the slightest incentive to make a special price to A & P at least beyond that which might in some circumstances be associated with the simple economies of bulk sale.

The examples of the exercise of countervailing power by Sears, Roebuck and A & P just cited show how this power is deployed in its most dramatic form. The day-to-day exercise of the buyer's power is a good deal less spectacular but also a good deal more significant. At the end of virtually every channel by which consumers' goods reach the public there is, in practice, a layer of powerful buyers. In the food market there are the great food chains; in clothing there are the department stores, the chain department stores and the department store buying organizations; in appliances there are Sears, Roebuck and Montgomery Ward and the department stores; these latter firms are also important outlets for furniture and other house furnishings; the drug and cosmetic manufacturer has to seek part of his market through the large drug chains and the department stores; a vast miscellany of consumers' goods pass to the public through Woolworth's, Kresge's and other variety chains.

The buyers of all these firms deal directly with the manufacturer and there are few of the latter who, in setting prices, do not have to reckon with the attitude and reaction of their powerful customers. The retail buyers have a variety of weapons at their disposal to use against the market power of their suppliers. Their ultimate sanction is to develop their own source of supply as the food chains, Sears, Roebuck and Montgomery Ward have extensively done. They can also concentrate their entire patronage on a single supplier and, in return for a lower price, give him security in his volume and relieve him of selling and advertising costs. This policy has been widely followed and there have also been numerous complaints of the leverage it gives the retailer on his source of supply.

The more commonplace but more important tactic in the exercise of countervailing power consists, merely, in keeping the seller in a state of uncertainty as to the intentions of a buyer who is indispensable to him. The larger of the retail buying organizations place orders around which the production schedules and occasionally the investment of even the largest manufacturers become organized. A shift in this custom imposes prompt and heavy loss. The threat or even the fear of this sanction is enough to cause the supplier to surrender some or all of the rewards of his market power. He must frequently, in addition, make a partial surrender to less potent buyers if he is not to be more than ever in the power of his large customers. It will be clear that in this operation there are rare opportunities for playing one supplier off against another.

A measure of the importance which large retailing organizations attach to the deployment of their countervailing power is the prestige they accord to their buyers. These men (and women) are the key employees of the modern large retail organization; they are highly paid and they are among the most intelligent and resourceful people to be found anywhere in business. In the everyday course of business, they may be considerably better known and command rather more respect than the salesmen from whom they buy. This is a not unimportant index of the power they wield.

There are producers of consumers' goods who have protected themselves from exercise of countervailing power. Some, like the automobile and the oil industry, have done so by

<hr>

[3] I am indebted to my friend Professor M. A. Adelman of the Massachusetts Institute of Technology for these details.

integrating their distribution through to the consumer— a strategy which attests the importance of the use of countervailing power by retailers. Others have found it possible to maintain dominance over an organization of small and dependent and therefore fairly powerless dealers. It seems probable that in a few industries, tobacco manufacture for example, the members are ordinarily strong enough and have sufficient solidarity to withstand any pressure applied to them by the most powerful buyer. However, even the tobacco manufacturers, under conditions that were especially favorable to the exercise of countervailing power in the thirties, were forced to make liberal price concessions, in the form of advertising allowances, to the A & P[4] and possibly also to other large customers. When the comprehensive representation of large retailers in the various fields of consumers' goods distribution is considered, it is reasonable to conclude—the reader is warned that this is an important generalization—that most positions of market power in the production of consumers' goods are covered by positions of countervailing power. As noted, there are exceptions and, as between markets, countervailing power is exercised with varying strength and effectiveness. The existence of exceptions does not impair the significance of the regulatory phenomenon here described. To its devotees the virtues of competition were great but few if any ever held its reign to be universal.

Countervailing power also manifests itself, although less visibly, in producers' goods markets. For many years the power of the auto-

mobile companies, as purchasers of steel, has sharply curbed the power of the steel mills as sellers. Detroit is the only city where the historic basing-point system was not used to price steel. Under the basing-point system, all producers regardless of location quoted the same price at any particular point of delivery. This obviously minimized the opportunity of a strong buyer to play one seller off against the other. The large firms in the automobile industry had developed the countervailing power which enabled them to do precisely this. They were not disposed to tolerate any limitations on their exercise of such power. In explaining the quotation of "arbitrary prices" on Detroit steel, a leading student of the basing-point system some years ago recognized, implicitly but accurately, the role of countervailing power by observing that "it is difficult to apply high cartel prices to particularly large and strong customers such as the automobile manufacturers in Detroit."[5]

The more normal operation of countervailing power in producers' goods markets has, as its point of departure, the relatively small number of customers which firms in these industries typically have. Where the cigarette or soap manufacturer numbers his retail outlets by the hundreds of thousands and his final consumers by the millions, the machinery or equipment manufacturer counts his customers by the hundreds or thousands and, very often, his important ones by the dozen. But here, as elsewhere, the market pays a premium to those who develop power as buyers that is equivalent to the market power of those from whom they buy. The reverse is true where weak sellers do business with strong buyers.

[4] Richard B. Tennant, *The American Cigarette Industry* (New Haven: Yale University Press, 1950), p. 312.

[5] Fritz Machlup, *The Basing Point System* (Philadelphia: Blakiston Co., 1949), p. 115.

17. Conflict and Cooperation in Marketing Channels

BRUCE MALLEN

Forces leading to conflict and cooperation within marketing channels are explored in this discussion, methods of control and cooperation are presented, and finally, some conclusions and hypotheses concerning marketing channels are advanced including one emphasizing the importance of the various institutions comprising a channel to act in unity.

The purpose of this paper is to advance the hypotheses that between member firms of a marketing channel there exists a dynamic field of conflicting and cooperating objectives; that if the conflicting objectives outweigh the cooperating ones, the effectiveness of the channel will be reduced and efficient distribution impeded; and that implementation of certain methods of cooperation will lead to increased channel efficiency.

DEFINITION OF CHANNEL

The concept of a marketing channel is slightly more involved than expected on initial study. One author in a recent paper[1] has identified "trading" channels, "non-trading" channels, "type" channels, "enterprise" channels, and "business-unit" channels. Another source[2] refers to channels as all the flows extending from the producer to the user. These include the flows of physical possession, ownership, promotion, negotiation, financing, risking, ordering, and payment.

The concept of channels to be used here involves only two of the above-mentioned flows: ownership and negotiation. The first draws merchants, both wholesalers and retailers, into the channel definition, and the second draws in agent middlemen. Both, of course, include producers and consumers. This definition roughly corresponds to Professor Breyer's "trading channel," though the latter does not restrict (nor will this paper) the definition to actual flows, but to "flow-capacity." "A trading channel is formed when trading relations, making possible the passage of title and/or possession (usually both) of goods from the producer to the ultimate consumer, is consummated by the component trading concerns of the system."[3] In addition, this paper will deal with trading channels in the broadest manner and so will be concentrating on "type-trading" channels rather than "enterprise" or "business-unit" channels. This means that there will be little discussion of problems peculiar to integrated or semi-integrated channels, or peculiar to specific channels and firms.

CONFLICT

Palamountain isolated three forms of distributive conflict.[4]

1. Horizontal competition—this is competition between middlemen of the same type; for example, discount store *versus* discount store.
2. Intertype competition—this is competition between middlemen of different types in the same

• SOURCE: Bruce Mallen, "Conflict and Cooperation in Marketing Channels," in L. George Smith, *Reflections On Progress In Marketing* (Chicago: American Marketing Association, 1964), pp. 65–85. Bruce Mallen, President, International Marketing Consultants, Inc.

[1] Ralph F. Breyer, "Some Observations on Structural Formation and The Growth of Marketing Channels," in *Theory in Marketing*, Reavis Cox, Wroe Alderson, Stanley J. Shapiro, Editors. (Homewood, Illinois: Richard D. Irwin, 1964), pp. 163–175.
[2] Ronald S. Vaile, E. T. Grether, and Reavis Cox, *Marketing in the American Economy* (New York: Ronald Press, 1952), pp. 121 and 124.

[3] Breyer, *op. cit.*, p. 165.
[4] Joseph C. Palamountain, *The Politics of Distribution* (Cambridge: Harvard University Press, 1955).

channel sector; for example, discount store *versus* department store.

3. Vertical conflict—this is conflict between channel members of different levels; for example, discount store *versus* manufacturer.

The first form, horizontal competition, is well covered in traditional economic analysis and is usually referred to simply as "competition." However, both intertype competition and vertical conflict, particularly the latter, are neglected in the usual micro-economic discussion.

The concepts of "intertype competition" and "distributive innovation" are closely related and require some discussion. Intertype competition will be divided into two categories; (a) "traditional intertype competition" and (b) "innovative intertype competition." The first category includes the usual price and promotional competition between two or more different types of channel members at the same channel level. The second category involves the action on the part of traditional channel members to prevent channel innovators from establishing themselves. For example, in Canada there is a strong campaign, on the part of traditional department stores, to prevent the discount operation from taking a firm hold on the Canadian market.[5]

Distributive innovation will also be divided into two categories; (a) "intrafirm innovative conflict" and (b) "innovative intertype competition." The first category involves the action of channel member firms to prevent sweeping changes within their own companies. The second category, "innovative intertype competition," is identical to the second category of intertype competition.

Thus the concepts of intertype competition and distributive innovation give rise to three forms of conflict, the second of which is a combination of both: (1) traditional intertype competition, (2) innovative intertype competition, and (3) intrafirm innovative conflict.

It is to this second form that this paper now turns before going on to vertical conflict.

Innovative Intertype Competition

Professor McCammon has identified several sources, both intrafirm and intertype, of innovative conflict in distribution, i.e., where there

are barriers to change within the marketing structure.[6]

Traditional members of a channel have several motives for maintaining the channel status quo against outside innovators. The traditional members are particularly strong in this conflict when they can ban together in some formal or informal manner—when there is strong reseller solidarity.

Both entrepreneurs and professional managers may resist outside innovators, not only for economic reasons, but because change "violates group norms, creates uncertainty, and results in a loss of status." The traditional channel members (the insiders) and their affiliated members (the strivers and complementors) are emotionally and financially committed to the dominant channel and are interested in perpetuating it against the minor irritations of the "transient" channel members and the major attacks of the "outside innovators."

Thus, against a background of horizontal and intertype channel conflict, this paper now moves to its area of major concern; vertical conflict and cooperation.

Vertical Conflict—Price

The Exchange Act. The act of exchange is composed of two elements: a sale and a purchase. It is to the advantage of the seller to obtain the highest return possible from such an exchange and the exact opposite is the desire of the buyer. This exchange act takes place between any kind of buyer and seller. If the consumer is the buyer, then that side of the act is termed shopping; if the manufacturer, purchasing; if the government, procurement; and if a retailer, buying. Thus, between each level in the channel and exchange will take place (except if a channel member is an agent rather than a merchant).

One must look to the process of the exchange act for the basic source of conflict between channel members. This is not to say the exchange act itself is a conflict. Indeed, the act or transaction is a sign that the element of price conflict has been resolved to the mutual satisfaction of both principals. Only along the road to this mutual satisfaction point or exchange

[5] Isaiah A. Litvak and Bruce E. Mallen, *Marketing: Canada* (Toronto: McGraw-Hill of Canada, Limited, 1964), pp. 196–197.

[6] This section is based on Bert C. McCammon, Jr., "Alternative Explanations of Institutional Change And Channel Evolution," in *Toward Scientific Marketing*, Stephen A. Greyser, Editor (Chicago: American Marketing Association, 1963), pp. 477–490.

price do the principals have opposing interests. This is no less true even if they work out the exchange price together, as in mass retailers' specification-buying programs.

It is quite natural for the selling member in an exchange to want a higher price than the buying member. The conflict is subdued through persuasion or force by one member over the other, or it is subdued by the fact that the exchange act or transaction does not take place, or finally, as mentioned above, it is eliminated if the act does take place.

Suppliers may emphasize the customer aspect of a reseller rather than the channel member aspect. As a customer the reseller is somebody to persuade, manipulate, or even fool. Conversely, under the marketing concept, the view of the reseller as a customer or channel member is identical. Under this philosophy he is somebody to aid, help, and serve. However, it is by no means certain that even a large minority of suppliers have accepted the marketing concept.

To view the reseller as simply the opposing principal in the act of exchange may be channel myopia, but this view exists. On the other hand, failure to recognize this basic opposing interest is also a conceptual fault.

When the opposite principals in an exchange act are of unequal strength, the stronger is very likely to force or persuade the weaker to adhere to the former's desires. However, when they are of equal strength, the basic conflict cannot so easily be resolved. Hence, the growth of big retailers who can match the power of big producers has possibly led to greater open conflict between channel members, not only with regard to exchange, but also to other conflict sources.

There are other sources of conflict within the pricing area outside of the basic one discussed above.

A supplier may force a product onto its resellers, who dare not oppose, but who retaliate in other ways, such as using it as a loss leader. Large manufacturers may try to dictate the resale price of their merchandise; this may be less or more than the price at which resellers wish to sell it. Occasionally, a local market may be more competitive for a reseller than is true nationally. The manufacturer may not recognize the difference in competition and refuse to help this channel member.

Resellers complain of maufacturers' special price concessions to competitors and rebel at the attempt of manufacturers to control resale prices. Manufacturers complain of resellers' deceptive and misleading price advertising, nonadherence to resale price suggestions, bootlegging to unauthorized outlets, seeking special price concessions by unfair methods, and misrepresenting offers by competitive suppliers.

Other points of price conflict are the paperwork aspects of pricing. Resellers complain of delays in price change notices and complicated price sheets.

Price Theory. If one looks upon a channel as a series of markets or as the vertical exchange mechanism between buyers and sellers, one can adapt several theories and concepts to the channel situation which can aid marketing theory in this important area of channel conflict.[7]

Vertical Conflict—Non-Price

Channel conflict not only finds its source in the exchange act and pricing, but it permeates all areas of marketing. Thus, a manufacturer may wish to promote a product in one manner or to a certain degree while his resellers oppose this. Another manufacturer may wish to get information from his resellers on a certain aspect relating to his product, but his resellers may refuse to provide this information. A producer may want to distribute his product extensively, but his resellers may demand exclusives.

There is also conflict because of the tendency for both manufacturers and retailers to want the elimination of the wholesaler.

One very basic source of channel conflict is the possible difference in the primary business philosophy of channel members. Writing in the *Harvard Business Review*, Wittreich says:

"In essence, then, the key to understanding management's problem of crossed purpose is the recognition that the fundamental (philosophy) in life of the high-level corporate manager and the typical (small) retail dealer in the distribution system are quite different. The former's (philosophy) can be characterized as being essentially dynamic in nature, continuously evolving and emerging; the latter, which are in sharp contrast, can be characterized as being essentially static in nature, reaching a point and leveling off into a continuously satisfying plateau."[8]

While the big members of the channel may

[7] Bruce Mallen, "Introducing The Marketing Channel To Price Theory," *Journal of Marketing*, July, 1964, pp. 29–33.
[8] Warren J. Wittreich, "Misunderstanding The Retailer," *Harvard Business Review*, May–June, 1962, p. 149.

want growth, the small retail members may be satisfied with stability and a "good living."

ANARCHY[9]

The channel can adjust to its conflicting-cooperating environment in three distinct ways. *First*, it can have a leader (one of the channel members) who "forces" members to cooperate; this is an autocratic relationship. *Second*, it can have a leader who "helps" members to cooperate, creating a democratic relationship. *Finally*, it can do nothing, and so have an anarchistic relationship. Lewis B. Sappington and C. G. Browne, writing on the problems of internal company organizations, state:

"The first classification may be called "autocracy." In this approach to the group the leader determines the policy and dictates or assigns the work tasks. There are no group deliberations, no group decisions . . . .

"The second classification may be called "democracy." In this approach the leader allows all policies to be decided by the group with his participation. The group members work with each other as they wish. The group determines the division and assignment of tasks . . . .

"The third classification may be called "anarchy." In anarchy there is complete freedom of the group or the individual regarding policies or task assignments, without leader participation."[10]

Advanced in this paper is the hypothesis that if anarchy exists, there is a great chance of the conflicting dynamics destroying the channel. If autocracy exists, there is less chance of this happening. However, the latter method creates a state of cooperation based on power and control. This controlled cooperation is really subdued conflict and makes for a more unstable equilibrium than does voluntary democratic cooperation.

CONTROLLED COOPERATION

The usual pattern in the establishment of channel relationships is that there is a leader,

an initiator who puts structure into this relationship and who holds it together. This leader controls, whether through command or cooperation, i.e., through an autocratic or a democratic system.

Too often it is automatically assumed that the manufacturer or producer will be the channel leader and that the middlemen will be the channel followers. This has not always been so, nor will it necessarily be so in the future. The growth of mass retailers is increasingly challenging the manufacturer for channel leadership, as the manufacturer challenged the wholesaler in the early part of this century.

The following historical discussion will concentrate on the three-ring struggle between manufacturer, wholesaler, and retailer rather than on the changing patterns of distribution within a channel sector, i.e., between service wholesaler and agent middleman or discount and department store. This will lay the necessary background for a discussion of the present-day manufacturer-dominated *versus* retailer-dominated struggle.

Early History

The simple distribution system of Colonial days gave way to a more complex one. Among the forces of change were the growth of population, the long distances involved, the increasing complexity of new products, the increase of wealth, and the increase of consumption.

The United States was ready for specialists to provide a growing and widely dispersed populace with the many new goods and services required. The more primitive methods of public markets and barter could not efficiently handle the situation. This type of system required short distances, few products, and a small population, to operate properly.

19th Century History

In the same period that this older system was dissolving, the retailer was still a very small merchant who, especially in the West, lived in relative isolation from his supply sources. Aside from being small, he further diminished his power position by spreading himself thin over many merchandise lines. The retailer certainly was no specialist but was as general as a general store can be. His opposite channel member, the manufacturer, was also a small businessman,

[9] The term "anarchy" as used in this paper connotes "no leadership" and nothing more.
[10] Lewis B. Sappington and C. G. Browne, "The Skills of Creative Leadership," in *Managerial Marketing*, rev. ed., William Lazar and Eugene J. Kelley, Editors. (Homewood, Ill.: Richard D. Irwin, 1962), p. 350.

too concerned with production and financial problems to fuss with marketing.

Obviously, both these channel members were in no position to assume leadership. However, somebody had to perform all the various marketing functions between production and retailing if the economy was to function. The wholesaler filled this vacuum and became the channel leader of the 19th century.

The wholesaler became the selling force of the manufacturer and the latter's link to the widely scattered retailers over the nation. He became the retailer's life line to these distant domestic and even more important foreign sources of supply.

These wholesalers carried any type of product from any manufacturer and sold any type of product to the general retailers. They can be described as general merchandise wholesalers. They were concentrated at those transportation points in the country which gave them access to both the interior and its retailers, and the exterior and its foreign suppliers.

Early 20th Century

The end of the century saw the wholesaler's power on the decline. The manufacturer had grown larger and more financially secure with the shift from a foreign-oriented economy to a domestic-oriented one. He could now finance his marketing in a manner impossible to him in early times. His thoughts shifted to some extent from production problems to marketing problems.

Prodding the manufacturer on was the increased rivalry of his other domestic competitors The increased investment in capital and inventory made it necessary that he maintain volume. He tended to locate himself in the larger market areas, and thus, did not have great distances to travel to see his retail customers. In addition, he started to produce various products; and because of his new multiproduct production, he could reach—even more efficiently—these already more accessible markets.

The advent of the automobile and highways almost clinched the manufacturer's bid for power. For now he could reach a much vaster market (and they could reach him) and reap the benefits of economics of scale.

The branding of his products projected him to the channel leadership. No longer did he have as great a need for a specialist in reaching widely dispersed customers, nor did he need them to the same extent for their contacts. The market knew where the product came from. The age of wholesaler dominance declined. That of manufacturer dominance emerged.

Is it still here? What is its future? How strong is the challenge by retailers? Is one "better" than the other? These are the questions of the next section.

Disagreement Among Scholars

No topic seems to generate so much heat and bias in marketing as the question of who should be the channel leader, and more strangely, who is the channel leader. Depending on where the author sits, he can give numerous reasons why his particular choice should take the channel initiative.

Authors of sales management and general marketing books say the manufacturer is and should be the chief institution in the channel. Retailing authors feel the same way about retailers, and wholesaling authors (as few as there are), though not blinded to the fact that wholesaling is not "captain," still imply that they should be, and talk about the coming resurrection of wholesalers. Yet a final and compromising view is put forth by those who believe that a balance of power, rather than a general and prolonged dominance of any channel member, is best.

The truth is that an immediate reaction would set in against any temporary dominance by a channel member. In that sense, there is a constant tendency toward the equilibrium of market forces. The present view is that public interest is served by a balance of power rather than by a general and prolonged predominance of any one level in marketing channels.[11]

John Kenneth Galbraith's concept of countervailing power also holds to this last view.

For the retailer:

In the opinion of the writer, "retailer-dominated marketing" has yielded, and will continue to yield in the future greater net benefits to consumers than "manufacturer-dominated marketing," as the central-buying mass distributor continues to play a role of ever-increasing im-

[11] Wroe Alderson, "Factors Governing The Development of Marketing Channels," in *Marketing Channels For Manufactured Products*, Richard M. Clewett, Editor. (Homewood: Richard D. Irwin, 1954), p. 30.

portance in the marketing of goods in our economy . . . .

. . . In the years to come, as more and more large-scale multiple-unit retailers follow the central buying patterns set by Sears and Penneys, as leaders in their respective fields (hard lines and soft goods), ever-greater benefits should flow to consumers in the way of more goods better adjusted to their demands, at lower prices.[12]

. . . In a long run buyer's market, such as we probably face in this country, the retailers have the inherent advantage of economy in distribution and will, therefore, become increasingly important.[13]

The retailer cannot be the selling agent of the manufacturer because he holds a higher commission; he is the purchasing agent for the public.[14]

For the wholesaler:

The wholesaling sector is, first of all, the most significant part of the entire marketing organization.[15]

. . . The orthodox wholesaler and affiliated types have had a resurgence to previous 1929 levels of sales importance.[16]

. . . Wholesalers have since made a comeback.[17] This revival of wholesaling has resulted from infusion of new management blood and the adoption of new techniques.[18]

For the manufacturer:

. . . the final decision in channel selection rests with the seller manufacturer and will continue to rest with him as long as he has the legal right to choose to sell to some potential customers and refuse to sell to others.[19]

These channel decisions are primarily problems for the manufacturer. They rarely arise for general wholesalers . . . .[20]

Of all the historical tendencies in the field of marketing, no other is so distinctly apparent as the tendency for the manufacturer to assume greater control over the distribution of his product. . . .[21]

. . . Marketing policies at other levels can be viewed as extensions of policies established by marketing managers in manufacturing firms; and, furthermore, . . . the nature and function can adequately be surveyed by looking at the relationship to manufacturers.[22]

Pro-Manufacture

The argument for manufacturer leadership is production oriented. It claims that they must assure themselves of increasing volume. This is needed to derive the benefits of production scale economies, to spread their overhead over many units, to meet increasingly stiff competition, and to justify the investment risk they, not the retailers, are taking. Since retailers will not do this job for them properly, the manufacturer must control the channel.

Another major argumentative point for manufacturer dominance is that neither the public nor retailers can create new products even under a market-oriented system. The most the public can do is to select and choose among those that manufacturers have developed. They cannot select products that they cannot conceive. This argument would say that it is of no use to ask consumers and retailers what they want because they cannot articulate abstract needs into tangible goods; indeed, the need can be created by the goods rather than vice-versa.

[12] Arnold Corbin, *Central Buying in Relation To The Merchandising of Multiple Retail Units* (New York, Unpublished Doctoral Dissertation at New York University, 1954), pp. 708–709.
[13] David Craig and Werner Gabler, "The Competitive Struggle for Market Control," in *Readings in Marketing*, Howard J. Westing, Editor. (New York, Prentice-Hall, 1953), p. 46.
[14] Lew Hahn, *Stores, Merchants and Customers* (New York, Fairchild Publications, 1952), p. 12.
[15] David A. Revzan, *Wholesaling in Marketing Organization* (New York: John Wiley & Sons, 1961), p. 606.
[16] *Ibid.*, p. 202.
[17] E. Jerome McCarthy, *Basic Marketing* (Homewood, Illinois: Richard D. Irwin, 1960), p. 419.
[18] *Ibid.*, p. 420.

[19] Eli P. Cox, *Federal Quantity Discount Limitations and Its Possible Effects on Distribution Channel Dynamics* (Unpublished Doctoral Dissertation, University of Texas, 1956), p. 12.
[20] Milton Brown, Wilbur B. England, John B. Matthews, Jr., *Problems in Marketing*, 3rd ed. (New York: McGraw-Hill, 1961), p. 239.
[21] Maynard D. Phelps and Howard J. Westing, *Marketing Management*, Revised Edition (Homewood, Ill.: Richard D. Irwin, 1960), p. 11.
[22] Kenneth Davis, *Marketing Management* (New York: The Ronald Press Co., 1961), p. 131.

This argument may hold well when applied to consumers, but a study of the specification-buying programs of the mass retailers will show that the latter can indeed create new products, and need not be relegated to simply selecting among alternatives.

Pro-Retailer

This writer sees the mass retailer as the natural leader of the channel for consumer goods under the marketing concept. The retailer stands closest to the consumer; he feels the pulse of consumer wants and needs day in and day out. The retailer can easily undertake consumer research right on his own premises and can best interpret what is wanted, how much is wanted, and when it is wanted.

An equilibrium in the channel conflict may come about when small retailers join forces with big manufacturers in a manufacturer leadership channel to compete with a small manufacturer-big retailer leadership channel.

Pro-Wholesaler

It would seem that the wholesaler has a choice in this domination problem as well. Unlike the manufacturer and retailer though, his method is not mainly through a power struggle. This problem is almost settled for him once he chooses the type of wholesaling business he wishes to enter. A manufacturers' agent and purchasing agent are manufacturer-dominated, a sales agent dominates the manufacturer. A resident buyer and voluntary group wholesaler are retail-dominated.

Methods of Manufacturer Domination

How does a channel leader dominate his fellow members? What are his tools in this channel power struggle? A manufacturer has many domination weapons at his disposal. His arsenal can be divided into promotional, legal, negative, suggestive, and, ironically, voluntary cooperative compartments.

Promotional. Probably the major method that the manufacturer has used is the building of a consumer franchise through advertising, sales promotion, and packaging of his branded products. When he has developed some degree of consumer loyalty, the other channel members must bow to his leadership. The more successful this identification through the promotion process, the more assured is the manufacturer of his leadership.

Legal. The legal weapon has also been a poignant force for the manufacturer. It can take many forms, such as, where permissible, resale price maintenance. Other contractual methods are franchises, where the channel members may become mere shells of legal entities. Through this weapon the automobile manufacturers have achieved an almost absolute dominance over their dealers.

Even more absolute is resort to legal ownership of channel members, called forward vertical integration. Vertical integration is the ultimate in manufacturer dominance of the channel. Another legal weapon is the use of consignment sales. Under this method the channel members must by law sell the goods as designated by the owner (manufacturer). Consignment selling is in a sense vertical integration; it is keeping legal ownership of the goods until they reach the consumer, rather than keeping legal ownership of the institutions which are involved in the process.

Negative Methods. Among the "negative" methods of dominance are refusal to sell to possibly uncooperative retailers or refusal to concentrate a large percentage of one's volume with any one customer.

A spreading of sales makes for a concentrating of manufacturer power, while a concentrating of sales may make for a thinning of manufacturer power. Of course, if a manufacturer is one of the few resources available and if there are many available retailers, then a concentrating of sales will also make for a concentrating of power.

The avoidance and refusal tactics, of course, eliminate the possibility of opposing dominating institutions.

Suggestives. A rather weak group of dominating weapons are the "suggestives." Thus, a manufacturer can issue price sheets and discounts, preticket and premark resale prices on goods, recommend, suggest, and advertise resale prices.

These methods are not powerful unless supplemented by promotional, legal, and/or negative weapons. It is common for these methods to boomerang. Thus a manufacturer pretickets or advertises resale prices, and a retailer cuts this price, pointing with pride to the manufacturer's suggested retail price.

Voluntary Cooperative Devices. There is one more group of dominating weapons, and these are really all the voluntary cooperating weapons to be mentioned later. The promise to provide these, or to withdraw them, can have a "whip and carrot" effect on the channel members.

Retailers' Dominating Weapons

Retailers also have numerous dominating weapons at their disposal. As with manufacturers, their strongest weapon is the building of a consumer franchise through advertising, sales promotion, and branding. The growth of private brands is the growth of retail dominance.

Attempts at concentrating a retailer's purchasing power are a further group of weapons and are analogous to a manufacturer's attempts to disperse his volume. The more a retailer can concentrate his purchasing, the more dominating he can become; the more he spreads his purchasing, the more dominated he becomes. Again, if the resource is one of only a few, this generalization reverses itself.

Such legal contracts as specification buying, vertical integration (or the threat), and entry into manufacturing can also be effective. Even semiproduction, such as the packaging of goods received in bulk by the supermarket can be a weapon of dominance.

Retailers can dilute the dominance of manufacturers by patronizing those with excess capacity and those who are "hungry" for the extra volume. There is also the subtlety, which retailers may recognize, that a strong manufacturer may concede to their wishes just to avoid an open conflict with a customer.

VOLUNTARY COOPERATION

But despite some of the conflict dynamics and forced cooperation, channel members usually have more harmonious and common interests than conflicting ones. A team effort to market a producer's product will probably help all involved. All members have a common interest in selling the product; only in the division of total channel profits are they in conflict. They have a singular goal to reach, and here they are allies. If any one of them fails in the team effort, this weak link in the chain can destroy them all. As such, all members are concerned with one another's welfare (unless a member can be easily replaced).

Organizational Extension Concept

This emphasis on the cooperating, rather than the conflicting objectives of channel members, has led to the concept of the channel as simply an extension of one's own internal organization. Conflict in such a system is to be expected even as it is to be expected within an organization. However, it is the common or "macro-objective" that is the center of concentration. Members are to sacrifice their selfish "micro-objectives" to this cause. By increasing the profit pie they will all be better off than squabbling over pieces of a smaller one. The goal is to minimize conflict and maximize cooperation. This view has been expounded in various articles by Peter Drucker, Ralph Alexander, and Valentine Ridgeway.

"Together, the manufacturer with his suppliers and/or dealers comprise a system in which the manufacturer may be designated the primary organization and the dealers and suppliers designated as secondary organizations. This system is in competition with similar systems in the economy; and in order for the system to operate effectively as an integrated whole, there must be some administration of the system as a whole, not merely administration of the separate organizations within that system."[23]

Peter Drucker[24] has pleaded against the conceptual blindness that the idea of the legal entity generates. A legal entity is not a marketing entity. Since often half of the cost to the consumer is added on after the product leaves the producer, the latter should think of his channel members as part of his firm. General Motors is an example of an organization which does this.

"Both businessmen and students of marketing often define too narrowly the problem of marketing channels. Many of them tend to define the term channels of distribution as a complex of relationships between the firm on the one hand, and marketing establishments exterior to the firm by which the products of the firm are moved to market, on the other . . . . A much broader more constructive concept embraces the relationships with external agents or units as part of the marketing organization of the company. From this viewpoint, the complex of external relationships may be regarded as merely an extension of the marketing organization of the firm. When we look at the problem

[23] Valentine F. Ridgeway, "Administration of Manufacturer-Dealer Systems," in *Managerial Marketing*, rev. ed., William Lazer and Eugene J. Kelley, Editors (Homewood, Ill.: Richard D. Irwin, 1962), p. 480.
[24] Peter Drucker, "The Economy's Dark Continent," *Fortune*, April 1962, pp. 103 ff.

in this way, we are much less likely to lose sight of the interdependence of the two structures and more likely to be constantly aware that they are closely related parts of the marketing machine. The fact that the internal organization structure is linked together by a system of employment contracts, while the external one is set up and maintained by a series of transactions, contracts of purchase and sale, tends to obscure their common purpose and close relationship."[25]

Cooperation Methods

But how does a supplier project its organization into the channel? How does it make organization and channel into one? It accomplishes this by doing many things for its resellers that it does for its own organization. It sells, advertises, trains, plans, and promotes for these firms. A brief elaboration of these methods follows.

Missionary salesmen aid the sales of channel members, as well as bolster the whole system's level of activity and selling effort. Training of resellers' salesmen and executives is an effective weapon of cooperation. The channels operate more efficiently when all are educated in the promotional techniques and uses of the products involved.

Involvement in the planning functions of its channel members could be another poignant weapon of the supplier. Helping resellers to set quotas for their customers, studying the market potential for them, forecasting a member's sales volume, inventory planning and protection, etc., are all aspects of this latter method.

Aid in promotion through the provision of advertising materials (mats, displays, commercials, literature, direct-mail pieces), ideas, funds (cooperative advertising), sales contest, store layout designs, push money (PM's or spiffs), is another form of cooperation.

The big supplier can act as management consultant to the members, dispensing advice in all areas of their business, including accounting, personnel, planning, control, finance, buying, paper systems or office procedure, and site selection. Aid in financing may include extended credit terms, consignment selling, and loans.

By no means do these methods of coordination take a one-way route. All members of the channel, including supplier and reseller, see their own organizations meshing with the others, and so provide coordinating weapons in accordance with their ability. Thus, the manufacturer would undertake a marketing research project for his channel, and also expect his resellers to keep records and vital information for the manufacturer's use. A supplier may also expect his channel members to service the product after the sale.

A useful device for fostering cooperation is a channel advisory council composed of the supplier and his resellers.

Finally, a manufacturer or reseller can avoid associations with potentially uncooperative channel members. Thus, a price-conservative manufacturer may avoid linking to a price-cutting retailer.

E. B. Weiss has developed an impressive, though admittedly incomplete list of cooperation methods (Table 1). Paradoxically, many of these instruments of cooperation are also weapons of control (forced cooperation) to be used by both middlemen and manufacturers. However, this is not so strange if one keeps in mind that control is subdued conflict and a form of cooperation—even though perhaps involuntary cooperation.

Extension Concept Is the Marketing Concept

The philosophy of cooperation is described in the following quote:

"The essence of the marketing concept is of course customer orientation at all levels of distribution. It is particularly important that customer orientation motivate all relations between a manufacturer and his customer—both immediate and ultimate. It must permeate his entire channels-of-distribution policy."[26]

This quote synthesizes the extension-of-the-organization system concept of channels with the marketing concept. Indeed, it shows that the former is, in essence, "the" marketing concept applied to the channel area in marketing. To continue:

"The characteristics of the highly competitive markets of today naturally put a distinct premium on harmonious manufacturer-distributor relationships. Their very mutuality of interest demands that the manufacturer base his distribution program not only on what he would like

---

[25] Ralph S. Alexander, James S. Cross, Ross M. Cunningham, *Industrial Marketing*, rev. ed. (Homewood, Ill.: Richard D. Irwin, 1961), p. 266.

[26] Hector Lazo and Arnold Corbin, *Management in Marketing* (New York: McGraw-Hill, 1961), p. 379.

Table 1.   Methods of Cooperation as Listed[27]

1. Cooperative advertising allowances
2. Payments for interior displays including shelf-extenders, dump displays, "A" locations, aisle displays, etc.
3. P.M.'s for salespeople
4. Contests for buyers, salespeople, etc.
5. Allowances for a variety of warehousing functions
6. Payments for window display space, plus installation costs
7. Detail men who check inventory, put up stock, set up complete promotions, etc.
8. Demonstrators
9. On certain canned food, a "swell" allowance
10. Label allowance
11. Coupon handling allowance
12. Free goods
13. Guaranteed sales
14. In-store and window display material
15. Local research work
16. Mail-in premium offers to consumer
17. Preticketing
18. Automatic reorder systems
19. Delivery costs to individual stores of large retailers
20. Studies of innumerable types, such as studies of merchandise management accounting
21. Payments for mailings to store lists
22. Liberal return privileges
23. Contributions to favorite charities of store personnel
24. Contributions to special store anniversaries
25. Prizes, etc., to store buyers when visiting showrooms—plus entertainment, of course
26. Training retail salespeople
27. Payments for store fixtures
28. Payments for new store costs, for more improvements, including painting
29. An infinite variety of promotion allowances
30. Special payments for exclusive franchises
31. Payments of part of salary of retail salespeople
32. Deals of innumerable types
33. Time spent in actual selling floor by manufacturer, salesmen
34. Inventory price adjustments
35. Store name mention in manufacturer's advertising

from distributors, but perhaps more importantly, on what they would like from him. In order to get the cooperation of the best distributors, and thus maximum exposure for his line among the various market segments, he must adjust his policies to serve their best interest and, thereby, his own. In other words, he must put the principles of the marketing concept to work for him. By so doing, he will inspire in his customers a feeling of mutual interest and trust and will help convince them that they are essential members of his marketing team."[28]

SUMMARY

Figure 1 summarizes this whole paper. Each person within each department will cooperate, control, and conflict with each other (notice arrows). Together they form a department (notice department box contains person boxes) which will be best off when cooperating (or cooperation through control) forces weigh

[27] Edward B. Weiss, "How Much of a Retailer Is the Manufacturer," in *Advertising Age*, July 21, 1958, p. 68.

[28] Lazo and Corbin, *loc. cit.*

heavier than conflicting forces. Now each department cooperates, controls, and conflicts with each other. Departments together also form a higher level organization—the firm (manufacturer, wholesaler, and retailer). Again, the firm will be better off if department cooperation is maximized and conflict minimized. Finally, firms standing vertically to each other cooperate, control, and conflict. Together they form a distribution channel that will be best off under conditions of optimum cooperation leading to consumer and profit satisfaction.

CONCLUSIONS AND HYPOTHESES

1. Channel relationships are set against a background of cooperation and conflict; horizontal, intertype, and vertical.

2. An autocratic relationship exists when one channel member controls conflict and forces the others to cooperate. A democratic relationship exists when all members agree to cooperate without a power play. An anarchistic relationship exists when there is open conflict, with no member able to impose his will on the others. This last form could destroy or seriously reduce the effectiveness of the channel.

3. The process of the exchange act where one member is a seller and the other is a buyer is the basic source of channel conflict. Economic theory can aid in comprehending this phenomenon. There are, however, many other areas of conflict, such as differences in business philosophy or primary objectives.

4. Reasons for cooperation, however, usually outweigh reasons for conflict. This has led to the concept of the channel as an extension of a firm's organization.

5. This concept drops the facade of "legal entity" and treats channel members as one great organization with the leader providing each with various forms of assistance. These are called cooperating weapons.

6. It is argued that this concept is actually the marketing concept adapted to a channel situation.

7. In an autocratic or democratic channel relationship, there must be a leader. This leadership has shifted and is shifting between the various channel levels.

8. The wholesaler was the leader in the last century, the manufacturer now, and it appears that the mass retailer is next in line.

9. There is much disagreement on the above point, however, especially on who should be the leader. Various authors have differing arguments to advance for their choice.

10. In the opinion of this writer, the mass retailer appears to be best adapted for leadership under the marketing concept.

11. As there are weapons of cooperation, so are there weapons of domination. Indeed the former paradoxically are one group of the latter. The other groups are promotional, legal, negative, and suggestive methods. Both manufacturers and retailers have at their disposal these dominating weapons.

12. *For maximization of channel profits and consumer satisfaction, the channel must act as a unit.*

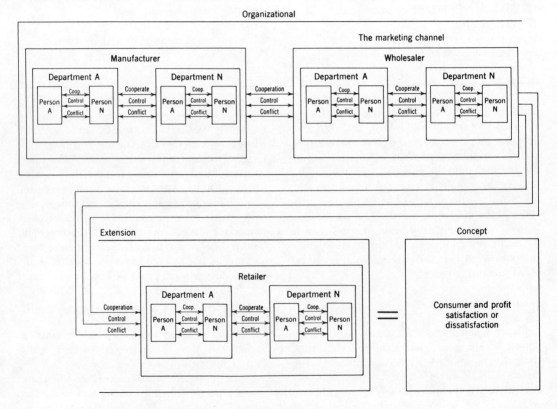

Figure 1

B. Vertical Price Relationships

18. Introducing the Marketing Channel to Price Theory

BRUCE MALLEN

Economic price theory has much to contribute to organized marketing thought. Likewise the reality of microeconomic price theory can be improved by its incorporation of marketing concepts.

Mallen reviews several price theories, which if properly integrated, could aid marketing theory as applied to the important area of marketing channels.

Most of the various areas of marketing such as promotion, advertising, selling, pricing, product development, and distribution can be enriched by economic theory.

But one area in particular has had very little integration with economic theory—the marketing channel. "The final price of an article is not a simple thing arrived at as a result merely of the interaction of the forces in play at the point of sale and purchase. It is compounded of a whole system of interlocking price relationships reaching back through the retailer, the wholesaler, the manufacturer, and all the other marketing agents who may have had a hand in the movement of the product to the point of ultimate sale. It is the final fruit of an elaborate price structure complicated by such conditioning and obscuring factors as quantity allowances, credit terms, delivery arrangements, and services rendered at each of the several stages through which the product passes in its often devious and tortuous way to the point of final sale."[1]

DEFINITION OF CHANNEL

Trade channels and channels of distribution are synonymous with marketing channels. Resource channels are also synonymous, but they involve marketing channels from a buying rather than a selling standpoint.

In a wide sense, channels are all the "flows" extending from the producer to the user. "A channel of distribution may be thought of as the combination and sequence of agencies through which one or more of the marketing flows move. . . . In its simplest form, a channel is limited to the movement of one unit of goods in one flow. . . . In its more complicated forms, the channel includes all combinations and sequences of all the agencies used in all the flows, possibly with an indication of the quantitative importance of each. It may apply to a whole class or type of goods and to a company, a trade, or an industry. In its most complex form, it describes typical or actual flows of broad classes of goods (say consumers' goods or industrial goods) or charts the marketing structure as a whole."[2]

This definition refers to the flows of physical possession, ownership promotion, negotiation, financing, risking, ordering, and payment; and

• SOURCE: Bruce Mallen, "Introducing the Marketing Channel to Price Theory," *Journal of Marketing*, Vol. 28 (July, 1964), pp. 29–33. Bruce Mallen, Senior Marketing Consultant, P. S. Ross and Partners, Canada.
[1] Ralph S. Alexander, "Marketing's Contribution to Economics," in Robert A. Solo, Editor, *Economics and the Public Interest* (New Brunswick: Rutgers University Press, 1955), pp. 71–72.

[2] Ronald S. Vaile, E. T. Grether, and Reavis Cox, *Marketing in the American Economy* (New York: Ronald Press, 1952), pp. 121 and 124.

it is accepted by many authorities.[3] Under this concept, such diverse agencies as railroads, warehouses, factors, advertising agencies, and marketing research agencies would be included as channel members.

However, the concept of channels to be used here involves only two of the above-mentioned flows: ownership and negotiation. The first draws merchants into the channel definition, and the second draws agent middlemen. If any major processing is undergone, the channel ends. For example, the route from cotton farmer to textile mill to garment manufacturer to consumer is not one channel, but several.

ECONOMIC MARKETS CLASSIFICATION

How can the marketing man's concept of a channel be injected into the economist's concept of a market? This is a crucial question, as the concept of a market place is central to micro-economic price theory.

Economists look upon a market as the exchange mechanism between buyers and sellers. Thus, the exchange mechanism between a manufacturer as a seller and a wholesaler as a buyer is one market. A second market is the exchange mechanism between the wholesaler as a seller and the retailer as a buyer. Finally, the exchange mechanism between the retailer as a seller and the consumer as a buyer is a third market. Thus, a manufacturer-whole-saler-retailer-consumer channel can be looked upon as a series of three markets.

The type of market can be defined according to its degree of competitiveness, which depends to a great extent on the number of buyers and sellers in a market. Some possible conbinations are shown in Table 1.

The classification of economic markets in Table 1 is based primarily on the degree of concentration and number of suppliers (manufacturers or middlemen) on the selling side, and the degree of concentration and number of middlemen on the buying side of the market.

1. The smaller the number and the greater the degree of concentration on the selling side, the less purely competitive and the more monopolistic that market becomes.
2. The smaller the number and the greater the degree of concentration on the buying side, the less purely competitive and the more monopsonistic that market becomes.

[3] David A. Revzan, *Wholesaling in Marketing Organization* (New York: John Wiley & Sons, 1961), p. 109.

Table 1. **Classification of Economic Markets**

Suppliers (sellers)	Middlemen (buyers)	Market situation
Pure competitor	Pure competitor	Pure competition
Oligopolist	Pure competitor	Oligopoly
Monopolist	Pure competitor	Monopoly
Pure competitor	Oligopsonist	Oligoposony
Pure competitor	Monopsonist	Monopsony
Oligopoly	Oligopsonist	Bilateral oligopoly
Monopolist	Monopsonist	Bilateral monopoly
Monopolist	Monopolist	Successive monopoly

3. Where this diminishing number and increasing concentration are "working" on both sides of the market, the closer that market moves to bilateral monopoly.

In an oversimplified way, it can be said that:

1. Pure competition means many sellers and many buyers.
2. Oligopoly means few sellers; monopoly means one seller.
3. Oligopsony means few buyers; monopsony means one buyer.
4. Bilateral oligopoly means few buyers and few sellers; and bilateral monopoly means one buyer and one seller.
5. Successive monopoly means one seller selling to buyers, each of whom is in turn the only reseller in the next market of the channel series.

The more monopolistic the selling side, the higher the price will tend to be; and the more monopsonistic, the lower the price.

Aside from the number of micro-units involved, these definitions include specifications for degree of product differentiation (none in pure competition); degree of resource mobility and ease of entry (complete in pure competition); and degree of artificial restrictions (none in pure competition).

Because of these other specifications, definitions of other types of markets not mentioned above arise, such as monopolistic competition (pure competition changed by product differentiation); but these will not be dealt with here.

THEORIES IN THE CHANNEL-PRICE AREA

Several theories and concepts should be adapted to a channel situation. These include vertical conflict, simple monopoly, successive monopoly, vertical price relationship, monopsony and oligopsony, bilateral monopoly and bilateral oligopoly, countervailing power, inventory theory, and price level theory.

Channel-price theory as derived from economic theory is useful in studying the conflicting interaction of channel member firms, but is not very useful in understanding their cooperative interactions.[4] Thus, while such theory concentrates on how the total channel profit is shared among members, it does not adequately show how cooperation is used in increasing the total.

Vertical Conflict

Palamountain isolated three forms of distributive conflict.[5]

1. Horizontal competition—this is competition between middlemen of the same type; for example, discount store versus discount store.
2. Intertype competition—this is competition between middlemen of different types in the same channel sector; for example, discount store versus department store.
3. Vertical conflict—this is conflict between channel members of different levels; for example, discount store versus manufacturer.

The first two forms, especially the first, are well covered in ordinary economic analysis. Horizontal competition is what usually is referred to as "competition," while intertype competition can be referred to as "distributive innovation."

Vertical conflict, neglected in usual microeconomic discussion, is the type which is of special interest here. Microeconomics usually treats this area simply (too simply) as the ordinary relationship between buyer and seller; but this overlooks channel member conflict.

"It is apparent that a principal factor differentiating vertical conflict from horizontal and intertype competition is that it is so directly a power conflict. Power relationships among horizontal competitors occasionally are significant, but this power usually is narrowly limited. . . . In the plane of vertical conflict,

however, power relationships are direct, obvious, and important to the extent that the market is imperfect."[6]

In essence, any type of channel market —where both buyers and sellers are channel members—is vertical conflict.

Simple Monopoly[7]

If one channel member is a monopolist and the others pure competitors, the consumer pays a price equivalent to that of an integrated monopolist; and the monopolist member reaps all the channel's pure profits; that is, the sum of the pure profits of all channel members. Pure profits are, of course, the economist's concept of those profits over and above the minimum return on investment required to keep a firm in business.

Assume that the retailer is the monopolist and the others (wholesalers and manufacturers) are pure competitors, as for example, a single department store in an isolated town. Total costs to the retailer are composed of the total cost of the other levels, plus his own costs. No pure profits of the other levels are included in his costs, as they make none by definition (they are pure competitors).

The retailer would be in the same buying price position, so far as the lack of suppliers' profits are concerned, as would the vertically integrated firm. Thus, he charges the same price as the integrated monopolist and makes the same profits.

If the manufacturer were the monopolist and the other channel members pure competitors, he would calculate the maximizing profits for the channel, and then charge the wholesaler his cost plus the total channel's pure profits, all of which would go to him since the others are pure competitors. The wholesaler would take this price, add it on to his own costs, and the result would be the price to retailers. Then the retailers would do likewise for the consumer price.

Thus, the prices to the wholesaler and to the retailer are higher than in the first case (retailer monopoly), since the channel's pure profits are added on before the retail level. The price to the consumer is the same as in the first case. It is of no concern to the consumer if the

[4] For the cooperative aspect, see Bruce Mallen "A Theory of Retailer-Supplier Conflict, Control and Cooperation," *Journal of Retailing*, Vol. 39 (Summer, 1963), pp. 24–32 and 51.
[5] Joseph C. Palamountain, *The Politics of Distribution* (Cambridge: Harvard University Press, 1955).
[6] Same reference as footnote 5, at pp. 52–53.
[7] Alfred R. Oxenfeldt, *Industrial Pricing and Market Practices* (New York: Prentice-Hall, 1951), Chapter 7, Part I, Section A.

pure profit elements in his price are added on by the manufacturer, wholesaler, or retailer.

Thus, under integrated monopoly, manufacturer monopoly, wholesaler monopoly, or retailer nonopoly, the consumer price is the same; but the prices within the channel are the lowest with the retailer monopoly, and highest with the manufacturer monopoly. Of course, the nonmonopolistic channel members' pure profits are not affected by this intrachannel price variation, as they have no such profits in any case.

Successive Monopoly[8]

Successive monopoly—that is, monopoly at two or more successive channel stages—can lead to a higher price than an integrated monopoly for the consumer and members, if no agreement is reached among the monopolists.

If there are two monopolies in a channel, such as a manufacturer monopolist and a wholesaler monopolist, the former may still try to gain all the pure profits of the channel, as described in the previous "monopoly" section.

Temporarily the price to the wholesaler would be the manufacturer's cost plus the total channel's pure profits. Under these circumstances, the wholesaler would have to charge the retailer the price the former paid the manufacturer plus his own costs. He could not add on pure profits as the manufacturer has kept them all for himself.

However, unlike the situation when the wholesaler was a pure competitor and was forced to receive no pure profits, this wholesaler can now cut back on the supply he will sell to the retailer, in order to maximize profits. This reduction in supply will increase the price to the retailer more than when the wholesaler was a pure competitor and only the manufacturer was a monopolist. The retailer must now pay not only the costs of the wholesaler and manufacturer, but also the pure profits of both.

The cutback in supply of the wholesaler will also reduce his purchases from the manufacturer, and cause the latter's profits to fall. The manufacturer may then recalculate his pricing policy to take account of his profit decline. He may make agreements with the wholesaler such that both their profits are maximized instead of allowing either of them to try to obtain all of the channel's pure profits.

[8] Same reference as footnote 7, at Chapter 7, Part II, Section B.

Vertical Price Relationship

The indeterminateness of the successive monopoly analysis (as the latter cannot predict price without knowing the nature of the members' agreement or disagreement), can be aided by an analysis by E. R. Hawkins.[9]

As well as assuming that the channel members know the shape of the final consumer demand curve, Hawkins assumes that they know the demand curves that they themselves face. (Of course, the consumer demand curve is the one faced by the retailer.) With this assumption he can arrive at the particular price at every level.

Monopsony and Oligopsony[10]

A monopsonistic or oligopsonistic channel member can obtain lower buying prices. His selling price depends on the market structure on his selling side. If it is competitive, he passes on his low buying price to the next level; and if it is not, he may simply increase his margin.

The mass retailer may be a monopsonist on some products and a competitor on others. He may also be a monopolist or competitor on his selling side, no matter what is his buying role.

Thus, he can be a monopsonist and a (seller) competitor with one product, and have a different combination with others. His role is often oligopsonist and competitor, and he would thus pass on his price savings to consumers.

Bilateral Monopoly and Bilateral Oligopoly[11]

Bilateral monopoly, where the selling channel member is a monopolist and the buying channel member is a monopsonist, is rare. Depending on the bargaining power of each, the price to the buying member may be lower or higher.

[9] E. R. Hawkins, "Vertical Price Relationship," in Cox and Alderson, Editors, Theory in Marketing (Homewood, Illinois: Richard D. Irwin, 1950), Chapter 11.
[10] Joe S. Bain, Pricing, Distribution and Employment (New York: Henry Holt and Company, 1953, revised edition), pp. 382–394.
[11] Richard B. Helflebower, "Mass Distribution: A Phase of Bilateral Oligopoly or of Competition?" in Robert D. Buzzell, Editor, Adaptive Behaviour in Marketing (Chicago: American Marketing Association, 1957); Fritz Machlup and Martha Taber, "Bilateral Monopoly, Successive Monopoly and Vertical Integration," Economica, Vol. 27 (May, 1960), pp. 101–117; Bain, same reference as footnote 10, at pp. 394–396.

One authority believes that price to the oligopsonist (or monopsonist) depends on who possesses the dominant bargaining power. If the monopolist (oligopolist) has it, then the price will be higher.

"It will be noted that the tendency of bilateral monopoly (between a monopolistic seller and a monopsonistic buyer who is in turn a monopolistic reseller) is to arrive at a price-quantity solution for the final market—to which the monopsonist resells—the same as would be reached if the monopolist and the monopsonist were members of a single firm with a monopoly in the final market. There are no added output restrictions because of the passage of the good first through a bilateral monopoly market on its way to the final market. . . . However, any monopolistic output restriction in a final market (where the buyer resells) will remain."[12]

But Wroe Alderson says that experience shows bilateral monopoly actually makes for a lower price to the consumer relative to monopoly.[13] It is from this ability to offer the consumer a low price, rather than the ability to exploit him with a monopoly price, that these large channel members derive their power.

Countervailing Power[14]

Countervailing power—the ability of a buying channel member to offset the power of a selling member when competition dissolves as a regulator—is similar to bilateral monopoly. However, proponents of this theory claim that big sellers automatically cause the rise of big buyers.

Various authors have discussed the validity of countervailing power.[15] In summary, it can be said that although there are various reasons for the rise of mass retailing and although these retailers are not always so effective in countervailing big producers, nevertheless countervailance is an important pricing-channel dynamic

Inventory Theory[16]

Inventory theory stresses the role of merchants' stocks in times of changing consumer demand:

1. The tendency of channel members to absorb increases in demand through inventory increases rather than price increases.
2. Their tendency to absorb demand decreases through price decreases rather than inventory decreases.

Price-Level Theory

It appears obvious that the level of prices (a macroeconomic rather than microeconomic concept) in one channel sector must influence the price level in another sector. However, this may not hold true for the short run.

One study concludes that short-run wholesale price index changes are not useful in predicting consumer prices, nor are they paralleled by retail price index changes.[17] Aside from purely structural differences in the make-up of these indexes, the difference is explained by the following: price variations of seasonal goods, differences in distribution costs at different channel levels, cumulating tendency of fixed percentage markup pricing, different competitive situations at different channel levels, varying level of inventories, desire of price stability, and different elasticities of buyers at various channel levels.

THE CHALLENGE TO THEORISTS

Quentin L. Coons' challenge to the economic theorist must be met.[18] And it must be met in a constructive fashion. There is a definite need to integrate marketing thought into economic theory—not only channel concepts, but concepts from all the marketing areas. Some of the attacks on marketing by economists are a direct result of this failure to integrate these concepts. Moreover, the meeting of this challenge will aid in the development of a marketing theory and increase the reality of economic theory.

[12] Same reference as footnote 10, at p. 485.
[13] Wroe Alderson, "Factors Governing the Development of Marketing Channels" in Richard M. Clewett, Editor, *Marketing Channels for Manufactured Products* (Homewood, Illinois: Richard D. Irwin, 1954), pp. 5–34.
[14] John K. Galbraith, *American Capitalism, The Concept of Countervailing Power* (Boston: Houghton Mifflin Co., 1956, revised edition), Chapter 9.
[15] For example, Alex Hunter, "Notes on Countervailing Power," *The Economic Journal*, Vol. 68 (March, 1958), pp. 89–103.

[16] Wilford J. Eiteman, *Price Determination* (Ann Arbor: Bureau of Business Research, Report No. 16, School of Business Administration, University of Michigan, 1949).
[17] Helen B. Jung and Theodore R. Gates, "Do Retail Prices Follow Wholesale Prices?" in Stanley C. Hollander, Editor, *Explorations in Retailing* (East Lansing: Michigan State University, 1959), pp. 48–51.
[18] Quentin L. Coons, "Marketing's Challenge to Economics," *Journal of Marketing*, Vol. 27 (July, 1963), pp. 11–15.

19. *Vertical Price Relationships*

E. R. HAWKINS

Unlike orthodox price theory, this paper assumes there are middlemen operating between the producer and consumer. This essay uses the theory of monopolistic competition to develop a theory which explains the interaction between prices at different levels of the marketing channel.

I. PRICES AT DIFFERENT LEVELS OF A CHANNEL

Although marketing men deal extensively with price problems and policies, it can scarcely be said that the study of marketing has developed any price theory. A vast amount of descriptive data has been accumulated; but few, if any, principles have evolved. Nor has the marketing literature on price policy received much illumination from economic theory. One reason is that much of the marketing material has been in the field of retail pricing, an area that has been ignored by orthodox economic theory.

John Stuart Mill explicitly stated that he was not dealing with prices in the retail market, and Alfred Marshall devoted only two pages and a footnote to retail prices.[1] Other economists, without being so explicit, have followed this lead. Economic theory in general has been written as though the producer sold directly to the consumer, in a market more like the wholesale than the retail market. The middleman has not been in the picture at all.

In recent years, hope of bridging the gap between economic theory and marketing has been offered by the development of the theory of monopolistic competition. This theory can

logically include advertising and sales promotion, since each seller is envisaged as being confronted with a negatively inclined demand curve and cannot sell all he wishes at "the market price." Unlike orthodox value theory, the theory of monolistic competition can deal with the discretion of the individual firm in establishing its price policies. And the retailer, who had to be excluded from the theory of pure competition because he is necessarily a monopolist by virtue of his location, can logically be included in the scope of the new theory.

Economists working with the theory of monopolistic competition have not, however, concerned themselves with the middleman and have continued to write as though goods were sold directly by the producer to the consumer. It is the purpose of this essay to use the theory of monopolistic competition to develop a theory of vertical price relationships, that is, the relationship between prices at different levels of the channel of distribution.

It is true that many economists themselves are losing faith in the theory of monopolistic competition, as well as in orthodox economic theory, and are directing their attention to realistic variables long known to marketing men.[2] But the field of marketing can contribute

• SOURCE: E. R. Hawkins, "Vertical Price Relationship," in Cox and Alderson (eds.), *Theory in Marketing* (Homewood, Ill.: Richard D. Irwin, 1950), Chapter 11. E. R. Hawkins, Johns Hopkins University.

[1] J. S. Mill, *Principles of Political Economy* (London: J. W. Parker, 1848), Bk. III, Chap. I, Sec. 5; A. Marshall, *Principles of Economics* (8th ed.; London: Macmillan & Co., 1927), pp. 451–52, 616 n.

[2] R. A. Lester, "Shortcomings of Marginal Analysis for Wage-Employment Problems," *American Economic Review*, XXXVI (1946), 63–82; and "Absence of Elasticity Considerations in Demand to the Firm," *Southern Economic Journal*, XIV (January, 1948), 285–89; H. M. Oliver, Jr., "Marginal Theory and Business Behavior," *American Economic Review*, XXXVII (1947), 375–83; R. A. Gordon, "Short-Period Price Determination in Theory and Practice," *American Economic Review*, XXXVIII (1948), 265–88; W.

to improvement of the theory by incorporating some of these variables in the formulation.

II. DEALER DEMAND

Under conditions of monopolistic competition, the rational retailer may be viewed as maximizing profits by equating marginal revenue and marginal cost in a situation in which there is a negatively inclined demand curve for each item he sells. It is often argued that retailers do not price in this fashion—that, instead, they apply the same percentage of markup to each item in the store or department. There appears to be some truth in both propositions. Retailers commonly use an average percentage of markup as a starting point in establishing prices, but the variations in observed markups as between different items are so numerous as to indicate that demand conditions are considered in setting the price.[3] For purposes of this discussion we shall assume that retailers do consider both demand and cost and attempt to price for maximum profit. With this assumption, we can them analyze the relationship between retail prices and prices at other levels.

It is obvious that the retailer's demand for goods sold by the wholesaler is derived from the consumers' demand curve confronting the retailer. The nature of this relationship may be seen in Figure 1.

The curve ANR is the net average revenue curve facing the retailer. It is the consumer demand curve minus any variable costs associated with the particular item, other than the cost of goods. Few retailers have made distribution cost analyses to measure these variable costs, and over realistic volume ranges it is likely that total costs do not increase appreciably with an increase in sales of one item; so ANR might be taken simply as the consumer demand curve. To this curve, draw the marginal revenue curve MR. The cost of goods to the retailer, AC_r, is identical with MC_r, unless the retailer is in a monopsonistic position. Now, if the retailer equates MC_r and MR, his demand

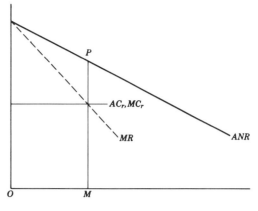

Fig. 1

prices must lie along MR, which is, therefore, the retailer's demand curve for the goods of the wholesaler.[4]

The wholesaler's demand may be similarly derived from the retailer's demand, and the whole structure of prices would appear as in Figure 2, which shows the simple case in which all dealers at the same level have identical or isoelastic AR curves and buy and sell at the same price. In this chart, AR_r is the aggregate consumer demand curve; MR_r is the summation of retailers' marginal revenue curves and is the aggregate retail demand curve; and MR_w is the summation of wholesalers' marginal revenue curves and is the manufacturer's average revenue curve. The manufacturer determines his production, OM, and his price, MP, by equating his own marginal cost and marginal revenue. When wholesalers are offered the goods at price MP, they equate this marginal cost with their marginal revenue and will buy quantity OM, reselling at price MP'. Retailers make the same kind of calculation; and, buying quantity OM at price MP', they will resell at price MP''. Where retailers' AR curves are not identical, the total demand facing the wholesalers will still be the summation of retailers' MR curves, although this may not be marginal to the aggregate consumer demand curve, and retailers will not all sell at the same price.

Fellner, "Average-Cost Pricing and the Theory of Uncertainty," *Journal of Political Economy*, LVI (June, 1948), 249–52.

[3] F. Machlup, "Marginal Analysis and Empirical Research," *American Economic Review*, XXXVI (1946), 519–54; and "Rejoinder to an Antimarginalist," *American Economic Review*, XXXVII (1947), 148–54.

[4] If the retailer's AR curve has appreciable changes in slope, the MR curve may contain "kinks," or may rise over part of its length. In this case, the MR curve is not directly the retailer's demand curve, since, for each case of multiple intersection of his MC and MR, he must determine which is the more profitable. The demand curve can be derived from AR by such a calculation.

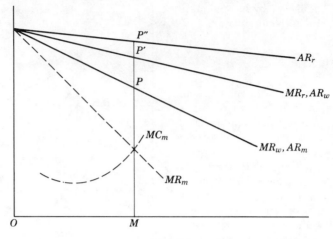

Fig. 2

III. IMPLICATIONS FOR THE MANUFACTURER

1. From this analysis, it is apparent that the dealer demand curve lies to the left of the consumer demand curve, which merely means that the manufacturer could sell directly to consumers at higher prices than to dealers, if consumers would buy as willingly from him. Of course, the manufacturer's cost of selling would be higher; the small volume of direct selling of consumers' goods suggests that in most cases the increase in cost would more than offset the increase in price.

2. More interesting and less obvious is the fact that the dealer demand curve is of different elasticity from the consumer demand curve. If the retailer's AR curve is a straight line, his MR curve will be less elastic throughout than the AR curve, at the same quantities. Of course, the MR curve may also be less elastic than the AR curve even if the latter is not a straight line. This means that, in this case, when the manufacturer reduces his price, dealers will not reduce their prices by the same amount. The prevalence of this condition seems to be indicated by the observed fact that retail prices do not move upward or downward as fast or as far as wholesale prices, although the explanation usually given is inertia and "stickiness" of retail prices. It should be noted that a policy of pricing on a fixed percentage of markup would not produce this result but would accentuate at the retail level any change in wholesale prices. Perhaps this is additional proof that retailers do not, in fact, price on a fixed percentage of markup, as is so often claimed.

It appears from this analysis that, when the manufacturer's MR curve is less elastic than his AR curve at equal quantities, a vertically integrated firm will more fully adjust retail prices to any change in cost at earlier stages of distribution. Figure 3 illustrates this. If the manufacturer has marginal cost MC_1 and is selling through retailers, his price to them will be MR and the retail price MP. If his marginal costs rise to MC_2, his price will be M_1D and the retail price M_1P_1. If the manufacturer were selling direct to consumers, however, his selling costs would be higher than in the case of sale to dealers. Although few manufacturers know the average variable selling costs associated with different volumes of an individual product, such costs do exist to a greater extent than is typically true in retailing. For purposes of comparison, let us assume that these marginal costs $M'C'_1$ are high enough so that, equated with marginal revenue MR_r, the retail price, MP, that would be established would be the same as in sales through dealers. If his marginal costs now rise by the same amount as assumed before, to $M'C'_2$, his retail price will rise to M_2P_2. This must be a higher price than the retail price M_1P_1 that would result if sales were made through retailers rather than directly, because in the latter case the higher marginal cost curve is applied to a more elastic marginal revenue curve than in the former case.

This kind of analysis may help to explain the observation that chain-store prices are more sensitive to wholesale price changes than are the prices of independent retailers.

But these conclusions apply only when the

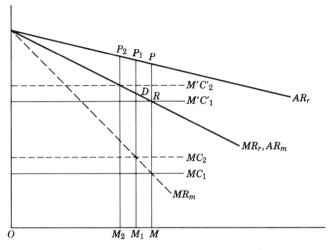

Fig. 3

manufacturer's MR curve is less elastic at equal quantities than his AR curve. Such need not be the case. In fact, if the AR curve loses slope appreciably, the MR curve may even become positive in certain segments. Likewise, if the manufacturer's marginal cost curve in direct selling were less elastic at equal quantities than in sales through retailers, then a rise in costs might, in the case of direct sale, increase the retail price the same as, or less than, in the case of sales through retailers. It would be possible to deduce the relationship between direct-selling prices and dealer prices for all possible elasticities of cost and demand.[5] This scarcely seems worthwhile in the absence of factual evidence as to the real elasticities in a given case. The general point may still be made, and with general significance, that vertically integrated organizations will not react to a primary price change in the same way as independent dealers, except in the unusual case where the elasticity of demand and cost give a coincidental result.

3. A complication arises if the retailer has, or thinks he has, an AR curve that is unaffected by competitors' price responses. Such a curve is generally more elastic than the total consumer demand for the manufacturer's product, since one dealer can take sales away from competitors by unmet price reductions. A single price-cutting dealer may therefore have a derived demand

[5] J. Robinson shows the geometry involved in all cases of change in demand or cost, under different conditions of elasticity (*Economics of Imperfect Competition* [London: Macmillan & Co., 1933], Chaps. IV and V).

curve for the product of the manufacturer that is more elastic than the total consumer demand curve. However, it is impossible that this should be true of all dealers, since, if they all attempted to price on AR curves ignoring competitors' responses, they would in fact move down along the aggregate consumer demand curve.

The pressure for resale price maintenance has come largely from dealers who want to enforce the oligopoly price equilibrium upon competitors who seek to expand their own sales at the expense of others.

IV. FAIR-TRADE PRICING

The manufacturer who establishes resale prices under fair-trade contracts has a double or triple pricing problem. He must determine not only his own price but also the prices of his dealers, and it is apparent that the relationships between prices at different levels must be properly adjusted. Suppose a manufacturer is selling to retailers at price MP (in Figure 4). The appropriate retail price is then MP', for that is the price at which retailers can sell quantity OM. If the manufacturer set the retail price at P_1, he would find he could not sell the volume OM, which had been calculated as the most profitable one. Similarly, although dealers would be receiving a larger markup per unit, their total revenue would not be so large as at the correct price. On the other hand, if the manufacturer set the retail price at P_2, dealers would sell quantity OM_2. They would make less profit than they would at price MP', and would ac-

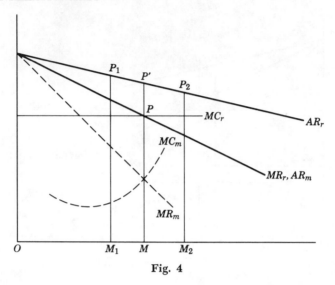

Fig. 4

cordingly sell above the fair-trade price, if permitted to do so by contract.[6]

If, however, retailers do accept the manufacturer's fair-trade retail price, either because of contract stipulation or because of pricing on estimated AR curves that do not allow for competitors' responses, then the vertical pricing problem becomes completely different. It is apparent that the manufacturer could allow the dealers zero, or even negative, margins if they would faithfully follow his stipulated retail price, sell all they could at that price, and buy that quantity from the manufacturer at whatever price he set. If zero margins were decided

[6] The California law—which has been copied substantially by Arizona, Illinois, Iowa, Kentucky, Louisiana, Maine, Massachusetts, Michigan, New Jersey, New Mexico, New York, North Dakota, Ohio, Oklahoma, Pennsylvania, Rhode Island, South Carolina, Tennessee, Virginia, Washington, and Wisconsin—authorizes the seller to impose a "stipulated resale price." The law drafted by the National Association of Retail Druggists—which has been adopted in Arkansas, Colorado, Georgia, Idaho, Indiana, Kansas, Maryland, Minnesota, Montana, Nebraska, Nevada, North Carolina, Oregon, South Dakota, Utah, West Virginia, and Wyoming (with some variations)—authorizes the setting of "minimum resale prices." See Zorn and Feldman, *Business under the New Price Laws* (New York: Prentice-Hall, Inc., 1937), pp. 299, 416–22. Even in states that have adopted the California law, however, many manufacturers use contracts that specify a "stipulated minimum price." E. T. Grether found that in January, 1935, average prices in independent stores were 5 per cent above the minimum contract prices ("Experience in California with Fair Trade Legislation Restricting Price Cutting," *California Law Review*, XXIV, 640).

upon, the manufacturer would establish his retail price by equating the consumer MR and his own MC, and would sell to retailers at that retail price.

The reason why this cannot be done, of course, is that at some point dealer resistance appears. If the margin becomes too small, dealers refuse to display or advertise the item, and may even drop it from their line. The adverse effect on the manufacturer's sales is something that he must consider in establishing his prices. In a moment, we shall examine the calculation that the manufacturer must make if he is willing to entertain the idea of active dealer resistance. Suppose, however, he plans to allow dealers margins just large enough so that they will be neutral toward his product, stocking it but neither pushing nor attempting to retard its sale. This is probably the most common situation in the market. In this case, the dealer demand curve is no longer marginal to the consumer demand curve but represents whatever margin below the fixed retail price is necessary to keep dealers neutral. This may well be a fixed and customary percentage of markup, in which case the dealer demand curve will be more elastic than the consumer demand curve, the dealer demand curve approaching the consumer demand curve at infinity. To this curve, the manufacturer draws a marginal curve, equates this with his marginal cost and arrives at price MP, with retail price MP'. (In Figure 5, a "neutral" markup of $33\frac{1}{3}$ per cent is shown as an example.)

It is possible, and even probable, that there is no one markup percentage that will keep dealers neutral, but a range. For example, re-

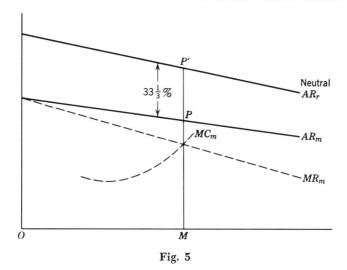

Fig. 5

tailers accustomed to a markup of 33⅓ per cent may remain neutral at any markup between 30 and 40 per cent. In this case, of course, the manufacturer should select the smallest neutral markup and regard that as defining his dealer demand curve.

We may now consider the effect of a dealer margin that does *not* keep dealers neutral in respect to the product. In Figure 6, the retail price MP' may be assumed as given, to begin with. To sell at this price, dealers will take different quantities, depending on the amount of margin allowed by the manufacturers' price to them. The quantities that they will take at different manufacturer's prices are shown by the dealers' demand curve AR_m, which is the manu-

facturer's average revenue curve associated with the retail price MP'. If the dealer markup is in the neutral range, dealers will take, and sell, the quantity indicated on the original consumer demand curve, AR_r. If the markup is smaller, dealers will discourage the sale of the product; and some will discontinue selling it, so that the quantities that they take, and sell, are less than shown on the original consumer demand curve for retail price MP'. On the other hand, if the dealer margin is large, they will push the item and will be able to sell the larger quantities indicated on the curve AR_m. The manufacturer finds his most profitable price to dealers in the usual fashion, by equating his MR and MC. In the situation shown in Figure 6, the manu-

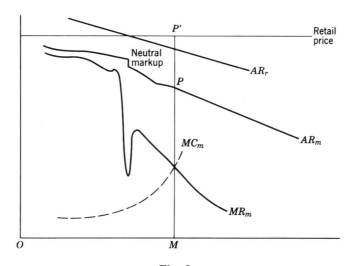

Fig. 6

facturer finds it to his advantage to allow dealers markups that are above normal.

For each possible retail price, the manufacturer has a different AR curve, representing the quantities he could sell to dealers at various markups for resale at that retail price. His final calculation must be to determine which retail price, with its appropriate price to dealers, offers him the largest profit.

The calculation that the dealer must make in each markup situation has been developed by the author elsewhere.[7]

V. MONOPSONY

We have noted that a monopolistic manufacturer might, in the short run, force dealers to sell at zero markup if the dealers had no alternatives. On the other hand, if dealers were to get together, openly or secretly, and boycott the manufacturer who does not offer adequate dealer margins, they might conceivably force the manufacturer to sell to them at prices that barely cover the manufacturer's costs. This would depend upon the manufacturer's alternatives, such as sales to different kinds of dealers or sales through his own retail stores.

The situation in which both parties are powerful, which is by no means uncommon, may be characterized as the case of monopsonistic-competitive buyers confronting a monopolistic-competitive seller. An example of this case is provided when an association of retailers faces a strong manufacturer with a well-advertised brand. Since the consumers expect retailers to

carry the brand, the manufacturer might force them to handle it at low profit margins. In the extreme case (if we exclude negative margins), the manufacturer might force dealers to sell the item at no markup at all. In Figure 7, the manufacturer would establish the retail price MQ by equating his own MC and the retailer MR. He would sell to retailers at this same price. The retailers, however, if monopsonistically organized, would attempt to buy quantity OM at price MR, which is just sufficient to keep the manufacturer in business. The area of bargaining is between the two prices, MQ and MR, the actual price depending on the alternatives of the parties and their relative knowledge and negotiating skill.

This extreme case is unlikely, however, because dealers' associations are seldom, if ever, strong enough to present the manufacturer with an "all-or-nothing" proposition. More common is the case of Figure 6, where the manufacturer can sell different quantities at various dealer markups and where any monopsonistic influence is shown merely by the more rapid rate at which the manufacturer's sales decline at markups that are below normal. The manufacturer's price decision is then made as discussed above.

With reference again to Figure 7, however, even if the monopsonistic association is a tight one, a compromise price can be established if we remove the assumption of a fixed retail price. Then the retailers' demand curve becomes MR_r, and the manufacturer finds his price to dealers, $M'P'$, by equating MR_m and MC_m. If dealers are monopsonistic, however, they will not agree to this price. Instead, they will recognize that, if they flatly name a price to the manufacturer and if he has no better alternative markets, he

[7] E. R. Hawkins, "Further Theoretical Considerations Regarding Fair Trade Laws," *Journal of Marketing*, IV (October, 1939), 126–34.

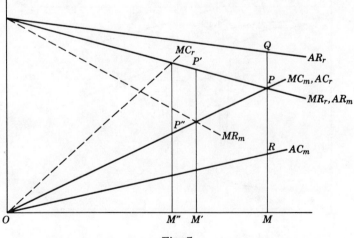

Fig. 7

will determine the quantity he is willing to sell at that price by equating it with his marginal cost. The curve MC_m is, therefore, his supply curve and the retailers' AC curve. The retailers' marginal cost, MC_r, equated with the retailers' own marginal revenue MR_r, establishes the price $M''P''$ as the one they are willing to pay, and the quantity OM'' as the desired quantity. The reasonable compromise price in this case is MP, for it is the only one at which both parties would agree on the quantity to be sold. That is, if either knew price MP to be the best he could get, he would want to deal in quantity OM; MP is the only price at which it is possible for both the manufacturer and the retailers to equate marginal cost and marginal revenue at the same volume. Also, the corresponding retail price MQ is the one that will extract the greatest total revenue from consumers, over the manufacturing costs. This price MQ is, accordingly, the retail price that dealers and the manufacturer would agree on if they got together and decided to maximize their joint profits. It is true that this price MP does not yield the manufacturer so much profit as his preferred price, $M'P'$, nor does it yield the retailers as much as their choice, $M''P''$. On the other hand, it is more advantageous to each of them than the price the other originally proposed, and it is a reasonable compromise price because they can agree on quantity.

VI. CONCLUSION

It is recognized that the foregoing conclusions apply only to the extent that manufacturers and dealers possess the necessary knowledge and seek maximum profits, and that, for many reasons, these assumptions are not completely true. Nevertheless, it is believed that there is sufficient validity in the assumptions to make the analysis meaningful, especially to those who are faced with the practical problems discussed and who have, to date, no theoretical principles on which to base a solution. It might be argued that the principles developed here constitute not "marketing theory" but economic theory. But economic theory applied to marketing problems may, in the end, turn out to be a large part of "marketing theory."

20. Mass Distribution: A Phase of Bilateral Oligopoly or of Competition?

RICHARD B. HEFLEBOWER

Do mass distributors pass along their oligopolistic powers to consumers in a competitive selling market? One of the key concepts required in answering this question is that of "bargaining power." Channel structure is another important idea which could aid understanding in this area.

That consumers benefit from mass distribution is quite generally accepted by economists, but both the source of those gains and the theoretical framework within which to place them are in dispute. Some contend that the benefits stem from the large, low-price retail organizations' ability to offset monopoly at the manufacturing level which is combined with such competition in reselling that the savings are passed forward to consumers.[1] Others emphasize the low operating costs of these mass distributors which competition forces them to reflect in prices to consumers.[2] Finally, some point out the more specific influence on suppliers' prices of mass distributors' actual or potential entry into manufacturing combined with the provision by them of lower priced alternatives for consumers.[3]

Parallel disagreement exists as to the theoretical framework most appropriate for analyzing the facts about mass distributors as buyers and resellers. Galbraith's "countervailing power" concept or dogma, according to one's liking, has been held to be nothing more than bilateral oligopoly (Stigler, pages 12, 13, and Miller, page 21). If it is, it would not follow, *ipso facto*, that consumers would benefit (Stigler, page 9). If chain stores buy advantageously as oligopsonists, are they not also oligopolistic resellers who would retain those gains for themselves? Others avoid this problem by arguing that chain stores buy primarily from competitive industries and sell in a competitive market; hence, their role falls under that expounded in competitive price theory (Stigler, pages 9, 13, and Miller, page 21).

THE ORGANIZATIONAL REVOLUTION IN DISTRIBUTION

There should be no mystery about what gave rise to chain store and mail-order distributors. They started as small ventures to take advantage of an attractive spread between the costs and expected revenues in the type of business they proposed to do. They could not have been a countervailing influence until their growth had substantially reshaped the buying side of the manufacturer-level market for consumer

• SOURCE: Reprinted from *The American Economic Review*, XLVII, No. 2 (May, 1957; Papers and Proceedings of the Sixty-ninth Annual Meeting of the American Economic Association, Cleveland, Ohio, December 27–29, 1956), 274–85. Copyright 1957. Used by permission. Richard B. Heflebower, Professor of Economics, Northwestern University.
[1] J. K. Galbraith, *American Capitalism: The Concept of Countervailing Power* (1952), p. 131.
[2] G. J. Stigler, "The Economist Plays With Blocs," *American Economic Review*, May, 1954, p. 12, and "Comment" by M. A. Adelman, *ibid.*, p. 33.
[3] Clair Wilcox, "On the Alleged Ubiquity of Oligopoly," AEA *Papers and Proceedings*, May, 1950, p. 71; J. P. Miller, "Competition and Countervailing Power: Their Roles in the American Economy," *ibid.*, May, 1954, p. 21; and R. B. Heflebower in *Monopoly and Competition and Their Regulation* (1954, E. H. Chamberlain, editor), pp. 126–127.

goods. That they did grow to their present stature reflects the success of two innovations:

1. Taking advantage of developments in transportation and communication, they co-ordinated wholesaling and retailing within one ownership rather than through market trans-actions. This organizational change, along with rationalization of the retailing operation, re-sulted in a new and substantially lower pro-duction function for carrying out the total distributive operation.

2. From their beginnings, the enterprises that blossomed into the mass distributors offered a new and less costly product, in the sense of less retail service, for which there seems to have been a tremendous latent demand. They pioneered in offering a lesser variety to choose from and in concentrating on volume items sold on low mar-gins,[4] and in selling not only for cash and with-out delivery but also with less prompt service. Preceding competition had vailed to provide for the sale of two or more such products at dif-ferent prices in the same store, or in varying types of outlets, to as large a degree as the mass distributors found that consumers wanted.

Because the new production function and the less expensive service reduced their operating costs far below those of rivals, the mass distrib-utors were able to thrive with much lower gross margins. The Federal Trade Commission report (pages 670–701) showed that in the 1929–31 period the gross margin of food chains, when weighted by the chain store volume, was 5 to 6 percentage points below the combined whole-saler-retailer margins. (The differences for drug-store items were far more striking.) Even ten years later, in 1941, the gross margin of food chains was about 12 per cent of retail prices lower than the combined margins of a retailer and full service wholesaler of groceries and about 7 per cent below that of a retailer-cooperative wholesaler channel.[5]

This lower store-wide margin is the signifi-cant test of the mass distributors' performance. It abstracts from their lower buying prices to the extent that they were obtained. By being a lower charge for an acceptable quality of re-tailing service, it makes irrelevant the accusation that consumers were deluded by prices on loss leaders as an index of the savings that could be obtained on other articles.

Such lower margins, which caused higher priced channels of distribution to lose volume, set in motion fundamental adjustments in dis-tribution. Self-service and cash and carry re-tailing of prepackaged goods has become general for foods and quite widespread for some other products. More important has been a funda-mental reorganization of distribution in most product areas where the retail firm is too small to perform what remains necessary of the whole-saler's function. Groups of retailers contract with a wholesaler for that service or form their own co-operative buying and wholesaling organization. The accompanying sharp re-duction in invoice cost to retailers (preliminary findings in a study now being made by the author indicate that the margins for such whole-sale operations are only a half or even a third or less of those of autonomous service wholesalers) is an indication of the savings from integration. Consequently, by an old-fashioned competitive adjustment, but one consisting primarily of a change in the organization of distribution and not by countervailance, an able retailer's prices can come close to and perhaps equal in some cases those of his chain store rivals.

STRUCTURE OF THE SUPPLIER-MASS DISTRIBUTOR MARKETS

So much for the organizational revolution spearheaded by the mass distributors; the next step is to describe the character of the markets in which they buy and their role therein. Here

---

[4] This is the rationale of Federal Trade Commis-sion's finding (*Chain Stores, Final Report on the Chain-Store Investigation*, 1934, pp. 67–71) that chains' margins were much lower when weighted by their volume in various products than when independent store weights were used.

[5] Office of Temporary Controls, *Economic Data Series*, No. 26, reports the average chain food store gross margin to have been 16.7 per cent of net sales in 1941 and that of the service wholesalers to have been 14.0 per cent. Independent retailer and co-operative and cash and carry wholesalers' margins for 1941 were not published, but the author recalls that the OPA survey showed an average margin (on sales) of between 16 and 17 per cent for the independent retailers and of from

5 to 7 per cent for these types of wholesalers. Be-cause a larger percentage of the chains' volume is made up of large-volume low-margin items, these store-wide differences in gross margins probably overstate differences in what consumers paid for identical commodities. But that there is a sub-stantial difference is shown by the lower retail margins on specific categories of food stores pro-vided for chains than for other than very large independent stores by the wartime OPA and the Korean period OPS. In the case of all but very large independent stores the retailer would, in addition, have had to buy from a wholesaler at an additional margin.

is where bilateral oligopolies may exist but there is no way of indicating adequately how a market is organized and operates except by intensive study of it. Concentration ratios, if industries are properly delineated, however, provide a list of oligopoly suspects.

Even on that basis (and using in most cases the census industry categories which are far from a satisfactory classification for this purpose), the food manufacturing industries cannot be blanketed into the nonconcentrated. The following all have concentration ratios of approximately 50 or above: sugar, shortening, margarine, salad dressings, soap, corn products, evaporated (excluding condensed) milk, cheese assembling, cookies and crackers, perishable bakery products, chocolate and cocoa products, breakfast cereals, salt, flour mixes, and baby foods.[6] On the basis of information provided to the author by a market research organization, it appears that these products constitute about 10 per cent of the dollar volume of the typical food store and about 33 per cent of dry grocery segment of that volume.[7]

The list of department and "hard goods" store products supplied by concentrated industries includes electrical appliances, tires and batteries,[8] hard surface floor covering, sewing machines, miscellaneous household furniture, small arms, photographic equipment, and vacuum cleaners. Undoubtedly still more products would be added if product definitions were confined to those relevant for price making.

Despite the length of these lists, which are longer than those cited by Stigler (page 12), the available information indicates that probably far more than half of the volume of mass distributors consists of products supplied by

less concentrated and distinctly competitive industries. Beyond the categories reviewed here, nearly all apparel and furniture suppliers can be bracketed in the competitive category.

The evidence as to the oligopsonistic position of the mass distributors is not very impressive either, since most supplying markets are national in scope. Concentration in food buying from manufacturers and assemblers of unprocessed foods has become substantial but not high. The four largest chains' total sales accounted for 19 per cent of total food store sales in 1955, as reported by the Department of Commerce. The largest ten handled 27 per cent. To get a total retail volume to compare with that of the department store type of mass distributors, department store volume must be combined with that of stores selling other lines handled by mail-order and low-price chain organizations. Of such a total, Sears Roebuck accounts for about 9 per cent and adding Ward's, Penney's, and Allied Stores makes the total for the four organizations to be 17 per cent of national volume.[9] For ten companies the percentage is 23. These are low concentration ratios.

Such product-wide and retail-outlet-wide data obscure an important and likely complementary relationship between firms of opposite size rankings on the two sides of the market. There is considerable evidence that mass distributors tend to buy from small manufacturers and large manufacturers to sell primarily to small firms in the distributive trades. Some business executives refer to this as the logical arrangement, for the mass distributor provides an outlet for the firms whose age and size are such that they have not successfully differentiated their products, or are unable to get stable operating rates through a large number of small orders. Even financing and product design may be provided by the buyer. Obversely, the small retailer sells under the aura of the manufacturer's brand, which also may enable him to obtain a higher margin. And the large manufacturer can get the stability of numerous orders from small resellers. But for a large manufacturer to rely on a few large mass distributors would place participants on each side of the

---

[6] Except for salad dressings, perishable bakery products, flour mixes, and baby foods, the concentration ratios are from Appendix II, Table II, "Study of Monopoly Power," *Hearings* of House Subcommittee on Study of Monopoly Power (81st Cong., Serial No. 14, Part 2-B). The exceptions just listed are for narrower categories than those used by the census. The author's judgment that they all have a concentration ratio of at least 50 is based on information from a variety of sources, mostly published.

[7] The percentage of food store volume is converted to a percentage of dry grocery volume by dividing by the ratio (.3) of grocery volume to all food store volume, as reported in the 1948 *Census of Business*, Volume II, *Retail Trade: General Statistics*, p. 16.02.

[8] Outlets built around the line of some other manufacture, such as manufacturer-owned tire stores or refinery-brand gasoline service stations, are mass distributors for present purposes.

[9] More relevant for these distributors than in the case of those selling food is the question of how adequately company-wide sales figures can be related to the store categories used by the Department of Commerce. Some checking with officials of mass-distribution type of department stores indicates that the percentages quoted above are too high by several points.

market in a precarious position in the event of a bargaining stalemate.

From this hasty review emerges a picture of manufacturer-distributive buyer markets with varied combinations and degrees of concentration or of nonconcentration on one or on both sides of the market. Even assuming that size distribution as crudely measured forecasts behavior, such a varied set of market organizations gives rise to a series of questions of which only a few can be explored here.

MASS DISTRIBUTORS AS BUYERS AND SUPPLIERS

The role of mass distributors as buyers is not shown solely by their size distribution; each of the following aspects of the supplier-mass distributor relationship potentially could have a strong effect on the cost of the goods they retail: (1) the multiproduct character of mass distribution; (2) the mass distributors as private branders; and (3) the mass distributors as potential entrants into the supplying industry.

1. There is a marked asymmetry between the horizontal scope of products handled by the mass distributor and that offered by the typical supplier, a fact which may affect relative bargaining power of these two parties. Whether it does depends on consumers' buying habits and the strength of their preferences for particular brands. In the case of "shopping goods"—furniture and most clothing, for example—where brand preferences are not strong, the advantage should lie with the mass distributor for he does not have to handle a particular supplier's product. Of a different sort are such products as appliances, tires, and batteries, for which there are well-known manufacturers' brands. But such brands are rarely handled by mass distributors for reasons that would take too much space to explore here. The mass distributors do, however, succeed with their own brands at times as will be seen under "2."

This leaves the convenience good category, or products bought frequently and in small dollar amounts. Most consumers either buy a basketful of such articles at a time or habitually return to the same store. Each article bought is part of a joint demand for the service of retailing a variety of articles at one time or over a period of time. If the consumer does not find the article she expects at a type of store—shortening in a grocery store or the brand she strongly prefers, Crisco—the quality of the retailing service is lessened in her view. She may go elsewhere

unless the price differential is sufficiently attractive.

This does not mean that a retailer of convenience goods is a mere order-taker. For many commodities consumers have no strong preference for one brand over several others and for some products, such as sugar, no brand preference at all. The manufacturer of such a line is a beggar at the retailer's office and fights for preferred space and selling effort once he is admitted. Even a strongly preferred brand can be put on the bottom shelf and one with a longer margin at eye level. All such alternatives are more promising for the mass distributor for he often can sell successfully under his own or "private label."

2. In most commodity fields mass distributors put their brand on a wide variety of products as more or less a routine matter, but their major economic influence is where differentiation (by the manufacturers) has been marked but can be eroded. Prior to that erosion, these cases are the epitome of textbook differentiation, whether the article be margarine, or coffee, or electrical appliances. But once the quality of such products has become generally satisfactory to consumers and an established part of the expenditure pattern of a large percentage of families, they are ripe for the "A & P" or "Sears" treatment. This involves purchasing (or manufacturing) the goods at an efficient operator's factory cost plus a few percentage points profit, placing the distributor's brand on the goods, and reselling the articles on a margin about equal to or perhaps above that actually obtained by independent retailers on manufacturers' brands.

The resulting retail price of the distributor's brand runs from as little as 5 to as high as 10 or even 15 per cent below that for well-known manufacturers' brands. Under the conditions specified, consumers flock to the low-price mass retailers' brands. Herein lies most of Sears' (and to a lesser degree other companies') influence on prices of appliances and tires and auto accessories and of A & P's (and other food chains') effects on coffee, margarine, and (quite recently) on frozen orange juice and instant coffee. This is clearly a dynamic process and one which has had a marked effect on the elasticity of the revenue curves of manufacturers.

While this private branding role has been powerful for a substantial number of commodities and of lesser influence for a larger number of other articles, it has had only nominal influence on cigarettes, candies, cosmetics, and drugs generally. The factory cost-retail price spread for these articles invites the treatment sketched above. But no such successful private branding move has been made either because no type of mass distributor has a large enough stake in the commodity—this may be the situation in cigarettes—or, more likely, because the consumer cannot be wooed by the price differential that is feasible.

3. Except in the type of case just considered, the mass distributor is a potential entrant into the supplying industry for in doing so it would have two advantages over most new manufacturers. (a) The mass distributor provides a ready-made reseller demand and merely by displaying the products under its own brand can move a large volume. (b) The mass distributor can supply sufficient capital to build a plant of efficient size.

Beyond that, the operating costs of the mass distributor's plant are often affected favorably by the limited product line it is called upon to manufacture compared to that autonomous suppliers ordinarily find it necessary to offer. In part, this is possible because mass distributors usually sell a smaller variety of items in a product line. Often, in addition, the owned plant makes a still narrower range of items and the mass distributor turns to independent sources for small-volume items in the product line.

Actually much of what full entry would accomplish can be attained by steps short of owning and operating manufacturing plants. The mass distributor may buy raw materials and contract for their processing into consumer goods. Or the same may be done on a cost-plus contract with a manufacturer which may cover a period long enough to amortize the supplier's investment in special equipment. These are the various degrees of entry which the mass distributor can execute whenever the supply situation is unsatisfactory.

Monopoly may or may not be the source of that dissatisfaction. Many of the food plants owned by chain food stores are in such competitive industries as jam and jelly manufacture. Department store chains own or develop sponsored suppliers of some furniture and apparel items. Either the supplying industries are inefficient or significant economies can be obtained by vertical co-ordination through ownership. Other cases, such as in bread baking, are composite of local market oligopoly, of an outmoded distribution method, and of union influence on wholesale distribution costs. Still others represent genuine monopoly of the sort which forced Sears and Ward into their early manufacturing ventures.

Regardless of the reason, wherever the product is important in volume and the prevailing margin between the costs of efficient manufacturing and retail price is inviting, the chains are in a position to move in. Their failure to do so is *prima facie* evidence that the supplying industry is competitive and efficient. That is, this conclusion is valid unless the product is unimportant or consumers are so strongly wedded to established brands that a large volume cannot be sold advantageously under a distributor's brand.

MASS DISTRIBUTORS AS RESELLERS

Much of what is written about competition in retailing misses the point about the mass distributors as sellers. There is, of course, the locational advantage of particular stores, but it is small because of the increased mobility of consumers as purchasers. Furthermore, it is a characteristic of independent stores as well.

The real issue is whether the revenue curve of the typical outlet of a mass distributor is sloped significantly because of consumers' preferences for that company's outlets. This seems unlikely given the price appeal basis of competition, which places mass distributors at the most competitive end of a continuum of retailers offering different combinations of product quality and price. Adelman comes to this view, but only after reviving for a moment the view of smallness and waste in distribution often derived from Chamberlin's large-numbers case. Added considerations include the mass distributors' invasion of each other's markets and the rather favorable entry and expansion possibilities for small operators in the multiproduct distributive trades. The latter has been aided by the success of small retailing firms in developing group buying or co-operatively-owned wholesale organizations which, together with other steps taken as retailers, enables them to acquire a production function and offer a type of retailing service which approaches that of the mass distributors. Finally, and overriding the preceding considerations, is the distinctly inelastic marginal cost curve of all types of retailers at volume rates in the neighborhood of those planned, a fact which makes each seller sensitive to loss of volume.

Cost pressure of this sort is more apt to affect prices when one recognizes the impediments to conjectural interdependence among multiprod-uct retailers. That such conjectural interdepend-ence must be appraised is indicated by the fact that concentration in retailing in particular urban markets is far higher than for the nation as a whole. This is most evident in food retailing. In 1948, for example, A & P sold more than 40 per cent of the foodstore volume in 23 cities and more than 20 per cent in 102 other cities. But even then conjectural interdependence would be inhibited for the product is a variable composite of the commodity and its brand, of the reputation of the store, and of the service it offers. It is difficult to conceive of conjectural independence as a significant restraint on alter-ing the variable components of such a product. Second, with the stores selling hundreds of com-modities and thousands of items, on any one of which the margins may be varied as a business-getting device, the difficulties of conjectures as to what rivals will do and the opportunities for independent actions are compounded.

Such considerations as have been reviewed here provide some but not full support to a con-clusion that whether mass distributors buy as oligopsonists or not, they resell in essentially competitive markets. Strength is added to such a conclusion by Adelman's view of the retailers' product as a retailing service for a broad cate-gory of goods and the price as the storewide gross margin. But neither what has been said here nor in the preceding papers constitutes adequate demonstration of the shape of the individual mass distributor's revenue curve. In the later discussion, nevertheless, the assump-tion is made that that curve in the moderately long run is not far from horizontal.

BILATERAL OLIGOPOLY
OR COMPETITION?

Since there is no well-articulated theory of bilateral oligopoly, the literature on bilateral monopoly must be drawn on for guidance. The latter indicates that the level of price to the final buyer and the division of profits between the monopolist (supplier) and monopsonist (distributor) will be influenced by the elasticity of the supplier's marginal cost curve, the elas-ticity of the marginal value product curve of the distributor-buyer as a reseller, and the relative bargaining power of the protagonists. No stand is taken here on the first of these. Whether the distributive buyer has the bargaining advantage or not, his marginal revenue curve—the unique component of his marginal value product curve

—is assumed to be so elastic that he tends to compete away his gains to the benefit of con-sumers. Where the bargaining advantage lies in markets that are properly denoted oligopolies depends on a variety of circumstances that can best be identified by use of the following cate-gories of market types.

1. Oligopoly-like Supplying Industries Selling to Generally Less Oligoposony-like Mass Distributors

These are the markets in which bilateral oligopoly influences on the prices which mass distributors pay their suppliers are most likely. But the above analysis suggests that two major subtypes should be identified:

(a) Those for which the mass distributors cannot develop a route around the demands of the suppliers. The obstacle may be the strength of consumer preference for manufacturers' brands which would inhibit private branding by the mass distributor, that there is no small-firm fringe of the supplying industry from which to buy, or that the product is not important enough for the mass distributor to become his own supplier.

Under these circumstances, the bargaining ad-vantage appears to be with the suppliers. Beyond the considerations just cited, which weaken the mass distributor's bargaining power, it seems probable that in a number of the sup-plying industries there is distinctly more con-centration and similarity of interests among sellers than in the corresponding distributive industry.

To the degree that mass-distributors' buying prices are above the competitive level in such cases, this does not mean a more than pro-portionately higher retail price. On the assump-tion that mass distributors' margins are at the competitive level, they could only "pass through" oligopolistic influences on the cost of goods resold.

(b) Those for which the mass distributor can escape the demands of oligopolistic suppliers. Among the methods of doing so are: buying from a small-firm fringe of the supplying industry, buying from oligopolists at discriminatory prices and placing the mass distributor's brand on the goods, or integrating into the supplying industry.

In this type of situation the bargaining power of the mass distributor exceeds that of the sup-plier because the asymmetry of breadth of commodity coverage strengthens the multi-product mass distributor's hand. It makes little difference whether one concludes that the opportunities for going around the oligopoly mean that the supplying industry is not in fact oligopolistic, or that the fear of entry or actual entry holds down the oligopolists' prices. The result, particularly where private branding is successful, is probably a competitive price to the mass distributor (or even lower as will be seen in a moment) plus a competitive distributive margin.

When the mass distributors have superior bargaining power, whether viewed as the outcome of a bilateral oligopoly or of these distributors' individual ability to award or take away a sizable increment of a supplier's volume, the stage is set for discriminatory prices. In the absence of effective legal restraints—discriminatory prices are the major target of the Robinson-Patman Act—or of such a degree of disappearance of the so-called "independent" sector of the distributive trades that manufacturers' supercompetitive profits in sales to them no longer counterbalance the low margins on sales to mass distributors, there could be a more or less enduring price structure favorable to the mass distributors.

2. Oligopoly-like Supplying Industry and Competitive-like Distributive Trade

Potentially the results of such a market are more like that of "1a" than of "1b"; the supplying industry can obtain prices above the competitive level but the distribution is done on a competitive margin. The resulting differences in retail prices would reflect only the differences in the cost of rendering differing qualities of retail services. But such a conclusion would be extreme, for such oligopsony-like buyers as mass distributors are more apt to and should be more successful in paring oligopolistic suppliers' prices than would a competitive buying trade. And of course the conclusion that mass distributors resell at a competitive margin may be invalid, but at most only to a small degree.

It is true that the retailer-owned co-operative organizations attempt some of the methods outlined under "1b" for escaping the level of prices charged by oligopolistic suppliers. To the extent that they succeeded, they move toward category "1b." It is the author's judgement that they have not yet been as successful in such moves as have the large mass distributors.

3. Competitive-like Suppliers Selling to Oligopsony-like Mass Distributors

The major issue with respect to markets of this sort is whether mass distributors are able to buy discriminatively and if so whether consumers benefit correspondingly. Under the assumption made earlier as to competition among sellers, discriminatory buying prices obtained by mass distributors would be reflected in retail prices. In the longer run, consumers would lose only if the reduction of volume by the smaller-scale retailers were to bring about such concentration among mass distributers that the assumption that they resell in a competitive market would become untenable.

Most manufacturing industries experience, however, periods of general excess capacity and much of the time some firms would like to sell more at the prevailing price. There is enough imperfection in these markets that (uniform) prices are not driven down along the marginal cost curve and opportunity for price discrimination exists. The likelihood of such discrimination is augmented by the size of orders that particular informed buyers can place.

But adjustments in the capacities of the supplying industry—facilitated, of course, by a rising level of demand—should eliminate such opportunities in time. If suppliers' profits are below the level necessary to induce investment, the capacity should fall relative to demand. Or if discriminatory prices are given some sellers, the movement of investment in a competitive industry (but not necessarily in an oligopoly) should be toward selling in the more profitable market segment and vice versa. Consequently the supply sources for buyers who had been getting discriminatory prices should dry up.

4. Competitive-like Suppliers Selling to Competitive-like Distributive Trades

This category is listed merely to round out the picture. It does not involve the issues to which this paper is addressed.

Only with respect to one of the above categories does the bilateral oligopoly framework assist analysis materially. It was not designed, of course, for categories "2," "3," or "4" because in each of them at least one side of the supplier-distributive trade market is competitive by definition. In category "1a," where the mass distributor is not able to escape the demands of suppliers, the bilateral oligopoly framework focuses attention on the significant variables.

These are the effect of relative bargaining power of the mass distributors on his invoice cost and of the elasticity of his marginal revenue on the size of his distributive margin. It might seem that in "1b" where bargaining power is reversed, bilateral oligopoly theory would be useful. But not only because of the embryonic state of that theory, but also because an expanded theory of competition would be distinctly adequate, the latter is to be preferred.

What is required and effective in such cases is to expand the concept of competition beyond that of mere price and output adjustments for a given product in a market with a given organization. Not merely is the product a variable, historically and for tactical purposes, but the organization is, also. Indeed, the adaptability of organization to profit opportunities has been uniquely important with respect to the distributive trades and their relation to, or participation in, the supplying industries.

All of this opens a large area of research. Where estimates of the significance of types of organization or of results have been given above, they are based on far from satisfactory data. For that reason, and because the validity of the assumption as to the elasticity of the mass distributors' revenue curves has not been demonstrated, no estimate was made of the net effect of mass distributors on retail prices. Testing that assumption will require appraisal of the whole spectrum of differing retail products and of the cross-elasticities of demand and of supply among them, particularly when those elasticities are viewed over a period long enough for organizational changes to be effected.

21. Vertical Integration in Marketing

ROBERT COLE

This paper records the advantages and disadvantages to firms and consumers of forward and backward vertical integration. Included in the advantages are decreased marketing expenses, control over distribution, easier branding, lower prices, better servicing. Included in the disadvantages are inflexibility and rigidity, increased inventory, managerial limitations.

POSSIBLE ADVANTAGES

To Firms That Adopt a Vertical Type of Organization

In attempting to summarize the advantages that may accrue to a vertically integrated firm, many offsetting factors are found. Thus, it is difficult to offer a complete set of advantages that are applicable to all firms or to the same firm at all times. There are outstanding variations among different types of industries, with widespread fluctuations in the age, the availability of capital, previous integration activities, and management ability of firms operating in the different branches of any industry. Recognition also should be given to the variation between purposes which motivate firms to integrate "forward" or "backward."[1] The direction of the integration movement and the purposes for the action have an important effect upon the advantages that such integration may secure for a concern. In addition, consideration should be given to the external factors[2] that often arise

and play a dominant role in determining whether a firm will be able to secure any of the advantages of a vertically integrated type of organization.

The following list of possible advantages that may accrue to a firm operating under a vertical integration type of organization has been compiled from information furnished by business executives and from data contained in published studies on the vertical integration movement.

1. Additional profit margins.
2. Decreased marketing expenses.
3. Stability of operations.
4. Certainty of materials and supplies.
5. Better control of product distribution.
6. Gratification of personal ambitions.
7. Quality control of products.
8. Prompt revision of production and distribution policies.
9. Better inventory control.
10. Ability to apply brand names to items produced and to enjoy the advantages therefrom.
11. Opportunity for increased research facilities.
12. Greater buying power.
13. Ability to secure better trained personnel.

To the Consumer

The vertically integrated type of organization may benefit the consumer in many ways. The question as to whether vertical integration actually does result in an advantage to the consumer should be carefully explored, in order to establish one of the basic criteria to measure the success of any integrated operation.

• SOURCE: Robert Cole, *Vertical Integration in Marketing* (Urbana, Ill.: University of Illinois, College of Commerce and Business Administration, Bureau of Business and Economic Research, 1952), from pp. 11, 28, 30, 96–98. Robert Cole, Assistant Professor of Marketing, University of Illinois.
[1] Transactions which increase vertical integration have been designated as "forward" or "backward," depending upon whether the stages of distribution or production that are combined under one control extend the acquiring firm's operations nearer to the ultimate consumer markets or nearer to the original raw material markets.
[2] These external factors include such occurrences as business cycle fluctuations, legislative action,

changing competitive conditions within the industry, periods of extreme currency inflation, and war.

Three possible advantages that vertical integration may furnish to the consumer are:

1. Lower prices.
2. Maintenance of quality.
3. Better servicing of products.

POSSIBLE DISADVANTAGES

To Firms That Adopt a Vertical Type of Organization

A vertically integrated organization may experience many disadvantages from such an arrangement. In fact, the possible disadvantages may have the effect of causing a firm to decide against combining two or more stages of distribution or production under its control. It should be recognized that the disadvantages listed will not always be viewed in the same manner by firms in the same industry. Nor will one concern look upon these disadvantages in the same light at different periods of time. Factors which may be influential in causing one company to decide against vertical integration may have little influence in the decision of another concern. The following list of possible disadvantages that may face a vertically integrated firm has likewise been compiled from information provided by business executives and from published studies.

1. Managerial limitations.
2. Inflexibility of operations.
3. Inability of some marginal firms to operate profitably in a vertically integrated setup.
4. Restrictions upon variety.
5. Disparity between stages of operation.
6. Difficulty in breaking into new fields of endeavor.
7. Increased inventory holdings.
8. Public opinion and governmental action.
9. Increased inequality in margins and "leaders."
10. Lack of specialization.

SUMMARY AND CONCLUSIONS

Vertical integration is not the panacea for all the ills of American business. It is not the "open sesame" to assured profits and continuous prosperity. But it is the means through which many firms in many lines of business have been able to provide the American consumer with goods of high quality at prices lower than would otherwise be available.

Many factors arise when an attempt is made to summarize the advantages that may accrue to a vertically integrated firm. Thus, it is difficult to set forth a complete set of advantages that are applicable to all firms or to the same firm at all times. There are outstanding variations among different types of industries, with widespread fluctuations in the age, availability of capital, previous integration activities, and management ability of individual firms. There is also widespread variation between the purposes which motivate firms to integrate "forward" or "backward." The direction of the integration movement and the purposes for such action have an important effect upon the advantages that such integration may provide for a concern. In addition, consideration must be given to the external factors that often arise and play a dominant role in determining whether a firm will be able to secure any of the advantages of a vertically integrated type of organization.

A vertically integrated organization may experience many disadvantages from such an arrangement. As a matter of fact, the possible disadvantages may assume such importance as to cause a firm to decide against combining two or more stages of distribution or production under its control. Consideration should be given to the fact that the possible disadvantages will not always be viewed in the same light by firms in the same industry. Nor will one concern look upon these disadvantages in the same manner at different periods of time. Factors that may be influential in causing one company to decide against vertical integration may carry little weight in the decision of another concern.

Some firms that have integrated backward toward the raw material sources have followed the policy of adjusting the capacity of the new stage assumed, in order that it will supply only a part of their needs. This backward taper of capacity necessitates the purchase of peak requirements of raw materials and other commodities. This action in itself, however, provides the vertical organization with market contacts, as well as with the variety of materials that can be assembled only from different sources. Some firms that have integrated forward toward the ultimate consumer have made use of noncompeting markets. This method of operation permits the avoidance of competition with old established customers and provides a diversity of products. Such action in itself makes the integrated concern less dependent on any one line of goods in times of reduced demand. Some firms in deciding to follow a vertically integrated plan of organization have acquired existing facilities, thus obtaining a ready-made organization experienced in the various aspects of the acquired activities. Whereas some firms have followed the techniques just described, other firms have done practically the opposite. Certain techniques have proved highly successful for some concerns but unsatisfactory for others.

The integrated cooperative and quasi-integrated voluntary groups have become a very strong element in the independent store picture, particularly in the grocery store category. They have been instrumental in enabling their independent retail store members to compete on fairly equal terms with retail units of integrated corporate chains. Under the cooperative and voluntary organizational plans, both retailers and wholesalers have learned how to work together better as a team. From this mutual understanding and interest, there has developed a large number of streamlined wholesalers (individually as well as cooperatively owned) who now are equipped to supply merchandise at low cost to retail merchants. These wholesalers also provide practical and needed services in store modernization, accounting, display, advertising, and storekeeping.

A growing recognition of vertical integration is evidenced by the Federal and state legislation that has been passed in an attempt to effect some degree of control over the expansion of this type of organization. Thus, a firm contemplating a vertically integrated system of operation not only must weigh all the possible advantages and disadvantages that can be expected to arise, but must also give detailed consideration to the Federal and state laws governing such action.

Vertical integration is one type of organization that has appeared in response to the cry that distribution costs are too high. Its operation is most successful in periods of rising prices, such as were experienced during the last ten years. But its importance in depression periods also is evidenced by the growth of many vertically integrated organizations during the 1930's.

This plan of organization is not a substitute for good management and executive ability but, coupled with these, it has enabled many firms to prosper and to give the American consumer a large share of the benefits derived from vertical integration. The question arises, however, at what point the American consumer ceases to benefit from lower prices and commences to be injured by the growth of integrated corporations. It is at this point that competition and monopoly clash, conflicting theories appear, and a decision has to be made as to the direction American business is to go.

22. Economic Factors Influencing Manufacturers' Decisions Concerning Price Maintenance

LOUIS W. STERN*

Stern explores the effect of the degree of sales concentration on price maintenance policy. He divides sales concentration into high, moderate, and low cases, and gives the implications of each. Usually, most channel members will have to cooperate if a price maintenance program is to prove successful. This requires compromise.

Although there has been some feeling in recent years that manufacturers no longer have any interest in retail price maintenance because of the ineffectiveness of fair-trade laws in many states, these feelings are unrealistic. Many manufacturers of consumer goods have been concerned with the deterioration of prices on the retail level, and have thrown their support behind the Quality Stabilization Act currently considered in Congress. If the premise can be accepted that certain manufacturers are very much interested in achieving some form of retail price stability for their products—and the support given to the Quality Stabilization Act seems to verify this—it might be asked whether, theoretically, manufacturers could expect to achieve compliance from retailers if they adopted a price maintenance policy.

The interrelations within the channel of distribution are extremely important influences on manufacturers' pricing policies. Manufacturers may decide not to adopt a policy of retail price maintenance because of chaotic competition on the retail level. The individual manufacturer may feel that his ability to enforce a minimum retail price is extremely limited if recognized mutual interdependence (and thus

stability of retail prices) will be undermined by mass merchandisers.

On the other hand, manufacturers may be discouraged from adopting a policy of price maintenance if price competition on their own level is intense. This would usually be the case in an industry typified by low or moderate concentration.[1] When concentration of sales is high, there is more chance that the extremely close interdependence among firms within an industry will encourage price maintenance. Under such conditions, deviation from the policy and the prices established may be negligible. A corollary to this hypothesis is, as Grether points out, that

---

[1] The following classification system, as developed by Joe Bain in his book, *Industrial Organization* (New York: John Wiley & Sons, 1959), pages 124–133, is employed in this article:

High Concentration (Type I-A)
Five to ten firms have 100 per cent control of the market.

Moderate Concentration (Type III)
The first eight sellers control roughly 70 to 85 per cent of total output, and the first four roughly 50 to 65 per cent, with the total number of sellers ranging from twenty or thirty to above one hundred in number.

Low Concentration (Type V)
The largest four sellers control on the average from 6 to 8 per cent apiece of the market (24 to 32 per cent combined) and the next four sellers 2 or 3 per cent apiece (8 to 12 per cent combined); nearly all remaining sellers control 1 per cent apiece or less of the market; the total number of sellers will ordinarily range from over one hundred to well over one thousand.

• SOURCE: *Journal of Retailing*, Vol. 41 (Spring, 1965), pp. 30–37.
* Assistant Professor of Business Organization, The Ohio State University. This article was submitted for publication prior to Dr. Stern's appointment to the National Commission on Food Marketing.

"The . . . best price maintenance possibilities exist where a small number of manufacturers have direct relations with selected specialty dealers of similar type and status and hence with homogeneous interests."[2]

The ability to adopt a successful price maintenance policy also rests largely on common interests among manufacturers and retailers, or in the exchange of benefits of price protection for the benefits of a secure market. Theoretical examples of several competitive situations follow; they serve to illustrate that the extent of concentration of sales may have a profound influence on the potential success of such a policy because of the direct effect of concentration on the power relationships within the channel. Emphasis has been placed on the manufacturers' viewpoint, for manufacturers make the final policy decisions.

THE HIGH CONCENTRATION CASE

At one extreme is the manufacturer whose individual brand enjoys a predominant share of the market within its industry. The manufacturer may feel that price maintenance is necessary because he believes it will assure promotional efforts for his brand by certain key retail outlets. But, because of strong consumer preference for his brand, the manufacturer may be able to forego potential patronage of outlets that reject his suggested minimum retail price. However, his brand must be distinctive enough so that its withdrawal would do some damage to a retailer. In such a case, the manufacturer may be able to dictate to retailers as a class.[3] The same reasoning applies to highly concentrated industries in which three or four firms enjoy a predominant share of the market.[4]

In these high concentration cases, middlemen may follow the manufacturers' policies, since it is assumed that the manufacturers' power may be sufficiently strong to be unaffected by antagonism of certain retailers. Such a situation would be ideal for a manufacturer who desires to adopt a price maintenance policy; and yet, in the business world, such overwhelming power is the exception rather than the rule. Furthermore, it is more likely that manufacturers' dominance will arise in a seller's market, i.e., when the available goods are sold before the demand for them (at the current prices) has been exhausted. The presence of a buyer's market weakens the manufacturer's position in the channel of distribution, with corresponding increase in the retailer's power, reducing the manufacturer's ability to control the market and to dictate price policy to retail level.[5]

THE MODERATE CONCENTRATION CASE

In the moderate concentration case, situations of bilateral monopoly are likely to be the rule.[6] As Bain points out,

"The significant measures of seller concentration in the distributive trades . . . are . . . within local competing groups in individual lines of distribution. The seller concentration picture . . . includes numerous cases of moderate and low moderate oligopolistic concen-

---

such as Union Carbide (Prestone) and Dupont (Zerex), have been able to achieve a high degree of price control among a multitude of service stations. Although the compliance has not been perfect, the high degree of market power gained through the effective advertising of these manufacturers and the close-knit structure of competition among them vis-a-vis the structure of competition on the retail level has, to a great extent, permitted them to direct retail pricing activities. Other highly concentrated industries where such price control is prevalent are the small arms ammunition and metal industries.

[2] Ewald T. Grether, *Price Control Under Fair Trade Legislation* (New York: Oxford University Press, 1939), p. 334.

[3] For an example of such channel power, see M. A. Adelman, *A & P: A Study in Price-Cost Behavior and Public Policy* (Cambridge, Mass.: Harvard University Press, 1959), p. 128, for a discussion of London Packing Company's successful campaign with V-8 vegetable juice.

[4] For example, in the sparkplug industry, where there is high concentration among producers and high competition among retailers, the manufacturers dictate pricing policy. See Ward S. Bowman, Jr., "The Prerequisites and Effects of Resale Price Maintenance," *University of Chicago Law Review*, XXII, No. 2 (Winter 1955). The antifreeze industry represents another example of high concentration where manufacturers of branded antifreeze,

[5] David R. Craig and Werner K. Gabler, "The Competitive Struggle for Market Control" (Philadelphia: *The Annals of the American Academy of Political and Social Science*, May 1940), p. 105.

[6] Under conditions of bilateral monopoly (or oligopoly) full control of price is in the hands of neither buyers alone, nor sellers alone. Express or tacit bargaining on price between buyer–seller pairs or between groups of buyers and sellers is generally the rule with some tendency for the respective power of each to offset that of the other. For a discussion of this concept, see Joe Bain, *Industrial Organization* (New York: John Wiley & Sons, 1959), pp. 140–143.

tration, together with the presence of a substantial competitive fringe of smaller sellers (especially in cities and metropolitan areas)."[7] This statement, along with the assumption of moderate concentration on the manufacturers' level, indicates the presence of monopoly power on both the retail and manufacturing levels, and suggests that

". . . retail price maintenance must involve to some extent the problems of bilateral monopoly."[8]

Situations of bilateral monopoly require compromise or acquiescence and exclude channel dictatorship. Obviously, in order to have successful price maintenance under conditions of bilateral monopoly, both manufacturers *and* retailers must desire such a policy. Basic agreement on the need for price stability permits movement toward an eventual compromise. The advantages of such a compromise to both sides are great because under conditions of bilateral monopoly,

". . . the interests of the seller and the buyer (reseller) are presumed to be in conflict. In the absence of agreement, output and price are indeterminate, and output (or prices) which will maximize joint return will not be reached. This is to say that vertical agreement makes possible the division of a larger pie irrespective of how it is sliced."[9]

There is some confusion, however, in attempting to apply the theory of bilateral monopoly to the practice of price maintenance. Although there may be monopsonistic power on the retail level, different retail factions operate in diametrically opposed ways to gain their ends. The small retailers who organize into associations may attempt to secure from manufacturers a final retail price incorporating a large percentage mark-up. Their monopsonistic power as a group may be used in a negative manner through informal boycotts to influence the final price.

On the other hand, mass distributors have as their goal buying at the lowest price in order to undersell competitors. In this form of bilateral monopoly,

". . . the buyer, instead of setting up a demand function, tries to select a price to be paid and a quantity to be purchased which, among all price-quantity combinations acceptable to the seller, are optimal from his (the buyer's) point of view. . . ."[10]

In fact, a strong, alert buyer who is constantly on the watch for a change in costs or prices on the manufacturing level which he can exploit, and who is able to force concessions, can collapse an existing structure of control, or prevent its inception.

"Whether these lower buying prices are transformed into lower selling prices will depend on the effectiveness of the horizontal and intertype competition confronting the monopsonistic buyer in his selling markets."[11]

The countervailing power of large buyers and large sellers may tend to blunt both monopolistic and monopsonistic tendencies. It appears that, especially in a buyer's market, the manufacturer is being squeezed by his distributive channel from two different directions. Ideally, the manufacturer's final adjustment would be to use price concessions, advertising, and retailer's margin adjustments up to a point of indifference, at which he would not care whether he spent the next dollar on price concessions to mass distributors, on advertising, or on higher margin allowances to smaller retailers, since in each case, it would pay for itself in increased revenue.

Obviously, the marginal analysis suggested above is extremely difficult to implement, as well as possibly self-defeating, since price concessions to the mass distributors may tend to negate larger retail margin to smaller-scale retailers. The balance is extremely delicate, and it is doubtful whether manufacturers can appease both distributive channels with one policy. Because manufacturers may have more knowledge about the demand for their particular products than the retailer, the retailers may relegate the pricing function to manufacturers without regret. The compromise must come in the markup allowed to retailers, and bargaining between manufacturers and retailers may re-

[7] Bain, *op. cit.*, p. 13.
[8] Ward S. Bowman, Jr., "Resale Price Maintenance—A Monopoly Problem," *The Journal of Business*, XXV, No. 3 (July, 1952), p. 148.
[9] Ward S. Bowman, Jr., "The Prerequisites and Effects of Resale Price Maintenance," *op. cit.*, p. 848.

[10] William Fellner, *Competition Among the Few* (New York: Alfred A. Knopf, 1949), p. 11.
[11] Joseph C. Palamountain, Jr., *The Politics of Distribution* (Cambridge, Mass.: Harvard University Press, 1955), p. 70.

volve around services offered by each in relation to the markup given or received.

The manufacturer's position is unsettled and complex. He attempts to maximize his profits, to price in line with his competitors, to allow a satisfactory markup for retailers, and to generate consumer demand by pricing low enough to attract patronage. Since retailers press continually to further their own interests, the result must be a compromise based on a common understanding, i.e., that both manufacturers and retailers want price stability in order to maintain a profitable equilibrium in their industries.

Furthermore, the differentiating abilities at the retailers' and manufacturers' levels are complementary. The ability of the manufacturer to differentiate his brand from others depends largely on the ability of retailers to perpetuate this differentiation through their services and promotions. Again, as Bowman points out,

"It is only when the existence of the monopoly power of each depends in some significant degree upon the monopoly power of the other that a result such as resale price maintenance becomes likely."[12]

The existence of mass merchandisers creates distinct problems for manufacturers seeking to adopt price maintenance policies. The increased bargaining strength of the mass merchandisers may create an obstacle for price maintenance in that such firms may not be willing to relinquish their price leadership policies. To counteract this threat, manufacturers may sometimes wish to support small retailers in competition with mass merchandisers by maintaining their profit margins. The manufacturers may believe that the large retail firms may not achieve monopsonistic buying positions if the smaller retailers continue to exist. Because the manufacturer's position is not wholly dominant in the moderate concentration case, he may be extremely anxious to prevent large retailers from gaining more bargaining strength.

Examples of moderate concentration situations include such industries as photographic equipment, electronic consumer goods (television, phonographs, etc.), electrical housewares, and pens and mechanical pencils. For instance, in the photographic equipment industry, the Subcommittee on Antitrust and Monopoly in its report, *Concentration Ratios in Manufacturing Industry*, noted that in 1958, 65 per cent

of the value of product shipped was manufactured by four firms, and that eight firms shipped 74 per cent. The photographic equipment field was (and still is) one of moderate concentration, even with the increase in foreign competition. Concentration of sales for specific lines of electrical housewares (toasters, mixers, vacuum cleaners, etc.) and writing instruments is approximately the same. On the retail level, the large department stores and discount operations share a majority of photographic equipment, housewares, and writing instrument sales. Although no specific statistics are available, interviews with executives of firms in these industries indicate that the larger outlets have usurped the position once held by the traditional service-oriented outlets.

In moderate concentration cases, the manufacturers have attempted to encourage some form of retail price stability by reducing the number of distributors selling the balance of their lines, dealing directly with retailers, entering into franchise arrangements with retailers, varying promotional allowances, reducing margins, discounts, and trade-in allowances, instituting consignment selling, and attempting to segment markets.[13]

THE LOW CONCENTRATION CASE

Manufacturers in a given industry may have very little monopoly power, and the industry itself may be one of low concentration of market control. Retailers may form associations enabling them to eliminate price competition and bend manufacturers to their will. (This would be theoretically compatible with the existence of low concentration among manufacturers.)

Manufacturers in such a situation may cooperate with retailers in an attempt to achieve price stability, but the task of attaining uniformity of price would then be difficult, to say the least. Coercion by retail associations is illegal even though it is occasionally practiced through the use of informal boycotts toward individual brands. Nevertheless, to achieve successful price maintenance, manufacturers must desire the elimination of price competition. In an industry with many firms and low concentration, it is difficult to prohibit smaller fringe firms from seeking competitive advantages through price cutting. Indeed, the policing efforts of retail associations would have to be

[12] Ward S. Bowman, Jr., "Resale Price Maintenance—A Monopoly Problem," *op. cit.*, p. 149.

[13] For a discussion of the last alternative mentioned, *see* page 163.

highly effective, and their informal boycotts complete.

Manufacturers in industries such as women's suits and coats, other garments, basic textiles, home furnishings, and wood products have negligible market power and therefore must play a relatively passive role in retail price stability. For example, there were 2,651 manufacturers of women's suits, coats, and skirts in 1958, and the four largest manufacturers together supplied only 3 per cent of the market. The presence of such a large number of sellers permits many pricing deviations. In addition, the atomistic nature of the structure of retail competition in the apparel field militates against price stability. Combined with low concentration among manufacturers, efforts made to encourage stability are, for the most part, futile.

THE ROLE OF RETAIL ORGANIZATION

The impetus for the adoption of price maintenance may often come from the retail level. However, a single retailer could not persuade an unwilling manufacturer to adopt such a policy, except perhaps under conditions of atomistic competition among manufacturers. Such persuasion must undoubtedly come from a group of retailers large enough and strong enough to affect manufacturers' total sales within an area. A manufacturer is likely to resist even then, unless he knows that other manufacturers competing with him will agree to adopt similar policies. If only one manufacturer of a particular commodity enters into a price maintenance agreement, competing manufacturers will be able to undersell him.

Retail price arrangements may be most effectively reinforced when organized retailers cooperate in establishing and policing such arrangements. In other words, there must be some cohesive, unifying influence at work among retailers besides the natural restraint imposed by their interdependence. Because of the chain-linking of individual markets, price disturbances in one market can encourage price competition in another. Therefore, any organization must be fairly widespread. In some lines of trade, such as drugs, the individual manufacturer may face strongly organized and extensive retail group pressure to adopt price maintenance policies.

Strong retail groups may be extremely beneficial to manufacturers who wish to adopt price maintenance policies. With effective organization, the manufacturer knows that his prices will probably not be cut by these groups. He can expect some assurance of price stability because of the degree of pricing tranquility in the channel. Without organization or cohesion among retailers there may always be the threat of price wars upsetting the established, stabilized prices in local markets.

RESISTANCE OF MASS MERCHANDISERS

Mass merchandisers may not be willing to part with their most important competitive weapon, i.e., lower prices. In fact, they may attempt to combat the price maintenance policies of manufacturers. Heflebower has shown that mass merchandisers may escape the demand of oligopolistic suppliers by:

1. buying from a small-firm fringe of the supplying industry;
2. buying from oligopolists at discriminatory prices and placing the mass distributor's brand on the goods; or
3. integrating into the supplying industry.[14]

It is obvious that there must be a clash between mass merchandisers using price leaders and manufacturers desiring price maintenance. In order to provide a firm basis for price stability, the manufacturers must persuade these mass merchandisers to reduce their price-cutting practices to the point where they no longer disturb the majority of individual markets. Should the clashes become too severe, the manufacturers of a given industry might discontinue distribution through these mass outlets. The only alternative might be to forego price maintenance altogether, with the possible consequences of retail price deterioration and eventual inducement of vigorous price competition on the manufacturing level. It is not likely that mass merchandisers will give up their major competitive weapon. If a strong buyer must charge the same price as weaker buyers, then his foremost monopolistic power within his marketing area is lost.

POSSIBLE COMPROMISE ALTERNATIVE FOR MANUFACTURERS

In a study of the policy of retail price maintenance[15] the writer found that attempts at seg-

[14] Richard B. Heflebower, "Mass Distribution: A Phase of Bilateral Oligopoly or Competition"? in *Explorations in Retailing*, ed. Stanley C. Hollander (Michigan State University, 1959), p. 202.
[15] Louis W. Stern, *An Economic Analysis of the Policy of Retail Price Maintenance from the Point of View of Consumer Goods Manufacturers* (unpublished Ph.D. dissertation, Northwestern University, 1962).

menting markets may be possible solutions, especially in the moderate concentration case. If manufacturers desire intensive distribution for their products, they must attempt to placate both the small-scale retailers and the mass merchandisers. They may attempt to segment the market between large price-cutting outlets and traditional service-oriented outlets by making certain higher-priced items available to the latter exclusively. Underlying this segmentation is the assumption that there are two types of customers for various products: price-oriented and quality-oriented. In reality, this method of distribution and of pricing is a form of price discrimination whereby a lower price is charged to the market typified by the more elastic demand.

This method has been used with some success in the photographic equipment and electrical housewares industries where slight variations of items stocked by mass merchandisers have been placed in small or key appliance or camera stores. These items are priced higher and the prices are maintained in these stores. A careful shopper would be able to tell that there is very little difference between the models that are price-maintained and those which are not. It should be noted that this is not a complete solution to the problem of retail price deterioration; it does, however, provide some means of pacifying the opposed factions in the distributive channel of many manufacturers.

Specifically, when introducing a new slide projector, the Mid-West sales manager of a major camera manufacturer explained to the author that the projector was designed for a specialty market and accordingly was not advertised in any mass media. Instead, it was advertised in specialty magazines which cater to particular groups of consumers. This projector was distributed to traditional service-oriented photographic equipment stores where price was maintained. Simultaneously, the company introduced two simplified and less expensive versions of the projector, sold primarily through discount outlets and advertised in mass consumer magazines. Realistically, the sales man-ager acknowledged that the price of the deluxe model might eventually be cut; when this happens, the company will bring out another high-priced specialty product which will again be sold through service-oriented camera retailers.

CONCLUSION

There are very few industries in the consumer goods field where the manufacturers almost completely dominate the channel of distribution. These manufacturers may be strong enough and may have sufficient solidarity to withstand any pressure applied to them by the most powerful buyer. Nevertheless, most positions of market power in the sale of consumers' goods are covered by positions of countervailing power, and this factor can greatly affect the ability of a manufacturer to institute price maintenance.

Situations of moderate concentration on both manufacturing and retailing levels are more likely in the business world. The interrelations within the channel are best explained by the concept of bilateral monopoly. As related to price maintenance, bilateral monopoly leads to different results when applied to different types of distributive channels. It must be modified to include the monopsonistic pressure of organized retailers attempting to gain higher final retail prices as opposed to the efforts of mass merchandisers seeking price concessions. It is important to recognize the potential impact of the two kinds of power thrusts directed toward the manufacturer. It appears theoretically impossible to discover which type of retailer will dominate in the struggle since the answer depends not only upon the relative strengths of the mass merchandisers and the smaller scale retailers, but also on the manufacturers' attitudes toward placating one side at the expense of the other. The adoption of a price maintenance policy by consumer goods manufacturers would, to a great extent, indicate that these manufacturers favor or require distribution by and cooperation from smaller retailers.

23. A Note on a Scale of Resale Price Control

BRUCE MALLEN

This short paper lists well over a dozen methods of resale price control, and indicates the relative strength of each. This ranges from complete control over resale prices by distributing direct to the consumer, to the very incomplete control of preticketing goods, or allowing price cuts so long as they are not advertised.

One of the most important ways that suppliers use to dictate policy to their retailer customers is resale price control.[1] There are many techniques by which a supplier may attempt to determine the retailer's selling price. Though they vary in strength, they can all be grouped under the heading, resale price control (RPC).

It is the purpose of this paper to survey these various techniques and arrange them along a scale of controllability. It should be realized, of course, that usually more than one technique is used simultaneously. For example, a supplier may only suggest a price, but use direct distribution in order to increase the chances of compliance.

Figure 1 shows the various methods roughly arranged along a scale proceeding from the complete control of a supplier who distributes direct to the consumer, to the supplier who distributes very indirectly and makes no attempt to control prices.

These methods can be used at one or more levels in the channel. Hence, a manufacturer can attempt to control the retailer's selling price but not the wholesaler's, vice-versa, or both.

Retailers, though restricted by RPC, still have the choice of carrying a RPC product or not. They usually also have a choice of charging the resale controlled price or a higher price.

Absolute
control

- Direct distribution to consumer
- Direct distribution to retailer
- Use of fair trade legislation
- Sale of goods on consignment
- Refusal to sell price cutters
- Distribution through exclusive franchises
- Threat to halt advertising allowances
- The threat of distributing directly
- Distribute to powerless small retailers
- Grant only small trade and quantity discounts
- Set resale price which would have existed anyway
- Advertise resale price to consumers
- Suggest or quote list or resale prices
- Preticket goods
- Avoidance of overstocking the middlemen
- Define only limits of price cutting
- Allow price cutting on some goods
- Don't allow the promotion of price cuts

No control

Fig. 1. The scale of resale price control.

• SOURCE: Bruce Mallen, "A Note on a Scale of Resale Price Control," *The Marketer* (Spring, 1964), pp. 10–11. Bruce Mallen, Editor-in-Chief, *The Marketer*.
[1] For a more general analysis of retailer-supplier dynamics see Bruce Mallen, "A Theory of Retailer-Supplier Conflict Control and Cooperation" (Journal of Retailing, Vol. 39, Summer, 1963), pp. 24–32.

Although resale price control is studied here from a supplier (manufacturer or wholesaler) viewpoint, it should be emphasized that the selling prices of any channel member may also be controlled from the retail end of the channel.

A discussion of specification buying by the mass retailer would further develop this point.

Direct distribution to the consumer makes the supplier in a sense the retailer, and so his price determination is done at the retailing level. Direct distribution to retailers puts the manufacturer one step closer to the consumer than indirect methods and so simplifies control.

The use of fair trade or resale price maintenance laws is a form of strong control. However, this method (though usually liked by small retailers) is on the wane in most industries and locations. The rise of the mass discounter has propelled its diminution.

Because a reseller may not alter the price of a supplier-owned good without the latter's permission, consignment selling is a method of resale price control. This method, of course, puts the supplier at the mercy of price changes and other non-price problems.

The refusal-to-sell-potential-price-cutters is an effective method of control. Another useful measure is distribution through exclusive franchises. The technique holds down the amount of retailers to a controllable number, and the amount of competition on the supplier's brand. This is usually coupled with an overt or subtle threat to withdraw the franchise if the retailer disregards the desired resale prices.

A threat to discontinue advertising allowances if suggested resale prices are not observed, may prove effective where fair trade has failed.

Simply the threat of direct distribution, rather than the actuality, may prove sufficient to control resale prices. This may imply a threat to do away with a level of middlemen entirely, or just to compete with them, by setting up a parallel direct channel. Thus, the threat of opening a manufacturer's retail outlet may in part control the prices of present retailers.

Distributing through small financially insecure retailers, who would not dare oppose the power of a supplier on price matters, could be considered a method of control, though risky.

A method of indirectly controlling resale prices is to limit the size of all the various discounts offered. If the retailer wishes to make a profit on these goods he cannot cut his selling price too far.

A supplier can control resale price very easily, if he makes them similar to what the retailers would have determined on their own.

Advertising resale prices to consumers is a method which, if not combined with another more powerful resale price control technique, can easily backfire. Price cutters could point to this higher advertised price for a favorable comparison.

The simple suggesting of list and resale prices is likewise a weak and even dangerous tool. Falling into this group are pre-ticketing, or the placing of resale prices on the goods, by the supplier. The latter method also leads into the problem of differing taxes, and mechanical difficulties, such as differing type of marking by retailers.

A supplier, by not overstocking his retailers can help prevent possible price cutting, and so in a sense control resale prices. One way is to desist from granting large quantity discounts.

Resale price control may; apply to only some of the products of a supplier, define only the limits of price cutting, and not control how high prices may be set. Indeed prices themselves may not be the object of control in some cases. Only the promotion and publicity of such price cuts may be frowned upon.

There are other methods of resale price control, one of the most bizarre schemes was when:

A large New York store cut the price of a well-known fountain pen. The pen company employed so called Bowery bums to line up at the counter to take advantage of the sale. To save fumigation costs the store called off the whole affair.[2]

[2] Ralph Alexander and Richard M. Hill, "What To Do About The Discount House," in *Marketing in Transition*, Alfred Seelye (Ed.), (Harper and Bros., New York, 1958), p. 43.

PART IV

Channel Models and Measurements

Marketing and operations research have made tremendous strides in the last quarter century. They have been applied with great sophistication to most of the variables in the marketing mix. One learns of advertising research, consumer research, product and price research, package research, sales forecasting and analysis, and so on. However, very little is heard of channel research. With the increasing interest in channel management and relations this will change. It is the purpose of this section to bring together some of the few contributions in the field of channel research and quantitative analysis.

There have been particularly few contributions from the management science area (operations research, decision theory, quantitative analysis) to the field of channel analysis. This is understandable as these quantitative techniques are only now becoming integrated into traditional marketing research (for example, *Research For Marketing Decisions* by Paul E. Green and Donald S. Tull, Prentice-Hall, Englewood Cliffs, N.J., 1966). However, the articles in this section are of high calibre. Balderston has been an important contributor in this area.

Channel evaluation and research, as with all areas of channel study, can be viewed as a managerial or social technique. The first category of channel research involves studying the channel from the viewpoint of one of the member micro-units, in order to increase the efficiency of that member's distributive operation. This category may be termed "managerial" channel research. Managerial channel research may itself be divided into two kinds of studies: (a) studies for the purpose of selecting and designing a distributive system for the firm, and (b) studies for increasing the efficiency of the system once it is in operation, i.e., channel relations studies. Managerial channel research may take the form of dealer-attitude studies, sales and distribution cost analysis, describing competitors' channels, describing and forecasting channel trends, consumer-attitude studies toward different outlet types, and so on. Two of the selections suggest the role accountants could play in this area.

The second category of channel research involves studying the channel from the viewpoint of the overall macrounit, in order to evaluate the total performance of the channel system in terms of its meeting the objectives of society and the entire economy. Cox's *Distribution in a High-Level Economy* (Prentice-Hall, 1965) is the prime example of this area of channel research. Another major contributor in this area of "social" channel research is Ralph Breyer who has developed such useful concepts as "nexus" costs and many others.

It is in the area of channel research that one expects to see the frontiers of channel knowledge pushed forward, not simply in the refinement of the research techniques themselves, but, even more important, in their findings.

A. Contributions of Management Science

24. *Design of Marketing Channels*

F. E. BALDERSTON

This paper discusses five topics concerned with channel design, i.e., the conscious choice of a channel pattern. These topics are the problem of determining the existence of a channel; the role of the channel; the point of view from which a channel is evaluated; the important elements in design for which analysis presently exists; and methods of evaluating channel models with insufficient analytic knowledge.

Marketing channels are institutional configurations for directing and supporting the flows, from production to use, of things of value. We discover a marketing channel by tracing what happens (or thinking about what can happen) to one or more units of one or more items en route from one or more origins to one or more destinations at one or more points in time. Marketing effort is important in general—and marketing channels exist in particular—because actuality refuses to meet the classical conditions laid down for effective economic organization.

Marketing channels are social systems—in Alderson's words, "organized behavior systems"[1] —which have technological, economic, sociological, and psychological features. When we speak of the *design* of marketing channels, this implies conscious choice of a pattern with foreknowledge of the results the pattern will deliver. Not much is yet known about how to undertake the task of designing comprehensively *any* complex system of social phenomena. Thus, ideas for the design of marketing channels are still fragmentary, and we will be able to make only limited statements; by the same token, of course, marketing scholars, concentrating on this problem, may inferentially contribute to much broader problems of pure and applied social theory.

We will comment on five issues in this essay on marketing channel design:

1. *How does one discover* the existence of a marketing channel?
2. *Why have channels?* That is, what are the functional requirements and operating features of the "natural" systems which grow up?
3. *For whose benefit* do we consider the channel to operate? That is, considering the issue of conscious evaluation, whose criterion do we employ —that of a "leading" firm; all firms participating; all households directly served; or "society"?
4. What are some critical design components for which analysis presently exists?
5. What can now be done to set up and evaluate marketing channel models even where our analytic knowledge is as yet incomplete?

MARKETING CHANNELS AS "NATURAL" SYSTEMS

Marketing scholars, over the last fifty years, have put prodigious effort into the development

• SOURCE: F. E. Balderston, "Design of Marketing Channels," in Cox, Alderson, Shapiro (editors), *Theory in Marketing* (Homewood, Ill.: Richard D. Irwin, Second Series, 1964), pp. 163–175. F. E. Balderston, Professor of Business Administration, University of California (Berkeley).
[1] Wroe Alderson, *Marketing Behavior and Executive Action* (Homewood, Ill.: Richard D. Irwin, 1957).

of concepts for identifying leading features of marketing channels and into detailed observations on channel behavior. One must go to Breyer for the essential contributions on two elements of a theory: (1) the recognition of institutional forces leading to norms of orderly behavior[2] and (2) the structural configurations, the resource-absorbing work of marketing channels and the problem of comparing costs of alternative channel arrangements for a given commodity flow.[3] We return at a later point to a discussion of the first of these, but the second involves the question of grouping the sequences of marketing activity, which in its turn depends on the nature of a fundamental adjustment process.

Various scholars have pointed to the presence of—and have suggested ways of thinking about —a central adjustment process which accommodates to one another a heterogeneous supply array and a heterogeneous (but differently distributed) array of demands.[4]

The Detection and Measurement of "Natural" Channel Systems

We will discuss four distinct elements of the adjustment process with a view, first, to providing a means of *detecting* marketing channels and then of explaining what they accomplish. First, there are sorting transformations which are required to bring items of an initially heterogeneous array into internally homogeneous classes. The class definition, in turn, may be in one or more dimensions. The question arises as to how each dimension is to be measured (whether by the absolute presence or absence of a defined attribute, or by the place of each unit within an ordinal ranking, or by the size of the unit in a cardinal measure). Also at stake is the question of sequence in which these tests of dimensionality are to be made. If each of n dimensions is independent of the

rest, then n tests can be applied in any arbitrary order. If not, the multidimensionality of the items needs to be treated in a manner such that one dimension dominates others and must be treated first.

Second, once homogeneity within sorting class is achieved, the process must bring about transformations of lot-size.

Third, transformations in time are required (this is "the inventory problem").

Fourth, transformations in space may be necessary.

Two distinct questions can be asked concerning each of the dimensions according to which the array might be sorted: (1) how far need the analysis go in the *extent* of each feature of the assortment? and (2) how "fine" does the measure need to be within any small interval of this measure of the assortment?

As an example of the first of these issues, let us consider the possible dimension of "commodity type," where there is a series of such types to be considered in the analysis of a marketing channel. One does not need to consider the possibility that *every* commodity produced in the economy will be attracted into the natural mode of operation of a channel system, as some commodities will be fundamentally irrelevant to the organization of the marketing channel that is under study. However, to use an example from field studies of the lumber trade, "softwood plywood" can be classified as a commodity different from "softwood lumber." One must be prepared to ask questions concerning the likelihood that these two commodity types will appear together in the sorting operation of business entities at various stages.

Another example of the question of the "fineness" of the dimensional measure can also be taken from this discussion of the lumber market. Within the generalized commodity type, "softwood lumber," there are numerous individual species which may be produced by a given sawmill or which can be drawn from different manufacturing sources into wholesale and retail assortments. For some purposes it is sufficient to examine "softwood lumber" regardless of species, but for others it may be necessary to label separately such species as Douglas fir, California redwood, western hemlock, or sugar pine.

Most descriptions of marketing channel configurations rest squarely upon a *prior* commodity classification in which the commodity dimensions are of fixed length and fineness. It is easy to see why scholars have chosen this

[2] Ralph F. Breyer, *The Marketing Institution* (New York: McGraw-Hill, 1934).

[3] Ralph F. Breyer, *Quantitative Systemic Analysis and Control: Study No. 1—Channel and Channel Group Costing* (Philadelphia, Pa.: R. F. Breyer, 1948).

[4] F. E. Clark and C. P. Clark, *Principles of Marketing* (3d ed.; New York: The Macmillan Co., 1942); R. S. Vaile, E. T. Grether, and Reavis Cox, *Marketing in the American Economy* (New York: The Ronald Press Co., 1952); especially chaps. v, vi, and vii; Alderson, *op. cit.;* and D. A. Revzan, *Wholesaling in Marketing Organization* (New York: John Wiley & Sons, 1961), especially chap. i.

approach rather than developing a *theory* of the emergence of the system of behavior. Such a theory would involve the simultaneous choice of the originating supply array (and its dimensional properties), of the final consumption array (and its dimensional properties), and of the intermediate adjustment process (with marketing tasks undertaken at a degree of complexity which would depend on the characteristics of the originating and absorbing distributions). In principle, one could empirically detect a marketing channel by tracing the forward movement of the samples of commodities in the originating array, somehow defined, or work backward by starting with samples from the ending array and finding their origins.[5] A third possibility involves investigating the flow properties of the channel system by studying a sample of the commodity handlings that occur during the course of the adjustment process, but until we know how to identify this process more effectively, we cannot specify the population from which such empirical samplings would be drawn.

The detection of marketing channels must now proceed more modestly than would be implied by the above, through fixing of at least some of the following elements:

1. The initial commodity array and the "final" arry;
2. The definitions of the sets of business entities (manufacturers, wholesalers with stocks, etc.) involved in necessary activities;
3. The specification of the *sequences* in which the various sets of entities will be linked together;
4. The specification of the *activities* which will be examined.

Suppose that all four of these features are fixed. Then we still have the problem of understanding how effort may be allocated, as the following example demonstrates. (See Table 1.)

Consider the channel arrangements for commodity x, in which

S_1 is the set of originating suppliers;
S_2 is a set of "intermediary" entities;
S_3 is the set of "final" entities;
F_1 is a functional activity, some total amount of which must be undertaken somewhere in the channel system;
F_2 is a second functional activity; and
F_3 is a third functional activity.

Table 1. Activity Coefficients, if the Elementary Functional Activity j Is Wholly Performed by Entities in Set i

	F_1	F_2	F_3
S_1	τ_{11}	τ_{12}	τ_{13}
S_2	τ_{21}	τ_{22}	τ_{23}
S_3	τ_{31}	τ_{32}	τ_{33}

In Table 2 we define *all* alternative channel sequences through which the above functional requirements could be met.

Given this framework, it is possible to state the problem of minimum cost or maximum revenue allocation of functional effort. Each activity (channel alternative) A_i has associated with it an unknown *level* of operation x_i and a net revenue per unit c_i. This net revenue coefficient would be derived by taking the gross margin per unit and subtracting the unit variable costs of performing the required functional activities in the manner indicated by the activity definition. The sets S_1, S_2, S_3 have given functional capacities E_1, E_2, E_3, respectively.[6] Each activity assignment (some combination of the F's in Table 2) has a unit requirement, a_{ij}, against each of the capacities. Thus, we can say in matrix notation, the problem is to find:

$$\text{Max } V = cX$$
$$\text{Subject to } Ax \leq E$$
$$\text{and } x \geq 0.$$

This linear programming formulation is clumsy and could be simplified for easier solution, but it demonstrates the basic structure of the problem of marketing theory more clearly than would a compressed statement of the optimization problem. This formulation shows that the assignment of functional efforts to particular levels in the channel system requires consideration of many combinatorial alternatives and of the costs associated with each one. Thus, the problem is inherently messy.

Scales of Operation at Critical Points in the Channel

A vital issue, not tackled in the above linear programming formulation, is the choice of a

---

[5] A gargantuan job of measurement of the individual flows of marketing effort, done by tracing backward from the point of final absorption, is reported by Reavis Cox and Charles S. Goodman in "Marketing of Housebuilding Materials," *Journal of Marketing* (July, 1956), pp. 36–61.

[6] If it is desired to break out separately the capacity requirements and technical coefficients for each functional activity, then for each set of participants, there could be *three* resource limits instead of one, and three *rows* of activity coefficients pertaining to each activity alternative.

Table 2. Definitions of Channel Alternatives

	A_1	A_2	A_3	A_4	A_5	A_6	A_7
S_1	$F_1F_2F_3$	0	0	F_1F_2	F_1F_3	F_2F_3	F_1F_3
S_2	0	$F_1F_2F_3$	0	F_3	F_2	F_1	0
S_3	0	0	$F_1F_2F_3$	0	0	0	F_3

	A_8	A_9	A_{10}	A_{11}	A_{12}	A_{13}	A_{14}
S_1	F_2F_3	F_2F_3	0	0	0	F_3	F_2
S_2	0	0	F_1F_2	F_1F_3	F_2F_3	F_1F_2	F_1F_3
S_3	F_2	F_1	F_3	F_2	F_1	0	0

	A_{15}	A_{16}	A_{17}	A_{18}	A_{19}	A_{20}	A_{21}
S_1	F_1	F_3	F_2	F_1	0	0	0
S_2	F_2F_3	0	0	0	F_3	F_2	F_1
S_3	0	F_1F_2	F_1F_3	F_2F_3	F_1F_2	F_1F_3	F_2F_3

	A_{22}	A_{23}	A_{24}	A_{25}	A_{26}	A_{27}
S_1	F_1	F_1	F_2	F_2	F_3	F_3
S_2	F_2	F_3	F_1	F_3	F_1	F_2
S_3	F_3	F_2	F_3	F_1	F_2	F_1

scale at which each of these transformations will be undertaken. For any one of the transformations considered individually, this depends upon the density distributions of the supply array and the intended demand array, and also upon the cost function for the transformation to be undertaken. The crudeness or fineness of the transformation may in turn be a matter of choice, and the degree of refinement may determine certain parameters of the cost function.

We are supposing the presence of a single basic adjustment process with the four elements previously mentioned, so that one of the issues to be determined is whether the technologies of these four subprocesses are independent and distinct or—what is more likely in most cases—whether they are interdependent, with the result that the choice of scale becomes a compromise among appropriate scales for the individual transformations.

In the "natural" system, each marketing agency—even if it is concerned only with a single commodity—may undertake many or few functional activities, each one of which may deserve treatment as a contribution to the adjustment between the supply array and the demand array for the commodity. Similarly, each activity may involve one or more of the kinds of transformation already mentioned.

These remarks bring us back to Breyer's concern with structural configurations. Put most briefly, the issue arises as to the number of stages needed in a sequence of agencies to treat these adjustment problems between the initial supply and the eventual demand arrays. The natural system is a continual contest regarding the number of stages and the allocation of efforts between one stage and another, precisely because of the large number of possible combinations of choices. The number of possibilities is so large that chaos could rule-no systematic and orderly behavior would emerge. Yet, we do find orderliness and finely coordinated behavior, and we need to know why and how it comes about and how it may be modified when new conditions arise.

Centralized and Decentralized Transaction Making

One of the most complex problems of overall channel design, if the designer were in a position to determine the entire structure of intermediary operations, would be to choose an appropriate degree of market centralization. Institutional studies of various central cash markets for agricultural products have shown these markets can become critically important both from the standpoint of logistics—the movement, handling and storage of commodities—and from that of information assembly, transaction making, and the creation of price signals which can be used both by the central-market participants and by those entities which choose not to involve themselves directly.

In order to analyze the alternatives, the channel designer needs to be able to compare the logistic efficiency of centralized and decentralized arrangements, and he must also be able to estimate the information-handling and computational burdens of the centralized and the decentralized schemes.

It is no accident that this issue resembles that of comparing the characteristics of centralized and decentralized national economics: many of the formal analytic problems are the same. Thus the theoretical work carried out in the latter area is relevant.[7] Empirical investigation of the information-processing features of centralized exchange markets is, however, very difficult to undertake. One effort in this direction has been reported tentatively and is continuing.[8]

In addition to the logistic and the informational features of centralized and decentralized markets, important problems of evoking the allegiance and the cooperative behavior of participating firms are encountered in making the market work effectively. Even if efficient logistics and information-handling would be achieved by a centralized market, once established, there are interesting questions as to whether a path of institutional development exists which will permit the formation of such a market. Some attempts to establish central-clearing schemes have been failures—and in one

such case known to this author, the resistance of wholesaling firms wedded to the decentralized pattern was a factor of some importance. In the presence of such institutional forces, the channel designer faces very great difficulties of predicting what it will take to evoke the needed response by potential participants in the market system.

Central markets are often quasi-public facilities and fall under extensive regulation—as, for example, SEC regulation of the securities exchanges. Marketing theory should consider whether these regulatory bodies have a theory of what they are doing, and why.

CRITERIA OF CHANNEL EFFECTIVENESS

The linear programming formulation presented above asserted that the objective was to *maximize total net revenues* to all members of the sets S_1, S_2, S_3, subject to the capacity constraints. The question of dividing the pie among the sets, and among the members of each set, was not considered.

In another and differently restricted model of communication networks, the focus was upon the determination of that number of wholesale intermediaries which would minimize the margin charged to the sets of manufacturers and retailers viewed as users of the intermediate market.[9] Since commodity flow through the channel was treated as given in this approach, the effective criterion was that of *minimizing cost to the channel's users*.

Neither of these approaches to the definition of a criterion, however, deals with a most significant underlying question: how much marketing service, and of what kinds, is it desirable for the channel system to deliver to the ultimate users of the products it handles, and how do the quantities and qualities of such service affect the amount of commodity output which will pass through the channel?

When it is couched in these terms, the criterion of channel effectiveness encompasses, but only with respect to the channel system that is under examination, many of the questions that have been discussed much more broadly under the heading of the productivity of distribution. Cox and Goodman addressed themselves to the measurement of the total amount of each functional activity performed in order to effect

[7] K. J. Arrow and L. Hurwicz, "Decentralization and Computation in Resource Allocations," R. W. Pfouts (ed.), *Essays in Economics and Econometrics* (Chapel Hill, N.C.: University of North Carolina Press, 1960); L. Hurwicz, "Optimality and Informational Efficiency in Resource Allocation," K. J. Arrow, S. Karlin, and P. Suppes (eds.), *Mathematical Methods in the Social Sciences* (Stanford, Calif.: Stanford University Press, 1960); T. Marschak, "Centralization and Decentralization in Economic Organizations," *Econometrics*, Vol. 27 (July, 1959), pp. 399–430; and G. Debreu, *Theory of Value, an Axiomatic Analysis of Economic Equilibrium* (New York: John Wiley & Sons, Inc., 1959).
[8] P. L. Schmidbauer, "An Estimation of the Quantity of Decision-Making Required by a Market," Working Paper No. 31, Center for Research in Management Science (Berkeley, Calif.: Center for Research in Management Science, July, 1961).

[9] F. E. Balderston, "Communication Networks in Intermediate Markets," *Management Science* (January, 1958), pp. 156–71.

delivery, to a sample site, of the major items in the bill of materials for a typical single-family house. They then sought to make a judgmental evaluation of the potential improvement of channel effectiveness which might be made in each of these dimensions of functional activity, taken separately.[10]

Marketing efficiency, in relation to cost, was the implicit criterion underlying this approach, but the authors did not seek to translate the separate measures of marketing work into either a "benefit" or a "cost" criterion. Further, while they obtained extremely detailed estimates of the amounts of functional activity undertaken in a marketing channel, their investigation could not encompass the comparison of the present system with other ways of combining marketing activities or of altering the scale of operations at some points in the channel.

The vexing question of the criterion is resolved rather easily, in principle, when attention is shifted from the global problem of channel design—including the specification of desired relations among all the entities involved—to the microproblem facing the individual firm, which is that of choosing a (possibly complex) distribution system to benefit its own operations, given some assumptions about the manner in which the "rest of the world" will function.

Not unnaturally, it is this perspective which dominates most of the literature of operations research in application to marketing problems. Frequently, the assumed criterion is that simplest of intellectual constructs, profit maximization. But there is no reason in principle why this analysis for the firm could not use a variant of utility maximization (to encompass other goals besides profits), or even a complex of goal statements to reflect a series of priorities and objectives which may not be capable of reduction to a single index measure. The important point is that, so long as the firm under analysis can be considered a single, unitary entity, the *source* of a criterion measure is simpler to define, and the character of the criterion is in principle more definite, than can be the case if channel designs must be evaluated subject to the combined judgment of the firms involved, or of "society."

CHANNEL DESIGN FOR THE INDIVIDUAL FIRM

The individual firm faces the channel problem in three ways, which differ from the preceding efforts at "global" analysis of an entire market-

ing channel as a system. First, the goals or objectives of one firm, no matter how far one chooses to complicate these beyond the assumed goal of simple profit maximization, are nevertheless simpler to identify, and simpler to apply in the evaluation of alternatives, than is the channel criterion problem when designing channels. Second, if the firm operates, or can operate, as a multiestablishment enterprise, some of the channel alternatives need evaluation in light of the relative efficiency of market participation and internal administrative controls. This is also a critical problem for the "global" channel designer, as the assignment of functional activities to different *loci* of operations often implies choices between one pattern of administrative efficiencies (or inefficiencies) and another—but the analysis of these problems in the case of the single firm is simpler conceptually.

The third difference between the single-firm channel problem and that of the "global" channel design is, however, a complicating rather than a simplifying difference. As was shown in a preceding section, models of a marketing channel system are generated by (1) identifying commodities or commodity groups to study and then (2) examining the various issues which arise in assigning functional activities to the participating entities. The single firm, however, is not necessarily restricted to participation in a single channel system. It may—to make matters most difficult of all—use the same facilities and manpower, at one or more establishments, to participate simultaneously in several marketing channels. While Breyer raised the question of how to define large systems involving several interdependent channels, the preceding review of design problems should be sufficient to indicate that even for the single channel the problems of analysis are as yet far from being solved.[11] The analysis of the single firm which is (or may consider becoming) involved in several channel systems will be considered briefly below, but for the most part we will confine attention to the elements of channel design for the firm that is involved only in a single channel system.

A series of problem areas, each of which is only a part of the problem of system design facing the firm, are reviewed in the following paragraphs. First, several approaches to problems of logistics and location are examined. A few other kinds of issue are then considered—chiefly, sales-solicitation alternatives and a brief note

[10] Cox and Goodman, *op. cit.*

[11] Breyer, *Quantitative Systemic . . . op. cit.*

on two problems of pricing which have channel design implications. Finally, we discuss briefly the problem of putting together the pieces of the puzzle in large-scale models which may enable the firm to discern simultaneously most of the important implications of channel design.

Logistics

A. Separated Markets. In one of the influential early articles on the application of linear programming to business problems, Henderson and Schlaifer discussed, among other things, the possibility of using the transportation-model linear program to determine what pattern of shipments a firm might most profitably make from m origins, under its control, to n distinct and mutually independent markets.[12] While the minimizing of total shipment costs was the main focus of attention, the authors did point out that additional market constraints could easily be built into the problem, to reflect either an estimated upper limit of the amount that market j could absorb or a *minimum* delivery amount which the firm might set as a matter of marketing strategy. The *source* of such maximum or minimum limiting constraints was not specified: they could be supplied by management judgment, by an analysis of trend in the historical pattern of shipments to each market, or by an attempt at analysis of the strategic interaction between the firm and its competitors in each market. The point, however, is that wherever these limits are known, they can be added to the model which optimizes shipping costs. This kind of constraint may be an important building block in the complex production-distribution models which are considered in our subsequent discussion of large-scale models.

In quite another context, the present author has considered problems of branch representation in each of a number of mutually independent submarkets.[13] Here also, policy constraints on minimum branch volume and environmental constraints on the maximum the local market can absorb can be included easily in the model.

B. Warehouse Location and Operation. Bowman and Stewart examined the question of where to locate warehouses and how big to make

each one of them to service local markets effectively, by examining the aggregate cost effects of a number of marginal considerations.[14] Choosing a "typical" geographical distribution of customer requirements, they first developed a branch-warehouse model, then fitted branch warehouses and a plant warehouse into the total marketing area. In an unpublished paper, Andresen and Lutz developed a macro approach to essentially the same problem.[15]

Besides such cost parameters as the carlot cost per mile and the LCL cost per mile, which must enter into such models as these, it is necessary to specify in some way the costs of storage and handling as a function of warehouse volume. As one example of potentially radical change in such cost functions, Meserole points out that high-speed data processing is modifying warehouse management by making possible the arbitrary assignment of goods to warehouse locations on a frequency-of-visit basis.[16] In the same sources, Magee discusses approximate cost functions for a physical distribution network.[17]

Despite enormous progress in the rigorous analysis of inventory systems, of which the most comprehensive treatment is that of Hadley and Whitin, there remain some critically interesting substantive problems for which optimizing rules are not yet well formulated.[18] At present, we cannot simply plug in a solution method for the general case of the n-commodity, m-stage inventory system, and thus dispose of the inventory management issue by means of one powerful optimizing rule.

C. Logistic Networks. The firm may wish to consider as channel alternatives the possible sequences of commodity flow from a source to a destination and choose the least-cost route which meets various capacity restrictions. For this purpose special algorithms have been developed to treat flows in networks. Ford and Fulkerson and Hadley lay out the basic analy-

---

[12] A. Henderson and R. Schlaifer, "Mathematical Programming—Better Information for Better Decision-Making," *Harvard Business Review*, Vol. 32 (May–June, 1954), pp. 73–100.

[13] F. E. Balderston, "Models of Multiple-Branch Organizations," *California Management Review*, Volume 4 (Spring, 1962), pp. 40–57.

[14] R. Bowman and E. Stewart, "A Model for Scale of Operations," *Journal of Marketing*, Vol. 20 (January, 1956), pp. 242–54.

[15] J. Andresen and R. Lutz, unpublished manuscript.

[16] W. H. Meserole, "Warehouses and Computers," in Wroe Alderson and Stanley J. Shapiro (eds.), *Marketing and the Computer* (Englewood Cliffs, N.J.: Prentice-Hall, 1963), p. 54.

[17] John F. Magee, "The Computer and the Physical Distribution Network," in Alderson and Shapiro (eds.), *op. cit.*, pp. 70–76.

[18] G. Hadley and T. M. Whitin, *Analysis of Inventory Systems* (Englewood Cliffs, N.J.: Prentice-Hall, 1963).

sis.[19] W. Jewell has extended this model to the case in which the flow is augmented or partly absorbed en route from the source to the destination, an extension which may improve markedly the prospects for handling important classes of marketing problems.[20]

Sales Solicitation; Pricing Rules. The problems of market coverage and adequate warehouse servicing have some analytic similarity to the problems of sales-force deployment, although different cost elements arise in the latter case. Artle and Berglund employ elaborate marginalist reasoning to determine whether a manufacturer would profit by using his own direct sales force or a series of wholesalers to secure sales coverage.[21] Andresen and Lutz also consider this question, in conjunction with the determination of an appropriate physical distribution scheme.[22]

Pricing policies are another important aspect of marketing channel relationships. Here, we refer only briefly to two issues. One, the question of the vertically integrated wholesaler's pricing in sales to "outside" customers versus the shadow prices it may charge to its own establishments at the same marketing level as the outside customers is considered by Hirschleifer.[23]

A quite different problem is faced by the firm which can set not only its own selling price but also the resale price of its customers. Curiously enough, the elaborate discussions of "fair trade" or "resale price maintenance" as an important issue of public regulatory policy do not seem to include much discussion of the manner in which the firm might choose an optimal fair-trade price, given the legality of such a policy and the availability of an enforcement procedure.

This question is a member of a class of pricing problems which arise in the firm's approach to its marketing channels, and a solution to a

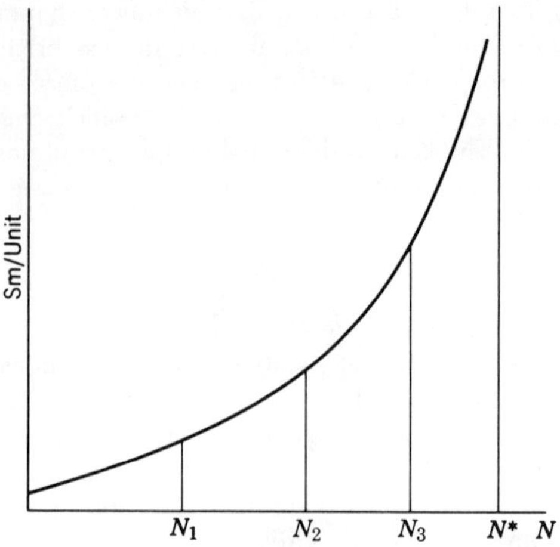

[19] L. R. Ford, Jr., and D. R. Fulkerson, *Flows in Networks* (Princeton, N.J.: Princeton University Press, 1962); and G. Hadley, *Linear Programming* (Reading, Mass.: Addison-Wesley Publishing Co., 1962), chap. x.
[20] W. S. Jewell, "Optimal Flow through Networks with Gains," *Operations Research*, Vol. 10 (July–August, 1962).
[21] R. Artle and S. Berglund, "A Note on Manufacturers' Choice of Distribution Channels," *Management Science*, Vol. 5 (July, 1959), pp. 460–71.
[22] Andresen and Lutz, *op. cit.*
[23] J. Hirschleifer, "Decentralized Decisions and Internal Pricing," in Graduate School of Business Administration, Stanford University, Seminar on Basic Research in Management Controls, *Proceedings*, forthcoming.

Fig. 1. Dealer response to different dealer margins offered by the manufacturer.

simplified case will be given. Suppose, first, that there is a maximum population of N^* "dealers" who may stock the manufacturer's product if the margin $\$M$ per unit is sufficiently attractive. (We presume that the manufacturer has first set a price to the dealer, P_n, that transport costs are zero, and that there are no quantity discounts.) There is a relation $N = f(M)$ of which the maximum value is N^*, the entire population of dealers. Figure 1 illustrates this function.

Consumers, however, react to the situation in two ways. First, they are negatively affected if P_c, the price they must pay, is high. Second, they are positively affected by the ease of availability of the product. The solid lines of Figure 2 show these two effects, in that for every number of dealers, quantity demanded falls as P_c increases, but, for each given level of P_c, the quantity demanded is greater, the greater the number of dealers.

Now we combine the margin relation and the consumer response relation in the dotted line of Figure 2, which shows the quantity sold at each price P_c, in view of the fact from Figure 1 that only a certain number of dealers will materialize at each level of margin.

Now, if the manufacutrer's marginal costs are constant over the entire relevant range, the profit-maximizing objective in the context of this fair-trade situation is that of choosing M so as to maximize sales quantity (P_M being fixed, by assumption). In Figure 2, the optimum fair-trade price is shown as P_c^*, at which price Q_{max} will be sold.

There are, to be sure, much more complicated pricing aspects of the firm's channel policy than

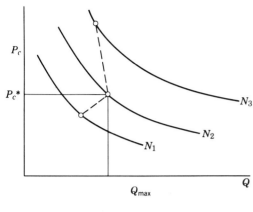

P_c

P_c^*

N_3

N_2

N_1

Q_{max}

Q

Fig. 2

the two considered in this section, but perhaps these examples illustrate the problem area.

Large-Scale Models. Some company research staffs have worked out extremely large-scale models of their production-distribution systems. Hadley refers to a sales district analysis involving four company plants and 2,500 jobbers, the solution of which required approximately two hours of IBM 704 time.[24] The present author has been told of at least one massive production-distribution model of the linear programming type which incorporated more than 30,000 variables. Both of these models

were optimizing (presumably, cost-minimizing) models.

Where analysis fails, there is always the comfort (slow, painful and expensive, to be sure) of computer simulation. The present author was a co-worker in one such study.[25] This model was developed in order to test hypotheses concerning the effect of information cost and market loyalty on the structure and performance of a market. It has since been adapted to the testing of alternative pricing rules and to an exploratory test of the desirability of replacing the set of wholesale intermediaries with a central clearing mechanism. The results are not yet fully analyzed.

The preceding review is not an exhaustive catalog of the work being done on various of the partial relationships entering into the firm's channel design problem, but it illustrates what kinds of relationships are available as inputs to new models for analyzing alternative marketing channel policies.

It is the author's view that much more work on channel design is both needed and feasible. This topic is central to our theories of the behavior of marketing systems, and in the context of the individual firm, it is of pressing practical importance.

[24] Hadley, *op. cit.*, pp. 433–37.

[25] F. E. Balderston and Austin C. Hoggatt, *Simulation of Market Processes* (Berkeley, Calif.: Institute of Business and Economic Research, Special Publications No. 1, 1962).

25. Simulating Market Processes

FREDERICK E. BALDERSTON and AUSTIN C. HOGGATT

This is a report on a simulation exercise performed on the marketing channel of the lumber industry. Balderston and Hoggatt show how this computer technique can increase one's understanding of the interrelationship of actions taken by channel members and can help one examine the organization and performance of a channel composed of multi-stages.

INTRODUCTORY COMMENT

The idea of simulation studies is to set up models which show the workings of very complex relationships—those which are too complex to be reduced to simple conclusions by means of mathematical or statistical analysis or ordinary reasoning. These models can then be used to generate predictions about the time-path of the system being studied.

This paper is a report of one such simulation study. Its purpose is to examine the intimate dynamics of a market, viewed as a complex system of behavior in which information is limited and costly.

A market can be characterized in many ways. The economic theorist views it as an arena for the interaction of prices, quantities, and similar variables. Students of marketing, regarded as one of the applied areas of business administration, often lay stress on institutional factors which modify these strictly economic relationships. Other social scientists—particularly sociologists and organization theorists—tend to regard markets as systems of decision-making in which the participants have a variety of roles. Finally, there is an emerging group of investigators (originally from engineering) who are interested in "systems engineering" and "system design." These investigators regard the

technology of the interaction system as particularly significant. For example, they may face the task of adapting alternative communication and information technologies for an individual enterprise or a market institution (such as a commodity or securities exchange). One might take the view that this study is an experiment in constructing a general system model.

The work that is reported here may be of interest to workers in all of these disciplines, as well as to those who are exploring the methodology of computer simulation. In this paper, we shall sketch the major components from each of these areas, show how the market model embraces a wide variety of features, review the major relationships that the model contains, and summarize the results of the investigation. The study is reported at greater length in our monograph, *Simulation of Market Processes* (Berkeley: University of California, Institute of Business and Economic Research, 1962). The monograph reports details of our measures on the model, the various hypotheses concerning its operating processes, and the results obtained. Those interested in the detailed structure of the model, its coding, value of parameters, and the resources required for this large-scale simulation study are referred to the appendices of the monograph.

Because this investigation describes and analyzes basic market processes, it is not primarily addressed to the business analyst whose interest is in the decision-making problems of an individual firm. From the point of view of the manager, the market as described here is a complex environment in which his

• SOURCE: Frederick Balderston and Austin Hoggatt, *Simulation of Market Processes* (Berkeley Institute of Business and Economic Research, University of California, 1962), Chapters 1 and 2. F. E. Balderston, Professor of Business Administration, University of California (Berkeley).

firm is impacted. With relatively minor modifications, a market model of the type described can be used to investigate such managerial questions as the short-run forecasting of price and other market variations in response to changes of final demand, the relative desirability of alternative patterns of vertical integration, and the pay-offs to alternative decision-rules. We do not, however, report such applications, and the reader concerned with business administration should rather look to this paper for general insight into market behavior and the methodology of computer simulation.

EMPIRICAL BACKGROUND OF THE STUDY

Summary of Research on Lumber Marketing Relationships on the U.S. Pacific Coast

In 1954–55, one of the authors, Balderston, began to collect data on patterns of trading and business operations among lumber manufacturers, wholesalers, and retailers on the U.S. Pacific Coast. A second such survey in 1957 provided further detailed information. These field studies helped to provide a picture of a market that was extremely decentralized: transactions occurred by means of specific bargains between a lumber mill and a wholesaler and a retailer. Wholesalers normally took the initiative in market communication; indeed, they were in a real sense specialists in accumulating and sending the information necessary to make the market function. Wholesalers did not, for the most part, carry intermediate inventories, but rather arranged to buy carlot amounts of lumber and sell them immediately to retail lumber dealers and industrial purchasers. Wholesalers also financed the intermediate market by making prompt payment to their mill sources and waiting for payment (for periods ranging from ten to ninety days) from their retail accounts.

We decided to use the empirical background of these field studies as a guide to research on the operation of markets in which information is limited and costly to obtain and transmit. Prior to this collaboration, one of the authors, Hoggatt, had written a doctoral dissertation, *Simulation of the Firm*, which employed computer simulation to study several problems in economic theory. This experience led us to believe that large-scale computer simulation would be an appropriate means of investigating our problem.

MAIN FEATURES OF THE COMPUTER SIMULATION

The Structure of the Market

Our model is stated as a computer program. Involved in it are three sets of participants in the market: manufacturers, wholesalers, and retailers. Communication between them is explicit rather than via a clearing mechanism, and initiative for the sending of all messages rests with the wholesalers. The right-hand columns of Figure 1 show the number of firms of each type, both at the beginning of the market's operation ($t = 0$) and at maximum number allowed in any period. We had to place maximum limits on the number of participating firms in order to fit the model into the high-speed memory of an IBM 709 computer. In the real market, of course, no such restriction exists. The proportions of the three types of firms were chosen so as to be approximately the same as the proportions existing in the actual market, but the scale of the market was cut down considerably. Even so, we may portray in the model all of the main featurers of operation and all of the accounting results of up to 105 firms, simultaneously.

Market Activities. In Figure 2 are presented the main flows of market activity between manufacturers, wholesalers, retailers, and final demand in this market. The commodity is shipped from manufacturers direct to retailers, who then sell to their local markets. As previously stated, communication is a special function of the wholesalers. They are in touch with both manufacturers and retailers, but no manufacturer is in direct contact with any other manufacturer or with any retailer, and no retailer is in contact with any manufacturer or with any retailer. The latter limitations are more severe than those found in actual practice, but it was very definitely characteristic of the market studied that contacts of the types we excluded were of minor importance. A mar-

	Number of Firms:	
	$t = 0$	Max.
Manufacturers	20	30
Wholesalers	10	15
Retailers	40	60
Final Demand	(One independent demand curve for each retailer)	

Fig. 1. The structure of the market.

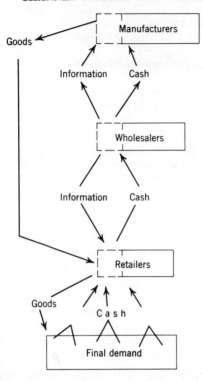

Fig. 2. Market flows of goods, information, and cash.

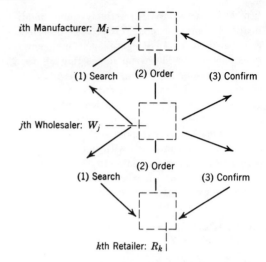

Fig. 3. Types of communication: Wholesalers first search, then order, then confirm.

ket group having a strong trade association or one in which oligopolistic interaction was significant would require different treatment in this respect than we have given here.

Types of Communication in the Market

Figure 3 summarizes the types of information flow that were represented in the simulation. Each "message" was sent by a wholesaler to a manufacturer or a retailer, and the wholesaler had to pay (unit message cost) for every message that he sent. These messages might be thought of as personal sales calls in some cases, telephone negotiations in other cases, and letters or teletype messages in still other cases. All of these messages are sent by wholesalers so that they can arrange transactions.

Steps in the Typical Transaction

Transactions occur in this market by means of the following procedure, outlined in Figure 4.

1. A wholesaler sends a *search* message to a manufacturer to determine what offer price the manufacturer has posted and what offer quantity he has available.

2. The wholesaler sends a *search* message to a retailer and obtains the retailer's bid price and bid quantity.

3. The wholesaler makes a test of the profitability of a potential transaction. If the test is met, he sends *ordering* messages to the manufacturer and the retailer, subject to confirmation from both sides.

4. If both sides confirm, the wholesaler sends a *confirming* message to each, the physical shipment goes immediately from the manufacturer directly to the retailer, and the wholesaler immediately pays the manufacturer the amount due to him. (The wholesaler does the financing of this intermediate market; he must wait until the end of the market period to receive the payment due him from the retailer.)

Thus, transactions are substantially *decentralized* in this market framework, and there is no clearing mechanism for the market as a whole. In fact, transactions occur at numerous offer prices and numerous bid prices within the same market period—a state of affairs which emphasizes the dependence of trading relations on strictly *localized* information.

Other Operating Features of the Model

Some additional features of the model will be mentioned briefly to indicate the scope of the interactions studied.

1. In our model each wholesaler has an opportunity to search and place orders in an attempt to complete one transaction. Wholesalers may then decide to try again and trading will continue

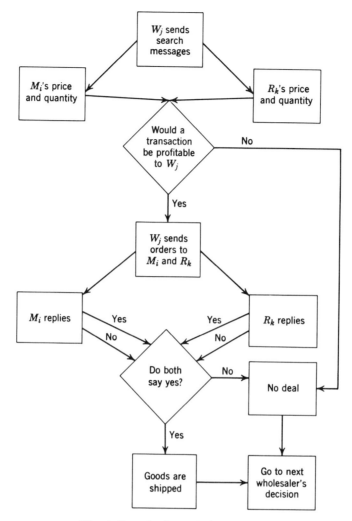

Fig. 4. Steps in the typical transaction.

until no wholesalers remain who wish to continue. We call each of these trial attempts a market *cycle*. A series of these cycles, terminating when wholesalers no longer wish to initiate search, we call a market *period*.

2. At the end of each market period, each manufacturer uses decision-rules to set his offer price, output rate, and offer quantity on the market for the next period, and each retailer sets bid price, bid quantity, and retail price and sales quantity into the localized (and monopolistically competitive) final market facing him.

3. At the end of each market period, insolvent firms (those having a negative cash position) go out of business. If average profits per firm in a certain class of participants are above an entry threshold, a new firm enters that class, up to the

maximum limits specified for the number of members of each class.

4. With probability less than one, each manufacturer and retailer adjusts physical plant upward or downward at the end of the market period to restore a desired ratio of plant to working capital.

Table 1 summarizes these additional operating features of the model.

Experimental Parameters of the Model

Unit Message Cost. An important parameter of the model is the unit cost of sending a message. This is subject to easy external control, and our runs of this market model involved, among other things, tests of the viability and

Table 1.   **Manufacturer's Decisions at End of Each Market Period**

1. Go out of business if cash is negative; otherwise,
2. Set offer price:
   a. Normal case (Sales rose when price was cut, or fell when price was raised.)
   $$\text{Price } (t+1) = \text{Price } (t) + \frac{\text{absolute change in price} \times \text{change in profit}}{\text{change in price} \times \text{scaling factor}}$$
   b. Perverse case (Sales fell when price was cut, or rose when price was raised.)
   $$\text{Price } (t+1) = \text{Price } (t) + \text{small random change}$$
3. Set output:
   $$\text{Output } (t+1) = \text{desired level of inventory} - \text{actual level of inventory}$$
4. Set offer quantity:
   $$\text{Offer quantity } (t+1) = [\text{output } (t+1) + (\text{inventory, end of } t)] \times \text{buffer}$$
5. Set preferences on wholesalers (*a* or *b* chosen depending on experimental control parameter SWPREF):
   a. By experience:
      (1) Compute, for each wholesaler,
      $$H = \frac{\text{number of transactions}}{\text{number of orders}} \times \text{total quantity shipped through this wholesaler}$$
      (2) Add small random factor to prevent ties.
      (3) Order wholesalers from highest value of H (best) to lowest value of H (worst).
   b. Order wholesalers by random choice.

Wholesalers' Decisions at End of Each Market Period

1. Go out of business if cash is negative; otherwise,
2. Set preferences on manufacturers
   a. By past experience (same rule as for manufacturers)
   b. By random choice
3. Set preferences on retailers
   a. By past experience (same rule as for manufacturers)
   b. By random choice

Retailers' Decisions at End of Each Market Period

1. Pay wholesalers amount due for purchases in period (t).
2. Go out of business if cash is negative; otherwise,
3. Set quantity sold into final market, to maximize expected profit.
4. Set bid quantity:
   Quantity $(t+1)$ = desired inventory in view of quantity sold into final market in period t − actual inventory
5. Set bid price:
   $P(t+1) = P(t) +$ [difference between bid quantity for $(t+1)$ and bid quantity for $(t) \times$ sensitivity parameter]
6. Set preferences on wholesalers:
   a. From past experience (same rule as for manufacturers)
   b. By random choice

Other Decisions, End of Each Period

1. Should there be new entry?
   $\left\{ \begin{array}{l} \text{Manufacturer} \\ \text{Wholesaler} \\ \text{Retailer} \end{array} \right.$

2. Should there be another period?
   $\left\{ \begin{array}{l} \text{Not if this is the last period} \\ \text{Not if market no longer has participants at some level} \end{array} \right.$

3. (On the average, every fifth period): Expand or reduce plant capacity.

efficiency of the market under different conditions of communication cost. Unit message cost, however, remained the same throughout any given run of the model.

Preference Orderings. Each transaction involves a specific triplet of market participants: one manufacturer, one wholesaler, and one retailer. The wholesaler selects the sequence of his contacts with manufacturers and retailers according to preference orderings on each of these classes of participants. Manufacturers and retailers are constrained in the model to accept only one order in any cycle. They use preference orderings for the purpose of determining which transaction opportunities to accept and which to reject.

We have studied the operation of the market under two alternative formulations of the preference ordering: (a) a preference ranking which each firm computes at the end of each market period on the basis of its specific experience with other market participants, and (b) a randomized preference ranking, generated separately for each firm at the end of each market period.

Manufacturers have preference orderings of wholesalers, but since they never deal with other manufacturers or directly with retailers, no preference orderings on these sets of participants are needed. Wholesalers have separate preference orderings on manufacturers and retailers, and retailers have preference rankings only on wholesalers. Each wholesaler sends search messages and attempts transactions with firms in the sequence governed by their positions in these preference orderings. When randomized preferences are used, the sequence of these market contacts is, of course, randomly determined.

The Market Cycle, the Market Period, and the Model "Run"

A market cycle is defined as an opportunity for each of the wholesalers, simultaneously, to attempt to arrange one transaction. Trading in such a market as the lumber market has this aspect of simultaneity. Our "market cycle" is an artificial construct which enables us to exemplify such simultaneity of behavior on the currently available digital computers, which are essentially serial machines.

The market period corresponds, in terms of parameter settings, to a calendar month of operations in the actual market which serves as our empirical referent. In the model, a size-

Preference Ordering

		Experience	Random
M e s s a g e c o s t	0	Run number 31	Run number 32
	12	Run number 29	Run number 30
	48	Run number 33	Run number 34
	192	Run number 35	Run number 36

Fig. 5. Runs of the model.

able and quite variable number of market cycles takes place during the market period.

Each run of the model is an observation of the market's timepath (exemplified in measures on a number of critical variables) under specified conditions. We restricted each run arbitrarily to sixty market periods, the equivalent of five years of market operation. Figure 5 lists the eight runs which serve as the basis for this paper.

The computer program labels its output according to run numbers. Each run was made with a specific set of parameters and was a maximum of sixty periods in length.

INTELLECTUAL ANTECEDENTS OF THE STUDY

Readers from our various audiences will all find echoes of their intellectual concerns in the model whose features have been summarized above. We shall now review the variety of intellectual developments that contribute to this study of market processes so that the rationale of the model can be understood.

Economic Features of the Model

The model not only contains the usual set of economic variables but also possesses four features that are of contemporary interest in economic theory: (1) it represents a multi-stage rather than a single-stage market; (2) the firms constituting the market face uncertainty and operate with limited information; (3) transactions occur by means of sequences of steps that are reminiscent of the Walrasian "tâtonnements" [1] though not identical with them; and (4) the system is dynamic in the strict, technical sense that its path develops, period by period, as a consequence of the interactions that occur. These aspects of the economic interpretation of the model will be discussed in turn.

Multi-Stage Market. Economic theory defines a one-stage market as a group of sellers of one or more related commodities confronting a group of buyers of those commodities. A multi-stage market, in contrast, involves a sequence of two or more transactions to move the commodity from points of production into the hands of final users. Thus, intermediaries whose major function is to buy and resell, in order to maintain connections between separated groups of firms, become of central importance in multi-stage markets.

There can be no doubt that multi-stage markets are of great empirical significance. It is all the more surprising, therefore, that little is said about them in the literature of price theory.

Theorists have set up a general argument concerning differences in price elasticity of demand at successive market stages. The final market possesses a demand function having given elasticity characteristics. Firms which serve this market make their purchases at the first prior, or "wholesale," marketing stage. Because these commodity purchases represent only one part of their costs, these firms generate total supply requirements at each possible purchase price which are less elastic, at each alternative purchase quantity, than the price-elasticity of demand at that quantity in the final market. The same argument extends backwards through the preceding market stages, until the raw materials stage is reached.

The theory has been used to explain why price fluctuations tend to have greater and greater amplitude, with changes in quantity demanded, at marketing stages that are increasingly remote from the final demand level.

This argument has obvious frailties as an explanation of vertical price structures since it requires quite special assumptions concerning cost functions, market structure, the distribution of inventories, inventory changes among market stages, etc. A related attempt at the explanation of demand responses at different marketing stages for the case of monopolistic competition is given by E. R. Hawkins [2].

Hawkins assumes a set of retail firms facing identical downward-sloping demand curves. Each of these firms makes purchase-quantity decisions based on its marginal-revenue curve, which is, of course, systematically less elastic than the average-revenue curve. It thus becomes possible to construct the demand curve facing the wholesaler by taking the aggregate of the retailers' marginal-revenue curves. Again, the same argument can be extended backwards to any number of prior stages, each of which then faces a less elastic demand at every quantity than the next stage.

These formulations, whether for pure or monopolistic competition, suffer from their dependence upon assumptions about elements of price and output decisions other than demands or costs relating only to the commodity that is being traced. A systematic theory of pricing and resource allocation through successive market stages still remains to be written.

The model we have used portrays these vertical price and output relationships in a more complex framework than that considered by Hawkins. Because transactions are decentralized, there is a *distribution* of prices at each market stage. We can therefore examine both the average transaction price at each stage and its dispersion or its range. We also observe how the average differentials between prices at successive marketing stages are affected by changes in the cost of market information. Our model therefore serves as a vehicle for further exploration of a number of problems of pricing and allocation in multi-stage markets.

Uncertainty, Limited Information. Explicit treatment of uncertainty and limited information in the economics of the firm and industry has been a central problem of economic analysis for two decades. It would exceed our purpose to review the entire course of these discussions, beginning with Knight [3] and proceeding through Hart [4] to the present time. The state of the theory as of a few years ago is summarized in the monograph, *Expectations, Uncertainty, and Business Behavior* [5].

Message Sequences Compared with Walrasian "Tâtonnements." In his classic work, Walras [1] suggested that the equilibrium price prevailing in each market could be arrived at by a series of adjustments, a process such as haggling or bargaining. For a long time, theoretical interest in the Walrasian system was focused on matters other than this problem of dynamic price formation. First came the increasing appreciation of the nature of general equilibrium: simultaneous resource-allocation balances in all (purely competitive) markets. Later, Leontief's input-output analysis was inspired rather directly by Walras. Now, however, contemporary theoretical interest in the stability of general equilibrium and in the computational burdens of the iterative approach to simultaneous equilibrium in all markets has forced a detailed reexamination of the precise mechanics of Walras' price adjustment process, or *tâtonnements*.

Uzawa [6] considers rigorously two different kinds of price adjustment process: simultaneous and successive. In essence, both types of adjustment require initial bids and offers as virtual market prices, the computation of excess demands and supplies at these two prices, the collection of modified price responses from both sides of the market, and the repetition of this adjustment until the bid price and the offer price are equalized at equilibrium.

The price adjustment processes in our market model differ from the above in the following ways:

1. Each bid price or offer price of an individual firm is held the same, is used in transactions throughout an entire market period, and is modified, by means of a feedback decision rule, only at the end of the market period. The new value is then used by the firm throughout the succeeding period.

2. Each transaction occurs solely through decisions by a specific triplet of firms—one manufacturer, one wholesaler, and one retailer—and is concluded at prices which are not necessarily the same as those appearing in other transactions. Thus, *distributions* of supply prices, purchase prices, and resale prices appear in the market, and we are interested in measuring not only the averages but the variances of these distributions.

3. Since no market clearing device exists *within* the market period, the entire market may be regarded, from the standpoint of the Walrasian theory of production and exchange, as being engaged in a search for equilibrium *over a series of market periods*. It would, of course, be possible to perform the intellectual experiment of *inserting* a market-clearing device into the model to perform the service of Walras' umpire, but this is emphatically not the kind of adjustment process that exists in the real-world market on which our model is based.

Market Dynamics: Iterative Interpretations. A very prominent concern among contemporary economists is to investigate the conditions of market equilibrium over time. It is impossible in short compass to review the entire scope of these developments. Uzawa's work, mentioned in the preceding section, is one contribution.

Arrow, Hurwicz, Debreu, Samuelson, and others have been concerned with three problems of dynamics which are somewhat related to our empirically based study:

1. What is the computational burden of an iteration leading to market equilibrium?

2. What processes may centralized and decentralized systems follow in approaching equilibrium adjustment?

3. What are the necessary and sufficient conditions for the existence of a stable dynamic equilibrium, if once achieved, and for the availability of a path to this equilibrium from a specified initial state?

Our model does not incorporate the usual restrictions which make it possible to construct theories of market dynamics. It is, in fact, intended to serve as a device for laboratory experimentation on a class of problems too complicated, as yet, for systematic theoretical treatment. Information is explicit and costly in the model, decision-sequences are easily traced, and the market's time-path can be derived for any interesting combination of initial conditions. Theorists may therefore have some interest in the consequences of this kind of exploration for their own approaches to further work.

Marketing Aspects of the Model

The applied field of marketing arose because enterprises faced two kinds of problems that were omitted by assumption from classical price theory: the problem of *organizing* an appropriate approach to the market, and the problem of *responding* to a variety of institutional restrictions in the system of social behavior represented by market dealings. We have seen that the treatment of informational and computational burdens of market operations, in the dynamic setting, has only recently become a major focus of work in economic theory. The need for a special field of marketing in the study of business behavior arose because complexities removed from economic analysis by assumption were, in fact, responsible for absorbing substantial resources and entrepreneurial attention in business life. "Marketing" became a study—at first in terms of judgmental, descriptive, and rough conceptual exploration—of the organization of business effort for market dealings and of the patterns of institutional structure which formed an environment for such efforts.

Numerous distinctive strands of background

therefore appear in the field of marketing. Breyer [7, 8] pioneered in the conceptual study of institutional complexes, their evolutionary properties, and their efficiency and cost performance.

Various writers, among them Fred Clark, Vaile, Grether, Cox, and Alderson, went beyond the conceptual assertion that different functional activities are performed in marketing organization and tried to define a central adjustment process. Clark called this process "concentration, equalization, and dispersion." Vaile, Grether and Cox called it "collecting, sorting, and dispersing." Alderson, in various versions, has defined it as a complex sorting and matching process.

None of these conceptual suggestions need be regarded as final; the proof of their usefulness must be in their power to interpret and predict marketing channel phenomena. What all the writers insist, however, is that *some organizing process exists for a complex of interactions in which no single decision-making entity has power, on its own, to control the nature of the system.*

Our simulation model incorporates explicitly a great many features of behavior that have been of interest to marketing scholars. Thus, we can use it to examine the organization and performance of the marketing channel.

It has been difficult to build a theoretical framework for the study of marketing channels. A brief account of a recent attempt to deal analytically with the communication features of an intermediate market may be instructive in showing how the problem may be conceived and how certain basic forces in the situation might be handled [9].

We begin by noting that a given group of suppliers (or manufacturers) may or may not find it efficient to use the services of wholesale intermediaries for communication with a given group of customers (or retailers). Initially, we regard the communication as consisting of a "link" which either exists or does not exist; if the link exists, it has a given cost per time period. Two alternative linkage systems are shown in Figure 6. This kind of diagram is to be found in practically every elementary marketing textbook, but it poses a very obvious analytic question: What market structure (i.e., for the case illustrated, merely what number of wholesalers) will emerge and what efficiency properties will it have?

We can answer these questions for the simple case that is defined by the following assumptions:

1. Each link has cost of q/time period, regardless of the amount of information flowing through it, distance, or other factors.

2. Commodity flow from manufacturers to retailers is given and constant.

3. Every manufacturer must be connected with every retailer directly or indirectly.

4. The number of manufacturers, M, and the number of retailers, R, are given and constant.

First, we examine the overall costs of various alternative networks. A system of *direct links* involves no intermediaries, each manufacturer being connected to every retailer [part (a) of Figure 6]. The total communication cost of such a system is

$$T_1 = q(M \times R) \qquad (1)$$

where M = number of manufacturers and R = number of retailers. Injecting one wholesaler

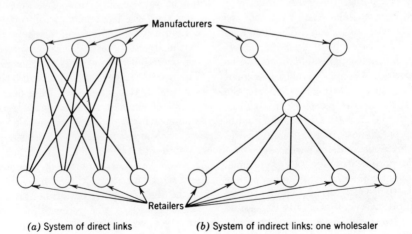

(a) System of direct links   (b) System of indirect links: one wholesaler

Fig. 6. Two alternative systems of communication linkages in a hypothetical market.

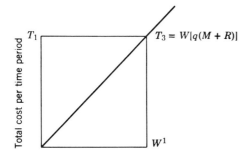

Fig. 7. Comparisons of total communication costs for two systems of linkages. Note: W = number of wholesalers; W^1 = number of wholesalers at which $T_1 = T$.

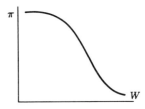

Fig. 8. A characterization of total economic profit to wholesalers. Note: Total amount of profit to wholesalers over and above all costs = $\pi = f(W)$. We can suppose that π falls as W increases.

into the situation [part (b) of Figure 6], we see that the total linkage costs become:

$$T_2 = q(M + R) \qquad (2)$$

Now suppose that additional wholesalers can enter the trade, but that each new one can only replicate the same network as was possessed by the first. The total linkage cost of the system can be expressed as a function of the number of wholesalers, W:

$$T_3 = W[q(M + R)] \qquad (3)$$

Figure 7 shows where this process has its limits. The greatest number of intermediaries that can be accommodated in the market is W'. At this number of wholesalers, the overall cost of indirect linkage is equal to the overall cost of a system of direct links.

Classical economic reasoning about incentives for entry and for changes in resource allocation can now be used to throw further light on the problem of optimal market structure. A single intermediary would possess monopoly power: indeed, he could absorb as economic profit, over and above all costs, most or all of the differential between his own costs and the costs of a system of direct links. This positive profit rate, when and if known about, would be the incentive to entry by new wholesale firms.

It is, however, normal to suppose that, as the number of firms offering the same service increases, competition among them reduces the potential economic profit for them all. Such a relation is shown, for a hypothetical case, in Figure 8.

The cost relation T_3 and the economic profit

relation $\pi = f(W)$ can now be summed to give us a function.

$$T_4 = W[q(M + R)] + f(W) \qquad (4)$$

This function represents the overall effective cost of the system *as viewed by its users*, that is, inclusive of economic profits arising from limits on the number of wholesalers. By simple differentiation, we can obtain a minimum of this cost function and find the number of wholesalers associated with this minimum. Diagrammatically, the situation is shown in Figure 9, the optimum number of wholesalers being W_0.

This theoretical model, therefore, has the useful characteristic of showing what we mean by optimal market structure and what conditions are required to bring about and maintain this optimum. In this sense, the model is an improvement over the simple structural diagram of Figure 6.

There are several respects, however, in which this model is seriously deficient as a guide to the formation of market structures in real cases, even where communication (and not a variety of other functional tasks) remains the central problem. We may list some normal properties

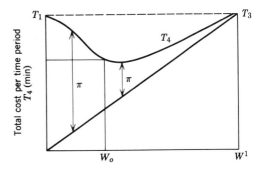

Fig. 9. Optimum number of wholesalers from the standpoint of the users of the market. Note: W_o = optimum number of wholesalers; W^1 = number of wholesalers.

of markets which violate the above restrictive assumptions:

1. Communication is intermittent and many methods with different costs may be used.
2. The communication system does not automatically connect together all members of the market.
3. The commodity flow depends on efficiency of communication and on intermediaries' margin.
4. Intermediaries have other tasks besides communication.
5. Numbers of manufacturers and retailers may be affected by the characteristics of the network.

The analysis just presented is static in character, but many interesting aspects of market communication are associated with *dyanamics*—time is important.

1. Market loyalties are significant.
2. Decisions are made in view of market experience and expectations.

If all these restrictions are relaxed at the same time, we create a system that is too large and cumbersome for solution by ordinary techniques of analysis. The simulation model presents an alternative avenue of attack on this problem.

Background of the Model in the Theory of Organization

We can take still another approach to conceptual characterization of a complex market. It can be viewed as a *decision system* in which informational inputs, behavioral and physical constraints, and criteria of choice determine the response of a decision maker at each local place in the system and in which the problem is to comprehend the interactions among these decision makers. Barnard, Simon, March, and other modern organization theorists have placed the decision-making schema at the heart of the study of the formal organization. If a market complex were indeed one organization, we could use directly the guidelines that these theorists have developed. The essential conditions for the existence of a formal organization are these: (1) there must exist a set of objectives which are, at least partially, perceived by all members of the organization as placing claims on their behavior; and (2) mechanisms must exist for the distribution of benefits for performance favorable to the purposes of the organization, and for the imposition of sanctions against inappropriate behavior. Because the organization theorist is loath to accept the *legal* boundary of the organization as the limit of its coordinative behavior, he often states that the

clienteles served by the organization are in fact part of it.

It is clear that a complex market is a system of behavior and that it has some of the properties of a single, formal organization. Two crucial features are, however, missing: recognition of common purposes and a mechanism for distributing rewards and penalties in accordance with the quality of performance in reference to such purposes. At best, we can say that the system of behavior represented by our model is a "quasi-organization," with laws of behavior which need not coincide with the minimum conditions of operation for a single organization.

First of all, our model fails to meet the specifications for a formal organization because its decision system is at the extreme of *decentralization*. Essentially no coordination demands are made upon members of the system with respect to any overall target. Secondly, even if, for example, a central clearing mechanism were inserted into the model to which all manufacturers and all retailers were required to respond, this would still not resolve the issue of commonness of purpose. Some degree of mutuality does in fact exist. If all of the manufacturers go bankrupt so will the wholesalers and retailers who, by our assumption that the model stands alone, depend upon these manufacturers for supply. Nevertheless, such underlying mutuality of interest is nowhere *operational* in the decision schema possessed by the individual firm.

What *is* present in our simulation model is a limited system of loyalties and priorities as a control on the transaction-making behavior of members of the market. This scheme of preference orderings could be strengthened in such a manner as to bring about *objective* mutuality of interest between, say, manufacturer number 3 and wholesaler number 7. Unless we went on, however, to modify the behavior of these two firms so that it represented more than the standard set of rules for bargaining possessed by *all* firms in the market, we would not really invade the basic character of the decision system itself. It is this which would require change, in the direction of greater overt coordination, before we could claim that the model had the properties of a single organization.

MAIN RESULTS OF THE INVESTIGATION

Our model contained a maximum number of approximately 16,000 variables and an uncounted number of relationships. Many of the latter were not in mathematical form but consisted of logical branches and decision trees to deal with various contingencies.

The model sets forth the full system of interactions which we considered to be important. Unfortunately, its complexity prevented analytic reduction. Therefore, our first concern in scheduling runs of the model was to establish its *viability*, that is, its ability, under plausible initial conditions and parameter settings, to generate behavior over time.

Viability: Tests and Interpretation

First, we report on the results achieved. In each of the eight runs of the model (Figure 5), the market continued to operate effectively for sixty periods—or the equivalent of five calendar years.[1]

It may appear transparently simple to demand that a model of this type merely exhibit persistent behavior, but this is a first requirement that may in fact fail to be met. We may then ask: What accounts for the viability of the model? Did the initial conditions and parameter settings of the model *guarantee* viability, thus removing strength from the assertion that the model's capability in this regard is a significant test of its usefulness, or can we claim that the model's viability is evidence that it illuminates important features of the real-world system which serves as its background?

Generally, stability of dynamic economic systems may first be approached in terms of the asymptotic character of such systems [10]. That is, do they eventually settle into a time-path having specified properties of convergence? This may mean that, after stability has been achieved, the main variables of the system repeat identically the same values through all succeeding periods. Alternatively, if stable *growth* of such a system is the desired property, stability may be interpreted as consisting of steady change over time, with proportional, or otherwise specified, changes in all variables.

Two additional features of dynamic stability need to be considered. First, there is the question of whether stability is considered as a *local* phenomenon: Is the system expected to reach an equilibrium state (after some adjustment interval) only if a *small* displacement is brought about, or is its adjustment process sufficiently powerful to accommodate massive changes in

[1] We have also run the model on other occasions for up to 99 periods without breakdown.

the position of the system? A second, and closely related interpretation has to do with the *initial* position of the system, not with its adjustment properties from other points in its time-path. If the system will eventually reach equilibrium from *any* initial conditions, no matter what they are, it is said to be *globally* rather than locally stable. This is a severe condition to impose.

Viability, in the sense in which we have used the term, is a quite weak condition on our dynamic system. It does not require that *equilibrium* be achieved but only that behavior should persist over a significant time interval.

For every one of the eight runs of our model, we specified the same set of initial conditions and parameter values, except for those parameters which control the unit cost of sending a message and the method of establishing preference orderings. In general, the remaining conditions were a close but necessarily idealized characterization of the real-world market. Certain of the initial relationships are "knife-edged" in character. For example, the wholesaler's spread between purchase price and resale price of the commodity was only 5%, which left little room to cover communication costs, overhead costs, and any errors of calculation or interpretation that might be present in the decision rules according to which the wholesaler operated. The initial conditions, then, tended to impose the requirement that the system commence operation under realistic circumstances leaving small margin for error.

A few parameters of our model had to be specified for completeness had no direct empirical referent. These were sensitivity parameters in certain of the pricing and output decision rules. It was clearly possible for firms in the real market to follow any of a wide variety of decision rules (and, of course, to follow them with imperfect consistency). We sought only to specify rules which would yield more or less representative behavior, which explains the extreme difficulty of parameter setting. We set the sensitivity parameter in the manufacturers' pricing rule to yield relatively large responses to changes in the situation, and the comparable parameter in the retailer's rule for setting bid prices to yield small responses. While this was roughly in accordance with observation, it is well to remember that our specification of these parameters may have had considerable effect on the viability of the model.

Another quite general question, still with reference to viability, concerns the nature of the adjustment process. It is well known that any given linear static system has a variety of nonlinear dynamic interpretations, depending on the specific character of the adjustment process.

Our approach to an adjustment process has little in common with strong convergent adjustments such as those requiring an adjustment rate proportional to the amount of excess demand at the disequilibrium price. Rather, we left adjustment to the quite complex interactions occurring in a decentralized framework having no clearing mechanism. This is closer to real life but farther from the known mathematics of systems or control theory.

Market Efficiency: Measures and Interpretation

Given that the model would "work," in the minimum sense of producing viable behavior, we next raised questions about its efficiency characteristics as a market mechanism.

The measures of efficiency and the empirical results from computer runs are reviewed in detail in Chapters 7, 8, and 9 of *Simulation of Market Processes*. Here we will discuss the measurement concepts and results in broad terms, concentrating on the efficiency properties of wholesale dealings.

At the beginning of a market period, an *ex ante* market offer curve can be constructed from offers of the individual manufacturers at the various prices they specify. A similar *ex ante* demand relation can be constructed from the bid quantities of retailers at their various bid prices. This, if they had the wit to know it, is the aggregate situation facing the wholesalers as a group. *Ex ante* imbalance in the market is present if the comparison of these two schedules shows excess quantity offered (or excess quantity bid for). Thus, we may use the excess supply, positive or negative, to indicate the degree of dynamic equilibrating tendency in the market.

Market information must be sought and paid for, and transactions can occur only in a decentralized fashion. The most efficient conceivable outcome for this decentralized system would be that all of the profitable bargains are taken up, going from best to worst, and stopping just at the point where the last transaction covered variable wholesale costs and no more. We measured the actual performance of the market relative to this standard by computing the market efficiency ratio.

Certain results were as one would expect: the efficiency ratio was systematically high at zero message cost and it fell as the unit message cost was progressively raised in successive runs.

Within a given run of the model, market efficiency generally fell off considerably during the most active adjustment interval (when, for example, new firms were entering), rose again after this process was mostly completed, and tended to oscillate in a rather narrow range thereafter.

Both the general level and the time-path of market efficiency were quite similar for all six of the computer runs that involved unit message costs of zero, $12, and $48. When message cost was raised, however, to very high levels in the final two runs of the model, there was a steep drop in market efficiency. Even so, the market gradually struggled toward a relative improvement of performance throughout these two runs.

Comparing the effects of experiential and randomized preferences, we see little difference in the profile of market efficiency at each level of unit message cost. Excess supply, however, is greater for randomized preferences at each level of message cost than for experiential preferences. From classical theory, we would expect greater efficiency to be associated with market processes that involve anonymity but this is not what we observe.

Size Distributions of Firms

A third class of results presented in this summary has to do with the size distribution of firms. There is an extensive literature in economics dealing with both theoretical and applied studies of the shape and causes of this distribution for different industries and kinds of firms. Most of these studies search for explanations of size distributions either in the differing amounts of entrepreneurial ability in different firms or in the differing amounts of resources initially available. We, however, find that skewed size distributions occur in our model as a result of *market* pressures on identically-endowed firms which are all employing the same decision rules. Further, these distributions depend on the preference rules employed and on the cost of information. We have shown that unequal size distribution may be a result of the operation of the market process itself. We do not need to call upon differing attributes of the individual firms in order to explain the phenomenon.

Related to this question of size distribution is a concept of market structure which we have called *segmentation*. Conceptually, a market segment is defined as a grouping of firms which trade with each other but do not trade with firms outside the group. Further details of this phenomenon are presented in Chapter 5 of *Simulation of Market Processes*.

The significance of market segmentation resides in the fact that the activity of the market is decentralized but not anonymous when nonrandom preference rules are employed. Market segments are an outgrowth of the failure of the system to be completely interconnected. Greater segmentation occurs as loyalties to market partners are emphasized or as costs of information are increased. Large firms are able to have connections with several market partners and, hence, reduce the number of market segments. With these concepts we link together the traditional economic interpretations and the sociological aspects of market process.

REFERENCES

1. Léon Walras, *Elements d'Economic Politique Pure*, translated by W. Jaffe as *Elements of Pure Economics*. Homewood, Ill.: R. D. Irwin, 1954.
2. E. R. Hawkins, "Vertical Price Relationships," in Reavis Cox and Wroe Alderson, eds., *Theory in Marketing*. Chicago: R. D. Irwin, 1950, pp. 179–192.
3. F. H. Knight, *Risk, Uncertainty and Profit*. Boston and New York: Houghton Mifflin Company, 1921; London: reissued 1948.
4. A. G. Hart, *Anticipation, Uncertainty, and Dynamic Planning*. Chicago: University of Chicago Press, 1940.
5. Mary Jean Bowman, ed. *Expectations, Uncertainty, and Business Behavior*. New York: Social Science Research Council, 1958.
6. H. Uzawa, "Tâtonnement in the Theory of Exchange," *Review of Economic Studies*, XXVII, 3 (June, 1960), pp. 182–194.
7. Ralph Frederick Breyer, *The Marketing Institution*. New York: McGraw-Hill, 1924.
8. R. F. Breyer, *Quantitative Systemic Analysis: Channel and Channel Group Costing*. Philadelphia: published by the author, 1949.
9. F. E. Balderston, "Communication Networks in Intermediate Markets," *Management Science* (January, 1958), pp. 156–171.
10. Peter Newman, "Approaches to Stability Analysis," *Economica*, N.S., 28 (February, 1961), pp. 12–29. (This article is a review of recent work on concepts of stability in dynamic economic systems.)

26. A Note on Manufacturers' Choice of Distribution Channels

ROLAND ARTLE and STURE BERGLUND*

This article tackles, with the aid of mathematical models and indifference formulas, the difficult decision of direct versus indirect distribution. The presentation concentrates on personal selling costs rather than the total marketing mix alternatives. The key question asked is: "What choice gives the lowest total cost and the maximum profits?"

GENERAL APPROACH

Many marketing problems are usually analysed in verbal terms only. For instance, different alternatives as regards the marketing routes, or channels, through which goods and services or their titles flow, are mostly considered in terms of "advantages" and "disadvantages." Recently, however, techniques aiming at quantification—such as linear programming and search theory—have been gaining favor. This essay purports to clarify, in quantitative terms, some of the considerations that may underlie a manufacturer's choice of distribution channels. We shall limit ourselves to a comparison of two alternatives, namely selling through wholesalers and selling directly to retailers.

There is a simple relationship that is sometimes used to explain why a manufacturer of products such as groceries, drugs, and dry goods, very often sells his goods through wholesalers. This relationship can be illustrated as follows:

Given four manufacturers and ten retailers, buying goods from each manufacturer, the number of contact lines necessary will be found to vary with the number of wholesalers, as the diagram shows. When selling directly each manufacturer contacts ten retailers, in all adding up to 40 contact lines. If the manufacturers turn to selling through a wholesaler, the necessary number of contacts reduces to 14. If the manufacturers sell their products through *two*

• SOURCE: Roland Artle and S. Berglund, "A Note on Manufacturers' Choice of Distribution Channel," *Management Science* (July, 1959), pp. 460–471.

* *The Stockholm School of Economics*

192

wholesalers, there will be 28 contact lines needed, and so on.

As is easily seen, however, this relationship rather simplifies too much. There are in fact differences in costs hidden in the diagram: any two contact lines may differ from the point of view of costs. This is obvious when, for example, the line between a manufacturer and a wholesaler is compared with the line between a manufacturer and a retailer. One may be used more or less frequently or with smaller or greater inputs per time than the other.

However, it seems to us that the above-mentioned relationship may serve as a fruitful starting point for further analysis. By splitting up each contact line into its components, functions, a much more realistic basis seems to be provided for computations of the inputs involved in different choices of distribution channels. The evaluation of each function may then be carried out in terms of standard costs, in order to facilitate comparisons between different alternatives. Further, the amounts of all the necessary inputs as well as the size and structure of the unit or standard costs applied to them may be adapted to those conditions that one may want to analyse.

For the sake of simplicity we shall limit ourselves to a study of the pure selling function, and we shall start with a practical illustration of the method. Other distributive functions, such as transportation, order routine, and handling of the goods, could be treated similarly. Obviously there is in reality a great variety of alternatives as regards channels of distribution. The examples described here are chosen because they are considered simple and sharply outlined.

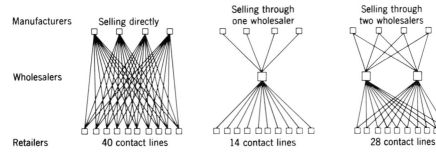

Fig. 1

PRACTICAL ILLUSTRATION[1]

Suppose there are ten retailers selling some particular goods in a town. The distance between any two neighboring retailers is on the average one mile.

Further it is assumed that there are four manufacturers supplying the ten retailers with their goods. Each manufacturer produces and sells one particular good. The factories are situated at different places, each place being some 15 miles away from the town where the retailers are located.

In the first case we shall assume that the manufacturers sell their products directly to retailers. Each manufacturer sends his salesman to call at each retailer some 50 times per year on the average. Thus each retailer is assumed to receive 200 calls per year by salesmen. Every call gives rise to an order of 25 units. Each of the four goods has the same price, namely $1.50 per unit, when sold to retailers. The total costs, per year, of the personal contacts will then be

A. The manufacturers' costs:

1. Assume that it will take the salesmen 20 minutes to drive in to a central point in the town and that their salaries per hour, amount to $4.50. The cost of the car is estimated at 12 cents per mile. To get to the central point some 50 times per year will then cost:

salaries:	cgk =	$75
motoring costs:	cfh =	$90
costs of each manufacturer:		
	$c(gk + fh)$ =	$165
total costs:	$ac(gk + fh)$ =	$660

2. Assume that it takes some four minutes to get from one customer to the next, on the average. The distance between the central point and the first customer is also assumed to be covered in four minutes. Total costs of travelling between the customers will then be:

salaries:	$bcgm$ =	$150
motoring costs:	$bchi$ =	$60
costs of each manufacturer:		
	$bc(gm + hi)$ =	$210
total costs:	$abc(gm + hi)$ =	$840

[1] In order to give the examples more clarity and generality, the computations have been given both algebraic and numerical form. The following symbols and assumed values of the parameters will be used in the examples:

Number of manufacturers	a		4
Number of retailers	b		10
Number of calls per retailer and manufacturer	c		50
Number of units per order and manufacturer	d		25
Price per unit, to retailers	e		1.50$
Distance between each manufacturer and a central point in the town	f		15 miles
Salesmen's salary, per hour	g		4.50$
Travelling costs per mile	h		0.12$
Distance between any two neighboring retailers	i		1 mile
Time to drive from factory to town	k hours	20	minutes
Time to drive from one retailer to the next	m hours	4	minutes
Fixed time per call	n hours	18	minutes
Time varying with number of order lines	o hours/line	0.6	minutes/line
Time varying with order value	p hours/$	0.8	minutes/20$
Salesman's waiting time per call	q	4	minutes
Number of contacts between wholesaler and each manufacturer	r		10
Wholesaler's or manufacturer's cost per contact between them	s		1 $
Fixed costs of manufacturing	t	20.000	$
Variable costs of manufacturing	j		0.90$/unit

3. On the basis of some empirical studies a regression analysis was carried out that showed visiting time to consist of the following parts: 18 minutes (fixed time) + 0.6 minutes per order line + 0.8 minutes per 20 dollar of sales.

These results need further validation. But if we do accept the equation as giving the approximate length of visiting time, the following computations will give total costs of calling at retailers:

cost of fixed time: $bcgn$ =   \$675
cost of time varying with the
    number of order lines: $bcgo$ =   \$22.50
cost of time varying with sales:
                              $bcdegp$ =   \$56.25
costs of each manufacturer:
            $bcg(n + o + dep)$ =   \$753.75
total costs: $abcg(n + o + dep)$ = \$3,015

4. The salesmen's costs of returning to their factories:

$$ac(gk + fh) = \$660$$

(The salesmen's costs of returning to their factories from the last customer are assumed to equal those given in point 1 above.)

B. The retailer's costs:

It is assumed that the salesman will have to wait some four minutes, on the average, until the retailer can spare the time to see him. The time the retailer spends will thus be given by the equation above, with the modification that the fixed time should be reduced by four minutes. Total costs of retailers will then be, assuming the retailer's time to be of the same value as the salesman's:

cost of fixed time: $abcg(n - q)$ = \$2,100
variable costs: $abcg(o + dep)$ =   \$315
total costs: $abcg(n - q + o + dep)$ = \$2,415

In the second case it is assumed that the manufacturers sell their goods through a wholesaler, located at the centre of the town. The wholesaler also calls at each retailer some 50 times per year on the average. His sales of each of the four goods are assumed to equal the manufacturers' sales in case they sell directly. The wholesaler's salesman has the same salary as the manufacturer's, that is \$4.50 per hour. The wholesaler orders his goods some ten times per year from each manufacturer. The contact between manufacturer and wholesaler is assumed to cost both one dollar per order irrespective of order size (contact by telephone).

Total costs per year can then be calculated as follows:
A. The manufacturers' costs:
The cost of receiving orders: ars = $\underline{\$40}$
B. Wholesaler's costs:
1. The cost of ordering from manufacturers, as above: ars = $\underline{\$40}$
2. The cost of driving to every customer (compare the first case, A.2.):
        salary: $bcgm$ = \$150
        motoring costs: $bchi$ = $\underline{\$60}$
        total costs: $bc(gm + hi)$ = $\overline{\$210}$
3. The cost of calling at retailers (the same formula as in the first case is assumed to apply):
        fixed time cost: $bcgn$ = \$675
        variable costs: $abcg(o + dep)$ = $\underline{\$315}$
        total costs: $bcg(n + ao + adep)$ = $\overline{\$990}$
C. Retailers' costs:
The calls of the wholesaler's salesman will cause the retailers to have the following costs:

$$bcg(n - q) + abcgo + abcdegp = \$840$$

Let us now, as *a third case*, assume that the manufacturers sell their products through *two* wholesalers. Suppose, for the sake of illustration, that only every second visit that the two wholesalers' salesmen make at retailers, results in a sale, but that all other conditions remain as above. Each wholesaler will then receive 25 one hundred and fifty-dollar-orders per year, on the average. In this case total costs will be computed thus:
A. The manufacturers' costs: $2ars$ = \$80
B. The wholesalers' costs:
1. The cost of ordering from manufacturers, as above: $2ars$ = \$80
2. The cost of driving to every customer (as in the second case, point B.2. but doubled, since there are now two wholesalers):

$$2bc(gm + hi) = \$420$$

3. The cost of calling at retailers (compare the second case, point B.3.):

$$2bcgn + 2ab\frac{c}{2}go + 2ab\frac{c}{2}degp = \$1,665$$

C. The retailers' costs:

$$2bcg(n - q) + 2ab\frac{c}{2}go + 2ab\frac{c}{2}degp$$
$$= \$1,365$$

Comparison between the three cases gives the following selling costs:

Case I	Case II	Case III
$2ac(gk + fh)$	$2ars$	$4ars$
$abc(gm + hi)$	$bc(gm + hi)$	$2bc(gm + hi)$
$abcg(n + o + dep)$	$bcg(n + ao + adep)$	$2bcg\left(n + \dfrac{ao}{2} + \dfrac{adep}{2}\right)$
$abcg(n - q + o + dep)$	$bcg(n - q + ao + adep)$	$2bcg\left(n - q + \dfrac{ao}{2} + \dfrac{adep}{2}\right)$
= \$7,590	= \$2,120	= \$3,610

Thus, under the conditions given, total contact costs of manufacturers and retailers will amount to $7,590, if manufacturers sell directly to retailers. Do they turn to selling through a wholesaler contact costs will decrease to $2,120. Costs rise, however, sharply when another wholesaler enters the stage: with two wholesalers contact will amount to $3,610.

Which Choice Gives the Lowest Manufacturing and Distribution Costs?

A manufacturer may sometimes consider it possible to sell more if he sells directly to retailers than if he sells through wholesalers. The fixed part of the cost of manufacturing would then be spread over a larger number of units sold: that is, manufacturing costs per unit would be reduced. The results might be a reduction in the total costs of manufacturing and selling, namely if the reduction in manufacturing costs would more than counterbalance the probable increase in selling costs. The question may then be raised: At what point will a rise in sales, when manufacturers sell directly to retailers, give the same total costs per unit as when manufacturers sell through wholesalers? Some answers to this question will be given in the following. To begin with, conditions earlier specified will be applied once again. It will further be assumed that manufacturing costs consist of a fixed part (that does not vary with moderate changes in the number of units produced) and another part that varies proportionately with the number of units. As before, the study will be limited to costs of personal contacts. Other selling costs will be neglected.

In principle, a rise in sales may be thought to come about through

(a) an increase in the number of calls upon customers, with sales per call remaining unchanged;
(b) an increase in sales per call, with the number of calls remaining unchanged; and
(c) some combination of changes in the number of calls and in sales per call.

We shall proceed by analysing each of these alternatives. Variable manufacturing costs will be neglected, since they will not affect results. Throughout it will be assumed that the fixed costs will amount to $20,000.

• *Example 1.* Suppose a retailer buys the same amount of each product each time a salesman calls upon him irrespective of whether the salesman comes slightly more often or slightly more seldom than what he used to. Let it further be assumed that he buys the same amount irrespective of whether the salesman represents

a wholesaler or a manufacturer. The question is then posed: how much should the manufacturers' salesmen increase their number of calls upon retailers in order to make the manufacturers' total costs (of manufacturing and personal contacts) just about as low as when manufacturers sell through a wholesaler?

Let the average number of calls that a salesman makes upon each retailer $= x_1$.

Let A stand for the expression:

$$ac\{2(gk + fh) + b[(gm + hi) + g(n + o + dep)]\},$$

i.e. the costs of selling in Case I, the retailers' costs not included, and B stand for the expression: $2ars + bc[(gm + hi) + g(n + ao + adep)]$, i.e. the costs of selling in Case II, the retailers' costs not included.

The four manufacturers in our example will then incur the following costs of manufacturing (fixed costs) and selling (costs of personal contacts), when selling directly to retailers:

$$T + \frac{x_1 A}{c}$$

or $20,000 + 4x_1 \cdot 25.875$

The unit cost will be calculated as:

$$\frac{T + (x_1 A / c)}{abdx_1} \quad \text{or} \quad \frac{20,000 + 4x_1 \cdot 25.875}{1,000x_1}$$

This figure is to be compared to the unit cost when selling through a wholesaler:

$$\frac{T + B}{abcd} \quad \text{or} \quad \frac{20,000 + 1,280}{50,000} = \$0.4256$$

The two unit costs are then put equal in order to solve the problem:

$$\frac{T + (x_1 A / c)}{abdx_1} = \frac{T + B}{abcd} \quad \text{or}$$

$$\frac{20,000 + 103.5x_1}{1000x_1} = \$0.4256$$

$$x_1 = c \frac{T}{T - (A - B)} \quad \text{or } x_1 = 62.1 \text{ calls.}$$

Thus we find that manufacturers must send their salesmen to visit retailers at least *63* times per year to get the same costs per unit sold as when selling through a wholesaler, provided that the wholesaler's salesman calls upon retailers some *50* times per year.

From an over-all, macroeconomic, point of view it might be argued that the retailers' costs of receiving salesmen should also be included. If they are, the break-even point will naturally be found to increase. In our example it would amount to 68.8 calls.

• *Example 2.* In this case it will be assumed that manufacturers let their salesmen call upon retailers the same number of times as the wholesaler does. Instead, manufacturers are assumed to aim at increasing order sizes. Here the problem will be: Which order size is required to obtain the same cost per sold unit (when manufacturers sell directly) as that which would have arisen, had manufacturers sold through a wholesaler?

Let the average number of units that a manufacturer sells each time his salesman calls upon a retailer $= u_1$ (order size).

Manufacturers will then incur the following costs when selling directly to retailers: $T + A + abcegp(u_1 - d)$ or $20,000 + 4,950 + 9u_1$.

The unit cost will be calculated as:

$$\frac{T + A + abcegp(u_1 - d)}{abcu_1} \quad \text{or} \quad \frac{24,950 + 9u_1}{2,000u_1}$$

The corresponding cost when selling through a wholesaler will be (as above):

$$\frac{T + B}{abcd} \quad \text{or} \quad \$0.4256$$

When the two unit costs are put equal, we find:

$$\frac{T + A + abcegp(u_1 - d)}{abcu_1} = \frac{T + B}{abcd}$$

or

$$\frac{24,950 + 9u_1}{2,000u_1} = 0.4256$$

$$u_1 = d\left(\frac{T + A - abcdegp}{T + B - abcdegp}\right)$$

of 29.6 units.

It should be observed that *abcdegp* represents the cost of selling time, varying with order value. It is identical in case I, II and III. If we call it *V*, we can write the expression:

$$u_1 = d\left(\frac{T + A - V}{T + B - V}\right)$$

The manufacturers' salesman must thus try to get at least *30* units per order, in order to compensate for the lower cost of personal contacts, when manufacturers sell through a wholesaler. This is to be compared to the order size that the wholesaler is assumed to get, namely *25* units (of each manufacturer's goods). In case retailers' costs of receiving salesmen are included

as above, the point of equilibrium will be found to lie at 31.3 units per order.

• *Example 3.* In reality a rise in sales is likely to come about through a combination of the two variables studied in isolated form above, namely number of calls and size of order. We pose the question: which combinations of the two will give the same costs per unit when selling directly as when selling through a wholesaler?

Let x_1 and u_1, as above, stand for number of calls and order size, respectively.

Total costs per unit when selling directly to retailers will then be:

$$\frac{T + x_1\left[\dfrac{A}{c} + abegp(u_1 - d)\right]}{abx_1u_1} \quad \text{or}$$

$$\frac{20,000 + 4x_1(24.75 + 0.045u_1)}{40x_1u_1}$$

Corresponding costs per unit when selling through a wholesaler will be:

$$\frac{T + B}{abcd} \quad \text{or} \quad \$0.4256$$

And so we get the following equation:

$$\frac{T + x_1\left[\dfrac{A}{c} + abegp(u_1 - d)\right]}{abx_1u_1} = \frac{T + B}{abcd}$$

or

$$\frac{20,000 + 4x_1(24.75 + 0.045u_1)}{40x_1u_1} = 0.4256$$

$$x_1 = \frac{cdT}{u_1(T + B - V) - d(A - V)}$$

or

$$x_1 = \frac{1,187}{u_1 - 5.88}$$

This equation can be expressed graphically as shown by Figure 2. The curve A shows all those combinations between number of calls and size of order that give the same added costs of manufacturing and selling, per unit.

The diagram in Figure 2 shows for example that *50* calls, each resulting in an order of *29.6* units on the average (= 1,480 units per manufacturer and year) give the same total costs per unit as *60* calls, each resulting in an order of *25.7* units on the average (= 1,540 units per manufacturer and year) or as *40* calls, each resulting in an order of *35.6* units (= 1,423 units per manufacturer and year). All these alternatives, relating to direct selling from the manu-

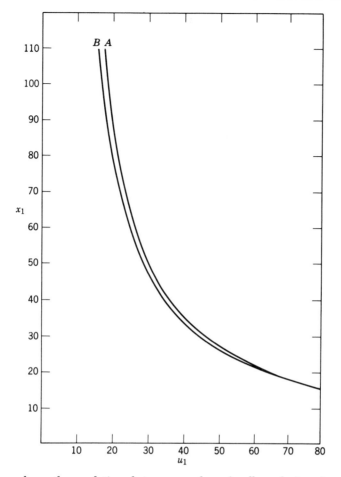

Fig. 2. The diagram shows those relations between number of calls and size of order that give, respectively, the same costs per unit (curve A) and the same contribution to profits (curve B), when selling directly to retailers, as when selling through a wholesaler.

facturer, render the same total costs per unit as when selling through a wholesaler.

If, in this case, retailers' costs of receiving salesmen are included, the relation between number of calls and size of order in the points of equilibrium will have the form:

$$x_1 = \frac{1{,}154}{u_1 - 8.24}$$

Which Choice Gives Maximum Profits?

• *Example 4.* The preceding examples, numbers 1–3, have illustrated the computation of an equilibrium point (or rather a set of points) where selling directly results in the same total costs per unit sold as when selling through a wholesaler.

If, on the other hand, the manufacturers aim at maximal profits by maximizing the contribution to fixed costs, a somewhat different method of computation is called for. The problem is here to compute the equilibrium point, where the dollar amount of this contribution is the same, whether selling directly or through a wholesaler.

Let us assume, as before, that each manufacturer and the wholesaler have priced their goods identically, viz. $1.50 per unit, when sold to retailers, and further that the variable manufacturing costs of each manufacturer amounts to $0.90 per unit.

When selling directly the total contributions will then be:

$$abx_1u_1(e - j) - x_1\left[\frac{A}{c} + \frac{V}{cd}(u_1 - d)\right]$$

for

$$(4)(10x_1u_1)(1.50 - 0.90) - (4x_1)(24.75 + 0.045u_1) = 4x_1(5.955u_1 - 24.75)$$

When selling through a wholesaler the contribution, computed correspondingly will be:

$abcd(e - j) - B$ or $30,000 - 1,280 = 28,720$

The equilibrium point desired can then be expressed in the equation:

$$abx_1u_1(e - j) - x_1\left[\frac{A}{c} + \frac{V}{cd}(u_1 - d)\right] = abcd(e - j) - B$$

or

$$4x_1(5.955u_1 - 24.75) = 28,720$$

$$x_1 = \frac{abcd(e - j) - B}{u_1\left[ab(e - j) - \dfrac{V}{cd}\right] - \dfrac{A - V}{c}} \text{ or}$$

$$= \frac{1,205.7}{u_1 - 4.16} \text{ calls.}$$

Table 1

Example 3			Example 4		
x_1	u_1	M	x_1	u_1	M
15	85.04	1,276	15	84.54	1,268
16	80.09	1,281	16	79.52	1,272
17	75.73	1,287	17	75.08	1,276
18	71.85	1,293	18	71.14	1,281
19	68.37	1,299	19	67.62	1,285
20	65.25	1,305	20	64.45	1,289
22	59.85	1,317	22	58.96	1,297
24	55.36	1,329	24	54.40	1,306
26	51.55	1,340	26	50.53	1,314
28	48.29	1,352	28	47.22	1,322
30	45.46	1,364	30	44.35	1,331
35	39.81	1,393	35	38.61	1,351
40	35.57	1,423	40	34.30	1,372
50	29.63	1,483	50	28.27	1,414
60	25.67	1,540	60	24.26	1,456
70	22.84	1,599	70	21.38	1,497
80	20.72	1,658	80	19.23	1,538
90	19.07	1,716	90	17.56	1,580
100	17.75	1,775	100	16.22	1,622
110	16.67	1,834	110	15.12	1,663

The table shows those relations between number of calls ($= x_1$) and size of order ($= u_1$) that give, respectively, the same costs per unit sold (example 3) and the same contribution to profits (example 4), when selling directly to retailers, as when selling through a wholesaler.

$M = x_1u_1$.

The curve B in Figure 2 shows all those combinations between number of calls and size of order that give the same contribution to fixed costs when selling directly as when selling through a wholesaler.

The Figure shows for example that in this case *50* calls, each resulting in an order of *28.3* units on the average (= *1,414* units per manufacturer and year) give the same contribution as *60* calls, each resulting in an order of *24.3* units (= *1,456* units per manufacturer and year) or as *40* calls, each resulting in an order of *34.3* units (= *1,372* units per manufacturer and year). These figures should be compared to those of the preceding example (*1,480*, *1,540* and *1,423* units respectively).

CONCLUSION

Since the aim of this paper has only been to present a method, no comments will be made here on the significance of the results of the numerical examples. But it seems as if these and similar examples could be developed in various directions and thus increase our understanding of the relation between such factors as order size, number of calls, quantity sold, the contribution to fixed costs, total costs per unit etc. It is probable, too, that by posing different assumptions about the number of calls and the order size of a wholesaler and by taking into account the fixed costs on the wholesaling and retailing level, one could make the examples more instructive and interesting.

As was pointed out earlier, it will be necessary to include in the computation other functions beside the selling function e.g. paper work, warehouse routines, transportation etc. If the costs of different alternative ways of distribution are given a general, algebraic form it should be easy to study the changes in costs, effected by specific changes in the methods of operation.

Also, we ought to get a more reliable picture of the effect of changes in methods of distribution by introducing into our calculations probability models, especially concerning the expected effects on sales volume.

In an economy, where the supremacy of selling directly or through a wholesaler is often discussed, the existence of an adjustable method of computation, like the one described here, may help to introduce into the discussion more exact and unbiased arguments.

27. Bayesian Decision Theory in Channel Selection

WROE ALDERSON and PAUL E. GREEN

The use of the "new" statistics is here applied to the channel decision area. Use is made of the normal distribution of sales for a given decision. The decision example used is sales agent versus direct distribution.

Many channel decisions are of the "make versus buy" class, for example, whether the firm should perform some part of the distribution process or whether the task should be "farmed out" to independent agents. In actual practice these decisions might be very complex, involving such considerations as comparative operating costs, sales effects on the product under study, effects on other products of the manufacturer, repercussions on other links in the distribution channel, and so on.

The problem which will be selected for illustration will be highly simplified. The purpose in choosing a relatively simple illustration is twofold. The first objective is to show that this general class of problems can be framed within a Bayesian model of the type designed earlier and thus round out the functional areas in which decision theory can be applied. The second objective is to introduce the concept of continuous prior distributions by means of a numerical illustration which is straightforward enough for simple exposition of this notion. Heretofore it has been assumed that the relevant states of nature were discrete; in fact, only a small number of states were usually assumed so as to make the problem easier to solve. In practice, however, the decision maker may visualize a large number of possible states of nature. When his continuous prior distribution can be represented by a mathematically tractable func-

tion (for example, a normal or Gaussian distribution) it is easier to apply the methods of continuous probability. If the decision maker's prior distribution cannot be so represented, the planner can always resort to a discrete analog of the underlying continuous distribution, using methods similar to those illustrated in the preceding chapters.

In this section, then, a Bayesian application is discussed in which the decision maker's prior distribution can be approximated by a normal distribution. It will be shown how such measures as the expected value of perfect information can be calculated under these conditions.

Assume that a manufacturer of a consumer packaged product has been using a sales agent to distribute his product to various retail food outlets, such as supermarket chain, independent food outlets, and so on. The sales agent's commission for performing this service amounts to 6 per cent of the sales price per case to retailers. That is, assuming the price to retailers is $10.00 per case, the sales agent receives 60¢ for each case sold.

The manufacturer has been considering the possibility of replacing his sales agent by an intracompany sales force. According to preliminary estimates, the cost incurred in distributing the product by means of his company's own salesmen would amount to only 50¢ per case, once the sales force was trained. Moreover, the manufacturer feels that use of a company sales force could result in a larger volume of sales than the sales agent is currently producing. Current sales, using the agent as distributor, amount to 100,000 cases, on an annual basis.

The manufacturer's marketing planner is asked to study the problem. He first looks at the costs associated with transition from sales

• SOURCE: Wroe Alderson and Paul E. Green, "Bayesian Decision Theory In Channel Selection," in their *Planning and Problem Solving In Marketing* (Homewood, Ill.: Richard D. Irwin, 1964), pp. 311–317. Wroe Alderson, Professor of Marketing and Paul Green, Associate Professor of Marketing, both of the Wharton School, University of Pennsylvania.

agent to company sales force. His estimates indicate that the fixed costs of hiring and training a group of salesmen (and phasing out the sales agent's services) are quite significant, amounting to $25,000. That is, if the salesmen did *not* produce additional business, it would take approximately two and a half years (ignoring the time value of money) to recoup the original transition costs on the basis of reduced selling costs alone:

$10(.06 − .05) 100,000 cases/year
$$= \$10,000/\text{year}.$$

The manufacturer believes, however, that use of a company sales force would produce additional sales. But, considering the vagaries of the market place and the possibility that the product may be superseded by newer products, he wishes to use a short time horizon (one year) in considering the payback of his original investment of $25,000.

The marketing planner next finds that the sales units required to justify the switch from sales agent to company salesmen amount to 250,000 cases over the one-year planning period:

$10(.06 − .05)$S_b$ = $25,000; S_b
$$= \text{breakeven sales}$$

$$S_b = 250{,}000 \text{ cases}$$

Any sales beyond 250,000 cases would, of course, make the transition more attractive, while if sales were less than 250,000 cases, an opportunity loss would be sustained. If S_b continues to stand for total sales required to break even (250,000 cases) and S represents actual sales in cases, the result is:

$$\$ .10(S_b - S) \text{ if } S \leq S_b$$
$$0 \qquad \text{if } S > S_b$$

as the manufacturer's conditional opportunity loss, assuming that he makes the transition from sales agent to company salesmen. For example, if sales are only 200,000 cases during the first year, the manufacturer suffers a conditional loss of $.10 (250,000–200,000) = $5,000. Notice that if actual sales S are only 100,000 cases (the amount anticipated by maintaining the sales agent's services) the conditional opportunity loss is equal to $15,000, since the salesmen would produce a $10,000 additional contribution to profit and overhead (through the 5 per cent cost of their services versus the 6 per cent sales agent commission) but their services would involve a transitional outlay of $25,000.

Now assume that the marketing planner attempts to elicit from the decision maker some estimates, given the use of company salesmen rather than the present sales agent. The decision maker estimates that first year sales, with the company sales force, would average 275,000 cases. He believes, however, that a 50-50 chance exists that sales could be less than 225,000 cases or more than 325,000 cases.

Now suppose it is assumed that the decision maker's estimates can be represented by a normal distribution. It will be recalled from elementary statistics that about one half of the area under the normal curve lies between the mean $\pm$ 0.67 standard deviations. Figure 1 shows the normal curve for this specific problem.

Note in Figure 1 that the decision maker has provided two pieces of information, namely, a

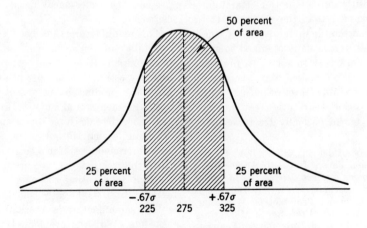

Fig. 1. Normal prior distribution of sales (sales in thousands of cases).

mean sales estimate (275,000 cases) and a probability equal to 0.5 that true sales lie between 225,000 and 325,000 cases. Thus, one half of the total area under the curve must lie outside these limits. This information can be used to solve for the standard deviation of this normal distribution, as follows:

$$.67\sigma(S) = 50,000 \text{ cases}$$

$$\sigma(S) = 75,000 \text{ cases (approximately)}$$

It will also be remembered from elementary statistics that

1. About 68 per cent of the total area under a normal curve lies between the mean ± 1 standard deviation.
2. About 95 per cent of the total area under a normal curve lies between the mean ± 2 standard deviations.
3. About 99.7 per cent (practically all) of the total area under a normal curve lies between the mean ± 3 standard deviations.

In this case the implication is that the decision maker cannot, for all practical purposes, conceive of first-year sales falling below 50,000 cases or being higher than 500,000 cases (275,-000 $\pm$ 3 (75,000)), given the use of a company sales force.

Inasmuch as the mean sales estimate of 275,-000 cases exceeds the breakeven requirement of 250,000 cases, the decision maker would (ignoring utility and time value of money considerations) change over to the company sales force.

Notice, however, that *should* sales turn out to be lower than S_b, the breakeven value of 250,000

units, the decision maker would suffer an opportunity loss. Also, notice that the size of this loss increases the further away that actual sales S are from breakeven sales S_b. For example, if $S \leq$ 225,000 cases (an event which can happen with probability .25), an opportunity loss of *at least* \$2,500 would be incurred. If actual sales $S \leq$ 125,000 (the mean minus two standard deviations), an opportunity loss of *at least* \$12,500 would be incurred.

Now suppose that the decision maker could obtain additional information of "perfect reliability" regarding true sales, assuming a change-over to company salesmen. The value of this information is conditional upon whether or not the decision would be *changed* on the basis of the new information. That is, the conditional value of perfect information can be summarized as follows:

$$CVPI = \quad 0 \text{ if } S > 250,000 \text{ cases}$$

$$CVPI = \$ .10(S_b - S) \text{ if } S \leq 250,000 \text{ cases}$$

That is, if the perfect information indicated sales exceeding 250,000 cases, the decision would not be changed from that taken in the absence of new information. If the perfect information indicated sales less than 250,000 cases, however, the *value* of this information would increase as the difference between true sales and breakeven sales increased. This relationship is shown (along with the prior distribution) in Figure 2.

In Figure 2 the expected value of perfect information is shown to increase linearly as the actual sales parameter moves to the left of the

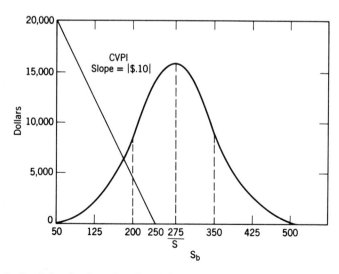

Fig. 2. Conditional value of perfect information (sales in thousands of cases).

breakeven sales level of 250,000 cases. EVPI equals zero, however, for all sales levels exceeding 250,000 cases since, in these cases, the original decision would not have been changed, given the new information. Note that the slope of the CVPI line equals $.10, corresponding to the additional 1 per cent commission saved on each $10 of sales per case. Finally, it is inferred that if sales actually amounted to zero cases, the *opportunity* loss through switching over to the company sales force would involve $25,000. That is, this alternative would produce a loss of $25,000 *more* than the loss sustained under using the sales agent.

To derive the *expected* value of perfect information one would have to multiply the conditional value of perfect information by the probability that true sales, given by the perfect information, would be a value falling respectively within each one of a set of tiny intervals in the range 0–250,000 cases; making such an approximation would be laborious, to say the least.

Fortunately, a short cut procedure, permissible through the use of a normal distribution of prior probabilities, can be used. The formula is

$$EVPI = C\sigma(S) \cdot N(D)$$

where C = absolute value of the slope of the $CVPI$ line; $\sigma(S)$ = the standard deviation of the normal prior distribution; and D of $N(D)$ is a measure of the absolute distance of the mean of the decision maker's prior distribution from

Table 1. N(D)—Loss Function*

D	.00	.01	.02	.03	.04	.05	.06	.07	.08	.09
.0	.3989	.3940	.3890	.3841	.3793	.3744	.3697	.3649	.3602	.3556
.1	.3509	.3464	.3418	.3373	.3328	.3284	.3240	.3197	.3154	.3111
.2	.3069	.3027	.2986	.2944	.2904	.2863	.2824	.2784	.2745	.2706
.3	.2668	.2630	.2592	.2555	.2518	.2481	.2445	.2409	.2374	.2339
.4	.2304	.2270	.2236	.2203	.2169	.2137	.2104	.2072	.2040	.2009
.5	.1078	.1947	.1917	.1887	.1857	.1828	.1799	.1771	.1742	.1714
.6	.1687	.1659	.1633	.1606	.1580	.1554	.1528	.1503	.1478	.1453
.7	.1429	.1405	.1381	.1358	.1334	.1312	.1289	.1267	.1245	.1223
.8	.1202	.1181	.1160	.1140	.1120	.1100	.1080	.1061	.1042	.1023
.9	.1004	.09860	.09680	.09503	.09328	.09156	.08986	.08819	.08654	.04891
1.0	.08332	.08174	.08019	.07866	.07716	.07568	.07422	.07279	.07138	.06999
1.1	.06862	.06727	.06595	.06465	.06336	.06210	.06086	.05964	.05844	.05726
1.2	.05610	.05496	.05384	.05274	.05165	.05059	.04954	.04851	.04750	.04650
1.3	.04553	.04457	.04363	.04270	.04179	.04090	.04002	.03916	.03831	.03748
1.4	.03667	.03587	.03508	.03431	.03356	.03281	.03208	.03137	.03067	.02998
1.5	.02931	.02865	.02800	.02736	.02674	.02612	.02552	.04294	.02436	.02380
1.6	.02324	.02270	.02217	.02165	.02114	.02064	.02015	.01967	.01920	.01874
1.7	.01829	.01785	.01742	.01699	.01658	.01617	.01578	.01539	.01502	.01464
1.8	.01428	.01392	.01357	.01323	.01290	.01257	.01226	.01195	.01164	.01134
1.9	.01105	.01077	.01049	.01022	$.0^29957$	$.0^29698$	$.0^29445$	$.0^29198$	$.0^28957$	$.0^28721$
2.0	$.0^28491$	$.0^28266$	$.0^28046$	$.0^27832$	$.0^27623$	$.0^27418$	$.0^27219$	$.0^27024$	$.0^26835$	$.0^26649$
2.1	$.0^26468$	$.0^26292$	$.0^26120$	$.0^25952$	$.0^25788$	$.0^25628$	$.0^25472$	$.0^25320$	$.0^25172$	$.0^25028$
2.2	$.0^24887$	$.0^24750$	$.0^24616$	$.0^24486$	$.0^24358$	$.0^24235$	$.0^24114$	$.0^23996$	$.0^23882$	$.0^23770$
2.3	$.0^23662$	$.0^23556$	$.0^23453$	$.0^23352$	$.0^23255$	$.0^23159$	$.0^23067$	$.0^22977$	$.0^22889$	$.0^22804$
2.4	$.0^22720$	$.0^22640$	$.0^22561$	$.0^22484$	$.0^22410$	$.0^22337$	$.0^22267$	$.0^22199$	$.0^22132$	$.0^22067$
2.5	$.0^22005$	$.0^21943$	$.0^21883$	$.0^21826$	$.0^21769$	$.0^21715$	$.0^21662$	$.0^21610$	$.0^21560$	$.0^21511$
3.0	$.0^33822$	$.0^33689$	$.0^33560$	$.0^33436$	$.0^33316$	$.0^33199$	$.0^33087$	$.0^32978$	$.0^32873$	$.0^32771$
3.5	$.0^45848$	$.0^45620$	$.0^45400$	$.0^45188$	$.0^44984$	$.0^44788$	$.0^44599$	$.0^44417$	$.0^44242$	$.0^44073$
4.0	$.0^57145$	$.0^56835$	$.0^56538$	$.0^56253$	$.0^55980$	$.0^55718$	$.0^55468$	$.0^55227$	$.0^54997$	$.0^54777$

* Reproduced, with permission from Schlaifer, R., *Probability and Statistics for Business Decisions* (New York: McGraw-Hill, 1959).

the breakeven value, expressed in terms of the number of standard deviations of the prior distribution.

$$D = \frac{|S_b - S|}{\sigma(S)}$$

$$= \frac{|250,000 - 275,000|}{75,000}$$

$$= 0.33$$

Table 1 shows $N(D)$, a loss function for the standardized normal curve. It shows the value of $N(D)$ for $D = 0.33$ to be .2555. The expected value of perfect information can now be calculated as follows:

$$EVPI = C \cdot \sigma(S) \cdot N(D)$$

$$= .10(75,000)(0.2555)$$

$$= \$1,916.25$$

In other words, the decision maker could afford to spend up to approximately $2,000 for perfect information which would indicate true sales, given the changeover to a company sales force for distributing the product to retailers. If the decision maker could not obtain perfect information (the more usual case) it is clear that the expected value of imperfect information would be less than $2,000. The $2,000 figure thus provides an upper limit on how much to spend for information.

Before leaving this illustration one should note that $EVPI$ is a function of the absolute value of the $CVPI$ line (0.10 in this illustration), the standard deviation of the decision maker's prior distribution and the absolute distance of the prior mean from the breakeven point. As common sense would suggest, the higher the opportunity loss of wrong decisions, the more one should be willing to pay for additional information about the consequences of his decisions. Moreover, the surer he is of the relevant consequences (small standard deviation of the prior distribution) and the better his preferred alternative is (distance of mean from breakeven value), the less valuable additional information becomes. Finally, one should remember that additional information assumes value *only if it changes the choice* which he would have made in its absence.

28. A Theoretical Framework for Channel Choice

HELMY H. BALIGH*

The firm's problem of choosing the channel to which it is to belong may be, for purposes of analysis, divided into two segments. At one stage, the firm attempts to find the most efficient channel, i.e., that channel which maximizes the firm's profits when it simply belongs in it. The solution to this problem results from a careful and rigorous analysis of the relation between the channel's structure and its efficiency, in which the concept of simple membership can be clearly defined. The second stage is the main topic of the paper. Here the question is for the firm to employ any given channel optimally by being more than just a simple member in it. The concept of control over the channel is used as an intermediate variable between the resources the firm employs, over those necessary for simple membership, and the profitability of a channel for the firm. The inputs which lead to control and, hence, affect revenues and costs are essentially within the realm of decision areas not normally viewed as part of the channel problem, e.g., advertising. Structuring the problem of optimal channel use by the determination of the combination of inputs leading to control, and the various constrained forms of this problem are analytically discussed.

THE CONCEPT OF A CHANNEL

The basic determinant of a firm's membership in a marketing channel is the presence of cooperation between it and another firm—cooperation that permits them to enter into an exchange transaction. Any two firms that cooperate to bring about the exchange of some good can be said to form either a channel, or a part of a channel, for that good. The classes from which the two firms are drawn are identified, in consequence, as the units which make up the marketing channel. Instead of stating that firm x_1 and y_1 form a channel, it is often convenient to state that the class of firms X and the class of firms Y make up the channel. The firms x_1 and y_1, come from the two sets, $X = [x_1,$ $x_2, \ldots x_i]$ and $Y = [y_1, y_2 \ldots y_i]$, where the x_i are similar to one another in certain respects and where the y_i are also similar to one another. Other types of firms linked by exchange of the product to either of these two types, X and Y, and which have not the same customers and suppliers as either of these two types have, are also members of the channel that includes types X and Y.

Each of the sets or classes of firms, X, Y, and Z is made up of firms which have certain characteristics similar to one another and different from those of the firms making up any other set. There is no one absolute way of choosing the relevant characteristics of firms that are to be used as determinants of membership in a set. There are, in fact, many ways of classifying firms, or making up sets of them such as X, or Y, on the basis of any group of desired criteria, and there are many levels of generality associated with different business firm classification schemes. The census has developed two basic schemes based on the type of operation of the firm and on the kind of business. Various authors have developed variations on these schemes for various purposes to which the

• SOURCE: Hemly H. Baligh, "A Theoretical Framework for Channel Choice," in P. D. Bennett, *Economic Growth, Competition and World Markets* (Chicago: American Marketing Association, 1965), pp. 631–654.
* Assistant Professor of Business Administration in the Graduate School of Business Administration, University of Illinois.

schemes are to be put. The important point to realize is that since decision making on the issue of channels is the aim, the determination of the membership of the sets of firms which make up a channel should be the best one for this purpose. Different classification schemes will render decision making on channels better or worse, and involve different costs of decision making. That scheme which permits the maximum difference between the returns to decision making and the cost of decision making should be chosen. In this choice problem, the critical characteristics of a scheme are its generality and the choice of criteria relevant to the issue at hand.

IDENTIFYING CHANNEL DECISION ALTERNATIVES

At the very most elementary level the problem facing the firm is the choice of a channel through which it is to sell or buy the product. To do so the firm has to have some comparable channel alternatives. Suppose that only 5 firms existed in the economy besides the firm in question and the final user of the product at hand. The question now is how many alternative channels made up of firms in existence could the firm employ to market its product. Conceptually there could be $\sum_{n=0}^{5} P^5_n = \sum_{n=0}^{5} \frac{5!}{(5-n)!}$ channel alternatives. Each alternative represents a set of individual firms in a given sequence with the number in the set varying from 0 to 5 in addition to the final user. One single set among these alternatives is that of the channel which includes only the firm facing the problem of channel choice, which now sells directly to the final user.

For purpose of the analysis below, firms are classified on the basis of their present location in the sequences of firms that make up existing channels. Thus, if channels are found in the form of the sets $[x_1, y_1, z_1]$, $[x_1, y_2, z_1]$, $[x_2, y_2, z_1]$, $[x_2, y_2, z_2]$, then all the above alternatives become just one, namely, the channel made up of the groups X, Y, and Z in the proper sequence $[X, Y, Z]$. This criterion is in effect that of the present channel level of the firm, i.e., that of wholesale middlemen. Criteria to distinguish between firms affect the profitability of the channel and may then be applied, thereby serving perhaps to distinguish between y_1 and y_2 such that one would end up with the two alternatives $[X, y_1, Z]$ and $[X, y_2, Z]$. Criteria that could for the moment be accepted as determinants of some

significance of channel profitability are the firm's type of operation and its assortment. The first is identified by the combination of input activities which it employs and which determine its output. Such input activities are inventory carrying, methods of sale, physical facilities for implementing exchange transactions and so on. The issue of assortment must be left till later, where it is shown to be a determinant of the profitability of a particular product's overall marketing program.

CHANNEL CONTROL

A firm in one level of the channel $[X, Y, Z]$, such as x_1 in the group $X = [x_1\ x_2, \ldots\ x_n]$, is said to control another firm in another level, such as y_1 in $Y = [y_1, y_2, \ldots\ y_m]$, if it makes, participates in, or influences some decisions of that firm. Simple membership of two firms in a channel does not involve, as such, any control relationship. Buying and selling alone do not produce control as meant here. Thus, the analysis of control defines positive control levels from the starting point of membership in a channel, which is now obviously compatible with zero control, and which is defined in terms of simple buying and selling relationships.

The extent to which one firm controls another is determined by the proportion of the latter firm's decisions which the former makes, and by the amount of influence on these decisions which it has. Such influence obviously can be measured along the scale of the probability that choice, and the communication of this choice, of an alternative by one is implemented by the other, and the probability that a change in this choice will also be implemented. It is not possible here to go into a detailed discussion of the theory of servo-mechanisms from which one could obtain the best and clearest concepts of control. It is, however, necessary to note that control is *not* defined by the ability to predict. It is defined by the ability to predict the *desired* outcome from the set of all possible outcomes which may conceptually be desired, and on the ability to improve or hold constant the level of the accuracy of the prediction of these desired outcomes.

In general, elements of managerial control can be said to exist if the product exchange transaction between two firms in different levels of the channel involves some enforceable limitations on the present and/or future marketing behavior of either or both of these firms. The elements of control also exist if the exchange transaction is entered into as a result of the consciously intended effects which the behavior of one firm has on the environment of the other. Two-way control relationships where x_1 controls in part some actions of y_1, and y_1 controls in part some actions of x_1, are undoubtedly possible within the framework of this concept of control.

To the firm trying to select a channel there is the problem of allocating resources among various inputs, one of which is the degree of control over the channel, and this is in turn attained by the allocation of resources to various means of attaining it. The costs of gaining control are not necessarily of the nature of out-of-pocket expenses. They may take the form of a limitation on the alternative choices in some or all of the marketing decisions thereby leading to the re-allocating of the controlled firm's resources. The returns to control are discussed in detail when the model of the channel problem is developed.

CONSTRAINTS ON CONTROL

In many cases it is not possible to gain a certain degree of control over firms at various marketing levels without destroying the essential nature of such a channel. Each kind of channel by virtue of its very nature (as will be shown presently), has a certain profit level which is determined by the degree of control exercised over it and by various other characteristics. The degree of control may at some point alter the nature of the channel, for example, by dictating the removal of an entire level. Since the identification of channels is based mainly on the kind and number of levels within it, such a change caused by increasing the degree of control would create a new channel. Talking about the profitability of the old channel at this level of control then becomes meaningless. The limit on the control of such a channel would then occur at some point before complete control. The resulting new channel will then have its own profit function for this and all other feasible levels of control over it, and this may differ radically from the profit function of the old channel under conditions of feasible control. The same analysis is applicable to negative control, i.e., allowing other firms to control oneself.

Consider the following situation where the channel $[X, Y, K, Z]$ is being considered. The profitability of this channel is some function of the control over it. At some level of control, any further increases in the degree of control entail the removal of the level k from the chan-

nel. If this degree of control were say .6 of the maximum, then this particular channel has a profit function identifiable only between 0 and .6 degree of control. At level .61 degree of control the channel would now become $[X, Y, Z]$, and this channel has a profit function that is identifiable over the range of 0 degrees of control to say .9. A maximum constraint on the control of a particular channel may then exist, and is beyond the controlling firm's power to alter regardless of the amount of resources it allocated to the attempts to alter it. It is in fact a constraint that stems from the concept of the problem. Other exogenously imposed constraints exist, and government regulations may involve such a constraint.

There are also constraints on control of a channel imposed upon the firm by its economic resources. Such constraints depend upon the resources the firm has available vis-a-vis its economic environment. Its ability to negotiate as determined by its economic power and its ability to inflict economic losses on the firms that do not accept various sets of the terms it imposes will determine this constraint. This negotiating and threat power depend in turn on a large number of factors *viz.* capital resources, size, degree of competition in the firm's level, cross elasticity of demand between its output and others, the effectiveness of its organization and so on.

Because of these constraints the solution of the channel and degree of control problem must proceed by examining how profits vary from channel to channel, how profits for a given channel vary as the degree of control exercised over such a channel varies, and how they vary as the allocation of resources to inputs which do not affect control varies.

GENERAL FORM OF THE CHANNEL MODEL

The discussion of the general form of the problem of channel choice leads to a model which involves the determination for each channel of a number of control variables. These variables are closely interrelated and are:

(a) The optimum combination of inputs to attain any given level of control over other firms and of control of other firms over one.

(b) The optimum degree of control to exercise over the channel for any given total sales and/or price level, and the optimum amount of control to allow others to exercise over one under the same set of constraints.

(c) The optimum combination of inputs associated with simple channel membership with **no** control relationship, for any given total sales or price level.

(d) The optimum number of firms to be included as active members in each level of the channel to which the firm in question belongs, and the optimum degree of control associated with each such firm.

(e) The optimum total sales level, or price, or combination of both for each channel.

(f) The optimum combination of channels or at least the identification of the most profitable channel.

It is possible to proceed with the solution of the model in a fashion that obtains each of these optima, holding other things equal, and then combine the steps to arrive at the most profitable use of any given channel. It is also possible to solve for maximum channel profits, directly obtaining the optimum value for each of the above listed variables in the process. Whichever method one uses, the decision must be made on the basis of the complexity of the problem at hand, and the costs of arriving at a solution. The presence of such costs as data collection and lost revenues while the problem is being solved may make it more advantageous not to solve the entire problem for all the control variables at once. It may be best to solve for each one sequentially, seeking out the functional relationships in a manner permitted by the available resources of the firm, and required to solve a multitude of other more or less pressing (costly) problems.

The model consists of a number of functional relationships which must be identified for each firm from its particular environmental circumstances. In essence these relationships are given to the firm in the short run, though possibly they are changeable in the long run. For purposes of concentrating only on the channel problem, and not on the firm's entire set of economic and non-economic (e.g. political) control variables, we assume that the exact form of the following functional relationships is given. Conceptually no problem exists in determining the exact forms for the equations, though empirically a number of issues arise which tend to limit the solution to sub-segments of the problem which contain the more easily identifiable functions.

The following are the functions in their general form; they refer to specific given identifiable and known channels:

(1) $S_i = f_i(D_{ij}, D^1_{ij}, J_{irj}, \bar{q}_{ij}, l_i)$

for: $j = 1, 2, \ldots j_{max}$
$\quad r = 1, 2, \ldots m$
$\quad i = i$

where: i = The channel in question
$\quad j$ = The level in the channel where there are $j = 1, 2, \ldots j_{max}$ levels other than that of the decision making form in the relevant channel.
$\quad S_i$ = Total unit sales by the final level, that selling to users or consumers, in the relevant channels. Given that inventory adjustments in the long run balance out, this figure can be viewed as identical for all levels.
$\quad J_{irj}$ = Inputs producing purely unconditional exchange transactions or simple membership in the channel. Each input J is of a particular kind, identified by the subscript r, and directed at a given level j.
$\quad D_{ij}$ = Average degree of control over firms in level j in channel i. This assumes that simple membership in a channel pure and simple means that $D_{ij} = 0$. It is also assumed that the distribution of control over individual firms is optimally allocated among them. Other things being equal, there is a unique relationship between D_{ij} and S_i
$\quad D^1_{ij}$ = Average degree of control by firms in level j of channel i over the decision making firm. All assumptions made for D_{ij} apply here.
$\quad \bar{q}_{ij}$ = Number of firms in level j with which the firm in question is directly or indirectly related by virtue of the selling or the buying of the product. The number refers to the firms in level j which are defined to belong to channel i on the basis of the earlier analysis of channels.
$\quad l_i$ = Price received per unit of product by firms in the final level.

(2) $\bar{q}_{ij}D_{ij} = g_{ij}(I_{is1}, I_{is2}, \ldots I_{isj}, \ldots$
$\qquad I_{isj_{max}}, q_{ij}, J_{ir1}, J_{ir2}, \ldots J_{irj_{max}}, D^1_{ij})$

for: $D_{ij} \leq k_{ij}$
$\quad s = 1, 2, \ldots n$
$\quad r = 1, 2, \ldots m$
$\quad i = i$

where: i = The channel in question
$\quad j$ = The level in the channel where there are $j = 1, 2, \ldots j_{max}$ levels other than that of the decision making firm in the relevant channel.
$\quad q_{ij}$ = Number of firms in level which could be but are not included in the chan-

nels by the firm. The total number of firms that meet the requirements of the definition of the level minus the number $\bar{q}_{ij}$ dealt with gives us q_{ij}.

k_{ij} = Maximum average level of control attainable over firms in level j, with assumptions on allocation of control to firms as before.

I_{isj} = Inputs producing control. The inputs are distinguished by kind, indicated by the subscript i, and levels indicated by subscript j.

$$(3) \quad (\bar{q}_{ij}, D^1{}_{ij} = g^1{}_{ij}(H_{it1}, H_{it2}, \ldots H_{itj}, \ldots$$
$$H_{itj_{max}}, q_{ij}, J_{ir1}, J_{ir2}, \ldots$$
$$J_{irj}, \ldots J_{irj_{max}}, D_{ij})$$

for: $D^1{}_{ij} \le k^1{}_{ij}$
$\quad t = 1, 2, \ldots w$
$\quad r = 1, 2, \ldots m$
$\quad i = i$

where: H_{itj} = Inputs producing (i.e., costs entailed by) control of level j over the firm. All other variables are as they are in equation 2 with appropriate changes from control over others to control of others over one.

It may be noted that any given I_{isj} may be an input that is of the same kind as J_{irj} or H_{itj}. Thus all may refer to advertising to a particular level. They are distinguished here essentially on the basis of the goal or output for which they are used, i.e., as a group of I, J, or H. They are distinguished from others in this same grouping based on output by their nature e.g. advertising or personal selling, i.e., as I_{i1}, J_{i1}, H_{i1} where the s subscript takes a given number. Finally they are distinguished by the channel level at which they are directed and by the channel in which they are employed, i.e., each sub group in the main group is distinguished by the subscript i and j.

Total revenue obtained from the use of any given channel is defined as the total revenue received by the last or final level in channel, and is equal to the product of the appropriate price and quantity (in units) figures. Thus:

$$(4) \quad R_i = l_i S_i$$
$$= l_i f_i(D_{ij}, D^1{}_{ij}, J_{irj}, \bar{q}_{ij}, l_i)$$
$$(4a) \quad = h_i(D_{ij}, D^1{}_{ij}, J_{irj}, \bar{q}_{ij}, l_i)$$

for: $j = 1, 2, \ldots j_{max}$
$\quad r = 1, 2, \ldots m$
$\quad i = i$

where: R_i = Revenues from channel i defined as total revenues of the level in the channel selling directly to the ultimate users or consumers.

The total costs of using a particular channel are:

$$(5) \quad C_i = b_i(S_i, D_{ij}, D^1{}_{ij}, J_{irj}, A_{irj},$$
$$B_{isj}, D_{itj}, c_i(S_i), \bar{q}_{ij})$$

for: $j = 1, 2, \ldots j_{max}$
$\quad r = 1, 2, \ldots m$
$\quad s = 1, 2, \ldots n$
$\quad t = 1, 2, \ldots w$
$\quad i = i$

where: C_i = Total cost of using channel i, including total costs of production of the product if any.

$c_i(S_i)$ = Total production costs
A_{irj} = Price of input J_{irj}
B_{isj} = Price of input I_{isj}
L_{itj} = Price of input H_{itj}

These input prices may be constant for the firm or they may vary as the firm's use of the inputs vary. If they vary, then we might have a relationship $A_{irj} = a_{ir}(J_{ir1}, J_{ir2}, \ldots J_{irj}, \ldots J_{irj_{max}}, I_{is1}, I_{is2}, \ldots I_{isj}, \ldots I_{isj_{max}})$ where I_{isj} refers to the same kind of input as J_{irj}, as for example, when both refer to advertising in a particular medium.

It is now possible to arrive at the conditions which will optimize the values of the variables under different constrained and unconstrained circumstances. One may, for example, minimize the costs of the inputs leading to control over all levels j_{max} in the channel, subject to the constraints that given average control levels be attained, and given the number of firms in each level to be controlled (or the number of potential members of the level which are excluded). Empirical investigation and research might show the relationships between the outputs and the inputs of the problem, and one would then need to do the following:

Minimize:

$$(6) \quad C_{i,1} \sum_{j=1}^{j_{max}} \sum_{s=1}^{n} B_{isj} I_{isj}$$
$$- \sum_{j=1}^{j_{max}} \lambda_{ij}[g_{ij}(I_{is1}, I_{is2}, \ldots I_{isj}, \ldots$$
$$I_{isj_{max}}, \overset{\circ}{q}_{ij}, \overset{\circ}{J}_{ir1}, \overset{\circ}{J}_{ir2}, \ldots \overset{\circ}{J}_{irj}, \ldots$$
$$\overset{\circ}{J}_{irj_{max}}, \overset{\circ}{D}^1{}_{ij}) - M_{ij}],$$

where λ_{ij} is a longrange multiplier.

Here g_{ij} is the function for $\bar{q}_{ij}D_{ij}$, and M_{ij} the level of $\bar{q}_{ij}D_{ij}$ required. All inputs J are held constant at $\overset{\circ}{J}$ values as are the values of $q_{ij} = \overset{\circ}{q}_{ij}$ and $D^1{}_{ij} = \overset{\circ}{D}{}^1{}_{ij}$.

A more general form of the problem of channel choice is that which requires the maximization of profits π_i defined as $R_i - C_i$, or as equation 4a minus equation 5. The solution, given the identity of the functional forms and relationships, would be in terms of setting values to all inputs, I_{isj}, J_{irj} and H_{itj}, to the number of firms $\bar{q}_{ij}$ in each level with which the firm is to deal, given the costs and conditions of producing the product if the firm is such a producer. The values so determined should then uniquely determine the degree of control levels, the total unit sales, the price, and the exact nature of the cooperative relationships between the firm in question and other levels of the channel. Finally when the optimum profit conditions for each channel are met it is possible to evaluate the channels. The simultaneous optimization for all feasible channels is the most complex form of the problem and can be obtained by activating the subscript i in all the equations of the model. The problem is complex enough for the moment and we will return to the multi channel case later.

Before investigating the general nature of the functional forms in equation 1 and 5 and attempting to identify them theoretically, and before identifying the empirical counterparts of the variables involved one issue needs discussion. It is necessary to see how the model might vary in its overall nature for firms of different kinds and with different goals.

CHANNEL CHOICE AND FIRM'S GOALS

The problem as formulated leads to an analysis of the exact nature of the variable I, J, H, $\bar{q}$ and the output that determines revenues, the relation of each to the degree of control the relation of this latter to costs and revenues, and the specification of what the firm's goals are. To this point it has been assumed that the firm wishes to maximize its profits, but nothing was said about the time at which or over which such profits are to be maximized. Given any date at which profit level is to be maximized the same formulation of the problem would apply, except that the actual solution may differ. However, the choice of a channel which is at present not the most profitable may indeed be the goal of a firm. Thus, such a goal can be seen as the

maximization of profits over the long run, a goal that is not necessarily compatible with that of short run profit maximization. The existence of such variations in goals when the time dimension is introduced necessitates a reformulation of the above model. It is no longer sufficient since it does not incorporate certain relationships between the variables.

The model in the general form outlined above is a static one. With the introduction of the dimension of time, the behavior of some variables can no longer be treated as independent of the behavior of others. The possibility now exists that over time the choice of a channel and the degree of control over it would affect the optimum level of control over other channels. Some channels may conceivably bear varying profitability levels to firms of varying ages with differing levels of market exposure for their products. A firm with little exposure may find a channel highly unprofitable at the present but highly profitable at some future time if used from the present to that time. Furthermore, the profitability of a channel may vary with the size of the firm and as this changes over time so would the profitability of that channel.

Finally the nature of competitive markets suggests that the choice of the optimum channel and the degree of control to exercise over it, or to have it exercise over the firm, will vary as competitors respond over time to such a choice. This and all the other objections to a static model suggest that for practical uses such a model ought to be reviewed periodically by firms, and that such review should depend for its frequency of occurrence on the rate of change of the firm's economic and institutional requirements.

CHANNEL CHOICE FOR FIRMS IN DIFFERENT CHANNEL LEVELS

The optimum channel, degree of its control, and the number of firms to be included in it by level may differ for firms in different levels in the channel. These firms may have different levels of constraints set by their capacities to invest in fixed plant. Differing assortments will dictate different requirements for firms. In general where such differences exist there will develop a competition among the firms in a channel for its control, or for designing the channel in their favor. Though channels are essentially based on cooperation, competition for gains at the expenses of other levels does exist among those very firms whose cooperation creates the channel. The model above applies equally for any firm in any channel level, but it does not explicitly expose the conditions that determine the outcome of this competition for channel control.

Two firms may find that the optimum channel for each includes the other, but that the channel differs in its other characteristics including the degree of control and the identity of the controller. This is a distinct possibility because of the channel requirements of various products, which products may be included in different combination in the two firm's assortments, and because of the different competitive conditions of the two levels in which the firms are found. Should this then be the case a struggle will develop between the firms in the two levels each attempting to attain its optimum. The result may not be the optimum for either, i.e., competition may render unattainable the optimum solution identified from the model centered around the requirements of a single product. The assumption made in the model is unrealistic and makes the situation not feasible. The resolution of the competition will depend essentially on the economic power of the two firms in the different levels. This power is determined in turn by the threat ability of each, i.e., the loss it can inflict upon the other by a total refusal to cooperate and enter into an exchange transaction. This, in turn, is determined by the competitive conditions in each firm's channel level (competition on the horizontal scale), and by the net difference in total profits between the unrestricted optimum channel and control level of each, and the optimum channel and control level when no cooperation exists between these two competitive firms at all. In general terms, other things being equal, the larger this difference between the optima the lower the firm's economic power since the lower will be its bargaining ability.

The solution of the problem of control and channel choice given the constraints mentioned may thus require the use of economic power for its implementation. Where the optimum is unattainable, economic power might well be used to approximate it as closely as possible. All this is done within the constraints on the choice already mentioned. The detailed elaboration of the channel and control model below permits the proper appreciation of the concept of economic power, and the model itself can be made to incorporate this variable without much difficulty. However, we must first consider the segment of the channel problem which ignores altogether any control possibilities.

REQUIREMENTS FOR SIMPLE CHANNEL MEMBERSHIP

When two firms agree to enter into an exchange transaction, they do so only because each expects to gain from the transaction. If, indeed, both gain, then there exists a total net gain which could be divided in any number of ways between the two firms. To the extent that each firm does not obtain all the gain from the transaction it has an opportunity cost equal to the amount of the total which it does not take to itself. Of the amount of gain received by the other firm, a portion constitutes the minimum requirements which it demands if it is to enter into an exchange agreement with the first firm. This latter is therefore required to forego these minimum requirements if it is to find the cooperation of any other firm or firms and to belong to a channel and exchange products and make profits.

The minimum requirements placed on the firm and, in fact, the total requirements or amount of potential gain from channel membership which the firm foregoes are dependent upon a large number of variables related to the structure of the channel, the nature of competitive conditions within and among the channel levels, and the characteristics of the product both economic and physical. To the individual firm, in any case, the total requirements can be viewed as constituting a sum total cost of the inputs used to meet it, where any input is substitutable for another. The firm receiving the requirements can be seen as being offered a value in terms of some final effect on its profits. The firm offering this value can be seen as having a large number of different input combinations all of which produce the same effects on the profits of the other firm and are hence of no interest to it. For every such effect on profits of the other firm which cooperates, or total value offered, a large number of combinations of inputs is possible, and the firm is free to choose that combination which best meets its goals and the requirements of the channel which are stated in terms only of the output of the combination. Thus there exists a set of inputs any combination of which has as an output a gain to other firms permitting the firm using these inputs to belong to the channel.

Channels, therefore, involve the firm in a basic number of costs and revenues that depend both on the very nature of the channel and on its utilization in terms of control and otherwise. The requirements leading to the incurring of these costs can be discussed under the assumption of a zero level of control as is done here. This permits the general nature of the effects of the channel *per se* to be easily distinguishable. It permits a clear view of the effects of the channel structure and of the numbers of firms in each level within it on the costs and revenues of one member firm.

The firm's problem may, therefore, be stated as one wherein complete ignorance of the issue of control levels is assumed, or one wherein such control is impossible under the circumstances. It is assumed that either all control inputs are set arbitrarily at a zero value, or that the optimum level of each is zero. The problem is now that of setting the levels of the remaining outputs associated with channel membership, with the aim of maximizing profits. The problem could just be stated as one of minimizing the costs of these inputs given some minimum revenue to the other levels. Thus, if the inputs in some given channel were J_{irj}, the revenues of firms in other levels were stated in terms of these inputs and in terms of the number of firms in each level $\bar{q}_{ij}$ with which the firm dealt, the firm would wish to minimize the cost of selling through this channel. It would wish to:

Minimize:

$$(7) \quad C_{i,2} = \sum_{j=1}^{j_{max}} \sum_{r=1}^{m} A_{irj} J_{irj}$$
$$- \sum_{j=1}^{j_{max}} \lambda_{ij} \overset{\circ}{\bar{q}}_{ij} k_{ij} - f_{ij} (J_{i11}, \ldots J_{irj}, \ldots$$
$$J_{im j_{max}}, \overset{\circ}{\bar{q}}_{ij}, \ldots \overset{\circ}{\bar{q}}_{ij_{max}})$$

where k_{ij} is the minimum level set on the returns acceptable to each firm in level j for belonging to this particular channel with the firm in question, $\bar{q}_{ij}$ is some given number of firms in each level and f_{ij} the function relating the returns to each firm in each level from membership in the channel as determined by the inputs levels set and to the number of firms in the level. Differentiating $C_{i,2}$ with respect to each J_{irj} and setting these partials equal to zero would give us $(r \times j_{max})$ equations in as many unknown inputs levels, and j_{max} equations in as many shadow prices λ_{ij} on the constraints.

To maximize profit the firm must solve for the J_{irj} and for $\bar{q}_{ij}$. The solution of this problem is not an unconstrained one, for there is some minimum level of returns necessary before a firm will in fact cooperate with the one wishing to maximize its profits. In effect, for any given group of firms $\bar{q}_{ij}$, the function f_{ij} must still attain some given minimum or no membership

in that channel and hence no revenues would be possible. In order to maximize profits it must be noted that beyond this constraint revenues are dependent on the number of firms in each level and the inputs levels. For profit maximization the problem is reformulated as maximizing π_i where,

$$(8) \quad \pi_i = F_i(\bar{q}_{i1}, \bar{q}_{i2}, \ldots \bar{q}_{ij_{max}}, J_{i11}, J_{i12}, \ldots$$
$$J_{i1j_{max}}, \ldots J_{irj}, \ldots J_{imj_{max}})$$
$$- C_i(q_{i1}, q_{i2}, \ldots q_{ij_{max}}, J_{i11}, J_{i12}, \ldots$$
$$J_{iij_{max}}, \ldots J_{irj}, \ldots J_{imj_{max}})$$
$$+ \sum_{j=1}^{j_{max}} \lambda_{ij}[\bar{q}_{ij} k_{ij} - f_{ij} (J_{i11}, J_{i12}, \ldots$$
$$J_{i1j_{max}}, \ldots J_{irj}, \ldots J_{imj_{max}},$$
$$\bar{q}_{i1}, \bar{q}_{ij}, \bar{q}_{ij_{max}})],$$

where F_i is the revenue function and C_i the cost function associated with the particular choice of the J_{irj} and the numbers $\bar{q}_{ij}$. Again for optimization we differentiate π_i partially (and set these equal to zero) with respect to $(r \times j_{max})$ inputs, j_{max} different $\bar{q}_{ij}$ and $j_{max}\lambda$'s—a total of $(r \times j_{max}) + 2j_{max}$ equations in as many unknowns. Given the suffi-second order conditions, it should be possible to solve for all J_{irj} and $\bar{q}_{ij}$ to maximize profits. We have assumed the minimum requirements of every level in the channel of the firm in question to be set at K_{ij} and to be attained and met as a result of the manipulation of the J_{irj} and the $\bar{q}_{ij}$ in a manner dictated by the function f_{ij}. In all cases k_{ij} is the minimum level which permits the firm only simple channel membership, and where all positive levels of control are assumed non-existent.

There is thus a point of maximum for each channel with respect to the input levels and the number of firms in each level. The inputs involved are of very many different kinds though, of course, in the particular case of any firm many will have no effects on revenues or in the function f_{ij}. They may, in effect, be totally ignored as useful control variables, which in turn would render the function to be maximized one that includes many fewer variables. In turn, obtaining the exact relationships between revenues, costs, and the function f_{ij} and all the control variables would become much easier to accomplish.

The inputs are essentially of the same kind, as is pointed out below, as those which are the producers of control. For purposes of exposition the decision on control is treated separately from that of simple channel membership. In some cases there is no possibility for controlling the channel, and in all cases control problems only become meaningful if simple membership is attainable. The kinds of inputs that produce the outputs which meet the requirements of other potential channel members in different levels include gross margins, advertising expenditures, inventory level, customer waiting time for service, credit terms, services offered, personal selling, store display and so on. The subscript r in J_{irj} refers then to the kind of input as distinguished from others in this fashion. Each r refers to a different source of costs for the firm.

Throughout, it is assumed that no further variation in these outputs and in the $\bar{q}_{ii}$'s will increase profits once we have solved the optimization problem. When this assumption is dropped, then increases in the levels of these inputs and variations in $\bar{q}_{ii}$'s (designed to gain control and improve total profits) may well cause a change in the optimum combinations of inputs and $\bar{q}_{ii}$'s for conditions of simple exchange and channel membership with zero control by all. This would occur, for example, if the prices of the inputs which are treated as J_{irj} and I_{isj}, i.e., as different in cases where $r = s$, but are in essence the same, (advertising, designated by $r = 2 = s$) should change as different amounts of each kind of unit is used by the firm. Some inputs are stated in terms of dollars and hence do not undergo changes in price. However, for all other kinds of inputs such changing prices mean that true optimum conditions can be obtained only by the simultaneous solution for all inputs J, I, and H, and for all $\bar{q}_{ij}$ and q_{ij}. The possibility also exists that the outputs which are treated as being different in the model, are not so and do in fact vary as a function of all the inputs rather than just some set J of these inputs. In any case, this interdependence raises no conceptual difficulties even though the zero control level as an output of any input is defined by the actual use of that input up to some level determined by the requirements of optimum profit *simple* channel membership.

The solution to these difficulties lies in treating simple membership in the channel as a concomitant of the decision on control levels, and not as a prerequisite to it. This would involve the simultaneous optimization of the levels of all inputs, those leading to control and those leading to simple membership and no control. Before this is done, however, it is best that the whole problem of control be clearly formulated, and this is best done at the firm stage with simple channel membership assumed

given with its costs and revenues invariant with respect to the decision on control.

CONTROL INPUT COMBINATIONS

Different levels of controls over any given channel can be obtained by varying the combination of the inputs leading to control. However, before this contention is supported it must be pointed out that some levels of control are not attainable without some minimum amount of a given input. This means that not all inputs are perfectly substitutable for one another over the entire range of feasible control levels. The first constraint on the total level of control has been considered and is incorporated in the equation for control. The second issue involves no added difficulties whatsoever, since any constraint on individual input levels (the minimum that must be used) could also be incorporated as a constraint in the equation. The issue can thus be ignored for purposes of simplicity (and is treated at the end of the section).

The inputs in equation 2 are not necessarily physical inputs. They involve sources of costs or expenditure. They refer to decision variables for the firm which lead it to incur costs. These costs are opportunity costs which may or may not be apparent in present day accounting reports. For example, if a firm, in order to gain some level of control over another firm, has to limit its own behavior in certain respects, it in effect allows the other firm to control it to some degree. This loss of freedom for the firm under consideration involves a cost; the cost associated with the removal of alternatives before it from consideration. By limiting its freedom of choice the firm incurs an opportunity cost, which is not an out-of-pocket expense, and its decision to incur this cost is, in effect, a decision to employ a certain kind of method to gain some measure of control. It is, in effect, using this input for an output in terms of control.

The inputs which singly or in combination produce control are many. Assuming for the moment that they are perfectly substitutable one can solve equation 2 for the optimum combination of such inputs as is shown below. First the nature of the inputs is discussed. The first such input is that of price reductions by the seller and price increases by the buyer. In both cases it is easier to view these as variations in the gross margins of firms in the channels.

Consider then the case of a wholesale middleman and a given channel which includes only two other levels, the manufacturers, and a retailer group. As a buyer, the wholesale middleman must offer any manufacturer some minimum price, and hence a minimum gross margin, to induce that manufacturer to sell the product to him. Similarly there is some minimum margin which any retailer must be allowed, given a final price to (or demand schedule of) final users. Each of these two margins can be viewed as a cost to the wholesale middleman, for one firm in one level, in this particular channel. It may be viewed as an opportunity cost which is independent of the degree of control exercised and which depends solely on the nature of the channel and the competitive conditions within the level, etc. The amount of total gross margin allowed firms x_i and z_i is the optimum requirement for membership in the set defining the channel and the number of firms in each of the levels the control of which involves added costs. It is not this basic cost or input that is meant here. It is the change in each of these two gross margin figures that is the input to the control of either of all x_i or all z_i. The basic requirements of membership in a channel give a zero level of control as the term control is defined. This gross margin amount could be treated as an input or an output of the channels under comparison and is treated as one of the inputs that do not lead to control. That is, it is not necessarily a given to the firm, but can be varied along with inputs of minimum requirements in such areas as personal selling, etc., none of which lead to control, but which affect the output of the channel and its sales.

The wholesale middleman could attempt to control the behavior of the manufacturer or the retailer by varying the gross margins he allows them, that is, the price he pays and receives. He could increase both or either, in return for a certain measure of control, over, say, the retailers' inventory levels, or the manufacturers' delivery schedules. But, increasing either or both margins means a higher price paid by the wholesale middleman, y_i, than is absolutely necessary. In either case he incurs an opportunity cost which is the cost of employing this input, or for setting the decision variable for prices at a given level different from that which would give a zero level of control, but be optimally sufficient to permit simple membership in that channel. Thus there are $s \times j_{max}$ inputs of this kind for each channel i with j_{max} levels in it, and there are j_{max} outputs in terms of control. In any one channel $[X, Y, Z]$, each x_i and each z_i may demand different minimum gross margins to induce them to belong to that channel. In

turn, each of them has a minimum gross margin required of him in order that he may belong to the channel. For the firm in question, y_i—the one whose channel problem is under discussion —it is the requirement of him in these gross margin terms which sets the starting point— sets the zero points—of the levels of the input of gross margins which it has to determine and which has outputs in terms of control D_{ij}, i.e., control in channel i over level j and firm $\bar{q}_{ij}$. For any given firm x_i, their variations from this minimum level required of the y_i indicates the levels of this input used to gain control over x_i. For an entire set $X = [x_1, x_2, \ldots x_n]$, the amount of this input (increases in gross margins) determines, in part, the average degree of control exercised over the entire membership of a level by the firm incurring the cost of this input viz. y_i. The exact situation holds for the set $Z = [z_1, z_2, \ldots z_n]$. In addition, the firm needs to solve for the number of firms in each of the sets simultaneously with its solution for the input amounts.

The problem of allocating the total amount of the input costs to the control over individual x_i and z_i is, of course, part of the channel problem. We have chosen to ignore it, that is, we have treated all firms in a level as sufficiently similar to warrant treatment of the whole level and not every individual firm as the simple element making up the channel. However, it may be pointed out that complicating the entire problem by treating firms individually does little to alter the basic nature of the model. The added issue is of the same form as all economic decision problems, and is one of allocating the degree of control attained over a whole level in the channel to the firms in it. It is assumed that this allocation is done optimally, as would be the case if all firms were identical in every respect, and all input amounts associated with each level were equally divided among these firms, thereby making the degree of control also equally divided. All inputs I_{isj} are total figures of input amounts optimally allocated to the firm $\bar{q}_{ij}$ dealt with in level j, and giving an average degree of control D_{ij} which also comes from a total control figure optimally allocated among all firms $\bar{q}_{ij}$.

If the firms are alike or sufficiently similar to permit simplifying the channel problem into one of choice of kinds of firms rather than individual firms, then this allocation problem becomes a fairly minor one. The assumption is, in effect, not critical, but deserves one more comment. The level of all, and any, inputs for each individual firm among the $\bar{q}_{ij}$, when optimized for all such firms by the decision making firm, assures the maximization of total output and hence of average output in terms of control over a given number of firms $\bar{q}_{ij}$. If it is difficult to imagine such optimal allocation, then some other assumption on the allocation of inputs among firms can be made, and the average degree of control D_{ij} associated with this particular allocation and combination of total input figures identified. That is, in developing the function with D_{ij} as the dependent variable, any allocation procedure can be assumed, but it must be assumed consistently for combinations of total input figures I_{isj}.

Besides gross margins two other inputs for the production of control over other firms in the channel are personal selling and buying efforts, and advertising. There again, we make the same assumption about minimum levels necessary for channel membership, beyond which all additions to inputs are reviewed as variables determining control.

Advertising produces control over other firms in other levels in the channel in a number of ways. Advertising to a group of firms, which buy directly from the firm which is working on its channel problem, in excess of the amounts needed for simple channel membership will affect many areas of these firms' decisions. This advertising, in excess of needs for simple information purposes or as a substitute for the buyers' costs of search, will lead to varying average degrees of control over firms' decisions on inventory levels, servicing facilities offered to their buyers, the extent of competing products carried, pricing, and so on. For every level in the channel the same amounts of direct advertising expenditures will produce varying outputs in terms of control over that level. The problem is therefore to optimize the input level of advertising to each level in each channel. The input I_{i11} may then refer to advertising ($s = 1$) to level j ($j = 1$) in channel i. There are of course problems in allocating this total figure I_{i11} to firms, areas, media, message, etc., and they must be solved, but they are not essentially channel problems. Total output thus depends on the level of input of advertising, on its allocation to the firms in any level (if any), on the number of firms dealt with in any level $\bar{q}_{ij}$, and on the allocation of total advertising to the levels in the channel $j = 1, 2, \ldots j_{\max}$, consumers of various kinds, retailers, wholesale middlemen of various kinds, and producers of various kinds.

Some examples of the relationship of advertising to a channel level and the control over it are obvious; some are subtle. Thus, advertising to retailers may, with varying force, permit the advertising wholesale middleman to convince the retailer of the superiority of his product and hence dictate to him the amounts he is expected to buy. A more subtle effect is that wrought by advertising to a level on the selling efforts which this level should put behind a product. Finally it is also true that advertising to consumers creates a control over their behavior and through that on the behavior of all other levels in the channel. The identical analysis applies to the input of personal selling.

To this point there have been identified the following inputs to control, in any given channel $\bar{q}_{ij}D_{ij}$ over level j in channel i:

I_{i11} = Gross margin (over optimum minimum necessary with no control in channel i) given to level 1;

I_{i12} = Gross margin (over optimum minimum necessary with no control in channel i) given to level 2;

$\cdot$

$\cdot$

$\cdot$

$I_{i1j_{\max}}$ = Gross margin (over optimum minimum necessary with no control in channel i) given to level $j_{\max}$;

I_{i21} = Advertising expenditures (over optimum minimum necessary with no control in channel i) directed at level 1;

I_{i22} = Advertising expenditures (over optimum minimum necessary with no control in channel i) directed at level 2;

$\cdot$

$\cdot$

$\cdot$

$I_{12j_{\max}}$ = Advertising expenditures (over optimum minimum necessary with no control in channel i) directed at level $j_{\max}$;

I_{i31} = Personal selling (over optimum minimum necessary with no control in channel i) directed at level 1;

I_{i32} = Personal selling (over optimum minimum necessary with no control in channel i) directed at level 2;

$\cdot$

$\cdot$

$\cdot$

$I_{i3j_{\max}}$ = Personal selling (over optimum minimum necessary with no control in channel i) directed at level $j_{\max}$;

q_{ij} = Number of firms not sold to over optimum necessary with no control.

For solving specific problems, rather than the general overall channel problem, the function

(9) $\bar{q}_{ij}D_{ij} = g_{ij}(I_{is1}, I_{is2}, \ldots I_{isj}, \ldots$

$I_{isj_{\max}}, q_{ij}, \overset{\circ}{J}_{ir1}, \overset{\circ}{J}_{ir2}, \ldots$

$\overset{\circ}{J}_{irj}, \ldots \overset{\circ}{J}_{irj_{\max}}, \overset{\circ}{D}'_{ij})$

(for $s = 1, 2, \ldots n$, $r = 1, 2, \ldots m$,

and $\overset{\circ}{J}_{irj}$ and $\overset{\circ}{D}'_{ij}$ given at some constant values)

must be identified for each level j in channel i. This entails an understanding of a complex relationship made up, in some fashion, of a number of individual relationships. The saving element is that all functional relationships identified to this point are stated in their most general form. In fact, there are many inputs, say I_{i4j} and I_{i5j}, etc., which have no effect on the control over some specific level, $j = 2$. This means that

$$\frac{\partial D_{i2}}{\partial D_{i42}} = \frac{\partial D_{i2}}{\partial I_{i52}} = 0$$

for all values of I_{i42} and I_{i52}.

One would not therefore include these inputs in the control equation in this case. One would only include those inputs for which the partials are not always zero or even only those with "significantly" large partials in the appropriate ranges.

Other groups of inputs can now be identified. There is no reason to suppose that all these inputs have been actually employed by firms. However, for any given known list, the problem's formulation permits optimization for the degree of control $\bar{q}_{ij}D_{ij}$ with or without constraints. Among such lists would be all services performed by one firm for another. If we allow now D'_{ij} to vary (i.e., control of other levels over one), then there is the whole area of the firm's many decision areas, where the input would be the degree to which one surrenders one's freedom of choice in any of these decision areas. Thus the input which a retailer might employ to gain control over the quality of the product produced by the manufacturer, may involve his surrendering of some freedom of choice in his decision on an assortment or a level of inventory, or an advertising expenditure level. Obviously, in this matter the inputs of this kind are as many as there are business decisions, and there are too many of these to consider in a practical situation. There is, however, no need to consider them all.

Some input costs are obviously much too high to allow their considerations; others have too small an output, i.e., a given $\partial D_{ij}/\partial I_{isj}$ may be extremely small for all values of the other inputs to make it worthwhile considering this input. For example, input I_{isj} may be that which refers to the firm's decisions on the form which accounting reports which the firm to be controlled should have. To the firm over which control is to be gained, this change in its accounting report may be of little interest and apparently of no value, and hence not an inducement to allow itself to be controlled. In this case, I_{isj} can be disregarded as an input for D_{ij}. For purposes of theory though, the optimum solution (where the cost of solving the problem) is not included, the list of I_{isj} for all i, s, and j, must include every input for which $\partial D_{ij}/\partial I_{isj} \neq 0$ for all values of the remaining inputs and I_{isj}.

One final set of inputs to the control level D_{ij} may be mentioned here because of their extensive present day use in the economy. These are the services which sellers render buyers (or vice versa), such as those which are to be found in voluntary chains. Here the wholesale middleman gains control over the choice of buying sources of retailers at a cost to himself. The cost is that of the inputs producing that control, *viz.* the services in the area of accounting, store layout, store display, pricing, etc. These services involve a cost to the wholesale middleman, and are thus the specific inputs which in some combination produce a certain level of control over a number of firms in some level in the channel. An example of services rendered by buyers to sellers is found in the relation between some chain store operations and producers.

OPTIMIZING THE COMBINATION OF INPUTS WITH CONSTRAINTS ON CONTROL LEVELS

To the firm, there is also the decision on how much control to allow firms in other levels to exercise over itself. To this firm this kind of control D'_{ij} involves inputs, the inputs being mostly of the kind of limitations on its freedom of choice. The firm must decide in fact the exact combination of the levels of these inputs which will produce control over its behavior. The returns to these inputs is related to the effects that their output, *viz.* D'_{ij}, has on total revenues and costs, just as it is for the control over other levels D_{ij}.

The optimum combinations of inputs needed to produce some required level $\bar{q}_{ij}D_{ij} = Q_{ij}$ can now be derived under varying circumstances. For example, we may wish to minimize the costs of attaining a given level of control over a given number of firms in a given channel. Essentially this is just determining the best way to attain any given feasible control level. If the price levels A_{irj} and B_{isj} are independent of input levels I_{isj} and J_{irj}[a] then for

[a] If $B_{isj} = f(I_{sj}, J_{irj})$ then we substitute the functional form into the total cost equations below. The problem is somewhat more complex, for we need to know these functional forms if we are to solve for the I, but the concepts of solution and formulation are unchanged.

a given channel i and a given level j within it the problem is to minimize

$$(10) \quad C_{ij3} = \sum_{s=1}^{n} B_{isj} I_{isj} + \lambda_{ij} [Q_{ij} - g_{ij}(T)]$$

where $g_{ij}(T)$ is the function given in equation 9 above, with a constant given value for $q_{ij} = \overset{\circ}{q}_{ij}$ (i.e., there is a given value for $\bar{q}_{ij}$).

Minimizing C_{ij3} as defined in equation 10 is not the solution of the problem of channel control which is itself only a part of the problem of channel choice. A more general problem is thus that of minimizing the cost of $\bar{q}_{ij} D_{ij}$ for all $j = 1, 2, \ldots j_{\max}$, subject to certain constraints on the D_{ij} and given values of q_{ij} and D'_{ij}. The total cost of control in all levels of channel i is given by the sum $\sum_{j=1}^{j_{\max}} \sum_{s=1}^{n} B_{isj} I_{isj}$ which is to be minimized given the constraints. For the problem viewed in this way one needs to minimize, therefore,

$$(11) \quad C_{i4} = \sum_{j=1}^{j_{\max}} \sum_{s=1}^{n} B_{isj} I_{isj} + \sum_{j=1}^{j_{\max}} \lambda_{ij} [Q_{ij} - g_{ij}(T)]$$

where $g_{ij}(T)$ for each j is the relevant function given in equation 9 above and with $q_{ij} = q_{ij}$, and Q_{ij} the chosen level of control over each level in channel i. Here $g_{ij}(T)$ is substituted for the function given in equation 9.

In equation 11 there are in effect $(s \times j_{\max})$ different inputs which are to be determined. Differentiating partially C_{i4} with respect to each such input and setting the partials equal to zero we have

$$\frac{\partial C_{i4}}{\partial I_{isj}} = B_{isj} - - \sum_{j=1}^{j_{\max}} \lambda_{ij} g'_{ij}(T) = 0$$

for all $s = 1, 2, \ldots n$ and $j = 1, 2, \ldots j_{\max}$,

and $\quad \dfrac{\partial C_{i4}}{\partial_{ij}} = [Q_{ij} - g_{ij}(T)] = 0$

for all $j = 1, 2, \ldots j_{\max}$.

There are $(s \times j_{\max}) + j_{\max}$ equations in as many unknowns. This solution should give the minimum cost input combination which satisfied these constraints.

To this point all formulations of the control level problem have held q_{ij} constant. It could, of course, be made into a variable to be set along with the inputs I. It will be recalled that q_{ij} is the number of firms not in level j but which if included in this channel i would be in level j. These firms are potential members of the channel in a given level clearly identified, by virtue of the fact that they meet the requirements of membership in the class of firms making up the given level. If, for example, level 3 in channel i were made up of drop shippers, then q_{ij} is the number of drop shippers of this product which are in fact *not* included in this channel level. The number q_{ij} is equal to the total number of firms eligible to be in this level minus the number actually in the level in the channel which is $\bar{q}_{ij}$.

The cost to the firm of a unit of q_{ij} (leaving out one firm in the level j from the channel in question) is discussed in detail below, and involves essentially the lost sales of the unit of q_{ij}. It is unlikely that this unit cost will be independent of the value of q_{ij} and hence we can let it be $\mu_{ij} = f(q_{ij})$. The problem is now to minimize

$$(12) \quad C_{ij5} = \sum_{j=1}^{j_{\max}} \sum_{s=1}^{n} B_{isj} I_{isj} + \sum_{j=1}^{j_{\max}} f(q_{ij}) q_{ij} + \sum_{j=1}^{j_{\max}} \lambda_{ij} [Q_{ij} - g_{ij}(T)]$$

where $g_{ij}(T)$ is the relevant function for each level j given in equation 9 above with q_{ij} a variable. The same method for minimizing this cost C_{i4} in equation 11 is used here. The variable q_{ij} is in fact an input of control, but one of a rather special nature, and for this reason it is discussed further below.

Yet another formulation of the issue of control is that of maximizing control levels $\bar{q}_{ij} D_{ij}$, subject to some limitations on the costs to be incurred in attaining that control. In any case, all sub-optimum solutions obtained from the limited problems formulated are based on certain assumptions. It is necessary to assume that the functions $g_{ij}(T)$ are continuous and have first and second order partial derivatives. This means that all outputs and all inputs are infinitely divisible, and that there are decreasing marginal returns at some point to the added use of one input when all others are held constant at some given level. When these assumptions are not justified in fact, and when their use as approximations is too inaccurate some tool other than the calculus must be found to obtain optimum input combinations. Finally it is quite obvious that various limited problems mentioned can be derived from the general case. The complexity of this latter probably means that in real situations it is indeed such subsystem formulations that would be the feasible ones for the decision maker to handle at any one time.

B. Evaluation of Channel Effectiveness

29. Evaluation of Channel Effectiveness

DAVID A. REVZAN

In this selection, channel effectiveness is evaluated. The objectives of each channel level's view, as well as the overall marketing view, are discussed. Revzan describes the types of tools available for channel evaluation and the basic components of channel analysis.

At the outset, it must be emphasized that far too many writers have viewed the evaluation of channel effectiveness only from the vantage point of the manufacturer.[1] That this view is emphasized should not be surprising since it is a continuation of a narrowness of perspective which all too often is present in the discussion of channels. Actually, the evaluation of channel effectiveness is, and should be, the concern of every primary agency in the channel—producer, wholesale middlemen, and retail middlemen. In addition, there is an over-all point of view which reflects the evaluation of the efficiency of the wholesaling sector within the entire marketing system. The objectives of the evaluation and the types of tools and techniques will vary according to the viewpoint thus indicated.

OBJECTIVES OF THE EVALUATION

Any discussion of the evaluation of channel effectiveness must take into consideration the objectives of each channel level's view as well as the over-all marketing view as noted. From the manufacturer's level, the principal objectives may be stated as follows: (1) To determine the contribution of the channel alternatives to the achievement of the company's over-all marketing program, in quantitative and qualitative units, (2) to determine, more specifically, the direct and indirect relationship between channel alternatives and the degree of market penetration of the company's product lines, area by area; (3) to determine the contribution of the channel alternatives to customer recognition and acceptance of the company's sales promotional campaigns; (4) to determine the contribution of the channel to the company's complete knowledge of the characteristics of the market it services; (5) to determine the contribution of the channel to the company's favorable or unfavorable cost-profit position, product line by product line, and market area by market area; and (6) to determine the contribution of each channel alternative to the degree of aggressiveness of the company's marketing program. Inherent in each of these are the implications for the managerial struggle for channel control noted above; and each of these may be subdivided into many appropriate subdivisions.

From the wholesale and retail middlemen's points of view, the following constitute the main objectives: (1) The extent to which the channel alternatives maximize the middleman's freedom

• SOURCE: David A. Revzan, "Evaluation of Channel Effectiveness," *Wholesaling In Marketing Organization* (New York: John Wiley and Sons, 1961), pp. 151–155. David A. Revzan, Professor of Business Administration, University of California (Berkeley).

[1] See, for example, R. M. Clewett (Ed.), *Marketing Channels for Manufactured Products* (Homewood, Ill.: Richard D. Irwin, 1954), Chapters 17, 18, and 19.

of managerial activity with respect to products handled, territory covered, and functional activities to be performed; (2) the extent to which the channel arrangement maximizes or circumscribes each middleman's freedom to expand; (3) the extent to which the channel arrangement permits the wholesale or retail middleman to enter the managerial struggle for control of the channel, if he so desires; (4) the extent to which the middlemen are permitted in the channel to maintain their type-of-operation identity, instead of being played off one against the other; and (5) the extent to which the wholesale and retail middlemen are permitted to realize either price spread margins or commissions or fees commensurate with their cost-profit requirements.

TYPES OF MANAGEMENT TOOLS AVAILABLE FOR CHANNEL EVALUATION

Before discussing the general framework of how the management tools may be used to evaluate channel effectiveness, an introductory description of the basic types of tools may be appropriate. The first management tool is the use of comparative sales analyses. These analyses involve the determination of the sales realized by the agencies in a particular channel structure, and the comparison of these results with some sales goals as established by the appropriate management unit. These types of analyses may be instituted by any agency level of the channel, with only the necessary changes of emphasis designed to meet differences in objectives as noted above.

Since much emphasis needs to be placed in the analysis of channel effectiveness on the relation of such effectiveness to cost and profits, it must be obvious that a second tool involves the use of special techniques of distribution cost accounting. In these analyses, distribution cost accounting may be used to evaluate the differential cost elements inherent in alternative channel structures; for measuring, similarly, alternative profit returns; for evaluating the cost of servicing various sales-size classes of customers; or for other types of problems to be discussed later.

A third family of tools may be included under the broad term of "marketing research." This may involve systematic analyses by the manufacturer or middlemen to test: (a) customer attitudes towards products and related services offered in the channel; (b) customer satisfaction or dissatisfaction with existing channel arrange-

ments, and attitudes towards suggested alternatives; (c) the determination of the trading area boundaries of wholesale and retail markets or of specific types of wholesale and retail middlemen; (d) the attitude of middlemen in the channel towards the manufacturer, his marketing policies, and his products; (e) the attitude, conversely, of the manufacturer towards each type of middleman; (f) the establishment of specific sales and cost goals for each agency in the channel. The tools under this heading frequently are combined with the other types to develop complicated marketing potentials to be derived from alternative channel arrangements.

THE BASIC COMPONENTS OF CHANNEL ANALYSIS

Given any particular channel arrangement and any given combination of analytical tools, the following represent the components of a necessary beginning analysis on which can be built a whole series of special studies:

1. The measurement of the size of the potential trading areas, using techniques which have been or will be described in detail.
2. The development of sales potentials for each of these trading areas.
3. The subdivision of (1) and (2) by product lines, if necessary, with accompanying measures of the estimated market penetration ratio of each line.
4. The subdivision of (1), and (2), and (3) by salesmen and salesmen's territories. This involves knowledge, by time-and-duty analyses, of how many customers a given type of salesman can adequately service per working day.
5. The calculation of the cost-of-getting-sales ratios, by product lines, salesmen, territories, etc., in terms of the direct, semidirect, and indirect components based on historical and estimated future bases.
6. The alternative costs, as in (5), for substituting possible channel alternatives.
7. The subdivisions of the cost estimates in (5) and (6) by various size classes of customers.
8. Finally, a comparison of actual sales, cost, and profit results with the budgeted potentials, together with a critical explanation of the reasons why the potentials have or have not been realized.

SPECIFIC STUDIES

The basic components outlined above are part of an analytical framework which can be undertaken by any business unit of sufficient sales size, adequate financial resources, and possessing sufficient insight into the marketing perspective so that it can keep its organizational executives well informed of the entire channel.

In actual practice, most of these units undertake at any given period of time only those special studies which reflect for each some scale of urgency. Thus, trading area boundary studies frequently are reduced in analytical content and cost by accepting such determinations made by others in the manner already described. The systematic determination of the boundaries of salesmen's territories and related quotas, while done most frequently by the manufacturing agencies, represents another grouping of specific studies in which the wholesale middlemen also can use many of the tools of marketing research in preparing complete studies; they may give the middlemen necessary data with which to check estimates prepared by the manufacturer for the use of the middlemen.

More manufacturers than wholesale middlemen are likely to make systematic cost studies of the contributions to profits and market penetration made by each sales-size category of customer. Yet such studies are very important for middlemen as well as for manufacturers in understanding the alternative yields available from each sales-size class by making selected channel pattern shifts. Again, more manufacturers than wholesale middlemen are likely to use the various techniques of sampling and interviewing in order to get reliable estimates of consumers' attitudes towards products as they move through the channel. This is true all too often even where the wholesale middleman or retail middleman, as the case might be, has his own brand affixed to the products. Sharp differences frequently are present between manufacturers themselves, or between manufacturers and middlemen, concerning the value of studies which present continuing measurement of total and individual product market penetration. The aggregates of such studies can become most valuable evidence in understanding why total budgeted sales may or may not be realized.

Sharp differences also exist between the awareness of individual managements as to the relationship between sales size of customer accounts, the number of invoices per account, the division of assignable and nonassignable items of cost by accounts, and estimated profits. Similarly, wide differences are apparent among management levels in the use of graphic relations between sales volume and profit volume. For manufacturers, careful distribution cost analyses must be made of the variable cost components of alternative channel arrangements if accurate estimates of net additions to profits are to be determined. These must include, as well, realistic estimates of sales, especially if middlemen, formerly used by the manufacturer, represent strong competitive lives in the shifts in channels. Finally, careful cost allocations must be made by all agencies handling multiproduct assortments, in order that realistic calculations may be made of the contribution of each item to gross and net profit.[2]

An additional type of analysis which requires much continuous research is the study of those marketing trends which have some significant relationship to channels of distribution. The appropriate personnel assigned to make such analyses in any organization must be well trained, first of all, in how to detect evidence of the existence of any change. This involves, in turn, professional acquaintanceship with the basic marketing literature; with those publications of the trade press specializing in the reporting of changes; with various statistical studies and professional studies of special aspects; and with provision for a continuous flow of oral and written reports about significant trends from the salesmen and branch executives in the various key centers of trade. From the evidence collected, careful analysis must be made of both the content and implication of each trend presented. The final aspect of such analyses must include careful recommendations as to whether the management can influence the direction of the trend or, on the contrary, can be dominated by the basic changes being generated.

All in all, the marketing organization (channel) aspects of many marketing problems have not been given, it would appear, the importance by the various agencies in the channel that they seem to require in view of the significance of channels. The channel is the managerial battlefield in which marketing strategy and marketing tactic activities of each business unit either succeed or fail. It would seem only logical, therefore, that a great deal of the marketing research being done recognize and emphasize this level of significance, and that the problems be so carefully defined as not to eliminate important channel aspects and implications.

[2] These statements are only suggestive of the kinds of analyses which need to be made and the types of analytical tools to be used. The next sections will examine certain aspects of these analyses in more detail in their internal management perspective. The evaluation of the over-all effectiveness of channels will be included in the concluding discussions of the efficiency of the wholesaling sector.

30. Modern Marketing and the Accountant

BRUCE MALLEN and STEPHEN D. SILVER

This paper pleads for a closer relationship between accounting and marketing, and outlines the areas in which such closer cooperation is essential. The authors include a useful and often overlooked clarification between sales and marketing, and sales analysis and marketing research.

Distribution cost accounting is an important and legitimate field of study for the accountant. However, the Canadian practitioner has paid little heed. Even the Canadian specialists in cost accounting have focussed only a little attention on marketing distribution costs.[1] Such indifference to a most important area of business is discouraging. Marketing usually accounts for over 40 per cent of the product's final cost to the ultimate user! This final cost includes the marketing costs of the manufacturer plus the total costs of the involved middlemen. The last includes retailers, wholesalers, transportation firms and so on.

A high degree of efficiency is vital in marketing, for it is here where a huge share of the costs are incurred. More important, it is *for* marketing that any costs (production, finance, etc.) are incurred. Marketing is the firm's "breadwinner." No significant revenues come in to cover costs and provide a profit until marketing moves the goods. In this sense, nothing happens until a sale is made.

It is the purpose of this article to show the importance of marketing in Canadian business and to describe the potential role of the accountant in providing assistance to the marketing executive via the specialized skills in which he is trained.

A description and perspective on the marketing function is first discussed, followed by a summary of its changing role in the past ten years. A brief explanation of marketing research and its subdivision sales analysis is included. The role of the accountant in marketing and marketing research is then analyzed together with a description of his most important technique "distribution cost accounting." There is at present a growing literature in the field of distribution costing. The authors have included a bibliography for those interested in further study.

THE NATURE AND IMPORTANCE OF MARKETING

The activity of marketing is to advise production on what and how much to produce, based on consumer needs, and to direct the flow of goods to users or resellers. Marketing thus includes or is directly involved in: personal selling, advertising, sales promotion, packaging, product development, pricing, marketing research, transportation, storage, wholesaling, and retailing.

A glance at the various activities listed above will indicate the vast range of marketing occupations in our economy. A sizable portion (in the U.S., over one-half) of the work force is engaged in marketing.

Marketing, indeed, consists of a tremendous share of the total activity of business. It, in fact, comprises three of the four utilities of "produc-

• SOURCE: Bruce Mallen and Stephen D. Silver, "Modern Marketing and the Accountant," *Cost and Management* (February, 1964), pp. 75–85. Bruce Mallen, Senior Marketing Consultant, P. S. Ross & Partners, Stephen D. Silver, Assistant Economist Canadian National Railways.

[1] See, for example, SICA's Special Study No. 3, *Distribution Costs—Their Control and Analysis,* by André Parent.

tion" described by economists. These are the utilities of time, place and possession. This means marketing provides goods "when," "where," and "to whom" they are wanted. Further, marketing directs and/or advises production on the fourth utility, that of "form." This means marketing helps production to decide "what" to produce.

The importance and cost of marketing is bound to grow. Indeed, it is inherent in a growing economy and one with a high standard of living. The larger an economy, the more specialized can its firms afford to be. This specialization leads to lower production costs, and so, through less expensive products, a higher living standard.

At the same time, however, specialized effort requires more exchange, more trading, i.e., more marketing. Thus, marketing costs as a percentage of total costs will grow. These costs will further be increased by the demands of consumers for more services, e.g., better packaging. This will surely cause the cost accountant to pay more and more attention to the marketing sphere.

Aside from the economic aspects, the importance of marketing in our society can be attributed, in part, to our democratic ideals. Every society must decide, for its fundamental philosophy, whether the individuals in that society are to have freedom of choice in their purchases or whether these choices are to conform to goals set by others, usually the government. Our democratic society has, by definition, picked the first alternative—freedom of consumer choice. This means that it is the push and pull of innumerable individual decisions on what to buy and sell which will determine the kinds of products to be produced.

It is the major (and most difficult) task of marketing to anticipate and interpret these free decisions so that the consumer can be served, and the company rewarded with profits. It is for this important task that the accountant can provide invaluable aid.

THE "NEW" MARKETING

Before the 1950's, the terms "marketing" and "sales" were synonymous and were used interchangeably, except by a very few companies. The sales function was simply to dispose of the goods produced by the manufacturing division. The emphasis was on selling what was made, rather than on making what would sell.

During the 1950's, however, with increased domestic and foreign competition, many new product innovations and developments, a shift from scarcity to abundance, a profit squeeze, a more discriminating buying public, and a tremendous growth in their discretionary income (giving consumers more freedom on spending decisions), the sales approach gradually began to give way to the marketing concept.

This concept is customer-oriented rather than production-oriented and states that: "Business exists and is rewarded for satisfying consumer wants." The desires of the customer rather than the production department are becoming the prime concern. Product management has developed as a coordination and control device to help ensure that all possible effort is directed to satisfying consumer wants and making a profit, right from the original conception of a product to its final consumption.

MARKETING RESEARCH

One of the pillars of the modern marketing concept is decision making based on accurate facts and information. The formal method of obtaining information is marketing research. The accountant's contribution, to be discussed in some detail further on, is an important phase of marketing research. Let us examine the five fundamental questions that marketing research asks.

(a) What is the potential market for a product and what will our company's share of this be in each period? Known as quantitative market research, this question involves a study of total industry volume and a forecast of the company's sales.

(b) Who are the present and potential customers? Known as qualitative market research, this question involves the study of the market's characteristics, e.g., age, location, size, etc.

(c) How can the company best appeal to this market? This area deals with motivation research, packaging research, pricing, and product research. It suggests appeals for promotion, selling and advertising.

(d) How can the company most effectively reach this market? Having answered the first three questions, it remains to find out the most efficient way of reaching the market. This involves transportation, channel, and media research.

(e) How successful is the firm's marketing program and what are its weak areas? It is this question that needs the accountant's specialized skills through his use of distribution cost accounting. It is to the latter question that we now turn.

SALES ANALYSIS

Sales analysis consists of a study of past sales performance as provided by internal sales records. These records, if properly maintained, offer an excellent and inexpensive source of information.

There are numerous ways in which sales data can be analyzed to provide marketing management with useful information. This data especially when placed on a comparative basis, can pinpoint trouble spots in the marketing program as well as within an individual salesman's performance. For example, analysis of one man's sales by product may show that he is doing relatively poorly with a particular product than most other salesmen. This especially presents a problem if the product happens to return a high margin. Further analysis by customer type (or size) may show that poor performance is concentrated among a certain class of buyer.

Thus, sales analysis, in the above example, has pinpointed for the marketing manager that a particular salesman is having difficulties with a specific product within a particular customer class. The reason for and the answer to the problem may now be apparent to the marketing manager. If not, he will undertake further study, perhaps in discussion with the customers concerned, to get at the exact reasons behind the problem which his sales analysis has uncovered.

Combining sales analysis with distribution cost analysis can provide an even more powerful analytic tool to the marketing manager. Cost analysis, as we shall later see in detail, will show the profit contributions or contribution to fixed cost which a man's performance pattern is making.

Thus, with the help of distribution cost analysis, the marketing executive, instead of having just a sales pattern picture, can have a profit pattern picture. He can, for example, uncover a situation as above, in which a particular salesman's profit contribution is poor for a particular product with specific customer types. This is especially useful, as a simple study of sales patterns may not reveal poor profit performance. For example, the poor sales pattern cited a few paragraphs above may actually provide a better profit performance than patterns whose sales performances are better.

It is to be kept in mind that modern marketing looks for "profitable volume," not simply more volume.

THE ACCOUNTANT IN MARKETING

Traditionally in Canada, cost accounting has placed the emphasis on the analysis and control of production costs, while little attention has been directed to the study of marketing distribution costs. Accountants seem to have a natural reluctance to enter the marketing sphere. This is unfortunate, since their specialized skills can be of great help to the marketing executive. Until recently, the marketing executive has had little recourse to sound accounting data on which to formulate important marketing decisions. The result is that the proper planning and control has suffered. The contribution which the accountant can make is to supply marketing executives with the necessary data and information so that they can plan, control and direct the various activities involved in the marketing process.

If businessmen in Canada are to operate as efficiently and as effectively as possible, there must be cooperation between the accounting and marketing groups. The accountant needs to know how the marketing man thinks and works, the problems he faces, and the type of information he requires. The marketing man, on the other hand, should be aware of the assumptions underlying accounting data, the type of information available, and the limitations inherent in using such. This all-important rapport can be achieved in various ways which vary from company to company. Yet, whatever company is involved, it is essential that top management play an important role in bringing this coordination about. For only if both the marketing team and accounting group subordinate their individual biases to the over-all benefit of the enterprise will each be able to contribute most effectively.

Methods for improving such cooperation include: (a) getting accounting personnel to sit in on top level marketing meetings; (b) rotating staff positions so that accounting and marketing men can spend some time in each other's departments; (c) having the accounting personnel accompany marketing men on their sales calls. Just as accounting and production men have joined forces in developing methods of production cost control, so must accounting and marketing executives work jointly in the control and analysis of distribution costs.

DISTRIBUTION COST ACCOUNTING

The accounting for distribution costs can be divided into two broad areas: (a) Cost Analysis and (b) Cost Control. Distribution cost analysis consists of determining the costs and the profitability of carrying out the various marketing activities. This information is used to discover more effective and more profitable ways of marketing. Distribution cost control, on the other hand, is the measurement of performance in the marketing field against predetermined standards and the execution of corrective action to eliminate unfavourable deviations.

Cost analysis is concerned with management planning, while cost control is concerned with seeing that the actual coincides with the planned. These two areas are the chief tasks of the marketing executive. The accountant can be of considerable assistance in this regard.

According to two pioneers in the field of distribution costing, Professors D. R. Longman and Michael Schiff, distribution cost accounting offers these advantages for the management of a business.[2]

(1) It forces a review of the company's basic marketing plan and its working organization, providing a new understanding.
(2) It shows how much expense and what kinds of expense are incurred for each activity of the business, and assigns responsibility for costs to specific individuals.
(3) It permits an evaluation of distribution methods.
(4) It spotlights inefficiencies in operating procedures.
(5) It facilitates over-all company budgeting procedures.

[2] D. R. Longman, and M. Schiff, *Practical Distribution Cost Analysis*, Richard D. Irwin, 1955, p. 72.

COST ANALYSIS

(a) By Functions

The first phase of distribution cost accounting consists of finding out the cost of performing each marketing activity. This requires a statement of the various activities of marketing performed by the firm. While these activities differ with individual firms, many are common to most. A typical list would include: (1) Direct selling, (2) Packaging, (3) Delivery, (4) Mail Orders, (5) Accounts Receivable and (6) Advertising.

In most corporations in Canada, the cost of these functions is seldom determined. Commonly used accounting systems classify costs according to their nature (e.g., salaries, depreciation) and not according to their function, i.e., the purpose for which they are intended. The natural classification may be adequate for financial reporting, or for the determination of the income tax liability. It is of little use to the marketing manager who wants a breakdown of the relative costs of the methods he is using or the customers he is serving.

The most economical way of obtaining functional data is by taking the natural expense accounts as found on the profit and loss statement and reclassifying them according to their function. Table 1 shows an Expense Distribution Sheet with the natural accounts broken down in two ways: (1) according to function (horizon-

Table 1. **Expense Distribution Sheet**

Natural Account	Total	Advtg.	Act. Rec.	Delivery	Packaging	Mail Order
Direct:						
Salaries	$ 2,600	$1,000	$ 500	$300	$ 600	$ 200
Pay charges	189	70	35	24	45	15
Stationery	255	50	90	10	5	100
Telephone	45	10	10	15	5	5
Postage	1,215	200	300	10	5	700
Advertising	5,000	5,000				
	9,304	6,330	935	359	660	1,020
Indirect:						
Insurance	250	50	50	50	50	50
Maintenance	500	100	100	100	100	100
Depreciation	1,000	200	200	200	200	200
	1,750	350	350	350	350	350
Total	$11,054	$6,680	$1,285	$709	$1,010	$1,370

tally) and (2) according to whether the costs are directly attributable to each function or whether they must be allocated according to some arbitrary base.

Using functional analysis offers four important advantages:

(1) *Appraisal.* It provides the basis for effective appraisal of marketing strategy and for cost analysis by product, customer, territory, etc. The full cost of any function including indirect charges can be determined. Different selling methods can be compared. The use of outside selling services can be evaluated. This valuable information is used generally, then, to evaluate present marketing methods in the light of possible alternatives.

(2) *Standardization.* It facilitates the introduction of a system of standards to be used in the control of costs.

(3) *Responsibility.* It enables management to pin responsibility for cost performance to specific individuals. Since the marketing functions should parallel the company organization, classification by function results in determining the cost which comes under the responsibility of each functional head:

(4) *Cost Performance.* It enables management to analyze the cost performance and thus the profit performance (when combined with sales analysis) of each market segment. Significant changes in the cost of each function can be determined and investigated. Referring to successive expense distribution sheets will give a skilled analyst much information as to which factors were the cause of material changes in various expenses.

(b) Other Classifications

Marketing costs can be classified further into other groupings to discover weak spots in the distribution policy and to forecast the effect of their elimination. The most frequently used groupings and analyses are by:

(1) Product group
(2) Method of sale
(3) Salesman
(4) Channel of distribution
(5) Customer group
(6) Territory

After the selection of the type of analysis needed, the accountant must then classify the various functional groups according to the directness with which they relate to a particular analysis. If terrorial analysis is chosen, the accountant must then determine which costs bear a direct relationship to each territory and which are indirectly associated (and so must be allocated arbitrarily). For example, direct costs which would relate to individual territories would include salaries and expenses of sales managers within each territory, automobile expenses for use within a given territory, commissions to brokers and agents, and so on. Indirectly related costs would include general sales executives' salaries, entertainment expense of the head office and the head office clerical staff expenses.

Analysis of costs of distributing in various territories could lead to discoveries of weaknesses. Possible corrective action could include:[3]

(1) Rearrangement of territorial boundaries
(2) Changes of methods in various territories
(3) Shifting of salesmen
(4) Abandonment of territories
(5) More emphasis on neglected lines.

This type of analysis can be of considerable advantage in the evaluation of the introduction of a new product. This can be seen from the following case study.

Case Study

A new product having a relatively high gross margin was introduced to one company's line. Because of its apparent high profitability, the executives promoted this new product quite vigorously. A detailed cost analysis was undertaken and the results were tabulated as shown in Table 2.

The new product, X was indeed contributing a profit. However it was a relatively small one in relation to the amount of effort expended. More detailed investigation revealed that the product was consumed in very small quantities and found its large market in small stores which typically were more expensive to serve. The buying habits of the consumers involved were discovered to be difficult to change and it was considered unlikely that a price decrease would be profitable because of the relatively high expenses.

In this particular case, the solution was to reallocate sales promotional effort to those areas where the sales manager thought it would be more effective, especially among the large buyers of fast-moving products. In the next year, the unit cost of distribution dropped from 65 cents

[3] J. B. Heckert, and R. B. Miner, *Distribution Costs*, Ronald Press, New York, 1940, p. 74.

Table 2.[4]   Margins, Distribution Costs and Profits By-Product Groups for Several Territories During One Year's Operations

Product Group	Unit Margin	Unit Cost of Distribution	Unit Profit or (Loss)
A	$ .46	$ .43	$ .03
B	.45	.53	(.08)
C	.24	.42	(.18)
D	.99	.64	.35
E	1.08	.58	.50
F	.76	.42	.34
G	.71	.79	(.08)
H	.96	.72	.24
X	1.31	1.25	.06
Average	$ .74	$ .65	$ .09

[4] Adapted from *How Manufacturers Reduce Their Distribution Costs*, Economic Series No. 72, U.S. Department of Commerce, Case 44, by Charles H. Sevin.

to 59 cents and the profit per unit increase from 9 cents to 17 cents.

It is obvious from the above example that proper cost analysis can be a very powerful tool in the solution of marketing problems.

NET PROFIT OR CONTRIBUTED MARGIN

In the analysis of marketing costs, two different schools of thought have developed. The first is known as the "Net Profit Approach." This school says that in determining the relative strength of a certain marketing segment (say products), all costs, including both fixed and variable, should be used. This method is similar

to the absorption method of allocating overhead in production accounting.

The second method is similar to the direct cost method of production accounting. It is known as the "contributed margin approach." This says that only the directly variable costs should be used in the analyses since fixed costs have no bearing on relative strength. Table 3 shows the difference in these two methods.

The advocates of the net profit approach would say that product *B* is the "weakest" product because it is not able to carry its share of the indirect or "inescapable" costs. The adherent to the contribution margin approach would say that since all products are contributing to the pool of fixed costs ($1,050) none

Table 3

	Total	A Product	B Product	C Product
Sales	$3,700	$1,000	$1,500	$1,200
Cost of Sales	2,200	500	800	900
Gross Profit	1,500	500	700	300
Direct Costs	500	100	300	100
Contribution Margin	1,000	400	400	200
Indirect Costs	1,050	350	600	100
Net Profit (Loss)	(50)	50	(200)	100

should be eliminated. Actually, both methods can supplement each other. Each method has its particular uses and advantages.

Professors Heckert and Miner feel that there are four distinct situations where the net profit approach yields fruitful results:[5]

(a) For regular and systematic reporting of historical costs. From the profit (or loss) information obtained, management can evaluate the relative strength of each segment.

(b) For special long-range studies of the relative profitability of individual segments.

(c) For budgeting costs in the manner in which management wishes them to be borne by each segment.

(d) For long-range pricing policies and the determination of mark-up policies.

The contribution margin approach, they feel, is appropriate in problems involving alternative courses in action of short run duration.

(a) For special studies of limited scope designed to aid management in making decisions in current tactical problems, such as pricing special orders and meeting competition in particular areas.

(b) For periodic reporting of data which management can utilize for immediate remedial action purposes.

COST CONTROL

Using the information generated from distribution cost analysis, the marketing executive and the accountant must develop a system of distribution cost control. The essence of control in this area is action which adjusts operations to predetermined standards. This action is based on information in the hands of the managers.

Any system of control consists of five prime elements:

(1) A definite plan of action to accomplish certain stated goals.

(2) Determination of standards to accomplish the plan.

(3) An information system to measure actual performance and compare the actual with the predetermined standards and then pass this information on to the relevant level of management.

(4) Analysis of the variances.

(5) The taking of corrective action. This means adjusting actual operations to the standards and/or the changing of the standards.

What role does the accountant play in the process of marketing control? He is not really a part of the planning process as such, nor is

it his responsibility to see that operations are brought closer to the standards. His role lies in the development and maintenance of the information system.

The key to the successful operation of the control system is information. The accountant must obtain the necessary information as quickly and as economically as possible, and transmit it to the relevant control point (i.e., the decision-making executive). Without the necessary data in the right place and at the right time, the system breaks down and the executive's job disintegrates into one of guesswork.

There are three main devices which the accountant uses in obtaining a proper information system.

(1) Budgets

The use of budgets for distribution activities is similar to that in other managerial fields. Budgeting serves to coordinate the entire operations of the firm. The finished budget serves as a declaration of the marketing executive's aims and ties in his effort with those of production and finance.

(2) Standards

The use of predetermined standards to control marketing costs is relatively new because of the difficulties inherent in trying to standardize such. These difficulties include the many psychological factors involved in distribution and the great flexibility present in distribution methods. For example, how much business should be secured by a given salesman in a given territory? Questions like these are extremely difficult to answer.

Yet, it must not be concluded that no standardization is feasible. Many marketing activities are as uniform and as routine as production work and lend themselves to standardization. These activities include order handling, warehousing, shipping, delivery, and clerical work. Even in areas such as advertising and personal selling, some sort of standards must be set. However, these are subject to considerable personal judgment and greater tolerance must be considered in the interpretation of the variances.

(3) Reports

Reports are the instruments by which all the information generated by distribution cost ac-

[5] J. B. Heckert, and R. Miner, *Op. cit.*, p. 32.

counting is passed on to the relevant level of management.

LIMITATIONS OF DISTRIBUTION COST ACCOUNTING

Distribution cost accounting, though an extremely valuable management tool does have some serious limitations, and these are among the reasons why many firms are not using it. Chief among these limitations are:

(a) High Cost

Except for the simplest of analyses, the accumulation of data and the development of an effective reporting system can be expensive. Many businessmen fear that the cost of instituting distribution cost accounting will exceed the benefits. Before any system such as has been described earlier can be introduced, a thorough feasibility study should be undertaken to compare the expected benefits and costs. In some cases extensive distribution cost accounting will not prove practical.

(b) Measurement Difficulties

Marketing research and analysis are filled with intangibles and uncertainties. It is extremely difficult to measure, and thereby standardize many of the operations. In addition, most marketing costs are indirect costs and the apportionment method of these indirect costs is usually arbitrary. This makes interpretation of such marketing information difficult.

(c) Personnel

Probably most serious is that few accountants in Canada at present are at home with the sophisticated techniques available in the field of distribution cost accounting. This is unfortunate, since the task of measuring and interpreting marketing costs then reverts to the marketing executive who has neither the time nor the training to institute proper accounting analyses.

Conclusion

The accountant has a valuable contribution to make to the vital area of marketing particularly with the technique of distribution cost accounting. In Canada, he has neglected the field. Marketing costs do, and will, outweigh production costs in many areas. With a growing economy, the growth of marketing costs both absolutely and relative to production costs is inevitable. The cost accountant must prepare himself then to apply his techniques to this area.

Under the "new" marketing, executives are very receptive to information provided by specialists; marketing research is today playing a most important role. Distribution cost accounting, as an area of marketing research, can and must share in this information gathering activity.

Notwithstanding its limitations, distribution cost accounting can, among other things, pinpoint and prevent troublespots, evaluate marketing performance, and facilitate control and the assignment of responsibilities. Marketing and accounting must get to know each other for their mutual benefit. At present they are almost strangers.

BIBLIOGRAPHY

The following is a list of books and articles which should prove informative and enlightening for those wishing to further their knowledge of cost accounting as applied to marketing.

W. E. Perry, "Distribution Methods and Costs," *N.A.C.A. Bulletin*, February 15, 1947.

J. A. Beckett, "The Art and Science of Distribution Costing," *N.A.C.A. Bulletin*, April 1951.

E. W. Kelley, "Marketing Needs Cost Control," *The Controller*, May 1953.

N.A.C.A. BULLETIN 19: "Assignment of Non-Manufacturing Costs for Managerial Decisions" (1951).

D. R. Longman, "The Values and Uses of Distribution Cost Analysis," *Journal of Marketing*, April 1957.

D. R. Longman, and M. Schiff, *Practical Distribution Cost Analysis*, Richard D. Irwin (1955).

J. B. Heckert, and R. B. Miner, *Distribution Costs*, Ronald Press (N.Y. 1953).

André Parent, *Distribution Costs—Their Control and Analysis*, Society of Industrial and Cost Accountants of Canada, Special Study No. 3.

31. The Accountant and Marketing Channels

ROBERT E. WEIGAND*

Weigand argues that accountants can play an important role in the area of marketing channel analysis. He indicates that this is becoming more important as the concept of managing the entire channel becomes more popular. His article suggests a few areas in which the accountant can aid management in this task.

The ability and willingness of wholesalers and retailers to buy, stock, sell, and deliver the product of a manufacturer has a significant and obvious effect on the profit of every firm that is involved in the transactions. Equally significant, but perhaps less obvious, is the view that decisions frequently must be made by the chief marketing executive in a manufacturing firm which are strategic to either modifying or adapting to other firms in the channel of distribution. Expressed differently, this suggests that the marketing executive often views the route taken by his firm's products as a variable which is subject to management in much the same way as is a sales force, an advertising budget, or the size of an inventory.

Still less obvious—and it is the thesis of this paper—is the thought that the limits of financial analysis extend beyond the confines of a manufacturing firm and should pervade the length of a channel of distribution. More specifically, considerable financial data is available to the manufacturer concerning the wholesalers and retailers to whom he sells. This data frequently is relevant to certain decisions which have a significant influence on the profit of the manufacturer. Ancillary to this thought is that the accountant often is qualified to aid the top marketing executive make strategic decisions which heretofore have been made with less than sufficient information and analysis. This article is, in short, recognition of a need for an interdisciplinary view of channel management. Two

specific recommendations are made concerning the type of financial information and analysis which would be helpful to the marketing executive.

There are two types of financial analysis or accounting service which are not within the scope of discussion here. First, sales and marketing cost analysis are valuable aids to marketing strategy but have been given considerable literary treatment by other writers. Accountants long have recognized that the net profit returned by two different channels may differ substantially, and they often present this information to the marketing executive. Second, a few manufacturers have helped their retail customers establish accounting systems and procedures as a "good-will" service. The purpose of this service is to make them stronger businessmen and consequently better customers.

The purpose of this article is not to clarify either sales or cost analysis or "good-will" services. Rather, it is to suggest (a) that channel relations are subject to management, (b) that analysis of financial data is helpful to the marketing executive in making many strategic decisions in this area, and (c) that the accountant often is well suited to gathering and analyzing this data. The inevitable conclusion, of course, is that the accountant can play a significant role in decisions made by the chief marketing executive; channel management becomes an interdisciplinary problem.

CURRENT VIEWS ON CHANNEL MANAGEMENT

The most common definition of a channel of distribution is that it consists of those institu-

• SOURCE: Robert E. Weigand, "The Accountant and Marketing Channels," in *The Accounting Review*, Vol. 38 (July, 1963), pp. 584–90.
* Robert E. Weigand is Chairman, Department of Marketing, De Paul University, Chicago.

tions which assume title to goods between producer and consumer. While this concept is often an accurate one, it does not adequately represent current thinking in many industries. Many ideas relative to marketing channels have been expressed in the literature, but three are particularly important here.

First, to an increased extent marketing writers have suggested that channels can be influenced or managed by a manufacturer. John A. Howard indicated[1] that the factors which determine a marketing executive's decisions are either controllable or non-controllable. The factors, according to Howard, which can be subjected to management include personal selling, advertising, price, location, product, and channels of distribution. The non-controllables include demand, competition, marketing law, the structure of distribution, and non-marketing costs. Of greatest interest in the development of this paper is the thought that through appropriate action the marketing executive can elicit cooperation from members of his channel. He is not forced passively to observe and accept the actions of channel participants.

In a related idea, Converse, Huegy, and Mitchell distinguish among marketing policies leading to what they call gravity, pressure, and suction channels.[2] In a gravity system the product is permitted to flow to its destination largely on the basis of a price appeal. To the business pursuing this policy additional marketing effort is considered unnecessary and even wasteful. The authors suggest that unprocessed agricultural products are the best example of commodities which move to the market by gravity although many raw materials and a few processed goods are also marketed in this way. In a pressure system an effort is made by the manufacturer, often through a quota system, to force the product downward through successive stages in the channel. For example, a manufacturer may establish a monthly volume which his retailers are expected to sell. The power to penalize for non-performance varies among firms. One of the most severe penalties for consistent nonperformance is loss of a valued franchise. In a suction system the manufacturer, often through advertising, attempts to pull the product through the channel by generating demand at the consumer stage. When pursuing

a suction policy the manufacturer leap-frogs his channel by directing a substantial share of his promotional effort at the final buyer. The latter two policies are complementary and often are used together. In each of the latter two views, the manufacturer would be attempting to "manage" the channel; in Howard's words, the channel would be a "controllable." The major automobile manufacturers and certain appliance manufacturers furnish good examples of firms which have combined the latter two ideas. Some have demanded performance of their distributors and dealers while simultaneously pulling the product through the channel through substantial expenditures on advertising.

The power which a large manufacturer can exert over a channel often is greater than a small manufacturer, but each has the capacity to make decisions which would influence a wholesaler's or retailer's willingness to cooperate. Many manufacturers, particularly those whose products have limited market appeal, have relatively little power; they may find that they must adjust to the power of others in the channel. Whether the extent of power is great or small is less important than recognition that the decisions of those in a channel are crucial to the profit position of a manufacturer. The nature and extent of information available to the chief marketing executive permits him to make effective and efficient decisions. Much of this information can be furnished by the accountant.

Second, to an increased extent in recent years, many participants in a channel have recognized the value of a continuing relationship over a period of time rather than for only a single transaction. Converse, Huegy, and Mitchell note that the "team" members of a channel under these circumstances, recognize ". . . a flow of duties and responsibilities both up and down throughout the team . . . each is linked through a complex of benefits and responsibilities."[3]

One of the purposes of such a long term team relationship is to reduce a variety of costs which are incurred when buyer and seller continually must seek either different sources of supply or new outlets. In addition, channel and market familiarity with the product and the problems accompanying the product often has a salutary effect on volume. The volume that is gained and the costs that are reduced more than compensate the channel participant for whatever flexibility may be lost.

---

[1] John A. Howard, *Marketing Management: Analysis and Decisions* (Homewood, Illinois: Richard D. Irwin, 1957).

[2] Paul D. Converse, Harvey W. Huegy, and Robert V. Mitchell, *Elements of Marketing* (Englewood Cliffs, N.J.: Prentice-Hall, 1958), pp. 587–590.

[3] *Ibid.*, p. 590.

The marketing executive's view of a channel is analogous to the manufacturing executive's view of plant and equipment. Conceptually each may be viewed as a long-term commitment to a particular course of action. Where desire for such stability of either manufacturing or marketing methods is present, it becomes substantially more important that the initial decision be the most effective and efficient that available information affords. Once again, much of this analysis is most easily performed by an accountant.

Third, there is great competition among manufacturers for the more favored outlets,[4] and the offering that any one manufacturer makes to wholesalers or retailers is usually weighed with great care. The alternative of offering the market substantially more than competition offers may occur only at substantially higher costs. For a manufacturer to offer less than competition is tantamount to market exclusion. Inasmuch as such decisions are often of considerable duration it is incumbent upon the chief marketing executive, and those assisting him, to weigh carefully the cost of long term channel decisions. And again, the accountant is in a position to furnish considerable help in making such decisions.

THE ACCOUNTANT'S ROLE

The ideas just presented suggest that marketing channels are as fully appropriate for implementation of managerial functions as are other areas of a business, that the relationship between buyer and seller frequently extends over a considerable period of time, and that the marketing mix offered to the channel is something of a compromise between volume desired and costs incurred. Implicit in all three views are the thoughts that channel decisions have a significant impact on long-term profits and that financial analysis should play an important role in such decisions. The following paragraphs suggest ways in which the accountant can contribute information that is relevant to channel relations.

Dealer Selection

In many of those firms which elect to sell to a single or limited number of dealers in a geo-

graphic area, a careful and rather extended analysis of the capital position of a prospective dealer is more important than where a strategy of widespread or general distribution is selected. Financial analysis, under these circumstances, must go considerably beyond the traditional review of reports prepared by the general or specialized mercantile credit agencies.

Where a manufacturer's product is sold through a single or relatively few outlets he generally expects both wider and more effective performance of the marketing functions. The cost of such performance obviously is greater than only the amount of capital that is invested in inventory. The role of the financial analyst is to evaluate a retailer's capacity to perform in the manner expected of him. For example, retailers often are expected to spend substantial sums on advertising the product, to train sales people on the technical featurers of a product, to train service personnel to make repairs, and to finance the consumer or arrange financing through local lending institutions. In addition the manufacturer is in a position to insist that the retailer carry a wider line of his products than the retailer might prefer if left to his own choice. These responsibilities are carried out properly only by those retailers who are in a reasonably strong capital position. The amount of capital necessary to assume such functional obligations is significantly greater than is necessary to purchase a single lot of goods where few responsibilities are attached to the purchaser.

In analyzing the suitability of a retailer to a manufacturer's marketing system the retailer's capital position is a major determinant. Review of a retailer's income statement or balance sheet does not indicate willingness to cooperate, but it clearly demonstrates his financial capacity to abide by the terms of an agreement. The marketing executive often does not possess the ability to understand financial data and must rely upon a financial analyst. A factor that is crucial to the above is the ability of a manufacturer to obtain access to sufficient evidence that a sound decision can be made. Part of the success in obtaining such data depends upon the skill of the analyst in knowing specifically what information is most relevant and the sources from which it can be pieced together if the wholesaler or retailer is not willing to cooperate. The thought is suggested here that access to certain types of data is not impossible in many instances; this is particularly true where buyer and seller acknowledge the importance of the right decision and where each expects to abide

[4] For an empirical analysis of the problem of obtaining suitable outlets see Joe Bain, *Barriers to New Competition* (Cambridge, Mass.: Harvard University Press, 1952).

by the decision over a considerable period of time. Crucial to such openness in negotiating a franchise agreement is appreciation of the commitments being made by each party. It would be naive to suggest that full disclosure is likely in most instances. This would be particularly true if the arrangement were not expected to continue over a relatively long period. To a retailer or wholesaler, however, the difficulties associated with loss of a franchise because of non-performance may be viewed as much more serious than to divulge a limited amount of financial data.

Product Profitability to Our Customers

A second area in which accountants can be of substantial service to the marketing division is in evaluating the profitability of a manufacturer's product from the point of view of the wholesalers and retailers who constitute the channel. Evaluating the profitability of products in a product line long has been a duty of the accountant; costs incurred are matched with sales income for each product or groups of products, and the result is analogous to a series of income statements.

The Sales Manager is continually faced with the thought that wholesalers or retailers also are attempting to determine which products in his own line are most profitable and deserve the greatest attention. In many instances, sales and cost analyses are a powerful tool to determine what will be purchased for re-sale; in other instances, a buying decision is made by wholesalers or retailers on the basis of little more than a hunch. The task of the Sales Manager becomes much easier when he has evidence that his own products are more profitable to the wholesaler or retailer than competitive products. The thought is suggested, therefore, that sales and cost analysis is not limited to determining which of a manufacturer's products are most profitable and which are being carried at a loss. This is, of course, the traditional view. Rather it should extend throughout the channel by evaluating the profitability of the manufacturer's product relative to similar products manufactured by competitors and carried by wholesalers and retailers. Expressed differently, the analyst must take the stance of a wholesaler or retailer who views with scepticism the claims of competing manufacturers that "My product will be more profitable to you than my competitor's." Many retailers will remain sceptical, but much of the information can be gathered

from largely incontrovertible sources. Such studies, in short, reflect the thought that delivered cost is increasingly recognized by buyers as only one of the determinants of profit.

When the Sales Manager can demonstrate the profitability of his firm's products vis-à-vis competitive products his selling task becomes substantially easier. The data becomes an effective selling tool because it replaces general statements with information that is considerably more objective. In many firms today (chain retailers are good examples) a multitude of buying decisions must be made quickly and on the basis of available evidence.[5] Formal sales presentations to buyers or buying committees obviously are more effective when accompanied by empirical data on stock turn, inventory investment, delivered cost, shelf space and other overhead commitments, because the mixture of these four factors constitutes the profit that can be made by a wholesaler or retailer on a product being considered. The presentation will only be effective if the mixture is at least as "sweet" as that offered by others. If sufficient information is available, the Sales Manager can know whether or not his product is competitive with others.

Such profit studies are not easy, but they can be sufficiently helpful that they are worth the time and money. To achieve the greatest accuracy the researcher would need access to certain records of the buyer. Such access is not always easy to obtain, but buyers often will show recent invoices to prospective sellers in the hope of obtaining an equally low or lower price. Evidence of stock turn also is difficult to obtain. It is available, however, from a few marketing research firms which specialize in gathering information on the flow of competing goods through retail outlets.[6] Shelf space devoted to competing products is readily observable. Overhead expenses are always difficult to determine and allocate; every cost accountant is familiar with this problem. The thought is suggested here that if the products are clearly competitive, overhead costs can be ignored and the study can safely be limited to direct costs. The researcher who elects to ignore overhead costs obviously must determine whether or not there are any real differences

[5] For a description of the multifarious factors considered by a chain buying committee, see Donald G. Hileman and Leonard A. Rosenstein, "Deliberations of a Chain Grocery Buying Committee," *Journal of Marketing*, January, 1961, p. 52.
[6] For example, A. C. Nielsen measures goods sold through grocery and drug stores.

in the way competitive products are handled; differences in both the amount and the location of shelf space, for example, have a significant effect on turnover and cannot be ignored.

For most manufacturers, such studies cannot be carried out by gathering information from every customer. The expense of such an approach would be prohibitive. Analysis on the basis of careful sampling, however, results in sufficiently accurate information to be helpful to the salesman. For those buyers who purchase in substantial volume special studies may be necessary since they may be unlike those who were sampled. Unhappily for the researcher, too, the conditions of a deal change so frequently that profit studies must be equally frequent. Fortunately, however, such studies become increasingly easy.

No suggestion is made here that such interdisciplinary studies as have been described are entirely new—at least conceptually—to American marketing thought. Sales Managers long have been aware of the interrelationship of gross margins, stock turnover, and overhead expenses; have attempted to see these factors from the viewpoint of their customers; and often have tried to gather whatever empirical evidence is available to present more objective sales arguments. But implementing these ideas has been a problem because few marketing or financial specialists are proficient in the other disciplines of business. In short, there is too little recognition that many financial analysts can make substantial contributions to channel management. When viewed in this manner, channel management might be described as less of a "marketing" problem and more of a "business" problem; the latter term reflects the contributions of more than a single discipline toward its solution.

Like the marketing executive, many finance specialists are willing to acknowledge that they do not understand the subtleties of other fields such as marketing. Therefore there is a real question as to who should undertake such studies as have been described here. The answer to this question is beyond the scope of this paper, but no doubt differs among firms. Indeed, in many firms the marketing research staff carries out continuing studies of its firm's relationship with its channel and submits policy recommendations to the top marketing executive. The crucial issue here is that accountants recognize that sufficient information to undertake profit studies is available, that buyers are aided by such information and may even insist on it, and that this is an area in which the accountant can be of considerable staff assistance to many marketing executives who lack any substantial training or experience in such analysis.

SUMMARY AND IMPLICATIONS

This article has been written from the point of view of a marketing specialist looking to another discipline for help. The area is that of management of marketing channels, and the thought has been suggested that financial analysis is a logical and increasingly necessary preliminary step to the most efficient decisions. Unhappily, there are few businessmen or academicians who can blend successfully the elements of various disciplines into a balanced decision. One of the first steps toward this blending is to identify the type of decisions where the need for such an integrated approach is most important. One such decisional area is channel management.

Various ideas concerning marketing channels have been expressed in the literature. Three important thoughts were that channels are often subject to management, that the relationship of firms in a channel may extend over a considerable time, and that the manufacturer must evaluate carefully what he offers the channel relative to what other manufacturers are offering.

Two specific suggestions of ways in which a financial analyst could be of assistance to the marketing executive were made. First, the financial position of a retailer is one of the more important of many factors that should be weighed in selecting new dealers. Substantial functional performance often is expected of wholesalers and retailers, and financial capacity is a major determinant as to whether such expectations will be fulfilled. Second, the marketing executive is aided by whatever reliable evidence he can gather that demonstrates that his product will result in more profit for a wholesaler or retailer than will the product of competing manufacturers. Gross margins, stock turn, inventory investment, shelf space and other overhead costs are relevant factors which, if properly evaluated, would indicate which of two or more manufacturers' product firms in the channel should stock for greatest profit. The accountant can imagine how much easier the salesman's task becomes if he can demonstrate to a wholesaler or retailer that handling his product will result in greater profit than if he were to purchase another manufacturer's product. Of course, the salesman has always suggested to potential buyers that this is true, but he seldom has had sufficient information to substantiate his claims.

The financial analyst can be of significant aid to the marketing executive in the two areas just described. There are no doubt many other ways in which a contribution can be made by the sophisticated accountant. Such problems as whether or not retailers are financially able to engage in cooperative advertising, the determination of marketing costs along alternative channels, and significant shifts in the financial position of various types of retailers can be of considerable help to the marketing executive. No small part of the success of such analysis rests upon the ability of the analyst to know what type of information would be helpful, and his ability to gain access to that which is not public information.

The most significant conclusion of this article is that the analyst who furnishes information such as was just described must be aware of the basic concepts of both marketing and finance. Solutions to the problems of channel management are interdisciplinary in nature. It is not a conclusion of this discussion, however, that the accountant is the only logical candidate for such work. An understanding of the interrelationship of marketing and finance is essential to the success of such work; and the individual who possesses such a balanced view probably differs among firms. It is suggested, however, that many accountants readily possess the ability to render valuable staff service to the chief marketing executive who often lacks financial training or experience. To the extent that this is true, the accountant is invited to join the party.

32. Breyer Study: Quantitative Systemic Analysis and Control

GEORGE SCHWARTZ

This selection is a summary and commentary on Breyer's pioneering study. Breyer takes a macroview of the channel and develops his analytical apparatus from this viewpoint. Included is the concept of "nexus" cost, i.e., channel costs which are incurred in duplicate form.

Like Professors Cox and Goodman, Professor Breyer has interested himself in the performance of channels of marketing, particularly the control of the operations of these channels. His study, *Quantitative Systemic Analysis and Control*, aims to develop concepts and quantitative methods of analysis designed to facilitate control of the operations of marketing channels with a view to increasing their efficiency.

THE SYSTEMIC APPROACH

Although Professor Breyer's study focuses on the control of marketing channels, he emphasizes that the study represents an example of the systemic approach to marketing. Breyer writes that this approach is "an approach to the study of marketing that is focused primarily on an integral part of the marketing institution (a 'system') that is of channel dimension and takes care of a full 'cycle' of marketing."[1]

In Breyer's opinion a channel or group of channels constitute marketing systems because an interdependence exists among the business units which comprise them. This interdependence arises out of the fact that the *raison d'etre* of the business units comprising a channel is to take care of "the full marketing channel,"

i.e., perform the marketing work necessary to move goods from producer to consumer.[2]

In Breyer's judgment the systemic approach is suitable for the study of all aspects of marketing. He states that the more important channel systems deserve individual study as "distinct operating units" of the entire marketing organization of an economy. Breyer goes on to write:

"The peculiar theoretical framework of each such major system needs to be developed; our body of marketing 'principles' needs to be reoriented to this pattern of systems, with a more realistic treatment of the channel structure of marketing; our research into price-making processes must not only strive to explain pricing and prices in terms of channels *in general* but it must strive to formulate the distinctive processes, and it is almost bound to be in some significant degree distinctive, for *each* of such major systems. This is not to argue that the *general* theory, the *general* principle, the *general* management methods, and so on, are not valid within prescribed and recognized limits and should be discarded, but rather that they need refinement that shapes them neatly to the actual situations in marketing. And the unalterable fact is that the marketing institution is made up of a variegated pattern of such systems, that they do the work of marketing, and that therefore

• SOURCE: George Schwartz, "Breyer Study: Quantitative Systemic Analysis and Control," *Development of Marketing Theory* (Cincinnati, Ohio: Southwestern Publishing Company, 1963), pp. 121–25. George Schwartz, College of Business Administration, University of Rochester.
[1] Ralph F. Breyer, *Quantitative Systemic Analysis and Control: Study No. 1—Channel and Channel Group Costing* (Philadelphia: published by the author, 1949), p. 8.

[2] The combined business units of marketing channels, Breyer writes, represent *unique systems* in that each possesses some peculiar pattern of sizes and concerns or product assemblies, or of geographical dispersion, or of common interests among the concerns, or distinctive combinations of such patterns.

both marketing scholars as well as practitioners must deal with these many different systems and not merely with a sort of amalgam of them whose analysis gives us findings that fit none of them truly. If the present study will serve in some way to make the students of marketing properly aware of this need for the 'systemic approach' to the practical and theoretical study of marketing, it will have fully served its purpose. . . ."[3]

The Nature of Systemic Control

In order to permit analysis and control of the operations of a channel system, Breyer's study aims to develop appropriate quantitative methods. These seek to measure the overall performance of marketing systems and to permit quantitative subanalyses of such systems which will uncover and measure points of weakness and strength.

When Breyer discusses channel control, he has in mind a specific type of marketing channel whose operations are to be analyzed and controlled. He has named this channel the unit marketing channel. This channel is composed of business units, engaged in marketing, having a distinct business identity or name or a distinct business location, regardless of common ownership. Thus, Breyer writes, a wholesale concern known as "A" and a retail concern known as "B," although owned by the same individual, are each given separate recognition as an integral part of the unit marketing channel even though they might occupy the same quarters. In Breyer's terminology a combination of two or more unit marketing channels constitute a unit marketing channel group.[4]

---

[3] Breyer, *Quantitative Systemic Analysis and Control: Study No. 1—Channel and Channel Group Costing*, pp. 8–9.
[4] Breyer uses the unit marketing channel rather than the "traditional" concept of the channel— an ordered series of types of trading concerns which move goods from producers to consumers— because, he writes, it has shortcomings for purposes of channel analysis and control. Among the shortcomings he cites are: (1) the types of business units employed are too crude for channel analysis and control, (2) the establishment of types of business units involves considerable arbitrary classification of trading enterprises, and (3) certain significant phases of channel control sometimes involve nontrading enterprises. These business units, however, Breyers states, are excluded from the traditional concept of the channel.

The unit marketing channel is composed of several constituent channels. The unit goods channel

Since most unit marketing channels consist of multiple ownerships, Breyer states, effective systemic analysis and control requires that the business units comprising these systems establish an authority with at least limited powers to manage the channel or channel group. As Breyer conceives it, such a managerial body would, "ideally," perform the following functions:

1. Establish the basic objectives for the channel system.
2. Determine the activities required to accomplish these goals.
3. Allocate these activities among the enterprises composing the system, i.e., determine which enterprises would perform specific activities such as, for example, packaging.
4. Establish a system for controlling the channel's operations.

Effective systemic control, Breyer believes, requires that the objectives established for the channel or channel group be paramount, with the objectives of the individual business units, whether independently owned or not, being derived from them. Actual control of the system's operations designed to achieve the overall objectives, he points out, requires that quantitative standards be established for the system as a whole. Actual performance of the system would then be compared against these standards and remedial action taken where warranted. Operating standards, Breyer emphasizes, should not be a mere sum of the standards of the individual enterprises composing the channel or channel group. For effective systemic control the standards for the individual establishments should be determined, at least in part, by overall channel considerations.

---

is a constituent channel that is formed by the "route" followed by the physical movement of the goods. The unit sales channel is formed by the "route" followed by the trading contacts. The unit selling channel is formed by the "flow" of the selling and/or buying effort. The unit transfer channel is formed by the "route" taken by the actual transfers of title to goods.

Breyer regards the enterprise marketing channel, a channel conceived in terms of specific, independently-owned business entities, as his primary channel concept. He holds this view because, he states, the enterprises composing the enterprise marketing channel are the initiating, financing, and risking agencies of marketing. The enterprise marketing channel, however, is not appropriate for quantitative systemic analysis and control, Breyer asserts, because such analysis and control needs to focus on individual business units regardless of common ownership.

Breyer is very much aware of the difficulty achieving effective systemic control. Among the difficulties he cites are:

1. Effective control of nonintegrated channels is likely to lead to larger profits for the aggregate system; however, since not all business units in the system are likely to benefit, the owners of such enterprises, Breyer believes, would probably be unwilling to cooperate with the system's managerial and control authority.

2. Even if the component business units cooperate, the nature of the situation is such that it is difficult to coordinate the successive activities of different and physically separate enterprises.

In Breyer's opinion a number of conditions facilitate the establishment of an effective channel control mechanism. Those that he cites are:

1. A high degree of integration in a channel or channel group.

2. A long record of cooperation among the independent owners in a channel.

3. Channels that are likely to persist for a long time and which are characterized by stable trading characteristics.

4. A situation in which most of the business units in a channel handle a limited number and similar group of products.

5. A reasonably large dollar volume handled in the channel by each of its business units and accounting for a significant percentage of each.

6. A minimum of independent nontrading business units which, because they usually have little at stake in any one channel, are not likely to cooperate effectively with any systemic arrangement.

7. A short and simple channel which, by making the task of analysis and control easier, increases the opportunity for such a program.

Principal Kinds of Systemic Cost Analysis

Breyer's study has led him to the conclusion that, with a few exceptions, the types of cost analysis which are significant for systemic control are the same as those which have been employed by individual business enterprises. Among these are product, customer, functional, and order-size cost analyses.

The one type of systemic cost analysis that has no counterpart in cost analysis for the single enterprise is what Breyer terms "nexus" cost analysis. This type of analysis determines the aggregate cost of complementary marketing activities of two business units of a specific channel, e.g., the selling work of a wholesaler directed at a retailer and the buying work of this retailer performed in making his purchases from the above mentioned wholesaler.

In order to compute costs for the various kinds of systemic cost analyses, the analyst first determines the relevant costs for the individual enterprises comprising the system being studied. Breyer states that the costing methods for this purpose are the familiar distribution cost analysis techniques used by individual marketing concerns. When this information has been obtained, the individual enterprise cost data are then added to establish the channel or channel group cost figures that are desired.

Breyer's first illustration shows how a cost analysis is made for a single, simple channel selling only one product to one ultimate consumer. In this example he shows how total channel costs for a single function, computation of costs for a channel segment, for various order sizes, and the like are carried out. He then demonstrates the costing methods that can be used when analyzing more complex channels having agents and nontrading institutions in them. Finally, Breyer discusses the techniques to be used in cost analysis for channels.[5]

The cost data for enterprises used in systemic analysis exclude the profits of the individual marketing firm. That is, systemic costs represent an accumulation of the operating costs of the enterprises which comprise a given system. Breyer views an entire marketing channel or channel group as an apparatus whose costs are those incurred by the owners of the various parts of the mechanism and not by the consuming public. Hence, Breyer writes, systemic costs serve to show the executives of the various business units their combined operating costs for moving goods from producer to consumer by means of the channel or channel group.

While Breyer is convinced of the utility to marketing of quantitative systemic analysis and control, the final comments of his study indicate that he is pessimistic as to the likelihood that this type of analysis and control will be widely accepted in the near future. His view stems essentially from two conclusions:

1. Channel and channel group costing apparently have little promise for the numerous channels which include small retail business enterprises.

2. The fact that most channels consist of multiple ownerships weakens the incentive to undertake quantitative systemic analysis and control since the benefits that each enterprise can gain are uncertain, depending largely upon its strategy and maneuvering within the framework of overall cooperation.

[5] See Breyer, *Quantitative Systemic Analysis and Control: Study No. 1—Channel and Channel Group Costing*, Chapters 5–7.

33. Marketing of Housebuilding Materials

REAVIS COX and CHARLES S. GOODMAN

This article is a report on a significant study in the field of describing and evaluating channel performance. Included is an inquiry into the amount and effectiveness of marketing required to assemble building materials and possible ways of improving this effectiveness. Cox and Goodman develop measures and analytical tools (the flow chart and product monograph) for purposes of this study.

THE NATURE OF THE PROBLEM

A Problem in Logistics

The physical substance of a house is a pile of materials assembled from widely scattered sources. They undergo different kinds and degrees of processing in large numbers of places, require many types of handling over periods that vary greatly in length, and use the services of a multitude of people organized into many different sorts of business entity.

The marketing of housebuilding materials may therefore be viewed as a vast exercise in logistics. For any given house, the parts of the process must be well enough performed and coordinated so that in the end all the separate pieces come together. These pieces must arrive at reasonably acceptable times, in a tolerable sequence, and at bearable prices upon the particular small piece of ground where a builder and his contractors combine them into a house some consumer can be induced to buy or rent.

Although the problem thus stated looks impossibly formidable, it is in fact solved over and over again as new houses go up in their millions. So often is it solved, and with such apparent ease, that we come to take the solution for granted and to forget how much effort and

ingenuity have gone into it. Yet, we need to look at it analytically now and again, asking ourselves such questions as: Has this problem of assembling the materials of a house really been solved effectively? Does every part of the work done contribute to the end sought rather than impede it? Could the end result be achieved with the expenditure of fewer resources?

This study we have summarized in this article undertook to answer such questions as these for a carefully selected illustrative house constructed by an operative builder in the Philadelphia area.[1] What we discovered, we believe, will interest students of marketing both for the substance of its findings and as an experiment in research methodology.

Measuring the Real Work Done in the Complete Channel

Anyone who ponders the matter will soon conclude that answers to these questions, if they are to be meaningful, must have at least two characteristics: (1) They must be stated in terms of real costs and products rather than in

---

• SOURCE: Reprinted from the *Journal of Marketing*, national quarterly publication of the American Marketing Association, XXI (July, 1956), 36–61. Used by permission. Reavis Cox, Professor of Marketing, Wharton School, University of Pennsylvania, Charles S. Goodman, Wharton School, University of Pennsylvania.

[1] Reavis Cox and Charles S. Goodman, *Channels and Flows in the Marketing of House-Building Materials*, Philadelphia: 1954, 3 vols., mimeographed.

The research and studies forming the basis for this report were performed pursuant to a contract with the Office of the Administrator, Housing and Home Finance Agency, authorized by Title III of the Housing Act of 1948, as amended. The substance of such research and studies is dedicated to the public. It is understood that the accuracy of statements or interpretations contained herein is solely the responsibility of the authors and publisher.

nominal monetary terms. (2) They must apply to complete channels rather than to such fragments of the whole as particular enterprises, industries, trades, or places.

That simple monetary estimates standing by themselves are not enough for present purposes is no doubt self-evident. Efficiency is a relation between work done and results achieved. For some purposes, money expenditures and revenues may serve well enough as input-output ratios. There are many situations, however, that require more direct comparisons of effort expended with results produced. Here, a search must be made for measures of work done other than money spent and measures of results achieved other than gross or net revenue obtained.

The need for analyzing the complete channel rather than some assortment of its constituent parts derives from the almost limitless number of combinations and sequences in which particular marketing processes can be passed around among places, agencies, and times. Two illustrations will serve to show how complex the assortments of choices are. One concerns millwork; the other, warm-air furnaces.

Much of this country's supply of wood millwork comes from the so-called "river mills." These are large factories along the Mississippi that enjoy milling-in-transit privileges on their materials. Shop lumber, starting from the Pacific Northwest, moves to these mills and thence, as manufactured millwork, to the yards of lumber or millwork dealers in the Philadelphia area. There it may compete with the millwork of a local manufacturer whose shop lumber or cut stock, though also originating in the Pacific Northwest, was bought independently from a local supplier.

If the river mill and its sources of lumber are under common ownership and the millwork is distributed in the building area through a direct factory branch instead of an independent dealer, we have an integration of extraction, processing, and marketing from tree to builder that further complicates comparisons. In such cases, it is rare to find that the quantity of marketing work can be determined accurately except by making a complete survey of all aspects of extraction, processing, and distribution, wherever they are found, and from the aggregate of effort thus described sorting out the marketing.

Warm-air furnaces offer another kind of complicated example. Manufacturing is divided among producers in many different patterns. Some make their own castings. Others buy castings from commercial foundries. Still others buy not only the castings but many other parts of the furnace from other manufacturers so that the "processing" which takes place in the "furnace factory" is principally or even entirely one of assembly. Then, there are manufacturers who do no assembling but ship each furnace as a package of parts for assembly by the distributor. Here, one of the principal acts of "production" is performed by the "distributor" in the middle of the course of "distribution" as conventionally conceived. In yet other instances, the manufacturer ships a partial furnace assembly, either set up or knocked down, and "manufacture" of the furnace is completely by the distributor or the heating contractor, who adds a steel jacket made from material of his own selection procured from sources altogether independent of the furnace factory. Clearly, to conceive marketing in conventional terms as commencing only when the furnace has been "finished" would prevent meaningful comparisons between alternatives and present a distorted view of the marketing work that must be performed to provide furnaces for houses.

Counting the Quantity of Marketing

For purposes of the present study, the most meaningful way of separating marketing from all the other activities performed in assembling the materials of a house has proved to be setting up an analogy or model of flows. That is, the tasks assigned to marketing in our economy are defined as taking the form of organizing and regulating a number of different but related flows. The marketing work done in each flow is measured by defining and counting one or more units of movement. In all, the following seven units have been counted:

1. The number of geographic places in which the materials are extracted, processed, or handled.[2]
2. The number of times the materials are loaded, moved, and unloaded during their progress from the places at which they are extracted to the building site.
3. The number of ton-miles of transportation performed for the materials in their progress from places of extraction to the building site.
4. The number of days taken to extract each of the principal materials, process it, and move it onto the building site.[3]

[2] A geographic place is defined as an identifiable city or town, although in a few cases it has been necessary to take a metropolitan area, a county, or a region surrounding some city or town.
[3] The time involved includes the time normally spent by these goods in the operating inventories of extractors, processors, and distributors and the time spent in transportation.

5. The dollar days of investment accumulated in the materials as they move from first extraction to final assembly at the site.[4]

6. The number of owning and nonowning business entities that participate in extracting, processing, and handling the materials as they move from places of extraction to the building site.[5]

7. The number of transactions arranged in moving the materials from places of extraction to the building site.[6]

Most obvious of the various flows is the physical movement of the materials through space. They start out in ore beds or as standing crops and timber. From their points of extraction, most of them move physically through a succession of processing plants and on to the building site. A few of them require no processing at all, and some go through only a single processing plant.

The first three of the measures indicate the amount of work done in moving the materials through space. They permit judgments as to whether there is an excessive amount of movement and particularly whether too many sources are drawn upon for materials, whether there is a great deal of crosshauling and backhauling, and whether such transportation as is done is performed at those stages of processing when the work can be minimized.

Another flow of these goods is that through time. The processes of extraction, processing, and marketing are spread over periods sometimes short but often long. Goods must be carried through these periods in the sense that at every instant they must be in the physical possession of someone and under the ownership control of someone.

The burdens imposed by the flows through time take a number of forms, among which the costs of investment, storage, and risk are important. Measures 4 and 5 give some indication of the size of these burdens for the products here under analysis. Counts based upon them permit meaningful comparisons between different materials and between different ways or getting a

given material. They also permit some evaluation of whether the total time required is as short as it could be and of the extent to which investment and storage are concentrated in those parts of each flow at which accumulated values are lowest.

A third set of flows arises from the fact that the activities of marketing are carried out by and between business entities. Much of the work of marketing is associated with bringing together these entities not only in the sense of an actual flow of orders (transactions in the legal sense) but also in the development of relationships that may become routinized once they have been established. The last two measures listed are intended to give some indication of the burden of work imposed by this third set of flows.

Taken together, these seven ways of counting provide the basic data used in measuring the marketing work done for the materials of a house as a whole and for subgroups of these materials.

ANALYTICAL TOOLS USED

Application of the counting procedures just outlined to a specific situation entailed selecting a house to be studied, breaking it down into a bill of materials, and tracing a sampled of these materials back from the building site to point of extraction along some meaningful channel or set of channels. The data were assembled into what we have called flow charts and product monographs.

The Bill of Materials

The House Studied. The kind of analysis visualized can be made only for specific lots of goods traced from specific points of origin to specific building sites. It soon became apparent that with the resources available we must choose between a superficial statistical study of many houses and a minutely detailed study of one house. Since our interests lay as much in concepts and procedures as in substantive findings, we elected to study one house in detail.

Several possibilities were reviewed in the search for a house that would be representative of current practice *as to its materials*. In the end an FHA "example" house used for appraisal work in the Philadelphia area was selected. The house so chosen is a two-story, single-family, detached, masonry dwelling with six rooms and one bath. It is of a type generally erected by both small- and large-scale operative builders and can readily be erected by a custom builder.

[4] A dollar day is the owning of one dollar's worth of material for one day.

[5] The nonowning agencies include both those who act as agents to bring about transactions of specific merchandise and others, such as carriers, who have operating control over goods owned by others. An entity is construed as a legal business unit together with any affiliates in the same ownership.

[6] Transactions are transfers of ownership of products. There are two types: (1) transfers between independent entities (purchase-sale transactions) and (2) transfers between affiliates (intrafirm allocations).

It thus permits investigation of the various channels through which materials are likely to find their way to a building site. Detailed specifications and bills of material were obtained from the FHA, and it was assumed that construction would take place on a site in the Philadelphia metropolitan area. Specification of a precise site within the area turned out to be unnecessary.

Erecting the example house in the summer of 1951 would have cost a builder in the Philadelphia area on the order of $9,300. Counting in the cost of the site and its improvements, builder's overhead and profit, architects' fees, and costs of marketing, the consumer would have paid about $13,250 for the property.

Other Houses. Two variants of the example house were also studied, one of frame construction and one of brick veneer. Except for a substantially higher accumulation of dollar days of investment in the frame house, such changes had little effect on our measures of the total marketing work. It must be emphasized that outwardly striking differences in houses, even as between geographic areas, are largely irrelevant to the present study because they generally rest not so much in the use of different materials as in different assortments of the same materials and in the design of the buildings.[7] Practically all of the houses built in this country are made from the same group of bulk materials. What is really new in a "new" house usually is another way of combining or treating the old list of materials, or a difference in the sequence of events such that assemblies formerly done on the site itself or in one kind of plant are transferred to another unit in the line of enterprises that make up the channel. Extremely uncommon are such events as the development of asphalt prepared roofing and the recent spectacular development of aluminum as a construction material.

Materials Studied. The components of the example house were classified into four broad groups: (1) forest products, (2) nonmetallic minerals and their products, (3) products of a single metal, and (4) miscellaneous and compound products.

This classification, based primarily on origins, turned out to be very helpful in analyses of the maze of products studied. It was particularly

useful in the formulation of estimates for products that could not be examined in detail.

Since thousands of items are used in even a modest house, it is fortunate that usable estimates of the amount of marketing work embodied in the bill of materials as a whole can be derived from detailed studies of fewer than 50 items.

In the first place, a relatively small number of materials provide a substantial portion of the total weight and value. Thus, the 43 materials finally selected for detailed analysis in the present study accounted for 95 per cent of the total delivered weight and for 81 per cent of the total delivered value of the entire pile of materials entering into the house.[8] Furthermore, a number of omitted products followed courses so similar to that of one or another of the 43 included as to enable very close estimates. Thus, porcelain-coated, cast-iron lavatories and kitchen sinks are made of the same materials and follow the same course of manufacture and distribution as cast-iron bathtubs.

Finally, it is not necessary to trace specifically each possible variant of every end product derived from a given basic material. Trees, for example, appear in the finished house as products varying endlessly in detail. For the most part, these differences are insignificant in their effects on marketing work. The wood products that go into a house fall into a few broad groups, and the products with each group follow pretty much the same course.

Flow Charts

The basic analysis is made in flow charts, one of which was prepared for each of the 43 materials studied intensively. Starting with the delivery of the material to the building site, such a chart traces the material and its antecedent materials back through the most likely sequence of events to its ultimate origin in mine, quarry, field, or forest. Data on the steps nearest the building site were obtained from builders and, more importantly, from contractors who provided materials for their own operations; these

---

[7] The characteristics of the example house are compared with construction practice in Philadelphia and other areas of the United States in Cox and Goodman, *op. cit.*, vol. 3, Ch. 7.

[8] The criteria used in selecting materials for detailed study were: (1) importance in weight or value, (2) representation of materials not analyzed, (3) raw material embodied, (4) type of processor, and (5) type of channel. The last three criteria were used to make sure that the goods analyzed included an example of every important raw material, every important type of processor, and every important combination of processing and marketing agencies into channels.

agencies were asked to name their usual sources for specific items. Contacts were made with these sources in turn, and their sources were determined. So materials were traced back step by step to their origins as extractive goods.

The kinds of establishments at each level were identified carefully. This turned out to be very important in grasping an understanding of the marketing considerations involved. For example, for one group of forest products, the survey turned up a supplier who, although called a "retail lumber dealer," catered exclusively to certain large builders. They accepted deliveries in substantial quantities and invariably took their discounts. The marketing services, margins, and costs of such a firm are materially different from those pertaining to "typical" dealers. It would have been erroneous to take an "average" cost of doing business or the "typical" practices of "retailers" as relevant to this situation.

The flow chart designates as "zero day" for a particular product the day on which it is delivered to the building site ready for incorporation into the house. Although each product has its own zero day, in the consolidated analyses all products are taken to be delivered on the same day.

Starting from zero, the flow chart counts back day by day to the day on which the product (or, more commonly, its principal antecedent material) was extracted from mine, quarry, forest, or farm. "Minus one" (-1) for each product is the day before delivery; "minus 30" (-30) is the thirtieth day preceding delivery; and so forth. The chart then records in parallel columns what happened to the product on each particular day. Every day intervening between extraction and final delivery is accounted for. If the product has more than one significant antecedent material, each one, in addition to the principal one, is traced back to its origin in a supplementary chart that indicates where it feeds into the main flow.

From the flow charts, one can determine for each product and each antecedent material analyzed where it was and what happened to it each day; when and where it changed form, who changed it, and how long it remained in each form; when and by whom it was loaded, unloaded, and moved, how far it was moved, and by what sort of carrier; who had operating control of the material and of the facilities used to move it, who had ownership of the material and of each transportation facility; the date of each change in ownership of the material; the value of the material at each principal

stage; and certain fees paid, notably those for transportation.

Since the number of possible permutations and combinations of specific places and entities is enormous, even for one product, every channel actually used by the industry for a specific bill of materials may properly be called a "one-time" channel.[9] Repetitive patterns appear in particular trades or industries, but the specific channel actually used for any particular unit of goods is likely to be unique or very nearly so.

So far as possible, each chart portrays the type of channel that is most important quantitatively for the product in question when it ends up on a site in the Philadelphia area upon which an operative builder constructs a house. In the aggregate, the charts thus portray a reasonable and apparently probable combination of the sorts of choices members of the building industries make repeatedly among alternatives open to them in the course of their daily work. As such, they form a workable basis for counting and computing the volume of marketing work.

Counts, Computations, Estimates, and Summaries. Counts and computations of the volume of marketing work done for analyzed products and analyzed antecedents were made directly from the flow charts. They were supplemented by careful estimates for the work embodied (1) in unanalyzed antecedents of the analyzed products and (2) in the materials and products that were not analyzed. The results then were summarized by products and product groups and for the entire house.

Product Monographs

Each product monograph is a narrative that supplements the flow chart. It consists essentially of five parts: (1) a description of the product, sufficiently detailed to make it readily identifiable in interviews with the trade; (2) a detailed description of the marketing channel selected for analysis; (3) variants observed in the marketing channels and an evaluation of their significance; (4) consideration of omitted antecedents, that is, materials which, though antecedent to the product, were of insufficient

[9] For a more detailed consideration of the "one-time" channel of marketing as a concept, see the discussion of what is called an "enterprise marketing channel" in R. F. Breyer, *Quantitative Systemic Analysis and Control: Study No. I,* "Channel and Channel Group Costing" (Philadelphia: 1949), pp. 21ff.

import to warrant supplementary flow charts; and (5) conclusions concerning the effectiveness of the marketing flows. The monograph summarizes much of the information used in developing the flow chart. It therefore serves as a useful supplement to the chart and provides breadth for the analysis.

THE MARKETING WORK EMBODIED IN THE MATERIALS FOR THE EXAMPLE HOUSE

To provide the materials for the "example house," the industries concerned moved onto one small spot of ground in the Philadelphia area 186 tons of products with a delivered value of $5,360 at 1951 price levels. The marketing work performed for the entire bundle of materials and for each of the 43 products analyzed is shown in detail in Table 1.[10]

Extension of the Flow Over Time

Extraction, processing, and assembly of these materials extended over periods varying from only 4 days for quarried stone to 412 days for the electrical service entrance box. Individual products varied widely among themselves not only as regards total time but also as regards distribution of that time among three periods: (1) the period between extraction and first off-the-site processing, here called preprocessing; (2) the period between first and last off-the-site processing, here called interprocessing; and (3) the period between last processing and delivery to the site, here called postprocessing.

For the 43 analyzed products as a group, 39 per cent of the time elapsed during preprocessing, 34 per cent during interprocessing, and 27 per cent during postprocessing. As between products, however, there were wide differences. Thus, for some products (for example, goods made from hardwoods and copper), there is virtually no preprocessing, since they move almost immediately from extraction into processing. Others (for example, fir logs and iron ore) may be held for several months in their crude state. Correspondingly, some products spend only a few hours in postprocessing (for example, central-mix concrete, oil tanks, and steel girders), whereas others are in this stage for months (for example, wallpaper and outlet boxes).

[10] Subtotals in Table I for the unanalyzed products were developed from detailed item-by-item estimates for each variable.

The reasons for such wide differences in over-all time and in the allocation of that time as among the three stages may be suggested by a few illustrations. As a group, forest products spend a long time in transit because timber can be found only at a far distance from Philadelphia. For example, Douglas fir, ponderosa pine, western cedar, and their manufacturers must move from the Far West to the East. The mileage for Douglas fir lumber is particularly large, since it moves over the long intercoastal water route. To save in weight and bulk, most of this movement takes place after at least preliminary processing. Furthermore, relatively long travel routes usually entail relatively long inventories as safeguards against interruptions, and they may require several intermediate handling or transshipping points at which inventories are maintained. The time is still further extended by the fact that loggers usually maintain inventories on the forest floor as protections against interruptions in felling and bucking because of the weather.

For yellow pine and oak, distances are much shorter than for the western woods; but processing time is longer because oak and yellow pine are air-dried for two to four months. Oak for hardwood flooring is kiln-dried in addition and then requires further time for manufacture into flooring.

The particularly long flow for the window units (387 days) is due to a combination of time-consuming processes. The northeastern pine used in the frames is air-dried for six months in a concentration yard before being manufactured into cut stock. The ponderosa pine sash moves slowly because the sash-and-door mills maintain large inventories of lumber, must schedule their work so as to get long factory runs, and need time to process and glaze the sash. Furthermore, it takes some time simply to assemble the numerous parts into the window unit.

Under these circumstances, it is hardly surprising that forest products are responsible for more than half of the ton-miles—although they represent less than one fifteenth of the weight delivered to the site—and for more than half of the dollar days of investment, although they represent only a little more than one third of the value delivered to the site.

In contrast, nonmetallic minerals and their products are simple. They require the assembly of at most two or three important components, and they pass through no elaborate complex of manufacturing processes. Most of them move short distances and face no seasonal interruptions to extraction, shipment, or manufacturing. The prevalence of direct marketing from manufacturer, or even from extractor, to contractor or builder still further reduces the danger of interruptions in the flow. There is thus no need for large inventories anywhere along the channel.

Where the Products Were Handled

The materials of the example house originated as raw materials and were handled in one way or another for processing, sorting, or storage at 148 different geographical places. They originated in 60 distinct and widely separated places, 42 of which confined their activities to extraction. They were processed in 110 places or nearly 2 for each place of extraction. Once finished, they moved directly into Philadelphia if they had not already come there for final processing. It thus seems clear that geographic complexities in the marketing of building materials are attributable more to the complexity of the house, which uses goods derived from many sources, than to complications in the marketing structures for individual products.

The products vary greatly among themselves as regards the geographical complexities of their marketing. Miscellaneous and compound products were handled in 65 places. They touched so many places chiefly because most of them moved through a complicated sequence of manufacturing processes performed by specialized manufacturers. In the later stages, some of them tended to become merely assemblies of parts made by others. Forest products were handled in 57 places. Here, a multiplicity of places is required to provide the different species of wood preferred for particular uses in the house. Also, the window units use a number of non-lumber materials and a complex system of subassemblies.

At the other extreme, products of a single metal moved through only 19 of the 148 places touched by building materials in their flow from extraction to the building site. Two factors account for this relatively small number. One is that iron and copper, the two principal basic metals involved, originate for use in Philadelphia in only a few places. The other is that, at least in the earlier stages, the processing of these materials is highly concentrated. The result is that most of these products are likely to have come from only a few mines and to have moved much of their way through processing operations in one or two plants, even though they emerge as end products outwardly quite different from each other.

The Products in Motion

The Timing of Transportation. In traveling from place to place during their flows, these products (and their antecedents) were loaded onto carriers, moved, and unloaded 424 separate times. Their travel added up to 49,667 ton-miles. This is equivalent to hauling a ton of goods back and forth between Philadelphia and Portland, Oregon, more than eight times. Another way of putting it is that the transportation done in moving these products through their flows is roughly equivalent to picking up the whole house and moving it from New York to Washington.

Two thirds of the 424 movements were made to carry an item into some aspect of processing or into use. One fourth of the trips moved goods into storage, principally in warehouses of distributors and contractors. About one tenth of the total were solely for change from one form of transportation to another, generally land to water or the reverse.

Some 28 per cent of the movements, involving 40 per cent of the ton-miles of transportation, took place in the various flows during preprocessing. Forty per cent of the movements, but only 9 per cent of the total ton-miles, took place during interprocessing. Thirty-two per cent of the movements, with slightly more than half of the ton-miles, occurred during postprocessing.

The contrast between movements and ton-miles is striking. Approximately two fifths of the movements connect various elements of processing, but these account for less than one tenth of the ton-miles. The movements during postprocessing are the sum of movements by some products from point of last processing directly to the site and for others from point of last processing to a distributive point in Philadelphia and from there to the site. For the 43 analyzed products alone, there were 77 movements after last off-the-site processing (80 if minor parts shipped separately are included), a consequence of the fact that most of these goods pass through a distribution yard or warehouse and some of them go through a contractor's warehouse or storeroom as well.

Clearly, then, most of the physical task of moving goods about is performed for building materials in the transportation of raw materials, of products that require no significant amount of processing, and of goods (such as lumber) where the finished product has received only the simplest of processing. Furthermore, the burden of transportation imposed by processing is primarily a matter of arranging for large numbers of shipments and of loading and unloading rather than one of movement itself. Any search for ways to reduce the costs involved must govern itself accordingly.

Where and How Goods Are Transported. As to where the transportation took place, nearly one half of the movements were between points outside the Philadelphia area, nearly one fourth were into the area, and slightly more than one fourth were between points within the area. Many of the movements within Philadelphia were deliveries of finished goods from factories, warehouses, and storage yards to the site; but some were from point of extraction to the site or to processing plants. Considerably more of the substance of this house comes to the site from nearby sources than might be supposed.

Only 4 of the 424 movements (less than 1 per cent) were movements out of the Philadelphia area of goods that involved subsequent backhauls after processing or combination with other materials. Each of the four is a raw material that came by sea into the port of Philadelphia, moved to a plant just outside the area, and came back into Philadelphia after processing.

Water transport by ocean, lake, and river accounted for only 9 per cent of the movements, but it accounted for 58 per cent of the ton-miles. Trucks, which provided 56 per cent of the movements, performed only 12 per cent of the ton-miles. Railroads performed 34 per cent of the movements and carried 30 per cent of the ton-miles. As would be expected with these bulky commodities, 57 per cent of the movements and 62 per cent of the ton-miles were performed by common or contract carriers, chiefly in long hauls. Nearly all the rest (173 out of 181 movements involving 17,893 out of 18,662 ton-miles) were performed in vehicles owned by the owners of the goods, chiefly short hauls in trucks.

Differences Among Products. As measured in ton-miles, most of the truck transportation was performed for the nonmetallic minerals and their products, and most of the rail and ocean transportation was for forest products. In number of movements, the miscellaneous and compound products ranked highest with regard to each of the three types of transportation. Lake transportation was confined almost en-

tirely to movement of iron ore for manufacture of the steel products and the iron and steel components of miscellaneous and compound products. Barges were used for only 4 out of the 424 movements, and they performed only 3 per cent of the 49,667 ton-miles. Though they carried heavy loads, they moved very short distances.

For forest products, the characteristic pattern of transportation was one long movement supplemented by several short ones. Western lumber and its products commonly made most of the distance from forest to building site in one long jump—3,000 miles or so if by rail, 6,500 if by water. Southern lumber and its products made one long jump, 500 to 700 miles, by rail. All other movements tended to fall within a range of 50 to 200 miles. Local deliveries from points within the Philadelphia area to the building site usually were less than 15 miles.

Among the nonmetallic minerals and their products, only one antecedent traveled as much as 1,000 miles to reach its processing plant; only two traveled as far as 500 miles in a single movement. The characteristic movement for these bulky products was less than 100 miles. For many of them, the accumulation of miles in all successive movements throughout the flow was not more than 100 miles. Ton-miles performed are nonetheless substantial because these products are heavy.

Only a little more than one third of the ton-miles for this group of products were performed by independent carriers; the rest were done either by owned carriers or by carriers under the operating control of the owners of the goods. The basic reason for this division is that producers and processors of many of these goods require specialized vehicles and keep them fully employed in their own work.

A striking characteristic of the products of a single metal is the wide variation among them as regards the relation between ownership of products and ownership of transportation facilities. In the steel industry, water carriers (whether on the Great Lakes or over the oceans) tend to be owned by integrated mining and refining companies. Railroad facilities, in contrast, are almost universally common carriers. Trucking is done for these products to a large extent by independent carriers up to the time when their dispersion begins from warehouses and terminals in Philadelphia. Most of the local haulage incident to dispersion is done in trucks controlled by the distributors, contractors, and builders. Sometimes, however, even these trucks are owned by fleet operators and used under lease or rental arrangements.

Business Entities Participating

The measures of the task of marketing thus far considered are derived from thinking of marketing as a physical flow. We now turn to the flow of ownership from entity to entity, beginning with extractors and ending with contractors or builders. The work involved in this flow has been measured by counting the business entities involved in the ownership flow and the number of transactions arranged among them. In addition, entities that handle the goods in some way but do not own them have also been counted.

Some 366 business entities constituted the channel for housebuilding materials and their antecedents. Of these, 148 were transportation agencies that did not take title to the goods; 217 of the remaining 218 did take the responsibilities of ownership.

Of the 217 owning entities, 76 per cent were extractors, fabricators, or processors of some product and 24 per cent were merchants of one sort or another, chiefly Philadelphia distributors who sell to contractors or builders.[11] About one sixth of the owning entities played their entire role for a particular product during preprocessing, about two thirds appeared during interprocessing, and another one sixth were not involved until postprocessing.

Practically all of the business entities that participated in the movement of building materials from extraction to the building site (357 out of the 366) took operating control over the goods. This includes both owners and nonowners. The nine exceptions were drop shippers, that is, merchants who take title to the goods but have them shipped directly to their own customers from their sources of supply. These appear chiefly in the flows for lumber, steel scrap, and some nonmetallic minerals.

Of the 366 business entities that participated in the processing and handling of the materials, 163 dealt with miscellaneous and compound products, 105 with forest products, 68 with products of a single metal, and 59 with products of nonmetallic minerals.[12]

[11] A firm may be a processor for one product and a distributor for another. Such duplications are eliminated from the totals.

[12] These figures add to more than 100 per cent because a number of entities that appear in more than one group have been counted only once each in the total for the house.

Transactions Arranged

The 217 business entities that participated in the ownership flow of building materials and their antecedents were connected into flows by the arrangement of 374 transactions. Of these, 330 were purchase-sale transactions and 44 intrafirm transfers. Of the 330 purchase-sale transactions, 156 took place during interprocessing, 125 during postprocessing, and only 49 during preprocessing. The burden of buying and selling evidently grows heavier as the products move forward in their flows. Of the 44 intrafirm transfers, however, 18 came during preprocessing and 21 during interprocessing. Only five involved the transfer of goods during postprocessing. Integration evidently has gone further in the earlier than in the later stages of the flow.

Dollar Days of Investment Accumulated

As a measure of the work in carrying goods through time, we have used the number of dollar days of investment accumulated in these goods as they move toward the building site. This accumulation does not measure marketing alone, since it depends upon the amount of value added by each stage of processing as well as upon two marketing factors—how long goods are in transit through their various movements, and how long they are held in storage between movements or between units of processing. The measure is a reasonably good indicator of the marketing burden, however, since, for most products, a given unit of processing is completed quickly once it gets under way. It thus serves to indicate roughly how effective the marketing mechanism has been in synchronizing successive and simultaneous stages of the various flows.

By the time they reached the building site, these products represented an accumulation of 305,774 dollar days of investment. This is equivalent to investing $1,000 for 306 days or approximately 10 months. It can also be described as equivalent to maintaining the end value of the materials at the site ($5,360) as an investment for 57 days or nearly 2 months. The investment burden is divided out among 217 owners of the goods and any lenders from whom they may have borrowed funds but must be taken care of in the aggregate by the construction industry and, in the longer run, by the buyers of the houses.

Approximately 56 per cent of the investment burden (172,238 out of 305,774 dollar days) is incurred after these products have moved into the Philadelphia area. The basic reason for this is not that the goods are held for very long periods but rather that their value has risen substantially. Dollar days accumulate rapidly and the investment burden is heavy in the later stages of each flow. Further support is given to these conclusions by the fact that 63 per cent of the dollar days are accumulated during post-processing and 29 per cent during interprocessing. Only 8 per cent are accumulated during preprocessing. If there are to be any substantial reductions in this task, they must be made in the later rather than in the earlier stages of the flows.

Forest products were responsible for 51 per cent of the dollar days; miscellaneous and compound products, for 30 per cent; products of nonmetallic minerals, for 10 per cent; and products of a single metal, for 8 per cent.

EFFECTIVENESS OF THE FLOWS FOR BUILDING MATERIALS

Organization of the Housebuilding Materials Industry

The present study confirms the common impression that even a quite unpretentious house is the end product of efforts exerted by a large number of organizations over a considerable time in many places. The participating industries are not dominated by a few distributors or a few manufacturers. Relatively little horizontal integration has developed. Vertical integration, which is most fully developed for products made from a single metal or other mineral, does not extend very far down into distribution except for the largest and the simplest products.

Whether the limitations on integration are to be construed as evidence of efficiency or the reverse is debatable. Although 366 separate business entities participate in the aspects of extraction, processing, and marketing covered by the study under review, the number of successive entities in any segment of the flow for particular products tends to be small. Numbers become large only as the product becomes complicated and requires a succession of subassemblies before being put together itself. An effective attack upon this aspect of the present organization of the industry must demonstrate that it is inefficient to have the separate gathering lines of the channels under multiple ownership and controls.

At various points in the channel, extremely specialized enterprises make their appearance.

Examples are the operating companies that mine iron ore owned by others and the so-called scrap "brokers" who buy prompt industrial scrap steel and resell it without ever handling it physically. Apparently the market for building materials in its many parts is sensitive enough to attract specialists of this sort whenever the opportunity offers.

Reducing the Amount of Transportation

The data assembled in the present study give no support to the accusation that there is much unnecessary transportation of building materials. Although a great deal of transportation is performed in connecting the numerous places at which materials are extracted, processed, and used, these data offer almost no evidence that the amount is excessive. On the contrary, there are many indications that housebuilders and their suppliers strive constantly to shorten and straighten the lines of physical movement for these materials.

The Use of Nearby Sources. Despite its reliance upon a large number of business entities working in a great many places and its need to connect these entities with the building site by intricate combinations of flows, the "industry" that built our example house is essentially a local industry. Nine tenths of the weight of this house originates as raw materials within 100 miles or so of the building site. Even if values rather than weights are measured, around one third of the total comes from relatively nearby sources. Builders reach out only when they must in order to provide the kinds of houses people want.

Further evidence in support of this conclusion is the indication that whenever nearby supplies become available, more distant sources of supply are likely to lose out. For example, Ohio has been giving ground for some years to nearby Pennsylvania points as the supplier of terra-cotta pipe to builders. Few examples were turned up of freight equalization that permits distant producers to deliver in the Philadelphia area at the social cost of excessive transportation. Those found are restricted to the less bulky parts of the house, where value per unit is relatively high and transportation costs are relatively low.

Early Elimination of Waste Materials. Evidence is mixed as to whether the burden of transportation is reduced as much as it might be by eliminating eventual waste materials early in the flows. Some of the materials fortunately suffer little or no loss in substance as they move from extraction to consuption. Examples are the limestone, gypsum, and clay used in such products as cement, plaster, and lath. Most of the products, however, involve a considerable reduction in substance, and the way the problem is handled differs widely from product to product. In copper, where the metal content of the ore may be as little as 1 or 2 per cent, the ore moves only for very short distances before being refined. Iron ore, on the contrary, moves hundreds or even thousands of miles before being refined, although half or more of its substance is waste. Forest products lose much weight in the early felling, bucking, and sawing operations but also may lose a good deal of additional weight all along the channel.

It follows that, by and large, the marketing organization performs a great many ton-miles for units of material that fall out as waste somewhere along the way. Whether the net effect is a true social waste cannot be decided without careful measurement of the several factors that in combination determine whether it is cheaper to move bulky raw materials than it is to move finished or partly finished products. Refined products weigh less but may be more expensive to carry per mile than their component materials. The size of the transportation task makes this an important area for further investigation.

Precutting and Prefabricating of Forest Products. A particularly complicated problem comes up with forest products. Much waste accumulates when logs are sawed into boards or dimension lumber, a process likely to be done in or near the timberlands and wood lots. More waste appears when lumber is cut to specific shapes and sizes that fit into the frame of the house or one of its component parts. Precutting or prefabricating would seem to offer opportunities for substantial savings in transportation (as well as in expensive cutting and shaping on the site), but the proposal runs counter to the principle of postponement, which we shall consider shortly, and so has not been widely adopted.

Precutting of lumber has developed to some extent on operative building projects. This may be done at a retail lumber yard or at some place, possibly the site itself, under the control of the builder. One objective is to reduce the waste resulting from an accumulation of small pieces cut off larger ones at the site. A more important objective, however, seems to be to increase the degree of specialization of operations. In the sawing operation, this leads to more effective

mechanization, concentration of sawing into longer runs, and the development of greater skills. Simultaneously, it concentrates the efforts of most of the carpenters at the site upon assembling the precut pieces, with savings in waste time and improvement of skills.

Crosshauling and Backhauling.[13] Crosshauling is rare—virtually insignificant—in the construction of houses by operative builders. Even branded fixtures and appliances come, in large measure, from nearby plants.

Backhauling is extremely rare in the flows of building materials that lead to a building site in the Philadelphia area. Among all the products and antecedents analyzed for the example house, only two were found that go through any appreciable amount of backhauling insofar as movements into and out of Philadelphia itself is concerned. One is gypsum, which comes into the city from Canada as a raw material, is sold to the mills that provide the Portland cement for the area, and reappears eventually as a minor ingredient in three different end products used for the house. The other is English ball clay, which is imported through Philadelphia and returns to the city as an ingredient of the water closet.

Backhauls were found at other points. An example is the shipment of glass from Pennsylvania to a Mississippi Valley sash manufacturer and back to Philadelphia as assembled sash. Such instances seem to be attributable to two causes: (1) A plant often benefits from being near the center of its market, and the market as a whole gains from this location even though some of its materials move through places to which they will return later on after processing. (2) Freight equalization and milling-in-transit privileges may negate the market effects of certain hauls. Over all, these situations are of minor importance in their effects on cost.

The Handling of Optimum Quantities

Shipment in Large Lots. An overwhelming proportion of the ton-miles performed for these building materials is done in truckloads, carloads, and bargeloads. Much of the work is in long hauls of raw or roughly processed goods that can be loaded, unloaded, and carried either

[13] Crosshauling exists when identical goods pass each other while moving in opposite directions along the same route. Backhauling exists where products are taken out of a place and later brought back into it either in the same or in a different form.

by the simplest sort of equipment or by more elaborate equipment that handles large quantities in bulk at low cost such as conveyor belts, ore unloaders, or hopper cars.

Particularly significant is the frequent appearance in the various flows of segments along which devices of one sort or another are used to consolidate shipments into carloads or truckloads. Lumber, for example, makes its long movements overland in carloads or truckloads; if necessary, an assortment of sizes will be made up to get the full load. Package deals for nails, which result in large consolidated shipments, are another example. Building-material dealers commonly make up truckloads by combining lath, plaster, and lime into single deliveries. Such efforts could be illustrated from almost any part of the channel. The result they achieve is not so much to reduce ton-miles numerically as to make them cheaper.

Minimizing Movements. Our survey provides less information upon which to base a judgment whether the number of movements, as distinct from the number of ton-miles and their cost, is minimized. It is of some interest that many of these products go through a combination of one long movement and several short ones. The long one may come in the early stages of processing, as with ore, or after processing has been completed, as with lumber. Once the material has been committed to a particular market such as Philadelphia, it seems to move directly into that market with no multiplication of loadings and unloadings. Most of the movements, however, are short ones that come after this stage. Whether there are too many, which means primarily too much work of loading and unloading for local deliveries, needs to be investigated further.

Reducing the Cost of Storage

The business of extracting, processing, and assembling the materials for the example house extended, as we have seen, over 412 days and required an investment in the goods themselves equivalent to investing $1,000 for 306 days. This indicates that an appreciable task of storage must be performed in the course of getting these materials together. Whether the task of storage can be reduced substantially is doubtful, although there is reason to doubt the effectiveness from this point of view of the work done during the last month or two in the flows of these materials.

The bulk of the storage is done when storage is cheapest, that is, in those segments of the flows where the goods have relatively little value in them and can be held in relatively simple facilities. For example, holding iron ore for months in a pile somewhere is relatively inexpensive as compared with holding furnaces or even girders and nails. It may be noted that whereas these materials are held for the largest part of their existence in the market as raw or semifinished goods, only 8 per cent of the investment burden arises in the raw stage and only 37 per cent in the raw and semifinished stages combined. For much of the bulk of the house, little storage is done even at the early levels of processing; the materials are simply left in the sand pits or quarries until shortly before they are wanted. Nevertheless, some question may be raised as to whether it would not be possible to reduce the amount of storage done and particularly that part done within the Philadelphia area for finished goods.

Application of the Principle of Massed Reserves. An extremely important economy in marketing is achieved by maintaining what are ordinarily called massed reserves. This means that stocks of goods are held for a group of distributors and users, or even for a community as a whole, by a few selected agencies rather than by each individual for himself. Ordinarily, this reduces the cost of storage because fluctuations in the flows into and out of individual establishments offset each other to some extent. Aggregate stocks can be smaller when they are centralized than when they are dispersed.

The building-materials industries have gone far in the desirable direction of applying this principle to their storage problems. This effort is particularly apparent at the level of wholesale or jobber distribution within the Philadelphia area. By and large, builders and contractors do very little storage in normal times. This job is done for them by dealers, distributors, and warehouses of various kinds. Even within the same firm, there are instances of the application of this principle, as in the operations of the wallpaper wholesaler who maintains his basic stock in a central warehouse rather than in scattered individual showrooms and stores.

Application of the Principle of Postponement. The principle of massed reserves is a special case of a more general rule that has been called the principle of postponement. This principle holds that, other things being equal, marketing costs are economized by deferring as long as possible the commitment of a unit of material to a specific use. A particular ton of iron ore, for example, should be maintained in the form and at the place that gives its owner the widest possible choice as to what shall be done with it. At the beginning of the flow, a fuel tank or length of black steel pipe is iron ore still in the mine that can be used for any one of hundreds of thousands (perhaps millions) of specific items and at any one of millions of points in space. At the other end of the flow, the specific fuel tank or length of pipe prepared to serve a specific purpose in a specific house on a specific plot of ground can be diverted to another site, house, or use only at considerable expense.

In practice, a material moves successively into narrower and narrower market areas and into forms that reduce the range of choice among uses to be made of it. Each narrowing choice imposes a penalty in that it either (1) cannot be reversed at all—as when a log has been made into plywood or when pieces of lumber have been cut into the parts of a stairway—or (2) can be reversed only at considerable expense, as when a girder is melted down and reworked into sheet steel or wire.

The principle of postponement holds that each successive narrowing commitment should be deferred as long as possible so as to reduce the likelihood and the cost of mistaken commitments. Many examples of the application of this principle can be found in the flow charts. Thus, the fuel tank is made from sheet steel only a short time before it is to be installed. This procedure delays committing the sheet to fuel tanks in general and to a particular type and size of tank, as contrasted with a multitude of other possible uses. In addition to reducing the risks of commitment, postponement offers the advantage that sheet alone is much less expensive to store and transport than is sheet plus the large volume of encased air that is in a tank. A smaller stock of sheet than of finished tanks is required because each sheet is potentially any one of several sizes and shapes of tank. Other examples of applying the principle of postponement are the dead storage of iron ore at transshipment points; the storage of galvanized sheets rather than duct work, which is made up at the last moment to fit the specific house; and the assembly of window sash and frames separately before they are put together.

Whether the principle of postponement has been applied as fully as it could be remains doubtful. This is true particularly as regards some of the compound products. These are assembled in factories, shipped as finished products (often for considerable distances), and stored in Philadelphia warehouses before going out to the site. As to the economies of the various alternatives open, a full judgment could be made only by a detailed consideration of specific cases. Perhaps this is an example of a situation in which higher-than-minimum costs of marketing are justified because they help make possible more-than-offsetting economies in manufacture. At least on the surface, however, they do not conform to the principle of postponement.

Flexibility of Marketing Methods

Responsiveness to Small Cost Differences. That the apparent lapses from the principle of postponement cannot make for much of an increase in end costs is indicated by much evidence concerning another aspect of marketing in this industry. This is, that the methods used are quite flexible and will shift in response to very moderate price or cost advantages. Thus, it is not difficult to convert the builder from one material to another for a given use. Perhaps the most conspicuous example in the present study is the virtual replacement of stone foundations by poured concrete foundations in the Philadelphia area during the period between selection of the house for analysis and completion of the field study. When the costs of stone and of stone setting went up, builders promptly and easily shifted to another type of foundation.

Further examples of flexibility may be found in changes that have taken place in the functions of wholesalers of some materials. For example, jobber applicators of mineral wool have in substance absorbed the tasks of their customers, at least insofar as insulation of old housing is concerned. The net effect is to reduce transactions, loadings, and unloadings. Similarly, current uncertainties as to whether the distribution of ceramic tile works best when contractor and wholesaler are combined into one business entity or divided into two are an evidence of willingness to experiment and change.

The Development of Drop Shipping. This flexibility extends into the willingness of enterprises within any flow to redistribute functions among themselves freely. A conspicuous case in point is the extent to which the practice of drop shipping has been adopted. Essentially a device to separate the flow of title or ownership from the physical flow of the goods, this practice appears whenever there are real advantages in having ownership and the resposibility for buying and selling pass through a middleman of some sort, but nothing is gained by having the goods pass physically through his hands.

Examples of drop shipping may be found at several levels of the various flows. Certain types of lumber move physically in carlots from mill to retailer. Prompt industrial scrap steel is drop shipped from the originating plant directly to the steel mill for the account of a "broker," who, despite his name, is really a merchant through whom the ownership flows. Such items as doors and mouldings are drop shipped from producer to retailer as a matter of routine procedure. Several products are commonly drop shipped directly from the manufacturer to the operative building site. They include bricks, granulated mineral wool, soil pipe, and water heaters. Under favorable conditions of location and requirements at a particular time, several other materials may forego their physical stop at what is "normally" their last point for handling and storage before going to the site. The same thing is done in substance, although not in name, when the retailer picks up doors at the jobber's yard and takes them directly to the building site rather than to his own establishment.

In other words, evidence has come up repeatedly that most of the supplying industries stand ready to ship physically to anyone who can use full carloads or truckloads of some product, making whatever rearrangements are necessary in the flow of ownership and passing the savings along to the receiver. The pressure for small advantages in price is great enough to force this in many transactions. Operative builders and their contractors do not, in general, have to pay for services they neither need nor want.

Labor-Only Contracts. There also is to be found what may be described as a reversal of drop shipping, since there is no generally accepted name for it. This is where the flow of the title is more direct than the physical flow of the goods. An example is the bitterly controversial arrangement under which plumbers or other contractors work for the builders on a labor-only basis. Here, the builder buys the materials, by-passing the contractor in the flow of title, whereas the actual goods are taken and installed by the contractor. Properly speaking, this is a way of reducing costs, although the trades concerned sometimes look upon it as a form of unethical price cutting.

The Availability of Meaningful Alternatives

Significant Choices. In all these matters, a very important fact is that members of the participating industries have a considerable assortment of meaningful choices open to them. Anyone in any flow who wants to absorb a task ordinarily performed by others can usually work out a transaction of the kind he wants with appropriate adjustments in price.

This fact is important because it strengthens a belief that seriously excessive costs in these various flows cannot long persist. The fact that the operators in these various markets are ordinarily numerous is important. Price competition is close and continuous for most products and services bought by operative builders. So there is a persistent willingness to bargain for arrangements that yield even small advantages.

Monopolies and Oligopolies. The presence of much indirect bargaining also indicates that the elements of monopoly in the market as a whole are rather limited. For a few products, the number of suppliers is unquestionably too small to result in any very close approximation to pure competition. In plumbing fixtures, for example, five companies dominate the national market; in gypsum products, two companies. One ready-mix concrete company and one steel company have long dominated the Philadelphia market specifically. Their degree of dominance is limited, however, since other suppliers are available to buyers. A formal determination of the effects of these situations lies outside the scope of the present study, but the fact that they exist should be noted.

Efforts to limit competition through the development of strong brands seem to have had relatively little success in building materials. Much of the material going into the example house either is not branded at all or carries brands whose only significance is that they identify the producer. Very few products were found in which brand preferences among operative builders were even moderately strong.

Continuing Relationships. There is some tendency to establish continuing relations between buyers and sellers even where independence is technically or theoretically complete. Contractors tend to concentrate their buying with a few houses. Similarly, each agency in the succession of segments back through the various flows is likely to have one or a few preferred sources of supply. There is thus no situation such that market forces result in a strictly random pairing of buyers and sellers, as is specified in the economist's definition of pure competition.

The connections between buyers and sellers are not tight and rigid. They ordinarily give way fairly easily when either party can get a real advantage from a change. Nevertheless, they exist. Complaints concerning "unethical" or "uneconomic" ways of doing business often afford evidence both of the existence of ties and of the fact that they are being broken.

An extremely significant aspect of the established relations between buyers and sellers is that they do not wholly shut the buyers off from the open market. It is customary in this industry for buyers, and more particularly for the operative builders and those who work with them, to test their markets regularly. Even though he has bought his supplies of some material from a particular supplier for a long time and fully expects to do so this time, the buyer will ask other sources for quotations. This is a device for "keeping the market in line." Everybody apparently expects that it will be done and accepts its desirability.

Finally, it should be remembered that, properly used, the crystallization of trade relations into stable patterns is an important way of economizing effort. In the economic theorists' perfect and frictionless world, no work is required to inform, persuade, and negotiate transactions between sellers and buyers. The real world is not so fortunate. In that world, all these things are done only at a cost—often a substantial cost. Once satisfactory arrangements have been made, there is thus every reason to convert them into routines. All that is required to keep them effective is to reconsider them from time to time, as in the tests just described for "keeping the market in line."

SOME SUGGESTIONS FOR "IMPROVEMENT"

The over-all significance of what has been said about the effectiveness of marketing flows for the materials in the example house becomes particularly great when attention is turned to various ways proposed for reducing the cost of housing. Familiar prescriptions are integration, modular dimensions, and prefabrication. A detailed channel analysis throws new light on these proposals.

Integration. "Integration" is a term of many meanings. What seems to be common to all of them is a reduction in the number of entities that participate in the flows through which building materials move from their points of origin through their points of processing to the point of construction. More specific is the implication that there are too many owners or too many planners in the successive phases of the flows.

The data from the present study do not support this criticism. There were only 163 separate identifiable business entities that participated substantially in the ownership flows for the 43 analyzed products and all their antecedents. This is an average of less than four per product. In the preprocessing and postprocessing parts of the flows, the number of entities is substantially smaller than the number of products. There is thus neither a large number of successive changes in ownership nor a large number of ownerships at each level of the ownership flow for the individual products. Where the number is even relatively large for a specific product, it is usually attributable to the complexity of the product.

Whether further reductions in the number of business entities at successive layers is economically feasible seems doubtful. The number of raw materials used is large; their physical points of origin are numerous and dispersed; and the differences in processes of handling and fabricating them are great. It must be remembered, furthermore, that these materials move into many types of construction in addition to the operative building of moderate-priced houses. Some of them are used for purposes having no connection with construction in any form. Thus, integration centered upon the end use of the products is not suitable in all instances. Only when the goods have been committed to houses, or even more specifically to medium- or low-cost operative built houses, does integration of this type seem to offer possibilities of real advantage.

The word "seem" is important. There is no certainty that putting various entities under one ownership will reduce significantly the amount of work they do in assembling the materials or will make the units of work done less costly. Each case would have to be studied carefully on its own merits to see whether combinations of ownership would in fact offer possibilities of eliminating ton-miles, dollar days, transactions, loadings, or unloadings or of making the planning of requirements easier. Alternatively, would they offer ways of reducing the amount of labor required for each of these units of work done?

Modular Dimensions. Another device often advocated is the universal use of modular dimensions. Modular dimensions are a method of standardization. They seem to offer advantages in manufacturing and in the actual construction of the house. Theoretically, they will help to set up longer production runs in the factories and reduce both the waste of materials on the site and some amount of cutting and fitting. In addition, they may permit the holding of smaller total stocks along the channel, reduce the work of sorting that enters into loading and unloading, and make for simpler procedures in pricing, buying, and selling. The fullest results along these lines are necessarily long term, however, since some provision must be made for non-module sizes as long as there is some demand for them either for construction or for alterations and repairs.

Prefabrication. Another possibility for increasing the efficiency of house construction is to introduce a larger element of prefabrication. In substance, this means a combination of two things: (1) The house should be brought to the site in a smaller number of pieces, each of which is an assembly of parts put together in a factory. (2) Lumber and other materials should be cut to size at a factory or yard rather than at the building site. Both kinds of prefabrication can affect all the variables in the present study.

It should be noted first that, in an absolute sense, there is already a great deal of prefabrication in the example house. What arrives on the site is not piles of logs, rocks, ore, clay, sand, and the like in their original form. Each of these materials has been processed, if only to the extent of cleaning and sorting. The true problem is thus not, as it is sometimes stated, "what would be the effects of introducing prefabrication?" but rather, "how can prefabrication be extended, and what would be the effects of extending it?"

Effects of Prefabrication Upon Units of Marketing Work. Much of the example house cannot be prefabricated by commercially feasible methods. This is true because more than 90 per cent of the weight of the house is in the products of nonmetallic minerals and some of these must be assembled on the site before a prefabricated house or prefabricated units can be put in place. Important in this regard are the foundation walls and the cellar floor. Most of the other products of nonmetallic minerals are used as an incident to the wet-wall construction of the interior walls and partitions, which must be done on the spot. Prefabrication can thus have no very significant effect upon the quantities here measured so long as it is restricted to what can be done with the house as specified in this study.

The effects of introducing large elements of prefabrication upon the quantities here measured must therefore be a composite result of changing both the specifications for the house and the point or points in the channels at which materials are assembled. If the house is placed on a full cellar with a cement floor, more than one third of the tonnage will evade prefabrication, no matter what is done to the rest of the house. The components of the foundation and cellar are made of materials that move short distances, however, so that they are responsible for only about 5 per cent of the ton-miles.

With more extensive prefabrication, ton-miles might drop, partly because it is likely that somewhat lighter materials would be used and partly because the waste accumulated in construction would be taken out earlier in the flow. This end result is not certain, however, since ton-miles are affected by distance as well as by weight, and transfer of the assembly task from site to factory might entail transportation through longer distances as the goods moved about among more factories in the course of processing.

What prefabrication would do to tonnages and ton-miles for an entire house cannot be determined without a detailed analysis of specific houses and specific types and degrees of prefabrication. The cost of the components delivered to the site presumably would increase, since a large part of the labor otherwise devoted to on-site assembly would have gone into the house at one or more factories. Furthermore, the time elapsed between extraction and delivery to the site would presumably increase so that a substantially larger number of dollar days would have been accumulated by the time the house arrived at the site. There is no way to tell how the number of places, movements, business entities, and transactions would be affected other than by making a detailed analysis of specific houses.

It is not unlikely, however, that the marketing work as thus measured would increase rather than decrease because of the introduction of one or more additional fabricating plants into the various flows. If the plants served large areas in order to achieve economies of large-scale processing, considerable backhauling would be likely. Marketing costs might also be substantially increased because higher rates per ton-mile are associated with more highly fabricated products. In short, an important part of the work associated with the marketing of the prefabricated unit may well be *in addition to*, rather than in lieu of, that of marketing the materials.

Further studies will be needed to test this hypothesis. All the present study can do is to indicate that because of the economies of effort extant in marketing materials in a direct line to the erection site, greater prefabrication might add substantially to the marketing work required as well as to the cost of doing it.

Present Elements of Standardization. As we have said, debates on these matters tend to overlook the very important fact that operative building, which provides the bulk of the medium-cost and low-cost housing in an area such as Philadelphia, already incorporates large elements of standardization. It is based upon purchase, sale, movement, and storage in large lots and emphasizes the use of a limited number of components from among those available. There is already a considerable degree of specialization by enterprises set up to serve this specific market. Examples were uncovered in the study here summarized of specialized distributors who will not sell to buyers who want frequent and small deliveries, or expect to be financed by long credit terms, or ask for special types and designs of material for individual houses. Alternatively, other distributors will do business with all kinds of buyers but vary their bases of trading and pricing. In either arrangement, the differences in cost are at least partially reflected in prices.

What this all comes down to is that conclusions derived from looking at custom building do not hold for the operative building considered in the study we have reviewed. There is room for much debate over the levels of quality, taste, and design provided by many operative builders. There is no room for debate as to whether the operative builders and their suppliers have already incorporated into their operations many of the marketing reforms proposed for them, or as to whether these changes already have had their effects upon prices and costs.

Channel Management and Trends

Parts II and III presented the concepts and theories of the channel field. Part IV did likewise for the research and analytical techniques. This final part moves into the applied areas of channel management and trends.

In Part V Section A (Channel Management), the reader will note papers by Berg, Warshaw, Brion, and Wittreich. Berg presents a program for designing the channel which includes: (1) factoring the strategic situation, (2) converting key factors into activity requirements (3) grouping tasks into work units, (4) allocating tasks to middlemen, and (5) designating structural relationships. Warshaw shows how a manufacturer may, through proper pricing policies, aid the distribution of his goods through wholesalers. This system includes suggestions for: (1) easing price competition among wholesalers, (2) taping diverse market segments, (3) setting reasonable discounts for the marginal (as defined) wholesaler, and (4) introducing the use of cost analysis at the wholesale level. Brion calls for increased coordination between channel members and lists the reasons and principal actions that should be taken to achieve this goal. Wittreich calls for a better understanding of the retailer on the part of large corporate suppliers. This includes a comprehension of the small retailer's goals and language.

In Part V Section B (Channel Trends) the reader will note papers by Tallman and Blomstrom, McCammon, and Mallen. Tallman and Blomstrom trace the development of various types of retailers, particularly discount stores and discuss the reaction of manufacturers towards the latter development. McCammon traces the development of voluntary, cooperative and franchise groups and provides the reasons underlying the growth of these centrally coordinated marketing systems. In the final selection, Mallen traces the growing strength of nonmetropolitan urban retail markets in Canada and the U.S.A. and predicts the effect this trend will have on various types of channel members. All selections in Section B are concerned with channel trends rather than simply channel level trends. In other words, it is the vertical effect rather than the horizontal effect alone that is here of concern.

A. Channel Management

34. Designing the Distribution System

THOMAS L. BERG*

The marketing executive needs some model of his distribution system to guide day-to-day trading operations. Organization theory might be used in constructing the model, for trade channels and internal company organizations are similar in important respects. Both deal with economic functions performed by interdependent human agents requiring motivation and coordination. Both involve continuous personal relationships, routinized tasks, and stable expectations of reciprocal performance. Despite the analogies, the idea that all distribution systems might be designed as organizational models has not been widely recognized nor warmly embraced. This study shows the idea to be technically feasible in the hope that one barrier to its acceptance will thus be removed. The complex process of channel model-building is depicted as unfolding in five separate but related phases. In demonstrating the feasibility of this approach, insights into the more intractable issues of practicality and morality are also revealed.

INTRODUCTION

Marketing management suffers from schizophrenia. Students of the firm are encouraging corporate psychoses identified by the classic syndrome: (1) loss of contact with company environments and (2) disintegration of the whole-properties of corporate organisms. The disease is amenable to treatment. This study is intended as a partial prescription, although it is not to be construed as any sort of a panacea.

To see the nature and origin of the malady in more concrete terms, it is necessary to understand how the total company is linked to its environment.

• SOURCE: Thomas L. Berg, "Designing the Distribution System," in W. D. Stevens (ed.), *The Social Responsibilities of Marketing* (Chicago: American Marketing Association, 1962), pp. 481–90.
* Thomas L. Berg, Assistant Professor of Marketing, Graduate School of Business, Columbia University.

The Firm as an Operating System

Any manufacturing enterprise can be viewed as an input-output system consisting of three parts: (1) the *internal organization* of the firm, (2) the company *environment*, and (3) various kinds of *external organizations* serving to link the internal organization with its economic milieu for the interorganizational transmission and processing of inputs and outputs.

Connections with suppliers, networks of financial intermediaries, and trade channels are examples of external organizations. Although they may not appear on company charts or in manuals, these should be regarded as logical extensions to the internal organization of the firm. Internal and external organizations are similar in that both deal with economic functions performed by interdependent human agents requiring motivation and coordination through communication. Both involve continuous personal relationships, routinized tasks, and stable expectations of reciprocal performance.

Failure to pay due respect to the systemic nature of the enterprise and to the fundamental similarities between internal and external organizations has resulted in schizoid thinking in management and marketing. Management theorists have been preoccupied with problems of *internal organization* and have failed to show how the firm is connected to its environment via externally organized linkages. An unnatural cleavage between internal and external aspects of structure has developed in the management literature.

"Administrative and organizational theories seem to have concentrated upon the administration of single organizations and have not specifically recognized that a system of separate organizations requires administration also. It is suggested . . . that that body of theory and research which contributes to an understanding of the administrative process in single organizations is pertinent to the administration of primary and secondary organizations."[1]

Over the years, a handful of people have come to suggest that the full development of organization theory awaits the day when management theorists explicitly bring environmental entities and external organizations into their analyses. The sire of this thought appears to be Chester Barnard.

"The conception of organization at which I arrived in writing *The Functions of the Executive* was that of an integrated aggregate of actions and interactions having a continuity in time. Thus I rejected the concept of organization as comprising a rather definite group of people whose behavior is coordinated with reference to some explicit goal or goals. On the contrary, I included in organization the actions of investors, suppliers, and customers or clients. Thus the material of organization is personal services, i.e., actions contributing to its purposes."[2]

Barnard's words have apparently fallen on deaf ears. Administrative theorists are concentrating more on refining theories of internal organization and less on extending and testing their notions in external realms. But the student

of marketing is equally responsible for the observable symptoms of schizophrenia.

In contrast to the management theorists' focus on internal aspects of business systems, marketers have been preoccupied with environmental forces and external trading channels without clarifying how these tie in to problems of internal administration and organization. Marketing academicians seem to appreciate the need of some model for building and operating trade channels, but few have recognized the potential role of organization theory in its design. Businessmen in marketing seem to know intuitively that channel-building is an organizational problem, although few acknowledge the need for a model to guide them in their organizing.

As a result, trends in management and marketing thinking become more and more divergent. To bring about some convergence, and to assure that both disciplines reverse the trend to schizophrenia, it is necessary to (a) persuade the internally-oriented administrative theorists to consider the application of their ideas to external-environmentals entities and (b) convince marketers to draw more heavily on internally-oriented theories for insights into building and operating external marketing systems. This study takes the distributive subsystem of the firm as an example of the applicability of organization theory to external systems.

The Distribution Subsystem

The term "trade channel" is often reserved to the network of external entities in a company's distribution setup. In this study, the term "distribution system" embraces all elements of the internal-external-environmental triad. Corporate marketing staffs and field salesforces are elements of internal organization, segments of ultimate consumer markets are the key environmental sectors, and retail merchants and other trade intermediaries make up the external organization. This study attempts to show that useful models of distribution systems can be designed with the help of organization theory.

Today, distribution systems are developed more by intuition than design. In part, this accounts for widespread cases of ineffective performance of trade management functions. Actual channel formation, budgeting for distribution, the setting of distributor's margins, the appraisal of dealer performance and similar management tasks could be performed more effectively if marketing managers had distributive models to guide them in the day-to-day

[1] Valentine F. Ridgway, "Administration of Manufacturer-Dealer Systems," *Administrative Science Quarterly*, Vol. 1, March, 1957, pp. 466–67.
[2] Chester I. Barnard, *Organization and Management*, Cambridge, Mass., Harvard University Press, 1948, pp. 112–13.

administration of trading functions and trading relationships.

For many reasons, the basic idea that distribution models might be designed by drawing upon organization theory has not been widely recognized nor warmly embraced. The notion is still a relatively new one accepted by a fairly small group of people. Those who have heard of the idea often seem not to have grasped its full significance. The understanding of some has been barred by the persistence of traditional perspectives on trade channels. Those congenial to the basic idea may not know how to push it to the level of operational reality. Lack of know-how simply prevents others from seeing that the approach is feasible. Those that agree to its feasibility may be reluctant to devote the time, energy, and cash to what inevitably is a difficult design job. Some apparently see the feasibility of the notion but do not regard the approach as useful on pragmatic grounds. Still others may object on philosophical bases, for when organization theory is pushed far enough into market relationships difficult questions concerning prevailing concepts of competition are bound to arise.

The purpose of this study is simply to overcome a few of these barriers to acceptance of the fundamental proposition. The chief test applied in the study is the test of feasibility. As a purely technical matter, organization theory *can* be meaningfully applied to external distribution systems, and not only to direct manufacturer-dealer organizations. In the process of demonstrating feasibility, insights into the more intractable pragmatic and philosophical issues are also revealed.

NATURE OF THE STUDY

This study focuses on the contactual, or trading, aspects of distribution as opposed to the logistics, or physical distribution, dimensions of the problem. It is nonsituational, i.e., the study is not restricted in scope to a particular product, institution, or historical period. It is addressed to marketers in manufacturing firms, although the ideas may also be of interest to others.

Few businessmen can yet verbalize their opinions and attitudes toward the application of organization theory to the design of distributive models. Therefore, personal interviews could not be used as a sole method of research. Information had to be gleaned piecemeal from a variety of sources—including protracted informal interviews with some 150 marketing executives and teachers, widely scattered secondary sources, and pure cogitation.

In effect, the study attempts to present elements of prudent practice within the unifying framework of organization theory. It does not describe any approach taken by a known manufacturer.

Elements in the Design Process

The process of designing a distributive model for a producer is envisaged as unfolding in five interrelated stages: (1) factoring the company-wide strategic situation, (2) converting key factors into functional prerequisites for the system, (3) grouping individual tasks into work units, (4) allocating tasks to appropriate functionaries, and (5) designing a structure of relationships to provide loci of distributive authority and responsibility within the work structure erected in the previous stages.

In the study, separate chapters are devoted to each of these elements and an integrating case is used to help synthesize the materials as the process unfolds.

Step One—Factoring the Strategic Situation. Early in the research, comparative studies of existing systems were undertaken with the aim of accounting for the sometimes marked inter-firm differences in distribution practices observable in many industries. Those variables were then abstracted which seemed to serve as decision-making constraints for a wide variety of the firms studied. These fell into two broad classes: (a) the nature and interests of various environmental entities as interpreted by top management, and (b) factors relating to the company's resource base. Environmental entities and company resources are related through broad marketing strategy to the functional necessities and structural features of distribution systems. Environmental entities include stockholders, employees and their unions, supplier interests, trade associations, governments, competitors, and ultimate consumers. The resource base refers especially to finances and manpower but also includes material, spatial, temporal, and other resources. In the study, these factors are arranged and presented in meaningful sequence, and illustrations are provided to suggest the possible impact of each variable on channel function or structure. The goal was to help the manager conduct a comprehensive position audit for his own particular firm in its unique competitive market setting in order to isolate key bits of information which might provide clues as to appropriate distributive structure in the specific case. The study thus offers a method of attack for factoring a firm's strategic situation as well as illustrating the potentialities for interfirm differences in distribution systems.

Step Two—Converting Key Factors into Activity Requirements. The research revealed that surprisingly few producers can meaning fully reply to the question, "What do you want your distribution setup to do for you?" It may be suggested here that until managers can verbalize the nature of the *work* they want performed by distribution systems, there can be little hope for real application of organization theory to trading networks.

Yet, the study offers guides for developing the inferential value of key factors uncovered in step one in sufficient detail to permit the generation of a fairly clear-cut list of activities to be performed by the yet-to-be-designed distribution system. At this point in the study, the integrating case is also introduced to illustrate how one firm actually posited its channel tasks in a simplified situation.

Step Three—Grouping Tasks into Work Units. This step involves a straightforward adaptation of organization theory, which alternatively depicts the process as one of a *division of labor* or of *grouping* tasks together in a meaningful fashion. No real problems of applying organization theory were encountered. However, there is clear evidence that the channel analyst might profit from taking this step very seriously. Traditional channel discourses, for example, have tended to stress specialization solely on the basis of function. Organization theory demands adequate attention to alternative modes of specialization, i.e., by product, by customer, by time, by location, by process, and by composite patterns of these basic varieties. All of the alternatives are relevant to distribution systems as well as to internal organization. Furthermore, channel planners perhaps stress short-term efficiency considerations too much in deciding what kind of task-split might be effected with the trade. Organizational theorists call attention to the needs for structural coordination, for promoting co-operation and reducing conflict, for recognizing the vagaries of local conditions, and other criteria for picking proper kinds and degrees of work specialization.

There is reason to assume that managers would uncover a much wider range of distribution alternatives and would probably end up by delegating more of the overall distributive job to tradesmen if they self-consciously applied the broader perspectives of organization theory to this step in the design of distribution systems. Finally, some varieties of organization theory focus first on the work and secondly on the worker. Classical institutional and commodity approaches to trade channels seem to have reversed the order of analysis.

Step Four—Allocating Tasks to Middlemen. In matching work and worker, the best procedural approach seems to be to begin with segmenting the end markets to be served and then to progress upward through a process of sequential segmentation in intermediate markets until the intervening work structure can be made to tie together with the producer's internal organization.

At each stage of this process of closing gaps separating the producer from his ultimate markets, a set of interrelated issues must be resolved.

All alternative middlemen must first be *recognized* as alternatives. This is less obvious and more difficult than it appears. Semantic traps, statistical fictions, informational gaps, trained incapacities, managerial impatience and other barriers to creativity befog and bury alternatives from view. Brainstorming and other alternative-producing techniques, of course, are relevant in overcoming this problem.

With the alternatives before him, the manager must sort out ineligible types of outlets, drawing upon earlier key factors, activity requirements, and preliminary grouping analysis for screening criteria. Next, the remaining eligible outlet-types can often be arrayed meaningfully in order of their apparent suitability to the producer, using the same criteria.

At this juncture, several additional types of questions often need to be answered before proceeding to another stage of the vertical channel stretch, e.g., whether there are economies of scale for each outlet-type, how many of each type will be required, and what areal coverage pattern should be used. Since many of the variables used to resolve the latter issues lend themselves to quantification, some companies have been able to program them for computer solutions.

This set of decisions, made at successive stages in bridging the vertical gap between customers and the producer, completes the steps involved in planning the structure of distributive *work*. Before going further, however, the study discusses principles and procedures which serve as possible checks on the adequacy of the activity structure erected thus far on paper. The final step is to define desired relationships between

individuals and institutions in the distribution
~~~~~~~~~~~~~~ loci of authority and respon-

natives involve outright contractual or other
specification of intended delegations, and these
steps may be supplemented by the provision of
facilitating and auxiliary service units (e.g., distributor training groups and dealer advisory
councils) which help all parties to hold the exercise of authority within responsible bounds. The
specific pattern of reservation-delegation devices
chosen by the producer will depend on the way
in which power has come to be institutionalized
in the particular work structure he has put together, on the relative size and bargaining
strength of producer and middlemen, on the
past history of cooperation and conflict with
similar patterns of tradesmen, and related
factors.

When the five steps of the model-building
process have been completed, the overall structure can then be described in charts and manuals. Job descriptions and man-specifications for
middlemen may also prove useful as guides to
implementation of the model.

CONCLUSION

In very skeletal fashion, these five steps to the
organizational design of distribution systems
represent the ground covered in this study.
Chester Barnard's basic idea is shown to be
operationally meaningful; as a technical proposition, organization theory can usefully be extended to the design of external systems. But
the task is just as difficult, frustrating, and time-
consuming as it is in internal analyses—perhaps
more so.

Yet the approach is practical for most firms.
Organization theory provides a systematic and
rational basis for superceding many of today's
intuitive approaches to channel-building. It is a
body of doctrine that respects the inherent
uniqueness of companies while providing guidelines for both orthodox and unconventional distribution systems. And it allows us to deal with
both the *work* to be done in the system and
the human *relationships* important to that
performance.

Step-by-step application of concepts from organizational theory helps in the discovery of
gaps in traditional ways of thinking about distribution. At the same time, it aids in uncovering
more distributive alternatives and in providing
criteria for choosing between them, it encourages
the challenging of old concepts which may have
outlived their usefulness, and it leads to a fuller
understanding of the implications of past, present, and future trading actions.

There are many additional ways in which administrative theory can be effectively used to
improve the management of distribution systems. Knowledge of institutional leadership and
control in internal realms needs to be further
extended, and perhaps modified, to apply in all
external systems. By breaking down the walls
tending to separate marketing from the field of
general administration, marketers can also find
themselves testing and improving administrative theory. The problem of choosing from alternative theories of organization still exists today.
Perhaps further attempts to apply these theories
to external systems could contribute to the uni-
fication of divergent threads.

This study was one test of organization theory
in an external setting. The conclusion is that
organization theory stands up better under analysis than does the marketer's concepts of
distribution.

Increased awareness of the general applicability of administrative and organization theory
to external systems may encourage further inter-

disciplinary contributions to marketing and management. Industrial relations specialists could collaborate with marketers, for instance, in exploring points of similarity and difference between employee-union relationships within the firm and the extra-firm relationships between merchants and their trade associations. Something akin to collective bargaining is said to take place in some trades with respect to the setting of distributor margins and other issues. It would be interesting to pursue this further. Sociologists are now attempting to apply insights from general studies of bureaucracy to manufacturer-dealer relations. The concept of reference group

behavior could perhaps be investigated more thoroughly for its relevance to trade channels. The anthropologist's idea of tangent relations and tangent institutions might provide further insights into the design and operation of distribution systems.

In short, recognition of the fact that organization theory offers immediate and practical help to manufacturers in the design of all distribution systems should open many doors for further research and remedy present tendencies toward schizophrenia in understanding business needs and company practices.

35. Pricing to Gain Wholesalers' Selling Support

MARTIN R. WARSHAW

Can a manufacturer do anything to increase the selling effort expended by his wholesalers? Is greater emphasis on direct sale the only way to gain greater promotional activity at wholesale levels?

The author shows that the manufacturer through his pricing policies may exert an important influence on wholesaler willingness and ability to sell.

A long-standing and frustrating enigma faced by many manufacturers utilizing wholesalers is how to gain their promotional support. This problem is important, first of all, because of the wholesalers' potential selling power. Moreover, the type of selling effort expended by wholesalers is both difficult and expensive to duplicate. Few manufacturers, for example, have sufficient sales volume, to say nothing of the time and resources, to match independent wholesalers with respect to unit distribution costs.

That the wholesaler's ability to grant promotional support to any one source is limited by the nature of his economic role is generally understood by marketing managers. However, the ways in which competitive frictions arising from the manufacturer-wholesaler relationship tend to depress wholesalers' willingness to sell is less well comprehended.

Nevertheless, manufacturer complaints of the ineffectiveness of selling effort by these intermediaries are widely heard. Although in many cases well deserved, such criticism does little to provide more and better sales effort at wholesale levels. The frustrated manufacturer, believing that the problem of gaining wholesaler support is unsolvable, often attempts to take over (either entirely or in part) the wholesaling job. This is a drastic decision, requiring long-term commitments of financial and human resources to de-velop an organization capable of performing wholesaling functions. Therefore, the thoughtful manufacturer first determines with certainty whether his own marketing policies and procedures are consistent with gaining the full measure of wholesaler response needed to attain his promotional objectives. Indeed, the assumption of typical wholesaling functions by a manufacturer should be considered only after he has made certain that his own marketing program is in order.

The area of pricing is of special importance in any such appraisal by a manufacturer of his marketing program. The policies formulated determine not only the prices which wholesalers pay for a given product, but also exercise a powerful influence over the prices at which these products can be resold.

The resulting spread between these levels is the effective margin from which the wholesaler derives payment for functions performed as well as his profit. Manufacturer pricing policy, therefore, not only has an effect on the wholesaler's ability to perform the selling function but also influences the wholesaler's willingness to allocate selling effort on a selective basis.

PRICING AND INTER-CHANNEL RIVALRY

Formulating effective pricing policy is especially difficult when the wholesale channel is used in conjunction with other channels of distribution. Although the objective of multiple-channel strategy is to maximize profits by tapping diverse segments of the market, these

• SOURCE: Martin R. Warshaw, "Pricing To Gain Wholesalers' Selling Support," *Journal of Marketing*, Vol. 25 (July, 1962), pp. 50–54. Martin, J. Warshaw, Assistant Professor of Marketing, University of Michigan.

segments are rarely served exclusively by a single channel of distribution.

The degree of overlap among these various channels determines the extent of rivalry which they face from one another. When overlap occurs between the direct channel and the wholesale channel, the resulting competitive frictions are especially acute. These frictions arise, of course, because wholesale intermediaries deeply resent competition with the very manufacturing sources they are attempting to serve.

Excessive inter-channel rivalry, with respect to the sale of any given product, reduces the profit potential for the wholesaler through the likelihood of price competition and the probable necessity of higher selling costs. Because wholesalers usually have so wide a range of lines over which to allocate their limited promotional resources, the threat is always present that they will redirect selling effort to those manufacturers who minimize the effects of competition from other types of resellers or from direct sale. The question is raised, therefore, as to the proper pricing policies for marketing managers faced with this critical problem.

Buying Distribution

Viewing the problem as one of "buying distribution" can be useful in developing effective pricing policies when utilizing multiple channels of distribution. The concept of buying distribution emphasizes the fact that the price paid to gain channel support must reflect not only the marketing job performed by the channel, but also the competitive environment in which the channel operates.[1] Buying distribution means that payments to diverse channels may vary. The manufacturer accepts different net receipts from individual channels, in each case paying the price needed to gain channel support.

Unfortunately, a policy of differential pricing to multiple channels of distribution may run afoul of the Robinson-Patman Act. The coverage pattern of one channel usually overlaps that of another, thus placing the channels in competition. In addition, as the price differentials needed to buy distribution reflect costs of selling *through* channels rather than *to* channels, they are cost justifiable only by coincidence.

The fact that the practice of buying distribution may run counter to current price legisla-

[1] See Charles N. Davisson, *The Marketing of Automotive Parts* (Ann Arbor: Bureau of Business Research, The University of Michigan, 1954), pp. 918 ff.

tion may limit its applicability but does not invalidate its conceptual value. Indeed, for the manufacturer engaged in concurrent distribution through the direct and wholesale channels, the legal problem need not arise, and an attack on the pricing problem in terms of buying distribution from wholesalers may provide valuable insights.

Given this perspective, it becomes evident that to gain promotional support from wholesalers margins granted must be adequate in terms of the marketing job to be assumed by them. However, these margins must also take into consideration the rivalry faced from other suppliers for wholesaler cooperation, as well as the intensity of competition faced by the wholesalers in selling for resale or for final use. Much of the latter rivalry may emanate from the manufacturer's own direct selling activities. Thus, the manufacturer himself may create competitive pressures which increase the price he must pay to buy wholesaler selling support.

Pricing to Market Segments

Pricing to market segments is another way to reduce interchannel frictions. Through varying prices to different groups of customers, the market may be broken into smaller portions, each of which differs in price sensitivity. One electrical appliance manufacturer interviewed by the author sold direct to governmental agencies, buying groups, and other large users where the price was set on a basis of competitive bids.

Wholesalers, on the other hand, were used to serve customers whose price demands were less pressing because the quantities which they purchased were relatively small. Prices charged to the wholesale channel covered full costs, while prices needed to gain orders on the basis of competitive bidding or direct negotiation covered out-of-pocket costs and made a contribution to overhead. By pricing so that each of the channels tapped an essentially different market segment, interchannel competition was greatly reduced. Although paying a higher price than many final users who purchased directly from the manufacturer, wholesalers were both willing and able to provide effective selling effort in the markets which they served.

Manufacturer pricing policy may, under certain conditions, place the wholesaler at a distinct advantage with respect to other channels of distribution. In one situation observed by the author, a manufacturer of electrical wiring priced himself out of the market with respect to replacement sales. Direct selling was confined to those original equipment manufacturers who customarily purchased in large quantities. Rivalry between the direct and wholesale channels was almost completely eliminated, and the manufacturer reported that his wholesale distributors were aggressively promoting his line in the market segment which they could serve most effectively.

In another case involving a manufacturer of industrial chemicals, company policy was to sell direct to carload users. However, recognition was given to the problem of forcing wholesalers to divest themselves of customers who had grown to be carload users; the wholesale channel was allowed to continue to serve these carload users if these customers so desired. Although drop shipments were made from the factory at the wholesaler's request, the discount on these shipments was about 5 per cent, which was considerably below the typical margins of 10 to 20 per cent allowed on less than carload sales from wholesalers' stocks.

The objective of this policy appeared to be to allow wholesalers to profit only from those carload sales which were an outgrowth of a long-standing association with the customer and not from large orders received by wholesaler solicitation of that market segment ordinarily covered by the direct channel. The situation illustrates how a company can use price policy to discourage wholesaler attempts to sell in the market segment reserved for direct sales solicitation. Further, this policy was instituted with full regard for distributor morale.

PRICING AND INTRACHANNEL RIVALRY

Pricing policy can also influence the intensity of indirect rivalry or competition among wholesale resellers within the channel. The size of the margin payment, for example, affects the number of wholesalers who can afford to carry a line and thus the intensity of distribution at wholesale. It is axiomatic that the larger the number of wholesalers used in any market area, the greater are the potential pressures of intrachannel competition.

These pressures, in turn, can reduce the profitability of the line for any one wholesaler. Thus, the manufacturer faces a crucial pricing problem of finding a payment level which will attract the number of wholesalers needed to provide adequate market coverage, while at the same time furnishing proper incentive for their full functional performance.

The solution to this problem would be greatly simplified for a manufacturer if all potential wholesale distributors had comparable expense ratios, performed the same functional tasks, and operated under similar competitive pressures. Given this desirable situation, the manufacturer could select one discount payment which would optimize the combination of coverage and promotion received from wholesalers in relation to the costs involved. Unfortunately, the real world is considerably more complex. Wholesale costs, functional performance, and competitive situations vary substantially. Therefore, it is necessary to examine several possible ways in which discounts can be established to minimize this problem.

The Marginal Approach

A logical attack on the problem of pricing to the wholesale channel requires an estimate of the distribution requirements imposed by the nature of the product and the way in which it is purchased. The manufacturer of convenience goods, for example, will find that his channel objectives will be heavily biased in favor of wide coverage, rather than intensive promotion at the wholesale level.

In contrast, the manufacturer of a consumer durable usually will find that his marketing mix places a considerable emphasis on both coverage and promotional push. Once having defined his *minimum coverage goals*, the manufacturer must decide how the total selling task should be borne. He must determine that portion of the selling job that he will perform and that portion he hopes to elicit from his wholesalers.

The wholesaler discount must be set in terms of the two requirements: *coverage* and *promotion*. The problem, of course, is to make one payment cover the wide variety of wholesaler needs and efficiencies. One possible solution is to set the distributor discount at a figure which will provide adequate compensation for his *average wholesaler*. Another solution is to set the discount so that it covers the needs of his *marginal wholesaler*.

Setting the distributor discount to cover both the functional and competitive needs of an "average" wholesaler who faces an "average" competitive situation has as its major disadvantage the fact that those wholesalers in the distributor organization who are below "average," as a result of higher than average costs or unusually difficult selling situations, cannot afford to meet the manufacturer's minimal coverage and promotional requirements. The result may be that the wholesaler will reduce the extent and quality of performance of the selling function.

Much more acceptable is the alternative, to set the distributor discount to provide the payment necessary to induce the marginal wholesaler to perform a full functional job. The "marginal" wholesaler may be the least effective wholesaler whose presence is required to provide coverage, or he may be a "key" wholesaler who is providing superior selling effort. If effective margin is reduced through increased costs of performing the wholesaling functions or through the impact of competition on price structures, the marginal distributor may drop the line, or may cut back to a less satisfactory performance. Either way, reduction in effective margin results in a less favorable combination of selling and coverage.

The Distribution Cost Analysis Approach

Wholesale margins can no longer be set on the basis of historical percentages of the sales dollar. Wholesaler complaints of margin inadequacy are heard by almost every manufacturer. When asked to provide more selling effort, wholesalers often reply that they already are providing more than they are being paid for. What is needed is a measurement of the reality of distributor needs, a method of quantifying the adequacy of margin payments.

Distribution cost analysis (the application of cost accounting techniques to marketing problems) may help on two counts. First, its usage might aid manufacturers to revamp margins and price structures to obtain the desired degree of distributor support. Second, the information gained from such cost analysis might help the distributor to see the adequacy of gross margins and, as a result, to understand why he should give the manufacturer his promotional support.

In one instance a manufacturer of grinding wheels felt that profitability of the line and not gross margin should be the criterion by which wholesale distributors appraised the relative values of lines carried and the selling support warranted. Therefore, accountants were sent to three important distributors to develop a procedure by which any distributor could measure the relative net profitability of product lines carried. The procedure was simplified and made available to all wholesale distributors of the company's products.[2] The suggested procedure covered the following steps:

1. Products or product lines to be analyzed were grouped and coded. Cost of sales as well as average inventory were calculated.
2. Natural expense items were related to the marketing and administrative functions of an industrial distributor.
3. Overhead expenses were allocated to operating functions.
4. Statistics were obtained to be used as bases for allocation of functional costs to product groups.
5. Functional costs were allocated to product groups.
6. A summary was then prepared showing total of costs allocated to each group as well as group gross profit contribution. The net result of these amounts was the net profit contribution before taxes of each group of products.

Although distribution cost analysis places emphasis on product profitability where it rightfully belongs, it is not without its limitations. These include, above all, a possible overemphasis on short-run profit contribution as an indication of the value of a product or group of products and the difficulty of correctly allocating functional costs to the various products. However, the approach does offer guidance to the manufacturer who must determine the relative adequacy of the margin he offers on his line. In addition to letting the manufacturer see what profit potential he is providing wholesalers, such information may also allow wholesalers to compare their operating expenses with those of other distributors.

IMPLICATIONS

Although pricing policy is but one part of a manufacturer's overall marketing program, pricing decisions can exert considerable influence over the willingness and ability of wholesale intermediaries to provide selective selling support. By understanding the wholesaler's role and by recognizing the effects of excessive competitive pressures, the manufacturer may adjust his own pricing policies to increase wholesaler promotional response.

Accordingly, the following suggestions should be useful.

(1) *When a manufacturer faces excessive rivalry from other producers for wholesaler support,*

[2] For an illustration of this approach in action, see "Accounting for Net Profits by Product Lines" (Worchester, Massachusetts: Norton Company, 1956). See also Charles H. Sevin, *Distribution Cost Analysis*, Economic Series No. 50 (Washington, D.C.: U.S. Government Printing Office, 1946).

or when wholesalers face heavy competition from other channels of distribution with respect to resale, the concept of "buying distribution" may provide an approach to effective manufacturer pricing policy.

Although the price paid to gain support from wholesalers under these circumstances may well exceed the cost of the functions performed, buying distribution may be more economical for the manufacturer than providing it for himself.

(2) Manufacturer pricing policy may also be used to tap diverse market segments.

The depressing effects of channel overlap upon wholesaler selling performance may be minimized by pricing, so that the wholesale channel serves a market segment which differs in price elasticity from segments served by other channels. In addition, manufacturer pricing policy can favor or discriminate against the wholesale channel to achieve desired patterns of distribution. These policies may deter wholesalers from intruding into markets reserved for direct sale, or they may encourage wholesalers to promote aggressively the manufacturer's product line by removing the fear of competition from direct sale.

(3) Although the proposal that distributor discounts should provide for full functional performance from the marginal wholesaler is conceptual, it can help the manufacturer to define the objectives of his distributor discount policy.

In practice, the concept may be dealt with experimentally. The gains in coverage and selling effort achieved by setting compensation for the least effective must be weighed against the cost of paying a premium to all wholesalers who are more efficient than the marginal firm. If premium payments are converted in some part to premium performances of the selling function at wholesale, all well and good. If, however, these extra payments are passed on by the more efficient wholesalers as price concessions, the net result is a further squeeze on the marginal wholesalers. Unfortunately, this is often the case.

(4) Manufacturers who want to escape the wholesalers' blanket condemnations for inadequate margins must assume responsibility for introducing wholesalers to the use of distribution cost analysis.

If sufficient cost data were collected from distributors, a manufacturer could provide figures on average handling, warehousing, and selling expense for his product based on the aggregate experiences of his distributor organization. Such data would inform the distributor if his costs were out of line, and furthermore would indicate to the manufacturer whether or not his margin was consistent with the costs of functional performance and the pressures of competition at the wholesale level. Although relative short-run profitability of a line should not be the sole criterion of its value to distributors, it is of considerably greater relevance than gross margin.

36. Marketing Through the Wholesaler/Distributor Channel

JOHN M. BRION

Increased automation, a trend to a rental economy, increased R&D, high volume break-even points, and increased competition all will pressure members of the channel towards increased cooperation. Brion discusses these trends and makes suggestions of how channel members should adapt to them.

COMMENT

The following statistics of Merchant Wholesale sales show that the per cent of total sales has remained relatively constant since 1939. Although the Bureau of the Census does not have comparable data extending beyond 1939, the available data indicate that the ratio of seventeen per cent held true in the late 20's. One might conclude the consistency of market share demonstrates a relatively permanent niche, or segment of merchandising, that lends itself to this kind of business.

Sales of Merchant Wholesalers Related to Total Sales in Manufacturing and Trade*

	Total Mfg. & Trade	Merchant Wholesalers	Per Cent of Total
1939	$133.4	$21.8	16.4
1948	437.3	76.5	17.5
1954	567.7	101.0	17.7
1958	648.2	115.6	17.8
1962	769.3	134.2	17.4
1963	803.5	140.0	17.4

* Billions of dollars, Minor changes in estimating methods after 1948.

But from the distributors' point of view, two questions immediately come to mind: Can the share be substantially improved? Are future markets going to be that much like past and present markets so that all they're going to have to do is more of the same?

These questions need to be answered together because they are so closely related. Wholesalers *can* increase their share but it will have to be largely by new techniques because future major markets are going to be based on different wants and precepts. If a manufacturer's distributors do not realize it he will have to help them do so; if they cannot fulfill their new functions alone, he will have to give them a hand, at least in getting started. There's plenty of evidence they can do the job.

Research and development and automation are placing an immense responsibility on marketing, for four reasons:

To find markets for new products;
To find markets to utilize an automated production capacity;
To increase the rate of consumption by present markets;
To level out the rate of consumption of present markets.

We can produce virtually anything in any quantity; we are held back only for want of markets, and our economy is repeatedly jarred by the way existing markets purchase. Indeed, any manufacturer knows an automated plant will be far more subject to jarring, in fact bankruptcy, with existing demand fluctuations than a non-automated plant.

The modern manufacturer, therefore, is going to be increasingly pressed to squeeze the water, the looseness, out of his channels to the buyer and to devise ways to make him buy consistently and commit himself over a period of time.

• SOURCE: John M. Brion, *Marketing Through the Wholesaler/Distributor Channel* (Chicago: American Marketing Association, 1965), pp. 53–57. John M. Brion, Marketing Consultant, New York City.

Fortunately he has the forces of plenty on his side (as well as in the form of competition). Through the ages people have wanted to possess goods and property because there was always a shortage, and thrift was sold as a virtue. To the extent that thrift contributes to survival or education it will continue to be, but where there is much more than is needed, the "virtue" is in conflict with our economic need of greater consumption for greater production. Even President Johnson in 1964 recently urged us to spend our increased income from tax cuts, not save it. But the most significant fact is that under conditions of plenty, material possession is a burden. The city man only asks for trouble when he buys a car, for all he needs to do is pick up a phone to have any model in top condition at his disposal; and we know that a corporation that buys a large computer not only ties up his money but may find it obsolete in a few years. Plenty is laying an important solution to our problems right in our laps, because the affluent society is beginning to realize that what it really wants is not possession but use to fulfill a function and function to save time and cost.

This realization is only in its beginning, fed by the rapidly expanding automation and followed closely by the sale of "use" and "function" to serve it, but the lag is too great. The sale of use and function, which is only touching a small part of the total marketplace, needs to be stepped up to stimulate the realization to a far greater growth rate in order to absorb the product of automation, if automation is to lead us to the millenium before it and poor tax policies drive our economic ship on the rocks— and selling it is marketing's job.

Marketing is naturally also obliged to help solve our immediate and most pressing problem, the profit squeeze, caused by this very plenty in the form of both national and international competition. It can make an immense contribution to its solution for all levels of distribution down the line through the very same method that needs to be applied as a medium for the above strategy—integration for greater efficiency and marketing effectiveness:

Integration of the supplier with his distributors;
Integration of the distributors with their customers;
Integration directly where the supplier sells directly.

This is, of course, nothing new to the more progressive manufacturers and distributors, and to them will go the increases in market share.

The others will have to settle for the left-over scraps.

To tick off the principal actions that the manufacturer should take, he should:

(1) Properly organize to manage the channel;
(2) Develop and sell distributors integrated marketing planning;
(3) Plan, establish, promote and continually work at the needed communications for both feedout and feedback;
(4) Offer competent distributor management assistance where needed;
(5) Provide marketing assistance and backup as needed to assure a total marketing effort, and
(6) Pay his distributors for the services to the customers he expects them to perform to better assure their execution.

His success with the channel will be strongly influenced by his understanding of wholesalers' strengths, weaknesses and problems. Particularly does he need to accept the realities that

(1) If he were to take over the wholesale function, the price of the complete control he seeks will be the higher investment required and poorer investment return as contrasted with manufacturing, a level the distributors are apparently willing to bear. There is also a virtual "diversification" into an unfamiliar industry, a fact that many large corporation executives do not appreciate until several years of branch warehousing deficits roll by.

(2) His own marketing job extends to and through the after-sale servicing of the final customer who uses his identifiable product, so if distributors are a part of his channel he is careless, even negligent, not to make full use of their resources and appropriately supplement them with needed services for which he is not paying. This entails the highest attainable integration with the distributors of not only marketing but communication, order processing, shipping and receiving, training and inventory-production tie-in, all of which has to be done at the expense of the independence of each.

(3) To a considerable degree the distributors' problems are his own problems. Ignoring them is worse than ignoring the promotion department's efforts for those products, for poor distributor performance can mean irretrievable loss of market share. The failure of individual distributors can mean loss of access to important areas. The fanning out of the upper part of the break-even chart may help to emphasize the profit-importance of the contribution of each distributor even though it may be a small per cent of total sales.

The integration of the distributors with their customers will inevitably be greatly assisted by this integration with suppliers because of the attendant improvement in marketing coordination and product flow. Procurement contracts (the more a distributor can contract to do for a customer the better) and leasing and installment buying are all forms of this integration, and they hit right at the very targets of increased consumption rate. They all provide for controlled disposition of the customers' income. Leasing has the added advantage of tending to force replacement therefore greater consumption. The merchandising of use instead of possession and function instead of items of hardware has to be the vehicle, and one or the other can be applied to virtually every product line.

The bulk of the economic problem of more consumption and level purchasing, to be sure, will be up to direct selling and retailing, the other 83% of the market, but the distributor channel with $140 billions of sales is certainly a significant part, especially to those who market all or most of their output through it. Any such manufacturer would be missing one of his great marketing opportunities by not constantly pushing his distributors along this line of thinking, because those who succeed in tying their customers to themselves will:

Have the greatest chance of getting the repeat business;

Be better able to feedback customer needs and suggestions for product improvement;

Be more willing and able to push new products and new uses;

Be able to submit their purchase requirements well in advance for production planning; and

Be more effective in absorbing demand fluctuation that cannot be tied down by such strategies.

And any distributor who ignores the trend stands a good chance of having less and less attractive franchises as the trend takes hold. Since most manufacturers prefer to concentrate on their strong suit of manufacturing and stay out of the business of inventory and credit, the opportunity for distributors as a group to up their 17.4% share is certainly there. Because the shift will be much to the manufacturers' advantage they would do well to encourage end-users to make the most of the available services.

Plenty and affluency obviously mean stiff competition, and one of the best competitive weapons will be to tighten up ship down the line, through stronger better partnerships. A larger share of the *product's* market will be the reward.

37. Misunderstanding the Retailer

WARREN J. WITTREICH

In this abridged article Wittreich states that there is a basic difference between the business philosophies and languages of the large company executives and those of the small or medium-sized retailer. The former is growth- and professional-minded, whereas the latter is stability- and vocational-minded. This difference leads to channel conflict. Retailers are not a homogeneous statistic but many different individuals; and they do not necessarily share the goals of the managements whose products they distribute.

There is no question that manufacturers generally acknowledge the *necessity* for communicating with the retail dealer. This is clearly evidenced by the dollars spent for advertising and promotion aimed directly at retail dealers (over and above dollars expended in personal selling effort) as well as the generally high number of articles and speeches which reaffirm management's recognition and interest in the problem.[1]

Yet, despite the large amount of such communicating and the importance attributed to it by management, within the complex distribution system of *all* owner-operated retailing outlets we generally find the same phenomenon: *the people who manufacture the goods and the people who move the goods into the hands of the ultimate consumer do not share the same business philosophy and do not talk essentially the same language.* Nevertheless, corporate management in the manufacturing organization (which obviously depends on the retailer for ultimate sales) continues to operate on the assumption that *there is no problem*—that it and the retailer have the same goals and use and understand the same words.

In this article, I shall explore these twin dimensions of the serious breakdown in the communications system between manufacturer and retailer. These dimensions I have identified as (1) the problem of *crossed purposes*, and (2) the problem of *confused languages*.

CROSSED PURPOSES

To understand the problem of crossed purposes, it is necessary to analyze and understand the differing points of view held by most members of corporate management, on the one hand, and by most retail owner-operators, on the other.

By and large, corporate management's point of view is characterized by a *growth psychology*. A key to understanding why this is so can be found in thinking about *who* gets to be top management.

Reams have been written about the characteristics of successful managers. For our purposes here, however, the most important finding about top managers is that generally they are people who identify their own personal goals with the goals of the corporation. While this fusion of personal and corporate goals can manifest itself in a number of ways, the essential fact remains that the people guiding our major corporations today are those individuals whose personal objectives in life are intellectually and

• SOURCE: Warren J. Wittreich, "Misunderstanding the Retailer," *Harvard Business Review*, Vol. 40 (May–June, 1962), from pp. 147–49, 159. Used by permission. Warren J. Wittreich, Vice-president, National Analysts.
[1] For example, see the editorial in *Sales Management*, October 20, 1961, p. 7; E. B. Weiss, "Outdated Ad Presentations to the Trade," *Advertising Age*, September 11, 1961, p. 122; W. J. Regan, "Full Cycle for Self-Service?" *Journal of Marketing*, April, 1961, p. 15; W. Lazar and E. J. Kelley, "The Retailing Mix: Planning and Management," *Journal of Retailing*, Spring, 1961, p. 34; "Ads Not Enough; Retailer Must Be Sold," speech by G. E. Mosley before the Boston Advertising Club and the Point of Purchase Advertising Institute, April, 1959.

emotionally intertwined with the goals of the organizations they command.

The significance of this rather obvious fact can best be understood against the broad background of our country's past history, present position, and expected evolution over the years ahead. The growth which is the keynote of modern management's thinking is in reality a part of the over-all growth which has characterized our country's history from the outset. Our society is riding the crest of a wave which began to gather strength hundreds of years ago and shows no signs of abatement—neither now nor in the foreseeable future. Our population, our government, and our corporate economy have grown, are growing, and will undoubtedly continue to grow in the future. In short, all of the basic elements of our over-all social structure are at this moment reflecting a basic, pervading, continuous thrust of expansion.

The consequence of this inexorable growth process for the individual corporation is the fact that the principle of growth is basic to the fused goals of top management and corporate organization. The age-old question of cause and effect—whether the leader produces, or merely manifests, the basic characteristic of the society—is unimportant. What *is* of importance is that our business leaders, as individuals, are characterized by an assortment of personal goals, all of which are focused on, contingent on, and superseded by the basic objective of achieving more tomorrow than was achieved today.

It really does not matter whether the individual's objectives in life are income, status, power, security, fame, self-satisfaction, or any other conceivable, understandable, and worthwhile human goal. What does matter is the fact that these goals are never finite—there is no satisfactory end point. Today's accomplishments quickly become history—rapidly become the plateau from which tomorrow's gains will be reached. *The psychology of our business leaders is a growth psychology;* the men who succeed to the positions of top management are men who are constantly striving for something more— for themselves and for the organization for which they are responsible.

Such is not the psychology of the typical retail dealer. Unlike corporate management, the individual retail dealer is characterized by a psychology essentially *static* in nature. Again, to understand the kind of thinking and philosophy which characterizes the dealer, we must understand the kind of individual who becomes an independent "owner-operator" retail dealer.

He is *not* the same kind of person that succeeds to the top management of a major corporation. He is a very different kind of person. Within the framework of this difference lies a large part of the fundamental problem.

While the various goals of the top corporate executive can be characterized as constantly evolving and never reaching a satisfactory terminal point, the goals of the typical retail dealer are far more circumscribed. Like the executive, the dealer's goals may also be income, status, power, security, fame, self-satisfaction, or other aims similar in kind to those of his corporate counterpart. However, regardless of the similarity of goals, the critical difference is that in the large majority of instances *there is a relatively easily defined end point to the objectives.* If money is a goal, at some not-too-difficult-to-define level of income this goal becomes satisfactorily achieved. If status is important, owning one's own business, becoming president of the local chamber of commerce, and other similar kinds of accomplishments provide the required satisfactions. If power is a drive of significance, the manipulation of a very few employees can usually satisfy the need. The same is true with other goals I could list here. The dealer's achievements can almost invariably be pegged at a clear and easily defined level of accomplishment. Once that level is reached, the fact that it has been reached provides the necessary degree of satisfaction as years go on.

In essence, then, the key to understanding management's problem of crossed purposes is recognition that the fundamental goals in life of the high-level corporate manager and the typical retail dealer in the distribution system are quite different. The former's goals can be characterized as being essentially dynamic in nature—continuously evolving and emerging; the latter, which are in sharp contrast, can be characterized as being essentially static in nature—reaching a point and leveling off into a continuously satisfying plateau.

CONFUSED LANGUAGES

The differences between the fundamental goals in life of most corporate managers and most retail dealers are only part of the over-all problem. The other part can best be summarized in a rather simple, but disturbing, sentence: *Corporate management tends to talk in a language comprehensible only to itself!*

Actually, this fact reflects a phenomenon which tends to characterize *all* new scientific-disciplines and professions. The field of management has been and is still undergoing the "pangs of professionalization," a process invariably accompanied by the development of a body of terms with meaning primarily (all too often, exclusively) for members of the professional "ingroup."

Misunderstanding the Retailer

As a professional psychologist, I can point to no better (or poorer) example of this phenomenon than that evidenced by psychology itself. Such terms as "ego," "id," "cathexis," "goal gradient behavior," "oral regression," "tension reduction" (regrettably the list is interminable) are meaningful and understandable to psychologists. To others they are relatively incomprehensible and all too often appear to be unnecessary gobbledygook.

While psychologists may be particularly prone to accusations of talking clearly and lucidly to no one but themselves, the same faults can be found in other scientific disciplines. Physicians, mathematicians, chemists, physicists, data-processing experts, and all other professional groups cannot escape the charge of professional lingo. Regardless of what the causes may be for this phenomenon, the simple fact remains that it exists. *Management is no exception.*

The language of modern industry revolves around words like *profit, profit margin, profitability, merchandising, marketing, promoting, quality control, delegation, line-and-staff function,* and all the other "modern" terms of the new science of management. Are these terms clear and meaningful? The answer is very definitely "yes" if we mean: Are they clear and meaningful to members of the management fraternity? However, if we raise the question as to their clarity and meaning for a very large proportion of individual owners of retail businesses, the answer is by no means "yes."

Manufacturers make the assumption that because "owner-operator" retailers are also "businessmen," the latter very quickly understand the words that corporate management uses with regularity. This assumption is no more valid than the assumption that such retailers share the same personal and business goals as does corporate management.

At times the differences in the meanings ascribed to words, or the kinds of words which are used most comfortably, may appear to be trite. In theory they may indeed be trite, but as the specific illustrative examples outlined below will indicate, in actual practice these differences can be critically important.

CONCLUSION

To some degree it is appalling that top-level management is so far out of contact with certain realities of the distribution system. In far too many cases, the retailer is nothing more than a statistic or some sort of depersonalized component of the "channels of distribution." There is no disputing the fact that large numbers of retailers constitute an impressive and essential set of statistics with which management *must* deal. There is no denying that management must *also* operate the total distribution system as effectively as possible. But it is equally true and important for management to recognize that these statistics—this "component of the system"—are made up of individual human beings!

Accomplishment of management's goals depends to a large degree on proper understanding of these human beings. To continue to operate on the implicit assumption that these people share the goals of management and understand the language with which management talks to them is simply wrong. Every bit of evidence with which I have had contact clearly indicates it to be wrong.

At the same time, no suggestion is being made that management should formulate policy solely in terms of what is good for, or meaningful to, the individual dealer. Setting policy for the distribution and marketing of products—like the setting of any other kind of basic corporate policy—requires an intelligent reconciliation of frequently conflicting or competing points of view. However, intelligent policies cannot be set if points of view are unknown or assumed to be something that they are not. If what is clear, worthwhile, and meaningful to corporate management is *not* viewed or understood in similar light by others on whom management depends for the accomplishment of its goals, then these goals cannot and will not be achieved in the most effective manner possible. In short, corporate management has a clear-cut responsibility *to itself* to achieve considerably better understanding of the retailer than exists at the moment.

B. Channel Trends

38. *Retail Innovations Challenge Manufacturers*

GERALD B. TALLMAN and BRUCE BLOMSTROM

This article explores the effect that new forms of retailing have on manufacturers' marketing channel policies. The discount store creates a particular problem for manufacturers who must also depend on the former's rivals for distribution. Tallman and Blomstrom feel that manufacturers have in general not met this challenge in the most economical manner.

In 1965 over 25% of the retail business in many lines of trade will move to consumers through stores which did not carry these products ten years earlier. The present rate of change in store locations, in the scrambling of retail lines, and in the development of new types of retail operations and of new shopping opportunities for consumers is probably as great as in any decade of our country's commercial history.

This relocation and reorientation of retail outlets represent a catching-up of retail institutions with the vast changes that have taken place in consumer living habits, location, and buying power since World War II. These changes have generated a major revolution in the kinds and quantities of goods purchased by consumers, and in the type and location of shopping which is convenient and attractive to them.

For manufacturers, the great growth and shift in retail stores now underway present serious problems in the choice of outlets. Most manufacturers of consumer products practice some degree of selective distribution in order to secure desired qualities in retail presentation of their products and to meet retailer requirements for some pro-

tection against excessive brand competition in the products carried. Through consumer acceptance of the combination of brands which the retailer carries may be a major factor in determining the customer pulling power of a store, few individual manufacturers enjoy strong enough consumer preference for their brands to assure that a high proportion of potential buyers will be deflected from customer-preferred shopping locations. Thus, the manufacturer must place his products in enough of the right kind of stores and locations if he is to achieve desired market goals.

On the other hand, for most products it is important that manufacturers be sufficiently selective in the number and compatibility of outlets used in order to gain retailer support for the brand.

Manufacturers have little problem in adapting their selling efforts to normal changes of ownership and management of stores, or the relocation or increase in numbers of familiar kinds of stores which are accepted as normal competition within the retail community. *But the emergence of a new kind of outlet has always presented a problem of major magnitude, particularly if the outlet is oriented to lower margins and lower retail prices.* This was true with the development of variety chains, of large general-merchandise, mail-order operations, of food chains, and of food supermarkets. The problem has been

• SOURCE: Gerald B. Tallman and Bruce Blomstrom, "Retail Innovations Challenge Manufacturers," *Harvard Business Review*, Vol. 40 (Sept.–Oct., 1962), pp. 130–141. Both, M.I.T. School of Industrial Management.

particularly acute with the development of discount selling of appliances following World War II and the current development of self-service supermarkets in the soft-goods field.

The decisions made will have a major effect on future sales and profits for manufacturers. We suspect that manufacturers' decisions will have considerably less effect on the rate of change in the retail marketplace. The growth and survival of stores in new types of locations with new combinations of product offerings and new balancing of convenience, service, and price appeals will depend more on the response of consumers, and on the skill with which retailers present themselves and adjust to consumer response, than on the choices made by manufacturers.

In this article, we shall document the growth of the discount department store and compare the development of this type of outlet with past innovations in retail institutions. We shall then report on the findings of a research study conducted among soft-goods manufacturers to determine their reactions to the growth of discount outlets. Finally, based on our conclusions from this research, we shall offer suggestions for manufacturer analysis in making decisions as to type of outlet.

DISCOUNT DEPARTMENT STORES

The development of self-service supermarket selling of soft goods (initiated in New England) and of "closed door" discount stores (on the West Coast) was first identifiable in about 1954. It is currently estimated that by the end of 1962 there will be 2,100 to 2,300 of these stores (with those built after 1959 averaging about 70,000 square feet of selling space each), doing an aggregate volume of about $6 billion to $7 billion in retail sales. The early growth and emergence into significance of this new type of retail operation was reported in the September–October 1960 Harvard Business Review.[1]

The growth of this type of retailing has continued; it is clearly the most dynamically changing force in retailing today. Its effect is seen not only in the continued rapid establishment of stores following this new pattern, but also in operational changes being adopted by traditional retailers. Though less readily measurable, it is apparently accompanied by a shrinking of activities for the few remaining general merchandising wholesalers and a loss of sales for small

[1] Gerald B. Tallman and Bruce Blomstrom, "Soft Goods Join the Retail Revolution," p. 133.

stores carrying women's and children's apparel, particularly in low- and medium-quality lines.

The "discount department stores," as they are commonly described, are of two general types:

(1) The closed-door stores allow only "members" access to the store through membership eligibility as defined by rather broad classifications of government employees, teachers, union members, or employees of government contractors. They carry a wide range of soft goods and apparel, but also give major attention to furniture, appliances, food, and automotive supplies. Several of the closed-door operations have recently opened their doors to the general public. Among the better known names under which closed-door stores operate are GEM, GEX, Fedco, and Fed Mart.

(2) The discount department stores, which first developed self-service for soft goods in New England and have subsequently spread across the country on an open-door basis, typically derive substantially more than 50% of their sales from apparel items. They use supermarket-type self-service, shopping carts, and central checkout for all but a few departments. The income class to which their merchandising appears to be directed is somewhat lower than for the closed-door stores.

Low operating margins achieved through volume sales and limited service expenditures for clerks, delivery, credit, and so on have allowed prices which average about 15% below those of the department stores and specialty shops with which discount stores compete in the sale of soft goods. Full-size food supermarkets are being established within many of the new large discount stores. Because of consumers' long experience in comparing food values between stores and because of the frequency of food store visits by the average family, these food departments are attractive to the soft-goods stores as traffic builders, and are frequently operated with planned narrow margins (or even planned losses) to maximize their drawing power.

The closed-door stores depend primarily on word of mouth and on mail promotion to their members to publicize the attractive values offered. The open-door discounters, however, make extensive use of local advertising media to give maximum publicity to the low prices and special values which they offer. Because their low prices are more apparent to both consumers and competing retailers, the open-door stores represent a thornier problem for manufacturers faced with the decision of whether or not to sell through these new type stores in competition with established dealers. The problem is especially acute in the case of well-known brands.

PAST INNOVATIONS

Retail innovations of importance comparable to that now found in the discount department stores have been the development from 1870 to 1890 of the early forms of the now "traditional" department stores, of general merchandise mail-order selling, (1890–1910), of the variety and food chain stores (1910–1930), and of the food supermarkets after 1930.

Each of these major retail innovations, when first developed, offered consumers lower prices than were generally available through previously existing retail outlets. Each, with time, has traded up the quality of its service, and with this its operating expenses and margins. This has been particularly true of department stores with the development over the years of more elaborate services and a greater emphasis on style merchandise.

Each innovation, however, offered the consumer something new besides lower prices:

• The department store offered a broader selection of kinds of merchandise under a single roof, the convenience and assurance of a fixed price, and the grouping of like goods into departments for more effective merchandising.

• The mail-order houses offered, particularly to rural patrons, a wider selection of merchandise than was available from local stores.

• Chains, particularly in the variety and apparel fields, brought the consumer a standardization of merchandise and a faster availability of new developments and styles from market centers.

• The supermarkets brought all kinds of food products into a single store, thus eliminating the necessity of visiting several specialty food stores in order to complete a shopping list, and, perhaps most important, introduced the consumer to the convenience and pleasures of self-service shopping.

The self-service soft-goods supermarkets, which are currently the most rapidly growing segment of retailing, have offered to consumers significantly lower prices for standard (not deluxe) quality merchandise. They have also adapted to the marketing of soft goods features which consumers have tried and liked in the food field namely, convenient access by automobile, ample parking, evening shopping hours, and the opportunity for browsing or buying at a pace determined by the customer rather than by the availability or attitude of clerks. One sees far more family groups shopping in these discount department stores than is typical of the department stores and the specialty shops with which they primarily compete.

In each period of innovation, established retailers have failed to realize that the new type of store was finding consumer acceptance on other than a price basis. This characteristic failure to comprehend the reasons for favorable consumer response has slowed the adjustment on the part of existing merchants to meeting the new competition, and has allowed the new institutions to secure a firm foothold.

At present, many consumers appear to like the shopping freedom provided by the soft-goods self-service outlets just about as much as they like the low prices. A dramatic confirmation of the appeal of self-service is developing in Dayton, Ohio, where a department store branch operation offers main-store quality and prices on a self-service basis. Volume is reported to be very satisfactory—although results are uneven as between types of merchandise.

The expansion of discount department store sales is proceeding at a pace unequalled by other major retail innovations during the period of their own most rapid expansion.

It seems unreasonable to expect that the growth of self-service supermarkets in the soft-goods field can continue to expand as equivalent operations in the food field have done during the second and third decades of their development. In the food field the total volume is substantially larger, and products are to a much greater extent standardized. By contrast, in apparel and soft goods, greater diversity of product, ever-changing fashions, the need for counseling, fitting, and other personal services, and higher average unit product price all suggest that there is much greater opportunity for continuance of service operations and for specialty store operators offering products of better or more distinctive style and faster styling turnover (at higher prices) than are feasible in large-scale, low-margin operations.

RETAILER RESPONSE

The past century has seen several dramatic innovations in retail operations which have had an impact on manufacturers and have raised the necessity for difficult choices in the selection of outlets. Each major innovation in retailing has threatened the existence or continued growth of some established retailers. A characteristic response to the threat has been for established retailers to use whatever dissuasive power was available to limit manufacturers' sales to the upstart operation. The threat and the reaction have been strongest when the retail innovation has allowed retail margins below those at which established retailers felt they could profitably survive. For example:

• The trade response to chain stores illustrates the conflict which low-cost innovation generates. The rise of chain stores was accompanied by shrunken volumes or the actual demise of thousands of independent retailers. Wholesalers and retailers had no doubt that the competition of the chain stores was the principal cause of their difficulties.

And so pressures were brought to bear against chain stores. Many suppliers were forced to boycott chain stores in order to retain independent stores as customers; national brands available to chain as well as independent stores were partially displaced by wholesaler brands, or by manufacturers' brands available only to "legitimate" dealers. Particularly in the smaller towns and cities, families whose economic welfare depended on the good will of their neighbors were pressured to stay away from the chain stores. Even the force of government was brought to bear when, under the prodding of independent retailers and wholesalers, anti-chain store legislation was passed by a majority of the state legislatures.

Licensing ordinances were instituted, differential taxation of multiunit retail operations was adopted, and fair trade (price maintenance) and loss leaders (unfair sales practices) laws were enacted to reduce the chain stores' advantages. At the national level the Robinson–Patman Act restricting the price differentials that manufacturers could offer to various classes of competing customers went through Congress as an "anti-chainstore bill."

• Another example, not quite so vivid, was the reaction to aggressive mail-order retailing. Though the effect of mail-order houses was more diffuse than the more immediate competition which the chain store offered to individual competitors, the retailing community brought significant pressure to bear against manufacturers who sought to serve *both* retail stores and mail-order houses. Furthermore, in many towns the municipal employees, teachers, preachers, and local bankers were led to understand that the

receipt of parcels from mail-order houses could be a source of embarrassment to them.

• The early supermarkets faced attempts to limit their store hours and their access to advertising media and to products. Eventually the entry of established chains into this field turned competitive efforts toward enulation rather than obstruction.

Understandably, the full history of pressures exerted on manufacturers by established retailers and wholesalers is not adequately recorded. In view of recent occurrences, however, it is not difficult to imagine that in their early years even the department stores felt pressure on their suppliers from the then-established wholesalers and retailers who feared the new type of competition that they represented.

MANUFACTURERS/RETAILERS

The development of new retail institutions, and the consistent reaction of consumers to them, have affected the nature of manufacturer-retailer relations. Traditionally, the manufacturer has taken the lead in getting products designed, manufactured, distributed, and sold across retail counters. He has usually acted as "captain" of the marketing team and as such has determined the product, its price, and the method of distribution. He has solicited the cooperation of subsequent members of the distribution chain to get these products into the hands of consumers.

By contrast, two retailing institutions—i.e., mail-order houses and, to a lesser extent, chain stores—have frequently taken this leadership role away from the manufacturer. In these instances they have expected of the manufacturer only efficient production of the goods which they (as captains, subject always to confirmation by consumer purchase action) would sell. Under these conditions the retailer, rather than the manufacturer, held the "consumer franchise" and was in a position to draw down most of the profit from successful product design and promotion.

The contest between manufacturers and large retailers for the dominant role in the marketing sequence becomes more intense as retailer buying power is increasingly concentrated in large organizations. The manufacturer's chances of retaining his traditional role and independence of action are greatly enhanced if he has a brand which consumers will prefer to buy by name and if he has the support of outlets that will provide favorable retail representation to his brand. It is concern over losing this support, as well as the loss of specific orders, that has made manufacturers sensitive to the complaints of established retailers whose sales are threatened by new types of retail operations.

MANUFACTURERS' REACTIONS

Manufacturers of convenience goods (food products, housewares, drugs and cosmetics, notions, and so on) and others who have generally practiced extensive, rather than selective, distribution have had few qualms about making their products available through the new discount department stores, although some brand-name manufacturers have insisted that their regular retail prices be maintained. The discount stores have also found appliance dealerships generally available. In the soft-goods field, however, many manufacturers, particularly those with branded lines, have refused to sell their products to the self-service supermarkets.

In the summer of 1961, we interviewed 78 major companies manufacturing products typically sold in the soft-goods departments of discount department stores (men's, women's, and children's apparel and domestics). About one half of the firms interviewed have brands with some degree of national advertising support. In conducting the interviews, we investigated both manufacturers' selling policies toward discount department stores and the ways in which manufacturers' operations have been affected (either voluntarily or involuntarily) by the burgeoning importance of the discount outlets. The key results of these interviews are discussed here.

Selling Policies and Sales

Of the firms interviewed, 61 reported that they offer some or all of their products to discount stores, while 17 stated that they were not then selling to discount stores. Table 1 indicates the general selling policies of these manufacturers classified as to whether or not the firms have some type of consumer-advertised brand.

A truly representative sampling of soft-goods manufacturers would presumably report a higher proportion of small firms which do no consumer advertising and sell freely to discounters. In a few instances manufacturers who claim not to sell to discounters find their goods being transshipped by traditional customers.

Soft-goods manufacturers, who have in the past carefully franchised their products to avoid undue competition among their customers and to secure maximum retail merchandising support, have generally refused to sell identical merchandise to discount operations. Only one of the manufacturers with an advertised brand makes all of his products available to discount stores. That manufacturer reports a very encouraging sales trend.

A number of the firms (48 of 61) that sell to discounters were willing to indicate the *share of their business* going to such customers. Of this number, 8 report that about 50% of their sales are to discounters; 14 report 20%; 15 report 5% to 15%; and 11 state that less than 5%

Table 1. **Selling Policies of Soft-Goods Manufacturers**

	Manufacturers who sell to discounters		Manufacturers who refuse to sell to discounters	Total
	Without limitation	With limitation*		
Manufacturers with consumer-advertised brands	1	22	13	36
Manufacturers without consumer-advertised brands	6	32	4	42
Total manufacturers interviewed	7	54	17	78

* Limitations include area restrictions, product disguise through changing or removing labels or changing style or fashion, selling a different price line, or changing the quality of goods sold.

SOURCE: Authors' survey date.

goes to discounters. Manufacturers report that both the size of individual orders and the frequency of reorders is substantially greater from self-service stores than from the average or traditional customers. For many manufacturers, sales to discount stores result in an increased concentration of business among a few customers. In the contest for dominance this is a source of worry.

Subject to Pressures

Whether or not they sell freely to discounters, most manufacturers report serious concern over the conflicting interest of their older customers, on the one hand, and the low-margin, low-price discounter, on the other.

About 75% of the manufacturers (45 of the 61) who reported selling to discounters say that at the time they began such selling they were subjected to pressure from established customers to discontinue the practice. Of these, 32 report that they suffered a temporary loss of volume; but they note a tendency for their old retail customers to renew the purchase of attractive merchandise once it has been clearly established that withholding purchases will not be effective in keeping the manufacturer's products out of the hands of discounters. Without exception, these 32 firms reported total volume to be at least as big as it was before they began selling to discounters, and most reported it to have grown.

None of the manufacturers interviewed would admit to an over-all reduction in sales; but the most enthusiastic claims of sales growth were made by firms that sell to the new self-service retailers. All of the firms presently selling to discounters expect this part of their business to grow in importance.

Reducing Conflict

A majority of the firms interviewed seek to restrict the effects of competition between discounters and their traditional customers by limiting the geographical areas in which they sell to discounters or by making some modification in products.

One pattern has been that of selling to discounters in areas like New England, the West Coast, and parts of the Middle West, where discounters already account for too large a part of the soft-goods volume to be ignored, while refusing to sell to discounters in other parts of the country, such as the South, where the development of self-service operations in soft goods has been relatively slow.

Another way of avoiding the conflict has been to sell to discounters only in areas where the manufacturer has had little or no prior representation. Area restrictions are becoming less manageable because the discount stores are so often parts of chains which are rapidly expanding into new territories. This makes selective distribution more difficult than when dealing with individual department or specialty stores. Chain operators of discount stores, or leased departments with outlets in several parts of the country, are increasingly unwilling to carry product lines on a restricted area basis.

Nearly three-fourths of the manufacturers who do sell to discounters report that, by one means or another, they differentiate the product made available to discounters from that sold to retailers following traditional markup policies. About half of these manufacturers state that they merely change the labels on their products. Since in soft goods so few brands have any meaningful degree of consumer recognition or preference, the mere change of label is not likely to affect consumer evaluation of the goods offered. The other half introduce some variation in style, fabric, or packaging when selling to discounters. In this process, some firms reduce the quality level from that sold to traditional outlets, but most state that they modify characteristics without changing quality level. Three report selling higher quality to discounters than to traditional customers.

Buying Relations

We find little evidence that discount-store buyers have yet abused the power which they may have by virtue of the fact that they represent a large part of manufacturers' total output, but the possibility is always there. Faced with rapidly expanding consumer patronage, on the one hand, and a degree of manufacturer reluctance, on the other, the discount-store buyers are considered by manufacturers to have been very "reasonable" customers. A common statement from manufacturers interviewed is that "discounters pay top dollar for merchandise and are less demanding than department stores in their bargaining relationships." Manufacturers say that the buyers for discount stores operate under less tightly organized merchandise control systems, are less frequently handcuffed by "open-to-buy" controls from store management, and are generally more flexible in dealing with the manufacturer. An interesting sidelight of the interviews is the reflection of a deep-seated antagonism against what are considered to be the arbitrary and high-handed buying practices of department stores.

There is, however, some evidence that the discount-store buyers are beginning to flex their muscles as buyers. We think the time may not be far off when discount-store buyers will become as unreasonable and hard to live with as "normal" customers.

Moreover, we believe the time is also coming when manufacturers who have refused to sell to discounters at a time when discounters were more or less humbly seeking sources of supply may well face some reverse discrimination. Some discounters, well entrenched with consumers and with acceptable sources of supply, are beginning to put into force their often stated intention to favor vendors who have supported them in their time of need and to refuse belated offers of previously unavailable brands. This may be particularly hurtful to the manufacturer whose brand has relatively little drawing power with consumers. However, we think it unlikely that discounters will allow old antagonisms to stand in the way of handling merchandise which can be bought under acceptable terms and which will have ready acceptance by consumers.

Effect on Operations

About half of the manufacturers state that they have had no major problems in servicing discount stores. Those who do have problems point most frequently to the fact that discounters seem to "want their goods yesterday." The heavy initial orders and frequent reorders, sometimes closer to the season than the manufacturers have been accustomed to, make the delivery of goods a major problem. More specifically, manufacturers report on the effect of discounters on inventory, costs, and sales-service:

• *Inventory*—One fourth of the manufacturers state that discounters have caused them additional storage problems, principally because of the duplication of lines to avoid identity with traditional customers. On the other hand, two manufacturers point out that they actually carry less inventory for discounters than for their regular customers because the discounters buy fewer different items.

• *Costs*—Only one fourth of the manufacturers interviewed mention that their costs have changed because of discounters, and these are evenly divided among those who claim cost increases and those whose costs have declined. Increased volume is the principal reason for a fall in costs. Changes in packaging and labeling, mainly to disguise the product, are the major causes of cost increases.

• *Sales Organization*—Barely 25% of the manufacturers note that they have made any changes in their sales organization as a result of discounters, but another 17% are considering one. Most changes were through the addition of personnel rather than a basic shift in the method of handling discounters.

Two manufacturers, both reporting dramatic sales increases, have begun to service the stock in discount stores, including taking inventory, writing the order, and setting up displays. Their sales to discount department stores are now about 50% of their total volume. Both expect their future growth to come primarily from the discount trade, while one states that the volume of business done by these stores is so great that what he is able to deliver to them every three to four weeks is actually sold within a period of one week. Three other manufacturers service the stock of discounters, but also have done so with their older customers; they report the same magnitude of sales success to discounters. All five of these manufacturers sell popular price merchandise, four of them having staple lines like men's or women's undergarments or hose.

One manufacturer who provides in-store servicing for all major customers and whose business with discounters now amounts to $15 million per year finds that such a complete merchandising program results in discounters buying primarily from one source, rather than from the large number of different suppliers typical for department stores. Moreover, he has been able to set up a plan for upgrading the stock carried in discount department stores and has just added, to his surprise, goods which sell at the fourth price level above those he originally sold to discounters. We believe that the success which these manufacturers have achieved through the adaptation of old and new selling practices to the discount department store trade is evidence of the potential which exists in this field.

Determining Policy

Whatever have been the manufacturers' decisions to date—to sell freely to discounters, to sell selected products only, or to refuse entirely —the decisions seem to have been made on an expediential basis with little systematic analysis of the long-run potential for low-margin, self-service soft-goods retailing. Though the application of supermarket methods in soft goods has been growing spectacularly for almost a decade, most manufacturers have remained uncertain as to its long-run future and how to adjust their own sales and operating policies.

The absence of orderly analysis is due in part to the division of the soft-goods manufacturing industry into a large number of relatively small firms whose success has depended more on their ability to keep abreast of style changes and to sell on a personal contact basis than on their ability to plan and develop long-range market representation. In neglecting long-range distribution analysis, the soft-goods manufacturers have not been alone. In marketing research, both academic and business attention has been focused more on problems of product innovation, promotion, and price response than on the adjustments in distribution required to accommodate changes in consumer income, living patterns, and shopping preferences.

The interrelated commitments and "choosing up of sides" implied in a manufacturer's choice of type of retail representation (particularly when selective distribution is used) make it impractical for either manufacturers or retailers to adjust channels of distribution as frequently as is common with promotional methods, product design, or price. This infrequency of opportunity for change carries with it the implication of longer range effects from major adjustments when they *are* made. Major retail innovations such as the development of mail-order houses, variety chains, food chains, food supermarkets, and soft-goods supermarkets have appeared infrequently; but when they do occur, the effect can be devastating on the distributors or manufacturers who do not accommodate their operations to the innovation.

Framework for Analysis

Even the fastest growing of these major retail innovations has taken a period of several years to achieve market significance. The dynamic growth of self-service supermarkets in soft goods has been available for observation over an eight-year period. Thus, there is more opportunity for an orderly analysis of future distribution prospects than there is, for example, for an analysis of changes in product fashions or promotion appeals.

Yet only one of the manufacturers interviewed appears to have made a through analysis of ways best to adapt its operational methods, products, price lines, packaging, inventory, and delivery system in order to serve the special requirements of large-volume self-service stores and to minimize the cost of mixing the product from factory to consumers via these institutions.

Our direct contact with manufacturers in the soft-goods field, supplemented by numerous conversations with discounters themselves and with trade editors in the field, leads to the conclusion that both those manufacturers who are actually jumping on the discount-outlet bandwagon and those who are standing to one side are following the dangerous course of *making expediential decisions based on current surface indications without probing into the long-range soundness of the new operations.*

Major retail innovations involve an "invention" of new means of performing the retailing function. They may be dependent on concomitant developments in products, in physical handling technology, and in organization at the wholesale supply level; but, *most important of all, they are dependent on changes in the income, location, and style of life of consumers.* Thus, it is important to make a detailed analysis of consumer action patterns and of the vulnerability/survival prospects of established outlets. Here are some specific suggestions:

(1) *Test against consumer buying patterns*—A manufacturer seeking to appraise the potential significance of a new form of retailing should first probe its appropriateness from the consumer viewpoint. Is the new innovation compatible with developments in consumer income, location, and living patterns as these may affect shopping patterns? Early in the development of self-service for soft goods, such inquiry might have indicated, for example, that:

• A large portion of the population, formerly at a low income level and with relatively little available discretion in both the kind of goods purchased or the place of purchase, had achieved a new freedom.
• These newly prosperous consumers were being poorly served by the small specialty shops in low income areas, and they had developed little affinity for department stores oriented to the already established middle- and upper-class consumers.
• Suburban locations, easy automobile access, ample parking, and long store hours would prove convenient for large numbers of consumers increasingly oriented to the automobile as a mode

of transportation, and frustrated by the crowding of downtown shopping areas.

• Consumer acceptance of self-service in food products represented a positive preference for self-service and not merely a desire for the lower prices associated with elimination of the costs of clerk "service."

Such a study might also consider the increasing physical and social mobility within our population. A useful portrayal of this mobility was given a decade ago in a series of articles by William H. Whyte.[2] This mobility may have an influence on loyalty to familiar retail establishments and on the willingness to sample the wares and methods of new kinds of stores.

(2) *Study the customers of pioneer stores*— There appears to have been remarkably little study of the types of consumers buying in discount department stores, the development of repeat-purchasing, interstore shopping, or the extent to which individual families take advantage of the wide range of products available in these stores.

There has also been little study of the aspects of these new stores which have positive pulling power to bring in consumers versus those aspects which customers merely tolerate in their search for bargins. Both manufacturers and retailers have a real stake in learning more about the consumers who patronize the new stores, where they previously bought similar products, and the share of total buying which consumers appear willing to do in these stores after they have had some experience with them. Only one of the 78 manufacturers interviewed is undertaking a direct study of consumer shopping as affected by self-service soft-goods supermarkets.

(3) *Study areas of highest saturation*—It is of greatest importance to manufacturers, to store operators, and to the financial community to identify more accurately the point at which the building of new discount department stores will saturate the market for this type of operation. In many areas in Southern New England, self-service soft-goods supermarkets are thickly enough established to make possible some measurement of the saturation point. Detailed analysis of sales trends in individual product lines and of the level at which long-exposed customers stabilize the share of their patronage given to the new type stores could provide useful information long before information on saturation becomes apparent in total store sales experience. Springfield, Massachusetts, and Lowell, Massachusetts, would be good locations for such saturation studies inasmuch as each has had a heavy concentration of stores for several years.

(4) *Appraise the survival potential of customers* —The growth of discount department stores has occurred during a period when consumer income and buying have been increasing in total. However, since 1958 or 1959, the annual increase in sales of the new-type stores has exceeded the average rate of total market growth ($1.0 to $1.25 billion a year) for the "general merchandise" and "apparel" classifications of stores. As a result of this transfer of volume, some older stores will go out of business and others will fail to achieve planned growth. Some of the traditional outlets will stagnate. Others will redirect their operations in order to serve some selected part of the market less directly affected by self-service competition. Still others will find some means of adaptation to offer consumers many of the advantages which they have recognized in the new self-service soft-goods stores. It appears reasonable to say that most of the volume of almost any manufacturer in the soft-goods field (except those in the very high-style and high-price lines) will move through stores whose operations are materially affected by this major retail innovation.

Few soft-goods manufacturers have made an orderly analysis to identify that share of their total business which is going through established retailers who are subject to direct competitive inroads from low-margin, self-service operations compared with those retailers who by virtue of operating methods or location are relatively insulated from such competition.

Obviously, much of the information necessary for the above kinds of analysis cannot be developed feasibly by individual firms. However, some of it exists from government-developed and/or industry-developed research. And for most manufacturers analysis of their own situations in the context of generally available information will yield bases for judgments far more sound than those presently employed.

Conclusion

The original self-service soft-goods supermarkets established in New England from five to eight years ago, located in an existing warehouse or mill building and frequently some distance from major traffic arteries and established shopping centers, were highly successful, but they represented a pattern from which the constructive evolution which has occurred could have

[2] *Fortune*, May, June, July, and August, 1953.

been expected. The majority of new stores of-fering soft goods on a low-margin, self-service basis have been substantially upgraded from the original prototypes in terms of store buildings and facilities, convenience and prominence of location, quality and completeness of merchan-dise offerings, and supporting services offered. A modest increase in expenses, margins, and prices has been associated with this upgrading, but there still exists a substantial—10% to 20% —gap between the prices offered in these self-service stores and those of the traditional retail-ers with which they principally compete.

Along with the improvement of store charac-teristics, locations, and merchandise, there has been an upgrading in the type of customer drawn into the store. The early stores were planned to appeal mainly to the working-class family. More recently, the self-service operations in soft goods have become established in, or adjacent to, first-class shopping centers in higher income suburbs.

We think that the evolutionary process within the self-service selling of soft goods, housewares and related items will continue. Additions to store services and merchandise (automobile care centers for tires, realignment, lubrication, etc. would be an example) may increase substantially the sales level at which general-merchandise, self-service stores will saturate a community.

Until now, these stores have been located primarily in the Pacific Coast, Southwest, North Central, Northwest, and Middle Atlantic sec-tions. From the success achieved in these areas, there would appear to be substantial opportu-nity for hundreds of new stores in other parts of the country. Development has also been largely in major metropolitan areas. It is rea-sonable to expect that some further development of self-service, general-merchandise operations will be found in the smaller towns and cities throughout the country.

We believe that the intrusion of low-margin, self-service retailing (other than in foods) has to date accomplished considerably less than half of its eventual growth. In the light of our research into manufacturer decision making thus far in this dynamic field, we would conclude that there is little assurance that the right decisions are being made with regard to product, price, promo-tion, and type of distribution outlet. Much fundamental information, as well as sophisti-cated analysis, has been lacking. Most neglected by manufacturers has been investigation of trends in the income, location, and style of life of consumers. How well do their present out-lets fit changing distribution patterns?

By the past record of one new major retail innovation every decade or so, the next "retailing revolution" may already be in incubation. Will manufacturers and existing retailers be ready to appraise its potential? If past records fore-shadow the future, the established firms will again allow a group of brash new innovators to sweep past them and to capitalize on the new approach.

39. The Emergence and Growth of Contractually Integrated Channels in the American Economy

BERT C. McCAMMON, JR.* and ALBERT D. BATES

This paper focuses on the development of contractual methods of achieving economies of scale and market power by marketing institutions. Three types of contractually integrated groups—voluntary groups, cooperative groups, and franchise programs—have been growing at rapid rates for the past 15 years. In some industries, these networks have become dominant.

INTRODUCTION

Marketing channels have been traditionally viewed as fragmented, potentially unstable, networks, in which vertically aligned firms bargain with each other at arm's length, terminate relationships with impunity, and otherwise behave autonomously. McVey, for example, argues that channels are a series of vertical markets,[1] rather than operating systems *per se*, and several economists, including Stigler and Coase, regard channel behavior as an extension of the theory of the firm.[2] These, and similar, constructs can be used effectively to explain the rationale of conventional marketing channels, which consist of relatively small and autonomous units. Unfortunately, they do not provide an adequate basis for analyzing the economies that can be achieved through vertical coordination of marketing activities.

Recent changes in the structure of distribution suggest that centrally coordinated systems are gradually displacing conventional marketing channels as the dominant distribution mechanism in the American economy. Furthermore, competition, to an increasing extent, involves rivalry between systems, as well as between the individual units that comprise them. Thus, centrally coordinated systems have emerged as a basic component of the competitive process.

There are at least three types of centrally coordinated systems—corporate, administered, and contractual—that compete for differential advantage in the marketplace. This paper is concerned, to some extent, with all three types of systems, but it focuses on the emergence and growth of contractual networks, with particular emphasis on the recent expansion of franchise programs and voluntary and cooperative groups. Consequently, the paragraphs that follow are selective rather than comprehensive in their coverage, and descriptive, rather than theoretical, in their content.

CORPORATE, CONTRACTUAL, AND ADMINISTERED SYSTEMS

Corporate marketing systems, which combine successive stages of production and distribution under a single ownership, have existed for an extended period of time, but their importance has risen in recent years as a result of mergers

• SOURCE: Bert C. McCammon Jr. and Albert D. Bates, "The Emergence and Growth of Contractually Integrated Channels in the American Economy," in P. D. Bennett (editor), *Economic Growth, Competition and World Markets* (Chicago: American Marketing Association, 1965), pp. 496–515. The research on which this paper is based was sponsored by the Marketing Science Institute.
* Associate Professor of Marketing, Indiana University.
[1] Philip McVey, "Are Channels of Distribution What the Textbooks Say?" *Journal of Marketing*, January, 1960, p. 61–65.
[2] See George J. Stigler, "The Division of Labor is Limited by the Extent of the Market," *Journal of Political Economy*, June, 1951, 11. 185–193; and R. H. Coase, "The Nature of the Firm" *Economica*, New Series, November, 1937, pp. 386–405.

and internal expansion. The Federal Trade Commission, for example, recently concluded that 22.5 per cent of the mergers and acquisitions consummated between 1949 and 1954 involved forward or backward integration.[3] Furthermore, many of the corporations, emerging from these consolidations, now operate manufacturing facilities, warehousing points, and retail outlets. Thus, they have combined the principal stages of production and distribution under a single ownership, which results in coordinated and concerted marketing activity. Sherwin-Williams, for example, operates over 2,000 paint stores, Hart Schaffner and Marx, a long established manufacturer in the men's wear field, owns over 100 clothing outlets; Sears has an ownership equity in production facilities that supply over 30 per cent of the company's inventory requirements; and large food chains obtain almost 10 per cent of their requirements from captive manufacturing facilities, many of which were acquired in the 1950's.[4]

Large corporations have also created relatively self-sufficient marketing systems through internal expansion, and this trend is particularly noticeable at the wholesale level. The authors analyzed the relative importance of primary channels in 72 industries for the 1939–1958 period. In 56 of these industries, a higher proportion of total output was distributed through manufacturer's sales branches and offices in 1958 than in 1939.[5] These facilities are frequently a partial or complete substitute for independent middlemen; thus the growing importance of manufacturer's sales branches and offices suggests that considerable vertical integration has taken place at the wholesale level since World War II. In summary, corporate vertical integration can be used as a device to coordinate marketing activities, and available data, though fragmentary, suggest that *corporate systems*, arising through mergers or internal expansion, have become more important in the American economy during recent years.

Administrative strategies, as opposed to ownership, can also be used to coordinate the flow of goods and services and thereby achieve systemic economies.[6] Individual enterprises, by exerting leadership, can often influence or otherwise control the behavior of adjacent firms within the channel, as a result, vertically aligned companies work closely with each other to achieve transportation, warehousing, data processing, and advertising economies, which reduce "total" costs within the system. Numerous manufacturing firms have historically relied on administrative expertise to coordinate reseller marketing efforts. Suppliers with dominant brands usually experience the least difficulty in securing strong trade support, but many manufacturers with "fringe" items have been able to elicit reseller cooperation through the use of liberal distribution policies, which take the form of attractive discounts (or discount substitutes), financial assistance, and various types of concessions that protect resellers from one or more of the risks of doing business.[7] Consequently, administrative strategies, of both a formal and informal nature, can be, and have been, used to reduce friction within channels and produce coordinated marketing effort. When these conditions prevail, the resulting channel may be designated as an *administered system*.

Finally, and most significantly, channel coordination can be effected through the use of contractual agreements. That is, independent firms at different levels can coordinate their activities on a contractual basis to obtain systemic economies and market impact that could not be achieved through individual action. *Contractual systems* have grown more rapidly in recent years than their corporate or administered counterparts, and this development, in retrospect, may be one of the most significant trends to emerge during the 1950–1965 period.

Contractual integration is an unusually flexible economic device, and thus there are a variety of possible affiliations from which individual firms may choose. Despite this diversity, the principal types of contractual systems can be classified as follows:

---

[3] *Report on Corporate Mergers and Acquisitions*, Federal Trade Commission, Washington, D.C., 1955, p. 7.

[4] For a brief, but useful discussion of vertical integration in marketing, "Vertical Integration," *Business Management*, January, 1965, pp. 47–49 and 78.

[5] Authors' calculations based on *Distribution of Manufacturers' Sales By Class of Customer*, 1939 and 1958, Census of Manufacturers, U.S. Department of Commerce, Washington, D.C.

[6] For an excellent discussion of administered marketing systems, see Valentine F. Ridgeway, "Administration of Manufacturer-Dealer Systems," *Administrative Science Quarterly*, March, 1957, pp. 464–467.

[7] For a more extended treatment of this subject, see Bert C. McCammon, Jr., "The Role of Distribution Policies in the Manufacturer's Promotional Mix," *Proceedings of the First Sales Promotion Management Seminar*, Association of National Advertisers, New York, 1965.

Contractual Sytems Involving
Backward Integration

Retail cooperative groups
Retail and wholesale buying groups
Retail promotional groups
Non-profit shipping associations (sponsored by consignees)
Retail resident buying offices (particularly those operated on a programmed basis or owned cooperatively)
Industrial, wholesale, and retail procurement contracts
Producer buying cooperatives

Contractual Sytems Involving
Forward Integration

Retail voluntary groups
Retail programmed groups
Retail franchise programs for individual brands and specific departments
Retail franchise programs covering all phases of licensee operations
Non-profit shipping associations (operated by shippers)
Leased department arrangements (particularly those involving subsidiaries of manufacturing and wholesaling enterprises)
Producer marketing cooperatives

These systems, as suggested above, differ in a variety of respects, but all represent attempts on the part of affiliated firms to achieve the efficiencies required in competitive markets, without totally sacrificing enterprise identity and autonomy.

REASONS UNDERLYING THE GROWTH OF CENTRALLY COORDINATED MARKETING SYSTEMS

Corporate, administered, and contractual marketing systems have grown in relative importance during recent years, and their development has been particularly rapid since World War II. In fact, these systems are becoming a principal element in the competitive process, and they are gradually displacing conventional marketing channels as the dominant distribution mechanism in the American economy. The growth of centrally coordinated systems can be attributed to several factors, although cause and effect relationships are predictably difficult to identify and measure.

Increased Capital Requirements and Higher Fixed Costs

The capital required to implement competitive manufacturing and marketing programs rose continuously between 1948 and 1965. Fixed costs, particularly those connected with the use of capital, increased, too. As a result, a growing number of firms were confronted by constantly rising break-even points, which forced them to maintain sales at unusually high levels in order to obtain adequate rates of return on investment. The need for assured volume encouraged the growth of centrally coordinated systems in which individual units can predict and/or control the behavior of others.[8]

The increases that occurred in capital requirements between 1948 and 1965 were impressive, indeed. Average investment per manufacturing employee, for example, rose from $8,089 in 1949 to $18,227 in 1960,[9] and comparable gains occurred in wholesaling and retailing, e.g., construction outlays for new supermarkets rose from $285,200 per unit in 1959 to $388,200 in 1964—a gain of 36.1 per cent—and average construction costs for new variety stores climbed from $238,800 to $341,300—an increase of 43.3 per cent—during the same period.[10] These illustrations tend to support Schultze's contention that capital related costs rose more rapidly than any other expense category following World War II. More specifically, he estimates that capital consumption allowances per unit of output increased by 112 per cent between 1947 and 1957.[11] Furthermore, he notes that other fixed costs, particularly those incurred to compensate "overhead" personnel, increased rapidly, too.[12] In short, the trend towards more capital-intensive operations has raised break-even points and created a need to maintain volume at unprecedented levels, which has encouraged the formation of centrally coordinated marketing systems.

Declining Profit Margins and Rates of Return on Investment

Internal Revenue Service data indicate that manufacturing, wholesaling, and retailing cor-

---

[8] For an extended and early treatment of this subject, see Oswald Knauth, *Business Practices, Trade Position, and Competition*, Columbia University Press, New York, 1956.
[9] *The Economic Almanac* 1964, National Industrial Conference Board, New York, p. 244.
[10] Authors' calculations and "Annual Survey of Construction and Modernization Expenditures," *Chain Store Age* (1959–1964 Editions).
[11] Charles L. Schultze, *Prices, Costs and Output for the Post War Decade: 1947–1957*, Committee for Economic Development, New York, 1960, p. 53.
[12] *Ibid*, p. 57.

porations experienced significant declines in operating profit margins and rates of return on investment between 1950 and 1962. For manufacturing corporations, net profits (after taxes) on net sales declined from 6.16 per cent in 1950 to 3.09 per cent in 1962, and net profits (after taxes) on tangible net worth decreased from 13.54 to 6.49 per cent during the same period. Operating profit margins (after taxes) for wholesaling corporations sagged from 2.17 to 1.05 per cent between 1950 and 1962, and their composite rate of return on tangible net worth declined from 13.06 to 6.67 per cent over the same interval. Finally, net profits (after taxes) as a per cent of sales for retailing corporations decreased from 2.84 to 1.11 per cent during the 1950–1962 period, and net profits (after taxes) on tangible net worth fell precipitously, too—declining from 11.82 to 5.83 per cent during the thirteen years in question.[13] These declines in relative profitability were the result of growing competition—of both a conventional and innovative nature—and rising costs. New approaches were clearly required to ameliorate these pressures, and thus a growing number of firms attempted to achieve economies and market impact through vertical affiliations and mergers.

Growing Complexity of Marketing Processes

Coordinating the flow of goods and services became increasingly more complicated between 1948 and 1965 due to the expansion in number of items, the increased emphasis placed on fashion merchandising, and the advances in management technology which occurred during this period. The number of items carried in a typical supermarket, for example, rose from 3,705 in 1950 to over 6,800 in 1963,[14] and variety stores, between 1956 and 1961 increased the number of housewares items stocked by 75 per cent; notions by 50 per cent; apparel by 40 per cent; drugs, toiletries, and stationery by 25 per cent; and confectionaries, cosmetics, and yardgoods, by 20 per cent.[15] Furthermore, a substantial number of merchandise categories, traditionally dominated by staple items, were

revitalized through the use of fashion programs, with children's ready-to-wear, domestics, and housewares being conspicuous examples of this development. Finally, significant advances were made in management technology and accompanying data processing systems. A variety of distribution cost accounting methods—including SOSCA, Merchandise Management Accounting, Production Unit Accounting, and others—were introduced between 1950 and 1965, mathematical models for inventory control and supporting computer programs, such as IBM's IMPACT System, were developed, too; and several relatively sophisticated decision criteria enjoyed widespread use. As a result of these factors, marketing in general, and retailing in particular, became increasingly more complex, and many enterprises were literally forced to merge or affiliate with large systems to obtain the specialized assistance and other services needed to compete in complex markets.

Potential Economies in Centrally Coordinated Marketing Systems

Centrally coordinated marketing systems also grew in importance, because they are the source of three types of economies, which are relatively difficult to obtain in conventional channels. First, centrally coordinated systems are often able to achieve scheduling efficiencies, because the requirements and intentions of member units can be predicted and/or controlled. There is also more data available for planning purposes in a centrally coordinated system than in a conventional channel. Consequently, manufacturing, warehousing, and promotional activities can be scheduled to minimize "total" costs. Second, centrally coordinated marketing systems also achieve economies by eliminating, simplifying, and repositioning marketing activities. Field selling costs, as an illustration, are often eliminated, or at least minimized, in centrally coordinated systems, and various activities such as ordering, financing, and billing are drastically simplified or reduced to programmed routines, which lowers expense ratios and "creates" more time for planning activities. Furthermore, certain functions can be shifted forward or backward within the system to achieve scalar economies. The marking of merchandise, for example, is often moved backward in centrally coordinated systems, because the originating supplier can perform this function at a lower cost per unit than resellers. In similar fashion, warehousing, data

[13] *Statistics of Income: Corporation Income Tax Returns* (1950–1962 Editions), Internal Revenue Service, Washington, D.C.
[14] Robert W. Mueller, *Grocery Business Annual Report*, Progressive Grocer, New York, 1964, p. 3.
[15] "Profit Engineering Demands Revaluation and Close Control of Assortments," *Variety Store Merchandiser*, August, 1961, p. 11.

processing, and other facilities are often relocated to obtain systemic efficiencies. Quite obviously, this repositioning can be accomplished more expeditiously in a centrally coordinated system than in a conventional channel. Third, centrally coordinated systems, in practice, often have substantial horizontal outreach which permits individual units to obtain economies of scale, or failing this, to achieve the savings that accrue to enterprises using existing facilities intensively.[16]

Other Factors and Summary

Other factors, such as the expansion and relocation of markets which occurred in the 1950's, also favored the growth of centrally coordinated systems. Furthermore, as new products were introduced or as new markets developed, various types of systems, particularly franchise networks, emerged to capitalize on these newly created opportunities.

In short, the 1948–1965 period was one that encouraged large scale undertakings and the formation of centrally coordinated marketing systems. Predictably, a response, counter-response pattern soon developed. That is, as one system achieved market power in a line of trade, others were quickly formed to counteract this competitive thrust. Consequently, all three types of systems experienced substantial growth between 1948 and 1965, with contractually integrated networks—particularly voluntary groups, cooperative groups, and franchise programs—expanding at the most rapid rate.

VOLUNTARY AND COOPERATIVE GROUPS

Current Status

Voluntary and cooperative groups have been in existence for an extended period of time. Several retail cooperatives were established in the food field before the turn of the century; the first drug cooperative was founded in 1902;[17]

[16] For a more extended discussion of channel theory, see Bert C. McCammon, Jr. and Robert W. Little, "Marketing Channels: Analytical Systems and Approaches," *Science in Marketing* (George Schwartz, Ed.), John Wiley and Sons, New York, 1965.

[17] For an excellent discussion of the history of contractual systems in the drug field, see William T. Kelley, "The Franchise System in Co-operative Drugstores," *Journal of Retailing*, Winter, 1957–1958, p. 185.

and a substantial number of voluntaries—including IGA, Red & White, Western Auto, Ben Franklin and others—operated on an extensive scale as early as the 1930's. Despite these historical precedents, voluntary and cooperative groups were largely confined to the food field prior to the middle 1950's. Since that time, however, voluntaries and cooperatives have expanded rapidly, particularly in drug, hardware, automotive, and variety retailing, and continued growth is predicted for the future.

Retailers affiliated with voluntary and cooperative groups normally operate their stores under the same name, contribute to a common advertising and sales promotion fund, adhere to comparable operating procedures, and purchase most of their inventory requirements from a sponsoring wholesaler (in the case of voluntaries) or from a retailer-owned warehouse (in the case of cooperatives). Conversely, the sponsoring wholesaler or warehouse offers a variety of supporting services to affiliated stores so that they can compete against chain outlets on a roughly equal basis.

Retailers belonging to voluntary and cooperative groups have been particularly successful in the food field since World War II. Their share of total food store sales rose from 32 per cent in 1950 to 49 per cent in 1963, while the share held by corporate chains climbed from 37 to only 41 per cent during the same period. Significantly, the proportion of total volume obtained by unaffiliated independents shrank from 33 to 10 per cent between 1950 and 1963.[18] Thus, independent retailers, purchasing from voluntary or cooperative warehouses, have become the dominant form of distribution in this important sector of the economy. On a dollar basis, voluntary group wholesalers increased their sales from approximately $3.2 billion in 1956 to over $6.5 billion in 1963, and cooperative warehouses boosted their volume from $2.0 billion to 4.2 billion during the same period.[19] Furthermore, several of these organizations now rank among the nation's largest merchandising enterprises. Super Valu's volume amounted to $412.2 million in 1964, and Fleming and Wetterau, two IGA affiliates, had sales of $261.7 and $120.0 million, respectively, during the same year.[20] Leading cooperatives such as Allied, Thrifty, Affiliated, Certified, and others,

[18] Mueller, *op. cit.* (1950 and 1962 Editions).
[19] *Ibid.*, p. 20.
[20] "The Best of Both Possible Worlds," *Forbes*, November 15, 1964, p. 48.

also obtain annual sales well in excess of $100 million.

Voluntaries and cooperatives have been active in the drug field since the turn of the century, but their growth has been relatively sluggish until recent years. Rexall and Walgreen, through their wholesale divisions, currently sponsor the most extensive voluntary programs. These organizations supply affiliated druggists with private brand merchandise and numerous supporting services, including financial, merchandising, advertising, and promotional assistance. In 1963, over 14,000 independent druggists were either Walgreen or Rexall "agency" outlets, and these stores, because of their number alone, are a significant competitive factor in the market.[21]

Conventional drug wholesalers began to sponsor voluntary groups in the early 1960's, and by 1963, approximately 8.4 per cent of these firms serviced affiliated outlets on a contractual basis.[22] Admittedly, many of the voluntary programs in the drug field are administrative devices for redistributing cooperative advertising allowances, but a growing number of wholesalers offer a substantial number of services to affiliated stores, and most trade authorities believe that existing programs will become increasingly more comprehensive. McKesson & Robbins, as an illustration, already provides numerous services to retailers affiliated with its Independent Druggist's League plan. Over 1,200 outlets, located in 26 major markets, participated in this program in 1963, and continued growth is planned for the future.[23] In total, an estimated 9,914 independent druggists participated in wholesaler-sponsored voluntary programs during 1963, and these outlets, in addition to those participating in the Rexall and Walgreen plans, represented approximately 47.5 per cent of all drugstores in operation during the year.[24]

The growth of cooperative groups in the drug field has also been impressive in recent years. Leader Drug Stores, Inc., which serves affiliated outlets in Cleveland, Buffalo, Toledo, and Pittsburgh, is the largest of the cooperative

groups currently in operation. This organization was formed by 34 independent druggists in 1949, and it has grown steadily since that time. Member stores currently account for 60 per cent of total drug sales in the Buffalo market, and the warehouse in Cleveland increased its volume from $7.5 million in 1962 to over $10 million in 1964—a gain of more than 33 per cent.[25] Significantly, the leading cooperatives in the drug field formed a national association on July 1, 1964. At the present time, the organizations belonging to the National Drug Cooperative Association service 850 affiliated outlets, which is over twice the number of stores operated by Walgreen, the largest chain in the field.[26]

The rapid growth of voluntaries and cooperatives in drug retailing is symptomatic of growing competition in the industry. Several major food chains, including Safeway, Kroger and Jewel, acquired drug subsidiaries during the 1950's, and each of these organizations operates over 100 outlets at the present time. Discounting has become a more important factor, too. Over 51 per cent of the discount department stores in operation contain drug departments, which generated annual sale of $380 million in 1964.[27] As a result of these and other competitive developments, a growing number of drug retailers joined voluntary or cooperative groups.

The voluntary and cooperative movement has also gained momentum in the hardware field. Trade authorities estimate that 10,575 hardware stores—or 35.9 per cent of the total—participated in wholesaler-sponsored programs in 1964.[28] Furthermore, a recent survey of 189 wholesalers indicates that 71 of these firms—or 37.6 per cent—sponsored voluntary groups in 1964, and 28—or 14.8 per cent—plan to develop such programs in the future.[29] Finally, large wholesalers in the hardware field, such as Ace and Cotter, offer a wide variety of services to affiliated stores, as is indicated in Table 1.

The voluntary group concept has been used extensively in the automotive field, too. There are several major programs that involve wholesaling enterprises exclusively, and a substantial

[21] *Fairchild's Financial Manual of Retail Stores*, Fairchild Publications, New York, 1964.
[22] Findings of a survey undertaken by the editors of *American Druggist* as reported in Bob Vereen, "Where is the Hardware Industry Headed?" *Hardware Retailer*, October, 1964, p. 69.
[23] Stanley Siegelman, "Corporate Portrait: McKesson & Robbins," *Drug News Weekly*, July 8, 1964, p. 8.
[24] Vereen, *op. cit.*, p. 69.

[25] "Independents Counterattack," *Drug News Weekly*, April 19, 1965, p. 4.
[26] Warren Moulds, "National Co-op Group Becomes Reality," *Drug News Weekly*, July 19, 1965, p. 1.
[27] *The True Look of the Discount Industry*, Super Market Publishing Company, New York, 1964.
[28] Bob Vereen, *op. cit.*, p. 65.
[29] *Ibid.*, p. 67.

Table 1. Services Provided by Voluntary Group Wholesalers in the Hardware Field, United States (1964)

Service Provided to Retailer	Percentage of Voluntary Group Wholesalers Providing Designated Service
Consumer circulars and/or catalogs	91.5%
Private brand merchandise	90.3
Monthly promotional specials	73.6
Store-wide promotional kits	73.6
Extended dating programs	69.4
Management and merchandising counseling services	68.1
Cooperative newspaper advertising programs	67.0
Member store identification programs	63.9
Store planning and modernization assistance	62.5
Inventory control systems	58.3
Drop-shipping program	55.6
Bin-tickets for inventory control	55.6
Sales training programs	51.4
Supply and installation of store fixtures	50.0
Catalog order service for consumers	48.6
Preprinted order forms	48.6
Sponsorship of retail advisory committee	44.4
Programmed merchandise deliveries	41.7
Preretailed invoices	31.9
Store location or relocation assistance	29.2
Consumer credit program	27.8
Window display service	22.2
Pool-car buying program	20.8
Centralized accounting service	6.9

SOURCE: "Where is The Hardware Industry Headed?" *Hardware Retailer*, October, 1964, p. 91.

number that extend to the retail level. The National Automotive Parts Association, founded in 1924, is the largest voluntary group in the industry. The program is sponsored by 45 warehouse distributors that service approximately 4,000 affiliated wholesalers. NAPA warehouses buy private label and nationally branded merchandise on a contractual basis from a limited number of resources for subsequent redistribution through affiliated jobber outlets. These warehouses also provide a variety of supporting services to automotive wholesalers, which enables the latter to compete more effectively in the marketplace. Gulf and Western's American Parts System, which supplies 450 affiliated jobbers, is quite similar to the NAPA program, as is the recently formed AllCar group, which consists of 12 warehouse distributors and an unannounced number of affiliated jobbers. These data suggest that approximately 20 per cent of

the wholesalers engaged in the distribution of automotive parts, accessories, and chemicals belong to voluntary programs sponsored by warehouse distributors.[30]

Voluntary groups are also active in the so-called "home and auto" field, which is an important part of the automotive aftermarket. This segment of retailing, which has grown rapidly in recent years, is dominated by a mixture of franchise and voluntary stores. Of the 33,000 home and auto stores in operation during 1963, approximately 16,300 held Firestone, Goodyear or Goodrich franchises. Over 4,900 of the remaining stores participated in voluntary programs sponsored by Western Auto, Gamble-Skogmo, and Coast-to-Coast Stores. In

[30] For an excellent discussion of the structure of distribution in the automotive field see, Charles N. Davison, *The Marketing of Automotive Parts*, University of Michigan, Ann Arbor, 1954.

summary, roughly 21,200 home and auto stores—or 64.2 per cent of the total—participated in franchise or voluntary group programs during the most recent year for which comprehensive data are available.[31]

Finally, voluntary group retailers are an important factor in the variety field, which has been traditionally dominated by large national chains and their regional counterparts. These organizations accounted for 71.5 per cent of total variety sales in 1964, and their market share has increased steadily since the early 1950's.[32] Retailers affiliated with the Ben Franklin program are the only other significant factor in the market at the present time. Over 2,400 variety stores participated in this program during 1964, and their aggregate volume amounted to approximately $300 million, which represented 6.0 per cent of total variety sales.[33]

Emerging Trends

There are several recent developments in the voluntary and cooperative field that have particular significance. First, a substantial number of voluntary and cooperative groups have expanded their private brand programs. Ben Franklin retailers, for example, obtained 15 per cent of their sales from private label merchandise in 1963.[34] Stores affiliated with the Super Valu program relied on private brands for 10 per cent of their volume in 1964, and IGA outlets exceeded even this percentage.[35] Furthermore, a substantial percentage of voluntary wholesalers in the hardware field inventoried private brands in 1964, as is indicated in Table 2. Consequently, this approach to merchandising has apparently become an established part of the voluntary and cooperative movement, and it could become increasingly more important in the future. Second, voluntary and cooperative wholesalers have diversified their inventories in recent years to better serve affiliated retailers, and this trend is particularly apparent in the food field. In 1963, for example, 93 per cent of all voluntary food wholesalers stocked health

and beauty aids; 49 per cent handled housewares, and a substantial proportion also carried garden supplies, small appliances, glassware and greeting cards.[36] Cooperative food wholesalers were equally as aggressive in their inventory diversification programs as were their counterparts in the drug, hardware and home and auto fields. Available data suggest that this trend will accelerate, rather than diminish, during the decade ahead, which indicates that intertype competition at the retail level may become more intense. Third, both voluntary and cooperative wholesalers are expanding the range of services offered to affiliated stores, and this development is particularly pronounced in the drug and hardware fields. Many drug wholesalers, sponsoring voluntary programs, routinely sign shopping center leases to secure prime locations for their accounts, and others provide a centralized accounting service. Voluntary hardware wholesalers are expanding their retail assistance programs at a comparable rate, which suggests that voluntary programs in these fields, at least, will become as comprehensive as those used in food retailing.

FRANCHISE PROGRAMS

Franchising involves a contractural arrangement between originating suppliers (manufacturers or service organizations) and affiliated outlets.[37] These agreements vary in scope and content, but all contain provisions in which the franchisee is given the right to sell a designated product or service, in a generally defined geographical area, in exchange for his promise to market the product or service in a specified manner.[38] Furthermore, the franchise agreement may cover the entire outlet, a department within the outlet, or a brand within the department. As is the case with other forms of contractual integration, franchising is a long established method of distribution. The Singer Sewing Machine Company, for example, developed an extensive and successful franchise network shortly after the Civil War; automobile manufacturers converted to a franchise system of distribution in 1911 which is still being used

[31] "The Anatomy of a Market," *Home & Auto Retailer*, July, 1965, p. 14.
[32] "Annual Report on the Variety Store Field," *Variety Store Merchandiser*, March, 1965, p. 23.
[33] A. J. Vogl, "Franchising: The New American Dream," *Modern Franchising*, September–October, 1964, p. 10.
[34] *Annual Report*, City Products Corporation, Des Plaines, Illinois, 1964, p. 8.
[35] "A Supermarket Chain that Isn't a Chain," *Business Week*, August 22, 1964, p. 82.

[36] Robert W. Mueller, *op. cit.*, p. 21.
[37] For an excellent discussion of the legal aspects of franchising, see Charles M. Hewitt, "The Furor Over Dealer Franchises," *Business Horizons*, Winter, 1958, p. 80–87.
[38] For an interesting analysis of the differences in franchise agreements, see Edwin A. Lewis and Robert S. Hancock, *The Franchise System of Distribution*, University of Minnesota, 1963.

Table 2. Private Brand Programs Sponsored by Voluntary Group Wholesalers in The Hardware Field United States (1964)

Merchandise Category	Percentage of Voluntary Group Wholesalers Stocking Private Brands in Designated Category
Traffic appliances	87.5%
Power tools	86.1
Power mowers and equipment	86.1
Hand tools	84.7
Lawn and garden supplies	76.4
Paint sundries	76.4
Hardware	75.0
Fishing tackle	65.3
Paint	61.1
Sporting goods	58.3
Lawn and garden chemicals	37.5

SOURCE: "Where is The Hardware Industry Headed?" *Hardware Retailer*, October, 1964, p. 87.

today; and the integrated oil companies, which obtain approximately 90 per cent of their volume from franchised outlets, adopted this method of distribution during the 1920's and 1930's.[39] As a result of these and similar programs, franchising systems have been an integral and important part of the marketing structure for almost 100 years. Franchising did not become a pervasive phenomenon until the early 1950's, however, when a growing number of companies entered the field for the first time.

Franchise programs, covering consumer goods and services, experienced particularly rapid growth between 1950 and 1965. Many of these programs, such as those sponsored by Fanny Farmer, Loft's, Russell Stover, Barton's, Barricini, and other candy companies, involve departmental franchises which are granted on a selective basis. There were approximately 15,000 franchised candy departments in operation during 1964,[40] and comparable expansion has occurred in other merchandise categories, including cosmetics, ready-to-wear, and vacuum cleaners. Franchise agreements, covering specific bands, which are normally merchandised

with competing brands, may have grown in importance too, but data regarding these programs are fragmentary. Certainly, individual manufacturers—including Maytag, Zenith, Magnavox, and Karastan—have strengthened their position in recent years through the use of intelligently conceived franchise programs. These developments, though significant in terms of marketing strategy, have had little impact on the structure of retailing. In sharp contrast, franchise programs covering all phases of an outlet's operations have dramatically affected competitive relationships, and these programs are the ones usually described by chroniclers of the "franchise movement."

Comprehensive franchise programs grew rapidly between 1950 and 1965, and they have become a particularly significant factor in the marketing of the following goods and services: laundry and dry cleaning services, soft ice cream, hearing aids, carpet and upholstery cleaning services, water conditioning systems, and swimming pools. Furthermore, a growing number of restaurants, motels, and part-time employment agencies are operated on a franchise basis (the relative importance of franchising in these and other industries as of the end of 1963 is shown in Table 3). On a national basis, trade authorities estimate that there were approximately 100,000 franchised outlets (excluded service stations and automobile dealers) in operation by the end of 1963. These enterprises generated aggregate

[39] For an analysis of the growth of franchise systems in the petroleum industry, see John Godfrey MacLean and Robert William Haigh, *The Growth of Integrated Oil Companies*, Harvard University Boston, 1954.

[40] "Store-Within-Store Franchises A Big Step," *Drug News Weekly*, March 29, 1965, p. 7.

Table 3.   Number of Franchised Outlets By Line of Retail Trade or Service Category United States (1963)

Line of Retail Trade or Service Category	Number of Franchised Outlets	Estimated Sales (millions of dollars)
Laundry and Dry Cleaning	35,700	$ 509
Restaurants and Rrefreshment Stands	24,590	1,410
Household Goods Moving Companies	5,000	1,000
Carpet and Upholstery Cleaning	4,000	100
Hearing Aids	3,500	70
Water Conditioning Systems	2,300	207
Swimming Pools	1,000	40
Part-time Employment Agencies	500	100
Total	76,590	$3,436

SOURCE: David B. Slater, "Some Socio-Economic Footnotes on Franchising," *Boston University Businss Review*, Summer, 1964, p. 19.

sales of over $5 billion and competed in at least 80 lines of trade under franchises granted by over 400 organizations, including Dairy Queen, Tastee Freez, A & W Root Beer, the Mary Carter Paint Company, Howard Johnson's, McDonald's System, Inc., and others.[41] Furthermore, most of the firms sponsoring, or affiliated with franchise programs were either founded after 1950 or have experienced their most rapid rate of growth since that time.

Franchising has expanded most rapidly in the food service field. At the present time, 10 of the 20 largest franchising organizations supply restaurants and soft ice cream outlets. The rapid growth of these programs can be effectively illustrated by examining the history of the soft ice cream industry. Only 100 outlets served this product after World War II, but by 1964 there were over 18,000 franchised dairy stands in operation.[42] Franchised restaurants have grown almost as rapidly, as indicated by the following corporate illustrations:

Chicken Delight, Inc. expanded from one franchise outlet in 1952 to over 511 in 1964. Furthermore, the company's total revenue, including sales, commissions, and fees, was over $40 million during the latter year.

McDonald's System, Inc. generated total sales of $100 million in 1964, after expanding from a small regional base 10 years earlier.

Howard Johnson's, a long established res-

taurant chain, accelerated its expansion through the use of a franchise program. The company serviced 675 restaurants in 1964, and half of these outlets were operated by franchisees.[43]

In summary, the franchise movement is well established in the food service field. There were over 24,590 franchised restaurants or road-side stands in operation by the end of 1963, and these outlets accounted for approximately 12.8 per cent of total food service sales.[44]

Franchised motels have become a significant competitive factor, too. There are three major types of contractual arrangements in this field: conventional franchise programs, co-owner franchise programs, and referral groups. Conventional franchise programs—such as those sponsored by Quality Courts Motels, Holiday Inns, and Congress Inns—involve contractual agreements between the sponsoring organization and affiliated motels in which the latter adhere to specified architectural standards, contribute to a common advertising and sales promotion fund, follow recommended operating procedures, and purchase most of their equipment and supplies from the franchisor. Co-owner franchise programs are virtually identical to their conventional counterparts, except that the sponsoring organization has an equity interest in affiliated units. TraveLodge, which developed the concept, Imperial 400, MoteLodge, and Hyatt Chalets, are the principal proponents of co-

[41] Steven S. Andreder, "License for Growth," *Barron's*, November 27, 1961, p. 3.

[42] "Franchise Selling Catches On," *Business Week*, February 6, 1960, p. 90.

[43] A. J. Vogl, *op, cit.*, p. 11.

[44] David B. Slater, "Some Socio-Economic Footnotes on Franchising," *Boston University Business Review*, Summer, 1964, p. 19–28.

owner franchise programs. Motels belonging to referral groups, the third type of contractual system in the field, constitute a loose economic coalition. These outlets often differ markedly in terms of their size, pricing practices, and operating methods. As a result, they do not project the unified image or maintain the consistency of service that is usually found in conventional or co-owner programs. However, referral group motels contribute to a common advertising and sales promotion fund, consolidate their orders to lower purchasing costs, and refer customers to affiliated outlets; thus they achieve systemic economies and substantial market impact. Best Western Motels, Superior Motels, and Emmons Walker are the largest of the referral groups currently in operation, and their growth has been unusually rapid in recent years. By the end of 1964, 1,723 motels were affiliated with conventional franchise programs, 544 participated in co-owner programs, and 2,324 were members of referral groups. These franchised motels contained over 279,500 rooms, which represented approximately 30 per cent of the industry's capacity at the end of the year.[45]

Franchising programs, as indicated above, tend to be offensive alignments. Sponsoring firms, by using this technique, can obtain extensive market coverage with a minimum capital investment. Similarly, franchisees tend to be entrepreneurs entering the market for the first time. As a result, franchising programs can significantly disrupt the competitive *status quo* in a relatively short period of time, and this innovative potential has been dramatically realized in the motel, restaurant, and dry cleaning fields, as well as others.

With respect to emerging trends, there are two significant developments that deserve particular emphasis. First, franchising will probably be used in a growing number of industries during the decade ahead, including home furnishings and ready-to-wear. Several pilot programs are already underway, and early results are encouraging. Second, multiple operations will probably emerge. TraveLodge and the Pure Oil Company, for example, are now developing TOURest units, which include a motel, service station and restaurant, all of which are franchised operations.[46] This type of arrangement has considerable appeal for affiliated operators because it broadens

their market base, and thus continued growth can be expected.

SOME UNRESOLVED PROBLEMS CONFRONTING MEMBERS OF FRANCHISE, VOLUNTARY AND COOPERATIVE GROUPS

The future growth of franchise networks and voluntary and co-operative groups may be somewhat inhibited, because these contractual systems have not solved several significant problems. First, there is the problem of management succession. The firms participating in franchise, voluntary, and cooperative programs are usually small scale enterprises operated by first generation entrepreneurs. Such organizations have historically experienced difficulty in ensuring continuity of capable management, and affiliation has not significantly eased this problem. As a result, the economic performance of franchise networks and voluntary and cooperative groups may deteriorate in the future due to a decline in the managerial capability of affiliated units. Second, the administrators of franchise, voluntary, and cooperative programs will probably continue to encounter difficulty in maintaining uniformity of operations throughout the system. Affiliated outlets, particularly in voluntary and cooperative groups, often differ markedly in terms of their store layouts, inventory assortments, pricing practices, and other characteristics. These variations are frequently difficult to eradicate, because member firms possess considerable autonomy, consequently, executives in contractual networks have much less control over marketing activities than their counterparts in corporate systems, which suggests that the former may have fewer opportunities than the latter to effect systemic economies. Admittedly, this lack of centralized control *may* result in prompter adjustments to demand and stronger management incentives at the *local* level, but such arguments lose much of their validity in the context of recent advances in data processing and executive development techniques. Third, financial limitations may dampen growth rates in the franchise, voluntary and cooperative fields. The firms affiliated with these systems tend to be undercapitalized, and virtually all of them depend on local sources of funds to finance their operations. As a result, they often experience difficulty in raising capital for expansion and modernization. Comparable units in corporate systems, on the other hand, have

[45] Ralph Dellevie, "Chain and Referral Groups," *Tourist Court Journal*, June, 1964, p. 8–12.
[46] Reuben Polen, "TOURest—New Concept Combines Three Basics," *Tourist Court Journal*, October, 1963, p. 16.

relatively easy access to the capital market, since their line of credit is based on the performance of the total system, rather than that of individual outlets. In addition, corporate systems offer lendors and investors the advantage of diversification of risk which the individual entrepreneur, operating at a single location, cannot. Fourth, voluntary and cooperative groups, in particular, have not been conspicuously successful in their attempts to compete in large urban markets. Affiliated outlets are typically located in small and medium size communities, which will decline in relative importance as the American economy becomes more urbanized. Consequently, the future growth of voluntary and cooperative programs is partially conditional on their ability to penetrate highly competitive urban areas. Fifth, and finally, franchisees and members of voluntary and cooperative groups have not solved their estate tax problems through affiliation. That is, entrepreneurs, interested in fragmenting and diversifying their holdings for estate tax purposes, cannot achieve this goal through contractual integration. Consequently, owner-mangers, desirous of diversifying their holdings, must still merge their operations with publicly owned corporations or negotiate an outright sale. If a growing number of affiliated entrepreneurs become concerned about estate tax problems, many may decide to liquidate their investments, and thus contractual integration may be a prelude to corporate integration.

The problems cited above are rather formidable, and each of them deserves careful study and additional research. Despite these reservations, however, franchise, voluntary, and cooperative groups will probably continue to expand in the future, since they have clearly demonstrated their ability to compete against corporate and administered systems. Furthermore, franchising has proved to be an effective device for obtaining consumer acceptance of new products, new services, and new methods of operation; thus, this distribution technique should continue to be of interest to prospective market entrants.

40. Retail Trade Flow Changes in Canada

BRUCE MALLEN

Mallen states that both in the United States and Canada, metropolitan retailing has become less effective over the years in generating trade from nonmetropolitan areas. He shows the effect this will have on channel members.

Retail trade in the metropolitan areas in the past three decades has definitely not kept pace with the population shift to these areas. Canadian metropolitan retailing has become less effective over the years in generating trade from nonmetropolitan areas. In 1931 metropolitan per capita retail sales were 188% above those of nonmetropolitan areas, but by 1962 the difference had fallen to only 44%.

The Metropolitan Areas'[1] share of trade had

• SOURCE: Bruce E. Mallen, "Retail Trade Flow Changes in Canada," *The Business Quarterly*, Vol. 29 (Winter, 1964), pp. 63–68. Bruce Mallen, Chairman, Department of Marketing, Sir George Williams University.

[1] The Dominion Bureau of Statistics defines a Metropolitan Area (MA) as a group of urban communities which are in close economic, geographic and social relationship. These usually consist of one major city and its surrounding suburbs. It is important to note that the declining power of retail trade in Metropolitan Areas vis-à-vis nonmetropolitan areas cannot be due to suburban shopping because the latter centres are included in the MA's.

There were, in 1961, 17 such DBS Census Metropolitan Areas. These included two additions since the 1951 Census: Kitchener, Ontario, (with a metropolitan population of slightly over 160,000 in 1963) and Sudbury, Ontario (with a metropolitan population of close to 120,000 in that year). Two large cities, Regina and Saskatoon, Saskatchewan, are not considered Metropolitan Areas, even though they are larger than some of the smaller MA's because they lack well defined satellite communities. Their respective 1963 populations of 120,000 and 104,000 actually make them larger than the two smallest Metropolitan Areas—Saint John, N.B., and St. John's Nfld.—which had populations of 99,000 and 97,000, respectively, in 1963.

not increased. It was 55% in 1930 and remains at this same percentage in 1962. This, in spite of the fact, for example, that Canada's half dozen largest cities have only in the past decade (1951–1962) moved from a 30% share of the Canadian population to a 38% share.

It appears that where a Metropolitan Area is directly surrounded by a basically rural area there results a flow of retail trade from this surrounding area to the Metropolitan Area. However, where a Metropolitan Area is directly surrounded by a nonmetropolitan urban area the inflow of retail trade to the MA is greatly restricted. This is because of the retailing facilities which nonmetropolitan urban populations can sustain.

As Canada becomes more urbanized, as the more rural areas are converted into nonmetropolitan urban areas, the MA's will be forced to depend less and less on trade inflow.

Implications to the Canadian Retailer

There are many consequences of importance to the Canadian retailer that follow from the above analysis and conclusion. Different types of retailers will be affected in different ways. The nature of the goods carried by the retailer will play a great part in determining how this growing strength of nonmetropolitan urban retailing will affect him. His location within the Metropolitan Area, whether it is downtown or suburban, is an important factor as well. Present retailers in these nonmetropolitan urban areas will also, of course, feel the effects of this marketing phenomenon. Chain stores, beyond a doubt, will react to the slow-down of trade inflow into the

Metropolitan Areas. Promotional and merchandising deals will have to be modified. Not only the retailers, but their suppliers, whether wholesalers or manufacturers, will be affected by the change in retail trade flow.

Since 1931 there has been a huge population growth which has strongly favored the Metropolitan Areas. "We must recognize that much of our population growth is occurring within a very few metropolitan cities. About half of the total increase in population in Canada between 1951 and 1956 (19.3%) occurred in 15 metropolitan areas. Approximately 40% of Canada's population in mid-1956 resided in metropolitan areas. The Report of the Royal Commission on Canada's Economic Prospects (The Gordon Commission) suggests that nearly two-thirds of our population will reside in these cities by 1980 and that perhaps 80% of us will be urban dwellers."[2] The 1961 Census of Canda population patterns certainly are in keeping with this trend.

THE ANALYSIS

The developed data presented in Tables 1 to 5 show for each of the 15 MA's: their share of population and sales of the province, their per capita sales both absolutely and relative to their province; and their per capita sales relative to their buying power.

Share of Population

Table 1 establishes the growing population shift to Metropolitan Areas. By 1962 almost half (47%) the population of those provinces containing the 15 MA's lived in these cities. In 1930 less than a third (30%) did so. Two specific Metropolitan Areas, Winnipeg and Vancouver, account for half of their respective provinces' population. Some areas, such as "oil-booming" Edmonton, have more than doubled their population shares since 1930.

Share of Retail Sales

The Metropolitan Area shares of provincial retail sales for 1930, 1941, 1951, and 1962 are shown in Table 2. The results show a very stable overall pattern going from around 55% in 1930, down to around 50% in 1941 and 1951, and back up to the 55% mark in 1962. This is in sharp contrast to the population movements

[2] Albert Rose, "Canada: The Design of Social Change," *The Business Quarterly*, Vol. 23, Winter, 1958, p. 208.

Table 1. Percentages of a Province's Population in Specific Metropolitan Areas

MA'S	1930	1941	1951	1962
Calgary, Alta.	11.5	11.2	14.8	21.5
Edmonton, Alta.	10.8	11.8	18.4	25.8
Halifax, N.S.	11.5	12.1	20.8	25.2
Hamilton, Ont.	4.5	4.9	5.7	6.4
London, Ont.	2.1	2.1	2.7	2.9
Montreal, Que.	28.5	34.2	34.4	40.5
Ottawa, Ont.	3.7	5.6	6.1	7.0
Quebec, Que.	4.6	5.9	6.8	6.8
Saint John, N.B.	11.8	11.4	15.1	16.1
St. John's, Nfld.	N.A.	N.A.	18.8	20.0
Toronto, Ont.	18.4	23.7	24.3	29.5
Vancouver, B.C.	36.6	42.4	45.6	48.6
Victoria, B.C.	5.6	5.4	8.9	9.5
Windsor, Ont.	2.9	3.2	3.4	3.0
Winnipeg, Man.	31.3	39.2	45.6	52.2
Overall	30.0	36.3	39.8	46.9

SOURCE: Developed from **Census of Canada** and **Survey of Markets** data.

of Table 1 which showed a share increase of over 1½ times. For example, Montreal's share of population increased from 28½% in 1930 to 40½% in 1962 at the same time that its share of sales declined from 57% to 50%. Winnipeg went from

Table 2. Percentages of a Province's Retail Sales Concentrated in Specific Metropolitan Areas

MA'S	1930	1941	1951	1962
Calgary, Alta.	24.4	23.5	21.5	27.5
Edmonton, Alta.	21.6	21.7	24.6	30.9
Halifax, N.S.	30.0	30.9	31.2	34.7
Hamilton, Ont.	6.3	6.2	6.2	6.3
London, Ont.	3.3	2.8	3.2	3.9
Montreal, Que.	56.8	48.1	49.7	49.8
Ottawa, Ont.	5.5	5.8	6.1	7.2
Quebec, Que.	7.4	7.7	8.0	8.4
Saint John, N.B.	25.0	24.5	21.7	16.7
St. John's, Nfld.	N.A.	N.A.	40.6	37.9
Toronto, Ont.	33.9	28.4	29.9	34.3
Vancouver, B.C.	49.4	46.8	52.4	53.3
Victoria, B.C.	10.8	11.9	9.4	10.0
Windsor, Ont.	3.5	3.8	3.5	2.8
Winnipeg, Man.	69.3	65.0	58.0	64.8
Overall	55.2	49.9	51.3	55.4

SOURCE: Developed from **Census of Canada** and **Survey of Markets** data.

a 31% to a 52% population share, but declined from 69% to under 65% in sales share.

These exhibits show that population shares for the MA's have increased substantially while retail shares have not increased at all.

Per Capita Retail Sales

Per capita retail sales in the MA's have more than doubled in dollar terms since 1930 when they were at $500 compared to 1962's $1,088. The 1962 figures ranged from $922 for Windsor, Ont., to $1,368 for London, Ont. Some cities, such as Edmonton and Quebec City, have almost tripled their per capita sales since 1930. Others such as Victoria, B.C., have only increased per capita sales by 1½ times (Table 3).

However, these increases in the MA's per capita sales over the years are small relative to the increases in nonmetropolitan per capita retail sales. This becomes obvious when relative per capita sales are studied. It should be recognized that much of the increases in per capita sales is due to increased prices or inflation. However, because the main purpose of this analysis is to compare per capita metropolitan sales to per capita nonmetropolitan sales—and because inflation has probably increased at the same rate in both types of areas—it would be of little value to deflate these figures.

Table 3. **Per Capita $ Retail Sales in Metropolitan Areas**

MA'S	1930–31	1941	1951	1962
Calgary, Alta.	$512	$584	$1,309	$1,248
Edmonton, Alta.	481	511	1,208	1,204
Halifax, N.S.	508	729	917	1,106
Hamilton, Ont.	442	524	985	1,005
London, Ont.	507	513	1,074	1,368
Montreal, Que.	452	436	869	1,000
Ottawa, Ont.	472	529	894	1,041
Quebec, Que.	366	417	709	1,008
Saint John, N.B.	438	481	795	1,020
St. John's, Nfld.	N.A.	N.A.	956	1,170
Toronto, Ont.	591	600	1,114	1,177
Vancouver, B.C.	498	527	1,070	1,114
Victoria, B.C.	692	841	981	1,070
Windsor, Ont.	388	514	924	922
Winnipeg, Man.	598	617	997	1,070
Overall	$501	$526	$ 983	$1,088

SOURCE: Developed from **Census of Canada** and **Survey of Markets** data.

Table 4. **Relative Per Capita Retail Sales for Specific Metropolitan Areas**

MA'S	1930–31	1941	1951	1962
Calgary, Alta.	307	296	180	163
Edmonton, Alta.	288	259	166	157
Halifax, N.S.	330	324	172	158
Hamilton, Ont.	198	185	125	112
London, Ont.	227	181	137	152
Montreal, Que.	374	274	201	155
Ottawa, Ont.	212	186	114	116
Quebec, Que.	302	262	164	156
Saint John, N.B.	250	253	156	151
St. John's, Nfld.	N.A.	N.A.	295	244
Toronto, Ont.	265	211	142	131
Vancouver, B.C.	205	205	137	125
Victoria, B.C.	285	327	126	120
Windsor, Ont.	174	181	118	103
Winnipeg, Man.	494	423	165	169
Overall	288	241	160	144

SOURCE: Developed from **Census of Canada** and **Survey of Markets** data.

Relative Per Capita Sales

The heart of this study is to be found in Table 4, in which retail sales per capita in Metropolitan Areas are compared with those in nonmetropolitan areas of the same province. This simple formula is:

$$\frac{\text{Per Capita Retail Sales for Specific MA}}{\text{Per Capita Nonmetropolitan Retail Sales for the Specific Province}} \times 100$$

It can be seen in Table 4 that the overall index for the 15 MA's has dropped consistently since 1930–31, falling from 288 in that year to exactly half, 144, by 1962. This means that Metropolitan Area per capita retail sales were 188% higher in 1930–31 than those in nonmetropolitan areas, and that the difference dropped to 44% by 1962.

The pattern of falling indices was relatively similar for most MA's in this three-decade period, falling by about ½. Only one city showed any signs of a strong upturn in 1962, namely, London, Ont. This may perhaps be explained by the Wellington Square Shopping Centre which opened in the heart of downtown London in August, 1960.[3]

While there is a high degree of consistency

[3] Joseph N. Fry, "Impact of a Shopping Centre," *The Business Quarterly*, Vol. 26, No. 2, Summer, 1961, pp. 89–96.

in the direction of change in the various areas, there is a wide spread in the magnitude of change. These variations are becoming smaller over time. For example, the biggest variation in 1930–31 was between Windsor, Ont. and Winnipeg, Man., where the former has an index of 174 and the latter 494—a spread of 320 points. In 1962, the biggest variation (excluding St. John's, Nfld.) was again between these two cities, but the spread was whittled down to 66 points. In 1962, Calgary and St. John's also had indices of over 160, while Ottawa and Hamilton were under 120.

The cities with the lowest and highest ratings can explain their respective positions in terms of their "hinterland." For example, Hamilton and Windsor have the lowest index numbers. Both are in areas of dense urban development—in fact, the most dense in Canada. This area is Canada's megalopolis.[4] Hamilton is surrounded by Burlington, Grimsby, St. Catharines, Oakville, Georgetown, Milton, and other urban areas. Windsor is surrounded by Leamington, Chatham, Wallaceburg, and Sarnia. But Windsor's biggest competitor by far, and the cause of its very low index rating, is that giant across the river—Detroit, Michigan.

Winnipeg and St. John's have the highest index numbers. Both are in provinces with little urban development outside of these MA's. The only town of any size in Newfoundland, with the exception of St. John's is Corner Brook. This town of 26,000 is over 500 miles west at the other end of the isolated island province. Winnipeg has only Portage la Prairie and Brandon to contend with, which together have a combined population of only slightly over 40,000. The first town is 60 miles to the west and the second is 140 miles in the same direction.

Per Capita Buying Power

Another approach to measuring the drawing power of MA's is to analyze the relationship between per capita retail sales and per capita income. This analysis reveals (Table 5) that the cities with the four highest percentages were the four most easterly MA's—St. John's, Halifax, Saint John, and Quebec City. This can probably be explained by the fact that the Atlantic Prov-

[4] Thayler C. Taylor, "7 Million Customers All In A Row," *Sales Management*, Vol. 91, No. 11, November 10, 1963, pp. 279–284; Edward G. Pleva, "The Marketing Corridors of Southern Ontario," *Marketing*, Vol. 67, No. 40, October 5, 1962, pp. 60–64.

Table 5. The 1962 Per Capita Retail Sales as a Percentage of Per Capita Effective Buying Power

MA's	Percentage
Calgary, Alta.	67.9
Edmonton, Alta.	74.9
Halifax, N.S.	82.7
Hamilton, Ont.	56.1
London, Ont.	72.1
Montreal, Que.	57.9
Ottawa, Ont.	63.1
Quebec, Que.	85.1
Saint John, N.B.	77.5
St. John's, Nfld.	99.2
Toronto, Ont.	60.3
Vancouver, B.C.	62.1
Victoria, B.C.	60.9
Windsor, Ont.	51.4
Winnipeg, Man.	67.5

SOURCE: Developed from **Sales Management's Survey of Buying Power**

inces and Eastern Quebec are the areas of lowest per capita income in Canada, and such areas tend to spend a greater proportion of their income on retail purchases. The two lowest percentages, shown by Windsor and Hamilton, can be explained by their urban "hinterland" and trade outflow (as explained in the previous section), and by their relatively high per capita incomes.

COMPARISON WITH U.S.A.

A similar study was completed on the retail trade flow in the United States.[5] In Canada, as stated above, metropolitan per capita retail sales were 188% above those of nonmetropolitan areas in 1931, and the difference had fallen to only 44% by 1962. For a comparable period in the United States these percentages were 83% and 30%, respectively. This indicates, together with the latest statistics, that although the relative retailing power of nonmetropolitan areas is stronger in the United States (and so the MA's retailing power is weaker) still the Canadian nonmetropolitan areas are rapidly catching up. Whereas in 1930 the spread between U.S. and Canadian index numbers was about 105 points, the spread today is probably less than 20 points.

[5] Eli P. Cox, "Changes In Retail Trade Flow," *Journal of Marketing*, Vol. 28, January, 1964, pp. 12–18.

CHANNEL MEMBERS

Type and Location of Retailer

Three categories of stores can be distinguished based on patronage motives:[6]

Convenience stores: those stores for which the consumer, before his need for some products arises, possesses a preference map that indicates a willingness to buy from the most accessible store.

Shopping stores: those stores for which the consumer has not developed a complete preference map relative to the product he wishes to buy, requiring him to undertake a search to construct such a map before purchase.

Specialty stores: those stores for which the consumer, before his need for some product arises, possesses a preference map that indicates a willingness to buy the item from a particular establishment even though it may not be the most accessible. (NOTE: As the term "specialty stores" is used in this paper, the definition is based on patronage motives not breadth of product line.)

As nonmetropolitan urban retailing has grown in sophistication there has been a pattern or evolution in which (1) the population of these areas which were always willing to use the convenience stores within their area, are now more and more willing to use the shopping stores within their area, and will perhaps eventually be willing to use their own specialty stores. Thus, it is for this reason that there is and will continue to be a restriction of retail trade outflow from these areas.

Convenience stores such as the food store, drug store, candy and stationery store, various service stores, etc., have, by the nature of the products they carry, always had the loyalty of their local market—whether it is a town or a neighbourhood within a larger city.

Shopping stores have until recently not had this kind of local loyalty. The nonmetropolitan urban consumer evidently has felt that her local retail facilities were insufficient in number of stores and in breadth of product line and variety to help her adequately construct her preference map. Therefore, she felt it necessary to expand her search into the Metropolitan Areas, in order to take advantage of their larger retail capacity.

Thus, such metropolitan shopping stores as clothing retailers, shoe stores, furniture and appliance outlets, most departments of department stores, etc., have benefited from a retail trade inflow from nonmetropolitan urban areas. Evidently, though statistics are not at this time available, it is this type of store which is beginning to lose its trade inflow in Metropolitan Areas and is beginning to gain local loyalty in nonmetropolitan urban areas.

Specialty stores are the next stage of this retail trade flow evolution, namely the consumers' growing local loyalty to the specialty stores (patronage motive definition). However, stores which engender this type of loyalty are still mainly located in the Metropolitan Areas, particularly the downtown. The high fashion clothing and jewellery stores and other specialty items are still located in the big cities. It will be quite some time, if ever, before the smaller cities will be able to prevent an outflow of this specialty trade to the Metropolitan Areas.

The implications to the various type of retailers of this three stage trade flow evolution is obvious. The present metropolitan convenience stores need not worry. They have not depended on an inflow of trade in the past, but only on their neighbourhood loyalty. And the specialty stores, as well, need not worry, although, an important percentage of their sales has come from trade inflow as mentioned above, it is highly unlikely that such inflow will dry up in the foreseeable future. Nonmetropolitan urban consumers will still make the special trip into the big city to purchase that high fashion item.

The outlet in the Metropolitan Areas which will be most affected in an adverse manner by the competition from nonmetropolitan stores is the shopping store. As the smaller city shopper learns to use the shopping stores in her own area the metropolitan shopping store will have to learn to depend almost entirely on the Metropolitan Area and surrounding rural areas for their sales.

The location of the metropolitan store will also determine the effect of this strengthening of nonmetropolitan urban retailing. In general, it may be said that suburban stores and shopping centres will be more adversely affected by these trends than the downtown shopping area. The downtown shopping area is fortified by its greater percentage of specialty stores and wider drawing power from all areas. However, the suburban shopping centres, many of which have been set up with the view of intercepting and gaining sales from the surrounding smaller towns

[6] Louis P. Bucklin, "Retail Strategy and the Classification of Consumer Goods,"—*Journal of Marketing*, Vol. 27, January, 1963, p. 53.

and cities can be put in a very embarrassing situation. It would be the wise shopping centre promoter and retailer who would review and try to measure the present dependence on surrounding cities and towns (excluding the Metropolitan Area suburbs themselves). Of course, it would also be the foolish shopping centre promoter and developer who would not take into consideration these important trends when thinking of opening a new shopping centre.

Combining the *type of store* and the *location of store* it can be said that the metropolitan retailers who would be most adversely affected by the strengthening nonmetropolitan urban retailing picture, would be those shopping stores located in suburban shopping centres which depend to an important degree on sales to consumers from surrounding towns and smaller cities.

Chain Stores

The growing strength of the nonmetropolitan urban retailing trade vis-à-vis the MA centres will most likely lead to a greater expansion of the chains into these towns and smaller cities. It is vital that the nonmetropolitan, urban, independent retailer reassess his present position in view of the dynamic merchandising and promotional abilities of these chains. A drive through the main streets of many of the towns and smaller cities would indicate to the observer the vulnerability of the small city retailer as the inflow of chains into his town becomes more and more prevalent. If these small independent retailers hope to survive, and there is a certainty that many of them will not, they must modernize their present merchandising techniques. Promotional policies, advertising appeals, store fronts, window displays, interior decor, the merchandise itself, must all be geared to meet this predicted chain-store influx.

The chain stores themselves will probably have to bring about certain modifications in their promotional and merchandise approaches. They will have to gear themselves to smaller city consumer psychology. Certainly they will have to learn what, if any, are the different needs of the smaller city consumer and what are the best forms of promotional appeals and merchandise to meet these needs. This may necessitate a greater decentralization of the buying and promotional functions in order to keep a flexibility between nonmetropolitan and metropolitan policies.

Suppliers

Suppliers, of course, will be affected by the need to recognize the growing importance of the nonmetropolitan areas and their somewhat different merchandising requirements. Suppliers will also be affected by the physical aspects of decentralized distribution and more decentralized sales forces.

The implications to the wholesalers are ambivalent and yet logical. In the towns the increased retail volume will lead to a growth in the importance of the wholesaler servicing these retailers. However, in the nonmetropolitan cities the growth in retailing power will most likely lead in the opposite direction, that is to the lessening of the importance of the wholesaler. Manufacturers are more likely to provide greater and greater service to the medium size city, lessening the need for the retailers' buyer trips into the Metropolitan Area. In addition, the retailer in the nonmetropolitan city will grow in size to a point where the direct contact and shopping trip becomes more and more economical. The influx of chain stores will, of course, accentuate the nonmetropolitan stores' buying direct from manufacturers.

It would seem then, that different types of retailers will be affected in different ways. Suburban shopping centre stores and nonmetropolitan independent retailers will probably suffer. Convenience stores and specialty stores will be little affected by this movement. Suppliers themselves will tend to have a more decentralized operation, chain stores will move in ever increasing strength into nonmetropolitan areas, and wholesalers in the nonmetropolitan cities will decline in relative importance.

Author's Note

This article excludes the cities of Sudbury, Kitchener, Regina, and Saskatoon, and restricts the analysis to the 15 original Metropolitan Areas of the 1951 Census. This is done for purposes of comparison and continuity and because the total effect of these four cities on the final results would be very small—their total population amounting to only 6% of the total population of the 15 Metropolitan Areas.

Other methodological problems involved: (a) Changing definitions of the areas included in specific MA's, (b) lack of DBS MA's prior to 1951 and, (c) a Retail Census conducted a year earlier (1930) than a Population Census (1931).

These problems are all handled so that a mini-

mum of inconsistency is involved and the effect on the final results and conclusions is negligible.

It has been decided not to adjust the 1951 definitions of MA's to correspond to the 1961 definitions or vice-versa. This is because, according to DBS definitions those suburbs included in the 1961 Census but not in the 1951 Census could not at that time be considered part of a Metropolitan Area and cannot therefore be legitimately analyzed as such. In addition, the increase in population and retail sales by adding back to 1951 MA's those suburbs now included in the same MA's for 1961 would be very small, and on a sales per capita basis would be negligible.

Because DBS did not define MA's before 1951, the 1941 figures included in this study use a close approximation, known as the "Greater Areas," e.g. Greater Montreal, as provided by The Financial Post Business Year Books and Market Surveys of the 1940's. No such definition was available for

the 1931 figures and only the 14 cities proper are used (St. John's, Nfld., 1931 and 1941 figures not available). This is not considered a serious understatement of their populations of 1931 because the suburban ring was a thing of the future at that time, and populations were highly concentrated in the centre city. Again, the effect on per capita sales figures for 1931 and 1941 because of the above small deviations are negligible.

The first Retail Census was actually conducted in 1930 and the Population Census in 1931. The per capita sales figures for 1931 were obtained by dividing the 1931 population figures into the 1930 retail trade figures. The resulting per capita figures would be little different if 1931 retail figures were available because of the very small changes in both population and trade in these two years. More detailed documentation on methods of calculation for any of the years under examination can be obtained by writing the author.

A Selective Bibliography

Part I

William R. Davidson, "Channels of Distribution—One Aspect of Marketing Strategy," *Business Horizons* (February, 1961), pp. 84–90.

Bert C. McCammon, Jr. and Robert W. Little, "Marketing Channels: Analytical Systems and Approaches," in George Schwartz (editor), *Science in Marketing* (New York: John Wiley and Sons, 1965), pp. 321–385.

Roland S. Vaile, E. T. Grether, and Reavis Cox, "Channels of Distribution," in *Marketing in the American Economy* (New York: Ronald Press Co., 1952), pp. 113–121, 124–127.

Part II

Wroe Alderson, "The Analytical Framework for Marketing," in D. J. Duncan (editor), *Proceedings: Conference of Marketing Teachers from Far Western States* (Berkeley: University of California 1958), pp. 15–28.

Wroe Alderson, "Scope and Place of Wholesaling in the United States," *Journal of Marketing*, Vol. 14 (September, 1949), pp. 149–155.

Seymour Banks, "Comments on Alderson's Index of Sorting Balance," *Journal of Marketing*, Vol. 15 (January, 1951), pp. 331–335.

Louis P. Bucklin and Leslie Halpert, "Explaining Channels of Distribution for Cement with the Principle of Postponement Speculations," *Economic Growth, Competition and World Markets* (Chicago: American Marketing Association, 1965), pp. 696–709.

Reavis Cox, "The Organization of Agencies Into Channels," *Distribution in a High-Level Economy* (Englewood Cliffs, N.J.: Prentice-Hall, 1965), pp. 71–84.

Roland S. Vaile, E. T. Grether, and Reavis Cox, "Collecting, Sorting and Dispersing," in *Marketing in the American Economy* (New York: Ronald Press Co., 1952), pp. 134–150.

Part III

Reavis Cox, "The Channel of Marketing as a Unit of Competition," in W. D. Robbin (editor) *Successful Marketing at Home and Abroad* (Chicago: American Marketing Association, 1958), pp. 208–212.

David Craig and Werner Gabler, "The Competitive Struggle for Market Control," *The Annals of the American Academy of Political and Social Science* (May, 1940), 84 ff.

George Fisk, "The General Systems Approach to the Study of Marketing," in W. D. Stevens (editor), *The Social Responsibilities of Marketing* (Chicago: American Marketing Association), pp. 207–211.

Werner Z. Hirsch, "Toward a Definition of Integration," *Southern Economic Journal*, Vol. 17 (October, 1950), pp. 159–165.

Helen B. Jung and Theodore R. Gates, "Do Retail Prices Follow Wholesale Prices?," *National Industrial Conference Board Business Record* XIV (June 1957), pp. 271–276.

James F. Kane, "Marketing Behavior and the Environment: An Ecological Study of the Adaptive Behavior of Marketing Agencies," in L. George Smith, *Reflections on Progress in Marketing* (Chicago: American Marketing Association, 1964), pp. 101–109.

Fritz Machlup and Martha Taber, "Bilateral Monopoly, Successive Monopoly and Vertical Integration," *Economica* (May, 1960), pp. 101–119.

David A. Revzan, "Managerial Struggle for Channel Control," *Wholesaling in Marketing Organization* (New York: John Wiley and Sons, 1961), pp. 143–150.

Louis W. Stern, "Channel Control and Inter-Organizational Management," *Economic Growth, Competition and World Markets* (Chicago: American Marketing Association, 1965), pp. 655–665.

Part IV

F. E. Balderston, "Communications Networks in Intermediate Markets," *Management Science* (January, 1958), pp. 154–171.

Richard C. Christian, "Three-Step Method to Better Distribution Channel Analysis," *Journal of Marketing*, Vol. 23 (October, 1958), pp. 191–192.

Richard M. Clewett, "Checking Your Marketing Channels," in *Management Aids for Small Manufacturers* (Small Business Administration, Washington, D.C., January, 1961), 4 pages.

R. Ferber, D. F. Blankertz, and S. Hollander, Jr., "Channel Research," *Marketing Research* (New York: Ronald Press Company, 1964), pp. 471–476.

Jay W. Forrester, "Industrial Dynamics: A Major Breakthrough for Decision Makers," *Harvard Business Review* (July–August, 1958), pp. 37–67.

William D. Kellner, "Evaluation of Supplier Performance," in Greyser, Stephen A. (ed.),

307

Toward Scientific Marketing (Chicago: American Marketing Association, 1963), pp. 503–512.

Lee E. Preston and Norman R. Collins, "The Analysis of Market Efficiency," *Journal of Marketing Research*, Vol. 3 (May, 1966), pp. 154–62.

Frank Rothman, "What Dealers Can Tell About Sales," *Printers' Ink* (March 29, 1963), pp. 66–68.

Charles W. Smith, "Are You Paying Too Much for Distribution?" *Dun's Review and Modern Industry* (January, 1958), pp. 42–43, 76–83.

Part V

James P. Cairns, "Suppliers, Retailers, and Shelf Space," *Journal of Marketing*, Vol. 26 (July, 1962), pp. 34–36.

Donald H. Granbois and Ronald P. Willett, "Patterns of Conflicting Perceptions Among Channel Members," in L. George Smith, *Reflections on Progress in Marketing* (Chicago: American Marketing Association, 1964), pp. 86–100.

William P. Hall, "Franchising—New Scope for Old Technique," *Harvard Business Review* (January–February, 1964), pp. 60–72.

Richard W. Hansen, "The Growth and Development of Cooperative Retail Chains and Their Marketing Significance," in L. George Smith, *Reflections on Progress in Marketing* (Chicago:

American Marketing Association, 1964), pp. 110–118.

Charles M. Hewitt, "The Furor Over Dealer Franchises," *Business Horizons* (Winter, 1958), pp. 80–87.

"Innovation in the Age of Distribution," *Industrial Distribution* (May, 1963), pp. 93–102.

Leonard J. Konapa, "What is Meant by Franchise Selling?," *Journal of Marketing*, Vol. 27 (April, 1963), pp. 35–37.

National Association of Manufacturers, *Dual Distribution and Allied Problems of Manufacturer-Dealer Relations* (New York: National Association of Manufacturers, Economic Series No. 84, 1961), 15 pages.

William H. Newman and Thomas L. Berg, "Managing External Relations," *California Management Review* (Spring, 1963), pp. 81–86.

Maynard D. Phelps, "Opportunities and Responsibilities of the Franchised Automobile Dealer," *Journal of Marketing*, Vol. 29 (July, 1965), pp. 29–36.

Valentine F. Ridgeway, "Administration of Manufacturer–Dealer Systems," *Administrative Science Quarterly*, Vol. 1 (March, 1957), pp. 464–483.

Thomas L. Stevens, "Here Comes Vertical Marketing," *Industrial Marketing* (September, 1963), pp. 123–124.

Martin R. Warshaw, *Effective Selling Through Wholesalers* (Ann Arbor: University of Michigan, Bureau of Business Research, 1961), pp. 171–181.

70
71
72
74
75
76
77
79
81
83